HOUSING IN THE TWENTY-FIRST CENTURY

WITHDRAWN

HOUSING IN THE TWENTY-FIRST CENTURY

ACHIEVING COMMON GROUND

Kent W. Colton

Published by the Harvard University
Wertheim Publications Committee

DISTRIBUTED BY HARVARD UNIVERSITY PRESS
Cambridge, Massachusetts, and London, England
2003

Copyright © 2003 by the President and Fellows of Harvard College

FIRST EDITION

ISBN: 0-674-01093-0
LIBRARY OF CONGRESS CONTROL NUMBER: 2003102541

PRINTED IN THE UNITED STATES OF AMERICA

10 9 8 7 6 5 4 3 2 1

This book is printed on acid-free paper, and its binding materials
have been chosen for strength and durability.

CONTENTS

PART III
FRAMEWORK FOR THE FUTURE

Introduction

Everyone needs a place to live. In the same way that such a declaration seems to state the obvious, we are often inclined to take our nation's housing stock — the physical places where people actually live — for granted. Yet at the very least, every one of 281 million Americans must have a place in which to lay his or her head on a pillow and sleep in every 24-hour cycle, a place in which to attend to bodily hygiene, and a place to store essential personal belongings. It is almost beyond imagination to envision the massive dimension of our societal life that is involved in providing habitation for 281 million Americans every day. Thankfully, the provision of housing sufficient for our national population does not have to be recreated every day. Its existence is the result of the cumulative process of housing design, construction, financing, sales, maintenance, and protection which has resulted in 120 million units of housing for the American people.

Dr. Kent Colton's book, *Housing in the Twenty-First Century: Achieving Common Ground,* discusses the history of housing over the last fifty years, the process by which national housing policy is made, and the challenges the nation faces looking to the future. As such, it highlights the important role housing plays in our society. The nation's housing stock spans a wide range of types, from shelter beds for the homeless to subsidized rental housing to owner-occupied mansions. And the occupations involved in providing that range of housing products include architects, engineers, land specialists, material manufacturers, transport drivers, construction craftsmen, financial specialists, public officials, real estate sales agents, appliance providers, decorators, retailers, property managers, and many others.

The sheer magnitude of the undertaking — providing housing for the nation — is dwarfed only by the importance of housing to our society. Housing is one of the most important engines of the American economy. Every month economists scrutinize housing starts, the sales volumes of new homes, and the prices of re-sold homes in search of insights into the overall health of the economy, because of the disproportionate volume that housing transactions represent in macro-economic activity. The performance of the housing sector commands the attention of the Federal Reserve System in its efforts to calibrate interest rates and manage the economy. The financial institutions that provide mortgages, including such intermediaries as the secondary market mechanisms, are now among the largest financial entities in the world. And evidence is clear that the depth and duration of economic recessions, as well as the peaks and lengths of expansions, depends in substantial measure on the vitality of the housing sector.

The economic importance of housing extends beyond the macro-economic sphere to its primary role in the personal finances of American families. The decision to purchase a home is for most American families the largest personal economic transaction they will undertake in a lifetime. That transaction provides opportunities for asset appreciation, for tax benefits, for leveraged borrowing, for creation of an estate, and for building the base for a future housing upgrade. Over time the equity that American families build up in their homes represents the largest component of personal net worth — accumulated wealth — in the nation.

But as vital as housing is in these economic and material dimensions, the most persuasive evidence of the importance of housing that I have seen is in the realm of the personal, of the psychological, even spiritual. Over the years I have had the opportunity to witness dramatic moments that make clear the importance of housing in peoples' lives. One such moment was the dedication ceremony of a Habitat for Humanity Blitz Build on a Native American reservation in South Dakota. As the traditional ceremony of presenting a Bible and the keys to the newly completed home neared conclusion, the homeowner, a single mother with two young children, stood anxiously on the front porch. The volunteers watching the ceremony from the front yard saw her begin to tremble and, after a few moments, to sob uncontrollably. Her children, frightened by their mother's tears, clutched her skirt and began to cry. Soon every Habitat volunteer and civic and business leader standing in that frontyard had moist eyes. It was simply too moving to hear that mother describe what a new home meant to her. After many hard years of living in sub-standard conditions, her spirit was overwhelmed by the prospect that her little children would have a warm place to pass the South Dakota winter, a bright place to study, a safe place to grow up. That moment — one of the epiphanies of my years as Secretary of the U.S. Department of Housing and Urban Development —reaffirmed for me the emotional significance of a safe, decent place to live for families in need.

Another moment of insight helped me reflect on the importance of housing to those of us who live in comfortable homes but perhaps take the role of housing in our lives for granted. That moment occurred a few days following the powerful Northridge earthquake, which struck Los Angeles on January 17, 1994. President Clinton dispatched a number of us in his Cabinet to Los Angeles within hours of the earthquake, which had occurred at 4:36 A.M. California time or 7:36 A.M. Washington time. Soon after arriving in Los Angeles in the cool twilight of that winter day, I received my first briefing on estimates of damage to the area's housing stock. It was estimated that 30,000 people could not return to their homes because the homes were either completely destroyed or were declared to be at least temporarily unsafe due to continuing aftershocks. That meant 30,000 people were living in their cars, under trees in the city parks, doubled up with neighbors or family members, in over-crowded shelters, in makeshift tents of plastic tarps, or around camp fires in public spaces. Poor families, middle-class families, senior citizens, parents with children, disabled persons, sick people — all were wrenched from their homes in the pre-dawn hours and tossed into the streets without articles of personal hygiene, changes of clothing, food or water, personal valuables or money, work papers or tools, school books, telephones for communication, televisions or radios for information, car keys, family records and phone numbers. It forced all of us who were working on getting people into some form of housing to reflect on how much we depend on our homes to stabilize the everyday routines of our lives. It made clear how much healthier a child is sleeping in her own bedroom rather than amidst the hacking coughs of groups of children with only a leaky tent for protection from a chilly Pacific rain storm.

It made me appreciate the precious shelter of the undamaged rooftops I drove past on the Southern California freeways, rows of homes I had never seen in precisely that way before.

It's for reasons such as these that the American people intuitively care about housing. It is because it is so important to our national well being that we have created an intricate structure of national housing policies. Over the last century, our national government — and more recently state and local governments and quasi-public institutions — have acted to establish standards for housing quality, to inspect the housing stock, to produce public housing, to encourage private development of rental and for-sale housing, to design tax policies to support housing, to create housing-specific financial instruments, and to offer mortgage insurance. The public interest has been guided by principles of safety and decency, of fairness and access, of adequacy of supply and affordability. Those principles are as valid today as ever.

The history of housing in America is the essential context for current policies that must be constantly reappraised and adjusted to reflect new populations, changing needs, breakthrough technologies, and financial innovations. Kent Colton's work is an important contribution to our understanding of the context of housing policy, as well as a thoughtful explanation of the new challenges that confront our nation's housing sector. The book also analyzes the process of reaching housing policy conclusions and the ability — or inability — of a wide range of public and private interests to achieve common ground.

Over the decades of a distinguished career in the housing field — in academic research and housing advocacy, in designing public policy and supporting private sector production — Colton has developed helpful perspectives concerning both the substance and the pathways of housing policies. More importantly for our nation's future, he is able to look ahead and establish guideposts for prospective housing initiatives. Because of the pervasiveness with which housing touches every American's life daily, a well-researched study such as Kent Colton has produced, which identifies ways to improve the condition of our housing and to expand our access to it, can deservedly be regarded as a major contribution to our national quality of life.

HENRY CISNEROS
Chairman and CEO, American City Vista,
Former Secretary of the U.S. Depratment
of Housing and Urban Development

Preface

On July 15, 1949 the Housing Act of 1949 (Public Law 81–171), was signed into law. The clear challenge to the nation was that every American should have a "decent home and suitable living environment." Since then we have made significant strides toward that goal, and the history of housing over the last fifty years is a remarkable story. However, the story is not complete. Important challenges remain, and new issues and problems have arisen. This book examines what we have learned as we look at housing in the twenty-first century. What have we accomplished over the past fifty years? What are the challenges we face looking to the future? And how can we be more effective as we develop and implement the nation's housing policy?

The story of housing is told in three parts. The first focuses on the substance of housing policy and examines fifty years of housing America. It provides an overview, and it identifies the challenges that we currently face and the areas that must be addressed as we move forward in the twenty-first century. The second focuses on the process of developing and implementing housing policy and understanding how we can better achieve "common ground." The third section outlines a framework for the future. As the title suggests, the book is based on the premise that both the substance and the process are important as we focus on national housing policy.

In dealing with housing policy, it is tempting to try to separate the substance of policy from the politics of the process. I understand why. If you are trying to set forth sound policy recommendations, you want to do so based on solid research and analysis, and let the politics fall where they may. In turn, when someone is involved in the day-to-day fray of implementing a policy or adjusting to the realities of the moment, there is little time, and often little will, to step back to do solid analytical work or to review how the decisions of the moment will impact other people or policies in the future. This book takes a strong position that both the substance and the process are essential for housing in the twenty-first century.

Also essential is the conclusion I have reached after more than thirty years working in the housing area — that a decent home and suitable living environment is not just a political or legislative slogan, and housing is far more than bricks and mortar. Housing truly matters in people's lives. It contributes to family stability and positive childhood outcomes. Stable housing improves the quality of neighborhoods and provides access to economic opportunity for individuals and families. Investment in housing — whether from the public sector or the private sector — usually leads to neighborhood strength and rising property values. Homeownership enables households to build financial resources as the house appreciates in value, and these resources can be tapped for other purposes. Housing makes up more than a third of the nation's tangible assets, and the majority of the wealth of many families is based on the value of their house. Housing is also a major contributor to the nation's economic growth and stability.

Over the last twenty years, I have had numerous opportunities to attend the ceremonial key exchange when a new home owner receives the keys to their house. With that magic moment comes new opportunity for a better life, stability in the home, and the gradual growth of family wealth. Soon after I came to the National Association of Home Builders I was asked to go to Frederick, Maryland near Christmas to speak to the local home builders, to install their officers, and to participate in one such key exchange. The event was described in the *Hagerstown Tri-State Morning Herald* with a headline which read "Frederick Builders Play Santa Claus." The article recounted how 200 people had worked to build a new two-bedroom home in thirty-two hours for an elderly woman — Lillian Fogle — who had been living in a dilapidated house with no indoor plumbing. I will never forget her comments. She said, "Oh! It's so wonderful. Oh my! It's like dying and going to heaven. It's funny, you know, how people get together and do things like this. And they were so pleasant. They even put me a Christmas tree up. It's really pretty." What did she like best? "Everything," she said, "especially the indoor plumbing."

FIFTY YEARS OF HOUSING AMERICA

In 1949, the nation faced a number of housing issues and concerns. With the end of World War II there were significant housing needs and opportunities. New families forming with the return of the GIs invigorated the economy and created a strong housing demand. However, the homeownership rate was only 55%, and significant portions of America's housing were in poor condition. Since the has been made passage of the Housing Act of 1949, remarkable progress has been made in many areas. This section of the book, divided into six chapters, will analyze what has transpired over the last fifty years.

Chapter 1 provides an overview of housing in America. It discusses the nature of the housing stock and when and how it was built. It focuses on the positive shift in the quality of the housing stock, noting that one of the primary goals of the 1949 act was a "decent home" and that significant progress has been made on the condition of the housing stock in the United States. The chapter also points out that affordability is the predominant housing problem in America today. Also discussed are the demographic factors that will influence housing in the future such as the baby boom and the echo baby boom, the aging of the population, and increasing immigration.

Chapter 2 discusses homeownership and single-family housing. The homeownership rate for the nation is currently at an all-time high. This chapter tracks the benefits of homeownership as well as the shifts in homeownership over the last fifty years, including both the progress we have made and the homeownership disparities and gaps that still exist in such areas as minority homeownership and inner city housing compared to the suburbs.

Chapter 3 serves as a parallel to Chapter 2 and focuses on multifamily housing and the importance of adequate and affordable rental housing. It reviews the nation's rental housing stock, including the full range of rental units from low- and moderate-income and public housing to luxury rental housing. The chapter also explores various approaches to financing multifamily housing and the changing demographics of multifamily housing.

Chapter 4 focuses on housing finance and the transformation that has occurred in the U.S. housing finance system. Over the last fifty years, we have seen significant shifts in the nation's housing finance delivery system. This has been particularly dramatic in the last two decades. In the early 1980s there was a serious question as to where the money to finance mortgage credit would come from in the future. Today the availability of mortgage credit for home loans is no longer a concern, due in large part to the growth and success of the secondary market for housing finance. The chapter also focuses on the fact that technology has already had a major impact on the housing finance system, and will undoubtedly continue to have a significant impact in the years ahead.

Chapter 5 discusses the role of government in housing, and at times it will overlap, by necessity, with the material covered as related to government progrms in Chapters 2, 3, and 4. It outlines direct expenditures and housing programs, primarily those overseen by the Department of Housing and

Urban Development (HUD). It explores how these programs have evolved over time and identifies some of the successes as well as the challenges as we look to the future. In addition, one of the primary means by which government policy has influenced housing has been through the tax code. Over the years, the federal government has provided significant support to home owners and some renters through tax expenditures. This chapter will review the nature and magnitude of federal tax expenditures related to housing.

Chapter 6 addresses the importance of housing in the economy and then outlines key challenges as we look to the future. A review of the developments over the past fifty years presents a story of success and achievement. Tremendous progress has been made in a number of areas, such as homeownership, the quality of the housing stock, the development of a strong tax and finance system to support housing, and the close link between the housing market and the nation's economy. It is fair to surmise that those involved in the passage of the Housing Act of 1949 would say that many of their expectations and hopes have been met, and in some cases, perhaps exceeded. However, over the past fifty years there have been important social and cultural changes, and the problems and challenges in the housing area have shifted and evolved. In many ways we now suffer from our own success, and significant issues remain. Chapter 6 will therefore focus on the challenges we face as we look to the future, such issues as meeting the needs of the housing "have-nots" and working families, overcoming the complacency that exists because of the nation's success in the housing area over the last fifty years, meeting the housing needs of a growing population, and dealing with the challenges of growth while at the same time protecting the environment.

ACHIEVING COMMON GROUND

By many standards, the United States today is the best-housed nation in the world. However, our very success in the past complicates our ability to address the problems of the future. Housing is no longer a top issue to many Americans. When the Housing Act of 1949 was passed, housing was an issue for a broad component of American society. The economic success of the last fifty years and the public policies implemented to address housing issues have led to a situation in which the public is now focused on other issues, such as homeland security, education, crime, and health care. In fact, to the extent that there is a public outcry related to housing, it tends to be oriented to issues such as sprawl, traffic congestion, and issues of growth that could actually work against trying to provide affordable housing. Also, the "have-nots" who are not being served, as well as many working families, young households, and immigrants who seek affordable housing, have relatively little political strength, and certainly far less influence than mainstream America, which is well housed and concerned with other issues.

In dealing with the challenges of the present and the future, then, one of the keys to success will be our ability to reach agreement — to achieve common ground. However, this ability is complicated by the ever present and perhaps growing trend toward partisanship. Partisan politics has long been a part of the American political system. Indeed, it is only natural in a democracy that a variety of special interests will strive to achieve what is most appropriate for their own good. However, by some accounts, and based on my own observations, partisan trends have heightened over the last decade. The impeachment challenge in 1999 brought partisanship to the forefront, but the trend toward hardened coalitions on the right and the left seems to be growing. If we are going to address the challenges the nation faces in the housing arena, it will require an effort to cut across traditional interests and differences.

As an academic, prior to spending over two decades working in Washington, it was tempting to believe that good analysis, vision, and public purpose would lead to sound housing policy. It was also tempting to decry the role of special interests in the process. As I was first approached about becoming the executive vice president and CEO of the National Association of Home Builders (NAHB), I thought to myself: Why would I want to represent a special interest group? Obviously, I changed my mind, and fifteen years at NAHB taught me that such a position was one of the best in Washington to focus on housing policy, and it also provided an opportunity to understand the role of interest groups in the political process. I further learned that although good analysis matters, other factors and realities must be considered as well in formulating sound housing policy. The problem is not the existence of special interests, per se. Special interests are a part of our democratic system. The problem is often the failure of the special interests to come together and to achieve common ground, and the failure to recognize and deal with significant market, political, and other realities.

Chapter 7 highlights the realities and the participants involved in achieving common ground on housing policy. It points out that the nation's housing focus has shifted over the past fifty years, and it identifies the various forces and players that are active in the housing market and the housing delivery system.

The reality is that because of the confluence of actors and forces, no one party is able to establish or dominate national housing policy. Rather, housing policy is sorted through issue by issue, whether at the national, state, or local level. National housing policy is the sum total of a series of smaller housing policy debates and efforts that focus on specific issues and cases. The book will therefore examine a series of case studies in formulating housing policy in Chapters 8 through 11.

Chapter 8 discusses Occupational Safety and Health Administration (OSHA) regulations for the home building industry. Overall the effort was a success, and one of the questions that is addressed is why this effort to achieve common ground was successful when so many others fail.

Chapter 9 is a case study of the challenges of achieving common ground on raising the loan limit for the Federal Housing Administration (FHA). Although a Congressional compromise was achieved, during the debate the discussion became bitter among several parties, and groups that generally work together were not able to agree. This led to lingering feelings of distress and animosity, which has complicated the ability to achieve common ground on other housing policy issues.

Chapter 10 is a case study on the inability to achieve common ground on wetlands regulations. The chapter explores the reasons for this failure and the result, which has been a series of lawsuits, regulatory disagreements, and a variety of efforts in Congress to change the law to make it more strict or more lenient.

Chapter 11 provides a case study on achieving common ground related to Habitat for Humanity. Since its founding, Habitat for Humanity International, working through its local affiliates, has built more than 125,000 homes and is on pace to celebrate the completion of their 200,000th house by 2005. Many of the homes have been built in the United States, but also in more than 83 countries around the world. In this effort, Habitat has brought together a wide range of groups and individuals in a common cause: providing affordable housing for low- and moderate-income households. This chapter will focus on how Habitat has achieved this common ground and what lessons can be learned from this experience.

FRAMEWORK FOR THE FUTURE

As we look to the future is the nation's housing glass half empty or half full? The answer is both. The last fifty years is a story of great success in meeting many of the challenges that existed in 1949. But the job is far from over! During this period we have also seen dramatic social and cultural change. With success comes complacency, and the urgency of the 1950s, 1960s, and 1970s no longer exists. Housing is not a top issue to many. Addressing the housing challenges of the twenty-first century will therefore be harder. Resources are limited, and the challenges of the very poor often go beyond housing. Further, a new battle has arisen related to housing, land use, smart growth, and environmental balance. New issues demand a new framework for housing policy discussions in the twenty-first century. Chapter 12 outlines this framework, and it includes two elements. The first draws on the lessons learned from the four case studies and identifies a set of principles helpful in achieving common ground. The second outlines ten building blocks that provide a framework for the future: homeownership; the production and preservation of affordable rental housing; creating a focus on the housing "have-nots" and working families; a strong housing finance system; a tax system to support housing; removing the barriers to build and remodel affordable housing; strong state and local leadership and the continued devolution of responsibility to the state and local level; a strong supporting and coordinating role at the federal level; harnessing the strengths of the private sector; and smart growth based on market realities.

As we address the challenges and issues of the twenty-first century, we must focus on both the process as well as the substance of housing policy. The nation's housing policy will not be dictated from the federal level. Rather, it will be framed incrementally through specific local, state, and national housing policy debates and the actions of both the private and public sectors. As this process continues, we can only hope that we will be able to more effectively achieve common ground.

Acknowledgments

I am deeply grateful to the many people who have contributed to this book. At the top of the list is my wife Kathryn, my children, their spouses, and my grandchildren. Their sincere encouragement, interest, and reassurance as I have worked on this book has made it a more worthwhile and thoughtful endeavor.

As I began to contemplate what I would do when I left the National Association of Home Builders, I was approached by Professor John Dunlop, Professor Emeritus at Harvard, and Nic Retsinas, the Director of the Harvard Joint Center for Housing Studies. They encouraged me to write this book, and without their wisdom and strong support it never would have happened. The thought of writing a book had crossed my mind several times, but their proposal turned an idea into reality. I gratefully acknowledge the financial support of the Jacob Wertheim Fellowship in Industrial Relations. The Joint Center for Housing Studies and Harvard University have also provided a wonderful place to work during this undertaking and a great environment for the exchange of ideas. At the Joint Center, John Dunlop, Nic Retsinas, Eric Belsky and Bill Apgar have all reviewed portions of the book, and their feedback has been extremely helpful. Through the Joint Center I have also been able to work with excellent research assistants. Amy Rowe played an essential role in working on the chapters on homeownership, the role of government in housing, and the case studies on wetlands and Habitat for Humanity. Amy was extremely thorough and very helpful with her research and writing. Kate Collignon was instrumental in her work on the chapter on multifamily housing, and the National Multi Housing Council (NMHC) provided additional financial resources in order to support the research in the multifamily area. Melonie Hurley was particularly valuable in developing an overview of the last fifty years of housing America as discussed in the first chapter of the book. And Thalia Brown has been essential in reviewing and updating the figures in the book and checking on the latest available information. Charles Field has been a valued friend and colleague over the years, and I also want to acknowledge his assistance in reviewing portions of the book and in helping to frame the concept of achieving common ground in the housing industry.

Of course my fifteen years of work at the National Association of Home Builders (NAHB) provides the background and context for the ideas in this book, and it is to the leaders and staff of NAHB that I dedicate this book. These people are far too numerous to name in their entirety, but they have had a great impact on my life and I want to express special thanks to the extremely qualified staff of the National Association of Home Builders, and to the many volunteers, elected leaders and executive officers of this great association. During a fifteen-year period, it was my privilege to work closely with eighteen presidents of NAHB including Pete Herder, John Koelemij, Dave Smith, Jim Fischer, Dale Stuard, Shirley Wiseman-Lach, Martin Perlman, Mark Tipton, Jay Buchert, Roger Glunt, Tommy Thompson, Jim Irvine, Randy Smith, Danny Pincus, Don Martin, Charlie Ruma, Bob Mitchell, and Bruce Smith. In addition, Leon Weiner a close friend and former President of NAHB, and to many the "conscience of the housing industry," was instrumental as a partner in working on national housing policy over the years. A special dedication and thanks goes to Leon and Helen Weiner for their friendship and for their amazing contributions to the housing industry.

While working at NAHB, one of my great pleasures was to help, along with others, to establish the National Housing Endowment (NHE). NHE is the philanthropic arm of the National Association of Home Builders. The endowment has already accomplished a great deal of good through the grants it has provided. In fact, this book has been the beneficiary of a grant from the National Housing Endowment, providing the support for the work of the research assistants highlighted above. A very special thanks goes to the men and women who have contributed to NHE and comprise the valued brain thrust for the National Housing Endowment.

A special acknowledgment also goes to Dionne Inman who has played an invaluable role in typing, editing, and producing this book. Dionne is a master with the computer, and she has patiently revised draft after draft, and worked closely with the editor of the book, Sue Hayes, in order to assure the successful completion of the production process.

Undoubtedly the book would not have been produced without the many contributions highlighted above, none, of course, more important than the contribution of the master — John Dunlop. But let me make it clear, the responsibility rests with me. If there are any mistakes, and I am sure there are, I take full responsibility. It has been a great joy to try to tell the story of housing in America over the last fifty years, both in substance and in process. However, I have undoubtedly missed many important points, and with this in mind, I hope that the book will serve as a framework for discussion as we look to the future.

HOUSING IN THE TWENTY-FIRST CENTURY

PART I

Fifty Years
of Housing America

Chapter 1

FIFTY YEARS OF HOUSING AMERICA: AN OVERVIEW

On July 15, 1949, the Housing Act of 1949 was signed into law and marked a new phase of housing in America. The resounding theme of the Housing Act was to provide "a decent home and suitable living environment" for every American. Housing had previously been an important issue for the nation, but, immediately following World War II, it became an even more central concern for many Americans. Wartime housing shortages, overcrowding, and decrepit housing conditions made housing a front-page, top-of-the-mind issue during the postwar period. In the years following the 1949 Act, housing remained a priority and great strides were made by the private and public sectors to improve housing options for American families. These advances are a significant accomplishment, and the success story will be told in this book. However, as we look to the future, a great deal of work remains.

GROWTH IN THE HOUSING STOCK

The second half of the twentieth century was an era of extensive growth for the nation's housing supply. Figure 1.1 highlights the number of housing starts by year from 1900 to 2001. It dramatically illustrates the housing growth following World War II, especially when compared to housing starts in the first half of the century. This is further illustrated in Figure 1.2, which outlines the housing inventory at the beginning of each decade and the remarkable growth which has occurred since 1940. Figure 1.3 shows a different version of housing stock growth, highlighting the amounts of the stock that were owner-occupied, renter-occupied and vacant over the same time period.

The most productive decade in terms of both the absolute number of

FIGURE 1.1
Total U.S. Housing Starts, 1900–2001

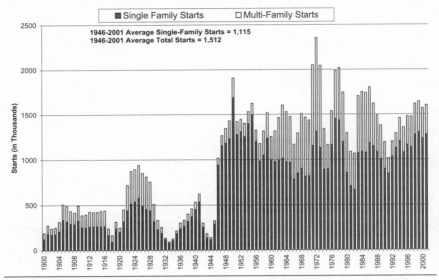

SOURCE: 1900–1999 data from Barbara Alexander, "The U.S. Homebuilding Industry: A Half-Century of Building the American Dream," John T. Dunlop Lecture, Harvard University, October 12, 2000. Other Data: U.S. Department of Commerce, Bureau of the Census.

new housing units and the growth rate was the 1970s. During this period the nation experienced a 29% increase in the housing stock — a growth of 19,700,000 new units. The 1950s had the second highest growth rate at a gain of 27% in the housing stock, although in terms of absolute new units created, the 1950s did not rank as high as later decades. The only decade that approached the 1970s in terms of actual units produced was the 1990s; in this period the housing stock grew by about 17,300,000 units, a 17% increase over the previous decade. In the 1980s, the pace of housing construction tapered off somewhat due primarily to recessions in the early 1980s and the early 1990s, but the late 1990s marked another high point for housing production. Economic prosperity and favorable interest rates were particularly important in achieving this housing boom. The 1990s included the nation's longest period of economic expansion, which began in March of 1991 and continued until the first quarter of 2001.[1] This expan-

---

[1]"The Durable Expansion," *New York Times,* February 7, 2000, A18. Ip, "New Data Paint Darker Picture of the Economy," *The Wall Street Journal,* August 1, 2002, A1–2. Revised data reported by the Commerce Department on July 31, 2002 indicated that the 2001 recession began in the first quarter of 2001.

FIGURE 1.2
Estimated Housing Inventory, 1940–2000

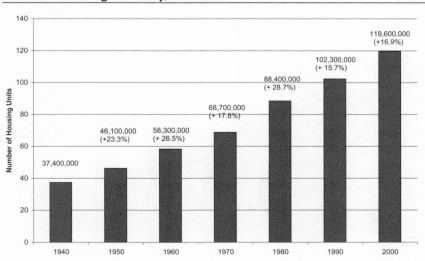

SOURCE: U.S. Census Bureau, Historical Census of Housing Tables and Housing Vacancies/Homeownership for 2000. (www.census.gov/hhes/www/housing/hvs/annual00/ann00t9.html).

sion produced a strong housing market, which in turn helped fuel economic growth.

Changes in the Housing Stock

There have been numerous housing cycles in the past fifty years, and throughout these cycles single-family homes have remained the most popular structure for new construction. Figure 1.4 outlines annual housing starts from 1940 to 2001; single-family homes dominate in terms of number of units built each year. Decennial census data reveal that single-family detached houses have remained relatively popular over time; they made up over two-thirds of the total housing inventory, 68.8%, in 1960. This percentage reduced somewhat to 60.62% in 1997.[2] Clearly the preference for single-family detached units remains, yet at the close of the twentieth century there was more variety in the housing stock. Figure 1.5 shows the types of housing units that make up the entire housing stock (vacant and occupied) as measured by the 1999 American Housing Survey,

[2] U.S. Census Bureau, "American Housing Survey 1997."

FIGURE 1.3
Housing Stock by Type of Occupancy, 1940–2000

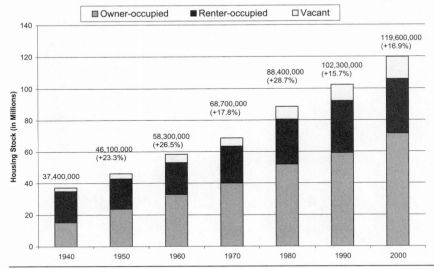

SOURCE: U.S. Census Bureau, Historical Census of Housing Tables and Housing Vacancies/Homeownership for 2000 (www.census.gov/hhes/www/housing/hvs/annual00/ann00t9.html).

with 61% single-family detached, 7% single-family attached, 9% two to four units, 16% five or more units, and 7% mobile homes or trailers.

Multifamily housing (structures containing two or more units) tended to be more sensitive to demographic and policy changes, and thus experienced radical upturns and downturns. For example, in 1972 multifamily housing made up 44% of the year's housing starts. Multifamily housing production dropped sharply after passage of the 1986 tax reform package (see Figure 1.4), which eliminated many of the tax advantages associated with multifamily construction. By 1992 multifamily units made up only 14% of the year's total starts. Although multifamily construction grew again in the late 1990s, multifamily production levels were only one-third of the 1972 peak and around half of the mid-1980s peaks (see Figure 1.4). These shifts can be explained primarily by tracking the needs and demands of the dominant population group, the baby boomers.[3] In the 1970s, multifamily housing units met the needs of young baby boomers who were just establishing their first households; later, single-family

---

[3] Throughout this book three generations will be referred to: The "baby boom" generation refers to people born between 1945 and 1964; "Generation X" refers to those born during the "baby bust" period from 1965 to 1976; The "echo boom" generation refers to those born after 1977.

FIGURE 1.4
America's Housing Stock Grew in Cycles, 1940–2001

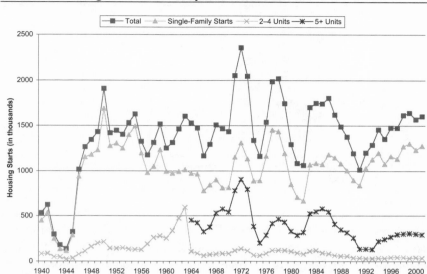

SOURCE: U.S. Census Bureau, Survey of Construction, C-20 (1940–1950 Census Bureau estimates).
Note: 1940–1963 data is for "2+ units" which includes 5+ units. This is separated out starting in 1964.

housing gained importance as baby boomers sought larger homes to accommodate growing families. By the end of the 1990s, single-family housing was firmly ensconced as the nation's dominant housing type. For example, in 2001 single-family housing comprised 80% of new housing construction.[4]

Another facet of the changing housing stock was the advent of manufactured housing, or mobile homes. Manufactured homes are built entirely in the factory under a federal building code administered by the U.S. Department of Housing and Urban Development (HUD). The Manufactured Home Construction and Safety Standards, commonly known as the HUD Code, went into effect June 15, 1976, and is the only federally-regulated national building code.[5] In the 1940 census, mobile homes were still not a significant housing type and were simply placed into an "other" category on the census. However, as revealed in Figure 1.6, mobile homes' popularity grew quickly. The inventory of mobile homes in the United States

---

[4] U.S. Census Bureau, "Survey of Construction," Table 2.
[5] "Mobile homes" is the term often used for the factory-built homes produced utilizing the HUD Code (since the 1976 law, houses built according to the HUD code are classified as manufactured housing). See: Manufactured Housing Institute. www.manufacturedhousing.org/CC_definition.html.

FIGURE 1.5
Types of Housing Units in the United States, 1999

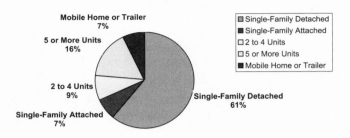

SOURCE: "American Housing Survey, 1999." U.S. Department of Housing & Urban Development & U.S. Department of Commerce.
NOTE: These percentages are for the total housing units in the United states (which includes both occupied and vacant units).

went from approximately 315,000 units in 1950 — less than 1% of the nation's total housing inventory — to 7.4 million units in 1990.[6] In 2001 the number of mobile homes in the housing stock reached 8.6 million, 7% of the housing stock.[7] Manufactured housing has been particularly popular at the edge of fast-growing metropolitan areas in the South and the West. In 1999, 55% of the nation's manufactured housing was in the South, and the region's 3.75 million mobile homes made up 10.3% of its housing stock. Further, 19% of the nation's manufactured housing was in the West, with 1.3 million units comprising 5.9% of the housing stock in the western region.[8] With continued migration to the South and the West, the importance of the manufactured housing sector is likely to continue.

Regional Distribution of the Nation's Housing

Patterns of regional housing development are manifested in the movements of the nation's population. The four regions referred to throughout this book are the Northeast, the Midwest, the West, and the South.[9] These

---

[6] U.S. Census Bureau, "Housing Then and Now."
[7] U.S. Census Bureau, "American Housing Survey 1999."
[8] Ibid.
[9] The states that correspond to each of the four regions as designated by the U.S. Census Bureau are: *Northeast:* Maine, New Hampshire, Vermont, Massachusetts, Rhode Island, Connecticut, New York, New Jersey, and Pennsylvania. *Midwest*: Ohio, Indiana, Illinois, Michigan, Wisconsin, Minnesota, Iowa, Missouri, North Dakota, South Dakota, Nebraska, and Kansas. *South:* Delaware, Maryland, District of Columbia, Virginia, West Virginia, North Carolina, South Carolina, Georgia, Florida, Kentucky, Tennessee, Alabama, Mississippi, Arkansas, Louisiana, Oklahoma, Texas. *West:* Montana, Idaho, Wyoming, Colorado, New Mexico, Arizona, Utah, Nevada, Washington, Oregon, California, Alaska, Hawaii.

FIGURE 1.6
Mobile Homes Gain Popularity, 1950–2000

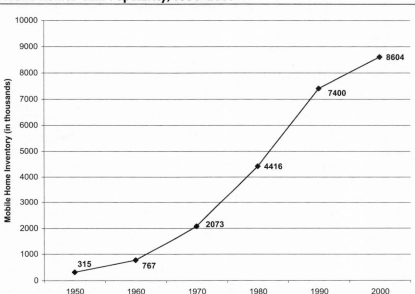

SOURCE: U.S. Census Bureau, Census of Population and Housing for 1950–1990 and Census 2000 Housing Characteristics.

four regions are used by the U.S. Census Bureau; a breakdown of each region by state can be seen in the map in Figure 1.7. Three key patterns of housing development have emerged in the United States over the past fifty years: (1) increased building in the South and the West, (2) migration from rural areas to more urbanized areas, and (3) movement away from central cities toward suburbs and outer fringes of metropolitan areas.[10]

Over the past fifty years, the traditional population centers of the Northeast lost popularity as sites for new construction diminished and new growth centers emerged in the South and West. The South has emerged as the regional leader in housing starts, and its housing growth rate has increased overall from 1959 through 2001. (See Figure 1.8) In 1959, 34% of new housing was built in the South, while the Midwest and the West each made up 24% of the new homes built. At that time, the Northeast still contained about 18% of new housing development. By 2001, the move away from the Northeast was apparent; the South was home to about half of the nation's new housing construction, while the Northeast's share fell to only

[10] McArdle, "Outward Bound," 4–5.

FIGURE 1.7
Census Regions and Divisions of the United States

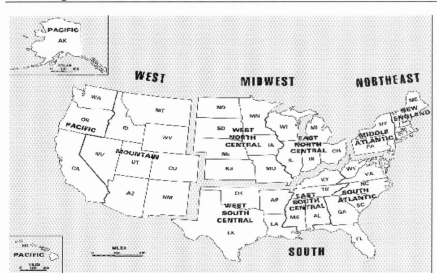

SOURCE: U.S. Census Bureau, "Geographic Areas Reference Manual" (www.census.gov/geo/www/garm.html).

9.3%. Meanwhile, the Midwest share fell slightly, while the West's share remained roughly the same. Figure 1.9, showing standing housing stock by region in 2000, confirms these trends. Given these trends and the fact that building in the South has dominated by such a large margin, it is likely that building activity will follow a similar trajectory in the twenty-first century.

The country's population moved increasingly toward urban areas in the latter half of the twentieth century. The proportion of people living in rural areas dwindled from 43.5% in 1940 to 25% in 1990.[11] Figure 1.10 indicates a strong population movement from rural to urban areas in the twentieth century. At the beginning of the century, 39.6% of the population was urban, and this increased to 75.2% by 1990. The figure shows that the decade with the largest rate of change was from 1940 to 1950, when the percentage of people in urban areas increased by 7.5%. Much of this movement away from rural areas was in fact a movement of people leaving farms, which also signifies movement into new occupations. Figure 1.10

---

[11] U.S. Census Bureau, "Urban and Rural Population, 1900–1990."

FIGURE 1.8
The South Led Housing Starts, 1959–2001

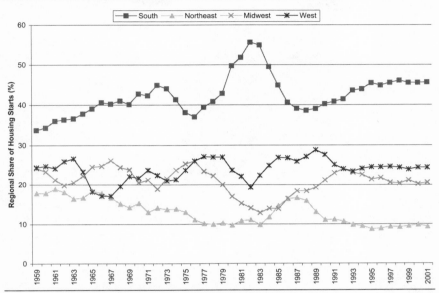

SOURCE: U.S. Census Bureau, Survey of Construction, C-20.

shows that from the 1970s through the 1990s, the movement from rural areas to urban centers tapered off significantly, although the overall trend of increasing urban population continued. This tapering off was largely due to a reconfiguration of the U.S. economy. Beginning in the 1970s, employment opportunities were expanded in lower density areas outside of the core city areas. This shift inspired the term *rural renaissance* and, though there was a brief pause during the 1980s, this renaissance continued strongly in the 1990s.[12] Industrial jobs declined throughout the U.S. around this time, and the economy evolved to provide more service-based employment options. The expansion of technology and transportation systems made moving employment centers into outlying areas more feasible. With this rural renaissance picking up speed again in the 1990s, it is highly probable that this shift in employment to outlying regions will continue.

In conjunction with the broad trend of population movement from rural to urban areas, there has been increasing population movement within

---

[12] McArdle, "Outward Bound," 2.

FIGURE 1.9
Most of U.S. Housing Stock was in the South, 2000

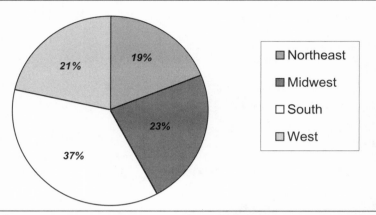

SOURCE: U.S. Census Bureau, Current Population Survey/Housing Vacancy Survey, Series H-111, 2000.

FIGURE 1.10
America's Population Shifted Toward Urban Areas, 1900–1990

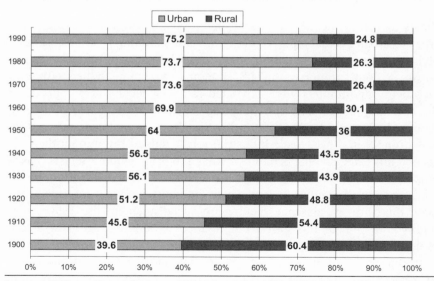

SOURCE: U.S. Census Bureau, "Urban and Rural Population, 1900–1990." Selected Historical Census Data: Urban and Rural Definitions Data. (www.censusdata/ur-def.html)
NOTE: The definition of urban/rural changed after the 1940 decennial census.

metropolitan areas themselves. The majority of new building in recent years has been outside the urban core. Thus a population movement from the urban core into the surrounding suburban regions parallels the overall population shift from rural to urban centers.[13] This is due to improvements in transportation and technology, which allows households to live farther away from the areas where they work, and also to the trends that inspired the rural renaissance mentioned above. New home building and ren ova-tion in urban areas is by no means consistent from city to city; cities with more land are more likely to have higher levels of construction than com-pact cities. The movement into the suburban belt of the metropolitan area has meant that suburban areas have been the site of much of the home building in recent years. Figure 1.11 shows that in 1997, far fewer permits were issued for building in the city cores than in the medium density (sub-urban belt) areas. In Figure 1.11, low density counties are those with pop-ulation density of less than 260 people per square mile, medium density counties have between 260 and 1825 people per square mile, and high density counties over 1,825 people per square mile.[14] The creation of the suburban areas and the focus on residential living outside of the central cities has fostered a great deal of discussion about suburban sprawl and its effect on the environment. It appears that the popularity of living in suburban areas and the concentration of building in such areas will con-tinue to increase and be a major topic of discussion. As Alexander von Hoffman writes: "Despite the indications of urban revival, a snapshot of building permit activity that took place in counties during 1997 indi-cates that the pattern of suburban growth that has dominated American urban growth since the nineteenth century will persist in the twenty-first century."[15]

Age of the Housing Stock

By the end of the twentieth century, the average American home tended to be older than in previous periods. Figure 1.12 displays the aging of the nation's housing units and indicates that by the end of the 1990s, the na-tion's housing stock was older than ever before. Although the nation's housing stock is constantly nourished by new growth, the size of the

---

[13] There are two terms used for this urban core, "large city" and "central city." Central city is the term used by the U.S. Census Bureau to define the largest city and any other cities in the metropolitan area of more than 250,000 people. Large city refers to the largest city and any others with a population of more than 200,000. For more information see: von Hoffman, "Home Building Patterns."

[14] Von Hoffman, "Home Building Patterns," 22.

[15] Ibid., 11.

FIGURE 1.11
Share of Permits by Region and County Density, 1997

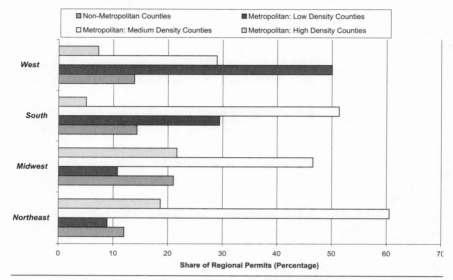

SOURCE: von Hoffman, Alexander, "Home Building Patterns in Metropolitan Areas." Working Paper Series, W99-9. Cambridge, MA: Joint Center for Housing Studies, Harvard University. 1999.
DATA: U.S. Census Bureau, "Series C-40 and County Population Estimates."

existing housing stock will obviously dominate any new construction; the result is that the housing stock continues to age. This phenomenon accelerated due to the intense housing growth that took place between 1950 and 1970. In addition, the increased longevity of homes is indicative of efforts to rehabilitate rather than demolish homes in poor condition. The share of homes lost each year to abandonment, fire, natural disasters, and other causes declined from just under 1% in the 1960s to about 0.25% in 1999.[16] Due to the fact that older units are prone to physical deterioration and obsolescence, the aging of the nation's homes signifies a greater future role for remodeling as well as for demolition in regions that are experiencing population loss.

At the time of the 1940 census the median age of housing units was twenty-five years. Only 16% of homes had been built between 1930 and 1940; this was largely due to the slowdown in housing construction during the Depression. At least 41% had been built more than thirty years earlier.[17] Housing production picked up in the 1960s and 1970s as older housing was

---

[16] Joint Center for Housing Studies, *Improving America's Housing,* 7.
[17] Devaney, *Tracking the American Dream,* 32.

FIGURE 1.12
Housing Has Been Aging Since 1980

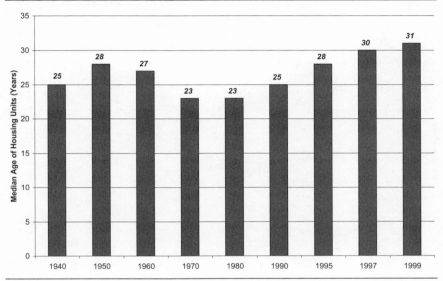

SOURCE: U.S. Census Bureau, "Decennial Census" and "American Housing Survey," 1995, 1997, 1999.

demolished. The median age of housing rose to twenty-eight years in 1950, dropped to twenty-seven years in 1960, then held at a steady twenty-three years in 1970 and 1980. In 1990, the median age returned to twenty-five years as the proportion of housing ten or fewer years old dropped to the 1950 level of 21%.[18] The aging became more pronounced during the 1990s. By 1993, the typical home was twenty-eight years old.[19] By 1997, the typical American home had a median age of thirty years, with owner-occupied houses younger than the median (twenty-nine years old), and rental housing older (about thirty-two years). More than 20% of them had been built in the 1970s, which was by far the most significant decade for home building. Even older were the 27.4% of homes built prior to 1950. By comparison, only about a quarter of the homes that existed in 1997 had been built after 1979.[20]

Remodeling enables the aging housing stock to adjust to contemporary preferences. It also allows owners to prevent deterioration caused by time and nature, thereby preserving the value of homes. As homes age, owners

[18] Ibid.
[19] U.S. Census Bureau, *Home Sweet Home*, 1.
[20] U.S. Census Bureau, "American Housing Survey 1997."

FIGURE 1.13
Total Remodeling Expenditures, 1965–2001

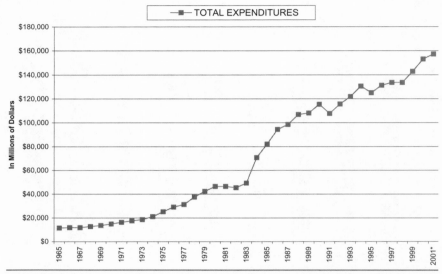

SOURCE: U.S. Census Bureau. Construction Reports: Expenditures for Residential Improvements and Repairs C-50. *2001 utilizes the 3rd Quarter Seasonally Adjusted Annual Rate.

spend more on maintenance and repairs to update their homes based on current space needs, the desire for additional amenities, and new styles and technologies. As illustrated in Figure 1.13, total remodeling expenditures has increased steadily, with significant growth starting in the mid-1980s. For example, in one study in 1995, property owners invested over $33 billion on major replacements in the home, such as furnaces, windows, doors, and roofs. They also spent over $35 billion on interior remodeling projects, $18 billion on exterior improvements (detached garages, swimming pools, patios, etc.) and about $5 billion to repair damage caused by natural disasters.[21] Figure 1.14 displays the amount spent on general maintenance and repairs, and Figure 1.15 contains information on additions and alterations to homes. Interestingly, additions and alterations — which generally represent efforts to remodel — continued to increase from the mid-1960s to 2001, while the amount spent on maintenance and repairs peaked in the early 1990s.

---

[21] Joint Center for Housing Studies, *Improving America's Housing*, 1.

FIGURE 1.14
Maintenance and Repairs, 1965–2001

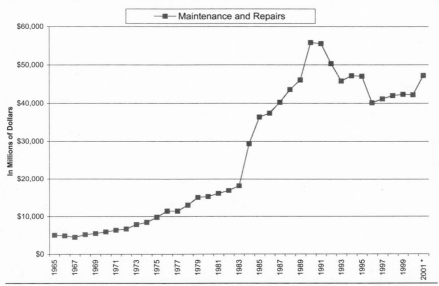

SOURCE: U.S. Census Bureau. Construction Reports: Expenditures for Residential Improvements and Repairs C-50. *2001 data uses the 2001 3rd Quarter Seasonally Adjusted Annual Rate.

Although remodeling spending tracks the general business cycle, it can be a less volatile sector than new housing construction. (See Figure 1.16) Home owners' spending on remodeling has grown about 1.8% annually over the past fifteen years, which is slower than the growth rate of the overall economy (2.7%) but faster than the 0.5% growth rate of home building.[22] The remodeling market tends to be less volatile because remodeling expenses, especially those for maintenance and repair, are often unavoidable, regardless of economic conditions. This spending by millions of property owners around the country reflects a long-term investment in the nation's housing supply and ensures that despite its aging, the housing stock will continue to meet the needs of Americans. With 120 million homes, the housing stock will continue to age. At the same time Americans' expectations of their homes are rising. Americans are demanding larger homes with more amenities, and their options are to renovate or sell their homes and buy something larger.

[22] Ibid., 6.

FIGURE 1.15
Additions and Alterations, 1965–2001

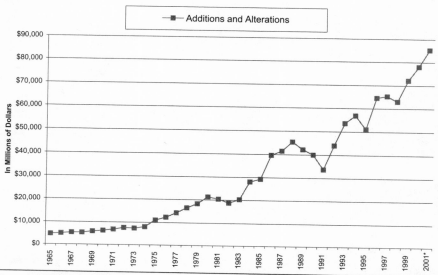

SOURCE: U.S. Census Bureau. Construction Reports: Expenditures for Residential Improvements and Repairs C-50. * 2001 data uses the 2001 3rd Quarter Seasonally Adjusted Annual Rate.

Housing Quality Improves

The amenities and features of American homes have improved significantly in the past fifty years. Although the majority of Americans today live in adequate physical environments, the 1940 census revealed serious problems with the nation's housing supply. Homes tended to be crowded, in poor condition, and many lacked adequate plumbing. About 18% of homes were considered to be "in need of major repair." However, improvements were rapid in the ensuing decades. In 1950, about 10% of housing units were found to be "dilapidated."[23] By 1960, the proportion of dilapidated units dropped to 5%, and by the century's end, serious housing problems were relatively rare. The American Housing Survey (AHS) uses a different set of criteria than did the decennial census, but the trend toward homes in good repair is still clear. According to AHS data, in 1997 only 7% of American households lived in homes with moderate or severe physical problems, such as lack of a complete kitchen, poor building or

---

[23] The 1940 census concept of "in need of major repair" was changed to "dilapidated" in the 1950 census. The two measures differed in their criteria, and therefore are not directly comparable.

FIGURE 1.16
Remodeling is Less Cyclical Than New Construction

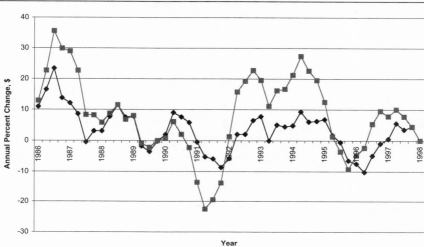

SOURCE: Joint Center for Housing Studies, Harvard University, "Improving America's Housing: The Remodeling Futures Program."

hallway maintenance, or frequent breakdowns in plumbing, heating, or electrical systems.[24]

Crowding is another area in which housing quality has improved, as indicated by Figure 1.17. In 1940, about one-fifth of American homes were deemed "crowded" (housing more than one person per room), and 9% were considered "severely crowded" (more than 1.5 persons per room). Crowding was especially severe in the southern states, where about one-third of all crowded homes were located. Following the 1940s, crowding decreased steadily until 1990, when severe crowding increased slightly to 2.1%, up from 1.4% in 1980. This increase was considered to be a result of domestic migration to cities, as well as increased immigration from abroad that tended to gravitate toward particular urban areas. For example, over one-fourth of all crowded units in 1990 were located in four metropolitan areas: Houston, Los Angeles, Miami, and New York.[25] However, from 1990 to 1999, rates of severe crowding again declined, to below 1% in 1999, as seen in Figure 1.17.

---

[24] U.S. Census Bureau, "American Housing Survey 1997."
[25] U.S. Census Bureau, "Housing Then and Now."

FIGURE 1.17
Crowding Has Decreased Dramatically

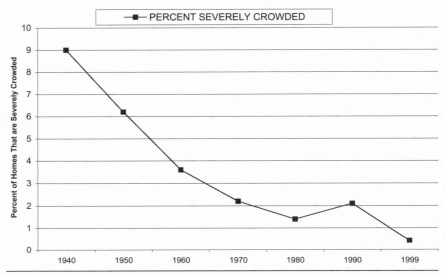

SOURCE: U.S. Census Bureau, Decennial Census & 1999 American Housing Survey
NOTE: "Severely Crowded" denotes a housing unit with more than 1.5 persons per room.

Plumbing is another indication of housing condition, and it has followed a similar trend of improvement, as shown in Figure 1.18. In 1940, nearly half of American homes lacked complete plumbing (defined as hot and cold piped water, a bathtub or shower, and a flush toilet). The problem was particularly acute in about ten states, many in the South, where 70% or more of homes lacked complete plumbing.[26] The proportion of homes lacking full plumbing dropped dramatically over the next fifty years, falling to about one-third in 1950, to one-sixth in 1960, and to only .46% by 2000.[27]

Houses Become Larger With More Amenities

American homes have grown dramatically both in terms of square footage and amenities. In the early postwar years, the typical American

---

[26] Ibid.

[27] According to the AHS, in 1997 about 2% of houses lacked complete plumbing facilities. U.S. Census Bureau, "American Housing Survey 1997." (Note: Definition differences between the decennial census and the 1940 census prevent direct comparisons on plumbing.)

FIGURE 1.18
Most Homes Gained Complete Plumbing Facilities By Century's End

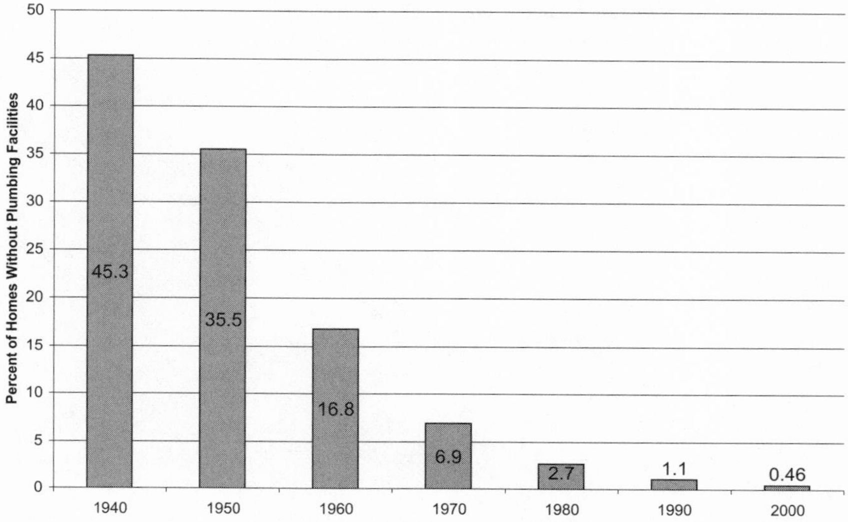

SOURCE: U.S. Census Bureau, Decennial Censuses (www.census.gov).

home was far smaller and more simple than it was by the end of the twentieth century. In 1947, the prototypical suburban subdivision was developed in Levittown, Pennsylvania, to meet the housing demands of war veterans and their families. The homes in Levittown paint a vivid picture of early postwar housing. As designed by William Levitt, they measured a mere 750 square feet, with two bedrooms, a living room, a kitchen, an unfinished second floor, and no garage. The price for such a home in the development's early years was just $7,990.[28]

The arrival of the new generation of baby-boom families, in conjunction with advances in construction and unprecedented economic prosperity, resulted in a dramatic rise in the size of homes. As the growth trajectory depicted in Figure 1.19 indicates, the size of single-family homes rose sharply, particularly from the mid-1980s onward. In 1970, the median living area in a newly built single-family home was 1,385 square feet. By 2000, the median figure had hit the 2,059 square feet, while the average size hit 2,273 square feet. Moreover, a significant percentage of new homes built in the late 1990s could be classified as large (2,400

---

[28] Lacayo, "Suburban Legend," 148.

FIGURE 1.19
Average Size of New Homes Grows by About One-Third, 1970–2000

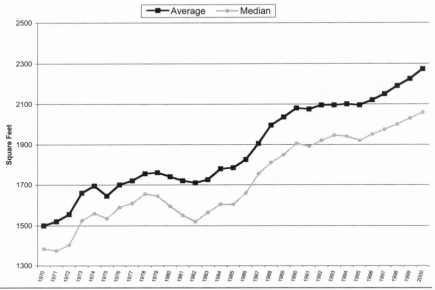

SOURCE: U.S. Census Bureau, "Construction Reports, Series C-25."
NOTE: New Homes include single-family houses and those built for rent.

square feet or greater): homes of at least 2,400 square feet made up 32% of new homes built in 1998, while those measuring at least 3,000 square feet made up 16%.[29] Interestingly, as the size of homes grew, the size of households actually shrank over the latter half of the century, and particularly in the last two decades. This phenomenon is displayed in Figure 1.20.

In addition to expanding in size, homes have also gained features that have come to be taken for granted by the end of the twentieth century. Figure 1.21 highlights some of the most notable changes. For example, bathrooms became more numerous. By 1997, more than half of new American single-family homes had two and a half or more bathrooms; in 1970, that figure was only 16%. Moreover, by the end of the century, it became quite rare for a builder to construct a home with fewer than two bathrooms. In 1970, 42% of new single-family homes had fewer than two bathrooms; by 1997, only 9% did. In 1999, about 34% of homes had four or more bedrooms; in 1970, only about 24% did. Likewise, air conditioning became

---

[29] U.S. Census Bureau, "Characteristics of New Housing: 1998."

FIGURE 1.20
Household Size Declines While Size of Homes Increase

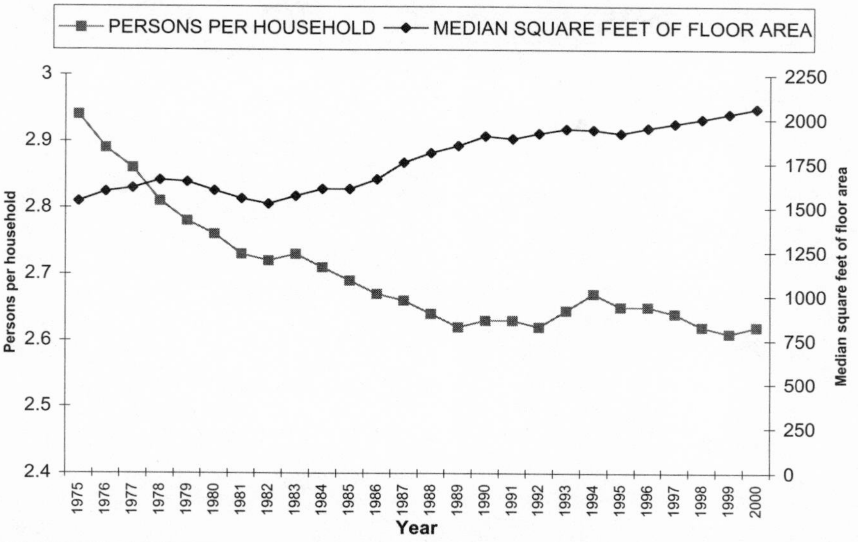

SOURCE: Size of home data from National Association of Home Builders (www.nahb.org/facts/forecast/af.html). Household size data from U.S. Census Bureau (www.census.gov/population/socdemo/hh-fam/htabHH-4.txt).

standard. In 1999, 84% of new homes had air conditioning; that figure was only 34% in 1970.

Automobiles became increasingly important for home owners by the century's end. In 1997, more than 90% of U.S. households had at least one vehicle at home for personal use. Even more revealing is the fact that 71% of home owners and 35% of renters had more than one vehicle.[30] In light of this trend, American homes gained more extensive parking facilities. In 1970, about 58% of new homes had garages; by 1997, 86% did. Carports had nearly vanished by the end of the century, and only about 13% of all new homes constructed had no garage or carport.[31]

By a number of standards, the United States currently has the best housing in its history. However, it is this very growth in size and amenities that has added to the challenge of ensuring affordability. With larger homes

[30] U.S. Census Bureau, "Housing Brief," 2.
[31] Ibid., 2.

FIGURE 1.21
New Single-Family Homes Are Increasingly Well Equipped

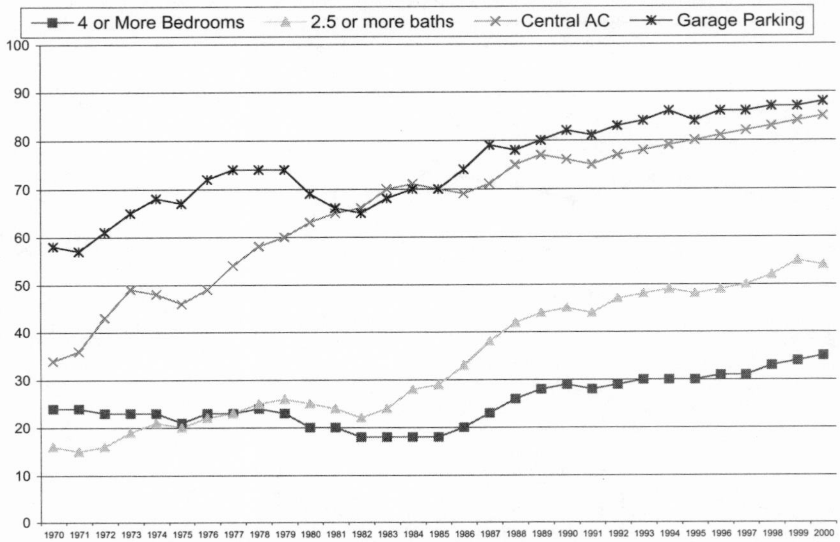

SOURCE: U.S. Census Bureau, "Construction Reports, Series C-25."

and added amenities, housing prices have risen. The nation's housing prices rose 28.5% between 1995 and the first quarter of 2000.[32] Also, annual appreciation increased 6.9% from the second quarter of 1999 through the second quarter of 2000.[33] The price of new single-family homes has increased sharply, as depicted in Figure 1.22; the median sale prices have risen noticeably almost every year since 1963. Based on consumer demand, houses are becoming increasingly comfortable and spacious, thus more costly. However, as Figure 1.22 shows, while home prices have risen, annual median incomes have risen at a much slower rate, making for a rather dramatic discrepancy between income and home prices.

The Housing Act of 1949 called for a decent home and suitable living environment for all Americans. The quality of America's housing has clearly increased significantly over the last fifty years, but the affordability of these homes continues to be a concern for many Americans.

---

[32] Freddie Mac, "Conventional Mortgage Home Price Index."
[33] Freddie Mac, "Conventional Mortgage Home Price Index: Press Release."

FIGURE 1.22
New Housing Prices Rose Sharply While Income Rose Moderately, 1975–1999

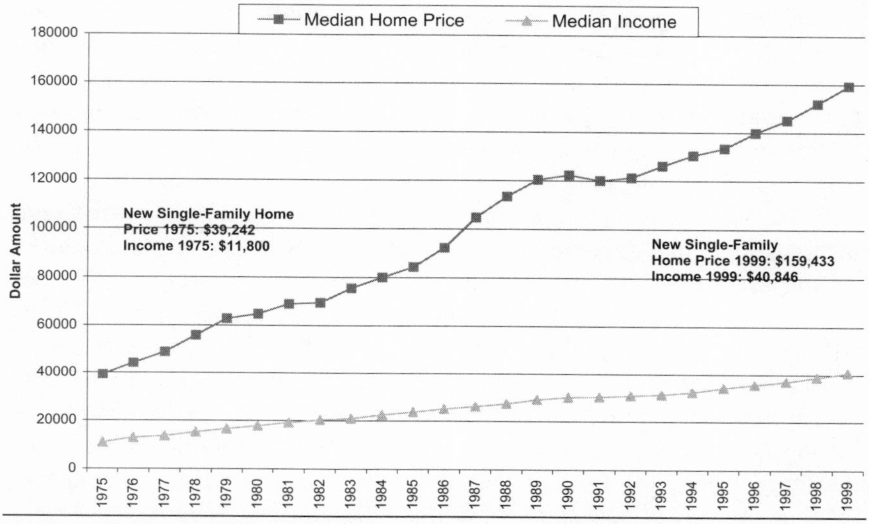

SOURCE: Median Sales Price Data from U.S. Dept. of Commerce (www.commerce.gov). Income Data from "Historical Income Tables—Households" (www.census.gov/hhes/income/histinc/h06.htm).

THE STORY BEHIND THE NUMBERS

To fully understand how and why the housing supply looks as it does today, it is important to examine some of the historical and social forces that have shaped housing production.

The Postwar Challenge

When the Housing Act of 1949 was passed into law, the nation was facing unprecedented housing challenges; housing demand was at new heights due to the return of World War II veterans, yet the housing supply had been ravaged by years of economic depression and wartime shortages. Housing was a high national priority and was viewed as a public crisis of the first order.

Even before millions of servicemen returned from overseas, a housing shortage had already developed. This was due to the fact that many households had experienced an increase in income, thus fostering a high demand for housing, which was not plentiful. The Great Depression had taken a dismal toll on the nation's housing stock, with construction at a near standstill. Demand had dropped precipitously as disposable income dropped by 39% from 1929 to 1932 and the nonfarm unemployment rate reached 36% in 1932.[34] In 1933, new housing starts fell to 93,000 units, less than one-tenth the number of units built in 1925. There was a surplus of available properties that families could not afford, a significant number of foreclosed properties, and a gross vacancy rate of 13.5%.[35] As previously noted, housing quality was abysmal.

World War II stimulated the economy, raising household income and thus housing demand; however, the exigencies of war prevented growth in housing production during that period. The wartime shortage of lumber and other materials, along with a national economic focus on the war effort, actually slowed housing production. In 1942, the War Production Board placed formal controls on new residential construction. Much of the housing that was built during the war years was designed as temporary housing in key war production centers. From 1941 to 1945, new starts totaled only 1,569,000 units of permanent housing.[36] In contrast, in 1946 alone the number of new starts was 1,015,000 units.[37]

Despite the stagnating supply, demand and the ability to buy a house began to grow during the war years. For example, nonfarm disposable personal incomes nearly doubled during the war, from an estimated $68 billion in 1940 to $133 billion in 1945 in current dollars.[38] Full employment (or full absorption of available workers) was increasing families' income, and at the same time, people were encountering lower mortgage debt burdens. Mortgage debt as a proportion of disposable income declined from 61% in 1932 to 18% in 1945.[39] With a rise in employment, personal savings also increased significantly. As families placed increased assets into government bonds and commercial bank accounts, the assets of lending institutions also rose. Banks began to favor mortgage and commercial loans, which provided greater returns than government bonds. Thus, incomes and savings helped stimulate the postwar housing boom. By 1945, housing vacancy rates had shrunk, and there was an estimated shortage of at least 3 million housing units.[40] In addition, the existing housing stock

---

[34] U.S. Census Bureau, *Historical Statistics,* vol. 1, 126.

[35] Doan, *American Housing Production,* 37.

[36] National Association of Home Builders, *The Future of Home Building,* 242. (*Note:* Estimates from U.S. Census Bureau and NAHB, 1940–1950.)

[37] Ibid.

[38] Doan, *American Housing Production,* 50.

[39] Ibid., 51.

[40] Ibid., 54.

was overburdened, with 2.6 million doubled-up households (two or more households sharing one housing unit).[41] At the same time, rent control and reduced production had reduced the turnover of desirable rental housing.

The Postwar Housing Boom

With surging housing demand and an inadequate housing stock, the stage was set for the postwar housing boom, which lasted from 1946 to 1956. A total of 16.8 million starts took place over the period, ranging from over 1 million in 1946, to 2 million in 1950. Figure 1.4 shows the sharp spike between 1946 and 1952. One of the most important outcomes of the housing boom was a rise in homeownership. The number of home owners increased by nearly 10 million, and the home owner ratio is estimated to have increased from 51% at the end of 1945 to nearly 59% in 1956.[42] This dramatic increase in homeownership is attributed to a number of factors, including the increase in real income during and after World War II, which made homeownership a viable option for renter households; the rise in income tax rates, making home owner deductions more significant; the shortage of existing housing; the high inflation rates, particularly in property values, and the low real mortgage interest rates, resulting in a strong incentive to buy real property; and the reduced production of rental housing due to rent control.

The housing boom was spurred by a number of demographic, economic, and historic factors. The return of millions of World War II servicemen, and their subsequent marriages, resulted in the formation of record numbers of new households. Other demographic influences included not only the baby boom's increase in population, but also a mass migration from the farms to urban areas. In addition, the economy was growing at a rapid rate and unemployment was low, which added to the demand for housing. Also, mortgage funds were available at lower interest rates than ever before, typically from 4% to 6%.[43]

Government programs helped to further spur demand. The GI Bill, passed in 1944, encouraged home ownership by authorizing mortgage guarantees through the Veterans Administration (VA) to help veterans to purchase, build, or improve homes. Through a variety of initiatives, the federal government began to take a major role in increasing home ownership by underwriting private mortgage debt. During the boom, the FHA

---

[41] U.S. Census Bureau, *Characteristics of Families,* 3.
[42] U.S. Census Bureau, *Historical Statistics* part 2, 646.
[43] Doan, *American Housing Production,* 60.

and the VA together insured or guaranteed $65 billion in resid
gage loans, with the VA guaranteeing nearly 60% of the
total.[44] The federal government supported 33% of the gros
nancing provided from 1946 to 1956.[45] Following the po
boom, vacancy rates resumed normal levels, and housing r
tinued at a healthy rate. Population growth stabilized as th
fect receded, although migration from rural areas continu

The 1970s: Boom and Bust

The next significant period of growth in the housing stoc
tween 1966 and 1973, one of the most active periods for Ame
production. The trend peaked in the early 1970s, with the highest annual
production totals yet recorded: in 1971, 1972, and 1973, housing starts exceeded 2 million.[46] Particularly strong gains were posted for mobile homes
and multifamily housing, including cooperatives and condominiums.

This expansion was primarily due to the large number of baby boomers
entering their twenties, forming their first households, and seeking their
first homes. Critical to this expansion was the phenomenon of "starter
homes"; this refers to a home buyer's tendency to initially purchase a
small "starter" home and to later replace it with a larger dwelling with
more amenities. This helps explain the popularity of condominiums, du-
plexes, and the like, which are typically more affordable than detached
single-family dwellings. Additionally, restrictive fiscal and monetary policies by the Federal Reserve, designed to combat rising inflation in the late
1960s, were relaxed in the early 1970s, which contributed to the increased
housing production seen in these years.

Following the building boom of the early 1970s, an economic downturn
took its toll on housing production. The downturn included high inflation
rates, exemplified by a 67% rise in the Consumer Price Index between
1974 and 1980, and restrictive monetary policies, including significant increases in interest rates, which held down housing production.[47] However,
although nominal (actual market) interest rates were high, real interest
rates (adjusted for inflation) were negative because the rise of inflation exceeded the increase in interest rates. The value of single-family homes increased in comparison with inflation rates, which also spurred consumers

---

[44] Ibid.
[45] Ibid., 61.
[46] See Figure 1.4.
[47] Doan, *American Housing Production,* 102.

to buy houses. Housing starts fell between 1973 and 1975, then rebounded, then fell again during the recession in the early 1980s.[48] In the years between these two dips, production increased due to expansionary monetary policies, negative real mortgage interest rates, and the expectation of rising property values. Homeownership increased to 64% in 1980, bolstered by the aging of the baby boomers, as well as by the investment incentives provided by rising residential real estate prices and negative real interest rates.

The 1980s: Another Roller Coaster Decade

In the 1980s, housing production went through a three-part cycle: stagnation, followed by rapid growth, and then another downturn. At the beginning of the decade, inflation controls by the Federal Reserve raised interest rates and depressed housing production. As highlighted in Figure 1.4, annual housing production bottomed out in 1982, at about 1.06 million new units. In the early 1980s, mortgage interest rates rose to new heights. In September and October of 1981, they rose as high as a market nominal rate of 18%.[49] As a result, a serious credit crunch took hold.

After 1982, starts began to rise rapidly when the Federal Reserve loosened monetary pressure, causing interest rates to drop and residential lending to increase. New production was spurred by the reduced supply of commercial and residential space, since a period of higher interest rates had caused a slower building pace during the late 1970s and early 1980s. Housing production was also facilitated by financial deregulation and 1981 tax changes that allowed real estate investors to use an accelerated rate of depreciation for real property, which particularly encouraged the construction of multifamily housing.

The boom that followed was dramatic, both in the housing and commercial sectors. Office space doubled to 2.5 billion square feet, the number of shopping centers rose 57%, and hotels by 43%. By the end of the decade, there were 12.5 billion square feet of new commercial property.[50] In the housing sector, production shot up significantly. In 1983, multifamily housing production exceeded the 600,000 mark for the first time since the all-time highs recorded in the early 1970s, and it maintained that pace until 1987. However, it soon became clear that overbuilding had taken place; the 1980s began with a national office vacancy rate of 5%, which by the end of

---

[48] Again, see Figure 4 for illustration of these roller-coaster turns.

[49] *See*: Federal Home Mortgage Corporation www.federalreserve.gov/releases/H15/data/m/cm.txt.

[50] "The 1980s: Too Easy Money," 40.

the decade reached 18%.[51] In the housing market, the effects of overbuilding were evident; the vacancy rate for rentals in buildings with five or more units reached a high of 11.4% in 1988, up from 7.1% in 1983.[52]

The housing slump that began in 1987 was the result of this overbuilding and of a collapse in real estate values, along with the Tax Reform Act of 1986, which, among other things, significantly reduced depreciation for multifamily housing and essentially curtailed the benefits of passive losses. Another factor in the housing slump was the savings and loan (S&L) disaster of the late 1980s, which was intricately tied to the change in tax law and the end of the real estate building boom. During the lending heyday of 1983 to 1987, S&Ls had taken on highly-leveraged loans for projects with risky fundamentals. The low real interest rates of the 1970s greatly reduced the effective cost of credit and gave a strong incentive to borrow for construction projects. The escalation of interest rates in the early 1980s caused solvency problems for lenders that had previously committed to long-term loans at much lower rates. When the real estate bubble burst in 1987, property values fell, vacancies increased, and S&Ls with significant real estate lending exposures suffered heavy losses, or failed.

S&L failures became more rampant in the 1980s than at any time since the Great Depression. More than 1,100 commercial banks failed or received federal financial assistance, representing nearly 8% of all banks operating at the beginning of the decade. Similarly, over 900 thrifts failed, representing 17.5% of all thrifts operating at the start of the decade. The widespread S&L failures brought about a credit crunch that caused the last few years of the decade to be marked by lower than usual housing production levels, particularly in the multifamily sector.

The 1990s: A Slow Start and a Strong Finish

Overall, the 1990s were strong years for housing production, in particular the late 1990s, abetted by a robust economy with effective mortgage interest rates and unemployment rates at their lowest levels since the 1960s. Homeownership climbed to a record 67.4% in 2000.[53] But, the early 1990s were not a promising start to the decade, as the credit crunch that began in the late 1980s continued to weigh down the housing market. Near-zero interest rates, driven down by aggressive monetary policies by

---

[51] Ibid.
[52] *See:* U.S. Census Bureau, "Housing Vacancy Survey," Series H-111.
[53] U.S. Census Bureau, "Housing Vacancies and Homeownership."

the Federal Reserve, helped to bring about an economic expansion, which began in March 1991 and started to affect the housing sector by 1993. Single-family housing expanded in the early 1990s, and in 1994 starts reached their highest level since 1978 (see Figure 1.4). However, in 1993 multifamily housing construction fell to only 162,000 new units — the lowest in more than thirty years and a 76% drop from the 1985 peak of 669,000 new units. This drop, in many respects, was due to the overbuilding in the multifamily sector that took place in the mid-1980s and to the 1986 changes in the tax laws related to multifamily housing. The recession in the early 1990s also had a major impact on multifamily housing construction.

By 1994, the economic recovery was under way in the housing sector and continued for the remainder of the decade. The growth rates for gross domestic product (GDP) and employment exceeded the first three years of the economic recovery. Interest rates were still among the lowest in fifteen years, contributing to a good housing market. Consumer confidence and spending rose as job security was enhanced. The economy flattened out again briefly in early 1995, with slower GDP growth, lower interest and adjustable mortgage rates, and a weakening overall economy. The economy soon took off again, continuing what turned out to be the longest economic expansion period in the nation's history. Housing production surpassed 1.6 million new units a year in 1998 and 1999.

Challenges Remain

While the U.S. economy remained consistently strong through the mid- and late 1990s, there was a growing problem with housing affordability. Starting in the 1980s, the major challenge in the housing sector shifted from the quality of the housing to its affordability. The affordability problem worsened throughout the 1990s, and today it is the nation's most urgent housing need. Rental prices have been increasing faster than inflation, the end result being a severe shortage in affordable housing. Shortages in certain urban areas are particularly stark. A 1999 HUD report on "worst case housing needs" notes an acceleration in the loss of housing units affordable to extremely low-income renters.[54] (Households with worst case housing needs are defined as unassisted renters with incomes below

---

[54] U.S. Department of Housing and Urban Development. "A Report on Worst Case Housing Needs in 1999." In fact, the number of units affordable to extremely low-income renters (those with 30% percent of area median income) dropped by 13% (or 750,000 units) between 1997 and 1999.

50% of the local median income who pay more than 50% of their income for rent or live in severely substandard housing.)

Perhaps the most striking aspect of the problem is the fact that a diverse array of households suffer from the affordable housing shortage. Low-income renters struggle to find decent, affordable housing, yet those with somewhat higher incomes who may rent or own are also struggling. Most important, moderate-income people who work and have steady, decent jobs are also finding it increasingly difficult to secure affordable shelter. Cushing N. Dolbeare writes that the urgency of housing needs goes beyond the problems of those with "worst case needs."

> [The] focus on the roughly five million households with worst case needs obscures the true scale of our housing problems. All too often the worst case number is cited as the measure of low-income housing need, instead of a fraction of the most critical needs. The arbitrary limitation of worst case problems to unsubsidized, very-low- income, renter households means that the definition excludes more than half of all households with these critical problems. It is time to put worst case needs in a broader context: the afford-ability and other problems of all households, regardless of their tenure.[55]

Thus the range of households who have affordable housing problems is far larger than is often depicted. Simultaneously, the number of households receiving direct assistance peaked in the 1990s and has since declined. Thus, larger numbers of households experience housing problems, and yet fewer households are receiving direct government assistance.

Given that a great deal of emphasis and discussion is often placed on the housing affordability struggles of the lowest-income renter households, it is important to also address the challenges of working families who either own or rent. The Center for Housing Policy/National Housing Conference has focused on the plight of working families across America. The center notes that, according to the 1997 and 1999 American Housing Survey, 13 million working families have critical housing needs, which means they spend more than half their income on housing costs and/or live in a severely inadequate unit.[56] Worse, 3.7 million of these are low- to moderate-income working families who have critical housing needs despite working steady full-time jobs,[57] many of which have opportunities for advancement.

---

[55] Dolbeare, "Housing Affordability," 4.
[56] Center for Housing Policy/National Housing Conference, "Paycheck to Paycheck," 6.
[57] Ibid., 8.

The problem tends to be most severe in the Northeast and on the West Coast, in cities such as New York, Boston, and San Francisco. While many households earn incomes that allow them to find quality, affordable housing, a significant portion of U.S. households are unable to do the same. Fifty years later, the question still remains as to how the standards set by the Housing Act of 1949 can be extended to more (and hopefully all) Americans.

DEMOGRAPHIC TRENDS

In addition to discussing the economic, political, and social factors that have affected the housing stock, it is important to highlight demographic forces such as the age structure of the population, immigration, household formation, and household composition. Demographic issues have clearly shaped America's current housing supply, and they will undoubtedly determine what kind of housing will be built in the future. Moreover, preferences change with the times, and these preferences translate into changes in the nation's housing stock. For example, the latter half of the twentieth century was marked by an increasing preference for living in the South and the West — the so-called "sunbelt." These preferences are mirrored by housing stock changes in these regions.

Population Booms and Busts

Cycles of population growth must be examined when discussing housing quality. Figure 1.23 shows overall population growth in the United States from 1940 to 2001. Figure 1.24 shows a tremendous increase in births from 1940 through the early1960s, then a leveling out, and then another boom in the 1980s. As noted in the previous section, the vast population increase due to the birth of the baby boomers (people born between 1945 and 1964) fostered both great demands and great opportunities in the housing sector. A housing stock that met the needs of the 24.4 million people born in the 1930s had to be supplemented by massive new construction when it came time to house the 40.5 million born in the 1950s.[58]

The late 1960s and early 1970s marked a "baby bust" period. The term *Generation X* generally refers to people born during the baby bust, from

---

[58] National Association of Home Builders, *The Future of Home Building,* 10.

FIGURE 1.23
U.S. Population Growth, 1940–2001

SOURCE: U.S. Census Bureau, Current Population Reports, Series P-25. Note: Actual U.S. Population is only measured during the Interim years are approximated using intercensal estimates. At the time of printing, population growth in the 1990s had not been adjusted for the actual 2000 count. Therefore, the actual count for 2000 has been omitted to better reflect actual population growth over time.

1965 to 1976. By 1973, total births fell to only 3.1 million from the 1957 peak of 4.3 million. By the late 1970s, baby boomers began to start their own families, and their children, born after 1977, were dubbed the "echo boom." The large size of the echo boom generation was largely due to the increased number of potential mothers from the baby boom cohort, along with moderate increases in fertility rates. In 1990, the number of births reached 4.16 million, nearly matching the 4.3 million record set in 1957, but the annual number of births began to fall after 1990.[59] By the end of the 1990s, as baby boomers reached the end of their childbearing years, births continued to fall. In 1997, the birth rate fell to its lowest point in U.S. history, 14.5 births per 1,000 people.

Household Growth

Residential construction demand is determined primarily by household growth, with the "headship rate," or the percentage of the population that heads households, as the key measure. Important social trends that deter-

---

[59] Ibid., 11.

FIGURE 1.24
U.S. Birth Rates, 1940–2000

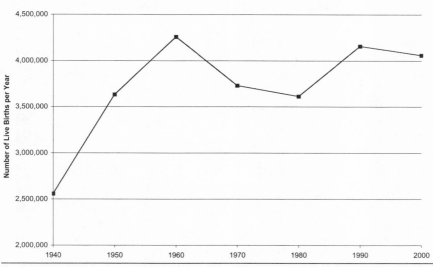

SOURCE: Ventura, S.J., J.A. Martin, B.E. Hamilton, Dr. Fay Menacker, M.M. Park, *Births: Final Data for 2000*. National Vital no 5. Hyattsville, Maryland: National Center for Health Statistics. February 2002.

mine headship rates are marriage rates, divorce rates, remarriage rates, and the age at which children leave home. In the 1970s, the headship rate rose dramatically due to substantial increases in the divorce rate and the tendency for single people to live alone. In the 1980s, the headship rate for those in older age groups continued to rise, while headship rates declined for those younger than thirty-five. Increasingly, adult children chose to live longer in their parents' homes. Headship rates are also greatly affected by the economy; the recessions from 1981 to 1982 and 1990 to 1991 resulted in sharply reduced rates of household formation. Unemployment and poor consumer confidence caused more people to live with family or friends during these economic downturns.

Projections by the Joint Center for Housing Studies in 1999 indicated that the number of U.S. households should increase by an average of 1.1 to 1.2 million annually from 2001 to 2010.[60] In Figure 1.25, NAHB expands on these projections and predicts that households should increase by an average of 1.25 million annually from 2001 to 2010. They also examine the details behind the projections for 2001 to 2010 compared to

---

[60] Joint Center for Housing Studies, *State of the Nation's Housing,* 9.

FIGURE 1.25
Annual Average New Home Demand (1990s and Projected 2001–2010 trend)

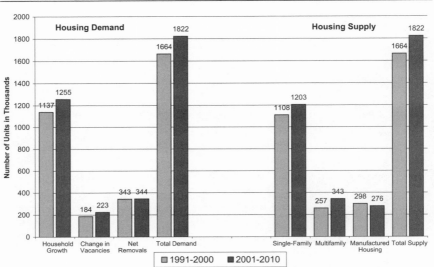

Source: National Association of Home Builders. "The Next Decade for Housing," NAHB Economics, Finance and Housing www.nahb.com, Home Builders Forecast, U.S. Bureau of the Census, 2001.

what actually occurred in the 1990s. In the 1990s overall housing demand led to the annual production of 1.365 million housing starts (including single-family and multifamily) and 298,000 manufactured housing units. In the next decade the annual demand will be even greater, with a demand for the production of 1.546 million housing starts each year (including single-family and multifamily) and 276,000 manufactured housing units. The demand for housing production in the decade of 2001 to 2010 is therefore projected to be almost 10% greater than for the decade of the 1990s.[61]

On the housing demand side, Figure 1.25 sets forth changes in vacancies, household growth, and net removals to identify housing demand from 1991 to 2000, and then compares that housing demand with projections for 2001 to 2010. Similarly, the figure looks at housing supply by housing type to project what type of housing will be built to meet the demands. In both the 1990s and in the projected first decade of the twenty-first century, total housing demand is equal to the total housing supply. The NAHB projects that immigration will contribute to about 25% of the growth between the 1990s and the decade of 2001 to 2010, and that another 65% will derive

---

[61] National Association of Home Builders, *The Next Decade For Housing*, 9.

from the movement of the population into ages with higher household headship rates. The remaining 10% of growth will result from the overall rise in headship rates caused by declining marriage rates and low remarriage rates.

Immigration

Foreign immigration is a key determinant of population growth in the United States. In the 1990s, net immigration (legal and illegal immigrants, minus emigrants) accounted for more than a third of net population growth. The aforementioned aging trend makes immigration particularly crucial: younger immigrants can help fill in the gaps where native population growth is weak. Figure 1.26 shows the flow of immigration to the United States while Figure 1.27 shows changes in the proportion of immigrants in the U.S. population.

The early part of the twentieth century was marked by high immigration levels, largely from southern and eastern Europe, as well as from Asia. However, highly restrictive immigration policies and the Great Depression resulted in a near elimination of immigration between 1930 and 1950. From 1930 to 1950, the foreign-born population of the United States declined from 14.2 million to 10.3 million, or from 11.6% to 6.9%

FIGURE 1.26
Immigration to the U.S. by Decade

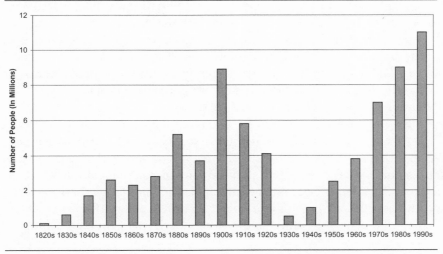

SOURCE: Passel, Jeffrey S. and Barry Edmonston, "Immigration and Race: Recent Trends in Immigration to the U.S.," and Joint Center for Housing Studies estimates from INS data.

FIGURE 1.27
Foreign-Born Population of the U.S.

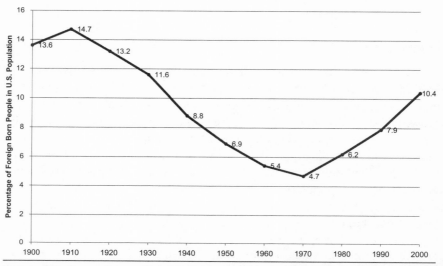

SOURCE: U.S. Census Bureau, Technical Paper 29, Table 1, (www.census.gov/population/www/documentation/twps0029/twps0029.html) and U.S. Census Bureau, "March Current Population Report P20-534."

of the total population. Immigration rose during the 1950s and 1960s, but it was still low by historical standards, and mortality was high among the foreign-born population because of its tendency to be older, a result of four decades of low immigration. In 1965, the Immigration Reform Act paved the way for increased immigration by eliminating per-country quotas that had restricted the number of immigrants from particular areas of the world. Still, in 1970, the foreign-born population dropped further, to 9.6 million — a record-low 4.7% of the total population.

After 1970, the foreign-born population of the United States increased rapidly due to large-scale immigration, largely from Latin America and Asia. It rose from 9.6 million in 1970 to 14.1 million in 1980 and to 19.8 million in 1990. By 1997, the estimated foreign-born population was 25.8 million. As a percentage of the total population, the foreign-born population increased from 4.7% in 1970 to 6.2% in 1980, and to 10.4% in 2000.[62] Figure 1.28 details the shifts in the national origins of immigrants in the

[62] Gibson and Lennon, "Historical Census Statistics," Table 1; U.S. Census Bureau, "Quarterly Report: July 1998."

FIGURE 1.28
Immigrants Were Mostly From Asia and the Americas, 1941–2000

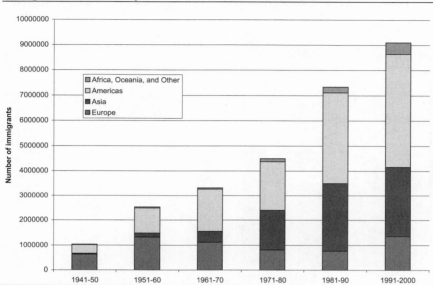

Legend:
- Africa, Oceania, and Other
- Americas
- Asia
- Europe

SOURCE: Immigration and Naturalization Service, *Statistical Abstract 2000.*

second half of the twentieth century. In 1940, over 60% of immigrants were European, with most of the remainder from the Americas. Asian immigrants made up less than 4% of immigrants. Strikingly, in the 1990s, half of U.S. immigrants were from the Americas and another 30.7% hailed from Asia. Between 1981 and 2000, the largest single source country for U.S. immigrants was Mexico, accounting for 23.8% of immigrants. The other top source countries during the same period were the Philippines (6.4%), China (4.7%), India (3.7%), and the Dominican Republic (3.6%).[63]

America's regions, states, and cities do not share equally in the effects of immigration. In fact, six states are home to over two-thirds of the foreign-born population, with California containing over one-third of the foreign born. Between 1971 and 1998, the top states of intended residence for new immigrants were California, New York, Florida, Texas, New Jersey, and Illinois.[64] As Figure 1.29 indicates, the West's share of the foreign-born

[63] U.S. Immigration and Naturalization Service, "Fact Sheet" (www.ins.gov/graphics/index.htm).
[64] U.S. Immigration and Naturalization Service, "INS Announces Legal Immigration Figures for FY 1998," (http://www.ins.gov/graphics/publicaffairs).

FIGURE 1.29
Immigrants Increasingly Tend to Move to the West and South

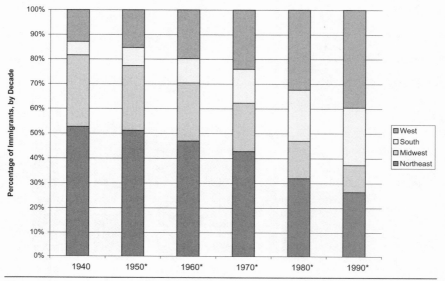

SOURCE: U.S. Census Bureau, Technical Paper 29, Table 14 (www.census.gov/population/www/docu-mentation/twps0029.twps0029.html).
*Indicates sample data.

population increased markedly between 1940 and 1990. By 1990, about 40% of the foreign-born population was in the West, while the Northeast's share fell from about half in 1940 to about a quarter in 1990.

Within these areas, new immigrants tend to gravitate toward large metropolitan "gateway" areas. In 1990, 67% of the foreign-born lived in one of eleven gateway metro areas (each of which had received 100,000 or more new foreign immigrants during the 1980s), compared to just 27% of the native born.[65] The great majority of these gateways are coastal or border ports of entry, including Miami, Los Angeles, San Francisco/Oakland, Houston, and New York. The other significant gateways are Chicago, Washington, D.C., San Diego, Boston, Dallas/Fort Worth, and Philadelphia. Within the gateway cities, immigrants are more likely than the native born to be clustered in the central city.[66] Looking ahead to the twenty-first century, it is likely that some of the immigrant base in the gateway cities

[65] McArdle, "Foreign Immigration," 8.
[66] Ibid.

will move away to other areas. However, although second-generation Americans are more likely to move away from the gateway areas than their parents, the impact of immigration in the years ahead will continue to be greatest in the key gateway communities.

Life Cycle Trends

In many ways, the trends within different age cohorts drive housing markets. In particular, the size or special needs of a given cohort impact the market. It is important to anticipate such needs to properly plan for adequate future housing supply. It is widely acknowledged that the baby boom generation has truly driven housing markets over the last thirty years due to the sheer number of people falling into this age category. As we look to the future and this generation continues to age and move into retirement, important shifts will be felt in the housing sector. In conjunction with this, it is also important to track the next large cohort, the baby boomers' children, the echo boom generation. Predictions of future housing demand will largely depend upon an analysis of the echo boomers and the aging of the baby boomers, the two largest age cohorts.

THE ECHO BOOMERS

As the echo boom ages in the next few years, the recent decline in the young adult population will begin to shift. By 2010, the echo boomers will account for more than one in ten owner households and four in ten renter households.[67] They differ from previous generations in several key ways. First, compared with the baby boom, the echo boom is more racially and ethnically diverse, and a higher percent are foreign-born, as represented in Figure 1.30. The echo boomers are also more educated than their parents were at the same ages, although they earn slightly less. In addition, more females of the echo boom generation are working. Echo boomers also tend to have greater financial resources than their parents did because they tend to have fewer siblings and wealthier parents. Finally, and perhaps most important, more of the leading-edge echo boomers live alone.[68] Because most of the population growth over the past fifty years has taken place in the South and the West, the echo boomers will probably have the greatest impact on the housing markets in these areas. They already make

---

[67] Joint Center for Housing Studies, *State of the Nation's Housing: 1999*, 9.
[68] Ibid.,10.

FIGURE 1.30
Leading Edge Echo Boomers Are More Diverse and Slower to Marry Than Original Boomers. Share of original and echo Boomers in each category at ages 18 to 22 (Percent)

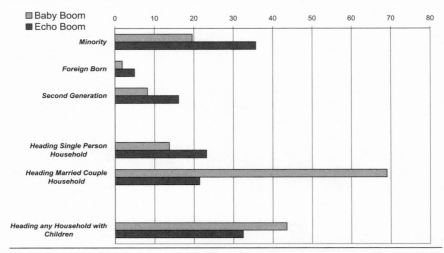

Source: Joint Center for Housing Studies, Harvard University. Household composition characteristics are from the 1968 and 1998 Current Population Surveys (CPS); echo boom rate and immigrant characteristics are from the 1998 CPS; baby boom rate and immigrant characteristics are from the 1970 Census PUMS files for people aged 20 to 24.

up a large share of the population in these two regions, and continued migration will only add to their concentration.

The Aging of the Population

While echo boomers will be a key component in housing demand in the twenty-first century, another trend will be even more significant: the aging of the population. Between 2000 and 2050, the elderly population in the United States will more than double, as shown in Figure 1.31. The driving force behind this trend is the aging of the baby boom generation; additional factors include longer life expectancies and a decline in births. In 2010, the first members of the baby boom generation will reach sixty-five; by 2030, the senior population is expected to reach 70 million, or a sizable 20% of the U.S. population.[69] By 2050, the share of people eighty-five

---

[69] Joint Center for Housing Studies, *Housing America's Seniors*, 3.

FIGURE 1.31
Elderly Population Will More Than Double, 2000–2050

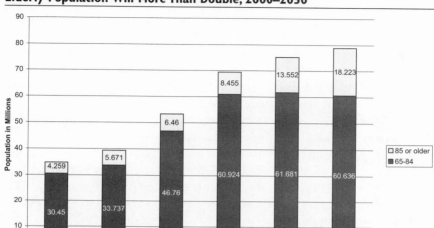

SOURCE: Joint Center for Housing Studies, Harvard University.
FROM: Day, Jennifer Cheseman, *Population Projections of the United States by Age, Sex, Race, and Hispanic Origin: 1995–2050.* U.S. Current Population Reports, Series P25-1130 (1996).

years or older will increase to nearly a quarter of the elderly population, compared with only one-seventh in 2000.[70]

This is partially due to people living longer and healthier lives. Life expectancy in the United States rose dramatically in the second half of the twentieth century thanks to factors such as medical advances and lifestyle changes. Men's life expectancy at birth increased from 65.6 years in 1950 to 73.6 years in 1997, while women's life expectancy at birth increased from 71.1 years in 1950 to 79.4 years in 1997.[71] The disability rate for persons aged sixty-five or older dropped by 14% between 1984 and 1994.[72] This kind of healthy aging will potentially increase seniors' ability to live self-sufficiently.

Unique characteristics of the growing generations of seniors will help to define their future housing needs. First, they are likely to have longer working careers, due to their tendency to live longer and their high educational attainment rates. Labor force participation for men over age sixty-five

---

[70] Ibid., 7.
[71] National Center for Health Statistics, *National Vital Statistics Report,* 17.
[72] Joint Center for Housing Studies, *Housing America's Seniors,* 15.

grew from 16.3% in 1991 to 17.1% in 1997.[73] Mandatory retirement ages have been largely eliminated, and private pension plans have removed many of the disincentives to continuing work past the age of sixty-five. Longer careers will probably impact the housing market by encouraging more seniors to remain in their current homes and/or communities, creating relatively less demand for assisted-living communities (although demand for such assisted-living arrangements will continue to grow due to the overall growth in the number of elderly households).

Baby boom seniors tend to have much better access to financial resources than previous elderly cohorts. In 1970, about one-quarter of Americans age sixty-five and over lived in poverty. By 2000, that dropped to one in ten.[74] In addition to Social Security, baby boomers retiring between 2010 and 2035 will be able to draw on large private pension funds, including individual retirement accounts, or IRAs, as well as 401(k) contribution plans. The increased wealth of seniors is likely to bring about high-quality senior communities, as well as a multitude of services for the senior population. In addition, baby boomers will be more likely to buy second homes than their parents were.[75]

Seniors live in a variety of settings and have different housing preferences although assisted living communities are often viewed as the most common retirement choice, surveys show that most seniors prefer to remain in their homes and in their communities. Figure 1.32 shows that most are able to remain in conventional housing. It is also important to note that smaller numbers of elderly from across the country are moving to popular retirement destinations such as Florida and Arizona.

One concern related to the aging of the population is that the smaller, post-baby boom populations will not be able to absorb the housing units left behind by the baby boomers and that the demand for new housing will drop. However, the number of young persons in the nation will exceed the number of elders in the first several decades of the twenty-first century, which implies that there will be adequate demand for housing. Larger numbers of young households ensures that the housing units vacated by older people will be filled and also increases the likelihood of continued new home building. This scenario is illustrated in Figure 1.33 which depicts the projected U.S. population in 2025. As the figure shows, the younger members of the U.S. population will exceed the older members.

---

[73] Ibid., 16.
[74] Ibid., 17.
[75] Ibid., 23.

FIGURE 1.32
Three Quarters of Seniors Live in Conventional Housing

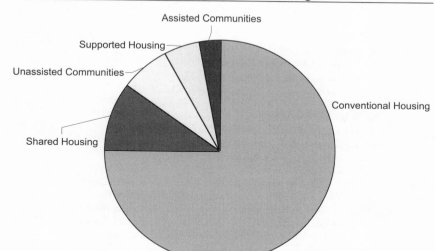

SOURCE: Joint Center for Housing Studies, Harvard University, Housing America's Seniors, 2000. Based on Joint Center tabulations of the 1993 AHEAD Survey. NOTE: Excludes persons living in long-term facilities such as nursing homes or other similar institutions.

It is interesting to contrast these projections to those of another highly industrialized nation, Germany. Figure 1.34 provides the same population information for Germany in 2025. Germany will have a far larger older cohort in the early part of the twenty-first century, and as it vacates housing units, it is very likely there will not be enough younger German households to consume existing housing stock, to build new housing, or to stimulate housing demand. The strength of the U.S. housing market forecast hinges on solid demand from younger households, but even more important is the strong demand from immigration discussed previously.

Conclusions

In reviewing the nation's housing over the past fifty years, we see that amazing progress has been made. Indeed, it is a story of major success. The quality of the housing stock today is unique in the country's history. The nation has successfully met many of the numerous housing challenges that existed at the end of World War II. Seriously dilapidated and crowded homes are a small minority of the nation's housing stock, and they are

FIGURE 1.33
Housing Demand in the U.S. in 2025

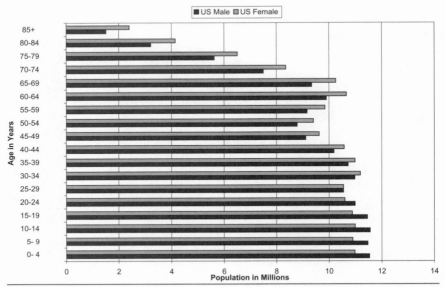

SOURCE: Housing America's Seniors, 1999. The Joint Center for Housing Studies, Harvard University.
DATA FROM: U.S. Census Bureau, International Data Base.

found primarily in inner cities and rural communities. The vast majority of homes have adequate plumbing and many contain two or more bathrooms. The challenges of immigration and of a swelling population in the baby boom era were met by large-scale building, creative financing, and the application of technology in the housing sector. Although single-family dwellings are a clear majority, the nation's current housing stock is diverse, so as to meet a variety of housing needs and desires. The numbers and demographic shifts discussed in this chapter are by and large very positive. Most Americans are well housed and enjoy an array of amenities in their homes.

As this chapter has shown, one of the major thrusts over the last fifty years of housing history has been to provide decent shelter for all Americans, and one of the primary features of public policy has been to provide an adequate supply of quality houses. The housing stock has been upgraded, and while maintenance, remodeling, and construction must continually occur, quality housing has become the standard in the United States at the beginning of the twenty-first century.

FIGURE 1.34
Housing Demand in Germany in 2025

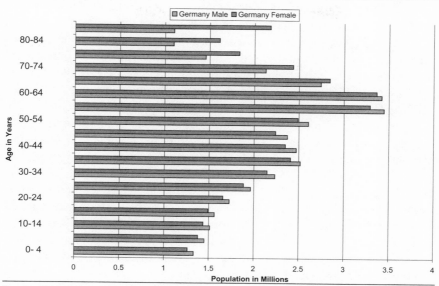

SOURCE: *Housing America's Seniors, 1999*. The Joint Center for Housing Studies, Harvard University.
DATA FROM: U.S. Census Bureau, International Data Base.

However, while housing quality has been a primary concern for the last fifty years, it has by no means been the only housing issue. The other major area of concern has been affordability. In the early 1980s, housing quality and affordability — especially for low-income households — was addressed in a report by the President's Commission on Housing. The report noted that all of the housing data related to quality pointed to continual improvement, with quality measured by the space available and the physical conditions of a housing unit. Even for lower-income families in the United States, the quality had greatly improved by the time the report was written, and it has continued to improve through the turn of the century.

Yet, this achievement in housing quality has come at an important price. The President's Commission on Housing highlighted that while adequate homes had become more plentiful, "the ability to pay for decent housing has become the predominant housing problem faced by the poor."[76] Further, while affordability is a question for many people, it disproportionately affects those households with very low incomes. As reported by the

[76] President's Commission on Housing, *Report of the President's Commission,* 3.

commission in 1982, over half of the very-low-income renters paid in excess of 30% of their income for housing.

The findings of the President's Commission on Housing were released about twenty years ago, and since that time the situation has only worsened. In the 1990s, housing costs rose at a rate greater than household incomes. In fact, many households in low-income brackets — many of which are minority households — are finding that it is more challenging to find a place to live at the close of the twentieth century than in previous decades. The number of affordable units has dropped in recent years, and in 1999 over 14 million owner and renter households spent more than half their incomes on housing.[77] At the same time, the stock of government-subsidized housing has shrunk as property owners are increasingly opting out of federal subsidy programs to secure higher market-rate rents. In the early 1980s, the President's Commission on Housing concluded that the emphasis on quality in the postwar years was very important and great strides had been made; continued emphasis on quality was important for the future, but the predominant problem was housing affordability. These conclusions are even more important at the end of the twentieth century: the emphasis of housing policy as we look to the future needs to be affordability, not just for very-low-income families, but for the many working families who pay large portions of their income on rent or home ownership.

The lack of investment in quality affordable housing for lower-income households signals that in coming decades many Americans will face serious housing problems. If housing prices continue to rise without comparable rises in income levels, there will be problems for both those unable to afford costly homes and for private home builders. Fortunately, many people in the housing sector have identified these on-going problems and acknowledge that changes need to be made. A number of organizations and individuals involved in housing are focusing their attention on affordability. If the nation is able to channel its energy and resources toward housing affordability in the same manner that it approached the housing quality issue after World War II, then another success story may be possible. However, there is still a great deal to be done to tackle these challenges. More people — private citizens, government at the federal, state, and local levels, and the various industries involved in providing housing for the nation — need to acknowledge that housing must consistently be a high priority. The potential to make progress exists; the challenge at the beginning of the twenty-first century is to turn this potential into reality.

---

[77] Joint Center for Housing Studies: 1999. *State of the Nation's Housing.*

Chapter 2

HOMEOWNERSHIP

Owning a home is an important goal for many Americans and is a central facet of American life. Homeownership has become particularly prominent and more widely accessible since the close of World War II. Remarkable progress has been made in terms of increased levels of homeownership, and this legacy of progress serves as a backdrop to this chapter. The homeownership rate is broadly defined as the proportion of households that own their own homes. Figure 2.1 displays the homeownership

FIGURE 2.1
Homeownership Rates in the United States, 1950–2001

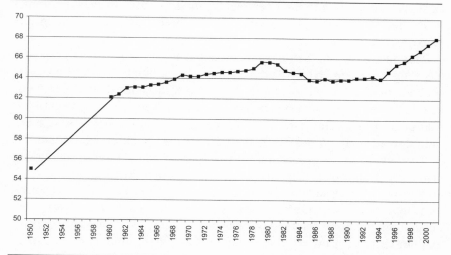

Source: 1950: U.S. Census Bureau, Historical Census of Housing Tables www.census/gov/hhes/www/housing/census/historic/owner.html; 1960–1999: "Housing Vacancies and Homeownership, Annual Statistics (2000)" (www.census.gov/hhes/www/housing/hvs/annual00/ann00t12.html).

Note: The U.S. Census Bureau reports two numbers for 1993 due to methodological revisions—the 1993 number on the chart is an average of the two. Also, there is no annual data available for 1951–1959, thus a straight line has been drawn on the chart between 1950–1960 data points.

rates in the United States from 1950 through 2001.[1] In 1950, the rate was 55%; fifty-one years later, it had risen to an impressive 68%. From 1950 through the late 1970s, the rate increased steadily. In the 1980s there was a decade-long leveling off and in some years a decline in the homeownership rate. However, this decline was reversed during the 1990s, and at the beginning of the twenty-first century homeownership was at the highest level in U.S. history.

When discussing the concept of homeownership and what it means in America, it is critical to recognize that homeownership is varied and complex. Homeownership varies dramatically from region to region, between urban and rural areas, among different racial and ethnic groups, and according to owner profiles. There is also a great deal of variety in the types of homes a person can own, including single-family detached homes, single-family attached homes such as townhouses, and manufactured housing (mobile homes). Homeownership is also linked to cultural ideas about what it means to be successful and independent in America. Owning a home can facilitate social mobility, but it can also restrict the geographic mobility of a given household over time. It is linked as well to a household's income and to the economy; a home is a large financial commitment and can restrict a household's spending, yet owning a home can translate into equity and become a primary source of wealth. Homeownership simultaneously provides a household with both freedom and responsibility.

America has a long history of and penchant for homeownership, and it has long been perceived as positive. Owning a home not only provides shelter, but it promotes economic and social well-being. This general attitude has often been supported by our political leaders, and as a result it has translated into a number of pro-homeownership public policies. In addition, homeownership is a key piece of American popular culture and one of the leading tangible signs of the "American dream." The concept of ownership, of control over one's living space, is associated with independence and prosperity. Buying a first home is often viewed as a rite of passage, and to many, it brings with it a wide range of intangible assets, such as better education for children, increased net worth, and a sense of community.

Both renter and owner households in the United States live in single-family detached housing. In 1997, 82.1% of owners and 24.6% of renters

[1] For the homeownership rate data in this chapter, "Historical Census of Housing Tables" U.S. Census Bureau is used for 1900–1950. From 1960 onward, "Housing Vacancies and Homeownership Annual Statistics (1999)" (U.S. Census Bureau, *www.census.gov/hhes/www/housing/hvs/annual99/ann99t12.html* is used.)

lived in single-family detached homes.[2] Clearly, there is a strong correlation between homeownership status and single-family detached dwellings. While it is important to bear this link in mind, it is equally important to note the ownership options which have continued to grow over the last fifty years.

HOMEOWNERSHIP IN HISTORICAL PERSPECTIVE

The ways in which people design, use, modify, and define their homes has changed significantly in the last fifty years, and homeownership has evolved in relation to these changes. In reviewing the history of housing and its ownership in the United States, it is important to bear in mind that many housing policies and innovations have been developed in response to housing need. Often, at the most basic level, housing policies are attempts to provide shelter for those in need or to rectify discrimination in housing or ownership patterns. The historical trends related to ownership and pro-homeowner policies provide an essential backdrop to understanding housing in the twenty-first century.

Homeownership Trends Prior to World War II

It has long been an American ideal to own land and a home, and to be self-sufficient. In 1900, close to half of all U.S. households were home owners, as evidenced by the homeownership rate of 46.5% reported by the U.S. Census Bureau.[3] This rate declined moderately until the early 1920s, when it was bolstered by a new phase of economic prosperity. During this period there was a great deal of building activity, and it tended to focus on single-family dwellings.[4] Between 1921 and 1928, the number of home-owners increased significantly more than the number of renters, the first time this had happened since 1880.[5] Figure 2.2 displays the homeownership rates for the twentieth century. It shows the rise in ownership during the 1920s, from 45.6% in 1920 to 47.8% in 1930. These gains were modest, though important given that the 1920s were preceded by small declines in homeownership and followed by the severe economic decline of the depression. In fact, it was not until after World War II that a majority of the families in the United States would become home owners.

---

[2] U.S. Census Bureau, "American Housing Survey, 1997," www.census.gov/hhes/www/housing/ahs/97adtchrt/tab3-1.html and www.census.gov/hhes/www/housing/ahs/97bdtchrt/tab4-1.html.

[3] U.S. Census Bureau, "Historical Census of Housing Tables."

[4] Doan, *American Housing Production,* 31.

[5] Ibid.

FIGURE 2.2
Homeownership in the Twentieth Century

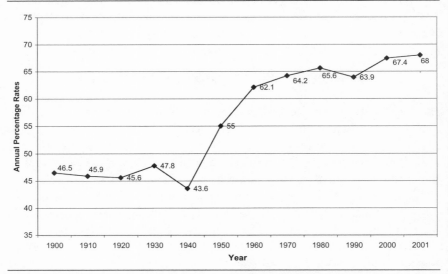

SOURCE: 1900–1950: U.S. Census Bureau, "Historical Census of Housing Tables" www.census.gov/hhes/
www/housing/census/historic/owner.html; 1960–2000: U.S. Census Bureau, "Housing Vacancies and
Homeownership Annual Statistics" (www.census.gov/hhes/www/housing/hvs/annual00/ ann00t12.html).

With the onset of the Great Depression, the ownership rates, as well as
general housing availability, affordability, and adequacy, spiraled downward. The economic downturn, affecting the United States and other nations around the world, resulted in widespread job loss and reductions in
income. An immediate result was foreclosures and evictions, both of
which soared.[6] With the lack of capital and demand to fuel home building,
the construction industry succumbed to the spreading crisis. The housing
finance system was pushed to its limits, and the mortgages financed in the
1920s could not withstand the series of changes and pressures brought on
by the economic upheaval. Figure 2.2 again reveals the devastating trend
of the 1930s, when the ownership rate declined from 47.8% in 1930 to
43.6% in 1940. The federal government stepped in on a number of fronts.
Two early attempts to ameliorate the situation were the Federal Home
Loan Bank Act in 1932 and the Home Owners Loan Act of 1933. Both of
these were targeted to help home owner households refinance existing
mortgages, pay taxes, and fund housing maintenance.[7]

---

[6] Hays, *Federal Government,* 85.
[7] These federal acts are discussed in greater detail in Chapters 4 and 5.

The next important development during this time of crisis was the passage of the National Housing Act in 1934, which established the Federal Housing Administration (FHA). This was more encompassing than previous federal efforts to help home owners or to help the housing finance system. In effect, the FHA restructured the way in which people borrowed money to buy a home by introducing the long-term, low-down-payment, fully amortized, level-payment mortgage.[8] In the following excerpt James Johnson describes the effects and the legacy of the FHA and how it affected the potential for homeownership:

> The 1934 housing act gave banks the guarantees and confidence to lend again. It gave home owners the chance to obtain a single mortgage covering a large portion of a home's appraised value. It extended the length of mortgages, usually to thirty years, and made monthly amortization of principle and interest a common part of homeownership. But the act accomplished much of this indirectly and gradually, only as its ripple effects were felt over the years.[9]

The FHA grew over time to support more widespread homeownership. However, it was not an immediate remedy for the dire circumstances faced by so many American households during the 1930s. Housing problems plagued the nation until the start of World War II. In 1940, the homeownership rate dipped to its lowest level of the century, 43.6%.[10] Despite federal and local efforts, people were unable to purchase homes during the depression years. Families tended to pool resources, consolidate into larger households and form fewer households, with many adult children remaining in their parent's homes. Anxiety about housing soared and ownership declined.

It is important to recognize the strong penchant for homeownership in the United States.[11] As Mary Lockwood Matthews stated in 1931 in her basic text on home economics, "A separate house surrounded by a yard is the ideal kind of home."[12] Or as Kenneth T. Jackson characterized it in his book *Crabgrass Frontier,* "The dream of a detached house in a safe, quiet, and peaceful place has been an important part of the Anglo-American past."[13] The depression, because of the policies and programs established during those years, as well as its psychological and cultural impact, only

---

[8] Hays, *Federal Government,* 85.
[9] Johnson, *Showing America,* 44–45.
[10] U.S. Census Bureau, "Historical Census of Housing Tables."
[11] For a fascinating discussion of the roots and evolution of homeownership and suburbanization in the United States, see Jackson, *Crabgrass Frontier,* especially 3–11; 45–72; 116–137; and 283–305.
[12] Matthews, *Elementary Home Economics,* 45.
[13] Jackson, *Crabgrass Frontier,* 288.

heightened this desire. Indeed, out of the depression came the foundation for the growth in homeownership over the next fifty years. Today's housing finance system and pro-homeownership policies were formed in a context of dire need and in an attempt to help people fulfill their basic need and desire for affordable shelter and a home of their own.

How the War Transformed the Nation's Housing

The outbreak of war around the globe in the early 1940s yanked the United States out of economic turmoil. Of course, the war itself was a new kind of turmoil, but the changes it fostered radically altered the nation's economic base. First, there was an immediate and imperative demand for products to fuel war activities such as building planes and ships. Second, as manufacturing centers were created to build such products, it was necessary to bring a supply of workers to these areas. The early 1940s saw huge demographic shifts as workers moved to the newly forming industrial centers. In particular, the West Coast attracted large numbers of people. Between 1940 and 1947, the combined population of California, Washington, and Oregon jumped by nearly 40%.[14] This situation promptly stimulated home building in these new war-production regions.

Interestingly, homeownership also increased during the war years. The data available is somewhat limited, yet it is clear that homeownership increased, and after the war it skyrocketed — thus launching the homeownership rate to well over 50%, where it would remain for the rest of the twentieth century. The Census Bureau reports that between 1940 and 1950, the homeownership rate increased dramatically from 43.6% to 55%.[15] This 11.4% increase is the largest in a single decade in the twentieth century, as outlined in Figure 2.3, which shows the shifts in homeownership rates by decade. The second highest period of growth was from 1950 to 1960, with a 7.1% increase. In 1945, the U.S. Census Bureau conducted a sample survey which showed that the number of home owners rose from 15,196,000 to 20,009,000 between 1940 and 1945; this means that the homeownership rate during this five-year span could have risen from 43.6% to as high as 53.2%.[16] While this 1945 sample survey is not as rigorous as the data from the 1940 and 1950 census, it indicates that significant change occurred between 1940 and 1945 in terms of owner-occupied homes in the United States. The largest rush into homeownership likely

---

[14] Albrecht, *World War II,* xxii.

[15] This is using decennial census data, from U.S. Census Bureau, "Historical Census of Housing Tables."

[16] U.S. Census Bureau, *Historical Statistics of the United States,* 646.

FIGURE 2.3
Percentage Rate of Increase or Decrease

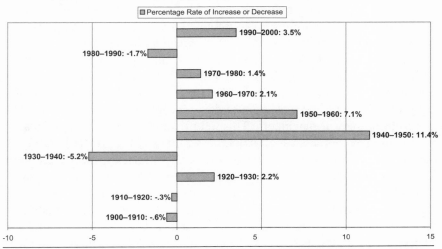

SOURCE: 1900–1950: U.S. Census Bureau, "Historical Census of housing Tables: Homeownership" (www.census/gov/hhes/www.housing/census/historic.owner.html); 1950–2000: U.S. Census Bureau, "Housing Vacancies and Homeownership: Annual Statistics" (www.census.gov/hhes/www/housing/hvs/annual00/ann00t12.html).

happened around the middle of the 1940s — coinciding with the passage of the GI Bill, the end of World War II, and the return of servicemen from overseas.

In the early 1940s, the homeownership increase was largely a result of people finding work in the war industries and the creation of new "defense homes" in manufacturing regions. These homes were created by the Defense Homes Corporation (founded by Congress in June of 1940) in the Washington, D.C. area and in other defense production areas for military officials and other workers involved in defense building for the country.[17] During this period, the federal government opened several other financial incentives for people to own a home. For example, the FHA was allowed to insure mortgages under more liberal terms, the number of years for loan repayment was extended from twenty to thirty, and in 1942 a new program, titled War Housing Insurance, was created.[18] These changes made it easier for families and individuals — especially those working in the war industries — to become home owners during the war years. The gains were

---

[17] Congressional Research Service Report. "A Chronology of Housing Legislation," 17.
[18] Ibid, 17–19.

moderate in comparison to the number of home owners added to the population around the close of World War II, yet it is important to note that ownership was on the rise even before the end of the war and the return of the GIs.

In many ways, the domestic building activity and the increase in home-ownership during the war significantly shaped the housing boom after the war. For instance, there was tension during the war years as to the type of housing to build — government public housing or more traditional private-enterprise building. The government essentially put public housing on hold during the war.[19] The focus was instead on defense housing and on building war machinery. This left private builders largely in charge of creating new homes, which helped pave the way for private building in the postwar period. From 1940 to 1949, 96% of the new units were built by independent builders.[20] The war also helped forge new relationships. Donald Albrecht notes that one of the most important new relationships was between military, scientific, and academic interests.[21] One outcome of this was the creation of new products, such as plywood and fiberglass. These items in turn were used to make the new defense homes efficient and moderately priced. The increase in new jobs and new housing communities translated into rises in homeownership.[22] These defense homes, designed to rapidly move people into their own homes, laid the framework for the development of postwar suburban housing communities. Prior to the war, many building companies, large and small, had focused on localized building; when the war began, the entire construction industry was asked to produce goods in a frenzy.[23] Home builders were asked to build near defense industries, to build rapidly, and to do so despite material shortages and supply restrictions. The shake up and movement during the war years meant that when the war came to a close, people would be settling in new areas and with new household patterns, thus poised for an increase in home building and homeownership.

The piece of legislation perhaps most crucial to making homeownership a widespread option was the GI Bill of Rights, passed by Congress on June 22, 1944. This bill was generated to help ease the return of servicemen to civilian life, the "dream home" being a central part of the envisioned postwar life. As servicemen fought overseas, home was idealized,

---

[19] Dreier, "Labor's Love Lost?," 330.

[20] Mason, *History of Housing,* 36.

[21] Albrecht, *World War II,*. xxiii.

[22] Again, although the data is scarce on homeownership during this period, it appears that there were gains from 1940 to1945 (as opposed to declines experienced during the 1930s), yet the bulk of the growth in ownership was experienced from 1945 to 1950.

[23] Mason, *History of Housing,* 34–35.

and the idea of living in a house in peace and safety became a vision for many. The GI Bill was also very practical. Without some type of financial assistance, the sheer number of troops returning home could easily overwhelm the nation. Even with preparation and attempts to build more homes, materials were scarce, and many government agencies were overwhelmed with the transition from war to peacetime. In 1945, veterans were returning home at a rate of 25,000 per week, and many found themselves living in temporary homes or trailers, or crowding in with relatives.[24] However, after initial difficulties, builders were able to venture into new projects with large-scale planning efforts.

The GI Bill established the Veterans Administration housing program, which offered federal guarantees for mortgages for returning servicemen. Over time, these came to be known as VA loans. Both VA and FHA loan programs made it possible for new households to build decent homes at an affordable price. These programs offer mortgage insurance backed by the federal government (see Chapters 4 and 5 for further detail). In essence, the government guaranteed the credit for veterans given the fact that they were unable to establish good credit while serving in the military. The loan guarantee program was a means of putting veterans on equal footing with their nonveteran peers.[25] This government backing provided a great deal of financial security and confidence, which in turn stimulated the private sector to raise capital for housing finance and building programs. The VA loans were also designed to offer very low down payments. Originally, up to 50% of the loan could be guaranteed, but not to exceed $2,000, and loans were limited to twenty years with a maximum interest rate of 4%. These loans could be used to purchase, construct, improve, or repair any type of residential property. In 1950, the legislation was changed so that 60% of the loan could be guaranteed, but not to exceed $7,500, and the loans were extended to thirty years.[26] These developments, in conjunction with the changes brought about by the war and wartime production, set the stage for a postwar boom in home building and ownership.

Rising to New Heights: The Expansion of Homeownership from 1945–1960

The postwar years were significant in the history of housing and homeownership. As described earlier, the bulk of the owners added from 1940

---

[24] Ibid., 45.
[25] U.S. Department of Veteran Affairs, "Legislative History."
[26] Ibid.

to 1950 were likely added around or shortly after 1945. This time period
saw the largest gains in homeownership in the twentieth century, as detailed in Figures 2.2, 2.3, and 2.4. Throughout the twentieth century, the
actual number of owners increased, although the ownership rate is, of
course, determined by the relationship of owners to other nonowning
households. Figure 2.4 depicts the rise in the number of owners in the
United States from over 7 million in 1900 to nearly 71 million in 2000.[27]
Between 1940 and 1950 alone, the number of owners rose by nearly 8.4
million. Figure 2.5 substantiates the argument that the largest gains in
homeownership were made around 1945 and shortly thereafter. It shows
that the amount loaned for one- to four-family houses between 1945 and
1946 rose from $4.9 million to $10 million, more than doubling the dollars owed on mortgage loans. This translates into more households taking
out loans and becoming home owners. The other significant leap in the
amount of money provided for home loans was between 1949 and 1950;
as seen in Figure 2.5, the amount lent for mortgages rose from about $11
million in 1949 to $16 million in 1950.

This era was marked not only by rises in ownership, but by broad
changes in attitude about community, leisure time, the economy, and job
opportunities. After the long Depression years and the war, Americans
were ready for new housing options, innovative designs, and stable communities. Homeownership was one way to make these desires a reality. Immediately following the war, new households formed, new jobs became
available, and there was a large amount of spending. A good economy and
solid incomes made it possible for people to purchase newly built homes,
and the construction of new homes, in turn, continued to fuel the economy.
This era is characterized by the formation of families and the birth of the
"baby boom" children. It is also characterized by a new relationship between private industry and the federal government. The government, which
had played a major role during the depression and wartime, continued to
play a large role in peacetime. Rising housing demands meant upward
pressure on construction costs, real estate prices, and rents, especially in a
situation where the time for housing construction was lengthy and additions to the stock of housing each year were modest.[28] In light of this, the
federal government intervened in a number of ways to keep home prices affordable. A partnership evolved as private industry expanded its capacity to

[27] U.S. Census Bureau, "Housing Vacancies and Homeownership: Second Quarter 2000."
[28] Doan, *American Housing Production,* 55.

FIGURE 2.4
Number of Home Owners in the United States, 1900–2001

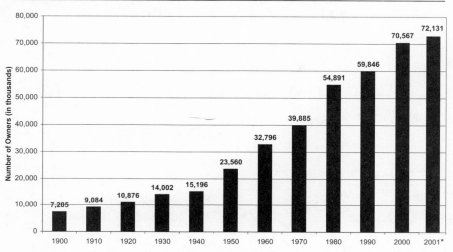

SOURCE: 1900–1970: U.S. Census Bureau, *Historical Statistics of the United States;* 1980–2000: U.S. Census Bureau, "Households by Tenure, Race, and Hispanic Origin."
*Number of owner-occupied units for First Quarter, 2001. http://www.census.gov/hhes/www/housing/hvs/q102prss.pdf

build and continued to build and profit from the strong demand, and the government made it feasible for more people to purchase these new homes.

The Housing Act of 1949 proved to be pivotal in the housing industry broadly, and for homeownership specifically. The major government program created by the act was the urban renewal program, which provided new funds for public housing, slum clearance, and redevelopment.[29] The act also expanded already existing housing programs. For example, it provided millions of dollars for FHA mortgage insurance, and changed and expanded the role of the Federal National Mortgage Association (FNMA), also known as Fannie Mae. Fannie Mae had been created in 1938 to serve the secondary market, meaning it was not a direct lending institution but rather an entity that worked with lenders to ensure that they did not run out of mortgage funds. Mortgage originators serving the primary market were allowed to sell mortgages in the secondary market to replenish their funds and generate new loans. When it was first established, Fannie Mae was only authorized to buy FHA-insured loans.[30] With the passage of the

[29] Von Hoffman, "A Study in Contradictions," 310.
[30] Fannie Mae, "Fannie Mae: Who We Are."

FIGURE 2.5
Mortgage Loans on 1- to 4-Family Homes, 1925 to 1950

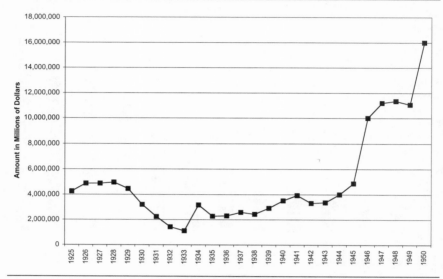

SOURCE: U.S. Census Bureau, Historical Statistics of the United States, 649.

Housing Act of 1949, Fannie Mae was authorized to act more broadly, purchasing mortgages for rental and cooperative housing, FHA mortgages on single-family homes, and VA-guaranteed mortgages.[31] Thus the act stimulated increasing homeownership across the nation.[32]

Policy makers in the ensuing decades have looked back to this act and acknowledged its goals and ideals while trying to forge their own new policies and meet shifting housing priorities.[33]

Throughout the 1950s, homeownership rates steadily increased, leaping from 55% in 1950 to 62.1% in 1960 — an increase of 7.1% (see Figure 2.3). Part of this increase was due to the sale of mobile homes. Mobile homes were one of the innovations resulting from new partnerships between science, government, and business; new materials created and used during the war now made new types of homes possible. The number of owned mobile homes (called manufactured homes since 1974) rose by 452,000 between 1950 and 1960.[34] Another part of the continued rise in

---

[31] Johnson, *Showing America,* 57.
[32] Von Hoffman, "A Study in Contradictions," 314.
[33] Ibid., 322.
[34] U.S. Census Bureau. "Census of Population and Housing" www.census.gov.

homeownership was that employment became increasingly decentralized, allowing people to purchase or build homes in outlying areas — newly created suburbs — where property was less expensive.[35] In the year 1950, more than a third of the 1.95 million new homes built were built in suburbia.[36]There was a rapid association between homeownership and suburban lifestyles where people owned single-family detached homes. During this span of time, the housing shortage dissipated as new homes were built and new ways of living were devised. There was a great deal of creativity and ingenuity as new partnerships were formed between builders and architects. New home decorating and architectural magazines were published. All of this added to the atmosphere of prosperity and helped increase the desirability of homeownership.

The decreased emphasis on public housing during the 1950s helped accelerate private housing production. Incomes were rising for the majority of American households, and many could afford the new homes being built. In conjunction with increased private building were new quality and safety standards for home building. The FHA established minimum housing construction standards that virtually became the norm.[37] Also, advances in building materials, delivery systems, installation, and prefabricated materials helped homes to be built and renovated more cheaply. This translated into more ownership options for more people. Notably, the period from about 1930 through the 1950s was the lowest point for immigration into the U.S. in the twentieth century. Newly-arrived immigrant households tend to be part of the renter population. In the early 1900s, immigrant households were a large percentage of the renter population, but given that fewer people immigrated to the United States during the war and in the 1950s, a smaller pool of people were likely to be renters during this period. With this decreased number of foreign-born immigrants and a favorable economy, fewer people chose renting as a housing option.

Consistent Homeownership Increases: 1960–1980

In the 1960s and 1970s, homeownership grew slowly but steadily. As Figure 2.3 shows, the rate increased by 3.5% from 1960 to 1980. Given the growing social and political unrest in the country in the 1960s, many of the housing initiatives around this time were formulated to manage

---

[35] Doan, *American Housing Production,* 74.
[36] Mason, *History of Housing,* 63.
[37] Dreier, "Labor's Love Lost?," 349.

growing urban social problems. The civil rights movement gave a growing voice to African Americans and other minorities in the United States, and then gave further momentum to women's and gay rights movements into the 1970s. Many people gained a new political voice and called for change, and part of this call for change included continued advances in housing options — especially for the poor and for minorities.

Thus Congress passed the Civil Rights Act of 1968, also known as the Fair Housing Act. This was the first major piece of legislation to address the problem of housing discrimination. It also tried to address the decline in urban neighborhoods and affirmed the 1949 commitment to "a decent home and a suitable living environment for every American."[38] While there were many parts to this legislation and a great deal of controversy surrounding some aspects of its formation and implementation, the pieces of the legislation relating to homeownership were particularly beneficial. The act (and its companion legislation in 1969 and 1970) was key in re-structuring the secondary mortgage market. The agencies that were created (or reformulated) during this time were Fannie Mae, Ginnie Mae, and Freddie Mac. Fannie Mae had been given a new role by the Housing Act of 1949, and it continued to be modified by various legislative actions through 1968. However, with this new act, Fannie Mae was transformed into a Government-Sponsored Enterprise (GSE), which operates as a private company with its own private capital. The goal was to allow the organization to move beyond its governmental loan limits to meet the need of a broader cross-section of American society.[39]

At the same time, the Government National Mortgage Association (GNMA), known as Ginnie Mae, was created to enhance the FHA's role in insuring housing for lower-income disadvantaged households. Ginnie Mae bought mortgages on higher risk low-income housing projects at a higher price, then resold them at market rates; the loss was absorbed as a government subsidy.[40] Ginnie Mae remains a government agency within HUD and deals exclusively with FHA-insured and VA-guaranteed loans. In 1970, as a companion piece of legislation to the 1968 act, the Federal Home Loan Mortgage Corporation (FHLMC) or Freddie Mac, was cre-ated as part of the Federal Home Loan Bank system. Then, in 1989, Fred-die Mac was given a similar charter to Fannie Mae, and today both GSEs function as stockholder-owned corporations. As GSEs, both companies

---

[38] Doan, *American Housing Production*, 83.
[39] Fannie Mae, "Fannie Mae: Who We Are."
[40] Hays, *The Federal Government*, 89.

are linked to the federal government in that they have a small line of credit with the Treasury, and they are regulated by the government; however, they are private companies that pay federal taxes and operate under separate stockholder-controlled boards. Both work to promote and increase homeownership, but they compete with each other in the secondary market arena, thus keeping housing costs and interest rates lower.[41] (The activities of Fannie Mae, Freddie Mac, and Ginne Mae will be discussed further in Chapters 4 and 5.)

The social and political turmoil at the end of the 1960s and in the early 1970s greatly affected a number of housing policies. Yet in the area of homeownership, the new legislation was particularly beneficial. The newly formed secondary mortgage market greatly expanded the means to finance home purchases. Homeownership rates continued to climb through the 1970s as baby boomers began to form households and purchase their first homes. Higher inflation rates during the 1970s made homeownership an important investment as a hedge against rising prices; and during this time, a home became more than just a place to raise a family, it offered a more secure financial future.[42] Also noticeable in this era was the rise in manufactured housing, condominiums and townhouses; each of these types of housing expanded the range of ownership opportunities. Condominiums and townhouses in particular offer options in urban, high-density areas where ownership is otherwise often limited. The number of American households entering into homeownership continued to rise through the end of the 1970s. In 1980, there were nearly 54.9 million home owners in the United States (see Figure 2.4) and the ownership rate had climbed to 65.6% — a dramatic increase from the wartime low of 43.6% in 1940.[43]

In short, during this period of time people had more options for buying a home in terms of both housing type and financing. This period of unprecedented success — extending from the late 1940s through the 1970s — was pivotal in shaping the ways in which homes were built, paid for, and used over time. Homeownership became even more entrenched as a cornerstone of the American way of life. Rising levels of ownership, however, did not mean that all housing problems had diminished. In fact, serious problems remained, and there were still groups of people who

[41] Freddie Mac, "12 Questions About Freddie Mac."
[42] Johnson, *Showing America*, 57.
[43] U.S. Census Bureau, "Households, by Tenure" (www.census.gov/population/socdemo/hh-fam/htabHH-5.txt, 7 August 2000).

were systematically shut out of homeownership due to racial/ethnic background, income level, or both.

From Stagnation to Soaring Rates: Homeownership in the 1980s and 1990s

The burgeoning homeownership rates the nation enjoyed through the 1990s were rather quickly shadowed by nearly a decade of declining rates from the early 1980s through 1995. Figure 2.4 shows that the gains in the number of home owners from 1980 to 1990 were moderate — just under 5 million — when compared to the gains in the preceding decade and later in the 1990s. One cause of this decline was that the inflation of the 1970s ultimately led to a sharp spike in interest rates, in some cases 14% or more for mortgages.[44] In addition, from 1970 to 1985 the proportion of the population classified as poor increased from 12% to a high of 14%.[45] At the same time, the stock of inexpensive housing shrank.[46] Most of the poor households were renters, and as their rents rose disproportionately to their incomes, the possibility of ever purchasing their own homes diminished. The "new poor" of the early 1980s did not achieve the same progress in home purchase that earlier generations of the poor did.[47] Many of these households were headed by women and tended to be concentrated in central cities. Also, the new poor were in service sector jobs that often had irregular work, few benefits, and — most importantly — less potential for upward mobility.

Unemployment rose during the early 1980s, further compounding housing problems and preventing homeownership. Both renters and home owners were struggling to find affordable housing. Also, the number of homeless people grew significantly. In the early 1980s the term *homelessness* was not widely known, and indeed no clear records of homelessness were kept.[48] However, people living on the streets became far more visible and further added to the growing array of housing problems. In response to growing homelessness and lack of access to adequate, affordable housing, many nonprofit organizations, some of which were religiously affiliated, were formed to address the problems at both the local and national

---

[44] Johnson, *Showing America,* 64.
[45] Clay, "Homeownership for the Poor," 7.
[46] Steinbach, "Hourglass Market," 570.
[47] Clay, "Homeownership for the Poor," 14.
[48] Hays, *Federal Government,* 245.

levels. For example, Habitat for Humanity was formed in 1976 and expanded in the 1980s to help build homes across the country with volunteer labor and donated funds.[49] This type of grassroots intervention shows the seriousness of the need and the strength of the belief that all people should have access to a safe and well-built home.

In 1990, the Cranston-Gonzales National Affordable Housing Act was passed. The act was stimulated by the recommendations of The Report of the National Housing Task Force, which was published in March 1988 and chaired by James W. Rouse and David O. Maxwell (it is often referred to as the Rouse/Maxwell Task Force).[50] It emphasized the role of state and local governments to provide affordable housing programs. The legislation had two key components. The first was the Home Investment Partnerships Act, known as the HOME program. Recommended by the Rouse/Maxwell Task Force, HOME is a block grant program designed to provide money to state and local governments for affordable housing. The block grants have matching fund requirements and must be used to develop or support affordable rental housing or homeownership programs.[51] The program helps construct new units and rehabilitate older ones for both ownership and rental housing. The HOME program encourages partnerships among private, public, and nonprofit organizations by providing incentives for profit and nonprofit developers to produce housing for low-income households, thereby filling a gap that the private sector often does not address.[52]

The second program was the HOPE program; HOPE stands for Housing Opportunities for People Everywhere. This slogan reflected a desire to move out of the slump of the 1980s and to work to give everyone access to quality housing. It was also a reaffirmation of pro-homeownership policies. The program was based on the fundamental belief that home- ownership would engender self-sufficiency and personal pride. There were three components to the program known as HOPE I, HOPE II, and HOPE III. HOPE I and II provided for conversion of existing multifamily rental housing to ownership and to resident self-management. HOPE III was designed to help single-family home buyers become owners in developments of one to four units owned or held by government organizations such

---

[49] Habitat for Humanity, "A Brief Introduction."
[50] Report of the National Housing Task Force, "A Decent Place to Live."
[51] Van Vliet, *Encyclopedia of Housing,* 228.
[52] U.S. Department of Housing and Urban Development, "Affordable Housing."

as HUD, state or local governments, public or Indian housing authorities, and the Department of Veterans Affairs.[53] In general, HOPE made it possible for either existing or recently purchased public housing (housing owned by government agencies) to be rehabilitated and sold to low-income, first-time buyers. In many cases, the property was sold to residents already living in the public housing; the idea was for the housing to be sold to tenant management organizations, eventually leading to individual ownership by the tenants. Many affordable housing programs had been cut by the federal government during the 1980s. The National Affordable Housing Act was a response to this and an attempt to help increase housing affordability and homeownership in the 1990s.

The downswing in homeownership rates and the general proliferation of housing problems during the 1980s and early 1990s shook the housing sector. Particularly harmful was the economic recession of the early 1990s. Difficult economic times meant that fewer households could gather money for down payments, and that owners were challenged to meet their monthly mortgage and general maintenance costs. However, this scenario changed rapidly as the economy began to recover and swiftly moved into a period of unprecedented growth facilitated by demographic shifts, new federal policies, and economic restructuring. These changes stimulated new home construction, remodeling, and a rise in home purchases. In 1995, the homeownership rate began making noticeable gains, thus breaking the series of declines endured since the early 1980s. In this same year, the National Partners in Home Ownership was established and coordinated by HUD. The goal of this partnership was to bring together public and private organizations to pool their ideas, energy, and resources to increase homeownership opportunities around the country. The organizations involved represented lenders, real estate professionals, Realtors, home builders, nonprofit housing providers, and federal, state, and local governments.[54] Members included the American Bankers Association, America's Community Bankers, Habitat for Humanity International, Fannie Mae, Freddie Mac, the Association of Community Organizations for Reform Now (ACORN), the Mortgage Bankers Association, the National Association of Home Builders, the National Association of Realtors, Homeownership Opportunities for Women, the National Association for the Advancement of Colored People (NAACP), the Mortgage Insurance

---

[53] Van Vliet, *Encyclopedia of Housing,* 238.
[54] National Association of Realtors, "Community Involvement."

Companies of America, the Urban Land Institute, the National Hispanic Housing Council, and the U.S. Department of Energy.

The end of the twentieth century saw homeownership surging to new heights, and this has continued into the early part of the twenty-first century. For the year 1999 the ownership rate climbed to 66.8%, in the year 2000 the rate rose again to 67.4%, and in 2001 it was at the highest level in U.S. history at 68%. This translates to more than 72 million home-owning households in the country at the end of 2001.[55] This is an addition of 12.3 million owners since 1990, and 17.2 million since 1980.[56] (See Figure 2.4.) The increase is due largely to a robust housing finance system and a booming economy in which people were spending a great deal, making home improvements, and building larger homes with more amenities. Continued commitment on the part of community organizations, nonprofits, and religious organizations has also helped families and individuals attain homeownership. Also, in the 1990s many lenders, along with Fannie Mae and Freddie Mac, widened the ways in which they provided loans to low-income households; some of the newer strategies included low or no down payment products, flexible underwriting standards, and improved risk assessment tools.[57] Additionally, advances in telecommunications and computer technology have enhanced the speed, access, and capabilities of lenders, and this has advanced the homeownership cause.

A strong trend toward ownership emerges from this overview, and it is clear that more households are living in adequate, safe homes that they own than in previous decades. Further, the historical evidence shows that homeownership has increased in popularity, has become more firmly linked to governmental policies, and is a pivotal aspect of the wealth of many households. In the twenty-first century, homeownership will continue to be a central goal for many Americans and will continue to be an important financial and political topic.

Nevertheless, the rising rates do not mean that homeownership is no longer an area of concern and will not be a challenge for some people in the future. Fundamental problems still exist concerning who has access to homeownership and who does not. Also, some owners find that ownership is overall more of a strain than a benefit. As noted at the beginning of this chapter, homeownership is complicated and each home owner is different. It is therefore important to examine how ownership impacts people

---

[55] U.S. Census Bureau, "Housing Vacancies."
[56] U.S. Census Bureau, "Households, by Tenure."
[57] Joint Center for Housing Studies, *State of the Nation's Housing 2000*, 2.

financially, socially, and psychologically when trying to decide if ownership is a wise option for a specific household.

A CLOSER LOOK AT THE BENEFITS OF HOMEOWNERSHIP

Homeownership provides benefits ranging from the personal to the political to the financial. For example, it is thought to improve commitment to
local politics and to forge strong community bonds. The seeds for such beliefs were planted in the early twentieth century, expanded during the recession, and solidified in the postwar era. As pro-home owner policies
have become the norm, academic researchers have tried to identify what is
unique about homeownership. The large majority of these inquiries has
determined that homeownership has a number of positive effects, although
some challenges have been identified. This section of the chapter highlights
the impacts of homeownership.

Foundations for Homeownership Benefits

An emphasis on the ownership of property as a positive activity has always been a part of American life. Ownership of land and home was one
of the primary goals of many early colonists. The Homestead Act and
other large governmental programs to offer land in western regions typified the settlement activity of the 1800s. This association of owning land,
and a home on the land, with freedom and creating individual value was
central to the nation's identity. President Lincoln equated the solidarity
and success of the nation with owning a home when he reportedly said:
"The state of a nation lies in the homes of its people."[58] By 1900, the interior of the continent had been extensively explored and the frontier regions linked to older settlements in the East. Immigration had swelled,
and the United States had firmly established an industrialized production
economy. Ownership remained a consistent goal, yet ideas about housing
were gradually shifting. In conjunction with industrialization, the middle
class began to grow, thereby increasing the demand for housing choices. It
was around this time that the ideal of homeownership became more firmly

---

[58] Although this statement has been quoted frequently by the National Association of Home
Builders and other publications, an origional citation for the quote has not been found.

linked to ideas of success and the American dream. Ownership was still the key, but the focus shifted from owning large tracts of land to ownership of homes in many forms, and in both urban and rural communities.

Political leaders began to give shape and direction to the importance of homeownership. In 1918, the Department of Labor introduced the Own Your Own Home campaign. Homeownership was in effect becoming a national goal. In the 1920s, key political figures, such as Herbert Hoover and Calvin Coolidge, publicly connected homeowership with the American dream and a good society. As Coolidge declared during his presidency: "No greater contribution could be made to the stability of the nation, and the advancement of its ideals, than to make it a nation of home-owning families."[59] Hoover introduced the Better Homes in America program to provide new ideas for home design and to promote better quality housing. The homeownership ideal was advanced greatly during the 1920s, an era in which the ownership rate rose for the first time in the twentieth century (see Figure 2.2). In the 1920s, the suburban ideal was a single-family detached dwelling which was often a two-story bungalow or a cottage with colonial design.[60] Housing organizations, many of which garnered federal support, were formed around this time to increase ownership around the country. They included the Better Homes in America movement mentioned above, the Architects' Small House Service Bureau, and the Home Modernizing Bureau.[61] There was increased emphasis on aesthetics, on commodities for the home, and on building — all of which would ultimately support a strong economy.

The national orientation toward homeownership was firmly established in the early decades of the twentieth century, yet it was still a goal far out of reach for most Americans. Although the sentiments were highlighted, and national leaders were boosting the idea of owning a home, the financial policies to make ownership a viable option for many were not in place until the depression years.[62] When Hoover became president, he continued the emphasis on housing. He stressed that "nothing contributes more to happiness or sound social stability than homes."[63] In December of 1931, he also organized the President's Conference on Home Building and Home Ownership, where his proposal for the Federal Home Loan

[59] Beyer, *Housing and Society,* 249.
[60] Hutchinson, "Building for Babbitt," 186.
[61] Ibid., 185.
[62] Retsinas, "Beyond the Bully Pulpit," 15.
[63] Sternlieb and Hughes, "Structuring the Future," 29.

Bank System was outlined and approved.[64] This and subsequent policies helped change the direction of housing finance in America. President Franklin D. Roosevelt continued this momentum by stating: "A nation of home owners, of people who won a real share in their own land, is un- conquerable."[65] Even though ownership levels dropped off during the de- pression years, when Roosevelt was in office, ownership remained an important ideal, and the restructuring of federal housing policies and pro- grams that took place during that time laid the foundation for the expan- sion of homeownership after World War II. In the postwar era, owning a home became one of the best ways to improve society and the quality of life for American families, and endorsements of homeownership by politi- cal figures advanced the idea that owning a home was a central part of the American Dream.

Economic Advantages

Owning a home is one of the primary means of wealth accumulation in the United States. Purchasing a home is a form of investment, while rent- ing a home is a form of consumption. Homes accrue equity, and the home owner has a store of capital to draw upon because she or he owns the prop- erty. Homeownership can be thought of as a wealth-building activity; it provides leverage in the economic system. Homes also often appreciate in price over time (although they can also decrease in value). If a home be- comes more valuable over time, the increases in value can more than off- set the costs of buying and maintaining the home.[66] This stands in contrast to the situation for renters, who put money into their housing, but it is not an investment they can draw upon.

In 1998, home equity made up the majority of wealth for most of the home owners in the United States.[67] Figure 2.6 indicates that for those households owning both stock and homes, home equity was a larger source of wealth than stocks. For three of the seven income brackets, own- ership equity made up over 70% of the household's wealth. For all house- holds except those in the highest income bracket ($100,000 and over), home equity is over 50% of their wealth. This shows that homeownership is doing far more than addressing a basic shelter need — it is a major method of financial investment for a large percentage of American fami-

---

[64] Doan, *American Housing Production,* 164.
[65] Jackson, *Crabgrass Frontier,* 190.
[66] National Association of Home Builders, *The Future of Home Building,* 123.
[67] Joint Center for Housing Studies, *State of the Nation's Housing: 2000,* 9.

FIGURE 2.6

Homeownership Is Largest Source of Wealth for Majority of Home Owners
Share of Home Owners with More Equity in Homes Than Stocks, 1998

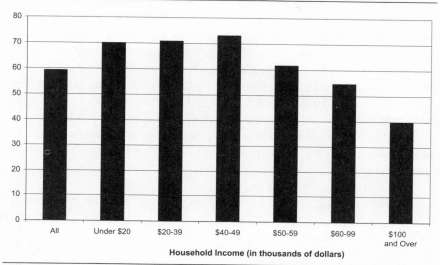

Household Income (in thousands of dollars)

SOURCE: Joint Center for Housing Studies, *State of Nation's Housing, 2000.*
DATA: Joint Center tabulations of the 1998 Survey of Consumer Finance.

lies. Home equity can also be an important form of wealth for lower-income and minority households. For example, the median wealth of low-income home owners under age sixty-five is about twelve times greater than that of low-income renters.[68] In addition, homes are often a major asset left to heirs, making owning a home a means of transferring wealth to children, relatives, or friends.[69]

Another way that owning a home provides economic benefit is through tax advantages. Although not originally linked to homeownership per se, the first income tax legislation paved the way for homeownership tax incentives, especially the mortgage interest and real estate property tax deductions. As Nicholas Retsinas writes:

> Any discussion of government programs that spurred homeownership will cite the New Deal, the tax-exempt bonds, and the secondary mortgage market. Yet equally critical was a codicil to the first income tax legislation in 1918. This early tax program excluded all debt income, whatever the source, and all other (state and local) taxes. In doing so, those who drafted this bill

---

[68] Collins, Belsky, and Retsinas, "Towards Tax Credit," 8.
[69] Alba, "Assimilation and Stratification," 1,315.

were not considering the issue of homeownership; indeed, at the time, most people were renters. But housing analysts credit the tax laws — the mortgage deductions — for propelling the steady increase in homeownership.[70]

Thus, there is a long history of a positive relationship between the tax code and homeownership in the United States.[71] Federal income tax policies support homeownership in several ways. These include the mortgage interest deduction, the real estate property tax deduction, the mortgage revenue bond program, the exclusion of house price appreciation from capital gains taxes, and penalty-free IRA withdrawals for first-time buyers.

Perhaps the most important (and most used) tax benefit for home owners is the mortgage interest deduction. Home owners with a mortgage can deduct the interest on up to $1 million in debt, which translates into significant savings. In a 1998 survey reported by the *Wall Street Journal,* 59% of home owners said that the mortgage-interest deduction on income tax was an important part of their decision to purchase a home.[72] Figure 2.7 shows the distribution of tax benefits from the mortgage interest deduction for 1998. Typically, the bulk of the benefits are gained when households itemize their tax deductions. Higher-income households tend to itemize their tax deductions more frequently because they have more expensive homes and larger tax liabilities.[73] This means that higher-income households tend to receive greater benefits from the mortgage tax deduction, although all home owners generally receive a financial benefit in some form.

The deferral of the capital gains tax is another important financial benefit of homeownership. Starting in the 1950s, home owners could defer the capital gains tax when selling their primary home; the seller then had up to two years to reinvest the money gained from the sale in a new home without incurring a tax liability.[74] In 1986, the passage of the Tax Reform Act changed the dynamics of investment in the housing sector. In many ways this act was detrimental to renter households and therefore, by comparison, helpful for households that owned a home.[75] Two important changes affected the after-tax cost of owner-occupied housing: first, the tax rates at which households deduct housing costs or upon which owner equity would be taxed if it were not invested in owner housing was reduced, and second, the pretax interest rate level was lowered.[76] Many home owners in

---

[70] Retsinas, "Beyond the Bully Pulpit," 16–17.
[71] Collins, Belsky, and Retsinas, "Towards Tax Credit," 4.
[72] "Tax Report," 1.
[73] Collins, Belsky, and Retsinas, "Towards Tax Credit," 5.
[74] Johnson, *Showing America,* 58.
[75] Hendershott, "The Tax Reform Act," 13.
[76] Ibid., 18.

FIGURE 2.7

Distribution of Tax Benefits for Mortgage Interest Deduction (FY 1998)

Income (Thousands)	Number of Returns (Thousands)	% of All Returns	Number of Returns taking Mortgage Interest Deduction (Thousands)	% of All Returns in Income Category	Value of Mortgage Interest Deductions (Millions)	% Value of all Mortgage Interest Deductions	Average Value per Return for Taking Mortgage Interest Deduction
Under $10	19, 763	14.75	14	1.4	$3		$214
$10-$20	25,158	18.78	354	5.5	128	1.00	371
$20-$30	20,397	15.22	1,134	14.7	466	2.63	411
$30-$40	16,189	12.08	2,375	24.8	1,238	4.83	521
$40-$50	12,434	9.28	3,080	42.1	2,270	16.32	737
$50-$75	19,469	14.53	8,201	65.3	7,667	21.34	935
$75-100	10,015	7.47	6,538	75.2	10,029	33.50	1,534
$100-$200	8,383	6.25	6,306	73	15,739	20.10	2,496
$200 and Over	2,129	1.58	1,554	22.1	9,438		6,073
TOTAL	133,938		29,548		46,977		

Source: Green, Richard, and Andrew Reschovsky, "Using Tax Policy to Increase Homeownership Among Low-and Moderate-Income Households": Final Report, submitted to Ford Foundation.
Data: Calculated from data provided in "Estimates of Federal Tax Expenditures for Fiscal years 1999–2003," Washington, D.C.: Joint Committee on Taxation, U.S. Congress, 14 December 1998.
Note: Figure 2.7 is also Figure 5.1 in Chapter 5.

the 1990s have been able to capitalize on the alterations made in 1986 and benefit from their ownership status. In 1997, the Taxpayer Relief Act allowed for further deferral of the capital gains tax in that after selling a home, the owner does not have to pay taxes on the money earned from the sale as long as the gain is less than $500,000. Thus, in many ways, homeownership in the 1990s is even more beneficial than in previous decades.

The benefits of homeownership are widespread and extend to most owners. However, typically home owners in the highest income brackets gain the most from the tax breaks. With this in mind, policy options have been developed to create increased incentives for low-income renters to become owners and also to help current low-income owners. Three provisions in the federal tax code help foster low-income homeownership. One is Mortgage Revenue Bonds (MRBs), which are tax-exempt bonds issued by state housing agencies to first-time buyers.[77] MRBs help lower monthly mortgage costs through subsidized interest rates. Also issued through state housing agencies are Mortgage Credit Certificates, which provide first-time home buyers with a nonrefundable income tax credit of 10% to 50% of their annual mortgage interest payments (up to $2,000 annually).[78] The third provision is the Low-Income Housing Tax Credit (LIHTC). The LIHTC is primarily a multifamily rental program, but on a very limited basis it has helped increase homeownership through lease-purchase programs. These provisions show that important pieces of the tax code reflect a commitment to help low-income home buyers. The mortgage interest tax deduction and other benefits help reduce a home buyer's housing costs, but such benefits do not help low-income people if they cannot afford the down payment, closing costs, and monthly mortgage payments, and if they do not itemize their federal tax deductions.

In summary, there are clear economic advantages to homeownership. Although not all home owners benefit from tax advantages and some houses lose value in depressed markets, overall, for the large majority of home owners, the mortgage interest deduction, house price appreciation over time, and the other positive factors discussed in this section make owning a home an excellent investment.

Citizenship and Community

One of the long-standing beliefs about homeownership is that home owners become better citizens. This appears over and over again in hous-

---

[77] Collins, Belsky, and Retsinas, "Towards Tax Credit," 8.
[78] Ibid.

ing literature and government policies supporting ownership. The premise is that home owners tend to be more civic-minded, participate more in local government, vote in elections, and become more involved in volunteer and community organizations. Participation in local affairs often begins with the basic incentive to protect one's property interests. Knowing about local politics and being politically involved can help a home owner influence local laws, schools, and community activities. The quality of a community is factored into the value of a home, thus there is a relationship between home owners being socially active and protecting (and possibly increasing) the value of their home.

A study by Denise DiPasquale and Edward L. Glaeser investigated homeownership as an endogenous variable that when linked with other individual characteristics seems to result in good citizenship.[79] They highlight two forms of actions, those that directly improve the quality of the neighborhood and those that improve social capital (connection to neighbors). The quality of the homes in a neighborhood directly impact one another, so forging relations with neighbors can help establish a neighborhood quality standard and can induce neighbors to work together to improve common areas. DiPasquale and Glaeser's findings show that home owners are 6% more likely to work to solve local problems.[80] The measures of civic participation used in this study are shown in Figure 2.8. The conclusion is that owners are generally more active citizens, as demonstrated by such factors as voting in local elections and knowing the name of their U.S. Representative and local school board head.

Another potential benefit stemming from homeownership is neighborhood stability. Neighborhood stability refers to the average length of tenure among residents.[81] Neighborhood stability does not necessarily mean that the neighborhood will be healthy, and increased tenure in a given locale is not always the best option for owners. Yet stability can generate positive effects, such as stabilizing property values. Also, if people live together in a neighborhood for a number of years, the social capital formed through their interactions with one another is likely to be stronger and more effective. Home owners maintain their residences for an average of thirteen years, while renters stay in the same residence for an average of only 2.5 years.[82] An important point related to housing tenure is that

---

[79] DiPasquale, and Glaeser, "Incentives and Social Capital," 356.
[80] Ibid.
[81] Rohe, McCarthy, and Van Zandt, "Social Benefits and Costs,"19.
[82] Ibid., 23.

FIGURE 2.8
Measures of Civic Participation

	Owners	Renters	Difference
Number of Non-Professional Organization Memberships	1.81	1.56	0.25
Know the Name of Local School Board Head	35.40%	26.00%	9.40%
Know the Name of US Representative	42.70%	32.40%	10.30%
Vote in Local Elections	74.80%	59.50%	15.30%
Garden	64.80%	53.20%	11.60%
Go to Church Regularly	4.04	3.68	0.36

SOURCE: DiPasquale and Glaeser, "Incentives and Social Capital," 354–384.

renters have less incentive to participate in civic improvements because they gain nothing from enhanced property values. If they participate, they expend the same effort and money as an owner, but receive few of the longer-term benefits.

The Personal and Psychological Level

Another aspect of homeownership that has a personal impact is the "sweat equity" factor. Sweat equity refers to the personal labor that the home owner puts into the building and/or the maintenance of the home. The idea is that the owner not only saves money by learning how to make needed repairs, gardening, painting, and so on, but also simultaneously gains a sense of responsibility, pride, and commitment and improves the value of the home. If necessary repairs or desired improvements are too challenging for the home owner to complete, sweat equity can take the form of researching and locating specialized repair companies. The process of hiring someone to make repairs on the home is also a learning experience and can foster good planning and management skills. It also can help hone interpersonal skills as the home owner learns how to negotiate with various people to modify the home.[83]

Homeownership can also be said to benefit owners on a psychological level. Many people associate homeownership with a sense of life satisfaction and pride. This satisfaction is with both the housing unit and its environs. As mentioned previously, homeownership has become equated with the American Dream. Recent studies by the Fannie Mae Foundation show that large percentages of both owners and renters believe that owning a home is an important life goal.[84] In addition, most renters would prefer to

---

[83] Green, and White, "Measuring the Benefits," 443.
[84] Fannie Mae, "National Housing Survey 1999."

be owners, with 62% of renters reporting that they rent as a result of circumstances rather than choice.[85] Homeownership is also thought to help enhance self-esteem. Considering that many households view ownership as a major life goal and an accomplishment, it is likely that self-esteem will be raised when one purchases a home.

While in most cases research shows that homeownership produces positive psychological effects, it does not produce these effects automatically for everyone. For lower-income people, for example, homeownership may provide satisfaction and increased self-worth. However, William Rohe and Michael Stegman argue that this has not been proven to be the case. They write: "Given that owners may stand to lose their equity in a foreclosure and that foreclosure can be a traumatic experience, low-income home owners may actually feel more insecure than low-income renters."[86] Also, people who own a home in a low-income, crime ridden area may not feel an enhanced sense of pride and stability. The benefits of homeownership may therefore be thwarted by larger problems. In essence, homeownership by itself is not enough, and other dimensions are also essential if the positive emotional, personal, and psychological benefits of homeownership are to flourish.

Organizations such as Habitat for Humanity can contribute to the personal and psychological aspects of home building and homeownership. People who own Habitat homes are involved with the home construction from the start and put in many sweat equity hours throughout the building process. Many of these people have lower incomes and may face some of the challenges noted above. Yet the process of building their own home, receiving appropriate counseling on homeownership, and meeting people who are forging new community relationships and revitalizing neighborhoods helps produce benefits that counteract some of the challenges. Millard Fuller, founder of Habitat, explains that Habitat is building much more than houses — the organization is bringing people together, building relationships, breaking down barriers, promoting understanding, and revitalizing neighborhoods.[87]

Homeownership and Children

Children have also been found to benefit from homeownership. Richard Green and Michelle White conducted a study that sought to determine

---

[85] Ibid., 6
[86] Rohe, and Stegman, "Effects of Homeownership," 175.
[87] Fuller, *More Than Houses,* xii–xiii.

whether children of home owners behaved in more socially desirable ways than children of renters. The two aspects of behavior that they examined were the likelihood of staying in school and of teenage children becoming pregnant. Green and White considered several reasons why ownership may potentially affect children: owners may tend to have different personality types than renters; they may have a stronger incentive to control their children's behavior so the children do not negatively affect house values; and home owners may gain skills (financial, maintenance, and learning skills for example) that can be applied to the job of parenting.[88] The study found that children of home owners are indeed more likely to remain in school and less likely to have children while they are teenagers, thereby supporting the idea that the status of home owning intrinsically makes a difference in children's lives.

While this study identifies a positive link, many scholars — including Green and White — acknowledge that more work needs to be done. Green and White's study controlled for a number of variables, but it is very difficult to isolate homeownership as the single cause of good behavior. Other variables such as family assets, neighborhood conditions, and peer influences may be responsible for their results.[89] A paper by Thomas Boehm and Alan Schlottmann examines the impact of housing on children's future outcomes by examining their educational attainment and housing choices as young adults. Boehm and Schlottman confirm that whether a child's parents were home owners is critical in determining whether he or she becomes a home owner.[90] Children of home owners tend to have better access to good schools and have greater educational achievement, which over time translates into increased earnings and opportunities for homeownership later in life.[91] Boehm and Schlottman confirm Green and White's suggestion that there may be many more indirect ways that housing choices affect children's well-being and productivity.

In a further study, Donald Haurin, Toby Parcel, and Jean Haurin examined the direct and indirect impacts of homeownership on child outcomes using data from the National Longitudinal Survey of Youth, maintained at the Center For Human Resources Research at the Ohio State University. The authors followed 1,024 children ages five to eight in 1988 through

---

[88] Green and White, "Measuring the Benefits," 443.
[89] Rohe, McCarthy, and Van Zandt, "Social Benefits and Costs," 29.
[90] Boehm, "Does Homeownership by Parents Have Impact?" 219.
[91] Ibid., 230.

1994, measuring child outcomes at four points in time. The specific outcome measures were achievement test scores in mathematics and reading and child behavior based on an index of behavioral problems.[92]

The authors went into the study with the hypothesis that homeownership impacts children in multiple ways. First, home owners have a stronger incentive to invest in their properties than renters, which could lead to increased property values and a better home environment. Second, home owners have greater residential stability because the transaction costs of moving are greater, which leads them to establish stronger community and social ties. Third, home owners enjoy a tax advantage compared with renters, which helps build wealth and should improve children's cognitive achievement and reduce behavior problems.

After analyzing achievement test scores over a seven-year period and controlling for the impact of many other factors, Haurin found strong evidence that homeownership leads to improved child outcomes. Specifically, for children living in owned homes, scores on math achievement tests were up to 9% higher, and scores on reading achievement were up to 7% higher.[93] Homeownership was also found to have a positive impact on child behavior. The authors developed an index of child behavior problems, and the cumulative impact was that homeownership reduced behavior problems by about 3%.[94]

Finally, the authors found that compared to renting, homeownership improves the quality of the home environment, even after controlling for many other social, demographic, and economic variables such as household wealth, nonlabor income, and wages of the father and mother. They estimated that the range of improvement in what they called "the cognitive/physical home environment of homeowners" was from 13% to 23% better — demonstrating that home owners tend to invest in their property more than those who rent.[95]

The Challenges of Homeownership

Throughout this section, homeownership emerges as a positive facet of American life. It is a benefit to individuals, families, and society. Yet is homeownership the right option for everyone? There are times in a

---

[92] Haurin, Parcel and Haurin, "Impact of Homeownership."
[93] Ibid., 23.
[94] Ibid., 24.
[95] Ibid., 21.

person's life when owning property — a home or otherwise — can be more of a hindrance than a benefit. It is important to examine situations in which homeownership may not be the best option or the only solution to a problem.

One consideration in purchasing a home is whether an individual or household is mobile. Home owning restricts mobility primarily because of the high transaction costs of selling a home. There are many steps involved in selling a home, and the process usually takes time. Renters do not encounter many of these transaction costs and are more able to change location rapidly. Homeownership keeps people in given locales, and this can be positive or negative, depending on the situation. For highly mobile households, such as those whose jobs cause them to move a great deal, homeownership may not be the best option. Nor is it practical for the many immigrants who continue to live between the United States and their country of origin.[96] Also, homeownership brings added responsibility. As previously noted, this can be a benefit in that it cultivates pride, helps owners learn how to make repairs, and encourages them to become involved in local activities to protect the value of their home. However, the responsibilities that come with owning a home can sometimes be overwhelming. For example, an older couple may not have the energy or skills to keep up with maintenance. Homeownership, then, may not be right for everyone, and a household must assess how capable it is to take on the responsibilities — financial and otherwise.

Despite the benefits of homeownership, it must not be viewed as an elixir for neighborhood problems.[97] Rather, one must carefully assess whether increasing homeownership is actually going to help eliminate problems in a given area. For example, encouraging residents of a low-income neighborhood to buy homes, with the hope that their newfound ownership status will yield more involvement in local politics, nonprofit activities, and upkeep of the neighborhood, will not always produce the desired results. The neighborhood may be run-down or deteriorated due to older housing stock, lack of high-paying jobs in the area, and a slow economy with falling property values. Encouraging people to purchase homes in these circumstances will not generate neighborhood stability and health. In fact, if people buy homes in troubled neighborhoods, the fact that they own can sometimes trap them in a decaying area where they can-

---

[96] Ratner, "Many Routes to Homeownership," 119–120.
[97] Rohe and Stewart, "Homeownership and Neighborhood Stability," 72.

not make improvements and are unable to sell their home. Homeownership may be part of a community solution, but is not the automatic or complete answer for solving household and neighborhood problems.

A PROFILE OF HOME OWNERS

What types of households are achieving high homeownership rates? Knowing where these households live, the types of homes they own, their educational backgrounds, their annual incomes, and more allows policy makers to determine how to break down barriers to ownership.

Dwelling Type, Income, and Education

The vast majority of home owners in the United States live in single-family detached homes. The option to own an apartment, single-family attached unit, or mobile home helps make ownership more accessible, yet there is a strong tie between homeownership and single-family detached

FIGURE 2.9
Household Dwelling Type by Tenure Status, 1999

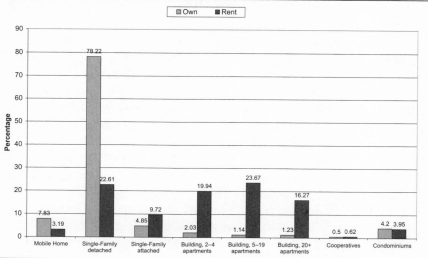

SOURCE: U.S. Census Bureau, American Housing Survey, 1999 (occupied dwellings only). (www.census.gov/hhes/www.housing/ahs/ahs99/ahs99.html).

homes. Figure 2.9 outlines the different dwelling types and the percentages of owners and renters who live in them. Fully 78.2% of owners live in single-family detached homes, with the next most popular option being mobile homes, at 7.8%. Still, 22.6% of renter households live in single-family detached units showing a significant preference.

Typically, households with higher incomes have higher homeownership rates. A higher income and the attendant ability to save money make it easier to manage the initial down payment on a home, closing costs, mortgage costs, and general home maintenance. In 1995, the median income of an owner household was $39,857, whereas the median income of a renter household was $21,981.[98] In essence, the median income of home owners is nearly double that of renters. Figure 2.10, which displays the percentages of owners and renters in each household income category, reveals that the higher the income, the more likely the household is to own its home. Further, households with income brackets of $60,000 or more had homeownership rates over 80%. The majority of home owners take out a mortgage to pay for their home. In 1995, 61% of home owners had a mortgage on their home, and the median outstanding principal was $48,466.[99]

Homeownership rates also rise among those with higher levels of education. Of householders who hold a graduate or professional degree, 76.7% are home owners; for those who did not graduate from high school, the homeownership rate is significantly lower, at 56.2%.[100] Figure 2.11 highlights that as the level of education rises, the homeownership rate rises correspondingly. People having a bachelor's degree or a graduate/professional degree have the highest homeownership rates, at 70% or higher. The next most important educational factor for homeownership is having vocational training. Among those with the least educational attainment (less than a ninth grade education or a twelfth grade education but no diploma), the percentage of renter households rises to more than 40%.

Education especially helps minority households to achieve homeownership. In most cases, the achievement of a higher-education degree by a minority person increases his or her chances of becoming a home owner at a rate faster than for a white person. Figure 2.12 illustrates this scenario. In all cases, achieving a degree increases the likelihood of ownership. But in the central city, Hispanics who have a bachelors degree are 30.6% more

---

[98] Russell, *Americans and Their Homes, 16.*
[99] Ibid., 44.
[100] U.S. Census Bureau, "American Housing Survey, 1997," (www.census.gov/hhes/www/housing/ahs/ahs97/tab29.html).

FIGURE 2.10
Homeownership by Household Income

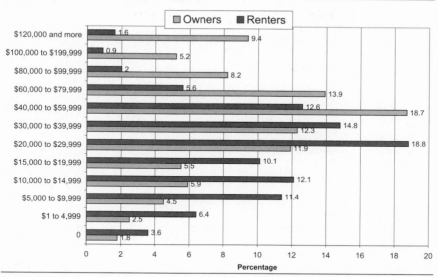

SOURCE: U.S. Census Bureau. American Housing Survey, 1999 (www.census.gov/hhes/www/housing/ahs/ahs99/ahs99.html).

likely to own a home than those with no high school diploma. For African Americans, the figure is 27.3%; for whites, 22.9%. In the suburbs, Hispanics with higher educational levels are an astounding 37.6% more likely to own. For whites, it's 28%, and for African Americans, 27.8%. So although white households have higher homeownership rates overall, in some circumstances, racial divides can be overcome through increased access to education. This suggests that an important policy route for increasing homeownership is to continue to support expanded educational opportunities, particularly for minorities.

Types of Households

A household can comprise a single person or many members, and it is important to look at different household types. The majority of owner households are married-couple families; this has been consistently true throughout the twentieth century. Of all married-couple families in the United States in 1996, 80.2% were home owners.[101] However, households

---

[101] U.S. Census Bureau, "Current Housing Reports."

FIGURE 2.11

Homeownership by Educational Attainment of Householder

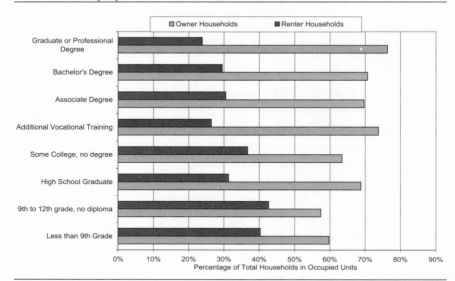

SOURCE: U.S. Census Bureau, "American Housing Survey, 1999, Household Composition—Occupied Units."

FIGURE 2.12

Homeownership by Educational Attainment of Householder by Race

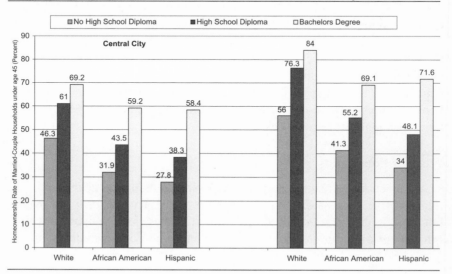

SOURCE: Joint Center for Housing Studies, *State of the Nation's Housing 1999.*

can also be single people living alone. Adult siblings living together can also form households in which incomes and resources are pooled. Unmarried, unrelated adults also form households and can become owners. Children are considered to be a part of a household. Historically, the U.S. Census Bureau has measured households by identifying a household head, traditionally defined as male. In other words, in a married-couple household, the male would be considered the head of the household.[102]

Given this statistical definition, it is not surprising that male-headed households are more likely to be home owners than female-headed households, as Figure 2.13 shows. There was little shift from 1977 to 1997, with female-headed households increasing by only 1.7%. Two major components of this are income and the presence of children. Men have higher incomes than women in the United States, and female-headed households are more likely to have children to support. This often creates a situation in which the female head is expected to work full time to earn money for the household and also to care for the children. Male-headed households with no spouse present are less likely to include children, and are therefore less affected by this kind of dual responsibility. Figure 2.14 displays the marital status of home owners over time; it confirms that married home owner heads are predominant among those who achieve ownership.

Another important part of the relationship between households and homeownership is the life cycle factor, as Figure 2.15 highlights. Ownership is greater during certain phases of life. In early adulthood, households often do not have a large enough income to make the initial down payment on a home or to meet monthly mortgage costs. Additionally, other priorities often take precedence, such as paying for higher education or the desire to be highly mobile and change residential location. For older households, owning a home can sometimes become a challenge because of all the maintenance involved. Also, some older householders may need assisted care, and living in their own homes may not be possible. Homeownership tends to be most important during the middle years of life, when many people have children and also have the money to make payments and the energy to maintain their home.

Home owners tend to be slightly older on average than other types of households. In 1995, the median age of home owners was fifty-one, whereas the median age for the average household was forty-six.[103] Figure 2.15

---

[102] Segal and Sullivan, "Trends in Homeownership," 57.
[103] Russell, *Americans and Their Homes,* 43.

FIGURE 2.13
Homeownership Rate by Gender of Household Head

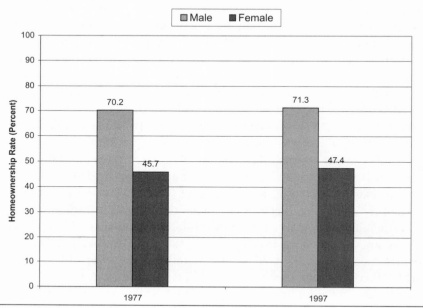

SOURCE: Segal and Sullivan, "Trends in Homeownership," 59.
NOTE: Author's tabulations of 1977, 1978, and 1983–97 March Current Population Survey.

categorizes homeownership by socioeconomic status as well as age. In all income brackets, the largest percentages of home owners are in the sixty-one to seventy age bracket. Also, all of the socioeconomic levels show a trend of increasing ownership through the age brackets until the trend reverses after age seventy and ownership levels begin to decline.

Regional Factors

Homeownership rates in the United States vary from region to region, with the highest rates found in the Midwest. In fact, as Figure 2.16 shows, the Midwest has since the 1960s consistently enjoyed the highest home-ownership rates. In the first quarter of 1970, the region was the first to have an ownership rate over 70%.[104] The homeownership rates for the four regions of the country as of 2001 were 73.5% in the Midwest, 70.1% in

[104] U.S. Census Bureau, "Homeownership Rates for the U.S."

FIGURE 2.14
Homeownership Rate by Marital Status of Household Head

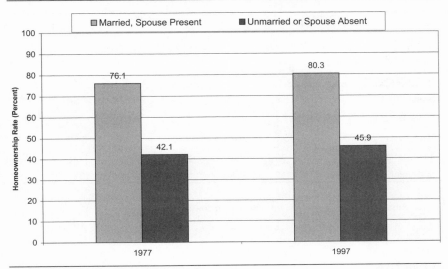

SOURCE: Segal and Sullivan, "Trends in Homeownership," 59.
NOTE: Author's tabulations of 1977, 1978, and 1983–97 March Current Population Survey.

the South, 64% in the Northeast, and 62.3% in the West.[105] Figure 2.16 also shows that the South's high homeownership rates have paralleled strong homeownership growth in the Midwest. In 1977, the Northeast surpassed the West and maintained this lead into the twenty-first century.

Figure 2.17 compares homeownership rates for all the states and Washington, D.C. (which has the lowest rate) from 1900 to 2000. In general, states that are less populated and have fewer urban centers tend to have higher homeownership rates. As of 2000, twenty-eight states had ownership rates at or above 70%, with Michigan leading at 77.2% and Maine and South Carolina sharing the second highest rate of 76.5%. Some states have had consistently high rates throughout the century, and others that now have high rates once had very low rates. Maine began the century with a high rate and has made steady progress. In contrast, Mississippi had a high homeownership rate of 75.2% in 2000, yet at the start of the century, it had a very low rate of 34.5%. The rates for New York and California are well below the national average, at 53.4% and 57.1% respectively. No single factor accounts for such contrasts, but demographic

---

[105] U.S. Census Bureau, "Housing Vacancies."

FIGURE 2.15
Homeownership by Age and Socioeconomic Status

Socioeconomic Index	Percent Homeowners in Householder Age Groups					
	<31	31–40	41–50	51–60	61–70	71+
Lowest Third	15.6	39.4	55.2	58.5	70.8	61
Middle Third	31.1	59.2	71.6	74.7	76	73.3
Highest Third	43.6	73.1	83.2	85.6	87.2	77.1
All Households	30	58.9	70.7	71.9	76.7	68.5
Total Number	3883	3388	1796	1352	1355	1230

SOURCE: Rossi and Weber, "The Social Benefits of Homeownership."

FIGURE 2.16
Homeownership Rates by Region, 1965–2001

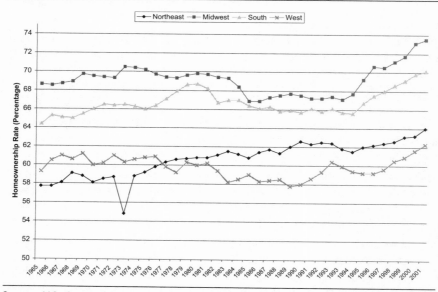

SOURCE: U.S. Census Bureau. "Housing Vacancies and Homeownership, Annual Statistics, 2000" (http://www.census.gov/hhes/www/housing/hvs/annual00/ann00t12.html).

FIGURE 2.17
Homeownership Rates by State, 1900–2000

	2000	1990	1980	1970	1960	1950	1940	1930	1920	1910	1900
AL	73.2	70.5	70.1	66.7	59.7	49.4	33.6	34.2	35	35.1	34.4
AK	66.4	56.1	58.3	50.3	48.3	54.5	N/A	N/A	N/A	N/A	N/A
AZ	68	64.2	68.3	65.3	63.9	56.4	47.9	44.8	42.8	49.2	57.5
AR	68.9	69.6	70.5	66.7	61.4	54.5	39.7	40.1	45.1	46.6	47.7
CA	57.1	55.6	55.9	54.9	58.4	54.3	43.4	46.1	43.7	49.5	46.3
CO	68.3	62.2	64.5	63.4	63.8	58.1	46.3	50.7	51.6	51.5	46.6
CT	70	65.6	63.9	62.5	61.9	51.1	40.5	44.5	37.6	37.3	39
DE	72	70.2	69.1	68	66.9	58.9	47.1	52.1	44.7	40.7	36.3
DC	41.9	38.9	35.5	28.2	30	32.3	29.9	38.6	30.3	25.2	24
FL	68.4	67.2	68.3	68.6	67.5	57.6	43.6	42	42.5	44.2	46.8
GA	69.8	64.9	65	61.1	56.2	46.5	30.8	30.6	30.9	30.5	30.6
HI	55.2	53.9	51.7	46.9	41.1	33	N/A	N/A	N/A	N/A	N/A
ID	70.5	70.1	72	70.1	70.5	65.5	57.9	57	60.9	68.1	71.6
IL	67.9	64.2	62.6	59.4	57.8	50.1	40.3	46.5	43.8	44.1	45
IN	74.9	70.2	71.7	71.7	71.1	65.5	53.1	57.3	54.8	54.8	56.1
IA	75.2	70	71.8	71.7	69.1	63.4	51.5	54.7	58.1	58.4	60.5
KS	69.3	67.9	70.2	69.1	68.9	63.9	51	56	56.9	59.1	59.1
KY	73.4	69.6	70	66.9	64.3	58.7	48	51.3	51.6	51.6	51.5
LA	68.1	65.9	65.5	63.1	59	50.3	36.9	35	33.7	32.2	31.4
ME	76.5	70.5	70.9	70.1	66.5	62.8	57.3	61.7	59.6	62.5	64.8
MD	69.9	65	62	58.8	64.5	56.3	47.4	55.2	49.9	44	40
MA	59.9	59.3	57.5	57.5	55.9	47.9	38.1	43.5	34.8	33.1	35
MI	77.2	71	72.7	74.4	74.4	67.5	55.4	59	58.9	61.7	62.3
MN	76.1	71.8	71.7	71.5	72.1	66.4	55.2	58.9	60.7	61.9	63.5
MS	75.2	71.5	71	66.3	57.7	47.8	33.3	32.5	34	34	34.5
MO	74.2	68.8	69.6	67.2	64.3	57.7	44.3	49.9	49.5	51.1	50.9
MT	70.2	67.3	68.6	65.7	64	60.3	52	54.5	60.5	60	56.6
NE	70.2	66.5	68.4	66.4	64.8	60.6	47.1	54.3	57.4	59.1	56.8
NV	64	54.8	59.6	58.5	56.3	48.7	46.1	47.1	47.6	53.4	66.2
NH	69.2	68.2	67.6	68.2	65.1	58.1	51.7	55	49.8	51.2	53.9
NJ	66.2	64.9	62	60.9	61.3	53.1	39.4	48.4	38.3	35	34.3
NM	73.7	67.4	68.1	66.4	65.3	58.8	57.3	57.4	59.4	70.6	68.5
NY	53.4	52.2	48.6	47.3	44.8	37.9	30.3	37.1	30.7	31	33.2
NC	71.1	68	68.4	65.4	60.1	53.3	42.2	44.5	47.4	47.3	46.6
ND	70.7	65.6	68.7	68.4	68.4	66.2	49.8	58.6	65.3	75.7	80
OH	71.3	67.5	68.4	67.7	67.4	61.1	50	54.4	51.6	51.3	52.5
OK	72.7	68.1	70.7	69.2	67	60	42.8	41.3	45.5	45.4	54.2
OR	65.3	63.1	65.1	66.1	69.3	65.3	55.4	59.1	54.8	60.1	58.7
PA	74.7	70.6	69.9	68.8	68.3	59.7	45.9	54.4	45.2	41.6	41.2
RI	61.5	59.5	58.8	57.9	54.5	45.3	37.4	41.2	31.1	28.3	28.6
SC	76.5	69.8	70.2	66.1	57.3	45.1	30.6	30.9	32.2	30.8	30.6
SD	71.2	66.1	69.3	69.6	67.2	62.5	45	53.1	61.5	68.2	71.2
TN	70.9	68	68.6	66.7	63.7	56.5	44.1	46.2	47.7	47	46.3
TX	63.8	60.9	64.3	64.7	64.8	56.7	42.8	41.7	42.8	45.1	46.5
UT	72.7	68.1	70.7	69.3	71.7	65.3	61.1	60.9	60	64.8	67.8
VT	68.7	69	68.7	69.1	66	61.3	55.9	59.8	57.5	58.5	60.4
VA	73.9	66.3	65.6	62	61.3	55	48.9	52.4	51.1	51.5	48.8
WA	63.6	62.6	65.6	66.8	68.5	65	57	59.4	54.7	57.3	54.5
WV	75.9	74.1	73.6	68.9	64.3	55	43.7	45.9	46.8	49.5	54.6
WI	71.8	66.7	68.2	69.1	68.6	63.5	54.4	63.2	63.6	64.6	66.4
WY	71	67.8	69.2	66.4	62.2	54	48.6	48.3	51.9	54.5	55.2

Source: U.S. Census Bureau, "Historical Census of Housing Tables Homeownership" (7 September 2000).

shifts, zoning laws, building requirements, and unemployment rates in each state can all help reveal why homeownership rates vary from state to state.

Citizenship and Race

Two other important categories to understand in terms of homeownership profiles are citizenship and race. A person's status as a citizen or a noncitizen and his or her racial or ethnic background play a part in determining the likelihood of becoming a home owner. First, citizens are far more likely than noncitizens to be home owners. Among foreign-born U.S. residents of all ages and years of arrival, citizens are twice as likely as noncitizens to live in owner-occupied housing."[106] In other words, immigrants who become citizens are far more likely to buy a home. Whether someone is foreign-born or native-born is far less important than whether he or she is a citizen. In 1996, 67.4% of native-born citizens were home owners, compared to 66.9% of foreign-born citizens.[107] There is little difference between these two statistics; the key element is that both groups have citizenship status in the United States. The percentage of foreign-born noncitizens who are home owners is 33.1%, revealing that immigrants who are not yet citizens, or who have chosen not to become citizens, are less likely to purchase a home.[108]

The speed with which immigrants move into homeownership is related to the wealth they were able to bring with them and also to the income they earn in their first jobs. Immigrants who are more wealthy upon arrival or who find high-paying jobs become owners more quickly. Those from more disadvantaged situations need to work for a length of time before homeownership is even a possibility. Immigrants from Europe and Canada have the highest rates of homeownership, those from Asia, the Caribbean, and South America have medium rates, and those from Central America and Mexico have the lowest rates. George Masnick points out in a recent working paper that Latino immigrants tend to lag behind in homeownership because they are younger and have less income when they arrive; this cohort also tends to lag behind in acquiring U.S. citizenship.[109]

Households with different racial backgrounds have very different homeownership profiles. In part this is due to a historical discrepancy relating to

---

[106] Masnick, "Citizenship and Homeownership," 3.
[107] U.S. Census Bureau, "Moving to America."
[108] Ibid.
[109] Masnick, "Citizenship and Homeownership," 24.

FIGURE 2.18
Homeownership Rates by Race and Ethnicity of Householder, 2001

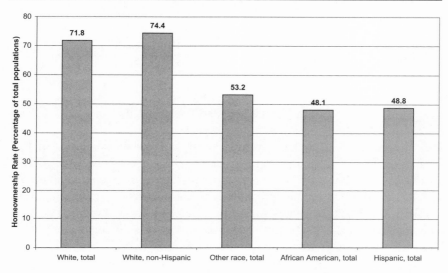

SOURCE: U.S. Census Bureau, "Housing Vacancies and Homeownership. Fourth Quarter 2001" (www.census.gov/hhes/www/hvs.html).

job access, wealth, and discrimination. Non-Hispanic whites have the highest homeownership rates in the country and have for the entire twentieth century. As shown in Figure 2.18, in 2001, non-Hispanic whites had a homeownership rate of 74.4%, while Hispanics had a rate of 48.8% and African Americans had a rate of 48.1%.[110] These discrepancies are linked to broader issues, such as where various ethnic/racial groups tend to live and what types of jobs they have. For example, poverty is three times more common among Hispanics than among non-Hispanic whites.[111] Certainly this reality affects the access Hispanic households have to ownership options. Despite the fact that a gap exists in ownership rates between racial groups, there has been some improvement in recent years.

A related point is that there is much variation within racial and ethnic categories. Economic and homeownership progress among Hispanics, for example, varies a great deal between the foreign and the native born, and again among Hispanics from various countries of national origin. For

---

[110] U.S. Census Bureau, "Housing Vacancies and Homeownership: First Quarter 2001" (www.census.gov/hhes/www/housing/hvs/q100prss.html).
[111] U.S. Census Bureau, "The Hispanic Population," 3.

example, Cuban Hispanics born in the United States have a homeowner-ship rate of 61.3%, while foreign-born Hispanics from Central and South America have a rate of 33%.[112] This shows that while broad categories such as "Hispanic" or "African American" are useful in some instances, it is important to take into consideration the true variety and fluctuation within racial and ethnic groups in the United States.

WHO ACHIEVES HOMEOWNERSHIP?

The foregoing home owner profiles reveal that certain segments of the population are not achieving homeownership. There is an evident "home-ownership gap" between low-income and high-income people and among people of different racial and ethnic backgrounds. Compounding this problem is the fact that many minorities are also in low income brackets, meaning they face affordability and discrimination challenges simultane-ously. In effect, there are those who have adequate housing and the option to own — the housing "haves," and those who do not. The people who are not being served can be thought of as the housing "have-nots."

Despite the seriousness of the problem, there are a number of changes that have been made to help more people gain fair access to housing mar-kets and to homeownership. In the 1960s, demands for social justice high-lighted the inequalities in housing and began a long struggle to even access to housing markets. In the 1990s, the Department of Housing and Urban Development and other organizations focused on decreasing own-ership gaps related to discrimination and affordability. Many of these gaps have persisted over time, yet some strides have been made to reverse the situation for the housing have-nots — especially in terms of opening up homeownership possibilities.

Housing Discrimination: Implications for Homeownership

Discrimination in the housing sector has historically been a problem. It continues to be a problem today, although important strides have been made. Discrimination tends to produce housing segregation — meaning people of the same racial and/or income background tend to live in the same neighborhoods. A related problem is redlining, or refusing to make

---

[112] Joint Center for Housing Studies, *State of the Nation's Housing*, 12.

credit available to households living in certain urban neighborhoods, unrelated to any objective determination of risk.[113] It is also important to note that while discrimination is often associated with race, it can also occur based on one's income status, sexual preference, age, or gender.

Discrimination related to housing has become far less overt over the past three decades, yet it still affects how, where, and when people are able to buy homes. In the 1990s, HUD repeatedly stressed fair housing and has worked to end racial segregation throughout the country. Part of the fair housing strategy is to provide more housing options for minorities in predominantly white areas. This integrationist strategy can be beneficial because it increases housing opportunities, yet it may also potentially serve to fracture minority communities. While minority leaders agree that non-whites should not be prevented from moving into white areas, they also note that integration breaks up neighborhoods that are a source of political solidarity, community, and culture for different minority groups.[114]

Another aspect of the segregation problem and the multiple housing markets is "steering" by realtors. Steering is when a real estate agent suggests to a person of a given race or ethnicity that he or she purchase a home in a neighborhood where there are other owners of that race or ethnicity. This is not to pinpoint real estate agents as the problem, but agents can have tremendous influence over where people choose to buy homes. In her paper on Anglo and Hispanic homeownership, Lauren Krivo notes that "realtors can prevent Hispanics from purchasing a home by withholding information on the availability of units, by showing homes only after repeated office visits and requests, or by showing fewer homes to Hispanic clients than they would Anglos."[115] The quality of the homes available to minorities and low-income households is often lower, and as a result such home owners do not feel all the benefits of homeownership.[116] A recent study by William Rohe and Michael Stegman shows that the housing condition (rather than being an owner or renter) often determines household satisfaction.[117] Thus low-income home owners may not feel many of the benefits of their ownership status. In many ways, the homeownership experience is different for minorities and whites. For example, homes owned

---

[113] Van Vliet, *Encyclopedia of Housing,* 462. *Note:* The term *redlining* itself comes from the practice of literally drawing red lines on city maps in the neighborhoods where people would not be eligible for credit.

[114] Hays, *Federal Government,* 269.

[115] Krivo, "Homeownership Differences," 325.

[116] Clay, "Homeownership for the Poor," 29.

[117] Rohe and Stegman, "Effects of Homeownership," 181.

by minorities tend to have lower values, and African American and Hispanic owners tend to be concentrated in central cities.[118]

The majority of potential home owners need to take out a loan to purchase a home, and minorities often have a more challenging time obtaining one. To counteract this trend, there has been significant effort regarding fair lending in recent decades. In 1975, the Home Mortgage Disclosure Act (HMDA) was passed to gather information on the geographic distribution of loans and the racial background of those applying for loans. The goal of HMDA was to record data on lending practices and to ultimately make the lending process more fair and not contingent on one's racial status. In 1977, the Community Reinvestment Act (CRA) was passed. It required the majority of lenders to assess and respond to the credit needs of their entire service areas.[119] Once HMDA data was collected and CRA implemented, it became more possible to identify discriminatory practices and to target companies that were practicing redlining in urban areas. Both pieces of legislation have helped directly address discrimination. In 1989, the Financial Institution Reform, Recovery, and Enforcement Act (FIRREA) expanded the terms of HMDA:

> [L]enders now had to report the race, income, and gender of each applicant as well as the census tract of the property. Such information must be reported for each type of loan (conventional or government insured — Federal Housing Administration, Department of Veterans Affairs, or Fannie Mae) and the purpose of the loan (single family, multifamily, home improvement, and non-occupant). FIRREA also requires lenders to report whether the loan was accepted or rejected and who purchased the loan if it was not retained in the lender's portfolio.[120]

HMDA data shows that minority households in the United States are more likely to be denied a mortgage loan than white households, although this data does not control for some important factors such as credit history.[121] Discrimination in the lending process continues to be a barrier for minority households. Yet progress has been made in recent years. Between 1993 and 1998, home purchase loans that went to African American households increased by 94.6%, and such loans for Hispanics increased by 77.7%.[122] Continued commitment on the part of the federal government to enforce fair lending policies has contributed to this progress.

---

[118] Simmons, "Homeownership Boom," 4.
[119] Martinez, "Housing Act of 1949," 474.
[120] Van Vliet, *Encyclopedia of Housing,* 231.
[121] Bogdon and Bell, "Making Lending a Reality," 1.
[122] Martinez, "Housing Act of 1949," 477.

But in addition, most lenders have come to realize that reaching out to historically underserved markets holds a great deal of business potential.

An important case of lending discrimination was found in what is known as the Boston Fed Study. This study was first released in 1992 and then published in 1996 in the *American Economic Review.*[123] It concluded that African American and Hispanic loan applicants were 82% more likely to be denied a mortgage loan than comparable white applicants. There has been a great deal of criticism about how the study was conducted and about important variables that were omitted; still, the study established the clear possibility that some lenders use different guidelines and/or underwriting criteria for minority applicants.[124] An earlier study titled "The Color of Money" examined lending practices in the Atlanta area in the 1980s and found that lenders were far more likely to lend to white middle-class applicants than to African American middle-class applicants. This study and the Boston Fed Study raised a great deal of attention and propelled further investigation. The dialogue has resulted in changes in lending practices, ultimately making people more aware of the situation and more able and willing to comply with federal regulations. For example, a recent article by Henry Buist, Peter D. Linneman, and Isaac F. Megbolugbe takes the Boston Fed Study information and looks specifically at lender compensation policies. Their findings do not negate discrimination as a factor, but rather point out that recent shifts toward using automated scoring systems to analyze lending risk do not allow for discriminatory treatment. Previously, discretionary, rule-based decisions for mortgage scoring left room for race and other characteristics to influence the decision to grant a loan. As the authors write, "Race and other protected characteristics simply are not part of the automated scoring systems, so that blatant differential treatment and statistical discrimination will be far less feasible. Moreover, basing the underwriting systems' decision models on loan performance and other risk management controls would, by design, pass any reasonable statement of an adverse-impact test."[125]

The Homeownership Gap

Larger percentages of people are home owners than ever before, and this means that minority groups are also seeing increased numbers of home

[123] Munnell, Tootell, Browne, and McEneaney, "Mortgage Lending in Boston: Interpreting HMDA Data," *American Economic Review,* Vol. 86, March 1996, 25–53.
[124] Bogdon and Bell. "Making Lending a Reality," 13.
[125] Buist, Linneman, and Megbolugbe, "Residential-Mortgage Lending Discrimination," 715.

owners. However, white households continue to gain as well, and the historic homeownership gap has shifted very little over time. The gap between whites and minorities is generally in the range of twenty-five percentage points. Figure 2.19 shows the ownership rates for various racial groups from 1983 to 2001, and homeownership levels have risen for everyone in the 1990s. Minority and white rates have both been on the rise in recent years as more people are able to save for down payments and to take out loans to purchase new homes. An article in *National Mortgage News* reported that more loans were funded to minorities in 1999 than in previous years, according to HMDA data. Loans increased 44.4% for Native Americans (26,123 loans), 18.3% for Hispanics (348,520 loans), 16.3% for Asians (155,442 loans), and 11.1% for African Americans (310,064).[126] These improvements show that strides are being made among minorities on the homeownership front.[127] However, as minority households gain, white households also gain, and the homeownership gap continues to be a reality.

In 1994, Henry Buist, Isaac Megbolugbe, and Tina Trent described the gap: "The roughly twenty-five percentage-point difference in homeownership rates seems to persist through time and across data sets and indicates that whites are about 58% more likely than African Americans or Hispanics to own their own residences."[128] In 2000, the Joint Center for Housing Studies of Harvard University reported in the *State of the Nation's Housing* that the since 1994, the homeownership gap has remained virtually unchanged. "Despite impressive growth in the number of minority home owners since 1994, the gap between minority and white homeownership rates holds at 25.8 percentage points — an improvement of just over one percentage point."[129] The report goes on to say: "If minorities owned homes at the same rates as whites of similar age and income, their homeownership rate would have been 60.8% in 1998 rather than 47.1% — a difference of nearly 3.5 million additional homeowners."[130]

Even when people of different racial backgrounds have similar characteristics, whites still maintain higher ownership rates. Lauren Krivo is just one of many academics who has explored the homeownership gap. In her study, she compared Hispanics with whites and found that Hispanics re-

---

[126] "Minorities Do Well on HMDA," 1. (See the HMDA website for more data: (www.ffiec.gov/hmda/).

[127] Minority gains have been particularly significant in the 1990s; this topic will again be addressed in Section VI which specifically discusses homeownership trends in the 1990s.

[128] Buist, Megbolugbe, and Trent, "Racial Homeownership Patterns," 92.

[129] Joint Center for Housing Studies, *State of the Nation's Housing 2000*, 16.

[130] Ibid., 17.

FIGURE 2.19

Homeownership Gap Between Whites and Minorities Remains over Time

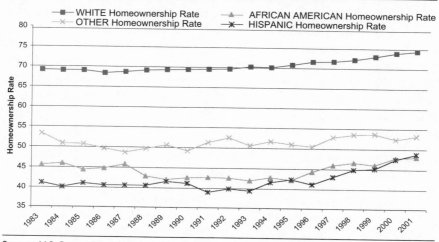

SOURCE: U.S. Census Bureau, Current Population Survey, March Supplement.

mained significantly less likely than whites to own homes even after controlling for socioeconomic, life-cycle, and geographic factors.[131]

Wealth and Income Limitations

Many minority groups and recent immigrants do not have the same wealth resources to pass on to their children as white, native-born families. Additionally, minority households are less likely to inherit homes from their parents or grandparents than white households. This lack of intergenerational assistance perpetuates the lower homeownership rates. Christopher Herbert notes the cyclical patterns that reproduce the homeownership gap: "If homeownership rates are not raised for the current generation of young black households, they will not have access to the primary form of wealth accumulation in this country. As a result, their children and grandchildren will have fewer financial resources than their white counterparts to draw on when they seek to become homeowners, and the shortfall in black homeownership rates will continue."[132] James Long and Steven Caudill

---

[131] Krivo, "Homeownership Differences," 325.
[132] Herbert, "Assessing the Potential," 22.

also confirm that African American couples in the United States are found to own a disproportionately low share of aggregate housing wealth.[133]

It has been noted that home owners receive tax advantages as compared to renter households. However, a number of studies report that higher-income home owners tend to receive greater tax advantages from their home owner status than their lower-income counterparts,[134] due largely to the fact that low-and moderate-income income taxpayers do not itemize deductions, thus reducing the tax code's potential to reduce housing costs.[135] In a recent article, Peter Dreier acknowledges that wealthy Americans primarily benefit from the tax benefits of homeownership:

> The nation's tax system allows home owners to deduct both mortgage interest and property tax payments from their federal taxes. Last year this cost Uncle Sam more than $63 billion in lost revenues. . . . These tax breaks disproportionately benefited those with the largest homes and the highest incomes. The wealthiest 1.5% of all taxpayers (those with incomes of $200,000) received more than one-fifth of the $63 billion in homeowner tax breaks. . . . Only 15% of families earning $30,000 to $40,000, and only 25% of families earning $40,000 to $50,000, received part of this homeowner subsidy.[136]

Another related problem is that when trying to encourage low-income households to become home owners, tax policies often do not address the true wealth and income restraints faced by low-income people, as a recent paper prepared for the Brookings Institution notes.[137] A number of recent federal policies — generated primarily by the FHA, Fannie Mae, and Freddie Mac — were designed to lower initial down payment costs and to make monthly mortgage payments more feasible. However, in many cases it is simply not possible for low-income people to make these payments consistently over time given their job access. Low-income people tend to have less stable jobs, and thus if they are home owners, they are more likely to face defaults on loans and to feel the burden of owning in difficult financial times.

Who Can Afford a Home?

The majority of the people who buy homes have to take out a loan. This means that what a household can afford is dependent on their savings to

---

[133] Long and Caudill, "Racial Differences in Homeownership," 83.
[134] Green and White, "Measuring the Benefits," 444.
[135] Stegman, Quercia, and McCarthy, "Housing America's Working Families," 12.
[136] Dreier, "Why America's Workers Can't Pay the Rent," 40.
[137] Collins, Belsky and Retsinas "Towards Tax Credit," 11.

cover down payment and closing costs, and their income to cover mortgage payments and upkeep.[138] Thus savings and income are the two primary factors that determine whether or not households can purchase a home. Figure 2.20 measures the percentage of individuals and families from both renter and owner households who could afford to purchase a modestly priced home in 1995. This figure makes two important points. First, it indicates that households that already own homes are far more likely to be able to purchase a home because they have more wealth and resources at their disposal than renter households. Second, it shows that the homeownership affordability gap by race is similar to the overall homeownership gap.

Recent research on housing affordability shows the widening wealth gap between high-income and low-income people. Incomes have risen in recent years, yet they have not risen uniformly across the population, with more growth at the upper end of the distribution than at the bottom.[139] In terms of housing, one of the primary problems for low-income households is that wages have not kept up with the changes in the housing market. In 1993, Peter Linneman and Joseph Gyourko noted that falling real wages combined with rising real home prices had by 1989 made lower-quality homes, which were affordable in 1974, unaffordable to many comparable households.[140] Gyourko and Linneman continue to point out the complexity of these problems:

> Virtually no new housing is being produced that is of low enough quality to be affordable to low-skilled households who want to become owners. While there is demand for such homes — perhaps of the quality of the original Levittown homes — strict building codes, approval delays, stringent low-density zoning, and impact fees may have made producing such housing economically infeasible by for-profit builders. Further, because the real wages of low-skilled workers continue to be eroded by an increasingly competitive global economy, we envision little help from the labor market. An important implication of this burgeoning affordability problem is that the strong rise in ownership that most demographers are predicting as baby boomers age will not happen, because many unskilled boomers will never be able to afford homeownership.[141]

The situation has shifted somewhat since 1993, and homeownership has risen in the United States. Yet the points made about incomes and about

---

[138] National Association of Home Builders. *The Future of Home Building*, 119.
[139] Segal and Sullivan, "Trends in Homeownership," 65.
[140] Gyourko and Linneman, "Affordability and the American Dream," 68.
[141] Ibid., 41.

FIGURE 2.20
Homeownership Affordability for a Modestly Priced House in 1995

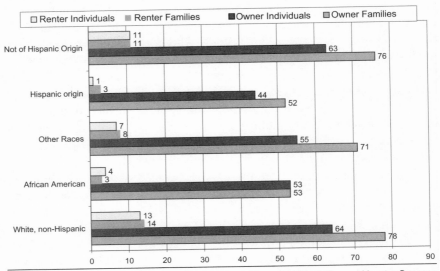

SOURCE: Savage, Howard A., "Who Could Afford to Buy a House in 1995?" *Current Housing Reports*, H121/99-1, U.S. Census Bureau August 1999, 3.
NOTE: Affordability relates to the ability to qualify for a conventional, 30–year mortgage with a 5% down payment.

investment in housing that is both affordable and desirable for low-income families are important. The National Low-Income Housing Coalition recently reported that there is no city in the United States where a family living on the federal minimum wage can afford to rent a typical apartment. In seventy metropolitan areas, minimum-wage workers would have to labor more than one hundred hours a week to afford market rents — that is, to pay no more than 30% of their income in rent.[142] Consequently, few low-income families can even think of becoming home owners. Also, although more families have become home owners over the last six years or so, many home owners at the lower end of the income spectrum continue to struggle financially.[143] As mentioned in Chapter 1, affordability is clearly the primary housing challenge in America.

---

[142] Dreier, "Why America's Workers Can't Pay the Rent," 38.

[143] Stegman, Quercia and McCarthy, "Housing America's Working Families," 12. *Note:* Critical housing needs are defined as households that spend more than half their total income on housing and/ or live in a seriously inadequate unit.

In response to this situation, organizations such as Fannie Mae and Freddie Mac have tried to devise new means of making homeownership more accessible to lower-income households. In 1992, Fannie Mae began conducting a National Housing Survey to determine Americans' attitudes toward housing and homeownership. The results showed that high down payments were the biggest challenge to ownership.[144] Since then, numerous programs have been devised to reduce the cost of the down payment on a home to between 3% and 0%. This type of targeted programming has helped to reduce the affordability problem. Additionally, advances in the loan application process have helped to speed the process and to more accurately determine the risk factor of the borrowing household; in many cases, this has led to increased homeownership. One of the most important advances in the mortgage industry has been automated underwriting. Automated underwriting uses a computerized analysis of a borrower's credit history to more accurately predict the risk of a borrower failing to pay back the mortgage. As the Fannie Mae National Housing Survey conducted in 1999 reports: "Automated underwriting and credit scoring have enabled the mortgage industry to more efficiently approve prospective home buyers' applications. Evidence shows that more families, not fewer, have been able to become home buyers faster, and with less hassle."[145] This illustrates that there have been a number of strong and effective efforts to expand homeownership opportunities for everyone, although much more remains to be done.

HOMEOWNERSHIP IN THE 1990S AND BEYOND

In the 1990s, homeownership rates in the United States rose to new highs.[146] This deserves special examination in light of how these changes may influence ownership levels in the twenty-first century. The 1990s also revealed a number of demographic changes that will likely affect the

---

[144] Fannie Mae, "National Housing Survey, 1999," 2.

[145] Ibid., 12.

[146] A recent working paper from the Joint Center for Housing Studies of Harvard University suggests that the rates may not have increased as much as data sources report, but were exaggerated by changes in methodology. The authors conclude that the ownership rates did rise during this time span — just not jump quite as much as some of the data sources indicate. For more information, see: Masnick, George S., McArdle, Nancy, and Eric S. Belsky, "A Critical Look at Rising Homeownership Rates in the United States Since 1994." Working Paper No. W99-2 Joint Center for Housing Studies, Harvard University, January 1999.

composition of the population and how households are formed in the coming decades.

Changing Circumstances

In the 1990s, many of the forces that shape the profiles of home owners began to shift. For the past three decades, the baby boom generation has dominated the housing markets, and in the 1990s, this cohort continued to have a major impact. In fact, the increase in homeownership rates at the end of the 1990s was due, in part to baby boomers in their late forties and fifties opting to buy homes.[147] However, members of Generation X and some echo boomers were just starting their first jobs, forming households, and making their first housing choices, and they began to have significant impacts as well. It is therefore important to note the ways in which these two younger generations differ from the baby boom cohort, because they will be at the forefront of the housing market in the future, and their housing choices may divert from those of their predecessors.

One of the major differences between the baby boomers and Generation X is that marriage is not a prerequisite for purchasing a home.[148] In the 1990s, there has been a significant rise in the number of single people purchasing homes. Figure 2.21 shows the percentages of home owners who live alone over time. Between 1940 and 1997, there was a 12.9% increase in owners living alone in their homes. Childless households had a 3% higher homeownership rate in 1997 than in 1977, while the rate for those with four or more children declined by more than 10%.[149] Initially, this appears to be a generational difference — more young householders today prefer to live alone. Yet it also means that although the numbers of households that are home owners has risen, it appears that the total number of people living in owned homes may be declining. Also interesting is that members of Generation X are starting out with higher homeownership levels than comparable baby boomers at the same age.[150] Another major difference in households in the 1990s is that increasingly they are dual-income households. This is true for both Generation X and the echo boomers. In some cases, having two incomes has allowed households to move more rapidly into homeownership.

---

[147] Throughout this book, three generations will be referred to: The "baby boom" generation refers to people born between 1945 and 1976; "Generation X" refers to those born during the "baby bust" period from 1965 to 1976; the "echo boom" generation refers to those born after 1977.

[148] Wellner, "Gen-X Homes In," 59.

[149] Segal and Sullivan. "Trends in Homeownership," 55.

[150] Wellner, "Gen-X Homes In," 58.

FIGURE 2.21

Percentage of Home Owners Living Alone Has Increased

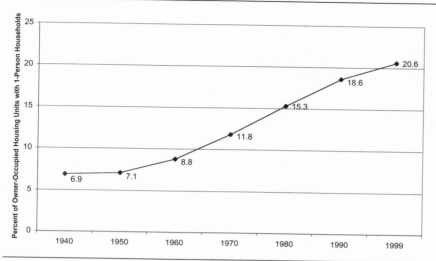

SOURCE: "Historical Census of Housing Tables—Living Alone" (www.census.gov/hhes/www/housing/census/historic/livalone) and "American Housing Survey 1999."

As mentioned previously, intergenerational assistance often facilitates movement into homeownership. Baby Boomers tend to be wealthier and have more wealth resources to pass on to their children to help with a variety of costs. This assistance helped new households in the 1990s and is expected to continue to help them well into the twenty-first century. Another shift that makes the 1990s unique is that minorities accounted for nearly 40% of the growth in home owners, as shown in Figure 2.22. Among the minority groups, Hispanics have seen the most significant leap in homeownership. The net growth in owners from 1994 to 1999 was 6.9 million, and in this time span, over one million Hispanic households became owners. African American households also made significant gains — adding close to one million more African American home owners over five years.[151]

This growth in minority homeownership is linked more broadly to rising levels of low-income ownership. The number of loans made to low-income home buyers from 1993 to 1999 surged by 94%.[152] Low-income households have increasingly been given opportunities to overcome their

---

[151] Joint Center for Housing Studies, *State of the Nation's Housing 2000*, 16–17.

[152] The loans to higher-income buyers in the same time span rose by only 52%, Duda and Belsky, "Anatomy of the Low-Income Homeownership Boom," 1.

FIGURE 2.22
Minorities Account for Nearly 40% of Home Owner Growth 1994–1999

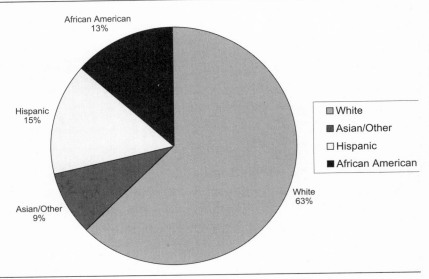

SOURCE: Joint Center for Housing Studies, *State of the Nation's Housing, 2000.*

wealth and income restraints to become home owners. Public policies such as the Community Reinvestment Act, fair housing laws, and affordable housing goals for Freddie Mac and Fannie Mae have helped provide such opportunities. Many of the low-income and minority households that entered into homeownership in the 1990s purchased their homes in suburbs and outside of poverty tracts.[153] The implications of this remain to be sorted out, and many low-income households still buy closer to the central business district than higher-income households. Regardless, the increases in low-income and minority homeownership do suggest a shift in buying trends.

The expansion of technology and telecommunications greatly changed the workplace in the 1990s. The trend toward a highly skilled knowledge- and service-based economy continues into the twenty-first century.[154] Any significant shifts in the job market — such as where people work, how often, how much they are paid — impact the housing sector. Increasingly, people are working from their homes, and this allows for flexibility in terms of where people are able to purchase homes, which in turn makes

---

[153] Duda and Belsky, "Anatomy of the Low-Income Homeownership Boom," 28.
[154] Stegman, "Recent U.S. Change," 1601.

more affordable choices available. Strides in technology and shifting ways of doing business have also allowed companies to choose varied locations for offices and production centers, again giving workers more housing options.

In the 1990s, people reported that they were more informed about the home buying process than in previous decades. This is partially due to targeted advertising and to the Internet. Today, potential buyers are able to quickly locate the information they need and then be prepared when going to request a home loan. In the past, lack of such information and understanding was cited as a major obstacle to home buying. At the end of the 1990s, one of the most significant challenge preventing people from becoming owners was a failure to understand the consequences of a poor credit rating. As reported in the 2000 Fannie Mae National Housing Survey, potential home buyers did not understand that poor credit can severely undermine one's chances of getting approved for a mortgage. Many of the survey respondents did not know that paying monthly bills late affects credit rating and hinders one's ability to get a mortgage.[155]

High Levels of Immigration

The arrival of millions of new people to the United States during the 1990s greatly affected the housing markets. As indicated by Figure 2.23, immigration reached its highest point ever in U.S. history in the 1990s. After peaking from 1900 to 1910 at 8.9 million people, immigration declined dramatically. However, after World War II, it began to rise again, and in the 1980s swelled to 9 million immigrants. In the 1990s, the numbers rose again by more than 2 million people, reaching upward to 11 million new immigrants flowing into the country that decade. The influx of new people also differed from previous waves of immigration to the United States. As depicted in Figure 2.24, the origins of the foreign-born population in 1960 vary dramatically from the origins of immigrants in 1990. The dominant shift has been a decrease in immigration from Europe and a significant rise in immigration from Mexico and Latin American countries. Figure 2.24 shows that the number of immigrants from Europe in 1990 dropped to 21.8% of the total, a decrease of 53.2% since 1960. Immigration from Mexico exceeded immigration from all the other Latin American countries combined; 23.3% of all immigrants were Mexican. Immigration from Mexico is often placed with immigration from other

---

[155] Fannie Mae, "National Housing Survey 2000," 10.

FIGURE 2.23
Immigration to the U.S. by Decade

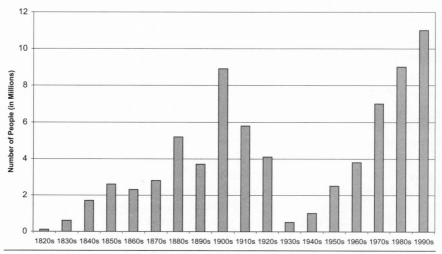

SOURCE: Passel, Jeffrey S., and Barry Edmonston, "Immigration and Race: Recent Trends in Immigration to the U.S.," and Joint Center for Housing Studies estimates from INS data.

Latin American countries, but it is important to recognize Mexico as one of the major sources of immigrants. Another recent shift in immigration is that people moving to the United States tend to be younger than previous generations of immigrants. In 1998, 19.6% of immigrants were fifteen years old or younger, 32.3% were fifteen to twenty-nine, 26.9% were thirty to forty-four, and 15.4% were forty-five to sixty-four.[156] Consequently, many do not come as married couples. They have tended to become renters and to form their first households after arriving in the country. The influx of large numbers of young people forming households means a growing pool of potential future home owners.

Another important factor in recent trends is that immigration has tended to concentrate in what are known as "gateway" cities. That is, recent arrivals generally cluster in metropolitan areas such as New York City, Los Angeles, Chicago, Houston, Miami, and Boston. Given their younger age and the fact that many are starting new jobs and beginning a new life in the United States, many recent immigrants do not cite homeownership as an immediate priority. However, it is a goal for many. Immigrants may face

[156] Immigration and Naturalization Services, "Legal Immigration," 10.

FIGURE 2.24
Regional Origin of Immigrants to the U.S. in 1960 and 1990

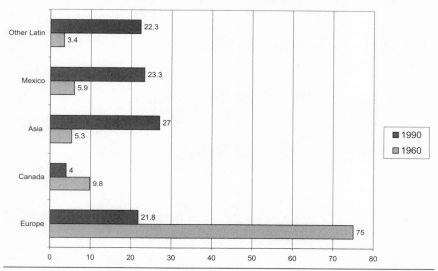

SOURCE: McArdle, "Foreign Immigration and Homeownership." Tabulations of the 1960 and 1990 Decennial Census, PUMS 1%.

discrimination based on their foreign-born status and their race or ethnicity. In this sense, immigrants and minorities in the United States may face similar challenges when purchasing a home. Often the details of purchasing a home — such as financing, the function of real estate agents, the time involved — are not as obvious or accessible to minority or immigrant households.[157] Figure 2.25 illustrates perceptions of the major obstacles to homeownership. The largest factor is purely financial — having money for a down payment — but certainly lack of knowledge, discrimination, and social barriers are impediments. When minority and immigrant households become owners, they often form community housing advocacy groups to assist if problems such as foreclosure arise or to generate emergency loan funds for home repairs.[158] These are examples of how immigrants and minorities are attempting to navigate the housing market. Expansion of such community groups and more extensive services to expedite and to provide knowledge about home buying could help tap the growing potential pool of immigrant owners.

[157] Ratner, "Many Routes to Homeownership," 137.
[158] Ibid., 132.

FIGURE 2.25
Perceived Barriers to Homeownership
Percent Rating Each Factor a Major Obstacle to Buying

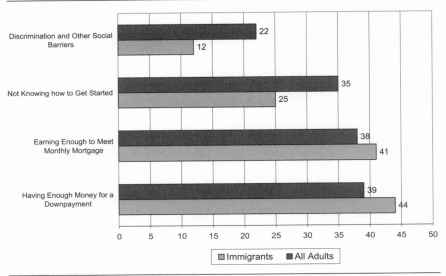

SOURCE: McArdle, "Foreign Immigration and Homeownership."
DATA FROM: Fannie Mae National Housing Survey, 1995.

Immigrants who have become citizens are more likely to live in owner-occupied homes than noncitizens living in the United States. Figure 2.26 shows this trend, and also points out that the longer immigrants have resided in the United States — regardless of citizenship status — the more likely they are to live in owner-occupied housing. In the past, immigrants have not equaled comparable native-born households in terms of home-ownership. However, the second generation — children of foreign-born parents — has tended to compare equally with native-born households in income, education, and homeownership. It is likely that this will also be true of the children of immigrants who moved to the country in the 1990s. Nancy McArdle summarizes the relationship between recent immigrants and homeownership:

> In some places [recent immigrants] have already made substantial impacts in the young buyer market and form a large proportion of the age group we traditionally look toward to become first time buyers. While not attaining the ownership rates of the same-aged, native-born whites, they do make

FIGURE 2.26

Percentage of Foreign-Born Citizens and Noncitizens Living in Owner-Occupied Households (by Age and Year of Entry into the U.S.)

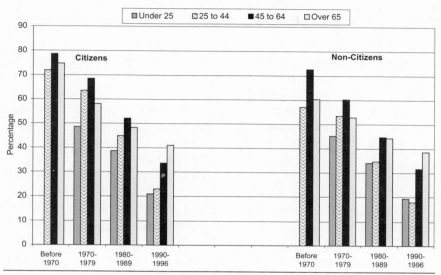

SOURCE: U.S. Census Bureau, Current Population Survey, 1996.
NOTE: There is no data for people under age 25 before 1970.

substantial progress as they remain in the U.S. over time. Furthermore, they expand the pool of potential first time buyers by extending the age group that we typically associate with first time buying into older ages. Certain groups of immigrants make very impressive gains toward homeownership indeed. However, the fact that immigrants as a whole do not attain the ownership rates of comparably endowed native whites and that they explicitly cite confusion about the home buying process and fears about discrimination, suggests that there is much to be done in order to allow this growing population to reach its full home buying potential.[159]

Certainly the recent surge in immigration has affected job markets, the kinds of homes people want to buy, and the cultural activities in many major U.S. cities. In a number of ways, the last decade marks a break with the past and shows a glimpse of the new composition of U.S. society. Immigration trends of the 1990s will likely continue into the twenty-first

[159] McArdle, "Foreign Immigration," 19–20.

century, and their effects on home buying markets will be felt in waves over the next several decades.

Population Projections

Looking carefully at trends over the last fifty years and specifically in the 1990s allows researchers to make projections about future household growth, and housing demand. As discussed previously, the fact that a large portion of immigrants in the 1990s were young means that there is great potential for household formation and home buying in this immigrant co-hort — which includes many minorities — in the upcoming decades. Also, it is likely that the trend of more owners living alone will continue to increase. A working paper done at the Joint Center for Housing Studies in 1996 projected that of the 6.9 million single-person households that will be added through 2010, more than a third will be age sixty-five and over.[160] This paper also notes that the aging of the baby boom generation will mean that the strongest household growth from 2000 to 2010 will be among fifty-five- to sixty-four- year-olds and the number of households with heads over age seventy-five will continue to rise. Also, the average age of householders will be greatly weighted toward the older end of the spectrum.[161]

Figure 2.27 is a compilation of population projections by race for 2001 and 2025, as calculated by the Population Projections Program of the U.S. Census Bureau. While these calculations show that white people will continue to be the majority, they will decline to only 62% of the total population by 2025. Hispanics will have the most impressive population gains by 2025, and are expected to continue showing strong gains throughout the twenty-first century.[162] If the homeownership gap between whites and minorities is maintained into the twenty-first century, this will have serious implications and will result in lopsided homeownership. As mentioned previously, the ownership gap between whites and minority groups narrowed by barely 1% in the 1990s, and the gap itself is around 25%. As minorities become a larger proportion of the U.S. population in the twenty-first century, it will be important to narrow this gap to continue to maintain high homeownership rates.

---

[160] Masnick, McArdle and Apgar, "U.S. Household Trends," 17.
[161] Ibid., 12.
[162] See: Population Projections Program, Population Division, U.S. Census Bureau (www.census.gov/population/projections/nation/summary/np-t5-b.txt).

FIGURE 2.27
Population Projections by Race for the US

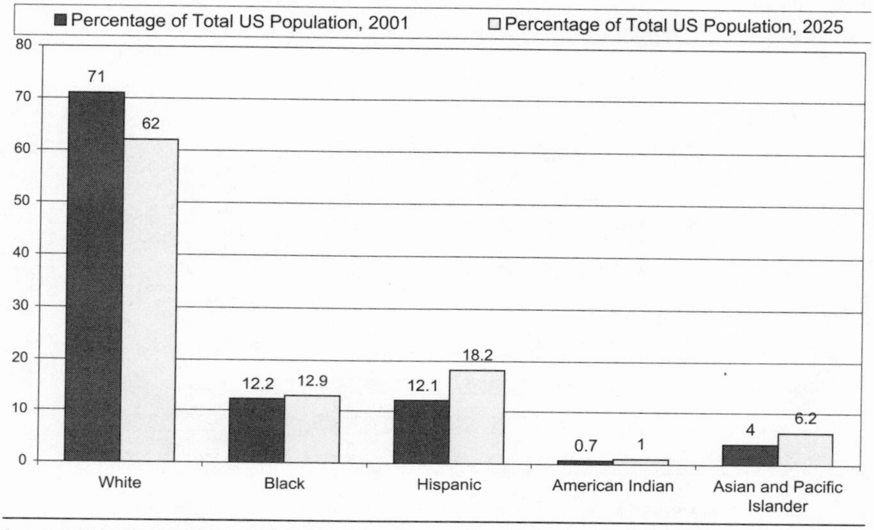

| ■ Percentage of Total US Population, 2001 | □ Percentage of Total US Population, 2025 |

SOURCE: U.S. Census Bureau, Population Projections Program, Population Division (www.census.gov/population/projections/nation/summary/np-t5-b.txt).

International Homeownership

Although homeownership in the United States is at an all time high, the U.S. homeownership rate is not the highest in the world. In fact, as illustrated in Figure 2.28, the U.S. is behind at least five other countries. Ireland leads the world with a homeownership rate above 80%, and Spain, Italy, Australia, and Britain all have rates above the United States. Naturally, many other factors are important to consider when comparing housing worldwide, such as the size and quality of the homes and cultural preferences. However, when the challenge is echoed that we can do better as a nation, it is worthwhile to realize that in the area of homeownership rates, other countries have been able to achieve a higher level.

Policy Suggestions for the Future

Based on the foregoing discussion of homeownership, it seems appropriate to highlight ten suggestions for homeownership policy in the twenty-first century.

FIGURE 2.28
International Homeownership Rates

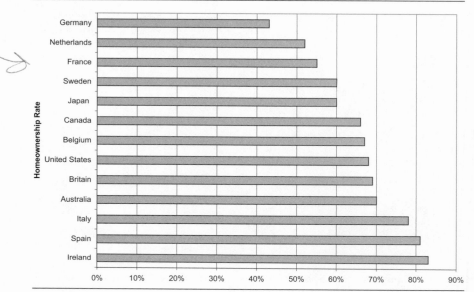

SOURCE: The Economist, "Going Through the Roof," March 30–April 5, 2002, 65. Data from European Mortgage Federation; IUHF; national statistics.

1. *Low down payments.* The down payment has long been cited as a major obstacle to ownership. Many families that would be able to meet the monthly costs of owning are prevented from buying a home because they cannot afford this initial down payment. Lowering the down payment on a home purchase was clearly helpful to first-time buyers in the 1990s. FHA loans have low down payments, so expanding access to such loans could be an important resource for first-time buyers. Continued efforts by Fannie Mae and Freddie Mac and others to lower down payment costs and to devise new financial tactics to assist in this area will greatly help the potential owners of the twenty-first century.

2. *Lower monthly payments.* Many home owners are challenged by the basic monthly costs of paying home bills, mortgage costs, and maintenance on the home. Such owners are forced to spend a large portion of their incomes on housing costs, leaving little for other basic necessities — such as health care — or for savings. Of all working families with critical housing needs, 76% (or 2.4 million

households) spend over half of their incomes on housing.[163] The majority of these households own their homes. This situation is most severe in high-cost areas such as New York, Los Angeles, San Jose, Washington, D.C., San Francisco, Tampa, Oakland, and Boston. Thus policies aimed at lowering monthly housing costs can help families use their incomes more efficiently.

3. *Tax credit for low-income home owners.* Formulating a new tax policy targeted for low-income households would help propel many renters into homeownership. President George W. Bush proposed a Homeownership Tax Credit in 2002 as a part of a program to raise minority homeownership and close the minority homeownership gap. A publication from Harvard's Joint Center for Housing Studies lists four ways in which tax polices could be created to foster homeownership for low-income people:

A. Provide a refundable income tax credit to cover closing costs and a down payment of up to 20% — the level at which mortgage lenders no longer require mortgage insurance.

B. Provide an income tax incentive for renters to save for a 20% down payment and closing costs in tax-free accounts or accounts matched by tax refunds.

C. Provide a tax subsidy to lenders for the difference between market and below-market-interest rates for first mortgages that fully finance closing costs and require only a small down payment.

D. Provide a tax subsidy to lenders for the difference between market and below-market-interest rates for second mortgages that capitalize down payment and closing costs into a below-market-interest-rate loan.[164]

4. *Education and home buyer training.* Expanding access to information about housing markets, how to save for a home purchase, and how to prepare to take out a loan is critical for first-time buyers. As the Fannie Mae National Housing Surveys showed in the 1990s, Americans are increasingly comfortable with the process of purchasing a home and getting a mortgage. This indicates that recent efforts must continue. In particular, financial institutions must continue to work on the key problems of potential buyers — the largest

---

[163] Stegman, Quercia and McCarthy, "Housing America's Working Families," 9.
[164] Collins, Belsky, and Retsinas, "Towards Tax Credit," 13–14.

of which is bad credit ratings. By providing ownership counseling sessions, lending institutions, nonprofit organizations, and in some cases the federal government, can help potential owners overcome barriers related to a poor understanding of the buying process.

5. *Immigrant home buying.* The points made above regarding education and training are especially important for immigrants because they face obstacles that native-born citizens do not. James Johnson provides three suggestions for conducting outreach to new immigrants:

   A. In the process of becoming citizens, immigrants should be exposed to the process of becoming a home owner. The Immigration and Nationalization Service (INS) and housing finance industry should establish links to help provide new immigrants who are studying to become citizens with the consumer information they need to buy a home in America.

   B. Although many immigrants have English skills, it is crucial to provide housing information in the immigrant's native language so that the buying process is understood in full.

   C. Training lenders and real estate professionals in cultural differences that affect the home buying process can help facilitate discussions between potential immigrant buyers and housing professionals.[165]

6. *Addressing Discrimination.* Substantial progress has been made in reducing discriminatory practices over the last several decades. In 1968, the Fair Housing Act made it illegal to discriminate in the sale (or rental) of housing on the grounds of race, color, religion, or national origin. Continued efforts to monitor lending institutions for discriminatory behavior are essential. It is also important to raise the awareness of underwriters, appraisers, Realtors, and lenders to the subtle ways in which they may discriminate, often unconsciously.[166]

7. *Utilizing new technology.* Advances in technology, particularly the use of computers and the Internet, have accelerated the lending process to make it simpler and less time-consuming. Activities such as credit scoring and underwriting can occur much faster and with higher levels of accuracy than ever before. Technology can

---

[165] Johnson, *Showing America*, 111.
[166] Ibid., 107.

also shorten the application process and make origination less expensive. Additionally, many consumers cite that they were able to locate information about the home buying process on the Internet. As the Internet continues to expand, it will likely further speed the mortgage process by allowing more buyers to prequalify for a mortgage, and to get final approval online.

8. *State and Local Involvement.* Increasingly, the activities that foster homeownership and create affordable housing have shifted from the federal level to state and local organizations. HUD block grant programs go to states and local governments. Many mayors, governors, and community leaders have made strong commitments to increasing homeownership in their regions. As we continue forward in the twenty-first century, it will be important to highlight and support these efforts at the state and local level.

9. *Nonprofits and creative partnerships.* In recent years, there has been a proliferation of grassroots organizations, many of which are religiously based, around the topic of housing. Many of them are important sources of support in their given locales, and partnerships between such organizations, the housing finance industry, and government can produce positive results. Such organizations help by, for example, counseling prospective buyers who do not initially qualify for a mortgage. Without support, many such people may feel frustrated and give up. Extending counseling programs run by national and grassroots organizations may help more of these households to reorganize and try again. [167]

10. *Removal of Regulatory Barriers.* As discussed in Chapter 1, houses in the United States have grown in terms of amenities and size over the last fifty years. Both of these trends increase the amount of labor materials needed to create, remodel, and maintain homes. Other factors that have driven up home prices include high property taxes, exclusionary zoning, building codes, rent controls, subdivision rules, and growth-control ordinances.[168] If some of the costs of building and of regulations could be reduced, homeownership would be more accessible. This will be key to unlocking the potential for increased homeownership in coming decades.

---

[167] Ibid., 135.

[168] U.S. Advisory Commission on Regulatory Barriers to Affordable Housing, "Not In My Back Yard."

CONCLUSIONS

Homeownership over the past fifty years has been a story of success. Homeownership in the nation rose rapidly with the close of World War II. From this period onward, the federal government and key government or government-sponsored financial institutions have been committed to making ownership a reality in people's lives. FHA and VA loans were innovative ways of helping a broader spectrum of Americans afford homeownership, and the development of the secondary mortgage market played an important role in advancing homeownership in the century. Today, more Americans own homes than ever before. People purchasing homes today also have a far greater range of options than any previous generation, and homes tend to be larger with more amenities. In discussing the Housing Act of 1949, Sylvia Martinez writes: "Perhaps one of the greatest national achievements of the twentieth century has been the democratization of homeownership. Owning one's home is no longer a privilege reserved for the elite. For most Americans today, the opportunity to own a home is implicit in the promise of 1949."[169] However, as technology, demographics, economics, and society continue to change, it will be worthwhile to continue encouraging homeownership with the expectation that ownership will benefit many additional Americans in the future.

This chapter has sought to explain the diversity of ownership across the housing sector and the many ways in which ownership can be beneficial to American families. Home owners are more likely to be satisfied with their homes and neighborhoods. Many owners feel that they have achieved a lifelong goal when they purchase a home. Research reveals that owners are more likely to be involved in civic, political, and volunteer activities in their local communities. Owners appear to have a more vested interest in their local communities and, for a variety of reasons, tend to remain in their homes for longer periods of time than renters.

The typical home owner tends to be more educated, and the majority of home owners are married couples. Citizens tend to have a far higher ownership rate than those who live in the United States as noncitizens. However, in reviewing the profile of owners, two problem areas emerge — affordability and discrimination. These challenges are not new, and in fact progress has been made in both areas. Yet challenges remain on these fronts in the twenty-first century, making it crucial for homeownership to remain a top priority in political arenas. In the coming years, it will be im-

---

[169] Martinez, "Housing Act of 1949," 468.

portant to build affordable new homes and to remove the barriers to building affordable housing. Continued advances in the mortgage market to help with issues such as lowering down payments will be significant for increasing homeownership. Also, the ownership gap between whites and minorities must be addressed, especially as the number of minorities rises in the twenty-first century. Reducing this gap will allow households that have traditionally been kept from ownership to become home owners. Continued efforts to enforce laws that prevent discriminatory lending and redlining will also be necessary.

The increased levels of homeownership over the last fifty years point to important progress. Owning a home provides social and financial benefits, and as we look to the future, homeownership should continue as an important part of the nations housing policy in the twenty-first century.

Chapter 3:

MULTIFAMILY HOUSING IN THE TWENTY-FIRST CENTURY

In response to demographic shifts and a variety of government-sponsored incentives, homeownership rates have risen over the last fifty years. Despite this national focus on homeownership, it is important to recognize that multifamily rental housing plays an essential role in meeting the nation's housing needs.[1]

Understanding the nature and composition of multifamily rental housing requires moving beyond the simple distinction between renters and home owners, and between single-family and multifamily housing. Not all renters live in multifamily rental apartments (structures with five or more units) — some rent single-family houses and units in smaller properties. Likewise, not all home owners live in single-family houses — some own condominiums and cooperatives in multifamily structures.

In 2000, there were 34.3 million rental housing units, and they comprised 32.8% of the nation's 104.7 million housing units. Of these rental units, approximately 33.4% were in single-family houses and 18% were in smaller buildings with two to four units.[2] The remaining 48.6% of rental housing units — totaling 16.7 million units and 15.9% of the total housing stock — were in buildings with five or more units each. Figure 3.1 provides a geographic representation of the housing stock in 2000 by tenure and structure size.

The housing industry generally defines multifamily rental housing — often referred to as apartments — as renter-occupied structures with five or more housing units, and this chapter will focus primarily on this segment of the housing stock. Apartment units comprise 48.6% of all rental

---

[1] Much of the research and analysis contained in the chapter was supported by the National Multi Housing Council (NMHC). Special appreciation is expressed to NMHC for their support, and for the personal support of Jack Goodman and Jonathan Kempner who were at the NMHC at the time the work was done.
[2] Schnare, "Impact of Changes in Multifamily Finance," 3.

FIGURE 3.1

Housing Units by Tenure and Structure Size: 2000

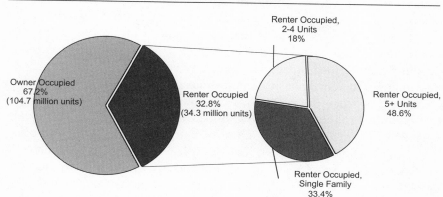

NUMBERS ADAPTED FROM: Schnare, "Impact of Changes in Multifamily Finance."

NOTE: According to Ann Schnare's estimates in March 2000, there were 104,705,000 total housing units, 34,336,000 rental units, and 70,369,000 owner-occupied units.

units, but because apartment *properties* contain at least five, and often many more, units they make up just 10% of all rental properties.[3] (Unless otherwise noted, apartments are defined in this chapter as housing units in rental properties with five or more units.)

Residents of multifamily rental housing are as diverse as the population itself. They span the income distribution, from households that could buy a home but choose instead to rent, to moderate-income renters, to lower-income households that rent out of economic necessity. Apartments also serve a variety of lifestyle needs. Upper-income households are attracted to the convenience and location of upscale apartments, often found in cities and high-end neighborhoods. Lack of maintenance, ease of relocation, and convenience of location and transportation are other factors that encourage households to choose rental housing.

Thanks in part to government-sponsored incentives, apartments have long served a critical niche within the housing market by providing essential affordable housing. In recent years, however, a variety of factors have

[3] Estimated from Simmons, *Housing Statistics in the United States,* 128. 1990 census data used in *Housing Statistics* presents data per household, rather than per building. However, it does indicate the number of units in the structure in which each household lives, broken into categories by building size. The total number of multifamily buildings was estimated by dividing the number of households per category by the mean structure size for that category. For example, the 4,283,000 renter households living in structures containing 5 to 9 units were estimated to represent 611,857 (4,283,000 / 7) multifamily buildings.

contributed to an ever-worsening shortage of decent, affordable rental housing for both lower- and moderate-income families. These factors include changes over the last two decades in federal housing programs, public tax and regulatory policies that have reduced incentives for private investment in apartments, and the stagnation of real income for some people. Recently, modest federal efforts have been made to increase affordable multifamily rental housing, but the impact also appears to be modest.

While apartments are best known for their affordability, in recent years the traditional stereotypes about who lives in apartments have been challenged by the growing number of discretionary renters and people who are at the higher-end of the market. Many of these are young professional and empty-nester households living in the inner city or the suburbs close to employment centers or subways, who are looking for better commutes and freedom from the burdens of homeownership. The apartment industry has responded to these nontraditional renters in ways that have revolutionized apartment living and made it more competitive with single-family housing. Improved designs, new technologies, increased amenities, and a focus on resident satisfaction are all helping to further apartment demand at the top end of the market.

In addition, growing concern over suburban sprawl has renewed both public and private interest in the role apartments can play in creating more livable communities. Recognized for their often more efficient use of infrastructure and service delivery, and their contributions toward reducing congestion and pollution, apartments are becoming an important ingredient in the smart-growth agenda.

THE BENEFITS OF MULTIFAMILY RENTAL HOUSING

Multifamily rental housing provides a broad range of benefits to both the communities in which it is located and the residents it houses. It provides economic benefits through its construction; it fills diverse and significant market needs; and it can enrich the communities where it is located.

Economic Benefits

The economic benefits of multifamily rental housing are felt at both the national and local level. The nation benefits from the construction of new apartments through the jobs created to build the housing and the products that go therein, and to design, finance, and manage the projects. For example, in 1997, the production of 341,000 multifamily units (in buildings with two or more units) nationwide generated 350,000 jobs, $10.9 billion in wages, and $5.4 billion in federal, state, and local taxes.[4]

Beyond job creation and tax revenue benefits at the local level, new apartment construction also produces ripple effects as the construction wages generated by the project are spent on local goods and services and as the new residents begin spending in the local economy. According to the National Association of Home Builders, a typical 100-unit apartment project generates, over ten years, 445 jobs, $23.2 million in local income, and $3.7 million in local taxes.[5] (See Figure 3.2)

Once the project is constructed, ongoing economic benefits are generated in the form of property taxes, employment for people who manage and maintain the building, and consumer spending by the renters. Another benefit is more efficient delivery of services from both the public and private sectors because of the greater densities found in apartment living. For example, senior citizens are often served better, and at less cost, when living in multifamily projects. Naturally, some of these efficiencies will depend on the scale of the development and the way projects are clustered, but the benefits that come from providing greater densities and economies of scale can be important both for the renter and for the community.

Market Need

Apartments serve several market needs. For many residents, apartments are the only affordable housing available. Because they are high density and spread land costs across more units, apartments are more affordable than single-family houses.

Apartments also serve the lifestyle needs of many people. First, the high-density nature of multifamily housing makes it easier for apartment owners to provide the amenities that attract upper-income households. Over the last few years, upscale apartments have added such things as high-speed Internet access, on-site business centers, fitness facilities, cyber cafés, and dedicated concierge services to make daily living more convenient for their residents. The lack of maintenance chores is a draw for many renters, while others are attracted by the ability to relocate for career and other reasons without incurring the costs of selling a home. Apartments, when well designed and monitored, can also provide important

---

[4] Colton, Crowe, and Emrath, *Benefits of Multifamily Housing,* 4.
[5] Ibid., 4–5.

FIGURE 3.2
Local Economic Impact of 100 Multifamily Home

	Year of Construction	On-Going	Over 10 Years
Local Income ($000)	$5,234	$1,798	$23,210
Local Taxes and Fees ($000)	$579	$308	$3,660
Local Employment (jobs)	122	46	445*

SOURCE: NAHB Local Economic Impact Model for a typical metropolitan area, as reported in National Association of Home Builders "Housing's Impact on the Economy," Report Submitted to the Millennial Housing Commission, November, 2001, p. 8. *SOURCE: Colton, Benefits of Multifamily Housing, 1998.

security benefits and protection from crime. They can offer location advantages not available in single-family developments. Multifamily housing tends to be closer to employment centers, public transportation, and neighborhood services.[6] This location advantage makes apartments a leading component in urban revitalization.

Community Benefits

Multifamily rental housing can create community-wide benefits, even for those who choose to live in single-family homes. Its presence can create pedestrian-friendly neighborhoods and make communities more pleasant places to live. Multifamily housing helps relieve traffic congestion and pollution by providing housing closer to the workplace and by creating the densities required to support public transit. Apartments also provide significant environmental benefits by using land more efficiently and making it possible to preserve open space.[7] By increasing the residential options available, apartments make it possible for citizens to remain in the same community throughout the different stages of their lives. Recent graduates are able to stay in an area when there is an affordable housing option, and empty nesters looking for a simpler lifestyle are not forced to relocate if a suitable apartment or retirement community is available.[8]

The local jobs and spending created by new multifamily construction add economic vitality to a community. Apartments support an area's con-

[6] Urban Land Institute, *Case for Multifamily Housing*, 5.
[7] Ibid.
[8] Urban Land Institute, *ULI on the Future: Smart Growth*, 23.

tinued economic development by housing workers living in the area. Without a variety of housing options, local employers find it difficult to attract the employees needed to expand, and prospective employers are discouraged from locating or creating new businesses in the community.

THE CHANGING COMPOSITION OF MULTIFAMILY HOUSING

The residents served by multifamily housing are indeed diverse. While they are often associated with urban, lower-income households, multifamily residents also include higher-income lifestyle renters and a broad "middle market." In absolute numbers, lower- and moderate-income households make up the majority of the market, but in percentage terms, the fastest-growing segment of the multifamily market is the upper-income lifestyle renter who rents by choice.

Multifamily Housing Stock

As noted earlier, the housing industry generally defines multifamily rental housing as renter-occupied structures with five or more housing units. While apartments are found both in cities and in the suburbs that surround those cities, they are traditionally, and correctly, associated with urban living. In 1997, 51% of central-city households rented their homes, compared with 27% outside of cities. Also, rental properties located in the central city are more likely to have multiple units than are properties in the suburbs or outside metropolitan areas. In central cities, 52% of rental units are located in multifamily properties. This compares to 42% in the suburbs and only 23% outside metropolitan areas.[9] Because of these facts, fully 60% of center-city residents live in apartments, compared to 27% of suburban residents and 13% of those living outside metropolitan areas.[10]

Apartments are more prominent in some areas of the country than others. The South has led the country's four regions in apartment construction since 1980, and has increased its rate of construction each year since 1992.[11] As a result, the South today surpasses the other three regions in apartment units. Its 4.2 million apartment units make up 29% of the

[9] U.S. Census Bureau, "American Housing Survey 1997."
[10] Goodman, "Changing Demography of Multifamily Housing," 37.
[11] Joint Center for Housing Studies, *State of the Nation's Housing 1999*, 23. The country's four regions are the Northeast, Midwest, South and West.

nation's total apartment stock, while its 11.1 million rental units are a third of the total. That said, the Northeast has the highest proportion of rental units located in multifamily structures, 50%, compared to the South's 37%.[12]

When people think of apartments, they often think of high-rise apartment buildings in lower-income neighborhoods. On the contrary, in 1997, apartments in buildings of fifty or more units made up just 22% of all multifamily units.[13] A greater proportion of households in lower-income neighborhoods live in apartments, but these units are less likely to be located in huge apartment buildings than are units in higher-income neighborhoods. For example, using the 1991 Residential Finance Survey, Bogdon and Follain found that while low-income census tracts (with median incomes below 80% of area median) contained 26% of housing units, they contained 38% of all multifamily units. They contained an even greater share — 48% — of multifamily properties, indicating that multifamily properties located in lower-income tracts tended to be smaller than properties in higher-income neighborhoods.[14]

Demographic Diversity of Apartment Renters

Just as the apartment housing stock defies stereotypes, so do multifamily renters. While apartment households are often perceived as being low-income, this characterization is inaccurate in many instances. In fact, the decision to rent rather than buy is often based on factors other than affordability. According to Fannie Mae's 2000 *National Housing Survey,* nearly a third of renter households (32%) report that they rent as a matter of choice and not economic necessity.[15] (See Figure 3.3.) These often educated and affluent households eschew the burdens of homeownership and are presumably attracted to the flexibility and convenience associated with apartment living, the package of amenities and services offered by apartments, or the proximity of many apartment properties to employment, entertainment, and retail centers.

When measured by group averages, the characteristics of apartment renters tend to reinforce many of the stereotypes. The average income of apartment households is below the national average; the 1997 median annual income for apartment renters was $21,000 compared to $35,172 for

---

[12] U.S. Census Bureau, "American Housing Survey 1997."
[13] Ibid.
[14] Bogdon and Follain, "Multifamily Housing: An Exploratory Analysis," 89.
[15] Fannie Mae, *National Housing Survey, 1999,* 12.

FIGURE 3.3
Why Do Renters Choose to Rent

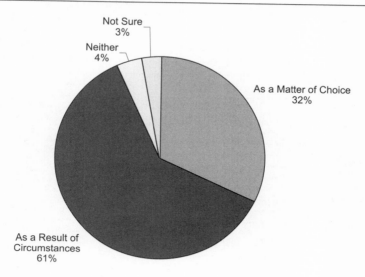

SOURCE: Fannie Mae, National Housing Survey, 2000.

households generally (see Figure 3.4). They are more mobile; 34% of apartment renters reported moving in the previous year, compared to 32% of other renters and 6% of home owners. They are more likely to be younger; 30% of apartment household heads were under thirty, compared to 14% of all households. They tend to be smaller households; 46% were one-person households, compared to 25% of total households. And they are more likely to be immigrant households. Nationally, just 3% of U.S. residents report having arrived here within the past ten years, but that figure triples among multifamily households. Finally, multifamily households are more likely than home owners to be people of color, 27% of multifamily renters are African-American or other nonwhite ethnicities, while those groups make up only 16% of all households nationwide.[16]

The broad view of apartment renters fails to capture their full diversity. Defying the view of apartment renters as low-income, highly mobile, and typically young are these facts:

---

[16] Data highlighted in this section and in Figure 4 is from the U.S. Census Bureau, 1997, found in Goodman, "Changing Demography of Multifamily Housing," 36.

FIGURE 3.4
Demographics of Multifamily Renters Versus All Households, 1997

	All Households	Multifamily Renters
Age		
Under 30	14%	30%
30–65	66%	54%
Over 65	20%	16%
Household Income		
Mean	$47,110	$29,603
Median	$35,172	$21,000
Race		
White	84.20%	72.70%
African American	12%	20.60%
Other	3.80%	6.70%
Hispanic Origin		
Yes	8.10%	14.90%
No	91.00%	84.20%
Household Size		
Mean	2.6	2
1 person	25%	46%
4+ persons	10%	5%
US resident less than 10 years		
Yes	3%	8.90%

ADAPTED FROM: Goodman, "Changing Demography of Multifamily Housing." 36, 42. DATA FROM: U.S. Census Bureau, 1997.

- Fully 3.5 million renters (of all housing types) earn 150% or more of the local area median income.
- 15% of multifamily renters remain in the same apartment for at least four years.
- 16% of multifamily renters are age sixty-five or older.[17]

One recent analysis by Jack Goodman offers a classification scheme that places apartment households into three broad groups: renters in affordable housing, lifestyle renters, and the middle market. (Figure 3.5.) *The affordable housing group* includes apartment renters who cannot afford to pay the market rent in their area and who must pay more than 30% of their incomes to rent decent housing. As shown in Figure 3.5, this group makes up nearly half (49%) of all apartment households and includes renters who live in privately-owned but federally-assisted housing and public housing. Fully 19% of all apartment renters and 39% of the affordable housing group live in assisted housing. These households are more likely than other multifamily renters to be nonwhite, and by definition have lower in-

---

[17] Ibid.

FIGURE 3.5

Resident Characteristics in the Three Markets for Multifamily Rental Housing

	Affordable Market		Middle Market	Lifestyle Market	All Apartment Households
	Total	Federally Assisted			
Share of all Apt. Householders	49%	19%	37%	14%	100%
Age of Householder					
Median	41	44	33	38	37
Mean	47	49	38	42	43
<30	26%	21%	39%	20%	30%
30-65	51%	48%	53%	70%	64%
65+	23%	31%	8%	10%	16%
Household Size					
Mean	2.1	2.3	2.2	1.4	2
1 person	50	43	31	65	46
4+ persons	17	19	14	0	5
With 1+ children	35	50	31	0	29
Household Income					
Mean	$11,795	$10,944	$42,752	$62,382	$29,603
Median	$10,444	$7,608	$32,100	$48,298	$21,000
Race					
White	66.70%	59.10%	74.20%	79.70%	72.70%
African-American	26.80%	34.80%	18.80%	11.90%	20.60%
Other	6.50%	6.10%	7%	8.40%	6.70%
Hispanic Origin	23%	14.60%	11.40%	8.10%	14.90%
Residency					
Moved in past year	30.10%	21.80%	38.70%	31.30%	33.40%
US resident less than 10 years	10.20%	NA	8.60%	6.90%	8.90%

SOURCE: Goodman, "Changing Demography of Multifamily Housing," 42. DATA FROM: U.S. Census Bureau, 1997.

comes. They are also older and less mobile than other apartment renters. Assisted-housing residents are even more likely than public-housing residents to be older and less mobile as well as to have at least one child.[18]

The lifestyle renters segment chooses apartment living for primarily nonfinancial reasons and in 1997 accounted for 14% of all apartment households. Lifestyle renter households meet three criteria: they are old enough to be established in the labor force and to have stopped being highly mobile; they have adult interests and schedules; and they earn enough to purchase a home if they choose to do so. They include renters twenty-five and older who are single or married without children and have incomes above the average required to buy a starter home. In contrast to the affordable group, the lifestyle renters have a median income of $48,928,

---

[18] Ibid., 40–41.

and 80% are nonminority, compared to 67% of affordable renters.[19] This renter-by-choice segment is also expanding. In 1998 and 1999, the fastest-growing segment of apartment renters was households making $50,000 or more a year.

The final group, the *middle market* makes up the remaining 37% of multifamily households. As a whole, middle market multifamily renters are younger and more mobile than affordable or lifestyle renters. There are several subgroups within this category. Younger, more mobile households make up approximately a quarter of the middle market. These renters may be recent college graduates or others who are on a track to earn enough money to purchase a home, but have not yet reached that point or are too mobile to settle down. Another important subgroup includes mature single women with no children, and they make up 12% of the middle market. The third subgroup consists of family households. Married couples with no children represent 7% of the middle market, couples with children, 17%, and single-parent households, 14%.[20]

Future Demand for Multifamily Rental Housing

Looking to the future, the demand for apartments is likely to continue to grow. Ultimately, such demand depends on demographic factors and the housing decisions made by households. Much attention has been paid to rising homeownership rates in the last half of the decade of the 1990s. However, as homeownership rates were increasing, the number of apartment households was also growing. In 1999, the number of people who rent apartments in buildings with five or more units was up 2.2%, while the total number of households grew just 1.4%. These seemingly contradictory trends have occurred because apartments seem to be picking up market from single-family house rentals or rental apartments in properties with less than five units. These two segments of the rental market benefit less from the renewed growth in young adult and single-person households than do apartments. Although homeownership may continue to increase, both economics and demographics suggest that future growth will be at a slower rate than has been recorded in recent years.[21]

Over the last few decades, apartment demand and homeownership rates have followed the life cycle of the baby boomers. In the 1960s and 1970s,

---

[19] Ibid., 41–43.
[20] Ibid., 43–45.
[21] Ibid., 47.

apartment demand increased as the baby boomers began to form their own households and enter the housing market — typically in a rented home. As this group aged, however, many transitioned to ownership. At the same time, the generation behind the boomers, the "baby busters," were a much smaller group, thus decreasing the number of people under thirty-five and the number of prospective first-time renters. Despite an 8.7% growth rate in the total number of households between 1991 and 1998, the number of renter households increased by only 2%.[22]

Going forward, however, demographic changes suggest that the pendulum may swing back to favor apartment living. Using Census Bureau projections and assuming that the housing choices of households of different ages and types do not change, Goodman projects that the demand for multifamily rental housing is likely to increase at a rate faster than the total number of households (see Figure 3.6). Whereas total household growth is projected to grow at a constant 1.1% from 2000 to 2010, the annual growth for apartment households is expected to increase from 0.9% from 1995 to 2000, to 1.1% from 2000 to 2005, and to 1.2% from 2005 to 2010. This simultaneous increase in multifamily rental housing demand and homeownership is possible because, as noted earlier, the overall declines in renting are the result of a decline in the number of apartment renters, but of declines in households who are renting single-family housing or multifamily housing with two to four units.

The growth in apartment renters will result primarily from the passage of the echo boomers (the children of the baby boom generation, born since 1977) into adulthood. For almost two decades, the number of households age twenty to twenty-nine decreased in absolute numbers. According to the Joint Center for Housing Studies, however, echo boomers are reversing this trend, contributing an average of 20,000 young households (eighteen- to twenty-four-year-olds) each year. Households headed by twenty-five- to thirty-four-years-olds will also increase substantially after 2005.[23] Both of these younger household groups have a higher propensity to rent. Many young adults are postponing buying a home until later in life. Between 1976 and 1997, the average age of first-time home buyers rose from twenty-eight to thirty-two.[24] This is likely due to young adults

---

[22] Joint Center for Housing Studies, *State of the Nation's Housing 1999*," 21; U.S. Census Bureau, *Statistical Abstract of the United States: 1992*, 46; U.S. Census Bureau, *Statistical Abstract of the United States: 1999*, 60.

[23] Joint Center for Housing Studies, *The State of the Nation's Housing 1999*, 2.

[24] Simmons, *Housing Statistics in the United States*, 245.

FIGURE 3.6
Projected Growth in All Households and Multifamily Households, 1995 to 2010

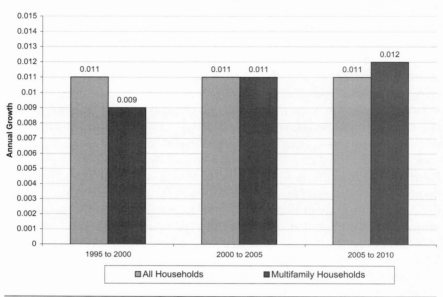

SOURCE: Goodman, "Changing Demography of Multifamily Housing," 46. BASED ON DATA FROM: U.S. Census Bureau, 1997, and Jennifer Day Cheeseman, *Projections of the Number of Households and Families in the United States, 1995 to 2010* (Washington, D.C.: U.S. Census Bureau, Current Population Reports, 1996).

pursuing higher education and postponing marriage, as well as greater mobility among young workers in today's economy.

A demographic shakeup in what constitutes the typical American household is also likely to boost apartment demand. Traditionally, the typical household has been a married couple with children. But these households have been decreasing in absolute numbers since the 1970s and now account for less than one-quarter of all U.S. households. The Census Bureau projects further declines in the number of traditional families. In their place are a growing number of single adults, single-parents, and childless couples. In fact, in the 1990s, households headed by single adults or single parents accounted for two-thirds of all new households. These smaller households have traditionally been attracted to apartment living and are likely to continue to be.

The precise housing tenure choices of the echo boomers are still evolving. On the one hand, echo boomers earn less than their parents' generation and are more likely to live alone, which could help encourage new apartment demand. On the other hand, more single echo boomers are buying homes than their parents did, and those who do marry are more likely to live in dual-income households, which promotes homeownership.[25]

Movement of the echo boomers into the overall rental market has also shifted the demographics of who rents apartments (see Figure 3.7). Echo boomers are more racially and ethnically diverse than their parents' generation: 12% are second-generation Americans, and 10% are foreign born. The proportion of minorities among young adult echo boomers — 34% — is more than double that for the baby boomers when they were of comparable age (17%). As a result, by 1998, 38% of all renters were minorities, up from 33% in 1990, and the proportion of immigrants rose from 13% to 16%.[26]

A final factor supporting increased demand for apartments is immigration. Foreign-born households today make up 10% of the U.S. population. While likely to double-up with other adult households when first arriving in the United States, immigrant households head out on their own once they get settled, increasing the total number of households in the market. Fully 25% of household growth through 2010 is expected to be from immigrant households.[27] Looking specifically at the impact of immigration on the overall rental market (renters in all property types), one study expects immigrants to account for 44% of the growth in all renter households between 1995 and 2010.[28]

In summary, the number of renters should increase sharply for the next decade as the echo boomers begin to form independent households and the twenty- to thirty-year-old population begins to increase after two decades of decline (see Figure 3.8). The continued aging of the postwar baby boom generation and the increasing propensity of these households to seek a simpler lifestyle and to shed their home owner chores could yield significant growth in renters aged fifty to sixty-four. Only the renter group aged thirty to forty-four is expected to decline sharply. That means that the fastest-growing segment of renters will be two very different sets of households: young adults with modest incomes, many of them minorities

---

[25] Joint Center for Housing Studies, *The State of the Nation's Housing 1999*, 10.

[26] For a discussion of these demographic drivers of housing demand, see Joint Center for Housing Studies, *State of the Nation's Housing 1999*, 10–22.

[27] Ibid., 9, 12.

[28] Goodman, *Changing Demography of Multifamily Housing*, 48, citing James H. Carr, "Multifamily Housing Demand into the Next Millennium: Growth, Diversity, and Opportunity," Paper presented at the Annual Meeting of the National Multi Housing Council, 16 January 16, Boca Raton, FL.

FIGURE 3.7
Baby Boomer and Echo Boomer Demographics
Percent in Each Catergory at Ages 18 to 22

	Baby Boom	Echo Boom
Population		
Minority	16.80%	34.00%
Foreign-Born	3.40%	10.10%
Second-Generation	9.80%	11.70%
Never Married	67.00%	88.40%
Women in Labor Force	52.30%	66.10%
Households		
Single-Person	13.70%	23.10%
Married-Couple	69.00%	21.40%
Any Household		
W/Children	43.50%	32.40%
Homeownership Rate	16.20%	15.20%
Single-Person		
Homeownership Rate	8.50%	11.40%

SOURCE: Joint Center for Housing Studies, *State of the Nation's Housing 1999*, 10.

and immigrants, and older, higher-income households that choose to rent rather than own for a variety of lifestyle reasons.[29]

This dual phenomenon is highlighted in Figure 3.9. Very-low-income households accounted for most of the growth in all renters (apartment renters in buildings with five units or more, and other renters combined) from 1985 to 1991 and from 1991 to 1997. But at the same time, approximately 250,000 of the new renters created between 1991 and 1997 had incomes that exceeded regional median income by 20% or more. In 1995 (the last year for which local income comparisons are possible), the incomes of more than 6 million renter households exceeded the local area median by at least 20%. In fact, nearly 3.5 million of these households had incomes that surpassed area medians by 50% or more.[30] Tracking this same phenomenon in apartments renters, Census Bureau population surveys between March 1998 and March 1999 found that the fastest-growing segment of apartment renters was those making $50,000 or more a year. In terms of the percentage change in 1998, apartment renter households making less than $20,000 actually dropped by 3%, those making $20,000

---

[29] Joint Center for Housing Studies, *State of the Nation's Housing 1999*, 24.
[30] Ibid., 22.

FIGURE 3.8
The Baby Boomers and the Echo Boomers Will Bolster the Ranks of Renters

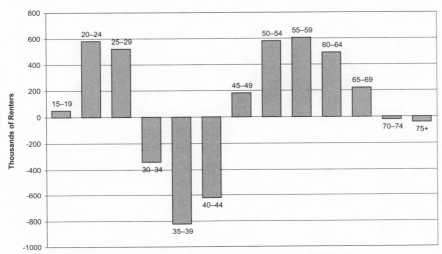

Projected Change in Renters by Age Group, 2000–2010

SOURCE: Joint Center for Housing Studies, *State of the Nation's Housing 1999*, 24.

to $49,999 rose by 4.2%, and those making $50,000 or more rose by 11.6%.[31]

The growth in higher-income apartment renters is even more evident when one looks at the characteristics of residents in newly-built apartments. Using unpublished data from the U.S. Census Bureau's American Housing Survey for 1995, the National Multi Housing Council found that 17% of households in newly built apartments had incomes of $55,000 or more, whereas overall, only 9% of apartment residents earned that much.[32]

AFFORDABLE HOUSING NEEDS AND THE ROLE OF MULTIFAMILY RENTAL HOUSING

The United States experienced an unprecedented economic expansion and housing boom in the 1990s. Unfortunately, not all households benefited

---

[31] National Multi Housing Council, "Growing Smarter with Apartments," 2.
[32] National Multi Housing Council, "Residents of Newly Built Apartments," 1–2.

FIGURE 3.9
Growth in Renters by Income Group, 1985 to 1991, and 1991 to 1997

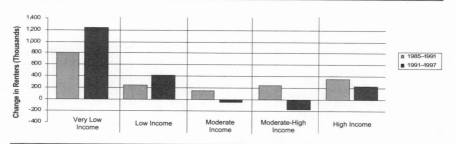

SOURCE: Joint Center for Housing Studies, *State of the Nation's Housing 1999*, 22.

NOTE: Very-low-income defined as less than 50% of regional median incomes: low is between 50% and 80%; moderate is between 80% and 100%; moderate-high is between 100% and 120%; high is above 120%.

equally from the rising tide of prosperity, and in many cases the economic growth actually served to exacerbate the nation's shortage of decent, affordable housing. In 1997, there were only seventy-six affordable apartments for every 100 extremely-low-income renter households.[33] And those low-income households lucky enough to find affordable housing were often paying a higher percent of their income for it in 1998 (27.7%) than they did in 1978 (25.5%), because rent increases during that period surpassed renter household income growth.[34] Home owners face housing problems of their own, but housing affordability and adequacy problems are a greater challenge among both apartment renters and other renters.

The Affordability Problem

According to tabulations by the U.S. Department of Housing and Urban Development (HUD) for the Millennial Housing Commission, 15% of all households (all renters and all owners) spent between 30% to 50% of their incomes on housing, and another 12% spent more than 50%.[35] These 27.9 million households were split fairly evenly with 13.4 million renter households and 14.5 million home owner households. However, affordability issues are generally discussed in terms of renters because a far greater proportion of renters pay more than they can afford for housing, 40% compared to 21% of home owners. And 18.5% of renters — 6.3 million

---

[33] U.S. Dept. of Housing and Urban Development, A-18.
[34] Joint Center for Housing Studies, *State of the Nation's Housing 1999*, 35.
[35] U.S. Dept. of Housing and Urban Development, *Rental Housing Assistance*, A-1.

FIGURE 3.10

Percent of All Households, Homeowners, and Renters by Rent Burden, 1999

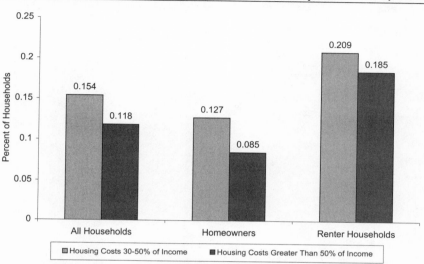

SOURCE: Special Tabulations from the U.S. Department of Housing and Urban Development of the 1999 American Housing Survey for the Millennial Housing Commission, 2002.

households — are severely burdened, paying more than 50% of their incomes for rent (see Figure 3.10).

The gap between the number of low-income renters and the supply of affordable units would be even wider were it not for federal housing subsidies. From 1975 to 1995, the proportion of low-cost housing units that were subsidized rose from one-fourth to over half.[36] (See Figure 3.11.) However, this increase did not result from an increase in the amount of subsidies provided, per se. Instead, it primarily reflects a decline in the total number of low-cost units over which to spread the existing subsidy dollars.

The physical quality of available affordable housing is another problem. In 1997, more than 1 million renter households (approximately 2.9% of all renter households — as shown in Figure 3.12 — and 6.7% of apartment renter households) lived in severely inadequate housing — housing with problems in plumbing, heating, electrical systems, upkeep, or hallways. More than 2.5 million renters (all types of housing) lived in housing that both cost more than they could afford and was physically inadequate

---

[36] Daskal, *In Search of Shelter*, 35.

FIGURE 3.11
Subsidized Housing Units as a Percentage of All Low-Cost Rental Units,
1975–1995

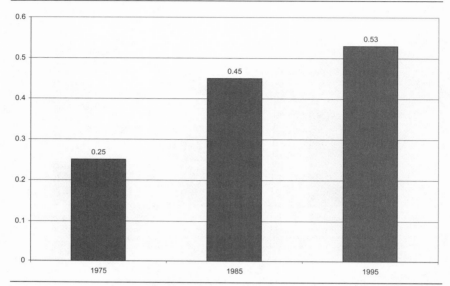

SOURCE: Daskal, *In Search of Shelter,* 35. Based on data from U.S. Census Bureau, "American Housing Survey 1995."

or overcrowded (with more than one person to a room).[37] Although these 2.5 million renters represent less than 17% of the total apartment renter population, their numbers are significant.

Housing problems are, not surprisingly, worst among households with the lowest incomes. In 1997, the overwhelming majority (nearly 70%) of extremely-low-income renters (defined as having an income below 30% of area median) without any housing assistance paid more than half their income for rent or lived in substandard housing. (See Figure 3.13.) Extremely-low-income households represented 21% of all unassisted renter households in 1997, but more than 69% of renter households with priority housing problems.[38] The nation's housing affordability problem looks even worse if one takes into account the approximately 700,000 individuals who are estimated to be homeless on any given night — a cumulative two million per year — and are not included in national housing

---

[37] U.S. Dept. of Housing and Urban Development, *Rental Housing Assistance,* A-1.
[38] Ibid., 29.

FIGURE 3.12
Prevalence of Problems among Families with Worst Case Needs

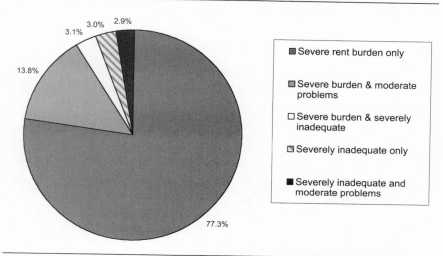

Source: U.S. Dept. of Housing and Urban Development, Office of Policy Development and Research, *Rental Housing Assistance*, 14.

surveys.[39] The significance of the problem is highlighted even more by the fact that 5.6 million renter households were receiving public rental assistance in 1997. Without this assistance, the shortage of affordable housing would be even greater.

In contrast to conventional wisdom, however, affordability issues are not restricted to low-income households. The Center for Housing Policy reports that more than three million moderate-income, working households had critical housing needs in 1997 (defined as spending more than half their income on housing and/or living in a severely inadequate unit.)[40] And their numbers are increasing. Between 1995 and 1997, the number of these households jumped 17%, or by 440,000. Overall, 14% of the nation's families have critical housing needs, and increasingly, "having a job does not guarantee a family a decent place to live at affordable cost."[41]

[39] National Coalition for the Homeless. Estimated by the National Law Center on Homelessness and Poverty, 1999, drawing from Burt and Cohen's 1989 estimate of 500,000–600,000 homeless nightly, and increased by 5% annually. National Law Center on Homelessness and Poverty, *Out of Sight — Out of Mind;* Burt and Cohen, *America's Homeless.*

[40] This is the same definition used by the U.S. Department of Housing and Urban Development in their "Report to Congress on Worst Case Housing Needs," March 2000.

[41] Stegman, Quercia, and McCarthy, *Housing America's Working Families,* 1–9.

FIGURE 3.13
All Unassisted Renter Households with
Priority Housing Problems by Income Group

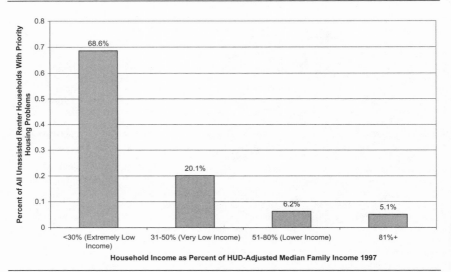

Household Income as Percent of HUD-Adjusted Median Family Income 1997

SOURCE: U.S. Dept. of Housing and Urban Development, *Rental Housing Assistance*, 29. Based on data from U.S. Census Bureau, "American Housing Survey 1997."

Central cities have more renters with severe housing problems than the suburbs, due to higher poverty concentrations. In 1997, 2.7 million households in central cities had worst case housing needs, compared to 1.8 million suburban households. However, housing affordability and quality is still a significant problem among suburban renters. In fact, very-low-income renters (with incomes below 50% of area median) in the suburbs are more likely to have worst case needs than their urban counterparts. More than 41% of unassisted suburban renters with very low incomes had worst case housing needs in 1997, compared with 37% of city renters with comparable incomes.[42]

Causes of the Expanding Affordability Gap

The growing affordability gap is the result of two trends: a shrinking supply of low-cost housing and an expanding demand from an increase in the number of low-income households. Although the nation's total hous-

---

[42] U.S. Dept. of Housing and Urban Development, *Rental Housing Assistance*, 36–37.

ing stock has grown substantially in recent decades, the stock of low-cost rental housing has declined. There were 4.9 million unsubsidized units renting for $300 or less in 1973, but by 1995, the inflation-adjusted number had been reduced to 2.0 million.[43] (See Figure 3.14.)

Even as the supply of affordable housing has fallen, demand has increased due to stagnating incomes and two recessions. Between 1975 and 1995, while home owners' monthly incomes rose by 10% (from $3,287 to $3,617 in 1998 dollars), renters' income fell 8% from $1,909 to $1,758.[44] At the same time, the gap between the "haves" and the "have-nots" widened. In 1970, the two-fifths of the population with the lowest incomes had 14.9% of national wealth, and the two-fifths with the highest incomes, 67.8%. By 1990, the gap had widened to 13.5% and 70.6%.[45] Also, between 1970 and 1995, the number of renter households earning less than $12,000 (1995 dollars) rose by 67%, from 6.2 million to 10.5 million.[46]

More recently, renters have benefited from the economic boom of the late 1990s. By 1998, monthly incomes had risen to $1,787 — the highest level since 1990. However, this is still below incomes of two decades ago, and reflects only a 1.6% increase from 1995, compared to the 5.6% increase experienced by home owners.[47]

The Role of Housing Subsidies

The gap between the number of low-income renters and the supply of affordable units would be even wider were it not for federal housing subsidies. As noted earlier, the proportion of all low-cost units that depended on subsidies to remain affordable rose from one-fourth in 1975 to over half in 1995.[48] (See Figure 3.15.) Yet, according to Goodman, as discussed earlier, by 1997 federally assisted renters represented only 19% of apartment renters.[49] This is because the increase in the percentage of properties that receive subsidies reflects a decline in the total number of low-cost units, as opposed to an increase in subsidized units. In fact, the country saw a retrenchment in housing subsidies in the late 1990s. Between 1995 and 1998, virtually no funding was allocated for new vouchers or

---

[43] For a further discussion of these trends see Daskal, *In Search of Shelter,* 30–40.
[44] Calculated from U.S. Statistical Abstract 1998, Table 718.
[45] Burchell and Listokin, "Influences on Housing Policy," 582.
[46] Daskal, *In Search of Shelter,* 32.
[47] Joint Center for Housing Studies, *State of the Nation's Housing 1999,* 35.
[48] Daskal, *In Search of Shelter,* 35.
[49] Goodman, "Changing Demography of Multifamily Housing," 42.

FIGURE 3.14
Supply of Unsubsidized Low-Income Rental Housing 1975–1995

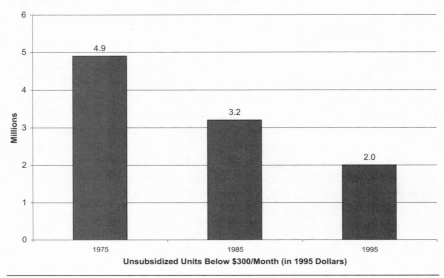

SOURCE: Daskal, *In Search of Shelter, 32*. Based on data from U.S. Census Bureau, "American Housing Survey 1995."

housing certificates, not even the amount required to keep up with increases in the low-income population that would be expected from overall population growth alone.[50] Furthermore, the focus of housing subsidies has shifted away from very-low-income households toward households with somewhat greater incomes. The Low-Income Housing Tax Credit has become the dominant federal subsidy program for new construction, and in 1996, public housing rules that had required preference for families with the most severe housing needs (who also were the poorest) were suspended.[51] In the last several years, the federal government has demonstrated a renewed, albeit modest, commitment to affordable housing. Congress funded 50,000 new housing vouchers in 1999 and 60,000 in 2000 (see Figure 3.16). In addition, approximately 79,000 new vouchers were funded in the fiscal year 2001 HUD budget.

---

[50] U.S. Dept. of Housing and Urban Development, *Rental Housing Assistance,* 50.
[51] Daskal, *In Search of Shelter,* 39.

FIGURE 3.15
**Subsidized Housing Units as a Percentage of All Low-Cost Rental Units,
1975 to 1995**

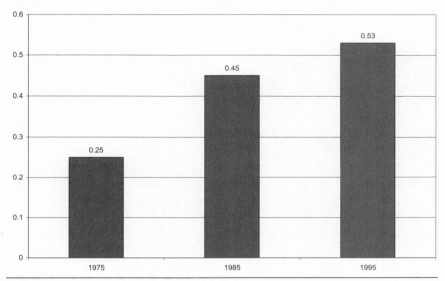

SOURCE: Daskal, *In Search of Shelter,* 35. Based on data from U.S. Census Bureau, "American Housing Survey 1995."

The Future Challenge

As we look to the future, the affordable housing gap presents a significant housing policy challenge. By any measure, the gap between the housing "haves" and the housing "have-nots" is growing. At the same time, the federal resources available to deal with this issue have essentially been frozen or declining for a number of years. Resources are growing in some state and local communities, but that growth is sporadic and varies widely.

After World War II, federal housing programs stimulated the production of low and moderate income housing with direct spending and tax incentives. However, in the last several decades, major shifts have occurred in the federal approach. Now, to the extent that public dollars are available, they are devoted primarily to housing vouchers and the Low-Income Housing Tax Credit (LIHTC). By themselves, these programs will not come close to meeting the affordable housing gap.

The production of affordable rental housing is essential if we are to meet this housing need. Higher-density construction splits land costs across

FIGURE 3.16
New Units of Federal Rental Assistance, 1978–2000

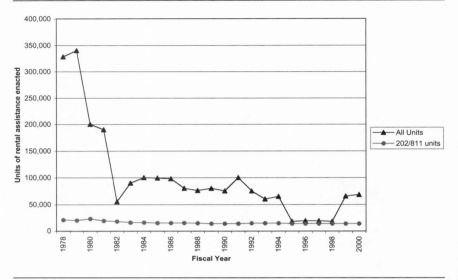

SOURCE: U.S. Department of Housing and Urban Development.

multiple units, and these units generally cost less than single-family housing, or even structures containing two to four units. However, with only limited federal, state, and local resources, the problems in addressing these
issues are huge.

The overall challenge is to provide housing affordable to working families, but in many communities, the economics simply will not allow developers and builders to construct units with affordable rents (for which
renters spend no more than 30% of their total income). It is possible to
build lifestyle, upper-end apartments, and such housing production will
indirectly address the affordability issue since people moving up may provide some "trickle-down" housing at a more moderate level. However, the
benefits of the trickle-down approach will be very small for working families. While some "smart growth" advocates are calling for greater housing
densities and rental housing solutions, regulatory barriers and local zoning
often discourage new apartment construction. In many areas, then, the
challenge is not just a lack of public financial support, but also finding a
way to deal with the "not in my backyard" phenomenon and to remove
regulatory barriers in such areas as zoning, building codes, and development processing.

Part of the solution to this problem is to unleash the private sector to work in concert with the public sector. For example, the LIHTC, the largest current publicly funded program for construction of affordable housing, continues to fund housing for low-income households and brings together a wide range of private and public players such as builders, financial entities, state housing-finance agencies, and local officials. Nevertheless, the LIHTC does not target the lowest-income households in greatest need, and it can only begin to address the problem since funding is constrained. New ideas and housing production programs at the federal level are essential, along with further creativity and resources at the state and local levels. Without additional support at the federal, state, and local levels, as well as a concentrated approach from the private sector, the nation's affordable housing crisis is likely to get worse, not better.

FINANCING MULTIFAMILY RENTAL HOUSING

Financing apartment communities — both existing buildings and new construction — is more complex than single-family financing, due to the greater diversity of properties and the perceived higher risk associated with apartments.[52] In addition, unlike single-family construction, no standardized debt instruments or financing process exists and multiple funding needs and sources are common. Financing needs include funding for rehabilitation acquisition, development, construction, long-term debt, refinancing, and equity. Funding for each may come from different sources, and sometimes multiple sources are required to meet a single need.

Funding for these types of debt and equity instruments is provided by traditional lenders, such as commercial banks, savings and loan associations, pension funds, and life insurance companies, and more recently, through the secondary mortgage market and the broader capital markets. Affordable housing properties also require additional subsidies or "gap financing" to bridge the shortfall between available debt and equity.

Early Days

Before the Great Depression in the 1930s, apartment properties were either owned, debt free, by individuals or small associations of individuals or financed by local banks or individuals. Until the late 1920s, the largest

---

[52] DiPasquale and Cummings, "Financing Multifamily Rental Housing," 91.

category of lenders in the United States was individuals, not financial institutions.[53] With the depression came the virtual collapse of the nation's housing finance system, necessitating more involvement from the federal government.

The first federal efforts came in 1933, when Congress passed the Home Owners Loan Act (HOLA) and established the Home Owners Loan Corporation (HOLC) to help refinance the mortgages of home owners threatened with foreclosure. In June 1934, Congress passed the National Housing Act, which created the FHA, and in 1938 the FHA Section 207 and General Insurance (GI) Fund were created to provide long-term loans for apartment properties. These loans were fully amortizable for up to twenty-five years, and offered loan-to-value ratios as high as 90% and interest rates of 5% to 6%. The Section 207 program was not nearly as important in multifamily finance as its single-family counterpart, Section 203(b), but it did establish an important framework for a federal role in apartment financing and provided the experience needed later to meet the market need for large-scale garden-style and high-rise apartments at the end of World War II.

As the GIs returned from World War II, there was a sudden and dramatic need for large-scale garden-style and high-rise apartments. Despite this new market need, the FHA continued to focus on smaller and more affordable properties. Eventually, a growing number of institutional investors, such as pension funds and life insurance companies, entered the multifamily loan market, and some of the nation's mortgage banking firms began originating apartment loans to sell to these investors. According to Vandell, most large loans were originated by savings associations, but life insurance companies were not far behind. Banks remained in third place until 1984, when they surpassed life insurance company balances.[54]

The Declining Role of the Thrifts

Over the last twenty-five years, the sources of apartment financing have changed and shifted. Until the 1980s, the savings associations — savings and loans and mutual savings banks, commonly known as thrifts — dominated multifamily finance. However, in the early 1980s, the country's thrift institutions faced a mounting crisis. The reliance of these institutions

---

[53] Vandell, "Multifamily Finance," 5.
[54] Ibid., 8.

on short-term savings deposits to invest in long-term, fixed-rate single-family mortgages put them in a tenuous position when interest rates began rising steeply in the 1970s, especially the later part of the decade. By the early 1980s, hundreds of savings and loans and mutual savings banks were close to insolvency and were being forced out of business.[55] To keep them afloat, Congress provided emergency assistance and deregulated thrifts, allowing investment in almost any type of income-producing property.[56] Many thrifts proceeded to expand heavily into apartment financing in the mid-1980s (see Figure 3.17).

Deregulation of the thrift industry made it possible for savings and loans to invest in unfamiliar — and more risky — projects. As a result, according to Brueggeman and Fisher, some thrifts with limited underwriting experience proceeded very aggressively in an attempt to establish market share, reasoning that if their risky enterprises failed, depositors would be protected by the Federal Savings and Loan Insurance Corporation (FSLIC).[57] The softening of the domestic energy market in 1986, however, created an economic slowdown in certain parts of the country — particularly in the Southwest — and sent a limited, but significant, number of thrifts into bankruptcy. The FSLIC repaid depositors, but by 1987 its reserves were severely depleted. In August of that year, Congress passed emergency legislation to provide the FSLIC with $10 billion in additional reserves. However, government regulators and Congress felt a more permanent solution was necessary to replenish not only the FSLIC reserves, but the reserves of the FDIC, which were also at an all-time low. In 1989, Congress passed the Financial Institutions Reform Recovery and Enforcement Act (FIRREA), which imposed new regulations on the thrifts, created the Office of Thrift Supervision (OTS), and created a special organization, the Resolution Trust Corporation (RTC), to take over and close insolvent savings and loans. The FIRREA regulations were designed to reduce the risk under which the thrifts were allowed to make investments, and prohibited them from making direct equity investments in real estate. FIRREA guidelines allowed for a 95% loan-to-value ratio for home owner mortgages, but loans for acquisition, development, and construction (AD&C) were limited to 70%. This severely restricted the availability of AD&C loans in certain regions. FIRREA also established minimum risk-based capital requirements and identified multifamily mortgages as being more risky than single-family mortgages.

---

[55] Meyerson, "Changing Structure of Housing Finance," 155–156.
[56] Brueggeman and Fisher, *Real Estate Finance and Investments,* 158.
[57] Ibid., 566.

FIGURE 3.17
Multifamily Mortgage Originations for New and Existing Properties,
1980–1996 (1996 Dollars)

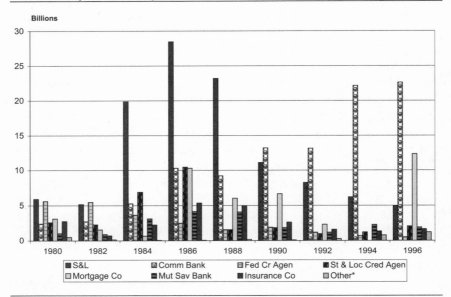

SOURCE: U.S. Department of Housing and Urban Development, *Survey of Mortgage Lending Activity,* annual tables, table 4.

During this time, an increasing number of competitors to thrifts sought to securitize their loan portfolios. This heightened competition contributed to a major reduction in the share of thrift loans in the multifamily finance market. In 1985, thrift institutions held 44% of multifamily debt held in portfolio, but by 2000 their share had dropped to only 16% (see Figure 3.18).

Another important source of multifamily debt has been commercial banks. In 1985 they held 12% of all multifamily mortgage debt outstanding. That number has gradually risen since then, and in 2000 they held 18% of all multifamily debt. Insurance companies lost holdings to thrift institutions during the 1980s, but since the late 1980s, their market share has remained near their 2000 level of 9%.[58]

With the diminishing role of the thrifts, the secondary mortgage market — led by Fannie Mae, Freddie Mac, and private conduits — has

---

[58] Schnare, "Impact of Changes in Multifamily Finance," 9.

FIGURE 3.18
Multifamily Mortgage Debt Outstanding (Percent Share)

Year	Commercial Banks	Thrifts	Insurance Co.	GSEs[1]	Private Conduits[3]	REITS	FHA/VA/GNMA	RTC/FDIC	FHMA	GNMA	Total	State and Local[5]	Other[6]
							Government Held		Securitized[4]				
80[1]	8%	39%	14%	5%	0%	0%	5%	0%	3%	1%	9%	7%	14%
81	9%	38%	14%	5%	0%	0%	5%	0%	3%	2%	10%	7%	14%
82	10%	38%	14%	4%	0%	0%	5%	0%	3%	2%	11%	5%	13%
83	11%	38%	13%	4%	0%	0%	5%	0%	4%	2%	11%	9%	12%
84	12%	40%	12%	4%	0%	1%	4%	0%	4%	3%	11%	10%	11%
85	12%	44%	11%	4%	0%	1%	3%	0%	4%	3%	9%	12%	11%
86	12%	46%	10%	5%	0%	1%	2%	0%	3%	3%	8%	12%	11%
87	12%	38%	8%	6%	0%	1%	1%	0%	9%	2%	12%	12%	11%
88	12%	40%	8%	6%	0%	1%	1%	0%	7%	3%	11%	14%	10%
89	12%	40%	9%	8%	0%	1%	1%	0%	7%	3%	11%	14%	9%
90	13%	37%	9%	9%	0%	1%	1%	0%	7%	4%	11%	14%	9%
91	12%	31%	10%	10%	0%	1%	2%	3%	6%	4%	15%	14%	8%
92	12%	27%	10%	11%	0%	1%	2%	5%	6%	3%	17%	14%	7%
93	13%	25%	10%	11%	1%	1%	3%	2%	7%	3%	16%	15%	6%
94	14%	25%	10%	11%	2%	1%	3%	2%	7%	4%	15%	16%	6%
95	14%	24%	10%	11%	3%	1%	2%	0%	7%	4%	14%	16%	7%
96	16%	23%	10%	13%	4%	0%	2%	0%	7%	4%	12%	16%	7%
97	16%	22%	10%	13%	6%	1%	2%	0%	7%	4%	11%	16%	8%
98	17%	20%	10%	13%	7%	1%	1%	0%	6%	5%	11%	16%	8%
99	17%	18%	9%	15%	11%	1%	1%	0%	5%	5%	10%	15%	8%
2000	18%	16%	9%	17%	12%	0%	1%	0%	5%	5%	9%	13%	8%

SOURCE: Federal Reserve Flow of Funds data as calculated by Schnare, "Impact of Changes in Multifamily Finance" 8–9.

1. Data for the two GSE's—Fannie Mae and Freddie Mac—include mortgages securitized by the agencies, as well as mortgages held in their investment portfolios. Procedures used to calculate GSE holdings changed in 1982. Numbers on GSE holdings in 1980 and 1981 are estimates.

2. Figures represent mortgage holdings at the beginning of each calendar year.

3. Data for private conduits include mortgages funded through CMBS issuances (and held by a broad range of investors).

4. Data for government-securitized mortgages refer to mortgages securitized by Ginnie Mae (GNMA) or Farmers' Home.

5. Data for state and local housing finance agencies refers to mortgages funded by tax-exempt multifamily bonds under the private activity cap.

6. Data in the "other" category includes mortgages funded by pension funds, as well as a variety of nontraditional mortgage arrangements, such as individual investors or seller-financing.

played an increasingly important role in multifamily mortgage finance. This will be discussed in greater depth later, but for now it is worth noting that in 1985, the two government sponsored enterprises (GSEs), Freddie Mac and Fannie Mae, accounted for only 4% of the mortgage debt outstanding, and by 2000, their share had climbed to 17%. The share accounted for by private conduits was essentially nonexistent until 1992, and by 2000 they accounted for 12% of the multifamily mortgage debt outstanding. (See Figure 3.18.)

The Federal Tax Code and Multifamily Rental Housing

Because private investors provide most of the equity for rental projects, return on investment is an important determinant for apartment construction. In the past, tax incentives for multifamily investments were an important determinant of investment return. Changes in these tax policies over time have had an important influence on the kinds of financing sources available to private developers. DiPasquale and Cummings identified three tax regimes that defined multifamily development: the era prior to the 1981 Economic Recovery Tax Act (ERTA); the period between 1981 and the 1986 Tax Reform Act (TRA); and today's post-Tax Reform Act regime.[59] (See Figure 3.19.) Through its effects on depreciation, required tax life, tax rate on income for investors, and tax rate on capital gains, each act changed the incentives for investors to fund apartments.

Congress passed ERTA as a response to the recession of 1981. To counteract relatively high income tax rates, ERTA accelerated depreciation rates and provided lenient initial expense write-offs and large construction and passive loss write-offs. These changes gave apartment investors significant tax breaks, which spurred new construction. Between 1981 and 1986, the strong economy brought many new participants into the apartment market, including new capital from foreign investors and new debt financing from the deregulated savings and loans. With an abundance of funding sources, the apartment stock surged over the first half of the decade. In 1985, multifamily housing starts reached nearly 600,000, their highest level since 1973 (see Figure 3.20).

By 1986 it became clear that the growth in the apartment industry stimulated by ERTA had resulted in the rental housing market becoming overbuilt, primarily among middle and higher-end units. To discourage apartment

---

[59] DiPasquale and Cummings, "Financing Multifamily Rental Housing," 87.

FIGURE 3.19

Changes in Tax Variables: 1960–Present

	Pre-ERTA	ERTA 1981–1986	Tax Reform 1987–Present
Depreciation Method	Double-Declining Balance	Double-Declining Balance	Straight-Line
Tax Life (years)	30-40	15-19	27.5
Tax rate on income for investors	0.5	0.45	0.28
Tax rate on capital gains	0.25	0.18	0.28

ADAPTED FROM: DiPasquale, *Financing Multifamily Rental Housing,* 87.

investment motivated solely by tax policy and not market need for new apartments, the Tax Reform Act (TRA) of 1986, among other things, eliminated much of the tax-favored status of rental housing. Specifically, the TRA increased the required tax life to nearly pre-ERTA levels, eliminated accelerated depreciation, and prohibited passive investors (including most investors in limited partnerships of rental housing) from offsetting ordinary income with losses from real estate investments.[60] The act also decreased income tax rates across the board. The TRA's combination of reforms and lower tax rates effectively discouraged limited partnerships, the most popular mode of investment in apartment housing at the time. This sent apartment starts plummeting (see Figure 3.20). However, the TRA also established the Low-Income Housing Tax Credit (LIHTC) to leverage private sector dollars to invest in affordable housing. By the late 1990s, construction under the LIHTC, discussed later, represented approximately 20% to 25% of multifamily construction nationwide.

These key events culminated in a shortage of both equity and debt financing for multifamily housing in the 1980s. Without tax incentives, investors had limited reason to invest equity in new projects, and with the new loan-to-value ratio and risk-based capital requirements that followed the thrift crisis of the 1980s, thrifts and commercial banks had little incentive to lend money for multifamily projects.

[60] Ibid.

FIGURE 3.20
Multifamily Housing Starts, 1969–2001

Thousands

SOURCE: U.S. Census Bureau, Census Construction Division.

Innovation and Adaptation in Multifamily Rental Financing

The crunch in both debt and equity financing in the 1980s required adaptation and innovation. Three responses stand out as key developments in multifamily financing and help define the industry today: secondary mortgage markets, commercial mortgage-backed securities (CMBSs), and real estate investment trusts (REITs).

SECONDARY MORTGAGE MARKETS

A secondary market provides mortgage originators with a venue to sell their mortgages to third parties in order to replenish their funds and make new loans. It also facilitates the flow of funds between geographic regions. A secondary mortgage market has always existed in some form for both single-family housing and apartments. Prior to the 1950s, large life insurance companies and thrifts provided a secondary market for mortgages.[61] In 1938, Congress established the Federal National Mortgage

---

[61] Brueggeman and Fisher, *Real Estate Finance and Investments,* 566.

Association, now known as Fannie Mae, to create a secondary market for government-insured residential (single-family) mortgages. In 1968, Fannie Mae was converted into a government-sponsored, private corporation, and the Federal Home Loan Mortgage Corporation (FHLMC), now known as Freddie Mac, was formed to further expand the secondary market. As government-sponsored enterprises (GSEs), both Fannie Mae and Freddie Mac provide a secondary market for conventional mortgages.

Freddie Mac and Fannie Mae became involved in the apartment industry in the late 1970s, when they began issuing securities that "pass through" to the security holders the regular interest and principal payments on a pool of mortgages. Although these early mortgage backed securities accounted for just 3% of multifamily originations from 1971 to 1975 period, their entry into the multifamily market spurred later innovations by the GSEs and encouraged other participants to begin serving the apartment market.

The earlier section on the thrift crisis discussed the changing sources of multifamily finance over the last twenty-five years. However, perhaps the most dynamic story has been the growth of securitization and the secondary market. According to Schnare, the GSEs purchases of multifamily mortgages began to accelerate starting with the thrift crisis. Between 1985 and 1990, Fannie Mae and Freddie Mac accounted for 17% of the net increase in multifamily debt, and by 1990, their combined market share was 9% (see Figure 3.18). The market share for the two GSEs had risen to 17% by 2000, and between 1995 and 2000, Fannie Mae and Freddie Mac accounted for about 30% of the overall increase in multifamily mortgage debt — roughly the same as commercial banks.[62]

COMMERCIAL MORTGAGE-BACKED SECURITIES

Commercial mortgage-backed securities (CMBSs), issued against mortgages on apartments and nonresidential properties by investment banks and other major financial institutions, have become a primary vehicle through which debt capital enters the multifamily market. The CMBS market first emerged in the mid-1980s, with an initial focus on apartment loans, for which Fannie Mae and Freddie Mac had already created a secondary market. However, CMBSs only really took off after 1991, when the Resolution Trust Corporation (RTC) was aggressively marketing the mortgage portfolios of failed thrift institutions. The RTC absorbed some of the initial risk in demonstrating to investors that private-sector

---

[62] Schnare, "Impact of Changes in Multifamily Finance," 11.

securitization of mortgages on apartments and other income producing property (often referred to as commercial property) was both feasible and potentially profitable. The CMBS market grew from $34.6 billion in 1990 to $176.6 billion by the end of 1997 — a change from 3.3% of outstanding commercial mortgage credit to 15.1%. The apartment industry benefited from this growth, along with office, retail, and industrial properties. By the end of 1997, the apartment market was one of the most heavily securitized markets ($86.1 billion, which was 25.5% of apartment mortgage credit outstanding),[63] although single-family mortgages remain the most securitized.

However, the CMBS market was brought to a virtual standstill in the fall of 1998, when the world financial markets were shaken by a default of Russian bonds. The resulting turmoil led to a "flight to quality" and a decline in the CMBS market. Despite this setback, CMBSs accounted for about 30% of the net increase in multifamily mortgages from 1995 to 2000, roughly the same as the two GSEs and commercial banks.[64]

REAL ESTATE INVESTMENT TRUSTS

Real estate investment trusts (REITs) are real estate companies or trusts — often organized or sponsored by a financial institution such as an insurance company, commercial bank, or mortgage banker — that qualify as "pass-through" entities under a certain tax status. As pass-through entities, REITs distribute to their shareholders nearly all of their earnings as well as capital gains from property sales. While the REIT itself pays no taxes on earnings, shareholders pay taxes on dividends and capital gains.

Three types of REITs have developed over the last century: equity trusts, mortgage trusts, and hybrid trusts. An equity trust acquires property interests. A mortgage trust purchases mortgage obligations, thereby becoming a creditor; mortgage liens are given priority to equity holders.[65] Hybrid trusts combine the benefits of equity and mortgage trusts. Mortgage trusts were responsible for early growth in the market. However, as many mortgage trusts ran into financial difficulty and were liquidated in the early 1970s, equity trusts became the dominant kind of REIT.[66] By 1999, equity trusts made up 95% of the total REIT market.[67]

[63] Vandell, *Strategic Management of the Apartment Business*, 5–6.
[64] Shnare, "Impact of Changes in Multifamily Finance," 12.
[65] Brueggeman and Fisher, *Real Estate Finance and Investments*, 661–663.
[66] Ibid., 675–676.
[67] National Association of Real Estate Investment Trusts 1999.

The collapse of the REIT market for mortgage trusts in the early 1970s, coupled with strong competition from other mortgage lenders and from limited partnerships, restrained the growth of REITs in the late 1970s and 1980s. But in the 1990s, REITs came to the forefront of the commercial and multifamily real estate market. Several factors created new interest in REITs. Key among them was the capital crunch of 1990 to 1993, during which debt and equity became scarce in the private market, forcing real estate owners to look to the public markets for financing needs. Another important event was the 1986 Tax Reform Act, which eliminated significant tax advantages for private real estate ownership, especially limited partnerships, by stretching out the depreciation period and restricting the ability to claim "passive losses" on real estate investments. These changes helped make public vehicles for real estate ownership and financing more attractive. As a result, total market capitalization of equity REITs grew from $11 billion in 1992 to over $125 billion at their peak in 1997 (see Figure 3.21). REITs have been even more important to apartment financing. Most

FIGURE 3.21
Growth of The Public Markets in Real Estate, 1982–1999

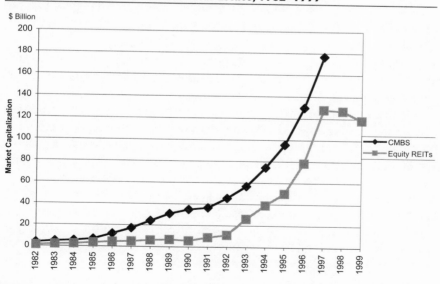

SOURCE: Vandell, *Strategic Management of the Apartment Business*, 8. Based on data from the Federal Reserve Board and National Association of Real Estate Investment Trusts.

industry analysts estimate that REITs now own 5% to 10% of all apartments nationwide and 15% to 20% of the apartments in properties of 100 or more units.

As REITs have grown increasingly important within real estate finance generally, and apartment development specifically, some have speculated that consolidation will continue until ultimately a few of the largest and strongest REITs dominate public equity markets. Others have countered that beyond a certain point, large size actually has disadvantages for REITs, and that new initial public offerings (IPOs) and spin-offs will preserve diversity among REITs. More likely, according to Vandell, two kinds of REITs will emerge within the market and exist side by side: aggressive, large national REITs and smaller REITs that focus on local and regional markets.[68] Thus, while it is unlikely that REITs will swallow the world, they will continue to fill an important role within multifamily housing finance.

The Financing of Small Multifamily Properties

Small multifamily properties account for a large share of unsubsidized affordable rental housing stock. In 2000, around 36% of the nation's rental housing units were in buildings with two to forty-nine units, and about 18% were in buildings with five to forty-nine units (see Figure 3.22). However, research has shown that smaller multifamily properties have more problems in receiving mortgage credit than larger properties, and when financing is found, the cost (in terms of the interest rate charged) is generally higher.[69]

One of the greatest barriers to providing financing for small properties is the underwriting process. The standard commercial underwriting used for larger commercial properties typically mandates a recent appraisal by a state-certified appraiser, environmental reviews, and attorney opinions and certifications. This process is prohibitively expensive for small properties.[70] Also, smaller properties often keep insufficient documentation related to their income and expenses. The principle source of financing for small multifamily properties has therefore been depository institutions, which apply a modified underwriting process and rely much more on the creditworthiness of the borrower to secure the loan.

[68] Vandell, *Strategic Management of the Apartment Business,* 9–10, 31.
[69] Schnare, "Impact of Changes in Multifamily Finance," 21–22; and Herbert, "An Assessment of Availability and Cost of Financing," ii–vii.
[70] Herbert, "Assessment of Availability and Cost of Financing," ii.

FIGURE 3.22

Estimated Distribution of Units by Tenure and Property Size: 2000

	Number of Units (thousands)	Percent of All Units	Percent of All Renter Occupied Units
Owner-Occupied Units	70,369	67.2%	
Renter-Occupied Units			
Single Family Rental			
One Unit	11,483	11.0%	33.4%
2 to 4 Units	6,168	5.9%	18.0%
Total	17,651	16.9%	51.4%
Multifamily Rentals			
5 to 19 Units	3,734	3.6%	10.9%
20 to 49 Units	2,468	2.4%	7.2%
Over 50 Units	10,485	10.0%	30.5%
Total	16,687	16.0%	48.6%
All Rental Units	34,338	32.9%	100.0%
Total Occupied Housing Units	104,707	100.0%	

SOURCE: Calculations by Schnare, "Impact of Changes in Multifamily Finance," 3. Based on U.S. Census Bureau's March 2000 Population Survey and the 1995–1996 Property Owners and Managers Survey.

   Because alternative sources of finance for multifamily properties is limited, smaller projects generally pay higher interest rates than larger ones. In fact, Herbert found that, compared to properties with 100 or more units, the average interest rate for properties with fewer than twenty units was 1.1% higher, and for properties with twenty to forty-nine units, 0.7% higher.[71]

   Herbert also found that, for the most part, small multifamily properties account for a relatively small share — consistently less than 5% — of the multifamily finance provided by the two secondary market GSEs. "For Freddie Mac, small multifamily properties have consistently accounted for less than 5% of their multifamily units; Fannie Mae has had similarly low shares . . . with the notable exceptions of 1995 and 1998."[72] When compared to the 18.1% share of the overall market for five- to forty-nine-unit buildings, (as shown in Figure 3.22), the GSE share falls well below the overall market. This is largely due to the many difficulties of providing a streamlined, efficient secondary market when the buildings involved are so diverse. As we move forward in the twenty-first century, one of the

[71] Ibid., 6–7.
[72] Ibid., vi.

challenges in the area of multifamily housing will continue to be financing for small multifamily properties.

Public Sector Involvement in Multifamily Rental Finance

The federal government influences the multifamily housing industry in a number ways. It regulates, finances, subsidizes, and in some cases operates apartment properties. It also provides tax incentives to encourage private apartment construction. Indirectly, it influences the industry by providing low-income households with income support (through welfare and housing vouchers), which translates into money for housing, and by promoting homeownership, which decreases demand for multifamily housing.

Public policy has historically focused on promoting housing affordability, primarily for low-income households. The goals and means of this involvement have shifted dramatically since the creation of the country's first public housing program in 1937. In the beginning, the government had a supply-side focus, constructing and managing its own affordable housing in the form of public housing. Later, it began providing incentives for the private sector to construct and operate the housing, and eventually, supply-side interventions shifted emphasis from subsidizing the construction of new affordable housing toward encouraging preservation and rehabilitation. Still later, federal efforts shifted to a demand-side focus that provided residents with rental vouchers to subsidize their rents. As federal resources have become scarce, some of the public activity in affordable housing has moved to the state and local levels, which has served to further expand the role of the private sector in affordable housing and has created a new role for nonprofits in multifamily housing.

THE FEDERAL SHIFT FROM SUPPLY-SIDE TO DEMAND-SIDE SUBSIDIES

The federal government began actively building multifamily housing in response to the Great Depression. By 1960, more than 400,000 units of public housing had been produced.[73] (See Figure 3.23.) Although public housing construction continued over the next several decades — tripling the number of units from 400,000 to 1.2 million between 1960 and 1980 — over time, the government turned to the private sector to meet the nation's affordable housing needs.

---

[73] Burchell and Listokin, "Influences on Housing Policy," 598.

FIGURE 3.23
Cumulative Number of Assisted Housing Units by Major HUD Programs

(End of Fiscal Year 1955–1994; Units in Thousands)

Fiscal Year (end of)	Public Housing	Section 236	Section 235	Rent Supplement	Section 8 (Including Voucher)	Total HUD Gross	Total HUD Net
1955	344	NA	NA	NA	NA	344	NA
1960	425	NA	NA	NA	NA	425	NA
1965	577	NA	NA	NA	NA	577	NA
1970	830	5	66	31	NA	932	NA
1975	1,151	400	409	165	NA	2,126	NA
1980	1,192	377	219	165	1,153	3,268	3,107
1985	1,355	332	200	46	2,010	4,140	3,943
1990	1,405	331	130	20	2,500	NA	4,386
1995	1,398	318	76	21	2,912	NA	4,725
1999	1,274	274	43	21	2,985	NA	4,597

SOURCE: Burchell and Listokin, "Influences on Housing Policy," 599. Data from U.S. Dept. of Housing and Urban Development, Division of Program Monitoring and Research, Office of Policy Development and Research, March 1994.

NOTE: Does not include approx. 150,000 units with Section 221(d)(3) and Section 202 below-market interest rates, but no additional subsidies, nor Community Development Block Grant-assisted units. Indicates number of subsidies to units (i.e., a single unit receiving dual subsidies would count as two units). Indicates the number of units subsidized (i.e., a single unit receiving dual subsidies would still count as one unit).

The U.S. Department of Housing and Urban Development (HUD) and Congress created several programs (Section 236, Section 221(d)(3), and Section 202, and Section 8) to provide private developers with low-interest mortgages to build rental housing. Key among these was Section 8, authorized in 1974, which paid developers the difference between fair market rent and the amount that qualified tenants — earning less than 80% of the area median income — could afford to pay for housing (25% of income, later amended to 30%). The number of units constructed with these kinds of subsidies grew from 400,000 in 1975 to more than 3 million by 1994.[74]

Beginning in the 1970s, however, the focus of federal affordable housing programs shifted to demand-side subsidies, largely through a modified Section 8 program for existing housing. The new Section 8 provided certificates and vouchers to residents with incomes less than 50% of the area median income to help them pay the rent in privately-held apartments. By 1994, approximately 1.3 million households received housing subsidies

---

[74] Ibid., 598–599.

through HUD (one million through HUD's Housing Certificate Program, and an additional 300,000 through Housing Vouchers).[75]

THE 1980s TO 1990s: FEDERAL RETRENCHMENT AND A FOCUS ON PRESERVATION

In the 1980s, after forty years of public involvement in creating and sustaining the nation's stock of affordable housing, the federal commitment to affordable housing was scaled back considerably. This was due in part to a growing suspicion that regulatory interference with the private market was at least partially responsible for the shortage of affordable housing. Another important factor was the recognition that federal resources to continue to construct new subsidized housing were no longer available.

Massive retrenchment of federal involvement in affordable housing followed, particularly in the area of new construction. New funds for subsidized housing fell by 60% between 1980 and 1990, from approximately $25 billion to $10 billion. Annual subsidized housing starts dropped even more steeply, by almost 90%, from 175,000 to 20,000. Total expansion of the HUD-subsidized inventory slowed to half the rate of the previous decade.[76] With no resources to construct new housing, federal efforts began to emphasize rehabilitation and preservation of the existing affordable housing stock and reliance on demand-side subsidies. Funding for existing or rehabilitated units made up 80% of HUD subsidies by the late 1980s, up from just 5% in the early 1960s.[77]

The shift to preservation was a response to both the loss of low-rent unsubsidized units (estimated at a reduction of 2.8 million units between 1974 and 1984) and the significant needs of the existing stock.[78] Public housing suffered from management and structural problems. By 1990, approximately 1.4 million public housing units were threatened by advancing age and depreciation, and it was estimated that $12.2 billion would be necessary to bring the entire stock up to acceptable physical condition. Aggravating this situation was the fact that admission policy changes made earlier to favor the poorest of households had caused the proportion of residents with special needs — such as drug addictions or violent criminal records — to grow dramatically. Average resident income fell lower and lower, forcing the federal government to allocate more dollars to keep public housing projects open and affordable. One response by HUD to this

---

[75] Gabriel, "Urban Housing Policy," 683.
[76] Burchell and Listokin, "Influences on Housing Policy," 599, 601.
[77] Ibid., 588.
[78] Gabriel, "Urban Housing Policy," 680.

situation was to begin to turn over ownership of some existing public housing facilities to the residents, first with a 1985 demonstration program and then later with the Housing Opportunities for People Everywhere (HOPE) program. The theory behind the program was that if public housing residents owned their units, they would have more incentive to take care of properties and to manage their finances efficiently.

Public housing was not the only affordable housing to reach a crisis point in the late 1980s. A similar situation was also developing in the privately-owned affordable housing built under the Section 236 and Section 221(d)(3) programs. A significant portion of the stock was in need of rehabilitation and recapitalization. More importantly, the affordability restrictions on these properties were beginning to expire. As originally built, the owners agreed to keep the properties affordable for ten to twenty years in exchange for below-market-rate loans. Once these periods expired, federal law allowed the owners to repay their mortgages, convert the properties to market-rate housing, and raise the rents, which threatened to further reduce the stock of affordable housing. Some of the affordability restrictions began expiring in the 1980s, but the majority did not come up until the 1990s.

In 1987, Congress acted to preserve these properties as affordable housing by passing the Emergency Low-Income Housing Preservation Act (ELIHPA). That was followed by the Low-Income Housing Preservation and Resident Homeownership Act (LIHPRHA) in 1990, and the Multifamily Assisted Housing Reform and Affordability Act ("Mark to Market") in 1997. All three acts provided incentives and requirements for owners related to keeping their properties affordable.[79]

THE SHIFT TO AN INCREASING STATE AND LOCAL ROLE FOR AFFORDABLE HOUSING

States and localities support affordable apartment development in three ways: through their local functions to oversee and set standards for housing construction; through their administration of federal programs; and increasingly, through funding and administration of their own programs.

State and local governments have always influenced housing markets through their authority to oversee and set standards for housing construction. This authority includes building codes, zoning and land use regulation, minimum housing standards, and real estate taxation.[80] They also

---

[79] Ibid., 680–681.
[80] Nenno, "Changes and Challenges," 10.

participate directly in multifamily affordable housing programs. Their original role was to implement federal programs, beginning with the creation in 1937 of local public housing authorities charged with managing federally-funded projects. This role expanded after the Housing Act of 1949, when local redevelopment authorities were established to administer federal community development activities under the Urban Renewal Program. Their responsibility for federal programs was solidified in 1974, when the Housing and Community Development Act created the Community Development Block Grant (CDBG) program, which allocates federal money directly to localities to support a broad range of housing and urban development activities.

Beginning in the 1970s, state and local governments began using the capacity and experience they developed over forty years of administering federal housing programs to take on a new role — as direct funders and developers of affordable housing. In many cases, this evolution was necessary to fill the void created by the gradual cutback in federal assistance.[81] According to Mary Nenno, by 1980, thirteen states had their own housing rehabilitation grant or loan programs, and fifteen had created tax incentives for housing. Between 1980 and 1989, an estimated 300 new state housing programs were enacted, and all but a few states had a housing finance agency.[82] Today, in addition to providing financing, states and localities also assess regional affordable housing inventories, develop lists of potential priority buyers for affordable properties that private owners seek to sell, provide technical assistance, assist in predevelopment and equity funding, train property managers, and provide buyers of last resort.[83]

THE LOW-INCOME HOUSING TAX CREDIT

Perhaps the most significant recent development in the public finance and taxation of affordable multifamily housing was the 1986 creation of the Low-Income Housing Tax Credit (LIHTC). Today, the LIHTC represents the largest federal commitment to affordable housing construction and rehabilitation. It also represents a clear redirection of public housing policy toward devolution, preservation, and a greater reliance on private investment.

---

[81] According to Nenno, "Changes and Challenges," "Between fiscal years 1981 and 1988, low-income housing assistance was cut by 75%, CDBG by 32%, and Urban Development Action Grants by 100%," 9.

[82] Ibid., 12.

[83] Gabriel, "Urban Housing Policy," 681.

The LIHTC offers private investors who provide the equity needed to build or rehab qualified housing properties with a ten-year federal income tax credit. These tax credits are first allocated to proposed projects through state and local housing finance agencies. Developers who receive the credits then sell them to private investors to generate equity for the property and to reduce the costs of construction or rehabilitation. In exchange for these credits, owners are required, for fifteen years, to maintain a portion of the units as affordable to households earning less than 60% of the area median income. In practice, most properties reserve all of their units for affordable housing in order to receive the maximum number of tax credits and to be able to combine tax credit equity with other state and federal subsidies.

The program has proven highly successful at both creating affordable housing and providing strong returns on investments. Competition for tax credits has increased as investors have become more familiar with the program. For example, the amount of private investment raised per dollar of tax credit rose from $0.47 in 1987, when the program began, to $0.62 in 1996. As investors have become more comfortable with the LIHTC program's minimal risk level, the internal rate of return (IRR) they require has fallen from 28.7 in 1987 to 18.2 in 1994 (assuming an eight-year pay-in).[84]

The LIHTC has been modified over the years, in some cases to reflect heightened public concern over preserving of the nation's affordable housing stock. In 1989, Congress was already grappling with the expiring contracts for Section 236 and 221(d)3 properties, so they extended the LIHTC's fifteen-year affordability period to prevent a similar situation from developing in that program. Properties that received credits in 1990 were required to remain affordable for thirty years, although some latitude was provided for partners to opt out under certain conditions. As competition for credits has increased, state and local housing finance agencies have been able to bolster affordability protections even more through their allocation processes. They now give preference to project proposals that commit to even lengthier affordability periods, relinquish their latitude to opt out, and/or agree to sell properties to nonprofit agencies interested in preserving affordability when affordability commitments expire. Some states also give preference to projects that target households with incomes even lower than required.

---

[84] Cummings and DiPasquale, *Building Affordable Rental Housing,* 46.

Begining with the LIHTC's inception through 1999, over 750,000 housing units have been constructed under the program, and their financing, design, and target populations have varied significantly according to state and local needs and preferences. On average, 62,500 units are created each year, representing approximately 20% to 25% of all multifamily housing construction.[85] However, the earliest LIHTC projects, those with the least affordability protections, began to expire in 2002, and dealing with these expirations is the next affordable housing public policy challenge.

MULTIFAMILY RENTAL HOUSING AND SMART GROWTH

The issue of growth management moved to the front of the political landscape in 1998, when voters passed some 200 separate ballot initiatives designed to curb the effects of suburban sprawl and preserve open space. With the economy soaring and crime rates falling, Americans increasingly began to turn their attention to quality of life issues such as traffic congestion, pollution, and overcrowded schools. With that change came a new focus on the role apartments play in housing the nation's population. Smart-growth strategies often place a high value on multifamily housing because of its greater residential density, because it uses existing infrastructure more efficiently, and because it is pedestrian-friendly.

Nonetheless, serious obstacles to promoting apartment housing in suburban neighborhoods remain, including overcoming community objections to new development and enticing more consumers to accept higher-density living. However, demographic and lifestyle trends have led to a growing number of young professionals and empty nesters who prefer the conveniences of apartment living. In addition, demographic trends and growth-related challenges are forcing communities to change their attitude toward apartment properties within their borders.

The Smart-Growth Dilemma

Over the last century, the U.S. population has steadily moved from urban areas to the suburban periphery. Within the last fifteen years, the suburbs have captured between 80% and 85% of newly constructed homes.[86] Evolutions in transportation — first streetcars and railroad lines

---

[85] Collignon, *Expiring Affordability,* 4.
[86] Von Hoffman, "Housing Heats Up," 3.

and eventually automobiles — made it possible for people to move farther from the city. The federal government reinforced this trend with legislation, such as the Federal Highway Act and the GI Bill, that supported infrastructure expansion and homeownership.[87]

With this mass movement to the suburbs, increasing amounts of land have been used at decreasing densities, although urban and suburban land still makes up only 3% of the 1.9 billion acres in the contiguous United States.[88] As an example of the move to the suburbs, between 1960 and 1990, the population of the greater Kansas City metropolitan area increased by 29%, but its land mass increased by 110%. Similarly, the land covered by the population of Chicago and Philadelphia grew 30% between 1970 and 1990 despite a population increase of less than 5%. Some have called Atlanta the most rapidly expanding settlement in history. Its size, end to end, increased from sixty-five miles in 1990 to 110 miles by 1997.[89]

The movement to the suburbs has been driven by consumer demand for more space, higher quality housing, safer and more effective schools, and other amenities perceived to be scarce within larger cities. Many households have individually benefited from the great urban exodus, but the movement has also created challenges for urban and suburban residents alike. Most visible among these are quality of life concerns such as loss of open space, traffic congestion, pollution, and the expansion of urban blight in some areas from inner cities to inner suburbs. In addition, there are fiscal issues such as the cost of infrastructure and the means to fund growing schools.

These concerns highlight a three-way dilemma related to smart growth. First, consumer preferences for the benefits the suburbs provide will continue to drive suburbanization, especially as long as positive alternatives are not available. Second, efforts to provide alternatives in the context of more efficient construction patterns must overcome fears that denser development will eliminate the benefits of suburban living. And third, government and regulatory efforts intended to slow down growth and sprawl often drive up housing and construction costs, further reducing the availability of affordable housing. True smart growth, then, must seek a balance between consumer preferences, the probability that extensive growth restrictions will limit housing opportunities for affordable housing, and the hope that reasonable land use will improve the quality of life for

---

[87] Urban Land Institute, *Future,* 5–6.
[88] National Association of Home Builders, *Smart Growth,* 9.
[89] Urban Land Institute, *Future,* 5.

generations to come. Apartments can play an important role in achieving this balance.

Smart Growth and Multifamily Rental Housing

Well-designed multifamily rental housing can help renew interest in downtown and urban living. It can also encourage new development to take on a more town-centered character by preserving open space and making it possible to locate housing within walking distance of shopping and public transit. In addition to meeting smart-growth guidelines, higher-density housing offers numerous advantages for individuals in addition to the lifestyle benefits discussed earlier. Land costs per unit are lower, making the housing more affordable and thus making it possible for moderate-income households to move into better neighborhoods. Higher-density developments within a suburban neighborhood also allow people to remain in the same community throughout the different stages of their lives.

Barriers to Smart Growth and Multifamily Development

Despite the intellectual appeal of apartments, significant barriers have long stood in the way of both building more apartments and attracting suburban-oriented households back into denser, more urban environments. Developers seeking to build apartments in suburban towns or urban communities have often faced tremendous legal and political resistance. Many suburbs have zoning laws that restrict residential development to single-family homes with large lots. In urban communities, the morass of regulatory constraints and uncoordinated government agencies can lead to costly delays or complete stoppage. When developers do appeal for zoning variances or local government cooperation, they often encounter intense local opposition and "not in my backyard" (NIMBY) responses. Communities resist development of multifamily housing based on a variety of often unfounded fears. Key among these are fears of rising local fiscal deficits as a result of apartment residents using public services, particularly schools; increased traffic and parking congestion; apartment residents who will differ from those already living in the community (by income, race, and/or culture); and potential increases in crime and decreases in property values.[90]

---

[90] Black, *Opportunity and Challenge,* 16–17; Burchell and Listokin, "Influences on Housing Policy," 573.

Objective research has refuted many of these fears. Apartment properties typically pay higher property tax rates than single-family homes, yet they place less demand on public services. The average apartment household consumes $1,647 in public services, compared to $2,361 for single-family home owners.[91] It is less expensive to provide public infrastructure and service such as police and fire protection to higher-density construction (see Figure 3.24). Apartment households place less demand on local school systems, with 36.1 children per 100 multifamily households versus 55.6 across all kinds of homes.[92] Apartment properties can also help municipalities accommodate growth without worsening traffic congestion because multifamily households generally own fewer vehicles and use public transportation more frequently. In fact, many choose where they live, at least in part, because of proximity to public transportation. While only 4% of single-family home owners use public transportation or walk to work, 19% of apartment residents do.[93] Finally, concerns that apartment properties will decrease the value of nearby single-family homes remain unsubstantiated. In fact, one study found that between 1987 and 1995, single-family homes located within 300 feet of a multifamily building appreciated just one-tenth of a percent less than the 3.2% appreciation seen among single-family homes without multifamily structures nearby.[94] Nevertheless, the costs of overcoming political resistance have discouraged many builders from even attempting to build apartments.

The Future of Multifamily Rental Housing and Smart Growth

Despite the barriers to smart growth, it is likely that a variety of factors, including economics, public policy pressures, demographics, and housing demand, will lead to greater urban and mixed-use development. Multifamily and rental housing will be an important component of this activity.

"Edge cities" — employment centers outside of center cities, surrounded by suburban development — are discovering that if they restrict residential development to large, expensive single-family homes, they do so at the expense of economic growth. Affordable multifamily housing

---

[91] Colton, Crowe, and Emrath, *Benefits of Multifamily Housing,* 6–7. From Paul B. Downing and Richard D. Gustav, "The Public Service Costs of Alternative Development Patterns: A Review of the Evidence," in Paul B. Downing, ed., *Local Service Pricing Policies and Their Effects on Urban Spatial Structures* (Vancouver, B.C.), University of British Columbia Press, 1977), table 8.

[92] Colton, Crowe, and Emrath, *Benefits of Multifamily Housing,* 6–7. From 1995 American Housing Survey. See also National Multi Housing Council, "Growing Smarter with Apartments," 4.

[93] Colton, Crowe and Emrath, *Benefits of Multifamily Housing,* 6–7. From 1990 U.S. Census.

[94] Colton, Crowe and Emrath, *Benefits of Multifamily Housing,* 5.

FIGURE 3.24
Capital Costs of Development of Alternative Residental Densities

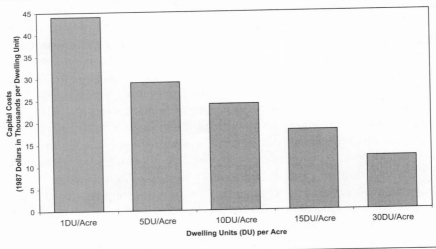

SOURCE: Colton, Crowe, and Emrath, *Benefits of Multifamily Housing,* utilizing data from the U.S. Census Bureau, "American Housing Survey 1995"

makes it possible for moderate- and lower-wage workers — such as teachers, nurses, police, administrative personnel, and restaurant and retail staff — to provide the services on which a locality depends on a day-to-day basis. Furthermore, employers of upper-income employees find they have to pay higher salaries to attract talent to areas with high housing costs. Without the affordable housing that higher-density and multifamily construction makes possible, localities jeopardize their own future development.

In the face of these kinds of pressures, as well as in response to fair housing concerns, strategies to encourage higher-density development have begun to emerge at the federal, state, and local levels. For example, the federal government has taken steps to promote higher-density development in some situations. State and local governments now have more flexibility in how they use the Federal Highway Trust Fund, including the ability to allocate these funds to improve urban transportation systems.[95] Brownfield redevelopment programs, created under the leadership of the U.S. Environmental Protection Agency, HUD, and the Department of

---

[95] Black, *Opportunity and Challenge,* 10.

Commerce, have helped remove disincentives for redeveloping sites contaminated by previous use.

Even without government intervention, demographic changes, as discussed earlier, are likely to increase demand for apartment housing within mixed-use areas. The fastest-growing household types between now and 2010 are smaller households — single-adult households, childless couples, and single-parent households — which have a higher propensity to select apartment living. The number of individuals seeking smaller housing units will further increase as the echo boomers move out of their parents' homes and the baby boomers become empty nesters.

If truly balanced smart-growth efforts gain strength, apartment housing should play an even more important role in urban and suburban development. Nonetheless, despite the linkage between smart growth and apartment development, and despite the demographic and public policy pressures supporting increased apartment production, there still remains a long road ahead to achieve greater consumer and community acceptance for apartment housing.

CONCLUSIONS

As the nation moves forward in the twenty-first century, multifamily rental housing will play an essential, and possibly expanded, role in housing our residents. The apartment industry currently provides housing to a wide diversity of renters who generally fall into three groups: lower-income residents of affordable housing apartments, higher-income lifestyle renters, and a vast middle market of moderate-income households. Both by necessity and by choice, a significant portion of the nation's households will look to multifamily housing to meet their housing needs.

Recently, much of the industry's attention has been focused on lifestyle renters. These households, defined as earning $50,000 or more, have been the fastest-growing sector of apartment renters in the decade of the 1990s. Such attention should continue in order to meet market demand, but the greatest housing needs are clearly in the affordable housing arena. Over the last two decades federal resources devoted to housing programs have leveled off or declined while the needs have grown. At the same time, public policies related to taxes and financial regulations have reduced the incentives for private investment in multifamily housing, particularly at the affordable end of the market. The result is a growing gap between the housing "haves" and "have-nots," and an increasing number of working families who cannot find or afford decent housing. Without a renewed commitment to provide federal, state and local financial support for new multifamily housing production, along with a sustained public/private housing partnership, it is likely that the affordable housing gap will continue to widen. In fact, increased multifamily housing production is essential in meeting the nation's housing needs.

To help counter the diminished federal role in affordable housing, the activities of state and local governments have grown, and the Low-Income Housing Tax Credit has provided a steady, albeit modest, level of new construction and rehabilitation for low- and moderate-income housing. Recent efforts by HUD and Congress have also resulted in a modest increase in the number of housing vouchers. At the same time, state and local regulatory burdens have grown in numerous communities, and the gap continues to widen between the need and the availability of affordable housing.

The challenge of suburban sprawl should provide an incentive for the development of multifamily residential alternatives in both suburban and urban locations. This can be achieved within the context of smart growth by recognizing the need to balance community growth and lifestyle concerns with the fact that growth controls raise construction and development costs and thereby limit the availability of affordable housing. Perhaps by learning from the successes and mistakes of the past, leaders and communities can achieve the mix of public policy guidance and private sector initiative necessary to support the role that multifamily housing must play in providing greater housing choice and meeting the nation's critical affordable housing needs.

Chapter 4:

HOUSING FINANCE IN THE UNITED STATES: THE TRANSFORMATION OF THE U.S. HOUSING FINANCE SYSTEM

By many standards, the United States has the best housing finance system in the world. However, the system has seen many changes and modifications over the last fifty years and throughout the twentieth century. One of its greatest certainties has been change. To understand where we are now, it is worth reflecting on the transformations that have taken place. Over the last century, the housing finance system has seen three major revolutions.

The first was a product of the Great Depression and the need to restructure a housing finance system that was in chaos. It included the creation of the fixed-rate mortgage, the development of a system of direct and indirect support from the federal government, and a linking of the public and the private sectors. The second revolution has taken place over the last twenty years. At the end of the 1970s and in the early 1980s, we once again faced a major disruption — a clear challenge to the nation's system of mortgage lending. Since then we have seen important changes and a phenomenal growth and development of the secondary market for housing finance. With this growth has also come a shift in the institutions that are originating and servicing mortgages, as well as a further evolution of the direct and indirect federal support surrounding housing finance in the United States. A third revolution is currently underway. It is tied directly to the rapid changes in technology taking place throughout society. Technology shifts and opportunities are driving numerous changes to the nation's housing finance system and will undoubtedly have a major impact on both the delivery system and its participants. It appears that the consumer will be a major beneficiary of the shifts. However, because change brings uncertainty, there are also concerns about where this revolution will lead, who the winners and losers will be, and the ultimate balance between the private sector, the public sector, and the three housing-related "government sponsored enterprises" (GSEs).

THE FIRST REVOLUTION: A STRONG SYSTEM OF HOUSING FINANCE RISES FROM THE ASHES OF THE DEPRESSION

The period from 1921 to 1928 witnessed a strong housing boom. Annual housing production accelerated from 449,000 units in 1921 to 937,000 units in 1925, the highest level recorded up to that point. In fact, given the challenges of record keeping at the time, 1925 might have been the first million-unit year for housing production, and 1926 the second. Production then declined slowly to 753,000 units in 1928, the last year of the post-World War I boom.[1] Housing production then dropped sharply to 509,000 units in 1929, heralding one of the darkest periods in the history of the country. As a consequence of the depression, housing production declined drastically year by year from 509,000 units in 1929 to 134,000 units in 1932. The decline in housing production included the collapse of multifamily starts from 238,000 units in 1928 and 142,000 in 1929 to a mere 9,000 in 1932, the lowest level ever recorded.[2]

Housing and the Great Depression

The first few years of the depression saw a significant drop in housing production, but even more important, a drastic fall in demand. From 1929 to 1932, the housing stock is estimated to have increased by 2.5 million units, compared to an increase of only 1 million households. The relatively large increase in housing stock was due mainly to a lag in the completion of structures started before 1929, and to the net conversions of existing structures to provide additional small units to accommodate families with reduced incomes. This relative increase in the housing stock in a rapidly deteriorating housing market was compounded by deflationary pressure, and the gross vacancy level went from an already high 8% in 1928 to 13% by 1932.[3]

In addition, the early 1930s was a catastrophic period for mortgage finance. People were confronted with unemployment and a sudden and drastic drop in personal income. This led to intense pressure on the ability

---

[1] Doan, *American Housing Production*, 29–31.
[2] Ibid., 33.
[3] Ibid., 33–34.

of people to pay for their housing. Extensive forbearance allowed many people with delinquent mortgages to remain in possession of their homes; between 1931 and 1935, thirty-three states actually passed laws providing some relief for delinquent mortgagors, including mortgage moratoria in twenty-eight states.[4] However, with no reserve funding sources available, mortgage lending institutions were unable to keep pace as borrowers defaulted on their loans, the value of housing assets continued to drop, and deposits were withdrawn in high volumes. Consequently, a large number of lending institutions failed. Outstanding nonfarm residential mortgage debt was squeezed down in what was the first recorded reduction, from a record $30.2 billion in 1930 to $27.4 billion in 1932. New lending came to a halt, and construction virtually ceased.[5]

The structure of mortgage debt which developed during the 1920s contributed significantly to the disaster. The large majority of mortgage loans at the time were on a short-term, renewable basis, frequently also involving higher-interest-rate junior or second mortgages. When the mortgage was due, if the homeowner could not pay the full amount of the mortgage, including interest, the mortgage was in default, and the homeowner lost the home. To make matters worse, the mortgage finance industry was highly fragmented and lacked any backup or reserve capacity, and a secondary market for housing was essentially nonexistent. The nation's system of mortgage debt was in collapse, and the stage was set for the first revolution in housing finance — the development of a system including not only a new, longer-term mortgage instrument for the home buyer, but also a new structure for financial institutions to provide and support the financing of housing.

Efforts at Reform

The first effort to reform the system came in July of 1932, while Herbert Hoover was president, with the passage of the Federal Home Loan Bank Act. The intent of the act was to provide a reserve system to support housing finance that would bring relief to troubled homeowners and lending institutions. It established twelve regional Federal Home Loan Banks supervised by a Federal Home Loan Bank Board. It also provided authority to borrow up to $215 million from the U.S. Treasury and for the newly created Federal Home Loan Banks to issue tax-free bonds as a source of loan funds (which became known as "advances") for the benefit of member

---

[4] Colean, *American Housing: Problems and Prospects,* 258.
[5] Doan, *American Housing Production,* 34.

institutions, which were largely savings and loan associations. The capital stock of the regional banks was to be owned by member institutions, each of which were required to purchase stock. Given the magnitude of the crisis and the normal start-up time for new institutions, the first year of the Federal Home Loan Bank Act produced few results. Only five regional banks were organized before the end of 1932, and few loans were made to distressed institutions.

The Foundation for a New System of Housing Finance

In March of 1933, when the Roosevelt administration took over, the banking and housing finance systems were in virtual collapse. To address the problems, two pieces of temporary legislation were enacted in June of 1933. The Home Owners Loan Act was meant to curtail the hemorrhage of mortgage debt, and Title II of the National Industrial Recovery Act was intended to provide federal financing for a program of low-cost housing and slum clearance, with the further purpose of stimulating employment in the depressed construction industry. The Home Owners Loan Act particularly focused on the housing finance system. It established the Home Owners Loan Corporation (HOLC) under the Federal Home Loan Bank System, created the year before. The HOLC was capitalized with $200 million in treasury funds and the authority to issue bonds up to $2 billion to finance operations for three years. The HOLC was to be, in effect, the lender of last resort, and it was authorized to refinance the mortgages of home owners threatened with foreclosure and to make cash advances to pay taxes and to fund necessary housing repairs. Owner-occupied properties of one-to-four units with a value up to $20,000 were eligible for HOLC loans, which were limited to 80% of appraised value, or $16,000. The maximum interest rate was 5% of the outstanding balance of the loan, and the loan was to be repaid in monthly installments for terms up to fifteen years (these terms were later increased to twenty years).

The Home Owners Loan Corporation pioneered, on a national basis, a long-term mortgage program with moderate interest rates and what were, for that period, high loan-to-value ratios. It not only played a key role in refinancing homes and slowing down foreclosures, but also set a precedent and a pattern for the remainder of the century. The HOLC received 1.9 million applications for loan assistance from June 1933 to June 1935, and it is estimated that this covered 40% of the approximate 4.8 million one-to-four-family properties that faced mortgage indebtedness at the time. Out of these applications, the HOLC made one million loans, aggregating $3.1 billion, refinancing about 20% of all outstanding mortgages on owner-occupied nonfarm properties — at a time when private mortgage debt was shrinking.[6] By 1935, the peak of activity, the HOLC held 12% of the country's outstanding residential mortgage debt, more than either life insurance companies or commercial banks.[7]

Approximately 20% of the HOLC borrowers defaulted, but this is not surprising in view of the fact that borrowers had to be threatened with foreclosure to be eligible for a loan. The HOLC was liquidated in 1951 — actually with a small profit to the federal government. Based on far more than this small profit, though, the HOLC was a great success. It saved the homes of three-quarters of a million families, provided relief to a range of hard-pressed mortgage lending institutions and a beleaguered mortgage finance market, and helped pave the way for our current system of housing finance. It established precedents for a long-term fixed-rate mortgage, for a national system of mortgage lending, and for a federal role in providing support for housing finance. As Thomas B. Marvell wrote in his 1969 book on the Federal Home Loan Bank Board, "The management of the HOLC has probably been the most important accomplishment of the Federal Home Loan Bank Board."[8]

The Establishment of the Federal Housing Administration

By early 1934, the HOLC was providing relief to distressed home owners in existing housing, and the Federal Emergency Administration of Public Works (PWA) was beginning to use government funds to build public housing through a program of low-cost housing and slum clearance authorized through Title II of the National Industry Recovery Act (the second piece of emergency legislation that was passed in June 1933). However, at that point private residential construction was still negligible. The Roosevelt administration and Congress were anxious to stimulate the private economy, and yet President Roosevelt wanted to minimize direct federal outlays in housing. This led to the passage in June 1934 of a third piece of housing legislation, the National Housing Act, which created the Federal Housing Administration (FHA) and established a key part of the foundation for the nation's system of housing finance. The act established the FHA, backed by a mutual mortgage insurance fund; continued the HOLC precedent of a long-term mortgage with moderate interest rates;

---

[6] Ibid., 39.
[7] U.S. Census Bureau, *Historical Statistics,* 647.
[8] Marvell, *The Federal Home Loan Bank Board,* 25.

authorized nationally charted mortgage associations (mortgage bankers) to purchase FHA-insured mortgages in the secondary market; and authorized the insurance of deposits for savings and loan associations. A number of innovative features were included in the act.[9]

- Perhaps the most innovative principle of the legislation was the insurance of housing loans and mortgages against default in order to encourage lending institutions to make funds available in a very adverse housing market. Operations for the FHA were financed through insurance premiums, fees, and interest on invested reserves rather than by the Treasury of the United States.
- Title I provided for the insurance of unsecured loans for the repair and improvement of nonfarm residential real estate up to $2,000.
- Title II, provided for the insurance of the unpaid balance of mortgages on small homes and rental projects. For homes (Section 203), the HOLC precedent was followed with the authorization of insurance on twenty-year mortgage loans up to 80% of the appraised value of $20,000 and a maximum interest rate of 5%. Insured loans were required to be "economically sound." A mutual mortgage insurance fund was established to insure this part of the program and it was supported by a premium of 0.5% of the outstanding loan balance, paid by the person buying the home — the mortgagor — to help cover operating expenses and insurance liabilities. Surplus funds were to be returned to the mortgagors under the mutuality principle.
- For rental projects (Section 207), the original language of the act provided for the insurance and mortgages on rental structures intended for occupancy by persons of low-income, owned by either public bodies or private limited dividend corporations.
- The act also provided, in Title III, for the authorization of nationally chartered mortgage associations to purchase FHA-insured mortgages in the secondary market, which eventually became an important innovation (leading to the creation of the mortgage banking industry).
- Finally, the act authorized the insurance of deposits for savings and loan associations. This provision was only reluctantly agreed to by the Roosevelt administration in order to secure the support

[9] For a discussion of these features see Doan, *American Housing Production,* 40–41.

of the savings and loan industry for the passage of the National Housing Act.

Another piece of permanent housing legislation, part of the New Deal, was the United States Housing Act (PL 412). It was passed in 1937, following Roosevelt's landslide victory in the 1936 election and the abandonment of the PWA Public Housing Program, which had been passed in June of 1933 on a temporary basis. This act was the beginning of the public housing program. It authorized federal support for a system of low-rent public housing to be built, owned, and managed by local housing authorities under state legislation. The United States Housing Authority was created to administer the loans, and financing was provided through sixty-year federal loans at a rate a half percent above the long-term rate of money for the government, as well as an annual contribution from the federal government to cover the debt service.

In 1938, Congress created the Federal National Mortgage Association, now known as Fannie Mae. In the absence of private initiatives, it was originally chartered under the Reconstruction Finance Corporation (RFC) as the secondary market facility for FHA-insured (and later VA-guaranteed) mortgages. Fannie Mae was given the power to borrow funds to buy mortgages from originators on the theory that it could access funds from areas where savings were high relative to mortgage demand, then use those funds to buy mortgages in areas where savings were low.

The Impact of the New Deal Response

In the short term, the response in the marketplace to these New Deal programs was slow. The ongoing problems included a surplus of existing housing, continuing mortgage and rental delinquencies and foreclosures, high construction costs in relationship to existing property values, unemployment rates in excess of 20%, and slow population growth. All of these challenges led to slow housing production throughout the remainder of the 1930s. Production crept up to 319,000 units in 1936, stagnated again in 1937, then advanced to 550,000 units in 1939. Nevertheless, the New Deal had provided the foundation for the housing finance system for the remainder of the twentieth century.

Once in place, these innovations provided the financing for the return of the veterans following World War II and for the tremendous burst of housing development and construction that took place over the next fifty years. Housing finance is the circulatory system for the housing delivery process, and without these changes to pump "new blood" into the system, the housing growth of the second half of the century would not have been possible.

In the revolution and housing growth that followed, the primary role of innovator was given to the FHA. Before the depression, the typical home mortgage ran for less than ten years, had a loan-to-value ratio of about 50%, and provided for repayment of interest only over the life of the mortgage, with a single "balloon payment" of the entire principal at expiration of the loan term. Built on the pattern of the HOLC, the FHA facilitated the use of a new type of mortgage loan: long-term, high loan-to-value ratio (and therefore low down payment), and self-amortizing, with repayment of both principal and interest at a fixed amount each month over the life of the loan. FHA did this, as noted above, by insuring such mortgages and assuming the risk of any loss due to default. Funds to pay the losses on defaulted mortgages came from the insurance premium levied on the mortgage holder. The system was intended to be self-supporting, with the insurance premiums equal to outlays for defaults plus administrative expenses.[10] FHA mortgage insurance is widely viewed to be a great success. More than 30% of all new homes built in the 1930s had FHA insurance, and FHA has undoubtedly contributed to the national rise in home ownership. Homeownership rose from 44% of all households in 1940 to 65% in 1976 and to 68% at the end of 2001.[11]

After World War II, a parallel program to the FHA was established by the Veterans Administration (VA) for servicemen. The main difference between the two programs was that VA guaranteed only a fraction of the loan amount (up to 60%, subject to a maximum dollar loss, which has been raised from time to time to keep pace with inflation). In addition, the VA program required no down payment and no mortgage insurance premium, since it guaranteed the loan rather than insuring it, but in reality these differences are minor compared to the basic similarities and intents of the programs — to provide support for home buyers and veterans to obtain long-term, fixed-rate mortgages at moderate interest rates.[12]

---

[10] Weicher, *Housing Federal Policies and Programs,* 111.

[11] For a further discussion of the role the FHA has played since it was established in the 1930s, see President's Commission on Housing, "Report of the Commission on Housing," 162.

[12] Weicher, *Housing, Federal Policies and Programs,* 112.

THE SECOND REVOLUTION: THE DEVELOPMENT
AND GROWTH OF THE SECONDARY MARKET

The Seeds of the Secondary Market

In the latter half of the 1960s, the country found itself in another period of challenge. With the war in Vietnam came civil disobedience, culminating in July 1967 with major riots in Newark and Detroit that involved federal and state troops. As a consequence of this unrest, President Lyndon Johnson established three commissions: the National Advisory Commission on Civil Disorder, which reported in March, 1968; the National Commission on Urban Problems (often called the Douglas Commission), which was established in 1967 and reported at the end of 1968; and the President's Committee on Urban Housing (often called the Kaiser Commission), which was appointed by the President in June of 1967 and concluded its work in December 1968. These three commissions provided the foundation for the Housing and Urban Development Act of 1968, enacted with virtually no opposition in the Senate and a wide margin in the House. Among other provisions, this act reaffirmed the policy set forth in 1949 Housing Act calling for "a decent home and a suitable living environment for every American family;" established the Section 235 program providing federal interest-rate subsidies for the production of one- and two-family properties for ownership by lower-income families; and established a series of provisions related to rental housing for low- and moderate-income families.

Almost hidden among the other provisions in the act was an important title, Title VIII, which planted one of several seeds related to a restructuring of the federal government's participation in the secondary mortgage market. As noted earlier, Fannie Mae (the Federal National Mortgage Association) had been created by Congress in 1938. As a part of the 1968 Housing and Urban Development Act, Fannie Mae was divided into two entities. The first, which retained the original name of Fannie Mae, was a government-sponsored private corporation (a government sponsored enterprise, or GSE) that held a government charter and a modest guarantee from the federal government but was also allowed to issue stock and trade as a private corporation. The second entity was a government corporation, the Government National Mortgage Association (Ginnie Mae). Its purpose was to operate some of the special assistance and liquidation functions of the former Fannie Mae, and also to provide an explicit government guarantee on mortgage-backed securities insured by FHA and VA. Fannie Mae, as a government sponsored enterprise, was authorized to issue securities backed by FHA and VA mortgages and guaranteed by Ginnie Mae.

In additional legislation passed in 1970, Congress created the Federal Home Loan Mortgage Corporation — for a time called the Mortgage Corporation and now called Freddie Mac. Freddie Mac was chartered by Congress to help increase the availability of residential mortgage financing. Its board of directors was the Federal Home Loan Bank Board, and the organization provided a secondary market for conventional residential mortgages owned and sold primarily by the savings and loan industry. Freddie Mac developed the first private mortgage-backed security for conventional mortgages, known as the PC (participation certificate); and the purpose was to buy mortgages from lenders and to pool them together and sell them as mortgage-backed securities. Thus, the seeds for linking the mortgage markets with the broader capital markets were planted in 1968 and 1970 with the restructuring of Fannie Mae and Ginnie Mae, and the establishment of Freddie Mac.

A New Crisis: Rising Interest Rates

The system of housing finance established during the depression worked well after World War II and during the 1950s, 1960s and 1970s — periods that had relatively stable interest rates. As long as interest rates were stable, savings and loan associations were able to borrow money from depositors and lend money for mortgages, and they became the dominant provider for mortgage credit (see Figure 4.1). In 1950, savings and loan associations and mutual savings banks together accounted for 36.9% of all residential mortgage debt outstanding, and by 1977 this number had risen to 54.2%. Life insurance companies, on the other hand, went from a 20.1% share of mortgage debt outstanding in 1950 to only 4.4% in 1977. Commercial banks' share remained relatively constant, going from 18.9% in 1950 to 14.99% in 1977 (see Figure 4.2).

However, when interest rates began to gyrate significantly in the mid-1970s, S&Ls found themselves "borrowing short" from consumers through short-term certificates of deposit (CDs), generally for six months, one year, two years, or five years. At the same time, the S&Ls were using this money to "lend long" in the form of longer-term mortgages — say, twenty years. When short-term interest rates rose, they were therefore paying more in interest for the money they were using to finance mort-

FIGURE 4.1
Residential Mortgages at Thrift Institutions
as a Percent of Total Mortgages Outstanding

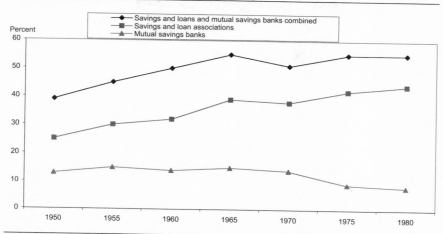

SOURCES: Federal Home Loan Bank Board; National Association of Mutual Savings Banks; and Board of Governors of the Federal Reserve System, Flow of Funds Accounts.

SOURCE: Figure 9.1 found in *President's Commission on Housing,* "Report of the Commission on Housing," 115.

NOTE: Federally related pass-through securities are included in both residential mortgages at thrift institutions and total mortgages outstanding.

gages than they were receiving from the mortgages, and this led to serious financial challenges for the S&Ls and for the housing finance system. In 1981, shortly after the election of Ronald Reagan as president, the President's Commission on Housing was created, and this author was asked to serve as the staff director for the commission. One of the purposes of the commission was to examine the country's housing finance difficulties. After a year of deliberation, the commission reached the following conclusions:

> Since the mid-1960s, the ability of the housing finance system to meet the needs of borrowers has deteriorated markedly on several occasions, and this system currently is in a serious state of disrepair. The volume of residential mortgage lending naturally reflects changes in financial market conditions because the sensitivity of demand for mortgage credit to changes in interest rates is high relative to interest rates sensitivity in other major sectors of the economy. However, the increasingly wide swings in residential mortgage and housing construction activity also are retraceable to structural shortcomings in the housing finance system.

FIGURE 4.2

Percent of Total Residential Mortgage Debt Outstanding by Type of Institution

End of Period	Depository Institutions			Life Insurance Companies	Federal and Related Agencies	Mortgage Pools[a]	All Others[b]
	Savings and Loan Assns	Mutual Savings Banks	Commer-cial Banks				
1950	24.14%	12.76%	18.87%	20.06%	2.73%	0.00%	21.45%
1955	29.85	15.18	15.49	20.68	3.31	0.00	15.48
1960	35.47	14.98	12.55	17.71	5.03	0.00	14.26
1965	39.72	15.56	12.57	14.90	2.90	0.02	14.33
1970	38.75	13.94	12.74	11.92	7.03	0.72	14.90
1975	42.19	10.79	14.03	6.29	8.49	4.96	13.25
1976	43.76	10.18	14.27	5.34	7.24	6.66	12.57
1977	44.70	9.51	14.89	4.37	6.27	8.29	11.97
1978	44.22	8.93	15.72	3.77	6.40	9.11	11.85
1979	42.83	8.20	15.93	3.52	6.60	10.77	12.15
1980	41.69	7.61	15.77	3.41	6.95	11.84	12.73
1981	40.53	7.23	16.11	3.17	7.02	12.67	13.27

[a] Mortgages in pools backing pass-through securities issued and/or guaranteed by the Government National Mortgage Association, Federal Home Loan Mortgage Corporation, and Farmers Home Administration.

[b] Includes mortgage banking companies, real estate investment trusts, private pension and retirement funds, State and local government credit agencies and retirement funds, credit unions, and individuals.

SOURCE: Data compiled by staff from information supplied by the Board of Governors of the Federal Reserve System.

SOURCE: Table 9.2 found in *President's Commission on Housing,* "Report of the Commission on Housing," 114.

As inflation accelerated and interest rates underwent unprecedented change, two major problem areas emerged in the housing finance system. First, the traditional process of mortgage lending and investment through primary and secondary market mechanisms began to deteriorate. Mortgage originators became less willing to write the types of loan agreements ordinarily offered to borrowers, and secondary market investors became reluctant to enter into traditional mortgage purchase contracts with originators. In addition, increasing proportions of real estate transactions were financed outside normal institutional lending channels, to the detriment of the health of the traditional mortgage finance institutions.[13]

Between 1960 and 1982, inflation, and the Federal Reserve's efforts to fight it, drove mortgage rates to unprecedented heights (see Figure 4.3). Mortgage rates were relatively low and quite stable until 1966, then high, volatile, and rising rates of inflation began to drive rates from one historic

---

[13] President's Commission on Housing, "Report of the Commission on Housing," 116.

FIGURE 4.3
Inflation Drives Up Mortgage Interest Rates

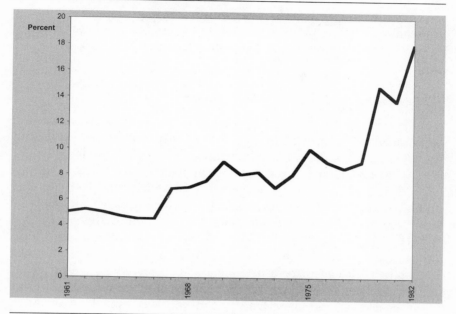

SOURCE: U.S. Department of Housing and Urban Development.

high to another with increasingly severe variations. During 1979 alone, mortgage rates fluctuated over a range of three percentage points. There were two major consequences of this increase in rates. First, households found it harder to sustain the cash flows necessary to pay for a house at market rates, and housing became less affordable. Second, thrift institutions (the dominant factor in financing housing) became less viable. Inflation outstripped expectations, and thrift institutions found that they had borrowed short and lent long, and they had loaned money for housing at rates that were insufficient to cover the costs of money they were borrowing from the savers at their institutions. Because they were forced to finance these mortgage loans by paying savers market rates reflecting the rate of inflation, the thrifts were caught in an earnings squeeze that hobbled them as a source of housing finance and threatened their long-term viability.

Due to this interest rate/institutional crisis, in 1982 the President's Commission on Housing concluded: "Inflation and unprecedented interest rate movements have fundamentally damaged the system of financial intermediation that so successfully supported American housing for more than forty years, and therefore a broader-based and more resilient system will be needed to supply the funds a strengthened housing finance industry will require."[14] Thus, the stage was set for the second revolution in housing finance: the development and growth of the secondary market.

The Development of the Secondary Market

In the early 1980s, the key housing finance question, as articulated by the President's Commission on Housing and many others, was where the money would come from to finance America's housing needs in the future. As the commission noted, the housing finance system had, since the 1960s, suffered increasingly severe financial shocks that had compromised its ability to serve the nation's housing credit needs.[15] The commission observed, "The nation can no longer rely so completely on a system of highly regulated and specialized mortgage investors and a single type of mortgage instrument if the strong underlying demand for housing credit is to be met." It called for a new legal and regulatory structure, and a broader-based and therefore more resilient housing finance system. In the future, it said, all mortgage lenders and borrowers should have unrestricted access to money and capital markets, and mortgage-market participants should have reliable ways of managing interest-rate risk.[16]

The commission's report went on to point out that the efficiency of the secondary market had improved in recent years because of widespread use of standardized mortgage documents, growth of private mortgage insurance, development of mortgage-issued securities, and efforts by securities dealers to develop primary and secondary markets for these instruments. It also noted that the greatest improvements had been made in markets for federally underwritten mortgages and pass-through securities, which had been principally the domain of mortgage banking companies rather than thrift institutions. The report highlighted that the secondary market for the trading of conventional residential mortgages remained relatively underdeveloped compared with other capital markets. The commission therefore outlined a series of recommendations to allow for the efficient operation of the conventional mortgage-backed security market (see Fig-

---

[14] Ibid., xxix.
[15] Ibid., 119.
[16] Ibid., 120.

FIGURE 4.4
Recommendations of the President's Commission on Housing Related to the Secondary Market

- The Internal Revenue Code should be amended to provide an exemption for conventional mortgage-backed securities (CMBSs) from taxation at the pool/issuer level, provided CMBSs meet minimum criteria.
- The Internal Revenue Code also should be amended to treat the recovery of market discounts on CMBSs on the basis as such discounts are treated on corporate securities.
- The Securities and Exchange Commission should promulgate regulations to provide specific and streamlined shelf-registration procedures designed for conventional mortgage-backed security issues.
- CMBS issuers should be permitted, but not required, to register as regulated investment companies.
- The Federal Reserve Board should amend Regulation T to allow for the purchase of privately issued conventional mortgage-backed securities on margin.
- Congress should extend the current provisions of the Federal Bankruptcy Code to all entities that sell mortgage loans, mortgage participations, or conventional mortgage-backed securities.
- The National Conference of Commissioners on Uniform State Laws should recommend amendments to relevant state blue-sky laws to exempt qualified conventional mortgage-backed security issuers from state registration
- States should be encouraged to create public conduit CMBS issuers that draw on the capacity and experience of their existing state housing finance agencies.

SOURCE: Colton, "Report of the President's Commission on Housing," 157.

ure 4.4).[17] The main premise was that mortgage-related securities issued for sale in the secondary market were disadvantaged from a legal, regulatory, and tax standpoint as compared with corporate debt obligations, unless the securities were covered by the guarantee of a federal or federally related agency. Recommendations were therefore set forth to exempt conventional mortgage-backed securities from taxation at the pool/issue level; to call on the Securities and Exchange Commission to promulgate regulations to provide specific streamlined self-registration procedures; for the Federal Reserve to amend Regulation T to allow for the purchase of privately issued conventional mortgage-backed securities on margin; and for Congress to extend the provisions of the Federal Bankruptcy Code to all entities selling mortgages or mortgage-related products. In sum, the recommendations were intended to produce the tax, legal, and regulatory environment necessary for the development of a broad and active conventional mortgage-backed securities market.

The commission report highlighted that Freddie Mac and Fannie Mae should play important roles in the development of markets for conventional mortgage pass-through securities. The report also recommended that federal policies should encourage the operation of Fannie Mae and Freddie Mac as private corporations, retaining only limited benefits arising

---

[17] Colton, "The Report of the President's Commission on Housing," 157.

from congressionally mandated commitments to housing. However, given concerns about the financial condition of Fannie Mae at the time (Fannie Mae had also borrowed short and lent long and therefore had significant problems similar to those of the thrift industry), the commission report called for both agencies to expand their efforts to support large amounts of newly issued pass-through securities.[18] This report therefore set the stage for an expansion of Freddie Mac's and Fannie Mae's activities in the mortgage-backed securities area, while at the same time opening the door to future discussions about the appropriate balance between the private sector and these two government sponsored enterprises. In a decisive step to deal with its portfolio imbalance, Fannie Mae initiated a program in 1981 to buy loans and issue mortgage-backed securities similar to the program Freddie Mac had already established. These efforts, coupled with numerous other programs, proved to be extremely successful. Fannie Mae moved from a position of instability to one of strong financial capacity, and Freddie Mac grew from a small institution buying mortgages and selling PCs into a major financial institution in the nation's capital market.

Many of the recommendations made by the President's Commission on Housing were incorporated in the Secondary Mortgage Market Enhancement Act (SMMEA) of 1984, enacted on October 3, 1984. Title I of the act, which was designed to enhance the development of the private mortgage securities markets, amended federal securities laws and preempted certain state laws. The major provisions may be summarized as follows:[19]

- Statutory limitations on investment in private mortgage-backed securities by federally chartered depository institutions were removed, leaving it up to the regulators to specify investment limits.
- Sales contracts made by brokers and dealers for forward or delayed delivery (within 180 days) of private mortgage-backed securities were specified to not involve extensions of credit to or by the brokers/dealers. This provision was intended to facilitate development of forward-delivery markets for fully private securities.
- State blue-sky and legal-investment statutes were preempted for high-grade, private mortgage-backed securities (those rated in one of the two highest categories by at least one nationally recognized statistical rating organization), subject to reversal by the states within seven years. Thus, such securities did not need to be registered with state supervisory agencies, and they could be purchased

---

[18] President's Commission on Housing, "Report of the Commission on Housing," 167–168.
[19] Seiders, "Residential Mortgage and Capital Markets."

by state-regulated financial institutions (such as pension funds and insurance companies) as if they were federally issued or guaranteed securities.

Title II of the act dealt with the secondary market programs of Fannie Mae and Freddie Mac. Provisions important to the competitive relationship between issuers of private mortgage securities and the government sponsored enterprises included the following:

- Limits on sizes of single-family mortgages that could be purchased by Fannie Mae and Freddie Mac were to apply to the total loan size even if only a portion of a loan (i.e., a loan participation) was purchased.
- Freddie Mac was prohibited from guaranteeing mortgage-backed securities issued by others.

The Growth of the Secondary Market

Based on these reforms, we have seen a major shift in the role and importance of the secondary market, as well as a shift in the role of lenders originating mortgage loans. Today, the availability of mortgage credit for home loans is no longer a major concern. Rather, the key questions are the affordability of the credit to the home buyer and how to qualify more people to buy homes. In addition, over the last ten years, a number of innovations, coupled with market forces and a strong economy, have helped lower the costs of mortgage finance for the home buyer. The nation's homeownership rate stagnated in the early 1980s due to the recession and problems in the housing finance system, but in the 1990s, with the support of a revitalized housing finance system and a strong secondary market, the homeownership rate swelled to record levels. In 1998, the mortgage market experienced its best year so far, with $1.45 trillion in new mortgage originations despite serious problems in the global financial markets. In 1999 the industry saw $1.3 trillion in new mortgage originations, and in 2000 $1 trillion in new mortgages were originated. In 2001 new mortgage originations rose again sharply to a new high over $1.7 trillion (see Figure 4.5).

The nation's current, robust housing finance system is a result of the second revolution in housing finance, the development and growth of the secondary mortgage market. Two important indications demonstrate how the housing finance system has changed over the last two decades. First, the changing role of the thrift industry and other mortgage finance originators,

FIGURE 4.5
Single Family Mortgage Loan Originations by Type of Loan

YEAR	CONVENTIONAL ($MIL)	(% DIST)	FHA/VA ($MIL)	(% DIST)	TOTAL ($MIL)	(% DIST)
1985	$245,771	84.81%	$44,013	15.19%	$289,784	100.00%
1986	$411,493	82.40%	$87,919	17.60%	$499,412	100.00%
1987	$399,232	78.71%	$107,998	21.29%	$507,230	100.00%
1988	$383,733	85.99%	$62,530	14.01%	$446,263	100.00%
1989	$394,118	87.02%	$58,789	12.98%	$452,907	100.00%
1990	$376,700	82.18%	$81,704	17.82%	$458,404	100.00%
1991	$499,875	88.93%	$62,199	11.07%	$562,074	100.00%
1992	$818,863	91.63%	$74,818	8.37%	$893,681	100.00%
1993	$895,381	87.79%	$124,480	12.21%	$1,019,861	100.00%
1994	$625,645	81.38%	$143,103	18.62%	$768,748	100.00%
1995	$564,750	88.32%	$74,686	11.68%	$639,436	100.00%
1996	$677,295	86.25%	$107,938	13.75%	$785,233	100.00%
1997	$756,882	88.10%	$102,242	11.90%	$859,124	100.00%
*1998	$1,297,500	89.48%	$152,500	10.52%	$1,450,000	100.00%
*1999	$1,138,800	87.01%	$170,050	12.99%	$1,308,850	100.00%
*2000	$896,000	88.60%	$115,320	11.40%	$1,011,320	100.00%
*2001	$1,578,000	90.45%	$166,670	9.55%	$1,744,670	100.00%

SOURCE: HUD Survey of Mortgage Lending Activity, 1985–1997, compiled by the National Association of Home Builders.

*Fannie Mae and Freddie Mac Estimates of total Single-Family Market, 1998–2001.

and second, the actual growth of the secondary mortgage market and the importance of mortgage-backed securities.

Thrift institutions, once the primary source of housing credit, no longer dominate the housing finance marketplace. The thrifts' share of mortgage origination fell from a high of 60% in 1976 to 21% in 2000, while mortgage banking companies' share grew from 14% in 1976 to 58% in 2000 (see Figures 4.6 and 4.7). Thrift industry problems with borrowing short and lending long, which started in the high and volatile interest-rate environment of the late 1970s and early 1980s, led to deregulation. But, without adequate examination and regulation, deregulation caused a severe crisis for the deposit insurance fund and in August of 1989 brought about government intervention through the Financial Institutions Reform, Recovery and Enforcement Act (FIRREA). The remaining thrift institutions are strong financially, but FIRREA and subsequent regulatory actions have restricted their housing lending, particularly for acquisition, development, and construction (AD&C) financing, and have weakened the housing focus of the thrift charter. Mortgage bankers stepped in to fill the void,

FIGURE 4.6
Single-Family Mortgage Loan Originations by Lender Types

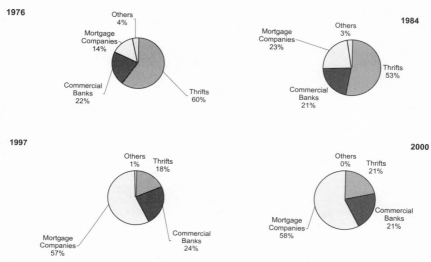

SOURCE: U.S. Department of Housing and Urban Development, Survey of Mortgage Lending Activity, 2000 data from Freddie Mac Research.

and the growth of the mortgage banking industry since the early 1980s, both in terms of absolute volume and market share, has been phenomenal.

As a part of FIRREA, the Federal Home Loan Bank Board was dissolved and replaced by the Office of Thrift Supervision (OTS), which was located in the Treasury Department. The OTS was given the power to charter federal savings and loan institutions and savings banks and to set capital standards for both federally and state-chartered institutions. With the Federal Home Loan Bank Board no longer in existence, a new governing structure needed to be established for the twelve Federal Home Loan Banks and Freddie Mac. FIRREA therefore created a new agency, the Federal Housing Finance Board (FHFB), to oversee the operations of the banks. In turn, Freddie Mac was given a federal charter almost identical to Fannie Mae's, with five members of the board appointed by the president of the United States, and the remaining thirteen board members selected by the Freddie Mac shareholders. Freddie Mac, which had been managed quite closely by the Federal Home Loan Bank Board, was now more independent, with the chief executive officer (CEO) also serving as the chairman of the new Freddie Mac board.

FIGURE 4.7
Single-Family Mortgage Loan Originations by Lender Type

YEAR	THRIFTS ($MIL)	(%DIST)	COMMERCIAL BANKS ($MIL)	(%DIST)	MORTGAGE COS ($MIL)	(%DIST)	OTHERS ($MIL)	(%DIST)	TOTAL ($MIL)	(%DIST)
1970	$16,961	47.66%	$7,797	21.91%	$8,906	25.03%	$1,922	5.40%	$35,586	100.00%
1971	$30,144	52.16%	$12,598	21.80%	$12,487	21.61%	$2,559	4.43%	$57,788	100.00%
1972	$41,793	55.09%	$17,710	23.34%	$13,326	17.57%	$3,036	4.00%	$75,865	100.00%
1973	$44,353	56.05%	$18,783	23.74%	$12,658	16.00%	$3,335	4.21%	$79,129	100.00%
1974	$34,861	51.64%	$16,128	23.89%	$13,026	19.30%	$3,493	5.17%	$67,508	100.00%
1975	$45,574	58.49%	$14,450	18.55%	$13,992	17.96%	$3,896	5.00%	$77,912	100.00%
1976	$68,328	60.58%	$24,501	21.72%	$15,744	13.96%	$4,212	3.73%	$112,785	100.00%
1977	$94,964	58.63%	$36,675	22.64%	$25,650	15.84%	$4,684	2.89%	$161,973	100.00%
1978	$99,331	53.68%	$43,924	23.74%	$34,448	18.62%	$7,333	3.96%	$185,036	100.00%
1979	$91,787	49.19%	$40,655	21.79%	$45,260	24.26%	$8,892	4.77%	$186,594	100.00%
1980	$66,530	49.74%	$28,778	21.51%	$29,419	21.99%	$9,035	6.75%	$133,762	100.00%
1981	$46,003	46.84%	$21,689	22.08%	$23,958	24.39%	$6,566	6.69%	$98,216	100.00%
1982	$38,784	40.00%	$25,188	25.98%	$27,995	28.88%	$4,983	5.14%	$96,950	100.00%
1983	$92,299	45.72%	$44,830	22.21%	$59,762	29.61%	$4,972	2.46%	$201,863	100.00%
1984	$108,872	53.45%	$41,941	20.59%	$47,589	23.36%	$5,304	2.60%	$203,706	100.00%
1985	$116,753	40.29%	$57,031	19.68%	$110,004	37.96%	$5,995	2.07%	$289,783	100.00%
1986	$207,182	41.49%	$108,613	21.75%	$175,986	35.24%	$7,632	1.53%	$499,413	100.00%
1987	$208,781	41.16%	$124,551	24.56%	$167,053	32.93%	$6,846	1.35%	$507,231	100.00%
1988	$188,871	42.32%	$101,863	22.83%	$148,004	33.17%	$7,525	1.69%	$446,263	100.00%
1989	$157,676	34.81%	$123,193	27.20%	$166,494	36.76%	$5,544	1.22%	$452,907	100.00%
1990	$138,990	30.32%	$153,285	33.44%	$161,153	35.15%	$5,010	1.09%	$458,438	100.00%
1991	$140,416	24.98%	$153,323	27.28%	$263,917	46.95%	$4,418	0.79%	$562,074	100.00%
1992	$218,792	24.48%	$232,065	25.97%	$437,604	48.97%	$5,220	0.58%	$893,681	100.00%
1993	$218,750	21.45%	$268,985	26.37%	$526,502	51.62%	$5,624	0.55%	$1,019,861	100.00%
1994	$152,381	19.82%	$199,996	26.02%	$408,141	53.09%	$8,230	1.07%	$768,748	100.00%
1995	$118,856	18.59%	$155,359	24.30%	$358,705	56.10%	$6,516	1.02%	$639,436	100.00%
1996	$155,611	19.82%	$178,548	22.74%	$445,739	56.77%	$5,335	0.68%	$785,233	100.00%
1997	$152,725	17.78%	$206,591	24.05%	$494,530	57.56%	$5,278	0.61%	$859,124	100.00%
1998	$311,129	23.66%	$200,932	15.28%	$802,939	61.06%	n.s.	n.s.	$1,315,000	100.00%
1999	$236,407	21.57%	$212,076	19.35%	$647,517	59.08%	n.s.	n.s.	$1,096,000	100.00%
2000	$185,445	20.72%	$191,172	21.36%	$518,385	57.92%	n.s.	n.s.	$895,000	100.00%

*Starting with 1985 data, mortgage origination and holdings data are not comparable to previous years' data because
of a change in HUD's survey methodology, which now captures greater mortgage origination activity by mortgage companies.
* Starting with 1998 data, mortgage originations are from the Home Mortgage Disclosure Act (HMDA), which represents
about 75% of all originations. The use of this data explains the difference between the numbers in this Figure and Figure 4.5
* n.s. refers to "not significant". Number was not readily available, however the amount is insignifiant.

SOURCE: 1970–1997, U.S. Department of Housing and Urban Development; 1998–2000 estimates from
Freddie Mac Research based on HMDA data.

NOTE: These estimates vary from the numbers in Figure 4.5 due to the fact that HMDA data only encom-
passes approximately 75% of the entire single-family mortgage market.

Juxtaposed against these developments in the thrift industry, the secondary mortgage market has matured in a way that has forever changed
the U.S. housing finance system. The secondary mortgage market linked
housing to the world's financial markets and filled the credit gap left by
the declining role of thrifts. The share of mortgages funded through the
secondary market has more than doubled from 27% in 1984 to 59.3% in

FIGURE 4.8

Share of New Mortgages Funded by the Secondary Market, 1984–2001

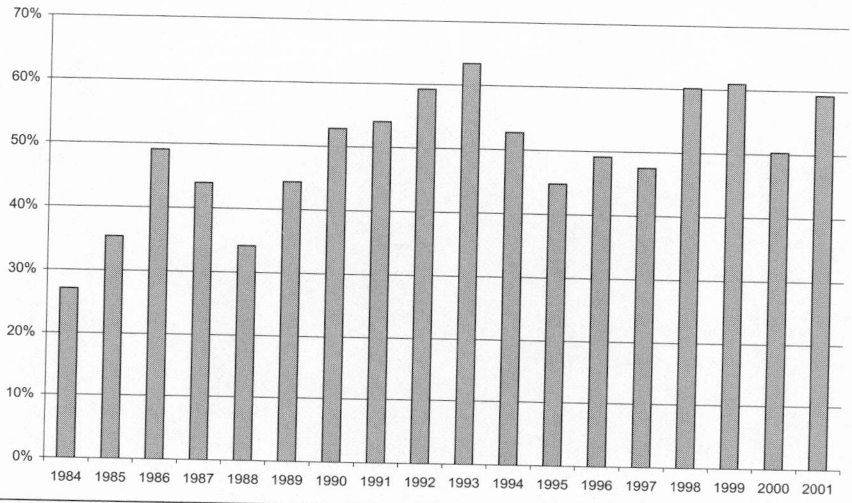

SOURCE: HUD, FNMA, FHLMC, GNMA, as compiled by NAHB. 1999–2001 estimates from Freddie Mac Research.

2001 (see Figure 4.8). Legislation enhancing the secondary mortgage market, coupled with a shifting regulatory structure, has played a key role in the development and growth of the secondary mortgage market, particularly through the activities of Fannie Mae and Freddie Mac, which have themselves grown remarkably since the early 1980s. At that time Fannie Mae was experiencing financial instability, and Freddie Mac was focused primarily on buying mortgages from savings and loan associations to help the liquidity of the thrift industry. However, Fannie Mae initiated a mortgage-backed securities (MBS) program and Freddie Mac dropped its nonmember fee (fifty basis points charged to institutions that were not members of the Federal Home Loan Bank system), and neither organization has looked back. (See Figure 4.9 for the recent growth of Fannie Mae and Freddie Mac's mortgage purchases.) They have fostered product and technological innovations that have expanded home ownership opportunities for a wide range of borrowers. The maturation of the secondary market has transformed the mortgage market from one dominated by portfolio lenders to one dominated by entities with close ties to the secondary market, such as mortgage banking companies, savings and loan associations acting as mortgage bankers, and the GSEs.

FIGURE 4.9

Fannie Mae and Freddie Mac Mortgage Purchases, 1997–2001

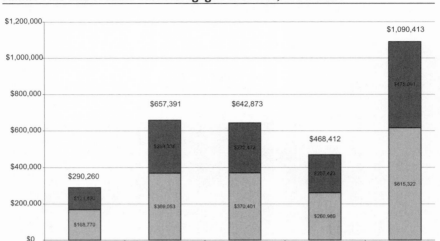

SOURCE: 1997 and 1998 data—U.S. Department of Housing and Urban Development, compiled by NAHB. 1999–2001 data—Freddie Mac, Financial Research Department

Further, the development of innovative securities structures has broadened the investor base, allowing more funds to flow into the mortgage market from the capital market and ultimately reducing mortgage rates for home buyers. The volume of mortgage-backed securities issued has increased dramatically, from $62 billion in 1984 to $1.2 trillion in 2001 (see Figures 4.10 and 4.11). All this secondary market activity has benefited consumers through lower interest rates — mortgage rates are generally thirty to fifty basis points lower on loans eligible for purchase by Fannie Mae and Freddie Mac than they are for "jumbo" loans that are above the "conforming" loan limits for Fannie Mae and Freddie Mac (see Figure 4.12).

Perhaps most important, the secondary market has maintained liquidity in the mortgage market in good economic times and bad. For example, during the liquidity crunch in the fall of 1998, when the bond market in Russia collapsed and numerous sources of credit around the world and the United States dried up, the volume of activity by Fannie Mae and Freddie Mac increased significantly in November and December. This is reflected in the more than doubling of Freddie Mac and Fannie Mae's purchase ac-

FIGURE 4.10

New Issues of Residential Mortgage-Backed Securities, 1984–2001

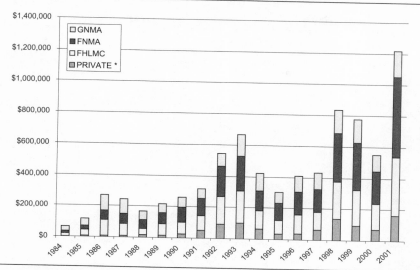

SOURCE: GNMA, FNMA, FHLMC, Salomon Brothers, Inside Mortgage Securities: 2000/2001: "Inside MBS and ABS," Issue 2002:5, February 8, 2002.

*Private securities data include non-agency whole loan CMOs and REMICS.

tivity between 1997 and 1998 (see Figure 4.9). The result was essentially no disruption in the flow of credit to housing despite major liquidity problems in other financial markets.

With the active expansion of the secondary market, the housing finance system, which was in serious challenge in the early 1980s, is now robust and vital. Indeed, it is a finance system that is by many standards the best in the world. The broader-based, more resilient system described in the President's Commission on Housing has been achieved. Figure 4.5 highlights single-family mortgage loan originations from 1985 through 2001, including both conventional and FHA/VA mortgages. It shows dramatic growth, from $290 billion in mortgage originations in 1985 to a high of $1.7 trillion in mortgage originations in 2001. Figure 4.13 outlines the total mortgages outstanding between 1991 and 2001. It shows significant growth from $3.95 trillion in 1991 to $7.39 trillion at the end of 2001. And finally, Figure 4.14 shows the institutions which hold this outstanding residential mortgage debt and how the share has shifted over time. In 1985, 48% was held by thrifts, with 15% held by banks, and only 5% held by

FIGURE 4.11
New Issues of Residential Mortgage-Backed Securities, 1970–2001

YEAR	GNMA ($MIL)	(% DIST)	FNMA ($MIL)	(% DIST)	FHLMC ($MIL)	(% DIST)	FHLMC & FNMA ($MIL)	(% DIST)	PRIVATE * ($MIL)	(% DIST)	TOTAL ($MIL)	(% DIST)
1970	$452	100.00%	$0	0.00%	$0	0.00%	$0	0.00%	$0	0.00%	$452	100.00%
1971	$2,702	97.65%	$0	0.00%	$65	2.35%	$65	2.35%	$0	0.00%	$2,767	100.00%
1972	$2,662	84.35%	$0	0.00%	$494	15.65%	$494	15.65%	$0	0.00%	$3,156	100.00%
1973	$2,953	90.14%	$0	0.00%	$323	9.86%	$323	9.86%	$0	0.00%	$3,276	100.00%
1974	$4,553	99.00%	$0	0.00%	$46	1.00%	$46	1.00%	$0	0.00%	$8,397	100.00%
1975	$7,447	88.69%	$0	0.00%	$950	11.31%	$950	11.31%	$0	0.00%	$15,151	100.00%
1976	$13,764	90.85%	$0	0.00%	$1,360	8.98%	$1,360	8.98%	$27	0.18%	$22,352	100.00%
1977	$17,440	78.02%	$0	0.00%	$4,657	20.83%	$4,657	20.83%	$255	1.14%	$22,741	100.00%
1978	$15,358	67.53%	$0	0.00%	$6,412	28.20%	$6,412	28.20%	$971	4.27%	$31,194	100.00%
1979	$24,940	79.95%	$0	0.00%	$4,546	14.57%	$4,546	14.57%	$1,708	5.48%	$24,288	100.00%
1980	$20,647	85.01%	$0	0.00%	$2,526	10.40%	$2,526	10.40%	$1,115	4.59%	$19,688	100.00%
1981	$14,257	72.41%	$717	3.64%	$3,529	17.92%	$4,246	21.57%	$1,185	6.02%	$55,827	100.00%
1982	$15,607	27.96%	$13,970	25.02%	$24,169	43.29%	$38,139	68.32%	$2,081	3.73%	$86,521	100.00%
1983	$50,736	58.64%	$13,340	15.42%	$19,691	22.76%	$33,031	38.18%	$2,754	3.18%	$62,396	100.00%
1984	$28,097	45.03%	$13,546	21.71%	$18,684	29.94%	$32,230	51.65%	$2,069	3.32%	$113,759	100.00%
1985	$45,980	40.42%	$23,649	20.79%	$38,829	34.13%	$62,478	54.92%	$5,301	4.66%	$269,157	100.00%
1986	$101,433	37.69%	$60,566	22.50%	$100,198	37.23%	$160,764	59.73%	$6,960	2.59%	$242,497	100.00%
1987	$94,890	39.13%	$63,229	26.07%	$75,018	30.94%	$138,247	57.01%	$9,360	3.86%	$165,258	100.00%
1988	$55,182	33.39%	$54,878	33.21%	$39,777	24.07%	$94,655	57.28%	$15,421	9.33%	$214,587	100.00%
1989	$57,067	26.59%	$69,764	32.51%	$73,518	34.26%	$143,282	66.77%	$14,238	6.64%	$259,284	100.00%
1990	$64,344	24.82%	$96,695	37.29%	$73,815	28.47%	$170,510	65.76%	$24,430	9.42%	$317,392	100.00%
1991	$62,630	19.73%	$112,933	35.58%	$92,479	29.14%	$205,412	64.72%	$49,350	15.55%	$544,627	100.00%
1992	$81,917	15.04%	$194,037	35.63%	$179,207	32.90%	$373,244	68.53%	$89,466	16.43%	$666,650	100.00%
1993	$137,989	20.70%	$221,444	33.22%	$208,724	31.31%	$430,168	64.53%	$98,493	14.77%	$422,098	100.00%
1994	$111,185	26.34%	$130,622	30.95%	$117,110	27.74%	$247,732	58.69%	$63,181	14.97%	$303,924	100.00%
1995	$72,765	23.94%	$110,456	36.34%	$85,877	28.26%	$196,333	64.60%	$34,826	11.46%	$408,937	100.00%
1996	$100,899	24.67%	$149,869	36.65%	$119,702	29.27%	$269,571	65.92%	$38,467	9.41%	$431,069	100.00%
1997	$104,091	24.15%	$149,429	34.66%	$114,258	26.51%	$263,687	61.17%	$63,291	14.68%	$834,859	100.00%
1998	$149,106	17.86%	$308,539	36.96%	$242,740	29.08%	$551,279	66.03%	$134,474	16.11%	$775,871	100.00%
1999	$149,285	19.24%	$300,689	38.76%	$233,031	30.03%	$533,720	68.79%	$92,866	11.97%	$549,818	100.00%
2000	$103,695	18.86%	$210,205	38.23%	$165,624	30.12%	$375,829	68.36%	$70,294	12.78%	$1,218,247	100.00%
2001	$167,029	13.71%	$513,717	42.17%	$378,079	31.03%	$891,796	73.20%	$159,422	13.09%		100.00%

* Private securities data include non-agency whole loan CMOs and REMICS. SOURCE: GNMA, FNMA, FHLMC, Salomon Brothers, Inside Mortgage Securities. 2002/2001: "Inside MBS and ABS," Issue 2002:5, February 8, 2002.

Fannie Mae and 1% held by Freddie Mac. By 2000 the thrift share had fallen to 19%, with banks rising to 27%, and the share held by Fannie Mae growing to 11% and the share held by Freddie Mac rising to 7%.

As an interesting note of comparison, it is worthwhile to look at the flow of dollars in Treasury debt compared to outstanding residential mortgages. Figure 4.15 highlights residential mortgage and treasury debt outstanding from 1945 to the third quarter of 2001. In 1945, mortgage debt was only 9.36% of total Treasury debt, but with the growth of housing activity following World War II, mortgage debt grew rapidly from $23.5 billion in 1945 to $273.3 billion in 1966. In 1966, mortgage debt surpassed Treasury debt, reaching 105.4% of Treasury debt. Since then, mortgage debt has remained above Treasury debt. In the 1980s, the federal deficit grew and the dollars needed to finance this deficit increased, so by the early 1990s mortgage debt as a percentage of Treasury debt actually fell as

FIGURE 4.12

Conforming Mortgage Rates for Freddie Mac and Fannie Mae Are Consistently Below the Rates for Jumbo Loans

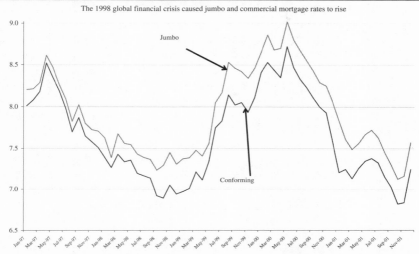

SOURCE: Fannie Mae and Freddie Mac.

low as 103%. However, in the later part of the 1990s, total Treasury debt began to drop while mortgage debt continued to rise, so by 2001, mortgage debt as a percent of Treasury debt had risen to a high of 184%.

Figures 4.5 through 4.15 show a robust mortgage finance market, one that is truly broad-based and resilient. Although questions have been raised by some as to whether the federal government and the government sponsored enterprises (GSEs) play too great a role, the overall housing finance system is strong, and mortgage rates have been reduced. Home buyers, then, have been one of the primary beneficiaries of the second revolution in the nation's housing finance system. A plethora of mortgage product innovations have given home buyers the tools to respond to a variety of interest rate environments. Adjustable-rate mortgages (ARMs), for example, provide a safety valve on loan qualifications and lower monthly mortgage costs when interest rates are higher. Conversely, when rates fall, no-cost refinancing programs save borrowers out-of-pocket transaction costs, enabling them to lower overall mortgage costs by refinancing into a lower-rate mortgage (either a fixed-rate mortgage or an adjustable-rate mortgage).

FIGURE 4.13
Billions of Dollars; Amounts Outstanding End of Period, Not Seasonally Adjusted

	1991	1992	1993	1994	1995	1996	1997	1998	1999	2000	2001	
1 Total Mortgages	**3951.8**	**4066**	**4206.1**	**4393**	**4604**	**4901.6**	**5216.7**	**5728.2**	**6283.3**	**6854.5**	**7391.9**	1
2 Home	2814.6	2984.1	3146.5	3330	3510.4	3721.9	3959.5	4327.5	4803.4	5225.9	5623.1	2
3 Multifamily residential	282.3	269.1	266.6	267.7	277	294.8	310.5	341	350.2	387.2	425.3	3
4 Commercial	775.8	733.1	712.3	712.3	732.1	797.7	856.5	963.2	1027.3	1132.5	1228.9	4
5 Farm	79.2	79.7	80.7	83	84.6	87.1	90.3	96.5	102.3	108.8	114.6	5
6	**3951.8**	**4066**	**4206.1**	**4393**	**4604**	**4901.6**	**5216.7**	**5728.2**	**6283.3**	**6854.5**	**7391.9**	6
7 Household sector	2714.6	2863.1	3001.1	3171.7	3344	3560.9	3801.7	4174.4	4558.9	4941.5	5305.9	7
8 Nonfinancial business	1232.4	1197.6	1196.1	1202.5	1236	1308.8	1368.3	1482.2	1609.4	1794.9	1957	8
9 Corporate	245.9	225.6	224.7	242.6	270.1	287.1	296.4	336.5	378.8	441.1	501	9
10 Nonfarm noncorporate	907.3	892.2	890.7	876.9	881.4	934.6	981.6	1049.2	1128.3	1245	1341.4	10
11 Farm	79.2	79.7	80.7	83	84.6	87.1	90.3	96.5	102.3	108.8	114.6	11
12 Federal government	0	0	0	0	0	0	0	0	0	0	0	12
13 REITs	4.8	5.4	8.9	18.7	24.1	31.9	46.8	71.6	76.7	82.9	83	13
14	**3951.8**	**4066**	**4206.1**	**4393**	**4604**	**4901.6**	**5216.7**	**5728.2**	**6283.3**	**6854.5**	**7391.9**	14
15 Household sector	145.2	136.8	126.3	115.6	109.5	109.4	108.9	109.2	110.2	111.3	112	15
16 Nonfinancial corporate business	59	60	52.3	56.4	57.9	54.4	50.4	46.4	60.3	55.3	51.5	16
17 Nonfarm noncorporate business	26	25.2	23.7	23.6	26.7	23.5	23.8	24.4	40.7	48.6	53.2	17
18 State and local governments	113.7	113.7	108.3	110.5	113.8	117.6	121.3	125.4	129.8	134.3	137.8	18
19 Federal government	98.3	86.4	85	71	57.8	50.3	45.7	44.9	77.7	76.9	75.3	19
20 Commercial banking	881.3	900.5	947.8	1012.7	1090.2	1145.4	1245.3	1337	1495.2	1659.3	1736.1	20
21 Savings institutions (1)	705.4	628	598.4	596.2	596.8	628.3	631.8	644.2	668.6	723.8	758.6	21
22 Credit unions	52.8	53.8	56	62.1	66.5	76	86	96.9	111	127.4	140.2	22
23 Bank personal trusts and estates	4	3.9	3.6	3.4	3.3	3.6	3	2.8	2.2	2.1	2	23
24 Life insurance companies	259.5	242	223.9	215.8	213.1	208.2	206.8	213.6	230.8	235.9	237.9	24
25 Other insurance companies	6.5	5.9	4.5	3.8	2.8	2.4	2.2	2	1.9	1.6	1.7	25
26 Private pension funds	18.2	14.5	14.5	18	19.4	21.2	23.6	27.2	13.5	15.1	15.9	26
27 State and local govt. retirement	16.9	16.5	14.5	15.2	15.9	16.7	17.6	18.6	21.5	21.5	23.7	27
28 Government-S sponsored	167.7	199.7	241	244.6	251	244.9	240.4	247.7	244.4	267.1	285.6	28
29 Federally related mortgage pools	1156.5	1272	1356.8	1472.1	1570.3	1711.4	1825.8	2018.4	2292.2	2491.6	2759	29
30 ABS issuers	110.3	172.9	217.8	255.3	289.4	350.6	441	605.5	655.5	740.7	844.4	30
31 Finance companies	63.3	65.8	62.7	66.9	72.4	82.7	87.9	102.3	145.8	172.3	187.4	31
32 Mortgage companies	60.3	60.5	60.4	36.5	33	41.2	32.1	35.3	35.6	35.9	36.9	32
33 REITs	7	8.1	8.6	13.3	14.1	13.8	22.9	26.3	23	16.8	15.6	33

(1) FHLB loans to savings institutions are included in other loans and advances.

SOURCE: U.S. Department of Housing and Urban Development. Fed. Flow of Funds, 3Q 2001.

FIGURE 4.14
Share of Residential Mortgage Debt Outstanding

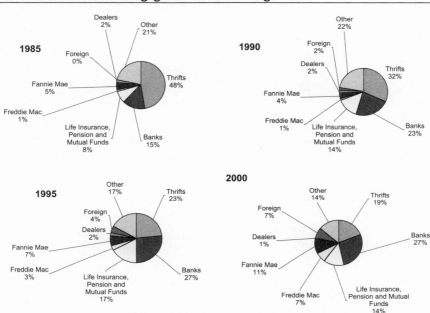

SOURCE: Freddie Mac, Financial Research Department

More recently, the market has developed a range of products to address one of the largest stumbling blocks to home ownership, the lack of a down payment. Following the lead of FHA, Fannie Mae and Freddie Mac now offer loans that reduce down payments and other front-end closing costs. For example, the Fannie Mae Flex 97 and Freddie Mac Alt 97 products require a down payment of only 3%, similar to the cash requirements in the FHA program, and these products can be combined with a grant or second mortgage to cover closing costs. Further, experimentation is underway with no-down-payment loans and 100% loan-to-value (LTV) ratios. All of these products allow more buyers to qualify for a mortgage.

It is also worth noting that in the last few years there has been a significant consolidation of financial institutions and of the institutions that are originating and servicing mortgages. With the various stages of bank reform, and with the desire of financial institutions to achieve greater efficiencies and consolidation through growth, the number of banks and savings and loan associations has plummeted. In 1984 there were 3,418 S&Ls, but by 2000, there were only 1,590 (see Figure 4.16). The same

FIGURE 4.15
Residential Mortgage and Treasury Debt Outstanding (Billions of Dollars)

| | Residential Mortgage Debt | | | | | | | |
PERIOD	Single-Family ($ Bil)	(%Dist)	Multifamily ($ Bil)	(% Dist)	Total Residential ($ Bil)	(% Dist)	Treasury Debt ($ Bil)	Mortgage Debt as % of Treasury Debt
1945	$18.60	79.15%	$4.90	20.85%	$23.50	100.00%	$251.20	9.36%
1946	$22.90	81.21%	$5.30	18.79%	$28.20	100.00%	$227.90	12.37%
1947	$28.00	82.84%	$5.80	17.16%	$33.80	100.00%	$220.70	15.31%
1948	$33.10	83.17%	$6.70	16.83%	$39.80	100.00%	$214.20	18.58%
1949	$37.40	82.74%	$7.80	17.26%	$45.20	100.00%	$216.70	20.86%
1950	$44.90	82.84%	$9.30	17.16%	$54.20	100.00%	$216.10	25.08%
1951	$51.50	82.93%	$10.60	17.07%	$62.10	100.00%	$215.80	28.78%
1952	$58.10	83.48%	$11.50	16.52%	$69.60	100.00%	$220.80	31.52%
1953	$65.70	84.45%	$12.10	15.55%	$77.80	100.00%	$226.20	34.39%
1954	$75.00	85.52%	$12.70	14.48%	$87.70	100.00%	$228.50	38.38%
1955	$87.50	86.63%	$13.50	13.37%	$101.00	100.00%	$228.40	44.22%
1956	$98.30	87.46%	$14.10	12.54%	$112.40	100.00%	$222.80	50.455
1957	$106.90	87.98%	$14.60	12.02%	$121.50	100.00%	$220.10	55.20%
1958	$116.70	87.55%	$16.60	12.45%	$133.30	100.00%	$229.00	58.21%
1959	$129.60	87.39%	$18.70	12.61%	$148.30	100.00%	$236.20	62.79%
1960	$140.80	87.13%	$20.80	12.87%	$161.60	100.00%	$234.00	69.06%
1961	$153.30	86.66%	$23.60	13.34%	$176.90	100.00%	$240.70	73.49%
1962	$167.40	86.24%	$26.70	13.76%	$194.10	100.00%	$246.80	78.65%
1963	$184.00	85.98%	$30.00	14.02%	$214.00	100.00%	$250.70	85.36%
1964	$201.30	85.33%	$34.60	14.67%	$235.90	100.00%	$255.90	92.18%
1965	$218.60	85.12%	$38.20	14.88%	$256.80	100.00%	$257.00	99.92%
1966	$232.00	84.89%	$41.30	15.11%	$273.30	100.00%	$259.30	105.40 %
1967	$245.30	84.56%	$44.80	15.44%	$290.10	100.00%	$268.20	108.17 %
1968	$262.50	84.46%	$48.30	15.54%	$310.80	100.00%	$277.60	111.96 %
1969	$280.70	84.07%	$53.20	15.93%	$333.90	100.00%	$276.80	120.63 %
1970	$294.90	83.07%	$60.10	16.93%	$355.00	100.00%	$289.90	122.46 %
1971	$321.50	82.10%	$70.10	17.90%	$391.60	100.00%	$315.90	123.96 %
1972	$361.00	81.34%	$82.80	18.66%	$443.80	100.00%	$330.10	134.44 %
1973	$404.00	81.27%	$93.10	18.73%	$497.10	100.00%	$336.70	147.65 %
1974	$438.20	81.42%	$100.00	18.58%	$538.20	100.00%	$348.80	154.30 %
1975	$477.70	82.60%	$100.60	17.40%	$578.30	100.00%	$434.90	132.97 %
1976	$540.30	83.64%	$105.70	16.36%	$646.00	100.00%	$503.70	128.25 %
1977	$633.60	84.75%	$114.00	15.25%	$747.60	100.00%	$560.90	133.29 %
1978	$743.80	85.62%	$124.90	14.38%	$868.70	100.00%	$614.90	141.28 %
1979	$861.50	86.47%	$134.80	13.53%	$996.30	100.00%	$652.10	152.78 %
1980	$964.70	87.15%	$142.30	12.85%	$1,107.00	100.00%	$730.00	151.64 %
1981	$1,038.40	87.975	$142.00	12.03%	$1,180.40	100.00%	$815.90	144.67 %
1982	$1,079.50	88.11%	$145.70	11.89%	$1,225.20	100.00%	$978.10	125.26 %
1983	$1,197.10	88.16%	$160.70	11.84%	$1,357.80	100.00%	$1,163.40	116.71 %
1984	$1,332.80	87.78%	$185.50	12.22%	$1,518.30	100.00%	$1,360.80	111.57 %
1985	$1,533.50	88.21%	$205.00	11.79%	$1,738.50	100.00%	$1,586.60	109.57 %
1986	$1,737.90	87.95%	$238.10	12.05%	$1,976.00	100.00%	$1,802.20	109.64 %
1987	$1,940.50	88.29%	$257.40	11.71%	$2,197.90	100.00%	$1,944.60	113.03 %
1988	$2,175.80	88.86%	$272.90	11.14%	$2,448.70	100.00%	$2,082.30	117.60 %
1989	$2,404.50	89.39%	$285.40	10.61%	$2,689.90	100.00%	$2,227.00	120.79 %
1990	$2,646.60	90.26%	$285.50	9.74%	$2,932.10	100.00%	$2,465.80	118.91 %
1991	$2,814.50	90.88%	$282.30	9.12%	$3,096.80	100.00%	$2,757.80	112.29 %
1992	$2,984.10	91.73%	$269.10	8.27%	$3,253.20	100.00%	$3,061.60	106.26 %
1993	$3,146.50	92.19%	$266.60	7.81%	$3,413.10	100.00%	$3,309.90	103.12 %
1994	$3,330.00	92.56%	$267.70	7.44%	$3,597.70	100.00%	$3,465.60	103.81 %
1995	$3,510.40	92.69%	$277.00	7.31%	$3,787.40	100.00%	$3,608.50	104.96 %
1996	$3,721.90	92.66%	$294.80	7.34%	$4,016.70	100.00%	$3,755.10	106.97 %
1997	$3,959.50	92.73%	$310.50	7.27%	$4,270.00	100.00%	$3,778.30	113.01 %
1998	$4,327.50	92.70%	$341.00	7.30%	$4,668.50	100.00%	$3,723.70	125.37 %
1999	$4,803.40	93.20%	$350.20	6.80%	$5,153.60	100.00%	$3,652.80	141.09 %
2000	$5,225.90	93.10%	$387.20	6.90%	$5,613.10	100.00%	$3,357.80	167.17 %
2001	$5,757.00	92.59%	$460.70	7.41%	$6,217.70	100.00%	$3,379.60	183.98 %

SOURCE: Federal Reserve Flow of Funds Accounts, U.S. Department of Housing and Urban Development.

FIGURE 4.16

Number of Savings Institutions and Commercial Banks Have Steadily Declined

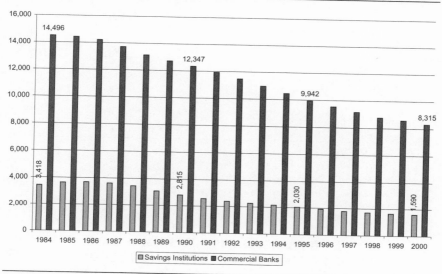

SOURCE: Federal Deposit Insurance Corporation, Historical Data on Banking, www2.fdic.gov/hsob.

pattern is true for commercial banks. In 1984 there were 14,496 banks, and by 2000 the number had dropped to 8,315 (see Figure 4.16).

Consolidation has also occurred in the mortgage banking business related to mortgage originations (see Figure 4.17). In 1990, the top twenty-five originators of mortgage loans among mortgage bankers had a 28% share of the market, but eleven years later, they had a 72% share. The same is true in mortgage servicing (see Figure 4.17). In 1990, the top twenty-five servicers held 21% of the market, and by 2001/2002 they held 67%.[20] This consolidation is likely to continue due to the greater efficiencies and lower overhead that come with size, and due to the ability through technology to process large volumes of mortgage loan activity. Publicly traded companies like these are expected to grow, and the technology facilitates, and in some ways drives, the growth. (See Figure 4.18 for a listing of the top ten originators and servicers in the mortgage industry in the first quarter, 2002.)

---

[20] For a further discussion of this phenomenon see Muolo, 'Top 10 Servicers Pass 50% Share," *National Mortgage News*.

FIGURE 4.17
Industry Background: Mortgage Banking Consolidation in the 1990s

Share of Market for Top Lenders

	1990	1993	1998	2001/2002
Top 25 Originators	28%	37%	55%	72%*
Top 25 Servicers	21%	30%	51%	67%**

SOURCE: *National Mortgage News, Quarterly Data Report*
Data for the years 1990, 1993 and 1998 are calendar years.
*This number is the Top 25 Originators for Fourth Quarter 2001
**This number includes the Top 25 Servicers as of March 31, 2002.

THE THIRD REVOLUTION: TECHNOLOGY AND
HOUSING FINANCE OF THE TWENTY-FIRST CENTURY

The last few years have seen dramatic changes in technology and housing finance. Technology has had a major impact on the way mortgages are originated, underwritten, processed, and serviced. The tremendous growth in mortgage originations and transactions in both the primary and the secondary market would have been extremely difficult without the processing capacities of new technology. Further, the Internet has expanded consumer knowledge, and offers opportunities that impact and improve the housing finance system.

Borrowers have benefited from technological innovations. Automated underwriting systems have resulted in faster loan qualifications and processing — the time from mortgage application to approval has been reduced from months to minutes. New credit and mortgage scoring systems have allowed the mortgage market to serve some of those with weaker credit histories. Fannie Mae and Freddie Mac have played an increasing role in developing this technology, and they have therefore expanded their points of entry when buying loans for the secondary market. Both Freddie Mac and Fannie Mae are quick to point out that because of charter and regulatory restrictions, they have no intention to become lenders. But there is no question that technology will bring change, both in the ways mortgages are originated and serviced and in the changing roles of everyone involved in the housing finance process.

FIGURE 4.18

Industry Background: Mortgage Industry Sees Emergence of "Mega-Servicers"

TOP ORIGINATORS 1st Quarter 2002		TOP SERVICERS 1st Quarter 2002	
Institution	$ Billions	Institution	$ Billions
1 Washington Mutual	71.0	1 Washington Mutual	739.4
2 Wells Fargo Home Mtg.	67.9	2 Wells Fargo Home Mtg.	512.5
3 Countrywide Credit Ind.	44.0	3 Chase Manhattan Mtg.	425.0
4 Chase Manhattan Mtg.	32.7	4 Countrywide Credit Ind.	355.0
5 ABN AMRO Mortgage	24.2	5 Bank of America	308.6
6 Bank of America	17.8	6 GMAC Mortgage	203.2
7 National City Mtg.	14.5	7 HomeSide Lending	171.3
8 GMAC Mortgage	14.1	8 ABN AMRO Mortgage	160.2
9 Cendant Mortgage	12.6	9 First National Mtg. Corp.	114.2
10 CitiMortgage, Inc.	11.4	10 CitiMortgage, Inc.	104.9
Top 10 Totals	$ 310.2	Top 10 Totals	3,094.3
Others	168.2	Others	2,662.7
TOTAL	$478.4	TOTAL	$5,757.0

Source: *National Mortgage News, Quarterly Data Report,* 1st Quarter 2002.

The question now is how quickly this technological revolution will take place and what form it will take. Who will be the winners? The losers? Change is clearly underway, and the pace is fast, but there is a tendency to exaggerate the actual level of implementation. Twenty-five years ago, it was common to predict that by the turn of the century we would be living in a "checkless, cashless society." There are more checks now than there were twenty-five years ago, but at the same time, most people are closely tied to some form of financial technology, such as Automated Teller Machines (ATMs), credit card processing, and electronic banking. Reading the newspaper or listening to selected consumer advertising, one might assume that electronic lending for mortgages is widespread. Undoubtedly it is growing and will continue to grow, but it is also clear that it will take time, and consumer acceptance will influence how rapidly change unfolds. Still, a third revolution in the nation's housing finance system is under way, and the ultimate impact will be profound.

The Status of Technological Change in Housing Finance

Depending on your perspective, electronic lending and e-commerce is either moving faster than expected or is slow to be adopted. Two headlines tell the story. The first on the front-page of the *Washington Post* real-estate section on January 1, 2000 read: "Online loans slow to build a following, ease of loan application process not enough for most buyers." The second, in a special section of the *National Mortgage News* twelve days later, stated: "E-commerce continues to gain a foothold in the mortgage industry." The latter story goes on to explain that over the last few years there has been a greater "comfort level" with the Internet and electronic communication. According to a study released at the beginning of 1999 by Forrester Research, about 1% of all mortgages were originated online. Further, the study estimated, less than 10% of all mortgage loans will be originated online by 2003. By comparison, a year earlier, Forrester Research had predicted that more than 25% of all student loans would be originated online in 2003.[21]

Online originations generally rose from the second quarter of 2000 to the first quarter of 2002. As Figure 4.19 shows, in the second quarter of 2000, the top ten online lenders originated $1.19 billion of mortgages, and the total market was $1.25 billion of online originations. By the first quarter of 2002 the number of originations for the top ten online lenders had risen to $77.7 billion and the total market for online originations climbed to $86.88 billion. Interestingly, over half of the online origination volume in the first quarter of 2002 was from two lenders — Countrywide and Washington Mutual — both are also major "brick and mortar" lenders using on-line lending as another way to serve the consumer. Online lending will undoubtedly continue to grow, but just because online lending is available, it does not mean that the consumer will shift instantly to such mortgage products. If consumers are to move to online lending, they will need to see a clear advantage, either in cost advantages, more rapid and efficient processing, or personal preference. Further, in the future it is likely the majority of online lending will continue to be done by large lenders who are already well established in the mortgage business and provide both "brick and mortar" and online services. Certainly new online lenders will emerge, such as e-trade whose volume rose from $316 million to $2.83 billion between the second quarter of 2000 and the first quarter of 2002, and they will continue to provide the consumer an electronic alternative to more traditional lending. However, the dominate force in mortgage lending will continue to be the top lenders listed in Figure 4.17 who will offer both online and traditional mortgage services.

---

[21] Forester Research, "E-Commerce Continues to Gain" *National Mortgage News*.

FIGURE 4.19

Retail (Direct-to-Customer) Online Originations, Sample of Firms

(Dollars in Millions)

Organization Name	Online Retail Originations							
	Q2/00	Q3/00	Q4/00	Q1/01	Q2/01	Q3/01	Q4/01	Q1/02
Countrywide Credit Industries	na	$4,904	$118	$10,546	$3,696	$3,516	$23,512	$20,588
Washington Mutual	na	$62	$154	$704	$890	$1,095	$6,107	$18,569
ABN AMRO Mortgage	na	na	na	na	$14	$94	$6,608	$16,527
Principal Residential Mortgage	$12	$3	$1	$1,279	$0	$10	$5,613	$4,897
Chase Manhattan Mortgage	na	na	na	na	na	na	n/a	$4,884
IndyMac Bancorp, Inc.	na	na	$184	$237	$204	$211	$3,632	$3,243
CitiMortgage, Inc.	$12	$18	$26	$642	$99	$107	$2,651	$3,186
E Trade	$316	$293	na	$571	$697	$702	$2,000	$2,831
First Union Mortgage Corporation	na	$15	$27	$71	na	$70	$1,843	$1,563
Resource Bancshares Mtg. Group	na	na	na	$667	na	na	na	$1,401
Top 10 Originators Total	$1,190	$6,085	$757	$14,717	$8,020	$8,033	$55,025	$77,689
Total Market	$1,248	$6,242	$1,657	$17,507	$9,515	$9,354	$60,483	$86,880

SOURCE: National Mortgage News, 2000–2002 data.

NOTE: These numbers are based on survey responses to the National Mortgage News by these organizations and therefore do not provide all online originations. Organizations are listed in order of their online originations for Q1 2002. na refers to data not available.

Every day new ideas, new opportunities, and new examples of technology in housing finance are introduced to the marketplace. For example, on March 16, 2000, Microsoft announced it was establishing a new corporation, HomeAdvisor Technologies Inc. (HTI). It was also announced that four companies would receive minority investments in the company, including Chase Manhattan Corporation, Bank of America Corporation, GMAC-Residential Funding Corporation, and Wells Fargo's Norwest Mortgage Unit. Freddie Mac also entered into a strategic agreement with HTI to provide HTI and the mortgage lenders using HTIs "front end" services with a host of mortgage-related products, including Freddie Mac's automated underwriting system, known as Loan Prospector. The new venture was supposed to have three components: a real estate transaction platform, a mortgage finance component, and a real estate listing service. The real estate transaction platform was intended to allow borrowers, as well as lenders, realtors, home builders, and other participants in the real estate transaction, to monitor the home buying and mortgage financing process from start to finish and to process the loan. Because it was done over the

Internet, it would have been accessible, through security codes, to all of the participants so everyone would have access to the same information. The mortgage component, through Freddie Mac's Loan Prospector would have allowed the home buyer to secure a firm commitment for the loan within a matter of minutes, and even seconds, after the appropriate data was entered into the computer. It was hoped that the new system would lead to reductions in the closing cost for the loan — even up to $1,000 or $1,500 per loan. To achieve these savings, HTI would automate and streamline credit checks, appraisals, and other aspects of the loan process. The third component of the system was a real estate listing service intended to allow home buyers to review and examine, on the Internet, homes for sale throughout the country.

The HTI system was never implemented with its full array of products, although several components did become operational. But it is one example of what is taking place or being talked about in the market, and it illustrates the effort to move the mortgage origination process to the point of sale, where the home buyer purchases the house, whether it is an existing home or a new home. Freddie Mac, the secondary-market entity involved in this situation, would not have been lending the money — that would have taken place through traditional lenders, whether mortgage bankers, commercial banks, saving and loan associations, credit unions, or mortgage brokers. However, any time a commitment is made up front for Fannie Mae or Freddie Mac to buy a loan in the secondary market, it both speeds the process and reduces the costs for the consumer. Essentially, all of the processing takes place automatically, and the new technology drives the information flow and the timing.

Technology Impacts

What are the potential impacts of technology in the housing finance system to the consumer, to the lender, and to government policy and regulation?

CONSUMER IMPACTS

The United States may have the best housing finance system in the world, but for a beginning home buyer, the process of obtaining a mortgage can still be a challenging, sometimes bewildering experience. It requires a myriad of forms and information, and often includes a back-and-forth trek between lender and borrower to exchange tax forms, background information, credit analysis, etcetera. Closing a loan is also very expensive, often 2% to 3% of the cost of the loan, depending on the state. (For a $100,000 loan, that means costs of $2,000 to $3,000.) Further, the origination process is often splintered into numerous steps that require the efforts of many players — title companies, appraisers, credit bureaus, and other third-party service providers. Data systems are often separate from company to company, and the same information is often required over and over again. Incompatibility among different computer systems makes collective data transfers cumbersome and sometimes impossible.

Technology has the potential to improve the home buying process for the consumer in a variety of ways. First, it can simplify and speed the process; second, it can make the process less expensive; and third, it can provide quick access to information and greater choice, at least for those consumers who are technologically literate.

For the borrower, as well as the lender, the mortgage origination process usually involves five steps: (1) filling out an application, (2) obtaining approval, (3) verifying information related to the mortgage, (4) for the lender, hedging the loan amount and interest rate, and (5) closing the loan. New information technology simplifies both the flow of information and the time required to process it. The consumer fills out the application once, and the same information can be used throughout the process. This simplifies the process for the home buyer and gives the computer-literate consumer on the Internet additional opportunities to be more independent and to influence and understand the process. It used to take days and often weeks for home buyers to find out if a loan was approved. Now buyers can find out in minutes and even seconds. Home buyers can also be pre-approved for a loan up to a certain amount, so they will know their price range.

Although it is widely believed that technology will reduce costs for the consumer, to date it is unclear to what extent this has actually materialized. The hope is that there will be a reduction in processing and closing costs, and perhaps even a reduction in the overall rate of mortgage loans. As noted earlier, closing costs are often 2% to 3% of the overall value of the mortgage. They fall into three areas: core costs, transaction costs, and loan program design costs (see Figure 4.20). According to Danforth, the core costs — the basic costs for processing the loan, such as legal fees or fees for appraisers — account for 45% of the cost of closing a loan. The transaction costs — which include the money spent to gather, receive, order, and file paper documents — account for 43%, and the loan program

FIGURE 4.20
Total Economic Costs of a Mortgage

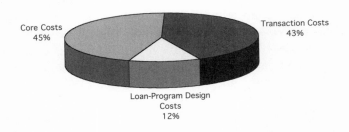

Core Costs
45%

Transaction Costs
43%

Loan-Program Design
Costs
12%

Source: *Secondary Mortgage Market,* April 1999, 4.

design costs for the lenders and investors are another 12%.[22] These cost components, according to Danforth, can then be further broken down as they relate to the five steps in originating a mortgage: application, approval, verification, hedging, and closing (see Figure 4.21). Nineteen percent of the costs relate to application, 14% to approval, 23% to verification, 14% to hedging, and 31% to closing.[23] Danforth proposes that costs can be saved in each of these areas, and if this is done, huge shifts will ripple through the market as lenders compete to offer faster and cheaper options. Overall, he believes that costs might be brought down by as much as 69%. Even a 50% reduction could mean savings of $1,000 to $1,500 on a $100,000 house; a "mere" 25% reduction could mean savings of $500 to $750. Although the specific elements of this type of cost model will obviously vary, it seems reasonable to conclude that over time technology can bring significant mortgage cost reductions to the consumer.

A third benefit to the consumer is greater access to information, and thereby greater understanding of competitive pricing on loan products and the nature and timing of the mortgage origination process.

However, the story is not all positive for the consumer. Some believe that a completely automated underwriting system becomes a "black box" that makes it hard for the consumer to understand why his or her application is turned down. If the loan is approved in minutes, everyone is happy. If the loan is not approved, the potential home buyer may be confused and frustrated. Further, for the consumer who is not computer literate, trying

[22] Danforth, "Online Mortgage Business," 4.
[23] Ibid., 7–8.

FIGURE 4.21
Cost Components of the Mortgage-Origination Process

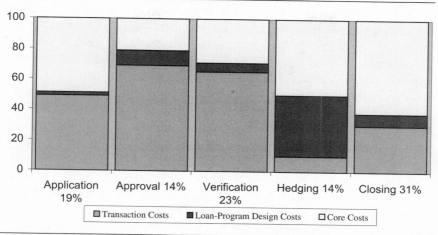

NOTE: Transaction costs cover gathering, receiving, ordering and filling paper documents. Loan-program design costs involve investor or lender requirements that specify, for example, the nature of loan-to-value ratios, appraisals and mortgage insurance. Core costs cover actual costs of services and products that occur during the process, such as loan officer's work (loan commission), legal advice, appraisal product and interest-rate hedging instrument.

SOURCE: *Secondary Mortgage Markets,* April 1999, 19.

to process a loan over the Internet can be intimidating or impossible. Finally, too many options can be overwhelming. One or two mortgage products with different rates and terms can be confusing. If consumers are offered a menu of dozens of mortgages from different lenders with different terms, rates, and prices, it will be difficult for some to make a choice.

IMPACT ON THE LENDERS AND OTHER MORTGAGE FINANCE PLAYERS

Technology increases the productivity of lenders and enhances their ability to provide expanded services at lower costs. Once the technological infrastructure is developed by the lender or other players in the housing finance market, with relatively low additional costs, the number of loans originated can increase substantially. In theory, these savings can be passed on to the consumer. Further, technology helps reduce the need for additional physical facilities or, in essence, "clicks" can be substituted for "bricks." However, the costs of marketing on the Internet can be high. One review of online lenders by Sandler O'Neill and Partners found that when it comes to spending money to generate loan applications, there are wide differences among lenders and the costs for some — especially those that are not established — can be high.[24]

Technology's greatest impact on mortgage lenders and other players in the housing finance process may be the shift that will occur related to roles and process. Technology will make some players in the market obsolete. For example, a variety of new systems automate or partially automate the appraisal process, possibly leading to reduced costs for the home buyer. However, with such systems, the role of the appraiser may shift over time, and there may be a diminished need for human appraisers. As GSE technology moves closer to the point of sale, lenders will face additional competition, perhaps from real estate agents who desire to be mortgage brokers or from home builders who are dealing with customers directly when they sell a new home and are therefore in a prime position to serve as the first point of contact in an electronic lending process. (Recognizing this advantage, a number of home builders have already established mortgage banking companies or affiliates.) Title companies currently play an essential role in buying a home. However, with nationwide automation, title companies will need to think carefully about their role if they are to preserve a position in the new world of electronic housing finance.

Another area in which technology will reduce costs is servicing. At a technology conference in 2000, as reported in the *National Mortgage News,* Richard Beidl of Tow Group, Needham, Massachusetts, indicated that "best of breed" servicers have already raised eyebrows by reducing the cost of servicing to between $40 and $50 per loan annually. However, he expects that within five years, the best mortgage servicers will reduce the cost of loan administration by even more — to $20 to $22 per loan.[25] The Internet and other technology advances in record keeping, information, and communication will allow the most efficient servicers to capture significant cost savings, he said. This will add to the consolidation noted earlier. Large-scale companies that have developed efficient technologies will continue to lower servicing costs, and therefore will compete very effectively with other companies. In turn, servicing is likely to become increasingly important as the housing finance process evolves. Large servicers will have large customer databases, which they will be able to use in a variety of "cross selling" situations. Large servicers will also be in a prime position to go directly to the home owner with a variety of products. When rates drop and refinancing demand rises, large servicers will go to

---

[24] Sandler O'Neill Research as reported in the *National Mortgage News,* 23.

[25] Beidle, as reported in *National Mortgage News.*

home buyers and offer to refinance their loans at a minimum cost to assure that owners keep their mortgages with the servicer. Companies not in a position to compete because they do not have the technology to rapidly and inexpensively process new loans will find themselves at a disadvantage.

GOVERNMENT POLICY AND REGULATORY IMPACTS

Government policies and regulations have become well established as a framework for the traditional loan origination and housing finance process. The new world of electronic lending creates new challenges for government policy and regulation. Issues related to Internet policy and electronic lending often transcend traditional industry boundaries. If regulations and statutes do not transfer easily to the electronic business environment, they may hinder progress toward electronic lending and its potential benefits. A few examples illustrate the challenge.[26]

BORROWER DISCLOSURE

Federal laws such as the Real Estate Settlement Procedures Act (RESPA), the Truth in Lending Act (TILA), and the Equal Credit Opportunity Act (ECOA) mandate disclosure of transaction costs, mortgage terms, and other information in order to protect home buyers. As a part of this, RESPA requires borrowers to sign documents attesting that they have received and reviewed these disclosures. The traditional system provides for disclosure through paper and ink documents. The Internet now offers alternatives, for example through posting documents on a website or delivering them via e-mail. How far the regulators, such as the Federal Reserve Board and the Department of Housing and Urban Development, will go in allowing lenders to use online methods to meet RESPA disclosure requirements is yet to be seen.

RESPA IN AN ONLINE ENVIRONMENT

When RESPA was enacted twenty-five years ago, its purpose was to assure full disclosure and to protect consumers from abuses related to high settlement charges. The statute, for example, prohibits referral fees. Confusion over the years about exactly what this rule intends has fueled a long-running controversy between lenders and realtors. Electronic lending contributes additional questions as to how RESPA can work in an online

---

[26] For a further discussion of government policy and regulatory impacts see Thomas, "Policy Thicket Complicates Efforts," *Secondary Mortgage Markets,* 9–15.

environment. The challenge from a regulatory perspective will be to protect the consumer while allowing the new technology to provide alternatives that will be more effective and less expensive for the home buyer.

COMMUNITY REINVESTMENT ACT

Under the 1977 Community Reinvestment Act (CRA) — in order to get regulatory approval for mergers and acquisitions — financial institutions must serve the local community before they expand their services in other areas, a principle, although controversial, that has been considered essential by community groups. What does this mean in a world of online lending in which the Internet transcends geographic boundaries? A growing number of financial institutions provide online banking services to people living outside the normal geographic areas served by their branches. One of the benefits of the Internet is that banking services can be provided nationwide without "brick" facilities. This creates challenges for both regulatory and depository institutions. Consumers may benefit from cheaper services provided by an online lender, but is it fair to give online and traditional lenders different sets of regulatory requirements?

STATE LICENSING

Once again, the Internet poses fascinating challenges as it enables a lender located in one state to serve borrowers in the other forty-nine states without establishing a local office with costly overhead. However, forty-eight states and the District of Columbia license mortgage lenders and mortgage brokers that do business within their state. Some of those states require a physical office within the state. State licensing allows authorities to defend consumers and curtail scams and illegal practices. However, the requirements of multiple registration may negate some of the savings lenders realize online. Maintaining a physical facility is expensive. In the new electronic environment, the question is whether such a requirement should remain.

PRIVACY

As the Internet expands, more personal information is captured — credit histories, buying habits, medical histories, personal financial data, etcetera. What should the rules be regarding the protection of such information, or the circulation of the information to third parties without consumer knowledge or consent? The information is valuable for marketing purposes and fundamental to providing customized online services. These are challenging issues. Electronic listing services have placed what used to be highly classified information at the hands of Internet users. But serious questions arise regarding the protection of this information from theft and reuse. Issues of privacy will be ongoing for many years and require careful government policy and regulatory consideration.

TAXATION IN AN ELECTRONIC WORLD

The amount of business and commerce conducted over the Internet is rising and is expected to grow substantially. Local and state governments are now able to tax a variety of business activities that take place within their jurisdictions. These governments could lose a significant portion of retail sales-tax revenues as more and more sales occur over the Internet. Yet, electronic businesses are concerned that if state and local jurisdictions start levying taxes, it will mean increased costs to the consumer. However, businesses that are not on the Internet say that it is unfair to force them and their customers to pay taxes when those on the Internet do not. Although Internet users would like to avoid any taxes, it is unlikely that complete laissez-faire will prevail. Over time the question remains, though, as to what type of taxes will be enacted, and at what level. The answer will obviously have an impact on electronically generated mortgage business.

CONCLUSIONS

By most standards, the United States has the best housing finance system in the world. It has evolved over the last seventy-five years, and the constant in this evolution has been change. The system collapsed in the late 1920s and early 1930s due to the pressures of the depression, but a new system rose from the ashes of economic turmoil. Federal depository insurance for financial institutions, the Federal Home Loan Bank System, the Federal Housing Administration, as well as Fannie Mae, Ginnie Mae, and Freddie Mac were all established over a forty-year period.

When interest rates skyrocketed in the late 1970s and early 1980s, the savings and loan industry found itself caught in an environment of rising interest rates where they had borrowed short and lent long. Change was essential, and a housing finance system largely dependent on thrift institutions evolved into a broader-based, more resilient system that linked housing to the broader capital markets through the secondary market. In the early 1980s, the primary question for our housing finance system was:

where would the credit come from to finance the nation's housing? The main answer was through the secondary market, mortgage-backed securities, and a wide range of secondary-market instruments.

New technology is now at the forefront of the third housing finance revolution. New technology often brings new opportunities and the potential to reduce costs and provide new instruments and programs to make housing more affordable. But it also brings new policy questions, market uncertainties, and possible shifts in the providers of housing finance. Two key perspectives in evaluating this transformation are whether this change will benefit the home buyer and whether it is safe and sound.

During the time this author worked at Freddie Mac as an Executive Vice President (1982–1984), Ken Thygerson, the President, Leland Brendsel, then the Chief Financial Officer (and now the Chairman and CEO), and this author were summoned to California to meet with some of the top savings and loan executives in the state. They were interested in promoting an adjustable rate mortgage (ARM) which was based on the cost of funds in their Federal Home Loan Bank District (the Eleventh District). With this mortgage, the interest rate to the home buyer would adjust based on the cost of funds for the Eleventh Federal Home Loan Bank District, and it would allow them to better balance their assets and liabilities.

They wanted Freddie Mac to agree to buy these mortgages in order to provide a secondary market and therefore greater liquidity for the ARMs. In addition, though, they wanted Freddie Mac to stop buying thirty-year, fixed-rate mortgages. From their perspective, the thirty-year, fixed-rate mortgage was a major competitor to the Eleventh District ARM they wanted to promote, and the secondary market allowed thirty-year mortgages to thrive and compete.

After careful consideration, Freddie Mac agreed to buy the Eleventh District ARM. However, fortunately for the consumer, they did not agree to stop buying thirty-year fixed-rate mortgages. As this experience illustrates, thirty-year fixed-rate mortgages still exist because of the secondary mortgage market, and the United States is essentially the only country in the world with such a consumer friendly mortgage product — a thirty-year fixed rate mortgage without prepayment penalties. Also, because of the growth and development of the secondary market, mortgage rates have been lowered due to a variety of market efficiencies. This is demonstrated by the difference in mortgage rates for conforming loans purchased by Freddie Mac and Fannie Mae compared with non-conforming mortgage loans (see Figure 4.12). One of the first considerations in evaluating new policy questions, or housing finance products, should be the impact on the home buyer. The secondary mortgage market and new technology have certainly helped to lower the costs and improve the access to mortgages for the buyer. As we look to the future, public policy should continue to encourage these benefits — especially for the home buyers that are in the greatest need.

Today, a unique system of public and private institutions meets the nation's housing finance needs. Some agencies are part of the federal government like the FHA and the VA. Others are quasi-public in the form of government sponsored enterprises (GSEs); still others are private but insured by the federal government and therefore closely tied to the federal government through the federal deposit insurance fund. Finally, some institutions are primarily private. For the institutions that have at least some link to the federal government, questions of safety and soundness are also paramount. The second major consideration in evaluating new policies or products, then, is that the federal government and the tax payer should be protected by sound regulation (while at the same time encouraging innovation and a focus on the consumer wherever possible).

The housing finance system sometimes leads to tension between the various players as institutions compete for products and market share, but overall it works remarkably well. Homeownership rates have risen dramatically over the last fifty years, and people travel from throughout the world to examine and try to emulate our housing finance system. Still, some would argue that the federal presence in housing finance is too great — that public institutions (such as FHA and VA) should be curtailed and the government sponsored enterprises (Fannie Mae, Freddie Mac, and the Federal Home Loan Banks) should be limited in their role or cut loose from their federal financial tie. This debate will undoubtedly continue into the twenty-first century. However, as we search for the delicate balance between the public and private roles in our system of housing finance, we should remember that it is impossible to turn back the clock. Further, issues of competition and tough debates will exist, but the key factors in evaluating policy choices should be the benefits to the consumer while assuring appropriate safety and soundness. Continued change is inevitable, but as we look to the future, it is important to build on the foundation of the past and not let concerns over increased competition constrain the potential benefits of our revitalized housing finance system to the home buyer.

Chapter 5:

THE ROLE OF THE FEDERAL GOVERNMENT IN HOUSING

For the first 150 years of the nation's history, housing was primarily the concern of individuals and, to some extent, state and municipal governments. This scenario changed dramatically during the Great Depression. In response to the devastation of the Depression, Congress enacted major housing initiatives, and federal support for housing has been maintained ever since. This support can be broadly organized into three categories: direct federal housing assistance programs; tax incentives for housing; and the nation's housing finance system.

A number of the federal housing assistance programs have already been discussed in the first four chapters of this book. However, because the federal role in housing is so broad — and at times confusing — this chapter summarizes the evolution and nature of that role in the three categories noted above. In addition, Appendix I provides a time-line outlining key federal housing laws and regulations.

DIRECT FEDERAL HOUSING ASSISTANCE PROGRAMS

Pre-Depression

Prior to the 1930s, the federal government had little involvement with the housing needs of American citizens. Government representatives were well aware that many Americans, especially recent immigrants in urban areas, lived in substandard housing, yet little was done to alleviate problems or lend formal assistance. In 1892, Congress passed a public resolution for the investigation of city slums, providing funding for the investigation of four cities.[1] Subsequently, recommendations were made

---

[1] Congressional Research Services Report, "Chronology of Housing Legislation," 1.

to clear slums and replace them with decent housing, but no formal action was taken.[2]

The 1930s: Responding to the Depression

With the crash of the stock market in 1929, thousands of Americans were left without employment and many were in financial ruin. People crowded together into housing units, and many became homeless. In response, the federal government began to take a proactive stance toward helping Americans with their housing needs. Housing legislation passed at this time included the Emergency Relief and Construction Act of 1932 and the National Industrial Recovery Act of 1933. The 1932 act authorized the *Reconstruction Finance Corporation* to make loans to corporations established to provide housing for low-income families or to reconstruct slum areas.[3] The 1933 act authorized use of federal funds to finance low-cost and slum-clearance housing.[4] The major reasons for federally sponsored slum clearance and housing construction in these depression years were to provide employment for construction workers and to improve public health.[5] Improvement of actual housing conditions was not the primary push for federal assistance, although it gradually became the principal reason in subsequent years. In 1935, Congress provided funds for an inventory of urban housing; results revealed the need for more sanitation facilities and improved housing conditions.[6]

These first steps taken by the federal government set the stage for the United States Housing Act of 1937. This act authorized the *Public Housing Program,* which provided publicly owned housing units for low-income households. Loans were made to local public housing agencies to assist in the development, acquisition, and administration of low-rent housing or slum clearance.[7] It was stipulated that all operating and utility costs should be covered by rental income, and that tenants' income could not exceed five times the rent.[8] These stipulations effectively meant that the lowest-income households could not be housed under this program because rents that covered operating and utility costs were too high.[9] Still,

---

[2] Coan, "Introduction to Federal Housing Programs," 2.
[3] Congressional Research Services Report, "Chronology of Housing Legislation," 2.
[4] Ibid., 4.
[5] National Association of Home Builders. *Low- & Moderate-Income Housing,* 36.
[6] Coan, "Introduction to Federal Housing Programs," 2.
[7] Congressional Research Services Report, "Chronology of Housing Legislation," 11.
[8] National Association of Home Builders, *Low- & Moderate-Income Housing,* 36.
[9] Ibid.

the legislation created the first major federal program for low-income households. Some of the building funded by the act was delayed due to the start of World War II, and some was constructed instead for war workers. Although not all of the units were completed, the program helped develop the expertise to operate public housing authorities.[10]

Post-World War II Activity

The end of World War II marked a turning point in U.S. housing policy. During the war years, the federal government's primary concern was to house those involved with the war effort. When the war ended in 1945, thousands of servicemen and servicewomen returned from overseas, creating a major housing shortage. The federal government was concerned for these returning servicepeople and their families, and also for the condition of U.S. cities. In 1941, a Temporary National Economic Committee was established. In its report to Congress it strongly recommended slum clearance and construction of low-cost housing.[11] This was further supported in 1945 when the Subcommittee on Housing and Urban Redevelopment of the Senate Committee on Postwar Economic Policy and Planning made similar recommendations for slum clearance. Thus, the prevailing focus for the federal government in the immediate postwar years was slum clearance and constructing housing to meet shortages around the nation.

The federal government's increasing interest in solving housing and urban problems led to the groundbreaking Housing Act of 1949. The act declared that the general welfare and security of the nation required a decent home and suitable living environment for every American family.[12] It called for government assistance for slum clearance and the elimination of substandard poverty housing. It also created the *Urban Redevelopment Program* (later known as the *Urban Renewal Program*). This program gave localities $1 billion in loans and $500 million in capital grants over a five-year period to help with slum clearance and community development programs. To be eligible for these grants, the designated project areas were to be predominantly residential either before or after redevelopment.[13] The program also increased the funds available for public housing

---

[10] Ibid., 37.
[11] Coan, "Introduction to Federal Housing Programs," 2.
[12] Congressional Research Services Report, "A Chronology of Housing Legislation," 32.
[13] Ibid.

and created new programs for rural housing. The Urban Redevelopment Program was viewed as an expansion of the slum clearance activities associated with the Public Housing Program,[14] and was successful in removing blighted sections of U.S. cities. However, it did very little to replace housing for low-income households, and for some it clearly exacerbated their housing problems.[15] Nevertheless, a significant number of public housing units were created in the 1950s and 1960s as a result of this program.

In the 1950s, the federal approach to supporting housing and community development expanded and evolved in new directions. In January of 1954, President Eisenhower directed a special message to Congress to continue and enhance federal commitments to preventing the spread of slums, to rehabilitate blighted areas, and to provide additional FHA mortgage insurance for housing those displaced by slum clearance.[16] Congress responded by passing the Housing Act of 1954. This act broadened the Housing Act of 1949, authorizing programs to clear and redevelop slums as well as to prevent their spread by rehabilitating blighted areas. It also authorized redevelopment of nonresidential areas.[17] The term *urban renewal* was designated as the new title for these expanded programs. Each community that received assistance was required to have a workable program for attacking and preventing slums and blight.[18] Congress also heeded the president's urging to increase the FHA mortgage insurance for those displaced by renewal activities by creating the FHA 220 and 221 mortgage insurance programs.

An Urban Renewal Administration was created within the Housing and Home Finance Administration to manage the urban renewal programs created by the 1954 act. The federal government worked hard during the 1950s to implement the programs authorized by the 1949 and 1954 housing acts. There was continued pressure to expand the scope of the renewal programs, and in 1959, after considerable struggle to pass similar bills, the Housing Act of 1959 was passed. It expanded the government's ability to redevelop nonresidential areas, authorized relocation payments for those displaced from an urban renewal area, authorized temporary loans for acquiring land prior to carrying out an urban renewal project, provided assistance for the development of *Community Renewal Programs* to enable

---

[14] National Association of Home Builders. *Low- & Moderate-Income Housing*, 36.
[15] Ibid.
[16] Coan, "Introduction to Federal Housing Programs," 3–4.
[17] Ibid., 4.
[18] Ibid.

communities to identify and coordinate the renewal of their slum and blighted areas, and expanded the *701 Urban Planning Grant Program* to encourage more metropolitan and regional planning.[19] The 1959 act also allowed local housing authorities to set income limits and rents for public housing; they could adjust rents downward for those with the lowest incomes while raising rents for higher-income tenants. This important change allowed the housing authorities to serve lower-income populations that had previously not had access to public housing.[20] The expectation was still that rental income would cover operating and utility costs.

New Directions in the 1960s

The 1960s saw an explosion in the number of federal assistance programs for housing and urban development. The Housing Act of 1961 further supported the Urban Renewal Program by, among other things, increasing federal money for urban renewal projects in communities of 50,000 or less and by providing support for mass transportation projects.[21] The Housing Act of 1964 expanded the assistance for code enforcement activities in urban renewal areas and allowed land in an urban renewal area to be sold at reduced prices for low- and moderate-income housing. It also provided federal grants to states to help train employees in economic and community development. The Housing Act of 1965 focused on continuing federal aid for urban problems. Title I of the act created the R*ent Supplement Program,* which allowed certain low-income households to use the supplements in privately-owned housing units. Also, the act authorized grants to local organizations to help finance water and sewer facilities, community centers, and beautification projects.

As further indication of the importance of national housing programs, the Department of Housing and Urban Development was established in 1965 to address housing and urban development policy concerns throughout the nation. This new department brought together all of the various federal programs related to housing and renewed the focus of national housing policy.

In continuing its commitment to problems in U.S. cities, Congress passed the Demonstration Cities and Metropolitan Development Act of 1966. This act authorized *Comprehensive City Demonstration Programs*

---

[19] Ibid., 5.
[20] National Association of Home Builders. *Low- & Moderate-Income Housing,* 37.
[21] Congressional Research Services Report, "Chronology of Housing Legislation," 93–95.

(more commonly known as *Model Cities*), which provided both grants and technical assistance to help communities renew the supply of low- and moderate-cost housing in entire slum neighborhoods. The grants could cover up to 80% of the cost of planning and developing a project. This was the first time a requirement was established in residential urban renewal areas for a substantial amount of low- and moderate-income housing.[22] The 1966 act also authorized HUD to work closely with and assist the housing industry in developing technology to reduce the cost and improve the quality of housing.

In light of worsening problems in U.S. cities, including urban riots, the federal government again devised new aid programs to help with community development and to alleviate serious economic, social, and class tensions in urban areas. The Housing and Urban Development Act of 1968 was a major piece of legislation crafted to address several prominent problems. One of its key aspects was the expansion of federal assistance to potential low- and moderate-income home owners. *FHA-insured home mortgage loans* were made available to such households and minimum down-payments established. The act expanded the scope of land acquisition, making it possible to acquire land for any public purpose (not just for public works and facilities), which was especially helpful in new communities.

The act also established important programs under *Section 235* and *Section 236*. Section 235 was a subsidy program that helped low-income households purchase rather than rent housing by offering a variable interest subsidy on low-down-payment, FHA-insured loans made by private institutions.[23] Notably, the government paid part of the mortgage interest under this program. Section 236 was designed to provide an interest rate subsidy to nonprofit or limited-dividend developers of affordable rental housing.[24] The projects were financed through private lending institutions with the mortgage interest rate being subsidized down to 1% and insured by the FHA. HUD paid the mortgagee the difference between the 1% interest rate and the market rate. Both the Section 236 and 235 programs were suspended in 1973, but by that time, hundreds of thousands of subsidized housing units had been built, providing needed housing for thousands of lower-income Americans. Finally, the Housing and Urban Development Act of 1968 set numeric goals for housing production. The Kaiser Commission (formerly the President's Commission on Urban Housing) had

---

[22] Coan, "Introduction to Federal Housing Programs," 9.
[23] National Association of Home Builders, *Low- & Moderate-Income Housing,* 38.
[24] Ibid.

recommended that housing goals be set in 1967, and the 1968 act followed through with the goal of creating 6 million units for low- and moderate-income families over a ten-year period.[25]

The final piece of legislation passed in the 1960s that significantly affected housing policy was the *Civil Rights Act of 1968*. Title VIII of this act addressed fair housing concerns, making it unlawful to refuse to sell, rent, or make a dwelling unavailable to any person because of race, color, religion, or national origin, or to deny a loan or other financial assistance for the purchase, construction, repair, or maintenance of a dwelling. The federal government was now committed to ensure that these fair housing provisions were followed and enforced throughout the country.

The 1970s: A Time of Reassessment and Consolidation

In the 1960s, government assistance for housing expanded at a rapid rate. By the 1970s, after these assistance programs had been in operation for a few years, their rapid growth and long-term budget implications began to raise concerns, and there was a call for a reassessment of the government's role and a review of how to best deal with housing and urban problems around the nation.

In the early 1970s, President Nixon pushed for new approaches to urban issues, and suggested that program consolidation and revenue sharing would be a more feasible and sustainable means of tackling housing and urban problems. The Housing and Urban Development Act of 1970 took some initial steps toward consolidating the various programs that had been enacted over the last twenty years.[26] Then, in 1973, Nixon suspended all housing assistance programs, including Sections 235 and 236, out of concern for their rapid growth and their long-term budget commitments.[27] Further, some of the programs suffered management, design, and implementation problems. Another critical issue was the increasingly negative image of public housing. The demolition of the Pruitt-Igoe high-rise development in St. Louis gained national media attention, and the bad press added to the pressure for the federal government to reassess its housing policy.

From 1971 to 1973, no housing or community development legislation was enacted for the first time in nearly ten years. Then, after two years of

---

[25] Ibid.
[26] Coan, "Introduction to Federal Housing Programs," 10.
[27] National Association of Home Builders, *Low- & Moderate-Income Housing,* 39.

consideration, the Housing and Community Development Act of 1974 was passed. It embodied the consolidation proposals advanced by the Nixon Administration for years.[28] The two critical components of this legislation were *Community Development Block Grants* (CDBG) and *Section 8*. CDBG represented a major shift in the way the federal government provided financial support for housing and urban programs. It offered 100% grants with which localities could create their own development programs — instead of having the federal government define the specific categories of development as a requirement for assistance.[29] This gave localities more flexibility to meet local needs. CDBG pulled together many of the urban assistance programs that had been funded separately, including Model Cities, Open-Space, Water and Sewer grants, 312 Rehabilitation loans, Urban Renewal and Neighborhood Development, Public Facility loans, and Neighborhood Facilities grants.[30]

Section 8 established a low-income housing assistance program. When Nixon suspended housing assistance programs in 1973, he established the National Housing Policy Review to consider the future of federal housing policy. The report it produced indicated that rent-burden was a major problem for many low-income households, even those living in standard housing. The new suggestion was to target households, rather than housing units, for assistance.[31] This recommendation was incorporated as Section 8 of the Housing and Community Development Act of 1974. It was the most comprehensive and versatile housing assistance program ever enacted — and one of the most expensive.[32] There were a few different approaches under Section 8. The first was the *Section 8 New Construction* program, which encouraged developers to build housing with the federal government subsidizing the rent of the lower-income tenants for twenty to forty years. This program helped to expand the housing stock and provide decent housing for lower-income tenants. The *Section 8 Substantial Rehabilitation* program was similar to the New Construction program except that it focused on revitalizing older structures and neighborhoods. The *Section 8 Existing* program allowed people to apply for a rent supplement-type subsidy that they could use in any unit that fell within the rent limit (meaning the rent on a given unit cannot exceed a specific maximum) and met the program quality standards.

---

[28] Coan, "Introduction to Federal Housing Programs," 11.
[29] Congressional Research Services Report, "A Chronology of Housing Legislation," 210.
[30] Coan, "Introduction to Federal Housing Programs," 12.
[31] National Association of Home Builders, *Low- & Moderate-Income Housing*, 39.
[32] Ibid., 40.

The Section 8 Existing program was effectively a form of *housing allowance*. This concept had been discussed by legislators in the 1930s and was again raised in 1967 by the Kaiser Commission. This committee had recommended that an experiment be conducted by the federal government to determine the effectiveness and desirability of a housing allowance system. This recommendation was authorized in 1970 as the Experimental Housing Allowance Program (EHAP); it was started in 1973 and was evaluated in 1980. The program was intended to assess how eligible households would respond to various versions of a housing allowance; to test how rental markets might be affected by an entitlement assistance program; and to determine what administrative complications might arise.[33] The EHAP resulted in some important conclusions. Many low-income households whose current residents did not meet program standards chose not to participate (unless only minor repairs were needed). Also, relatively few participants moved or sought major improvements from their landlords (contrary to expectations). Lastly, most of those whose current residences qualified continued to live there and used the subsidy to meet other pressing needs.[34]

In 1979, Congress passed the Housing and Community Development Amendments. Title I of this legislation created the *Urban Development Action Grants* (UDAG). These grants were made to cities or urban counties that did not meet HUD's minimum standards for eligibility, but did contain sizeable pockets of poverty in which at least 70% of residents had incomes below 80% of the median or at least 30% of residents had incomes below the national poverty level.[35] This was the last major legislative step taken in the 1970s, a decade that witnessed the greatest consolidation, redefinition, and expansion of housing assistance in the nation's history.

The 1980s: A Change in Direction

The increase in housing assistance in the 1970s was followed by a significant decrease in the early 1980s. The arrival of the Reagan administration, plus new criticisms of the 1970s programs (like Section 8 New Construction and Section 8 Existing), led to yet another round of reassessment and a change in the federal approach. The President's Commission on Housing was established to review the situation and make new recommendations, which it did in a 1982 report.

[33] Ibid.
[34] Ibid.
[35] Congressional Research Services Report, "A Chronology of Housing Legislation," 248.

One of the major findings of the President's Commission on Housing was that affordability was the primary problem for most households, not housing quality, although quality was still an issue for some low-income families. Based on this report, the Reagan administration suggested that a voucher program replace all parts of the Section 8 program. (Housing vouchers were tested in the EHAP in the 1970s.) The housing voucher system was similar to Section 8 Existing, yet had three major differences: it relied exclusively on the existing stock to meet the housing demands of the recipients; a voucher recipient was free to rent, at his or her own cost, a more expensive unit than would be permitted under Section 8 Existing; and the amount of the voucher subsidy was based on a "standard" rent in each locality, rather than on the rent actually paid by the tenant.[36] In 1983, Congress agreed to adopt the voucher program on a demonstration basis while reducing the Section 8 Existing and Moderate Rehabilitation programs.

The general thrust of the Reagan administration was to cap future housing assistance programs and, when possible, make cutbacks. The emphasis was to make it possible for low-income households to find housing in the existing stock, rather than have the federal government increase the housing supply. Despite this, some production programs persisted, albeit in a modified form. One key example of a new-style production program was the *Rental Housing Development Grant* (HoDAG), created under the Housing and Urban-Rural Recovery Act of 1983 for the rehabilitation and development of privately owned rental properties. HoDAG was a one-time grant used by a developer in the form of a grant or reduced-interest-rate loan to help subsidize construction or rehabilitation. These competitive grants were awarded to cities or counties based on criteria such as comparative severity of housing shortage.[37] The HoDAG subsidy was not particularly large, therefore only 20% of the units in a given project were required to be affordable (i.e. affordable to people with incomes below 80% of area median).[38]

The Housing and Community Development Act of 1987 provided an interesting new program known as the *Nehemiah Housing Opportunity Grants*. Title VI established the Nehemiah housing program and Nehemiah Housing Fund to provide grants to nonprofit organizations to help moderate-income families become home owners in lower-income

---

[36] National Association of Home Builders, *Low- & Moderate-Income Housing,* 41.
[37] Congressional Research Services Report, "A Chronology of Housing Legislation," 274.
[38] National Association of Home Builders, *Low- & Moderate-Income Housing,* 41.

neighborhoods. In 1988, the Indian Housing Act amended the United States Housing Act of 1937 by establishing a housing assistance program for Indians distinct from the public housing program. Also, Section 202 of the Indian Housing Act was designed to help Indian families on reservations become home owners, including the option of owning cooperatives.

The 1990s: The Block Grant Approach

In the latter part of the 1980s, there was a growing sentiment that the HoDAG Program was not adequately meeting low- and moderate-income housing needs around the country. In 1987, the U.S. Senate created the National Housing Task Force, often referred to as the Rouse/Maxwell Task Force because it was chaired by James W. Rouse and David O. Maxwell. The task force was privately funded, but its members were chosen in consultation with Senator Alan Cranston (D-California), and Senator Al D'Amato (R-New York). In 1988, the task force produced a report, entitled "A Decent Place to Live," that revealed several critical housing problems faced by low-income households around the country and spurred the formulation of new housing legislation.

In 1990, the Cranston-Gonzales National Affordable Housing Act was passed. This act implemented many of the recommendations made by the National Housing Task Force. The legislation emphasized the role of state and local governments in the creation of affordable housing programs and created the *HOME program,* which was designed to foster government-private partnerships to create affordable housing. The HOME program provides annual grants to larger communities and to states for a broad range of housing assistance efforts including new construction, rehabilitation, and rental assistance.[39] The HOME program is essentially a block grant program similar to the CDBG program. One important difference is that HOME imposed matching requirements.[40] However, the HOME program was significantly modified by the Housing and Community Development Act of 1992 in order to ease these matching requirements, thereby making it more possible for communities to utilize the HOME program.[41]

A second component of the Cranston-Gonzales National Affordable Housing Act was the *HOPE program.* HOPE stands for "Housing Opportunities for People Everywhere." The program was designed to convert

---

[39] Coan, "Introduction to Federal Housing Programs," 15.
[40] Van Vliet, *Encyclopedia of Housing,* 228.
[41] Coan, "Introduction to Federal Housing Programs," 16.

public housing units into units to be purchased by low-income residents. The HOPE program had three components, *HOPE I, HOPE II,* and *HOPE III.* HOPE I and II provide for conversion of existing multifamily rental housing to homeownership and to resident self-management. HOPE III was designed to help single-family home buyers become owners in developments of one to four units owned or held by government organizations such as HUD, state or local governments, public or Indian housing authorities, and the Department of Veterans Affairs.[42] In 1992, Congress established the *HOPE VI program* under which HUD provides competitive grants to public housing authorities for the revitalization of severely distressed public housing.[43]

In 1998, a public housing reform act, called the Quality Housing and Work Responsibility Act (QHWRA), was passed by Congress as part of HUD's fiscal 1999 appropriations act. This legislation focused on reducing poverty in public housing, ensuring that the lowest-income families have access to public housing, helping families in public housing transition from welfare to work, and rewarding high performance by public housing agencies.[44] The act also focused on reforming and merging the Section 8 and voucher programs, specifically allowing public housing agencies to implement Section 8 homeownership programs.[45] Finally, emphasis was placed on revitalizing the public housing stock.

TAX INCENTIVES FOR HOUSING

The federal tax code provides major incentives for both rental and owner-occupied housing for people in all income brackets. In fact, tax incentives are one of the most important developments of federal housing policy and complement direct housing assistance programs. Tax incentives also represent a significant revenue commitment on the part of the federal government.

---

[42] Van Vliet, *Encyclopedia of Housing,* 238.
[43] Lore, "Challenges and Opportunities for Federal Role," 8.
[44] U.S. Department of Housing and Urban Development. "Public Housing Reform Act."
[45] Ibid.

Tax Incentives for Home Owners: Mortgage Interest Deduction, Property Tax Deduction, and Deferral and Exclusion of Capital Gains Tax

One of the great incentives for Americans to become home owners is the mortgage interest deduction. A home owner can deduct the mortgage interest expense on up to $1 million in mortgage debt. The deduction can be made on both a primary residence and a second home. This is a significant savings for home owners, although those who itemize their tax deductions benefit most. Taxpayers who itemize deductions on their federal income tax returns are able to reduce their taxes by the amount of their annual mortgage interest times their federal marginal tax rate.

Typically, higher-income households itemize their tax deductions, usually because they have nonhousing deductions and more expensive homes. The mortgage interest deduction may not be as important for moderate-income households when making the decision to purchase a house. Nevertheless, all home owners receive some financial benefit from the deduction. Figure 5.1 shows the distribution of tax benefits from the mortgage interest deduction. Households in the $100,000 to $200,000 income bracket clearly benefit most with 33% of the benefits, although those in the $75,000 to $100,000 range and those in the $200,000 and over range also receive significant benefits.[46]

Another important deduction is the property (or real estate) tax deduction. Home owners are able to deduct the property taxes that they pay on their house to local or state governments, which often translates into important savings. The mechanics are similar to the mortgage interest deduction. Taxpayers who itemize on their federal tax returns are able to reduce their taxes by the amount that they pay in property (real estate) taxes times their federal marginal tax rate. Once again, higher-income households tend to itemize their deductions and thus will benefit more from the property tax deduction.

A third important deduction is the deferral and exclusion of the capital gains tax. This began in the 1950s and allowed home owners to defer the capital gains tax when selling a primary home. The owner then had up to two years to reinvest the money gained from the sale of the home into a new home without incurring a tax liability. In 1997, the Taxpayer Relief Act changed the law to allow individuals to exclude taxes on up to $250,000 (couples, $500,000) in capital gains from home sales every three years.

---

[46] Green and Reschovsky, "Using Tax Policy to Increase Homeownership."

FIGURE 5.1

Distribution of Tax Benefits for Mortgage Interest Deduction, FY 1998

Income (Thousands)	Number of Returns (Thousands)	% of All Returns	Number of Returns taking Mortgage Interest Deduction (Thousands)	% of All Returns in Income Category	Value of Mortgage Interest Deductions (Millions)	% Value of all Mortgage Interest Deduction	Average Value per Return for Taking Mortgage Interest Deduction
Under $10	19,763	14.75	14		$3		$214
$10–$20	25,158	18.78	354	1.4	128		371
$20–$30	20,397	15.22	1,134	5.5	466	1.00	411
$30–$40	16,189	12.08	2,375	14.7	1,238	2.63	521
$40–$50	12,434	9.28	3,080	24.8	2,270	4.83	737
$50–$75	19,469	14.53	8,201	42.1	7,667	16.32	935
$75–100	10,015	7.47	6,538	65.3	10,029	21.34	1,534
$100–$200	8,383	6.25	6,306	75.2	15,739	33.50	2,496
$200 and Over	2,129	1.58	1,554	73	9,438	20.10	6,073
TOTAL	133,938		29,548	22.1	46,977		

SOURCE: Green, Richard, and Andrew Reschovsky, "Using Tax Policy to Increase Homeownership Among Low- and Moderate-Income Households," Final report, submitted to Ford Foundation.

DATA: Calculated from data provided in "Estimates of federal Tax Expenditures for Fiscal Years 1999–2003," Washington, D.C.: Joint Committee on Taxation, U.S. Congress, 14 December 1998.

NOTE: Figure 5.1 in this chapter is also Figure 2.7 in Chapter 2.

Tax-Exempt Financing and Private Activity Bond Housing Program

There is a long-standing positive relationship between homeownership and the federal tax code. Many of the benefits noted above, though, tend to go to higher-income home owners, so federal programs have also been developed specifically to direct tax incentives to lower- and moderate-income households. These tax incentives are designed to help lower-income households become owners and to help current low-income home owners.

Mortgage Revenue Bonds (MRBs) are tax-exempt bonds issued by state housing agencies for first-time buyers. MRBs reduce new home owners' monthly mortgage costs through subsidized interest rates.[47] State housing agencies began issuing MRBs in the 1970s, and the activity increased in subsequent decades. Figure 5.2 breaks down MRB activity from 1993 to 2001, displaying the number of loans closed and the total issuance. 106,000 loans were closed in 2000 and 86,882 were closed in 2001, up from around 50,000 in 1993.[48] MRBs can be used to purchase new or existing homes, and are restricted to families that meet income limits, typically no greater than either the statewide or area median income. Further, the cost of a MRB-financed home cannot exceed 90% of the average home price in the area.[49]

Another tax provision for low-income home buyers is the Mortgage Credit Certificate. These certificates are provided to first-time home buyers through state housing agencies in the form of a nonrefundable income tax credit of between 10% and 50% of the borrower's annual mortgage interest payments (up to $2,000).[50]

There are also tax strategies designed to help with affordable rental housing. Multifamily bonds issued by state housing agencies are tax-exempt. Developers receive favorable interest rates with multifamily bonds, which reduces their expenses and makes it possible to set lower rents. Through 2000, multifamily bonds funded over 800,000 units. Figure 5.3 shows the breakdown of the expected units, actual units, and dollar amount for multifamily bonds from 1994 to 2001. Annual originations for multifamily bonds in 2001 were expected to be 61,600 units with a value of $3.43 billion.[51]

---

[47] Collins, Belsky, and Retsinas, "Towards a Targeted Homeownership Tax Credit," 8.
[48] National Council of State Housing Finance Agencies, Annual Reports.
[49] Green and Reschovsky, "Using Tax Policy to Increase Homeownership," 56.
[50] Collins, Belsky, and Retsinas, "Towards a Targeted Homeownership Tax Credit," 8.
[51] National Council of State Housing Finance Agencies, Annual Reports.

FIGURE 5.2
Mortgage Revenue Bonds

Year	Loans Closed	Total Issuance
1993	49,225	$5,315,548,310
1994	92,167	$9,168,846,839
1995	103,282	$8,000,664,645
1996	N/A	N/A
1997	104,311	$9,280,654,259
1998	97,857	$8,756,121,540
1999	117,095	$10,316,618,573
2000	106,455	$10,767,892,177
2001	86,882	$9,329,243,868

SOURCE: National Council of State Housing Agencies, Annual Reports, 1992–2001.
NOTE: N/A refers to not available.

Rental Housing Taxation

Tax policies have been an important determinant for how investors and private developers proceed in the creation of rental housing units. As discussed in Chapter 3, prior to 1986, tax code incentives for creating multifamily rental housing were a key reason for private developers to create such housing. They provided needed returns on the investment, thereby lessening risk. These tax incentives were provided in particular by the Economic Recovery Tax Act (ERTA), passed in 1981 in response to recession. These tax code provisions encouraged new construction. However, with a strong economy and significant investment in rental housing, the rental housing market actually became overbuilt in the 1980s. By 1986, concerns had risen about the emphasis on building multifamily housing for tax benefits with little regard for actual market needs. The Tax Reform Act of 1986 sharply changed this scenario by virtually eliminating the tax-favored status of rental housing. This legislation had the net effect of significantly discouraging apartment investments and construction for a long period of time.

FIGURE 5.3
Multi-Family Bond Activity

Year	Expected Units	Actual Units	Dollar Amount
1994	40,091	13,098	$2,266,896,000
1995	54,831	13,918	$2,841,330,006
1996	65,741	15,634	$2,665,571,123
1997	40,341	21,630	$2,577,172,297
1998	41,679	N/A	$2,131,535,942
1999	45,156	22,172	$2,632,764,624
2000	52,279	35,516	$3,151,703,979
2001	61,609	33,156	$3,434,734,411

SOURCE: National Council of State Housing Agencies, Annual Reports, 1992–2001.
NOTE: N/A refers to not available

1986: Low-Income Tax Credit

While the 1986 Tax Reform Act took away many investor incentives for creating rental housing, it simultaneously created the Low-Income Housing Tax Credit (LIHTC). Today, the LIHTC represents the largest federal commitment to affordable housing construction and rehabilitation. As discussed in Chapter 3, the LIHTC provides a ten-year federal income tax credit to private investors (both individuals and corporations) who provide the equity needed to build or rehabilitate housing.

To receive these credits, the owner of the multifamily housing property is required to maintain a designated portion of the units as affordable. This means that at least 20% of the apartments in each unit must be rented to households with incomes below 50% of the area median, and at least 40% rented to households with incomes below 60% of the area median.[52] In the original legislation, the units tagged as affordable had to remain affordable for a fifteen-year period. In 1989, this fifteen-year period was extended in an attempt to preserve the life of the affordable housing stock.

The credits are first allocated to state and local housing finance agencies for proposed projects. Then they are allocated to developers, who in turn sell them to private investors to gain equity for the property and to reduce the costs of construction and rehabilitation. After receiving the credits, the developer is responsible for gathering the financial resources for the pro-

---

[52] Green and Reschovsky, "Using Tax Policy to Increase Homeownership," 57.

ject. One of the primary means of doing so is by using LIHTC in conjunction with other assistance programs (such as Section 8 vouchers or HOME).[53] The National Council of State Housing Agencies estimates that about 67% of allocated LIHTC units receive other subsidies.[54] The LIHTC is the largest, most important program for affordable housing at present, and it brings together numerous groups in partnership to create affordable housing. Since 1987, the General Accounting Office (GAO) estimates, the program has produced around 752,000 units.[55]

HOUSING FINANCE

The nation's housing finance system is characterized by close ties between the public and private sectors, and a number of institutions, developed over time, provide federal support for this system. Chapter 4 outlines the transformation of the nation's housing finance system, whereas this section highlights some of the key organizations, agencies, and regulators involved in the housing finance system from a federal perspective — whether they are directly or only indirectly tied to the federal government.

Mortgage Insurance and the FHA

The National Housing Act of 1934 created the Federal Housing Administration (FHA). As a part of FHA, Congress enacted two major programs to provide mortgage insurance for housing — Section 203b for single-family housing and Section 207 for multifamily housing. Both programs insured longer-term, level-payment fully amortizing mortgages. Before the creation of the FHA, large down payments were typically required to purchase a home, and mortgages had very short repayment terms.[56] As Kenneth Lore explains: "The full faith and credit guaranty provided by FHA induced lenders to offer low down payment, long-term mortgages at more affordable rates. FHA credit enhancement attained a leading role in the single family market and its underwriting standards established national norms with respect to housing construction and design and mortgage loan

---

[53] Green and Reschovsky, "Using Tax Policy to Increase Homeownership," 59.

[54] National Council of State Housing Finance Agencies, *1999 Annual Report.*

[55] Estimates, General Accounting Office, Resources, Community and Economic Development Division, April 2001.

[56] National Association of Home Builders, *Low- & Moderate-Income Housing,* 59.

terms."[57] In 1938, lenders were given the option of assigning defaulted mortgages to the FHA instead of foreclosing on them.

Through the close of World War II, the FHA focused on insuring single-family loans. However, with the end of World War II, there was a major boom in multifamily housing construction. The federal government created a new insurance program, Section 608, to encourage private developers to build rental housing by insuring multifamily mortgages with loan-to-value ratios up to 90%.[58] In 1950, Congress ended the Section 608 program because the immediate housing shortage caused by the return of servicemen and servicewomen from World War II was over. In the 1950s, the demand for multifamily housing was strong. During that time, the insurance of market-rate mortgages was the primary federal role in multifamily finance.

Federal Home Loan Bank System

In 1932, Congress enacted the Federal Home Loan Bank Act to create the Federal Home Loan Bank system. Essentially, this was a reserve system designed to support housing finance, specifically residential mortgage lending and related community investment. The act established twelve regional Federal Home Loan Banks (FHL banks), which were supervised by a Federal Home Loan Bank Board (today, the FHL banks are supervised by the Federal Housing Finance Board). Each of these FHL banks was authorized to borrow from the Treasury and issue tax-free bonds.

Today, the FHL banks have over 7,000 members/shareholders, including commercial banks, thrifts, credit unions, and insurance companies.[59] They are supported by private capital and do not receive any direct taxpayer assistance. Each of the twelve FHL banks have an Affordable Housing Program (AHP) for the creation of low- and moderate-income single-family and multifamily housing. These AHPs provide subsidized interest rate advances and direct subsidies to member institutions.[60] Each of the FHL Banks also administers Community Investment Programs (CIPs), which focus on helping households whose incomes fall within a designated bracket (not to exceed a certain percent of median area income) purchase homes.[61] Finally, in 1997, several of the FHL Banks started Mortgage Partnership Finance (MPF) programs which provide member financial in-

---

[57] Lore, "Challenges and Opportunities for Federal Role," 1.
[58] National Association of Home Builders, *Low- & Moderate-Income Housing,* 60.
[59] Lore, "Challenges and Opportunities for Federal Role," 13.
[60] Ibid., 14.
[61] Ibid.

stitutions an alternative to using the secondary mortgage market (through Freddie Mac and Fannie Mae). With the MPF program the lender retains the credit risk and customer relationship of their loans while shifting the interest rate and prepayment risk to the FHL Bank. Mortgage lenders originate loans for the FHL bank (although the loan is closed in the lender's name) and the FHL bank provides the funding for the closing and owns the loan at the point of origination.[62]

Fannie Mae

Under the National Housing Act Amendments of 1938, the Federal National Mortgage Association (FNMA or Fannie Mae) was created. Fannie Mae was authorized by Congress to purchase, service, or sell any mortgages (or partial interests in mortgages) insured by FHA. The creation of Fannie Mae marked the creation of the secondary market, which allowed for greater flows of mortgage money. In 1954, Fannie Mae became a mixed-ownership corporation owned in part by private stockholders.[63] Under Title VIII of the Housing and Urban Development Act of 1968, Fannie Mae was made a government-sponsored enterprise (GSE) and became a privately-owned corporation.

Over time, Fannie Mae's range of services has increased dramatically. In 1970, Fannie Mae was authorized to purchase conventional home mortgages. By the early 1980s, Fannie Mae was able to purchase two- to four-family home loans and multifamily housing loans.[64] In 1992, Congress enacted legislation for Fannie Mae and Freddie Mac to set goals related to affordable housing (regulated by HUD) in the following areas: low- and moderate-income housing; central cities, rural areas, and other underserved areas; and housing affordable to very-low-income families and low-income families in low-income areas.[65] Fannie Mae responded by launching the Opening Doors to Affordable Housing initiative as a means of targeting housing finance toward housing projects for lower-income Americans. Also in 1992, Fannie Mae became the largest issuer of mortgage-backed securities, surpassing the two other primary government-sponsored enterprises (Freddie Mac and Ginnie Mae).[66] Fannie Mae also purchases mortgages and holds them in their portfolio — naturally hedging for interest rate risk.

---

[62] Ibid.
[63] Fannie Mae, "Our History."
[64] Ibid.
[65] Lore, "Challenges and Opportunities for Federal Role," 14.
[66] Fannie Mae, "Our History."

Freddie Mac

The Emergency Home Finance Act of 1970 created the Federal Home Loan Mortgage Corporation (FHLMC or Freddie Mac). Freddie Mac was chartered to purchase and securitize conventional loans originated by savings and loans.[67] Like Fannie Mae, Freddie Mac provides a continuous flow of funds to mortgage lenders. Freddie Mac operates by purchasing mortgages from lenders and packaging them into securities which are in turn sold to investors, or they will hold the mortgages in portfolio (while hedging for interest rate risk). This continuous flow of credit provides home owners and renters with lower housing costs and better access to home financing.[68] The mortgage lenders then use the money they gain from selling loans to Freddie Mac to fund new mortgages for home buyers and apartment owners. Just as stock and bond markets put investor capital to work for corporations, Freddie Mac puts private investor capital to work for home buyers and apartment owners.[69] Freddie Mac purchases both single-family and multi-family loans.

Freddie Mac was under the regulation of the Federal Home Loan Bank Board until 1989. With the 1989 passage of the Financial Institutions Reform, Recovery and Enforcement Act (FIRREA) in response to the savings and loan crisis, the Federal Home Loan Bank Board was dissolved and its functions split among several agencies and organizations. At that time, Freddie Mac's charter was altered to be very similar to Fannie Mae's, and it became a privately-owned corporation with private stockholders, while at the same time remaining a government-sponsored enterprise (GSE).

FEDERAL FINANCIAL REGULATORS

Behind many of the federal programs that support housing are offices and organizations that regulate all activity related to housing. These regulatory groups represent yet another facet to the federal government's extensive support of housing finance initiatives around the country. Although not all of these regulators are directly committed to housing, all have a major impact in one way or another.

---

[67] Lore, "Challenges and Opportunities for Federal Role," 12.
[68] Freddie Mac, "About Freddie Mac."
[69] Freddie Mac, "Twelve Frequently Asked Questions About Freddie Mac."

Federal Housing Finance Board

The Federal Housing Finance Board (FHFB) regulates the twelve regional Federal Home Loan Banks. As noted, the FHL banks were created in 1932 to improve the supply of funds to lenders specializing in loans for home mortgages. In addition to supervising the FHL banks, the Federal Housing Finance Board has regulatory authority and supervisory oversight responsibility for the Office of Finance.[70]

The Federal Housing Finance Board ensures that the FHL banks carry out their housing and community development finance mission. It also ensures that the FHL banks remain adequately capitalized and that they are able to raise funds in the capital markets.[71] An independent regulatory agency, it is part of the executive branch of the U.S. government. The board consists of five members, four appointed by the president for seven-year terms with the fifth member being the HUD secretary. The Federal Housing Finance Board is supported by assessments from the twelve FHL banks, which themselves are privately capitalized, government-sponsored enterprises.[72]

Office of Thrift Supervision

The Office of Thrift Supervision (OTS) is an office of the Department of the Treasury. OTS was created as part of the Financial Institutions Reform, Recovery, and Enforcement Act (FIRREA) of 1989 to replace the Federal Home Loan Bank Board. OTS is the primary regulator of all federal and several state-chartered thrift institutions (including savings banks and savings and loan associations). OTS has the power to charter federal savings and loan institutions and savings banks and to set capital standards for both federally and state-chartered institutions. It is funded by assessments and fees levied on the institutions it regulates.[73]

Office of the Comptroller of the Currency

The Office of the Comptroller of the Currency (OCC) is an office in the Department of the Treasury and was established in 1863. The OCC charters, regulates, and supervises all national banks. The office is headed by the

---

[70] Federal Housing Finance Board, "About Us."
[71] Ibid.
[72] Ibid.
[73] Office of Thrift Supervision.

Comptroller of the Currency, who is appointed by the president with the approval of the Senate for a five-year term. The comptroller is also a director of the Federal Deposit Insurance Corporation (FDIC) and a director of the Neighborhood Reinvestment Corporation.[74] OCC examiners analyze banks' loan and investment portfolios, funds management, capital, earnings, liquidity, sensitivity to market risk, and compliance with consumer banking laws, including the Community Reinvestment Act. They also review internal controls, internal and external audit, and compliance with law.[75] The OCC is responsible for helping banks develop new products and practices, and for ensuring that all Americans have fair and equal access to financial services, which is of vital importance for those seeking a mortgage for the purchase of a home.

Federal Deposit Insurance Corporation

The Federal Deposit Insurance Corporation (FDIC) insures the deposits in all national banks. An individual is covered up to $100,000 at each bank. The FDIC was created in the 1930s as part of the response to the depression, in which thousands of people lost the money in their bank. With the passage of FIRREA in 1989, the role of the FDIC was expanded. The cap on the amount to be insured in each account was raised to $100,000. Further, as a result of the S&L crisis, which brought about FIRREA, the Federal Savings and Loan Insurance Corporation (FSLIC) was folded into the FDIC. Thus the FDIC currently insures deposits in both savings banks and S&Ls. Banks and S&Ls are private institutions, but they also have a direct tie and support from the federal goverment through the FDIC.

Office of Federal Housing Enterprise Oversight

The Office of Federal Housing Enterprise (OFHEO) was created by the Federal Housing Enterprises Financial Safety and Soundness Act of 1992. OFHEO is an independent entity within HUD and it is headed by a director who is appointed by the president for a five-year term. The primary mission of OFHEO is to monitor and ensure the capital adequacy and financial safety and soundness of Fannie Mae and Freddie Mac.[76] These two government-sponsored enterprises are the nation's largest housing finance institutions. OFHEO develops a risk-based capital standard, prohibits excessive executive compensation, and issues regulations concerning cap-

---

[74] Office of the Comptroller of the Currency, "About the OCC."

[75] Ibid.

[76] Office of Federal Housing and Enterprise Oversight, "About OFHEO."

ital and enforcement standards.[77] OFHEO is funded through assessments of Freddie Mac and Fannie Mae.

The legislation that created the OFHEO also stipulated that certain affordable housing goals be met by Freddie Mac and Fannie Mae. The Department of Housing and Urban Development serves as the "housing mission" regulator for Fannie Mae and Freddie Mac and as such sets the specific affordable housing goals for the two institutions through the federal regulatory process.[78]

CURRENT STATUS OF FEDERAL DIRECT EXPENDITURES AND TAX EXPENDITURES

Direct Expenditures

The federal government dedicates a significant amount of money to housing support every fiscal year. The Department of Housing and Urban Development represents housing and urban interests within the executive branch and allocates a variety of direct federal spending. Figure 5.4 provides an overview of direct housing assistance outlays for HUD from 1979 to 2001. In the latter half of the 1990s, direct housing assistance has remained relatively consistent from year to year. For fiscal year 2001, HUD provided $33.649 billion in program outlays. Figure 5.5 depicts the budget outlays by program. Support for Section 8 is nearly half of HUD's budget for direct assistance, at over $16 billion, making Section 8 the largest housing program by far. Public housing and CDBG also have a significant portion of the budget at nearly $7.5 billion and $5 billion respectively.

The Rural Housing Service (RHS), a branch of the U.S. Department of Agriculture, also provides significant direct support for housing across the nation. RHS operates a range of programs to support affordable housing and community development in rural areas. In fiscal 2001, RHS committed $1.052 billion to rural housing programs. Figure 5.6 shows the budget outlays for RHS in fiscal 2001. As with the HUD direct assistance programs, the RHS program that uses the bulk of the total budget is a type of rental assistance program, known as the Rural Rental Assistance (RA) program. The RA program provides the landlord with the difference between the tenant's contribution (30% of adjusted income) and the monthly rental rate, including the cost of all utilities and services.[79]

---

[77] Ibid.

[78] Ibid.

[79] Housing Assistance Council, "Information about Rural Housing Assistance Programs."

FIGURE 5.4
Federal Budget HUD Outlays, Housing Assistance, 1979–2001 (in Millions)

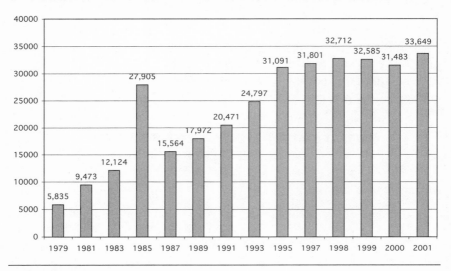

SOURCE: Budget of the U.S. Government.

Given that much of HUD's and the RHS's direct expenditures for housing go for rental support, it is worthwhile to look more closely at the status of the nation's direct rental subsidies. First, there are three forms of direct rental subsidies: public housing, tenant-based subsidies, and private-project-based subsidies. Figure 5.7 provides a breakdown of the nation's total subsidized units. The figure indicates that the private-project-based subsidies are the largest form of assistance. However, current trends indicate that the allocation for tenant-based subsidies will likely increase in upcoming years as the other two forms of subsidy decrease. Looking more closely at direct rental-project subsidies, Figure 5.8 provides a further analysis of the project-based housing programs. Section 8 provides the most support for project-based subsidies through its financial support of new and rehabilitated housing. Finally, Figure 5.9 shows the relationship between existing and new rental commitments made by the federal government from 1977 to 2000. The 1970s were the high point for federal commitment to new rental construction, and since then there has been relatively little new construction. It is also interesting to note that existing rental housing declined substantially in the mid-1990s, but increased dramatically in 2000.

FIGURE 5.5
HUD Budget Outlays for Select Programs, FY 2001 (in Millions)

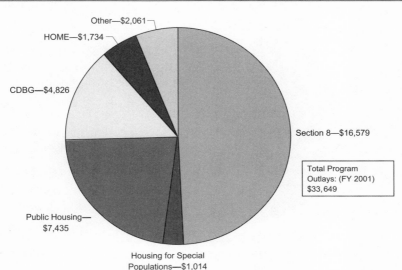

Other—$2,061

HOME—$1,734

CDBG—$4,826

Section 8—$16,579

Total Program
Outlays: (FY 2001)
$33,649

Public Housing—
$7,435

Housing for Special
Populations—$1,014

SOURCE: Belsky and Brown. "Federal Housing Assistance."
DATA SOURCE: HUD, Office of the Budget, "Congressional Justifications for 2001 Estimates."

Tax Expenditures

One of the primary means by which the nation has supported housing has been the tax code. Over the years, the federal government has provided significant support to housing through tax expenditures, primarily for homeownership, but also for rental housing. Generally speaking, the direct expenditures discussed above tend to benefit low- and moderate-income households, while federal tax expenditures tend to benefit middle- and upper-income households. Further, tax breaks tend to be most beneficial for home owners, especially given that the two largest tax expenditures — namely the deduction of mortgage interest and the deduction for local property taxes — only effect home owners.

In fiscal 2001 federal housing tax expenditures totaled $121.2 billion dollars. Figure 5.10 shows how this $121.2 billion is broken down according to program and policy. The mortgage interest deduction is by far the largest form of federal support at $64.51 billion dollars. The next largest portions go to the property tax/real estate tax deduction at $22.41

FIGURE 5.6
RHS Budget Outlays for Select Programs, FY 2001 (in Millions)

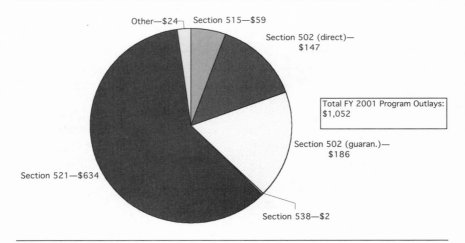

SOURCE: Belsky and Brown. "Federal Housing Assistance."
DATA SOURCE: Budget of the U.S. Government, FY 2002, Appendix.

billion and the exclusion of capital gains at $19.09 billion. Again, each of these benefits home owners, not renters. They represent a combined $106.0 billion dollars. Figure 5.10 also shows that the LIHTC costs the federal government $3.22 billion, and the exclusion of bond interest for both owners and rentals combined totals around $1 billion in tax expenditures.

Tax policy has obviously had an impact on such areas as the homeownership rate, the construction of single-family housing, the production of low-income and rental housing, and consumer choice related to investments in housing as compared to other investments.

Total Federal Housing Expenditures

Considering both direct and indirect federal expenditures, the housing sector receives a significant amount of federal support. Recognizing that there are analytical concerns in simply combining tax expenditures for housing and direct housing expenditures (like trying to add apples and oranges), it is still interesting to look at the two together. If fiscal 2001 HUD program outlays of $33.65 billion (Figure 5.5) are combined with the fiscal 2001 tax expenditures of $121.2 billion (Figure 5.10), housing received $154.75 billion in federal support in fiscal 2001.

FIGURE 5.7
The Nation's Direct Rental Subsidies, 1999

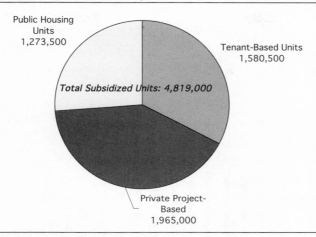

SOURCE: Belsky and Brown. "Federal Housing Assistance."
DATA SOURCE: General Accounting Office, Resources, Community, and Economic Dev. Divisions, estimates based on various sources, 1999.

FIGURE 5.8
Project-Based Housing Programs, 1999

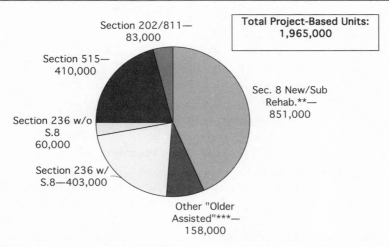

SOURCE: Belsky and Brown. "Federal Housing Assistance."
DATA SOURCE: General Accounting Office, Resources, Community, and Economic Development Divisions, estimates based on various sources, 1999. *Number of Units adjusted for overlap to account for multiple subsidies. **Sec. 8 New/Sub Rehab. Includes approximately 207,131 Sec. 202 Direct Loan Properties. *** "Older Assisted" includes Section 221(d)(3) BMIR, Rent Supplement, Section 8 PD and Section 8 LMSA units.

FIGURE 5.9
New vs. Existing Rental Commitments

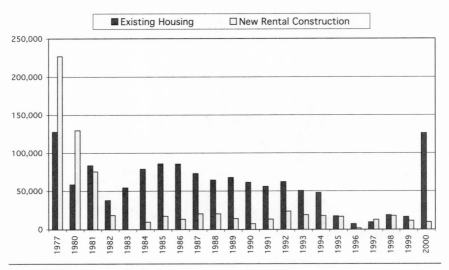

SOURCE: Belsky and Brown, "Federal Housing Assistance."
DATA SOURCE: The Green Book, U.S. House of Representatives, Committee on Ways and Means, 6 October 2000.

It is worth noting that compared to the functions of transportation, agriculture, education, and health and medical care, only health and medical care receives greater support than housing. As outlined in Figure 5.11, budget outlays in fiscal 2001 by function were $55.2 billion for transportation, $26.6 billion for agriculture, $57.3 billion for education related services, and $390.1 billion for health and medicare. Thus, since the close of World War II and the passage of the Housing Act of 1949, which declared that every American should have a decent home and suitable living environment, significant federal resources have been directed, and continue to be directed, toward housing.

As another way of portraying federal spending for housing, Figure 5.12 outlines past and projected spending for federal tax expenditures, assisted-housing budget authority, and assisted-housing outlays. The figure shows that in 1976 direct assisted-housing spending was the largest portion of federal housing spending, with budget authority exceeding both tax expenditures and assisted-housing outlays. However, since 1984, tax expenditures have made up the largest portion of the total amount committed to housing by the federal government.

FIGURE 5.10

Federal Tax Expenditures for Housing, FY 2001 (in Billions of Dollars)

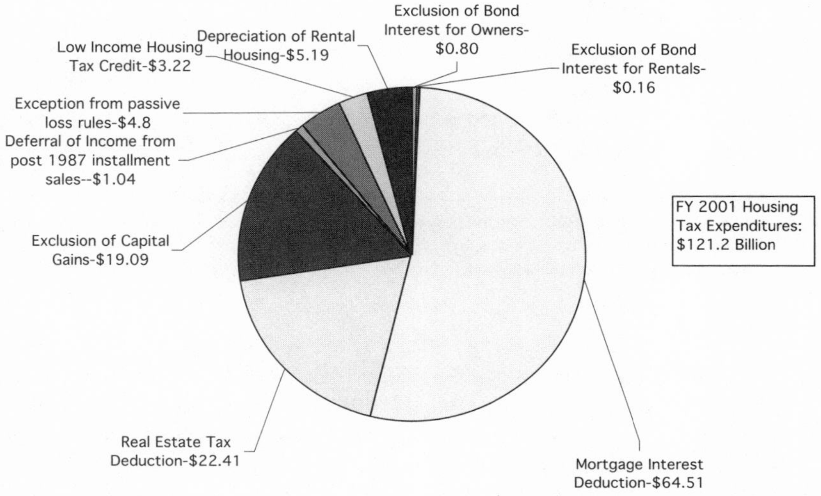

Low Income Housing Tax Credit-$3.22

Depreciation of Rental Housing-$5.19

Exclusion of Bond Interest for Owners-$0.80

Exclusion of Bond Interest for Rentals-$0.16

Exception from passive loss rules-$4.8

Deferral of Income from post 1987 installment sales--$1.04

Exclusion of Capital Gains-$19.09

FY 2001 Housing Tax Expenditures: $121.2 Billion

Real Estate Tax Deduction-$22.41

Mortgage Interest Deduction-$64.51

SOURCE: Analytical Perspectives, Budget of the U.S. Governments, FY 2003.

THE ROLE OF HUD AND THE GROWING IMPORTANCE OF STATE AND LOCAL ACTIONS

The creation of HUD in 1965 signified a further federal commitment to housing and urban development. The government established a cabinet level department to provide expertise and research, and to operate programs in housing and in urban and community development. Today, HUD is particularly involved in helping to increase homeownership, maintain and expand the affordable housing stock, oversee a wide range of direct housing expenditure and insurance programs, and ensure equal housing access for all Americans.

However, over the last three decades, there has been a growing emphasis on a decentralized approach to housing and community development initiatives. From the close of World War II through the 1960s, the federal government expanded its housing assistance programs and its financial commitments to housing and urban issues. By the early 1970s, the financing and operation of housing programs from the federal perspective was increasingly called into question. An alternative approach was devised

FIGURE 5.11
Federal Outlays in Other Policy Areas (by Function)

	$ Billions
Transportation	55.2
Agriculture	26.6
Education, Training Employment and Social Services	57.3
Health and Medicare	390.1

Spending is actual number for 2001. See: http://www.whitehouse.gov/omb/budget/fy2003/pdf/hist.pdf
These numbers are budgetary calculations from the Office of Management and Budget which examine federal spending by function rather than agency

that would disperse much of the responsibility for planning, financing, and operating housing programs. This decentralized, or federalist approach was first implemented with the CDGB program in 1974. State and local governments are given authority to devise local programs, and also are responsible for partially funding the projects. They have created departments, housing authorities, and community partnerships to address local housing concerns.

Two key entities that have been established and expanded as a result of this "devolution" are the state housing finance agencies (HFAs) and community development corporations (CDCs). CDCs specialize in local areas and focus on specific neighborhood needs. They are designed to be a grassroots network that addresses a range of housing and housing-related community needs. The state housing finance agencies have proven in recent years to be a highly effective means of delivering federal housing assistance. For example, state HFAs administer the private tax-exempt Housing Bond and Housing Credit Programs.[80] State HFAs have issued $158 billion in MRBs to finance more than 2 million first-time, low-income home buyers, and $42 billion in multifamily housing bonds for 800,000 apartments, and administer 40% of all HOME funds.[81] Given their pivotal role, HFAs are in an excellent position to assess the housing needs of the citizens in their states. It is likely that HFAs and CDCs will play an even greater role in the future.

In coming decades, HUD will continue to be a key player in federal housing support. According to its own statement of "mission and history,"

---

[80] McEvoy, "Statement of National Council of State Housing Agencies," 3.
[81] Ibid., 3–4.

FIGURE 5.12
Federal Spending for Housing, 1976–2006

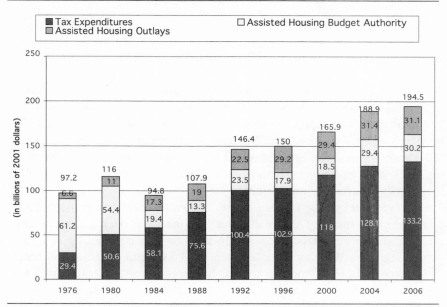

Source: Cushing N. Dolbeare, "Changing Priorities: The Federal Budget and Housing Assistance, 1976–2006," National Low-Income Housing Coalition, May 2001. "Assisted Housing" is a government function as defined by the Office of Management and Budget and includes spending for housing programs in addition to HUD.

HUD currently focuses on the following program areas: 1. creating opportunities for homeownership; 2. providing housing assistance for low-income persons; 3. working to create, rehabilitate, and maintain the nation's affordable housing; 4. enforcing fair housing laws; 5. helping the homeless; 6. spurring economic growth in distressed neighborhoods; and 7. helping local communities meet their development needs.[82] HUD administers and oversees numerous housing programs that will continue to be important components of the overall provision of housing around the nation.

However, as housing programs continue to "devolve," state and local agencies and institutions will become increasingly important. In the final analysis, housing issues are generally local or, at times, state issues, and the needs of each community and state vary widely. The federal government can provide national programs and incentives, but the real solutions

---

[82] U.S. Department of Housing and Community Affairs, "Mission & History."

often come at the local level, community by community and housing development by housing development.

CONCLUSIONS

Since the depression, the federal government has played a significant role in shaping the nation's housing through a wide variety of actions. A number of direct housing programs have been established, and over the years they have shifted and evolved. Significant tax expenditures have encouraged both homeownership and rental housing development. The nation's highly developed housing finance system comprises both direct and indirect links to the federal government.

However, over the last three decades, state and local governments have taken on larger housing responsibilities, and there has been a growing emphasis on a decentralized approach to housing and community development initiatives. With the establishment of the CDBG program and other block grant programs, more emphasis has been placed on state and local governments to devise local programs, and almost every state has established a state housing finance agency and other state housing departments to administer the Low-Income Tax Credit, CDBG funds, the HOME program, and many other housing-related activities. Significant resources are provided from the federal government, but much of the implementation is at the state and local levels.

This development — coupled with the realization that the nation now faces new and very different housing challenges than it did in 1949 — provides the opportunity for a new housing policy framework to match the challenges and the realities of the twenty-first century.

Appendix I

SELECTED FEDERAL LEGISLATION AND EXECUTIVE ORDERS RELATED TO HOUSING IN THE UNITED STATES, 1932 TO 2000

Year	Legislation	Critical Housing Components	Brief Description
1932	Federal Home Loan Bank Act		• Created a reserve system to support housing finance. Twelve regional *Federal Home Loan Banks* were established and supervised by a Federal Home Loan Bank Board. • Home Loan Banks were given authority to borrow from the Treasury and issue tax-free bonds.
1934	National Housing Act (Public Law 73-479)	• Title I: Property Improvements (housing renovation and modernization) • Title II: Mutual Mortgage Insurance (insurance of mortgages on one- to four-family homes) • Title III: Government National Mortgage Association	• Created the *Federal Housing Administration (FHA),* headed by a federal housing administrator and backed by mutual mortgage insurance fund. • Under Title III, a national mortgage association was created to provide a *secondary market* for home mortgage by the purchase and sale of first mortgages. • Continuation of long-term mortgages with moderate interest rates (which began under the HOLC, Home Owners Loan Corporation). • Authorized insurance deposits for savings and loan associations.
1937	Housing Act of 1937 (Public Law 75-412)		• Authorized the *Public Housing Program.* • Loans given to local public housing agencies for development, acquisition,

			or administration of low-rent housing or slum clearance projects.
1938	National Housing Act Amendments of 1938 (Public Law 75-424)	• Amended Title III	• Created the *Federal National Mortgage Association (FNMA).* • FNMA was authorized to purchase, service, or sell any mortgages or partial interests in mortgages insured by FHA.
1949	Housing Act of 1949 (Public Law 81-560)	• Title I: Slum Clearance and Urban Redevelopment (later known as Urban Renewal)	• Expressed a vision for housing in America; goal was to provide a "decent home and suitable living environment" for all American families. • Provided loans to localities for slum clearance, community development, and redevelopment projects. • Dual objectives of providing housing for low-income families and redeveloping urban areas.
1954	Housing Act of 1954 (Public Law 83-560)	• Title VII: Section 701: Comprehensive Planning Assistance (Urban Renewal was designated as title for these expanded programs.)	• Expanded the Housing Act of 1949 and provided more support and funding for urban renewal. • *Section 221 (d)(3):* enacted as part of this housing act. Allows HUD to provide mortgage insurance to finance rental or cooperative multifamily housing for moderate-income households. Public agencies, nonprofits, limited-dividend cooperative organizations, private builders, or investors can obtain these mortgages. Note: Section 221 (d)(4) was enacted in 1959 and serves virtually the same function as Section 221 (d)(3).
1959	Housing Act of 1959 (Public Law 86-372)	• Title II: Section 202: Senior Citizen Housing (direct loans)	• Authorized FHA administrator to make direct federal loans for rental housing for the elderly to private nonprofit corporations.
1964	Housing Act of 1964 (Public Law 88-560)	• Title III: Section 312: Rehabilitation Loans	• Title III authorized the FHA administrator to make low-interest-rate federal loans to owners or tenants of homes or business

			property in urban renewal areas to finance the rehabilitation of buildings that could meet new codes and not be demolished.
		• Title VIII: Part 1: Federal-State Training Programs	• Title VIII gave federal grants to states to help train employees and to develop skills necessary to economic and community development.
1965	Housing and Urban Development Act of 1965 (Public Law 89-117)	• Title I: Rent Supplements • Title VII: Community Facilities	• Title I created a new program by which rent supplement payments were made available for privately owned housing rented to low-income individuals or families who were elderly, handicapped, displaced by governmental action, occupants of substandard housing, etc. • Title VII authorized grants to local organizations to finance neighborhood facilities such as youth centers.
1965	Department of Housing and Urban Development Act (Public Law 89-174)	• Creation of the Department of Housing and Urban Development (HUD)	• Established the *Department of Housing and Urban Development (HUD)* to be headed by a secretary of housing and urban development. Secretary of HUD advises and suggests policy strategies to the president with respect to housing and urban development issues. • Transferred the functions, powers, and duties of the Housing and Home Finance Agency, the Federal Housing Administration, and the Public Housing Administration to the secretary of HUD. • Transferred the Federal National Mortgage Association (FNMA or Fannie Mae) as a corporate entity to HUD.
1966	Demonstration Cities and Metropolitan Development Act of 1966 (Public Law 89-754)	• Title I: *Model Cities* • Title X: Sections 1010 and 1011: Urban Research and Technology	• Title I authorized HUD to provide both grants and technical assistance to help communities either rebuild or restore entire pieces of cities by planning and developing former slum and blighted areas. The grants could cover up to 80% of the cost of planning and developing a project.

			• Title X authorized HUD to work closely with and assist the housing industry in developing technology to help reduce the cost and improve the quality of housing.
1968	Civil Rights Act of 1968	• Title VIII: *Fair Housing*	• Made it unlawful to refuse to sell or rent or to make unavailable a dwelling (or services and facilities linked to that dwelling) to any person because of race, color, religion, or national origin. • It also made it unlawful to deny a loan or other financial assistance for the purchase, construction, repair, or maintenance of a dwelling because of race, color, religion, or national origin. The legislation made HUD responsible for administering the Fair Housing provisions.
1968	Housing and Urban Development Act of 1968 (Public Law 90-448)	• Title I: Home-ownership for Lower-Income Families • Title IV: New Communities • Title VIII: Federal National Mortgage Association partitioned into Fannie Mae and the Government National Mortgage Association (Ginnie Mae) • Title XI: Urban Property Protection and Reinsurance • Title XIV: Interstate Land Sales	• Title I helped foster home ownership among lower-income households by helping make FHA-insured home mortgage loans available to such households and establishing minimum down payments. • Title IV authorized HUD to guarantee obligations issued by private developers to help finance the land acquisition and land development costs of new communities. • Title VIII partitioned the Federal National Mortgage Association into two separate corporations, one to be known as the *Federal National Mortgage Association (FNMA or Fannie Mae)* to conduct secondary mortgage market operations, and the other to be known as the *Government National Mortgage Association (GNMA or Ginnie Mae)*. FNMA became a government-sponsored privately owned corporation. • Title XI authorized HUD to provide private insurers with reinsurance against losses due to riots or civil disorders.

- Title XIV made it unlawful for any developer to sell or lease any lot in any subdivision (defined as one with 50 or more lots for sale as part of a promotional plan).
- *Section 235*: First major subsidy program that helped low-income households purchase rather than rent housing. Private builders produced predominantly new homes, which were financed through private lending institutions and the mortgages insured by the FHA at market interest rate. HUD made interest subsidy payments to the mortgagee.
- *Section 236*: Designed to produce new and substantially rehabilitated rental units for low-income households. Allowed private nonprofit and limited-profit developers to produce housing; projects were financed through private lending institutions and mortgages were insured by the FHA. Mortgage interest payments were made to the lenders as if the interest rate of the mortgage was equal to 1%, and HUD paid the mortgagee the difference between 1% and market rate.
- Note: Both Section 235 and Section 236 were suspended in 1973.

1969	Housing and Urban Development Act of 1969 (Public Law 91-152)		• Focused on low- and moderate-income housing programs. Expanded capabilities of GNMA and FHA insurance programs.
1970	Emergency Home Finance Act of 1970 (Public Law 91-351)	• Created Federal Home Loan Mortgage Corporation (FHLMC or Freddie Mac).	• Created *Federal Home Loan Mortgage Corporation (FHLMC or Freddie Mac)* as a private corporation to operate in the secondary market to help increase availability of residential mortgage financing (similar to Fannie Mac).

• Freddie Mac is authorized to purchase and make commitments to purchase mortgages on residential property from any Federal Home Loan Bank, the Federal Savings and Loan Insurance Corporation, any other member of a Federal Home Loan Bank, or any financial institution that has deposits or accounts which are insured by a Federal agency.

1970	Housing and Urban Development Act of 1970 (Public Law 91-609)	• Title V: Research and Technology • Title VII: National Urban Policy and New Communities	• Title VII declared that the federal government had to assume responsibility for the development of a national urban growth policy. • In conjunction with this goal, developed a *Community Development Corporation* within HUD. The corporation was authorized to guarantee bonds to private developers and state land development agencies to help finance new community development programs.
1974	Housing and Community Development Act of 1974 (Public Law 93-383)	• Title I: *Community Development Block Grants (CDBG)* • Title II: Assisted Housing *Section 8*: Lower-income Rental Assistance • Title III: Mortgage Credit Assistance Section 306: Compensation for Substantial Defects Section 307: Coinsurance Section 308: Experimental Financing • Title VI: Mobile Home Construction and Safety Standards • Title VIII: Miscellaneous	• Title I fundamentally changed the way in which the federal government provided financial assistance to communities for physical development. The *community development block grants* provided a single program of 100% grants with which localities could formulate their own development plans and programs (instead of having specific categorical development programs determined by the federal government). • Title II revamped lower-income housing assistance programs, in effect rewriting the United States Housing Act of 1937. • *Section 8:* Established a low-income housing assistance program. A major goal of the program was to refocus federal housing policy away from putting lots of low-income households in the same units in

Section 802: State
Housing Finance
Agency Coinsurance
Section 809: National
Instituted of Building
Science (NIBS)
Section 810: Urban
Homesteading
Section 811:
Counseling and
Technical Assistance

specific communities. Section 8 has
evolved a great deal since 1974.
Initially it provided subsidies that
reduced the interest rate to finance
low-income housing. Yet as rents
increased over the years to cover
operating costs, this became less
helpful for low-income households.
The program was expanded to
include tenant-based assistance with
both certificate and housing vouchers.
The voucher program allows
households to rent anywhere they
choose as long as the housing meets
HUD's rent and quality standards and
the landlord agrees to participate
in the program. The other expansion
of the program was project-based
assistance, which attached the Section
8 subsidies to particular housing units.
- Title III allowed national banks and
federal savings and loan associations
to provide more and broader
consumer home mortgage credit
assistance.
- Title VI established construction and
safety standards for mobile homes.

1974   Emergency
Home
Purchase
Assistance
Act of 1974
(Public Law
93-449)

Provided GNMA the authority to
purchase certain residential mortgages.
In some cases, the president could
direct GNMA to purchase loans when
inflationary conditions and related
governmental actions were having a
severely disproportionate effect on the
housing industry.

1975   Emergency
Housing Act
of 1975
(Public Law
94-50)

- Title I: Emergency
Homeowner's
Mortgage Relief

Title I provided relief for homeowners
facing foreclosure of mortgages on their
principle residences in two ways:
through loans from private financial
institutions, and through payments from
HUD to the mortgagee for debt service
on the mortgage for up to $250 per
month for up to two years.

1976	Housing Authorization Act of 1976 (Public Law 94-375)		This legislation authorized additional funding for various housing assistance programs and for operating assistance to public housing. It broadened the FHA insurance program.
1977	Housing and Community Development Act of 1977 (Public Law 95-128)	• Title I: Community Development • Title III: Federal Housing Administration Mortgage Insurance and Related Programs • Title IV: Lending Powers of Federal Savings and Loan Associations; Secondary Market Authorities • Title V: Rural Housing • Title VI: National Urban Policy • Title VIII: Community Reinvestment Act	• Title I helped to broaden scope of the CDBG program. • Title III increased the maximum mortgage amounts that could be insured and decreased down payment requirements for purchasing homes for specific mortgages insured under Sections 203, 220, etc. • Title IV liberalized lending powers of federal savings and loan associations and authorized HUD to require that when GNMA purchased mortgages while trying to stabilize the housing industry, such purchases promote homeownership opportunities for moderate-income families and finance rehabilitation of older dwellings. • Title VIII stated that banks and savings and loan associations were required to meet the credit as well as deposit needs of the communities in which they were chartered to do business, including an affirmative obligation to help meet the credit needs of local communities. This also required federal financial supervisory agencies to assess the institution's record in meeting such needs, including those of low- and moderate-income neighborhoods.
1978	Housing and Community Development Amendments of 1978	• Title I: Community and Neighborhood Development and Conservation • Title II: Housing Assistance Programs • Title IV: Congregate Services • Title V: Rural Housing	• Title I revised the Section 312 rehabilitation program to give priority to loan applications from low- and moderate-income persons (defined as those with incomes not exceeding 95 percent of area median) who own the property and will live in it after rehabilitation. • Title II gave further assistance to rental projects in order to protect the

- Title VI: Neighborhood Reinvestment Corporation
- Title VII: Neighborhood Self-Help Development
- Title VIII: Liveable Cities
- Title IX: Miscellaneous

insurance fund against claims because of foreclosures and to preserve the low- and moderate-income housing stock.

- Title IV established a program supporting congregate services for elderly and handicapped persons to continue living independently and not be institutionalized.
- Title VI established a Neighborhood Reinvestment Corporation as a tax-exempt nongovernmental agency to institutionalize and expand the work of the Urban Reinvestment Task Force in revitalizing housing in older urban neighborhoods.
- Title VII recognized that urban neighborhoods are a national resource and therefore should be conserved and revitalized, especially through the work of neighborhood organizations (voluntary, nonprofit, represented by and accountable to neighborhood residents).
- Title VIII declared that the encouragement of development and/or preservation of artistic, cultural, and historic resource is an important and appropriate function of the federal government, especially in terms of assisted housing and community development activities. The primary purpose of this title was to assist organizations that foster more suitable living environments through expansion of cultural opportunities, particularly for low- and moderate-income residents of deteriorated neighborhoods.
- Title IX, among other things, required HUD to investigate the extent of housing displacement resulting from housing and community development programs and to devise ways to minimize such involuntary displacement.

1979	Housing and Community Development Amendments of 1979 (Public Law 96-153)	• Title I: Community and Neighborhood Development and Conservation • Title II: Housing Assistance Programs • Title III: Program Amendments and Extensions • Title IV: Interstate Land Sales • Title V: Rural Housing	• Title I made *Urban Development Action Grants (UDAG)* available to cities or urban counties that did not meet the minimum standards established by HUD. • Title V reauthorized several rural housing programs and altered the definition of "low income" to mean 80 percent of the median income for the area.
1980	Housing and Community Development Act of 1980 (Public Law 96-399)	• Title I: Community and Neighborhood Development and Conservation • Title II: Housing Assistance Programs • Title III: Program Amendments and Extensions • Title IV: Planning Assistance • Title V: Rural Housing • Title VI: Condominium and Cooperative Conversion Protection and Abuse Relief	• Title I amended defining data for metropolitan areas to use CDBG funds and promoted energy efficiency. It also required more information for UDAG applications for historic preservation purposes. • Under Title II a new section was added to the United States Housing Act of 1937 that provided a Comprehensive Improvement Assistance Program (CIAP) for public housing; this program provided grants on a competitive basis to public housing agencies to improve physical conditions and management of public housing units. • Title III, among other things, changed all references in laws *from "mobile homes" to "manufactured homes."* • Title IV centered around the defining of National Policy Objectives—plans and strategies to promote community conservation activities, increase housing and employment choices (especially for lower-income families, women, the elderly, and handicapped persons), and encourage energy conservation and orderly growth and development. • Title VI adopted the vision that lending practices allowing rental housing to be converted into condominium or cooperative

			ownership and adversely affected lower-income, elderly, or handicapped persons should be discouraged. • Title VI included provisions for consumer protection related to such developments of rental property into condominiums or cooperative units.
1981	Housing and Community Development Amendments of 1981; Title III of the Omnibus Budget Reconciliation Act of 1981 (Public Law 97-35)	• Subtitle A: Housing and Community Development Part 1: Community and Economic Development Part 2: Housing Assistance Programs Part 3: Program Amendments and Extensions Part 5: Rural Housing Part 6: Multifamily Mortgage Foreclosure Part 7: Effective Date	• Extended CDBG, UDAG, Urban Homesteading, and Rehabilitation Loan programs. • Reauthorized ongoing assistance programs at substantially reduced level from previous years.
1982	Garn-St. Germaine Depository Institutions Act		• Allowed S&Ls to diversify their assets to increase profits. • This act allowed investment in the following assets: commercial, corporate, business, or agricultural loans (10%), consumer loans (30%), loans secured by non-residential real estate (40%), and personal property (10%).
1983	Housing and Urban-Rural Recovery Act of 1983; Titles I through V of the Domestic Housing and International Recovery and	• Title I: Community and Neighborhood Development and Conservation • Title II: Housing Assistance Programs • Title III: Rental Housing	• Title I made the primary CDBG objective to benefit low- and moderate-income people. It also increased ability of small cities to compete for UDAGs. • Title III adopted programs to make grants for rehabilitation of privately owned rental properties and for new development of such properties. Title

	Financial Stability Act (Public Law 98-181)	Rehabilitation and Production Program • Title IV: Program Amendments and Extensions • Title V: Rural Housing	III also created Housing Development Grants (HoDAG).
1984	Housing and Community Development Technical Amendments Act of 1984 (Public Law 98-479)		• This legislation primarily adopted technical and clarifying amendments to legislation related to CDBG programs and housing assistance programs.
1984	Secondary Mortgage Market Act		• Incorporated many of the recommendations made by the President's Commission on Housing. • Expanded the role of Freddie Mac and Fannie Mae, especially in relation to mortgage-backed securities.
1986	Tax Reform Act		• Eliminated a great deal of the tax-favored status of rental housing. • Decreased income tax rates. • Established the *Low-Income Housing Tax Credit (LIHTC)*. The goal of LIHTC was to put private investment into affordable housing. LIHTC offers private investors who build affordable housing a 10-year income tax credit.
1987	Steward B. McKinney Homeless Assistance Act (Public Law 100-77)	• Title IV: Housing Assistance Subtitle A: Comprehensive Homeless Assistance Plan Subtitle B: Emergency Shelter Grants Subtitle C: Supportive and Housing Demonstration	• Subtitle A of Title IV gave assistance to states, metropolitan cities, and urban counties to prepare a *Comprehensive Homeless Assistance Plan (CHAP)* describing the need for assistance, available facilities and services, strategy for meeting needs, and how federal assistance would be used. • Subtitle B provided grants for emergency shelter and to renovate, rehabilitate, and maintain structures for essential services, and required that grant recipients use the

Subtitle D: Supplemental Assistance for Facilities to Assist the Homeless Section 441: Section 8 Moderate Rehabilitation of Single Room Occupancy Units for Homeless Individuals

- Title V: Identification and Use of Surplus Federal Property

designated buildings as homeless shelters for at least 3 years.

- Subtitle C made competitive grants available for "supportive housing," meaning housing and supportive services to help homeless people move into transitional and permanent housing.
- Title V required HUD to collect information on underutilized properties and determine their suitability for use as facilities for the homeless.

| 1987 | Housing and Community Development Act of 1987 (Public Law 100-242) | • Title I: Housing Assistance
• Title II: Preservation of Low-Income Housing
• Title III: Rural Housing
• Title IV: Mortgage Insurance and Secondary Mortgage Market Programs
• Title V: Community Development and Miscellaneous Programs
• Title VI: *Nehemiah Housing Opportunity Grants*
• Title VII: Enterprise Zone Development | • Title II sought to protect the prospective loss of low-income rental housing units.
• Title V further targeted CDBG funds toward lower-income households and also required that recipients of CDBG or UDAG funds have a relocation plan and appropriate benefits for people displaced from their homes.
• Title VI established the Nehemiah housing program and Nehemiah Housing Fund to provide grants to nonprofit organizations to assist moderate-income families in becoming home owners in lower-income areas.
• Title VII authorized 100 areas to be designated as enterprise zones where state and local governments would agree to increase services and activities to reduce the burdens on businesses and workers in the given zone. |
| 1988 | Indian Housing Act of 1988 (Public Law 100-358) | • Title II: Assisted Housing for Indians and Alaska Natives Section 201: Lower-Income Housing on Indian Reservation Section 202: Mutual Help Homeownership Opportunity | • This legislation amended the United States Housing Act of 1937 to establish an assisted housing program for Indians distinct from the public housing program.
• Section 202 was designed to help Indian families on reservations become home owners, including owners of cooperatives. |

1988	Fair Housing Amendments Act of 1988 (Public Law 100-430, which amended Title VIII of Public Law 90-284)	• Title VIII: Fair Housing and Fair Housing Enforcement	• This legislative amendment strengthened the enforcement of the provision of Title VIII of the Civil Rights Act of 1968. It altered administrative and legal procedures relating to complaints of discriminatory action.
1988	Stewart B. McKinney Homeless Assistance Amendments Act of 1988 (Public Law 100-628)	• Title IV: Amendments to Title IV of the Stewart B. McKinney Homeless Assistance Act	• Title IV added provisions to help prevent the homelessness of people threatened with loss of their home due to sudden loss of income. It also authorized funding for technical assistance in operating and providing services to homeless persons. Required HUD to provide Congress with a report evaluating the impact of local rent control on the rate of homelessness and the supply of housing in major cities.
1988	Anti-Drug Abuse Act of 1988 (Public Law 100-690)	• Title V: User Accountability Subtitle C, Chapter 1: Regulatory and Enforcement Provisions Subtitle C, Chapter 2: Public Housing Drug Elimination Subtitle C, Chapter 3: Drug-Free Public Housing Subtitle D: Drug-Free Workforce Section 5301: Denial of Federal Benefits to Drug Traffickers and Possessors	• Provided severe criminal penalties for people distributing illegal drugs.
1989	Department of Housing and Urban Development	• Title I: Reforms to HUD • Title II: Housing Preservation	• Title I included a new declaration of ethics for HUD, management reform, and Federal Housing Administration reform.

Reform Act of 1989 (Public Law 101-235)	• Title V: National Commission on Severely Distressed Public Housing • Title VIII: Section 8 Rent Adjustments	
1989	Financial Institutions Reform, Recovery and Enforcement Act (FIRREA)		• Deregulation of the thrift industry caused a crisis, and the federal government intervened through FIRREA. • FIRREA imposed new regulations on the thrifts and greatly restricted thrift housing lending; as a result, the mortgage banking industry stepped in and began to deal more with the housing sector. • Created the Resolution Trust Corporation (RTC) to take over and close insolvent savings and loans. • Limited loans for acquisitions, development, and construction (AD&C loans). • FIRREA dissolved the Federal Home Loan Bank Board and replaced it with the Office of Thrift Supervisions (OTS). Dissolving this board meant that a new structure was needed to manage the 12 Federal Home Loan Banks, thus the Federal Housing Finance Board (FHFB) was created as an independent agency. Freddie Mac was given a legislative charter similar to Fannie Mae's and was made a government-sponsored enterprise (GSE)
1990	Cranston-Gonzalez National Affordable Housing Act (Public Law 101-625)	• Title I: General Provisions and Policies • Title II: Investment in Affordable Housing *(HOME Investment Partnership Act)* • Title III: Homeownership • Title IV: *Homeownership and*	• Title II established the *HOME program* to expand affordable housing and to expand government-private partnerships to create more affordable housing. The program focused on rehabilitating older units and constructing new ones for ownership and rental. • Title III established the National Homeownership Trust Act within HUD and expanded the abilities of

Opportunity for People Everywhere (HOPE)
Subtitle A: HOPE for Public and Indian Housing Homeownership
Subtitle B: HOPE for Homeownership of Multifamily Units
Subtitle C: HOPE for Homeownership of Single Family Homes
• Title V: Housing Assistance
• Title VI: Preservation of Affordable Rental Housing
• Title VIII: Housing for Persons with Special Needs
• Title IX: Community Development and Miscellaneous Programs

the FHA and secondary mortgage market.
• Title IV created the HOPE program, which essentially was designed to convert public housing units into units to be purchased by low-income residents, thereby increasing homeownership.
• Title VI (Low-Income Housing Preservation and Resident Homeownership Act or LIHPRHA) established a permanent program for preservation of assisted housing in danger of being lost from the low-rent stock through prepayment of selected mortgages.
• Title VIII helped create supportive housing for the elderly, people with disabilities, the homeless, and people with AIDS.

1992	Housing and Community Development Act of 1992 (Public Law 102-550)	• Referred to as the Annunzio-Wylie Anti-Money-Laundering Act	• Strengthens penalties for depository institutions found guilty of money laundering. • Established regulatory structure for GSEs within HUD. • Advanced commitment to reduced risk of lead-based paint poisoning.
1994	Multifamily Housing Property Disposition Reform Act of 1994 (Public Law 103-233)		• Provides Section 8 assistance in connection with the sale of HUD-owned multifamily rental housing projects.
1996	Housing Opportunity Extension Act of 1996		• Set up Section 8 Contract Renewal for Multifamily Properties • Increased CDBG limits and permitted use for homeownership activities

	(Public Law 104-120)	• Set aside a portion of rural housing funding for underserved areas as well as non-profit entities. • Provided loan guarantees for multifamily projects in rural areas. • Allowed FHA mortgage insurance to be used for home equity conversion mortgages. • Limited GNMA guarantees of Mortgage Backed Securities. • Extended Multifamily-housing finance through a risk-sharing pilot program and an HFA pilot. • Ensured safety and security in public housing. • Made public housing available to the elderly and disabled.
1998	Quality Housing and Work Responsibility Act of 1998 (Public Law 105-276)	• Called for reform of Public Housing and Tenant-Based Assistance Programs. • Established the Family Self-Sufficiency program • Repealed federal preferences for tenants left this in the hands of local PHAs. • Merged the Section 8 Certificate and Voucher programs into one. • Required conversion of distressed public housing to tenant-based assistance. • Set up a home rule flexible grant demonstration. • Required a Public Housing Agency Plan for each PHA. • Established community service and family self-sufficiency requirements for residents.
2000	American Homeowner-ship and Economic Opportunity Act of 2000 (Public Law 106-659)	• Provided for homeownership assistance for working families • Promoted the use of Section 8 for homeownership (down payment assistance). • Provided for Native American/ Hawaiian Homeownership assistance and loan guarantees

- Clarified rules regarding Private Mortgage Insurance cancellation and termination.
- Eliminated annual reporting requirement and other amendments for manufactured housing.
- Promoted rural housing homeownership with guarantees for refinancing, and limited partnership eligibility for farm labor loans.
- Expanded and preserved funding for housing available to the elderly and disabled.
- Established maximum payment standards for enhanced vouchers
- Allowed use of section 8 vouchers for opt outs.

Primary Sources:
Congressional Research Services Report, "A Chronology of Housing Legislation and Selected Executive Actions, 1892-1992." Prepared for the Committee on Banking, Finance, and Urban Affairs and the Subcommittee on Housing and Community Development, House of Representatives (Washington, D.C.: U.S. Government Printing Office, December 1993).
Willem van Vliet, *The Encyclopedia of Housing* (Thousand Oaks, CA: SAGE Publications, 1998).
Housing and Development Reporter, The Housing and Community Development Electronic Library (CD-Rom), West Group, February 2002.

Chapter 6

KEY CHALLENGES AS WE LOOK TO THE FUTURE

The developments of the last fifty years, as outlined in the first five chapters of this book, present a picture of success. Tremendous progress has been made in housing America. The quality of the housing stock has improved dramatically, the homeownership rate has risen substantially, and over the last fifty years the nation's supply of housing has grown vigorously. From 1950 to 2000 there were seventy-seven million new private housing units added to the overall stock. The total housing inventory in 1950 was just 46.1 million; in 2000 it was 119.6 million, a gain of over 159% in fifty years. (See Figure 1.2, Chapter 1).

The people involved in the passage and administration of the Housing Act of 1949, calling for a "decent home and suitable living environment for all Americans," would no doubt feel that many of their expectations and hopes have been met and, in some cases, exceeded. Housing plays a key part in the social fabric of society, and the level of housing activity in the United States is in many ways the envy of the world. Housing plays a significant role in the nation's economy, and its importance is outlined below in the first part of this chapter.

However, important social and cultural changes have occurred over the past fifty years, and housing problems and challenges have shifted and evolved. Significant issues remain, and new problems have developed. In many cases, these new problems, which will be discussed in the second part of the chapter, are very different from those faced in the 1950s, and some of them have been spawned by the nation's success in the housing arena.

HOUSING AND THE ECONOMY

Housing investment and consumption are a significant part of the nation's economy, and housing is the cornerstone of household wealth for many families. The production of housing has an important impact on the gross domestic product, both in terms of direct housing construction and indirect impacts. Housing has often played a primary role in leading the economy into and out of a recession. However, the role of housing in the economy may be changing as home builders learn to exert greater control over inventories. Further, small interest rate drops trigger greater refinancing activity, and some consolidation is taking place in the housing industry as measured by the level of production by the nation's largest home builders. Over time, investment in the stock market has surpassed housing as a share of household wealth, but for the majority of home owners, especially those with middle or moderate incomes and those who are minorities, housing is their largest asset.

Housing and Economic Activity: Direct Effects

Gross domestic product (GDP), the measure of the nation's total production of goods and services, includes products for consumption and capital goods produced as an investment for future production. Housing is a major part of both current consumption and private investment. In 2000, for example, the combination of consumption and investment spending on housing represented 14% of GDP. The share has been fairly constant over the past fifty years, as shown in Figure 6.1.[1]

HOUSING INVESTMENT

In the 1980s and the 1990s, the construction of new homes as a part of the investment component of GDP typically accounted for about 4% of the GDP (Figure 6.1). For example, in 2000, residential fixed investment (RFI) totaled $425 billion, or 4.3% of GDP. Overall, residential investment represented 24.05% of gross private domestic investment (See Figure 6.2). New conventional single-family and multifamily structures accounted for $249 billion, or 59% of RFI. The other major components of RFI include improvements to existing homes ($102 billion), real estate commissions ($55 billion), manufactured housing ($11 billion), and

---

[1] National Association of Home Builders, "Housing's Impact on the Economy,"1.

FIGURE 6.1
Housing's Share of GDP

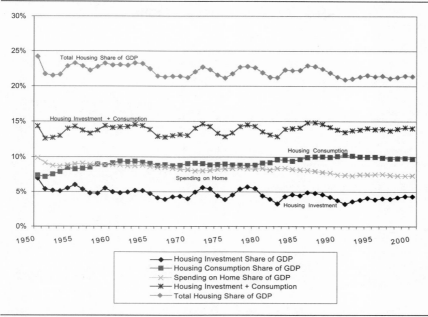

SOURCE: Commerce Department as reported in National Association of Home Builders "Housing's Impact on the Economy," Report submitted to the Millennial Housing Commission, November, 2001, p. 4.

equipment such as appliances for rental housing ($9 billion).[2] RFI is one of the more volatile components of GDP. In the past twenty-five years, the RFI share of GDP has ranged from 3.2% in 1982 and 1991 to 5.7% in 1978. The most recent peak was in 1999, when it was 4.4% (see Figure 6.1). The value of investment in new residential structures does not include the value of raw land, but it does include the value of land development.

Unlike investment in conventional homes and residential structures, whose construction is counted as fixed investment as the work occurs, investment in manufactured housing is measured when the completed unit is shipped. It is noteworthy that new conventional single-family and multi-family structures outweigh manufactured housing to a much greater extent in terms of residential investment than in numbers of units. The average

---

[2] Appliances purchased by home owners are included in personal consumption expenditures rather than residential investment.

FIGURE 6.2
Housing's Share of the Economy

Gross Domestic Product - Investment
[Billions of dollars]

	1930-39	1940-49	1950-59	1960-69	1970-79	1980-89	1990-99	2000
Gross domestic product (GDP	77.6	203.5	404.3	718.3	1,664.8	4,066.0	7,338.7	9,872.9
Gross private domestic investment	6.7	21.8	63.3	111.7	284.2	682.4	1,153.3	1,767.5
Residential	1.7	6.4	21.9	32.8	83.6	178.2	286.7	425.1
Residential Gross Invest/GDP	2.15%	3.16%	5.42%	4.57%	5.02%	4.38%	3.91%	4.31%
Residential/Gross Private Invest	24.81%	29.55%	34.63%	29.40%	29.42%	26.12%	24.86%	24.05%

Gross Domestic Product - Consumption
[Billions of dollars]

	1930-39	1940-49	1950-59	1960-69	1970-79	1980-89	1990-99	2000
Gross domestic product	77.6	203.5	404.3	718.3	1,664.8	4,066.0	7,338.7	9,872.9
Personal consumption expenditures	59.3	123.0	252.8	443.3	1,039.2	2,623.8	4,902.6	6,728.4
Housing PCE	9.0	13.6	33.3	64.9	148.2	394.8	730.7	958.8
Owner-occ nonfarm --space rent	4.2	6.9	20.6	42.3	99.7	274.0	523.5	702.7
Tenant-occ nonfarm --rent	3.8	5.1	9.8	18.0	39.0	101.5	173.1	209.3
Rental value of farm dwellings	0.7	1.1	1.7	2.5	4.0	5.0	6.0	7.7
Other	0.3	0.6	1.1	2.1	5.5	14.3	28.1	39.1
PCE Housing/GDP	11.64%	6.68%	8.23%	9.04%	8.90%	9.71%	9.96%	9.71%
PCE Housing/PCE Total	15.22%	11.05%	13.16%	14.64%	14.26%	15.05%	14.90%	14.25%

Gross Domestic Product -Spending on Home
[Billions of dollars]

	1930-39	1940-49	1950-59	1960-69	1970-79	1980-89	1990-99	2000
Gross domestic product	77.6	203.5	404.3	718.3	1,664.8	4,066.0	7,338.7	9,872.9
Personal consumption expenditures	59.3	123o	252.8	443.3	1,039.2	2,623.8	4,902.6	6,728.4
Spending on Home PCE	8.3	17.3	36.4	61.6	137.4	328.8	544.8	727.4
PCE Spending on Home/GDP	10.69%	8.50%	9.00%	8.58%	8.25%	8.09%	7.42%	7.37%
PCE Spending on Home/PCE Total	13.99%	14.07%	14.40%	13.90%	13.22%	12.53%	11.11%	10.81%

Housing (Investment and Consumption and Spending on Home) as Share of GDP

	1930-39	1940-49	1950-59	1960-69	1970-79	1980-89	1990-99	2000
PCE Housing + Res Invest+PCE Spending on Home/GDP	24.48%	18.34%	22.65%	22.18%	22.18%	22.18%	21.29%	21.39%

SOURCE: Bureau of Economic Analysis as reported in National Association of Home Builders "Housing's Impact on the Economy," Report submitted to the Millennial Housing Commission, November, 2001, p. 5. Plus additional Millennial Housing Commission Calculations.

PCE=Personal Consumption Expenditures

new single-family unit represents about four times as much investment as the average manufactured housing unit, and the average multifamily unit, about twice as much.

HOUSING CONSUMPTION

The housing sector's output for consumption consists primarily of the services — the shelter and the security — provided by the existing housing stock. The payment of rent by tenants is part of consumer spending on services. In 2000, renters spent $209 billion for nonfarm housing services. This represents the services of appliances and furniture provided by property owners, but mainly the rent for the use of the structure. The portion of rents paid in 2000 that is attributable to appliances and furniture is about $6 billion. When utilities are included in the rent, the value of those utilities is excluded from the total rent and counted as consumer spending for energy.

The estimated rental value of owner-occupied homes is also counted as consumer spending on housing services — home owners are considered to be renting from themselves. In 2000, imputed rent for nonfarm owner-occupied housing was $710 billion.[3] This treatment of owner-occupied housing is unique. The purchase of consumer durables such as cars, computers, and appliances is treated as current consumption, rather than investment. Arguably, households that buy cars or other durables could be said to be making investments and leasing use of those assets to themselves, but only residential structures are treated that way. In part, this is attributable to the fact that housing is more durable. Also, a shift toward homeownership would otherwise show up as a decline in GDP.[4]

In total, personal consumption expenditures for housing services in 2000 were reported as $959 billion, representing 9.7% of GDP and 14.3% of total personal consumption expenditures (see Figure 6.2). The housing consumption share of GDP has remained relatively constant over the last fifty years, from a low of around 7.2% in 1951 to a high of 10.3% in 1991. Averages for each of the past five decades are generally around 13% to 15% (see Figure 6.2).

HOUSING SPENDING

Another important housing related direct expenditure is the amount of money consumers spend to purchase goods to go into the home. Such spending in 2000 was reported at $727 billion, representing 7.4% of GDP and 10.8% of total personal consumption expenditures (Figure 6.2). The share of housing spending has drifted down slightly over the last fifty years from a 9.0% share of the GDP in the 1950s to a 7.4% share of GDP in the 1990s.

TOTAL HOUSING SHARE OF THE GDP

If all three components which comprise housing's share of the GDP are added together, the result is dramatic. In 2000 the total housing investment and consumption was 14% of the GDP, and when housing spending of 7.4% is added, the overall total housing spending rose to an impressive 21.4% of GDP (Figure 6.2). In essence, then, over one fifth of the entire GDP is comprised of housing related expenditures. In addition, this level of housing activity has been amazingly consistent over the last fifty years.

---

[3] Imputed rent is the payment owners would have to make if they rented a unit comparable in quality to the one they own.

[4] National Association of Home Builders, "Housing's Impact on the Economy," 2.

In the 1950s it was 22.65%, and in the 1990s it was only slightly lower at 21.29% (Figure 6.2).

LOCAL ECONOMIC AND REVENUE IMPACTS

The economic impact of housing and home building is also felt at the local level. Among other areas, the impacts relate to jobs, income, and local government revenue. (See Figure 6.3.) According to the National Association of Home Builders, the construction of 100 single-family homes generates $10.7 million in new income for local business and workers in the year of construction and another $2.9 million every year thereafter. Building 100 new homes creates 257 jobs in the community where the homes are built and seventy-five jobs every year thereafter in support of the new households. In ten years, the local economic impact of building 100 single-family homes is $37 million.[5] Similarly, construction of 100 multifamily units generates $5.2 million in local income in the year of construction and another $1.8 million every year thereafter. This translates into 122 jobs the first year and forty-six additional jobs every year thereafter. In ten years, the local economic impact of building 100 apartments is $23 million.[6]

The economic and job impacts are broad. As one might expect, the construction sector accounts for a substantial share of the impact, but wholesale and retail trade, business and professional services and numerous other industries are also affected (see Figure 6.3). Local governments realize new revenues as well, as builders pay fees and as businesses expand and pay fees and taxes. Building 100 new single-family homes generates additional local taxes and other revenues of $1.2 million in the year of construction and $472,000 every year thereafter. Similarly, 100 new multifamily units generate $579,000 in local government revenue the first year and $308,000 every year thereafter. Permit and impact fees are the largest component of local government revenue generated during the construction period, totaling $535,000 for every 100 single-family and $270,000 for every 100 multifamily homes in a typical community. Residential property taxes are the largest component of ongoing effect, totaling $177,000 a year for every 100 single-family and $106,000 for every 100 multifamily homes built. Still, residential property taxes account for only a little over one-third of the ongoing, recurring impact, and other sources of new rev-

---

[5] Ibid., 6–7.
[6] Ibid.

FIGURE 6.3
Local Income Generated by Building 100 Homes

Industry	Single Family			Multifamily		
	Benefits Year of Construction	Recurring Impacts	10-year Impact	Benefits Year of Construction	Recurring Impacts	10-year Impact
Construction	$5,792,000	$161,000	$7,241,000	$2,796,000	$90,000	$3,697,000
Wholesale and Retail Trade	$1,501,000	$643,000	$7,288,000	$10,000	$8,000	$86,000
Business & Professional Services	$737,000	$268,000	$3,149,000	$19,000	$13,000	$148,000
Health, Educ. & Social Services	$640,000	$467,000	$4,843,000	$57,000	$53,000	$589,000
Local Government	$463,000	$209,000	$2,344,000	$31,000	$19,000	$221,000
Finance and Insurance	$393,000	$417,000	$4,146,000	$654,000	$420,000	$4,855,000
Real Estate	$260,000	$115,000	$1,295,000	$189,000	$124,000	$1,425,000
Personal & Repair Services	$183,000	$118,000	$1,245,000	$122,000	$215,000	$2,276,000
Automobile Repair & Service	$150,000	$110,000	$1,140,000	$83,000	$76,000	$839,000
Eating and drinking places	$150,000	$115,000	$1,185,000	$16,000	$20,000	$219,000
Other	$135,000	$36,000	$459,000	$515,000	$142,000	$1,935,000
Communications	$125,000	$81,000	$854,000	$72,000	$92,000	$989,000
Utilities	$69,000	$51,000	$528,000	$69,000	$78,000	$854,000
Entertainment Services	$57,000	$73,000	$714,000	$27,000	$51,000	$541,000
Transportation	$43,000	$20,000	$223,000	$311,000	$241,000	$2,721,000
Services to dwellings / buildings	$37,000	$19,000	$208,000	$233,000	$144,000	$1,673,000
Manufacturing	$21,000	$13,000	$138,000	$27,000	$12,000	$142,000
Total	$10,755,000	$2,915,000	$36,990,000	$5,234,000	$1,798,000	$23,210,000

SOURCE: NAHB Local Economic Impact Model for a typical metropolitan area, as found in National Association of Home Builders "Housing's Impact on the Economy," Report submitted to the Millennial Housing Commission, November, 2001, p. 7.

enue for local governments are also generated. Figure 6.4 provides a distribution of these revenues.[7]

HOUSING CYCLES

Housing construction's contribution to GDP typically varies with the business cycle (Figure 6.5). In the past, housing has usually led the economy into and out of recession. Contraction in the home building and remodeling industries alone, for example, contributed more than one-third of the drop in GDP in the 1990–1991 recession, and expansion contributed nearly 30% of GDP growth in the year following the recession. In the nine business cycles since 1945, housing starts began to decline an average of twenty-five months before the onset of a recession and turned up an average of five months ahead of the broader economy.

Housing's role in business cycle contractions and expansions, in terms of both timing and magnitude, also depends on fiscal and monetary policy, as well as home builder inventory management practices. In the past, interest rates have climbed in advance of a recession, then dropped sharply during the recession, and home builders have accumulated large stocks of unsold but completed homes. Based on these circumstances, housing cycles in past years have been volatile and have contributed significantly to recessionary pressures. As discussed in Chapter 4, mortgage credit flows added to these cycles — especially in the 1950s, 1960s, and 1970s, when mortgage credit was rationed by capping the rates that thrifts could offer on deposits.

In the 1990s, however, home builders kept inventories of new homes under better control, and interest rate policy was far more positive for housing. If this pattern continues, housing's traditional role in the contours of business cycles may change somewhat. In fact, as much of the economy began to slow down in 2000 and 2001, with interest rates low and demographic demand strong, housing activity remained strong, and in the first two quarters housing played an important role in slowing the economy's fall into a recession. Following the catastrophic terrorist events of September 11, 2001, the nation's economic situation shifted dramatically, and a recession could no longer be avoided. Still, in 2001 and 2002 housing remained one of the few bright spots in the economy. This was illustrated in the March 30–April 15, 2002 issue of *The Economist* with the cover headline: "The Houses that Saved the World." The article spoke not only of the role of housing in the United States, but in the world: "If there is one single

---

[7] Ibid., 8.

FIGURE 6.4
Revenues and Taxes to Local Governments

	Single Family			Multifamily		
	Year of Construction	Recurring Impacts		Year of Construction	Recurring Impacts	
Residential Permit / Impact Fees	$535,000		$535,000	$270,000		$270,000
Utilities & Other Govt. Enterprises	$150,000	$110,000	$1,140,000	$70,000	$50,000	$575,000
Business Property Taxes	$134,000	$70,000	$764,000	$70,000	$66,000	$734,000
General Sales Taxes	$99,000	$19,000	$270,000	$49,000	$18,000	$225,000
Other Fees and Charges	$67,000	$24,000	$283,000	$34,000	$19,000	$224,000
Hospitals	$52,000	$31,000	$331,000	$25,000	$18,000	$203,000
Other Taxes	$41,000	$14,000	$167,000	$20,000	$11,000	$132,000
Income Taxes	$24,000	$7,000	$87,000	$12,000	$5,000	$63,000
Education Charges	$21,000	$6,000	$75,000	$10,000	$4,000	$46,000
Transportation Charges	$18,000	$5,000	$63,000	$9,000	$3,000	$38,000
Specific Excise Taxes	$16,000	$8,000	$88,000	$8,000	$8,000	$86,000
License Taxes	$2,000	$1,000	$11,000	$1,000	$0	$5,000
Residential Property Taxes	$0	$177,000	$1,593,000	$0	$106,000	$1,059,000
TOTAL GENERAL REVENUE	$1,159,000	$472,000	$5,407,000	$579,000	$308,000	$3,660,000

Source: NAHB Local Economic Impact Model for a typical metropolitan area, as found in National Association of Home Builders "Housing's Impact on the Economy," Report submitted to the Millennial Housing Commission, November, 2001, p. 8.

FIGURE 6.5
Three Recessions: Growth in the Year Before and After the Trough

	1974-75 Recession		1981-1982 Recession		1990-91 Recession	
	Year Before Trough	Year After Trough	Year Before Trough	Year After Trough	Year Before Trough	Year After Trough
Gross Domestic Product	-3.8%	6.1%	1.9%	6.5%	-0.9%	2.5%
Personal Consumption	0.6	6.0	2.9	5.4	0.1	2.9
Residential	-24.4	26.7	4.9	38.1	-16.6	9.7
Single Family	-15.0	40.9	14.9	63.6	-22.9	18.7
Multifamily	-56.1	-31.7	4.9	54.1	-25.3	2.4
Other	-10.1	33.6	-3.1	8.7	-7.2	2.0
Government	1.7	0.8	3.8	-2.7	1.6	-3.4
Unemployment Rate	5.1	7.7	8.2	8.5	5.3	6.8
Capacity Utilization	85.3	77.1	76.4	78.0	82.6	79.5

SOURCE: NAHB Local Economic Impact Model for a typical metropolitan area, as found in National Association of Home Builders "Housing's Impact on the Economy," Report submitted to the Millennial Housing Commission, November, 2001.

factor that has saved the world economy from a deep recession it is the housing market."[8]

All of this is not to say that housing cycles are over. Housing activity will still rise and fall from year to year based on overall economic growth, interest rates, and demographic demand. However, as long as demographic demand remains strong, housing should remain an important driver for the nation's economy since home builders have become more careful in not allowing inventories to grow too high and the housing finance system is far more robust in meeting the needs of the home buyer and the housing industry.

Housing and Economic Activity: Indirect Effects

Housing also contributes to the economy indirectly through the refinancing behavior of home owners. Home equity is a principal part of many people's wealth, and when owners tap into this wealth or lower their debt costs by refinancing, the consumer dollars that are made available can affect consumer spending and the broader economy. Freddie Mac's

---

[8] "Going Through the Roof," *The Economist,* March 20–April 15, 2002, 65.

Primary Mortgage Market Survey reveals that in recent years, about half of refinancing households take out a mortgage more than $5,000 larger than the mortgage they are retiring. On average, they take out about $18,000 more than needed to pay off their existing loans, and they take the difference in cash. The half of refinancing households that do not take out a larger mortgage realizes significant monthly savings on mortgage payments, and some of these savings are spent on other consumer goods.[9]

As in housing construction, the role that refinancing plays in the economy varies across the business cycle. When interest rates drop, it triggers refinance activity. In the past, it took interest rate declines well in excess of 100 basis points to spur owners to refinance in significant numbers because the transaction costs were higher. Now, interest rate changes as small as fifty basis points can motivate borrowers intending to hold their mortgages for several years to refinance. In 2001, for example, with rates dropping fast and refinances expected to reach at least $700 billion, refinancers probably cashed out about $70 billion in equity. An uncertain, but undoubtedly significant, portion of these returns contributes to short-term spending. In 2001, savings to home owners — assuming a 100-basis-point spread and $700 billion in refinances — would amount to at least $3.5 billion. These refinance savings and equity extractions, if all spent in the same year, would add nearly 0.75% to GDP growth.

Finally, capital gains on home sales add liquidity to the economy. The Federal Reserve Board has estimated that for the past few years, capital gains on an average home resale, net of transaction costs, have exceeded $25,000. With existing home sales now running at well over five million per year, realized capital gains are putting an additional $125 billion into the bank accounts of consumers. Again, the amount varies with market conditions. In booming markets with rapid house price appreciation, both the number of sales and the amount of gain are typically higher than in stalled markets. Federal Reserve Board Chairman Allan Greenspan has concluded that in the short run, the propensity to spend some portion of the extracted home equity is higher than for the capital gains on stocks.

Home owners can also use their homes to finance current spending by taking out home equity loans and lines of credit. Like cash-out refinances, home equity loans are sometimes used for short-term consumption, although many are used to convert higher-cost consumer debt into lower-cost

---

[9] The amount of the reduced housing cost depends on the spread between the interest rate on the new and retired mortgage as well as the level of those rates.

mortgage debt. In the 1990s, home owners demonstrated their desire to cash out on home equity in a booming market and to see the home as a store of wealth to be "tapped" rather than "trapped." As a result, the share of home equity compared to overall value in the economy reached record lows in the 1990s, dropping nearly 10% from 1990 to 2000, even as home values surged (Figure 6.6).

Housing Wealth

Housing constitutes more than one-third of the nation's tangible assets (Figure 6.7), and equity in the home (as measured by the value of primary residences) accounts for nearly 30% of the nation's household wealth (Figure 6.8). As one would expect, owners have greater wealth than renters, and in large measure, owners' greater wealth is attributable to the fact that they have higher incomes and they can accumulate more non-housing wealth. Nevertheless, housing is a central contributor to the wealth held by home owners. When last measured in 1998, nearly 60% of home owners with stock holdings had more home equity than stock equity

FIGURE 6.6
Despite Rising Prices, Home Equity Fell as a Share of Value in the 1990s

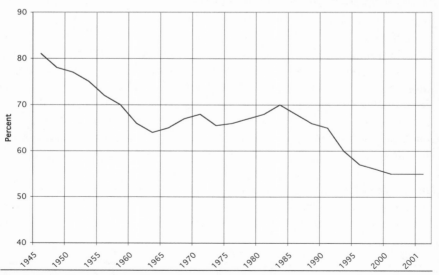

SOURCE: Federal Reserve Flow of Funds of Accounts, Table B. 100.

FIGURE 6.7
The Nation's Tangible Assets — 2001

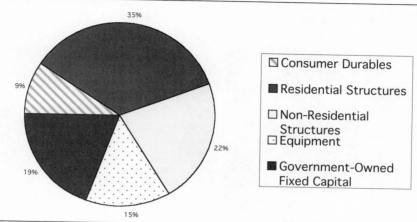

SOURCE: Bureau of Economic Analysis, Survey of Current Business, September 2001.
NOTE: The value of land is not included in the value of residential and non-residential structures.

(Figure 6.9), and the percentage was even higher for home owners with household income below $50,000.

Housing wealth is an especially important form of wealth for low-income and minority home owners (Figure 6.10). Half of nonelderly home owners with incomes under $20,000 held 69% or more of their wealth in home equity, while half of home owners with incomes of $50,000 to $60,000 held 38% or less of their wealth in home equity. Similarly, while half of African American home owners held 57% or more of their wealth in home equity and Hispanics an even higher 71% or more, half of white home owners held 40% or less of their wealth in the form of home equity.

Housing wealth is also an important source that can be tapped to meet other demands. This is evidenced by the heavy home equity borrowing that occurred through refinances and second mortgage loans and lines of credit in the 1990s. Not only does such financing provide borrowers with lower rates than personal loans (because home equity debt is secured), but it also allows borrowers to deduct mortgage interest payments up to $125,000 of their original indebtedness at the time of home purchase, and more if the proceeds are used for home improvements.

A more subtle way in which housing wealth contributes to the economy is through its role in capital formation. Home equity is often used to start a small business or as collateral for a small business loan. About 2.5% of

FIGURE 6.8
Value of Primary Residences Still Nearly 30% of All Household Assets;
Financial Assets are 40%

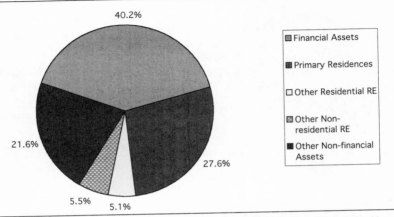

SOURCE: 1998 Survey of Consumer Finance as tabulated by the Harvard Joint Center for Housing Studies.

FIGURE 6.9
Home Equity Still Makes Up the Majority of Wealth for Most Homeowners
Share of Homeowners with More Equity in Homes than Stocks, 1998

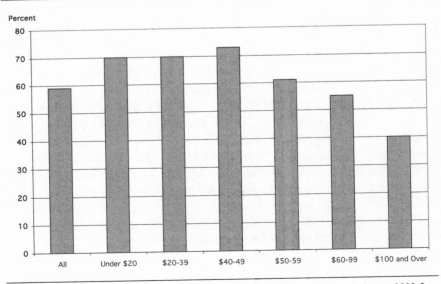

SOURCE: Harvard Joint Center for Housing Studies, *The State of the Nation's Housing Report*, 2000, 9.

FIGURE 6.10
Income and Wealth of Owners and Renters: 1998

	Owners			Renters	
	Median Income	Median Home Equity	Median Net Wealth	Median Income	Median Net Wealth
TOTAL	43,581	57,000	132,130	20,000	4,200
AGE					
Under 35	42,557	19,000	40,649	19,000	2,600
35 to 64	52,702	55,000	145,100	23,000	5,480
75 and Over	23,311	80,000	169,750	12,000	6,220
RACE/ETHNICITY					
White	46,621	60,000	148,920	22,000	5,800
African American	28,878	29,000	67,280	13,000	1,061
Hispanic	33,446	43,000	70,000	19,000	2,000
Other	54,729	70,000	163,800	23,000	7,750
INCOME					
Under $20,000	12,162	47,000	70,100	9,800	1,000
$20,000-49,999	32,432	30,000	104,650	30,000	8,050
$50,000 and Over	74,999	65,000	288,500	63,000	51,300

NOTES: Hispanics may be of any race. Other includes Asians and Pacific Islanders, Native Americans, and all other racial groups not shown separately.
SOURCE: Harvard Joint Center for Housing Studies tabulations of the 1998 Survey of Consumer Finance.

white home owners and 7% of African American home owners who cashed out during refinancing or who took out second mortgages in 1998 reported doing so for investment purposes (including money for businesses, stocks, or other investments).

Finally, housing wealth helps even out (but does not erase) disparities in wealth distribution. Housing wealth is more equally distributed than other forms of wealth (Figure 6.11). In 1998, the top 1% of stock holders held 35% of the stock wealth, while the top 1% of home owners held only 13% of the home equity. Furthermore, when minorities are able to become home owners, housing investments help to reduce racial disparities in wealth (Figure 6.12).

Consolidation in the Home Building Industry

Since the end of the housing recession in 1992, the largest builders' share of total housing starts has grown significantly (see Figure 6.13). In 1992, the share captured by the top 100 home builders was 12.2%, and by 2001, it had doubled to 24.5%, while the share captured by the top twenty-five rose from 7.1% to 15.8%, and by the top ten, from 4.5% to

FIGURE 6.11
Housing Wealth More "Equally" Distributed

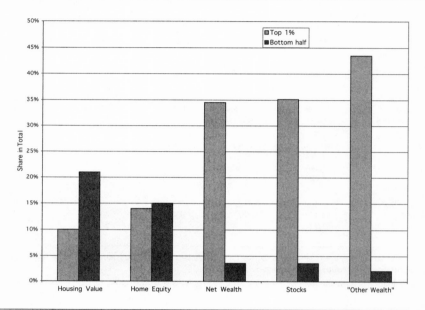

SOURCE: 1998 Survey of Consumer Finance as tabulated by the Harvard Joint Center for Housing Studies.

10.8%. The share of single-family starts built by the largest builders is even greater (see Figure 6.14). By 2001, the top 100 builders claimed 27.8% of single-family starts, the top twenty-five were up to 20.1%, and the top ten, 13.9%.

In years past, the starts accounted for by the major builders has tended to rise when times were good and drop off during periods of recession (see Figure 6.15). However, based on the consistent rise during the 1990s, the trends of the past may no longer be valid, and the large home builders are likely to continue to get bigger. In the 1980s, it seemed unlikely that one builder would ever build 20,000 units in a single year but it happened in 2000. It is certainly possible that by the end of the first decade of the twenty-first century, the largest builders could build between 40,000 and 50,000 units per year, or even more.

Much of this growth has occurred through acquisition, and the largest home builders have all made significant acquisitions. Although being large does not by itself assure profitability and significant variations still

FIGURE 6.12
Homeownership Helps Reduce the Racial Gap in Distribution of Net Wealth

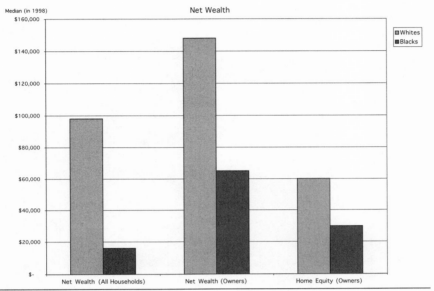

SOURCE: 1998 Survey of Consumer Finance as tabulated by the Harvard Joint Center for Housing Studies.

occur in local and regional markets, it is very likely that the larger home builders will continue to increase in size. New technology and information systems provide opportunities to achieve greater efficiencies and economies of scale through consolidation. For example, company-wide information systems — built internally in the company or adapting systems developed by others — allow for greater efficiencies in scheduling subcontractors or suppliers, keeping track of inventory, and matching supply and demand. Such standardized systems help drive down costs and achieve greater efficiencies in the timeliness of and access to data.

Size also often brings improved access to financial markets — even when the economy slows down — and therefore means better financial ratings and a lower cost to finance the development of land and the construction of houses. Credit ratings and rates often improve for companies that are less regional and more national in scope. Further, operating economies of scale provide purchasing opportunities for larger builders to buy in bulk and therefore reduce costs. The potential exists for larger

FIGURE 6.13

Share of Total Starts Built by the Largest Home Builders

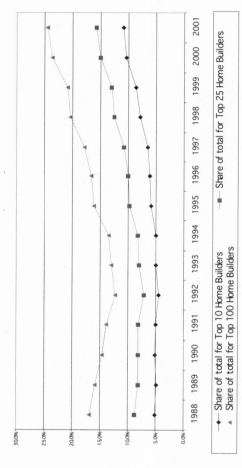

Legend:
- Share of total for Top 10 Home Builders
- Share of total for Top 25 Home Builders
- Share of total for Top 100 Home Builders

	1988	1989	1990	1991	1992	1993	1994	1995	1996	1997	1998	1999	2000	2001
Share of Total for Top 10 Home Builders	5.1%	4.9%	5.1%	5.0%	4.5%	5.0%	4.9%	5.9%	6.2%	6.5%	7.9%	8.7%	10.4%	10.8%
	75,675	67,361	61,382	50,876	54,264	64,670	71,960	79,294	88,969	95,216	127,173	144,529	164,877	173,410
Share of Total for Top 25 Home Builders	8.7%	8.1%	8.2%	8.1%	7.1%	8.0%	8.2%	9.8%	10.0%	10.8%	12.5%	13.0%	15.0%	15.8%
	129,826	111,456	97,540	81,891	85,316	102,613	119,976	131,785	145,100	159,181	202,275	215,940	238,561	252,873
Share of Total for Top 100 Home Builders	16.8%	15.9%	14.6%	13.8%	12.2%	13.0%	13.4%	16.2%	16.7%	17.9%	20.4%	20.9%	23.7%	24.5%
	250,400	218,200	174,096	140,322	146,461	167,687	195,847	218,475	240,868	264,457	329,664	348,202	376,739	393,376
Total National Starts	1,487,000	1,376,000	1,193,000	1,015,000	1,200,000	1,285,000	1,457,000	1,351,000	1,444,000	1,476,000	1,616,000	1,665,000	1,592,000	1,603,000

SOURCES: 1988–1990 data from *Builder* magazine, based on single-family and multifamily starts by home builders to total national housing starts, 1991–2001 data from *Builder* magazine, based on single-family and multifamily closings by home builders to total national housing starts, 1999–2001 data from *Professional Builder* magazine, based on single-family and multifamily closings by home builders to total national housing starts. Total national starts data from U.S. Census Bureau.

FIGURE 6.14

Share of Single Family Starts Built by the Largest Home Builders

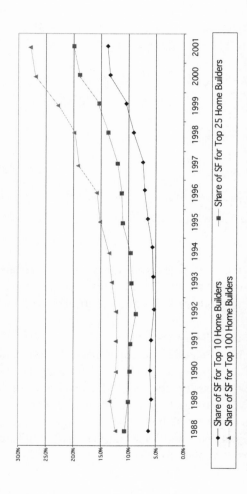

	1988	1989	1990	1991	1992	1993	1994	1995	1996	1997	1998	1999	2000	2001
Share of Single-family for Top 10 Home Builders	6.2%	6.0%	6.2%	6.0%	5.3%	5.7%	5.8%	6.8%	7.2%	7.7%	9.2%	10.8%	13.7%	13.9%
	67,499	59,798	55,178	50,876	54,264	63,840	69,702	73,011	82,394	86,927	116,651	143,840	164,221	176,840
Share of Single-family for Top 25 Home Builders	10.8%	10.0%	9.3%	9.3%	8.1%	8.8%	9.3%	11.0%	11.1%	12.0%	13.4%	15.3%	18.5%	20.1%
	116,720	100,736	83,426	78,264	83,787	99,229	111,484	117,839	126,115	136,315	170,579	204,316	222,217	255,933
Share of Single-family for Top 100 Home Builders	12.3%	13.1%	11.9%	11.8%	11.8%	12.8%	13.7%	15.1%	16.1%	19.3%	19.6%	22.6%	27.0%	27.8%
	132,900	131,745	106,134	99,008	121,323	143,557	164,234	183,658	218,448	249,388	301,450	323,088	335,899
National Single Family Starts	1,080,000	1,003,000	895,000	842,000	1,030,000	1,123,000	1,198,000	1,073,000	1,140,000	1,134,000	1,270,000	1,333,000	1,198,000	1,273,000

- ◆ Share of SF for Top 10 Home Builders
- ▲ Share of SF for Top 100 Home Builders
- ■ Share of SF for Top 25 Home Builders

SOURCE: Single-family data from *Builder* magazine; national single-family starts data from U.S. Census Bureau. Also note that 1988–1990 data based on single-family starts by home builders to national single-family starts; 1991–2001 data based on single-family closings by home builders to national single-family starts.

FIGURE 6.15
Share of All Single Family Starts Over Several Decades

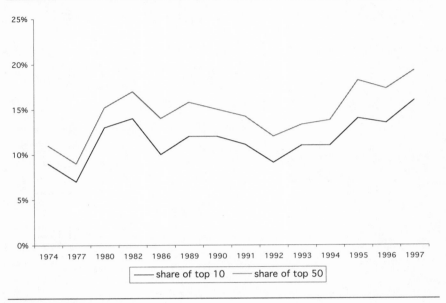

SOURCE: *Builder* Magazine

builders to establish strategic alliances to buy products at the best prices. The Internet further enhances the opportunities for such alliances.

Still, the home building industry will continue to include a large number of small firms due to regional variations, ease of entry into the market, and the cyclical nature of the business. Other industries are even more consolidated. For example, in 2001 the top ten mortgage bankers accounted for 65% of the mortgages originated and 54% of the mortgages serviced, whereas in 2001, the top ten single-family home builders accounted for only 13.9% of the single-family homes built throughout the country. The very nature of the home building process necessitates significantly different regional patterns, and local markets will continue to have a major impact on both preferences and demand.

CHALLENGES IN THE TWENTY-FIRST CENTURY

As we look to the future, the housing challenges we face are very different from those we faced after World War II. Six major challenges will be discussed in this chapter: meeting the needs of the housing "have-nots" and working families; meeting the housing needs of a growing population; overcoming the complacency of our own success; overcoming regulatory barriers that delay and add costs to housing; dealing with the challenges of growth and the environment; and achieving common ground.

Meeting the Needs of the Housing "Have-Nots" and Working Families

Despite progress in home ownership rates, housing quality, and the general strength of the economy in the last several decades, people have been left behind, and serious challenges remain in providing housing for the poor, households with low and moderate incomes, and working families. Increasing numbers of households do not have access to decent and affordable housing, and the number of households with significant housing needs is close to an all-time high. In 1988, William Apgar and James Brown — coauthors of the Joint Center for Housing Studies at Harvard and MIT, *The State of the Nation's Housing Report* — highlighted their presentation by noting "this report paints a picture of America clearly divided between housing 'haves' and housing 'have nots.'"[10] The same issue is still relevant today.

In the *1997 Report to Congress on Worst Case Housing Needs,* issued by the U.S. Department of Housing and Urban Development in April 1998, Secretary Andrew Cuomo noted that robust economic growth between 1993 and 1997 notwithstanding, the number of very-low-income households with worst case housing needs remained at an all-time high of 5.3 million. (Households with "worst case" housing needs are defined as unassisted renters with incomes below 50% of the local median income who pay more than half of their income for rent or live in severely substandard housing.)[11] Secretary Cuomo went on to say that the stock of rental housing affordable to these households was shrinking and that since 1995 Congress had eliminated funding for new rental assistance.

Although a strong economy in the latter 1990s helped many households, those in worst case housing experienced only modest improvements. In the 1999 report on worst case housing published by HUD, the number of worst case families fell by about 440,000, or 8%. This drop occurred because the income of very-low-income renters rose more quickly

---

[10] Apgar and Brown, Press Release introducing *The State of the Nation's Housing,* 1988, Joint Center for Housing Studies of Harvard University, Cambridge, MA, p. 1, March 17, 1988.

[11] U.S. Department of Housing and Urban Development, "Rental Housing Assistance," 19.

than their gross rent. Still, 4.9 million households had worst case needs for rental assistance — a critical problem that requires ongoing high-priority attention.[12] In 1999, 4.86 million households had worst case needs, compared to 5.38 million in 1997. Worst case needs impact 13.3% of renters and 4.7% of all U.S. households. In 1999, these households comprised 10.9 million people, among them 2.6 million children, 1.4 million elderly, and 1.3 million disabled adults.[13] The 2001 *The State of the Nation's Housing* report, prepared by the Joint Center for Housing Studies at Harvard University, highlighted that over 14 million American households — about one in eight — were severely cost burdened, spending more than 50% of their incomes for housing. The number of households that had at least moderate cost burdens was even higher, with three in ten households paying 30% or more of their income for housing. In addition, the Joint Center found that 2 million households lived in homes with serious structural problems, and nearly one-fourth of these households had high cost burdens, spending more than 50% of their incomes for housing.[14]

A further study by the Center for Housing Policy of the National Housing Conference, published in June 2001, found that in 1999, the number of American families with critical housing needs hovered around 13 million — one out of seven — families, including millions of working families.[15] Despite the strong economy at the time, from 1997 to 1999 the number fell by just over 1% (see Figure 6.16). (In this report, a family is defined as having a critical housing need if it spends more than half of its total income on housing and/or lives in a severely inadequate unit.)

Although the overall numbers held more or less steady over that two-year period, the composition of families did shift somewhat (see Figure 6.17). The proportion of elderly, nonworking families was roughly unchanged, a little over 28% (3.8 million). However, the proportion of nonelderly families unemployed and/or dependent on welfare fell by 3%, as did the proportion of marginally employed — those whose income is less than the equivalent of one full-time wage earner. These groups now make up 3 million and 2.5 million, respectively, of the 13 million total. The strong economy may have allowed some previously unemployed workers to find jobs. Meanwhile, and perhaps most striking, low- and moderate-income working families rose to 28.5%, or 3.7 million, of the

---

[12] U.S. Department of Housing and Urban Development Office, "A Report on Worst Case Housing Needs in 1999," 1–2.

[13] Ibid., 2.

[14] Joint Center for Housing Studies, *The State of the Nation's Housing: 2001,* 22–23.

[15] Lipman, "Paycheck to Paycheck," 6–7.

FIGURE 6.16
Working Status of All Households with Critical Housing Needs, U.S., 1997 and 1999 (000s)

	1997		1999	
	Number	Percent	Number	Percent
Elderly, Not-Working [1]	3,736	28.3	3,756	28.9
Non-elderly, Not Working [1]	3,499	26.5	3,030	23.3
Marginally Employed [2]	2,939	22.3	2,515	19.3
Low- to Moderate-Income Working Families [3]	3,021	22.9	3,712	28.5
Total [4,5]	13,195	100.0	13,013	100.0
Percent of all U.S. Households	14.0		13.7	

[1] The "not working" categories comprise households with less than $2,678 in salary and wage income.

[2] "Marginally employed" is defined as households with at least $2,678, but less than $10,712 in salary and wage income.

[3] "Low- to moderate-income working families" are those with at least $10,712 in salary and wage income, total income below 120 percent of the area median, and salary and wage income accounting for at least half of total income.

[4] This table does not cover all U.S. households. For 1997, of those with critical housing needs, the largest excluded group consists of those with incomes greater than 120 percent of the area median (roughly 392,000 households).

[5] For 1999, of those with critical housing needs, the largest excluded group consists of those with incomes greater than 120 percent of the area median (roughly 709,000 households).

SOURCE: Barbra J. Lipman, "Paycheck to Paycheck: Working Families and the Cost of Housing in America," "New Century Housing Center for Housing Policy/National Housing Conference, Volume 2, Issue 1, June 2001, p. 32 1997 and 1999 American Housing Survey.

FIGURE 6.17
Working Status of All Households with Critical Housing Needs

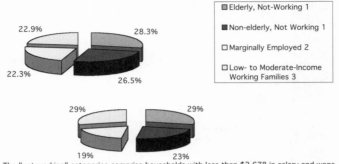

■	Elderly, Not-Working 1
■	Non-elderly, Not Working 1
□	Marginally Employed 2
□	Low- to Moderate-Income Working Families 3

1 The "not working" categories comprise households with less than $2,678 in salary and wage income.
2 "Marginally employed" is defined as households with at least $2,678, but less than $10,712 in salary and wage income.
3 "Low- to moderate-income working families" are those with at least $10,712 in salary and wage income, total income below 120% of the area median, and salary and wage income accounting for at least half of total income.

SOURCE: Barbara J. Lipman, "Paycheck to Paycheck: Working Families and the Cost of Housing in America."

total number of families with critical housing needs, as compared to about 23%, or 3 million, previously.[16]

For the vast majority of the 3.7 million working families with critical housing needs in 1999, cost was the primary problem. About eight out of ten of these families were paying more than half of their income for housing, while the other 20% lived in severely inadequate housing. A small fraction of families faced both problems (see Figure 6.18).[17] When we refer to the housing "have-nots," people often think of individuals and families without work, or of the elderly. This study points out that housing affordability is an issue for working families as well. The result is that many people who provide the bulk of services in many communities — teachers, police officers, firefighters, laundry and restaurant workers — cannot find affordable places to live.

A comparison of the supply of affordable housing in different income groups to the demand from different household income groups helps to further illustrate the nation's housing challenge — especially for extremely-low-income households earning less than 30% of median income. Figure 6.19 shows that there are 8.51 million extremely-low-income

[16] Ibid., 6.
[17] Ibid., 8.

FIGURE 6.18
Critical Housing Needs of Low- to Moderate-Income Working Families

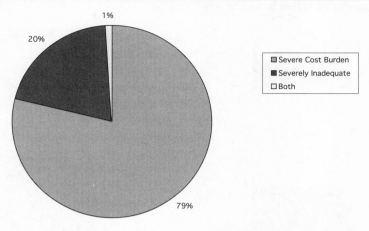

SOURCE: Barbara J. Lipman, "Paycheck to Paycheck: Working Families and the Cost of Housing in America," *New Century Housing Center for Housing Policy/National Housing Conference,* Volume 2, Issue 1, June, 2001, p. 8.

households and only 6.7 million housing units which are affordable to these households — a gap of close to two million housing units.

This housing challenge is exacerbated by a dwindling supply of affordable rental housing. Despite an overhang of market-rate multifamily rentals from the overbuilding of rental housing in the 1980s (discussed in Chapter 3), market forces in the 1990s failed to produce enough new or "filtered down" units to prevent losses of affordable rental housing. Between 1997 and 1999, HUD estimates, the number of units affordable to extremely-low-income (less than 30% of area median) households fell precipitously, by 750,000 units, or 13%. Nearly 7% of the homes affordable to very-low-income (less than 50% of area median) households were lost. Meanwhile, higher-income people determined to spend less than 30% of their income on housing increasingly crowded out the remaining affordable rentals. Even the supply of directly assisted private and public housing dwindled in the second half of the 1990s. After three decades of net additions, more than 175,000 assisted homes were lost.[18]

---

[18] Belsky, paper for the Millennial Housing Commission.

FIGURE 6.19
The Supply-Demand Gap Mostly Effects Extremely-Low-Income Households (millions of households and units)

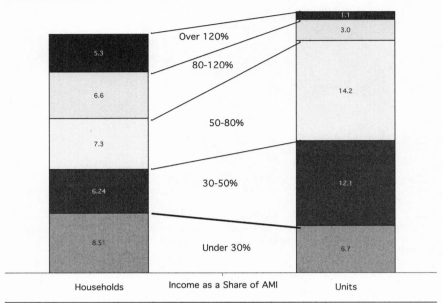

SOURCE: HUD Tabulations of the 1999 American Housing Survey prepared for the Millennial Housing Commission.

Figure 6.20 highlights a further area of concern related to housing supply. Between 1985 and 1996, the moderate-income rental supply experienced significant losses. These losses were greatest in the 80–100% of area median income (AMI) category, but there were also losses in the 60–80% of AMI and 100–120% of AMI categories.

The homeownership gap discussed in Chapter 2 is also a problem. Homeownership is growing, but the homeownership rate for minority households is significantly below that of white households. For example, in 2001, the overall homeownership rate was 68%, but when it is separated by race and ethnicity of households, a very different picture arises. For the white population, the rate was 71.8%, and for white non-Hispanics, 74.4%. For African Americans it was 48.1%, for Hispanics, 48.8%, and for all other races, 53.9%. In essence, the African American and Hispanic homeownership rate is around 25% below that for white Americans. (See Figure 2.18, Chapter 2).

FIGURE 6.20

Affordability Pressures are Mounting as the Moderate-Income Rental Supply Plummets

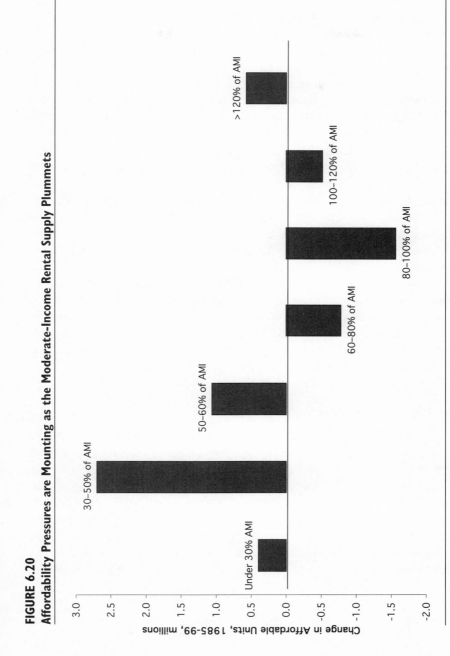

SOURCE: HUD tabulations of the 1985 and 1999 American Housing Surveys prepared for the Millennial Housing Commission.

Meanwhile, homelessness remains a serious concern. Although the precise number of homeless people is elusive, national estimates converge around 650,000 homeless people using homeless assistance programs during an average week, and an average of 2.9 million people using homeless assistance programs sometime during a year's period.[19] The problems of homelessness are exacerbated by a wide range of social, health, and mental health concerns, but high housing costs clearly contribute to the number of homeless, and to the number of near homeless living in tenuous housing arrangements with relatives or friends.

The nation's housing challenges are further exacerbated by the fact that federal direct housing support reaches a diminishing number of those who are in need. Further, some individuals are not only poor, they are geographically segregated, and this causes serious concentrations of poverty, poor housing, homelessness, and discrimination. Unfortunately, residential segregation by income and race is still a problem, and poor and working families earning the minimum wage are often socially and economically isolated from higher-wage employment opportunities. These issues are complicated, and often the challenges relate not only to housing problems but to welfare, income, education, health care, mental health, and a variety of social services. However, the problems cannot be ignored just because they are difficult. As we move forward in the twenty-first century, these issues require ongoing public policy focus and attention and resources from both the public and the private sectors.

Meeting the Needs of a Growing Population

Meeting the needs of the housing "have-nots" in the twenty-first century is a significant challenge, but it is not the only challenge. It is complicated by the fact that the nation's overall population and housing demand is growing substantially — through births, the aging of the population, and immigration. In 2000, the population (based on the 2000 census) reached 281.4 million, an increase of 32.7 million people, or 13.2%, since 1990. For the first time in the twentieth century, all states gained in population, and the decade set a record for absolute growth. The West grew the fastest, by 19.7%, followed by the South, at 17.3%, the Midwest, at 7.9% and the Northeast by 5.5%. The growth in households between 1990 and 2000 was close to 12

---

[19] Burt, *Helping America's Homeless,* The Urban Institute, 34–50. The fact that these two figures are so different is significant. There is tremendous churning among the homeless population. While during an average week there are about 650,000 using homeless assistance, over the course of a year, because people exit and enter homelessness, the annualized figure is nearly five times greater.

million.[20] The demand generated by this household growth led to an increase in the nation's housing stock of 17.3 million units — from 102.3 million in 1990 to 119.6 million in 2000 (see Figure 1.2, Chapter 1).

Looking to the future, U.S. Census Bureau projections indicate that the population could grow by 25 million people to a total of 305 million by 2010[21] (see Figure 6.21). The National Association of Home Builders projects that the number of households will grow by 12.55 million between 2001 and 2010, which means that there will be over a million more households formed in that decade compared to the 1990s. Since all of these households will need a place to live, it will undoubtedly create a strong demand for new housing construction — almost 10% stronger than in the 1990s (see Figure 1.25). The question then arises as to how we will meet the housing needs of a growing population. Where will these people live? Where will they find affordable housing? How will they get to work?

Looking even further into the future, the Census Bureau projects that by 2025, the U.S. population could increase by as many as 63 million people to 344 million total[22] (see Figure 6.21). This growth compares to the current population of Great Britain or France — and all this within twenty-five years. Almost half of this growth is projected to be in three states. California is expected to be hardest hit with 17 million, then Texas with 7 million, and Florida with nearly 6 million. Many other states will see increases of at least a half million people. Once again, the questions arise: Where will these people live, and how will they find affordable housing?

This population growth is further complicated by illegal immigration. The projections noted above include growth from immigration — both legal and illegal — but obviously, the level of illegal immigration is very difficult to project. The U.S. Census Bureau estimates that about 8 million illegal immigrants live in the United States.[23] However, the number of illegal immigrants is rising rapidly, and the actual figure may be significantly higher. This is an additional strain on housing resources.

The challenge in the twenty-first century, then, is not only to meet the needs of the housing "have-nots" and working families, but to also meet the general needs of a growing population. And naturally, those who have greater resources will tend to push out those that do not. Barbara Ehrenreich

---

[20] U.S. Census Department data as presented by Eric Belsky.

[21] The 25 million figure is the midpoint of the middle series and highest series estimates of the U.S. Census Bureau Population Estimates Program.

[22] The 343 million estimate is a conservative figure slightly higher than the 338 million of the U.S. Census Bureau middle estimate, but well below its high estimate of 380 million.

[23] *Wall Street Journal,* 25 October 2001, 1.

FIGURE 6.21
U.S. Census Population Projections (in millions)

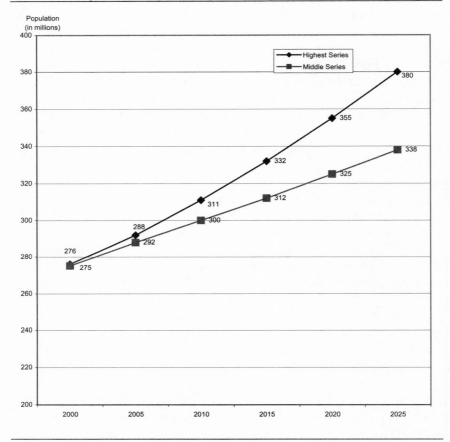

SOURCE: U.S. Census Bureau, Population Projections Program. www.census.gov/population/
projections/nation/summary/np-t1.txt.

said it well in her book *Nickled and Dimed.* "The problem of rents is easy for noneconomists, even a sparsely educated low-wage worker, to grasp; it's the market, stupid. When the rich and the poor compete for housing on the open market, the poor don't stand a chance. The rich can always outbid them, buy out their tenements and trailer parks, and replace them with condos, McMansions, golf courses, or whatever they like. Since the rich have become more numerous, thanks largely to rising stock prices and executive salaries, the poor have necessarily been forced into housing that is more expensive, more dilapidated, and more distant from their places of work."[24]

Overcoming the Complacency of Our Own Success

A majority of the U.S. population is now well housed, and the home-ownership rate has risen dramatically, as highlighted in Chapter 2. However we suffer from our own success. Public sentiment is generally focused on concerns other than housing, such as homeland security, education, crime, and health care. The 70 million existing homeowners "have" their housing, and this leads to the "not in my backyard" (NIMBY) phenomenon. Against the backdrop of this success and the recognition that other issues are more prominent in the minds of the American public, housing the "have-nots" may be harder to achieve in the twenty-first century than it was in 1949.

The fact that housing is no longer a top issue is illustrated by several surveys. In December 1992, Bonner and Associates commissioned a survey by the Gallup Organization of members of Congress.[25] Twenty-eight percent of the members of Congress (not their staffs) responded. They were asked to rank a series of issues by importance, with the top two categories being "critical" and "very important." Of the eighteen issues on the list, housing came in dead last, with only 6% of Democrats and 2% of Republicans deeming it "critical." When the "critical" and "very important" categories were combined, housing came in seventeenth with only term limits lagging behind. By comparison, 97% of members of Congress ranked jobs and health care issues as either "critical" or "very important," and 96% ranked the federal budget deficit as such. Only 29% felt that way about housing issues, and 21% about term limits. Given that limiting the length of their terms is not a high priority for very many members of Congress, there is little solace in knowing that housing was not ranked last.

In a July 1997 survey of 400 national opinion leaders commissioned by the National Association of Home Builders, respondents were asked to indicate which issues they felt should receive the greatest attention in Washington: the federal budget deficit, health care, the economy, housing, crime and drugs, or public education. Only 2% of respondents chose housing as

---

[24] Ehrenreich, *Nickled and Dimed*, 199.
[25] "Bonner and Associates Survey," The Gallop Organization, Inc.

the primary issue. The survey was repeated in January 1999, with an identical result. However, these same opinion leaders did feel that homeownership was important. Eighty-four percent of the people surveyed owned their own home, and 49% felt the federal government should do more to promote homeownership, while 30% felt that the level of federal promotion was the right amount and only 13% felt that less should be done. Of respondents who had children at home, an even higher number, 56%, compared to 41% of those who did not have children living at home, felt that more should be done to promote homeownership. Overall, this group felt that homeownership was important to the community, and that important values stemmed from homeownership that added to the safety of the community and the quality of education. However, it seems that because these opinion leaders already were by and large home owners, they were generally unconcerned about housing for others (except perhaps their own children), and housing was not a top priority.

Housing, then, is not a top-of-the-mind issue, and it will be difficult to address the housing needs of the "have-nots" highlighted earlier, and even the housing challenges of a growing population. Paradoxically, despite the fact that housing is no longer a top issue to Congress or many of the American public, each year (as discussed in Chapter 5) large federal expenditures are allocated to housing, both through direct housing programs and indirect programs that provide tax benefits such as the mortgage interest deduction, the low income tax credit, and the property tax deduction. The housing industry and others interested in housing the nation will, therefore, have to work hard to maintain the resources allocated for housing, and particular effort will be required to increase them. Although political support for the Mortgage Interest Deduction remains strong, meeting the needs of the housing "have-nots" and America's working families will be a far more difficult challenge.

Regulatory Barriers That Increase the Cost of Housing

Among the greatest housing challenges in the twenty-first century are regulatory barriers (related to such areas as zoning, land use controls, building codes, the process of approving bulding permits, etc.) at the local, state, and federal levels which add significantly to the cost of housing. As the Advisory Commission on Regulatory Barriers to Affordable Housing reported to HUD Secretary Jack Kemp and President George Bush in 1991, "Millions of Americans are being priced out of buying or renting the kind of housing they could otherwise afford were it not for a web of government regulations. For them, America — the land of opportunity — has become the land of a frustrating and often unrewarded search for the affordable home."[26] Regulatory barriers affect middle-income workers such as police, firefighters, teachers, and other vital workers, who often live miles from the communities they serve because they cannot find affordable housing. Also affected are workers who are forced to live far from their jobs and commute long distances; low-income and minority people, who, as noted earlier, have an especially hard time finding suitable affordable housing; and the elderly, who have difficulties finding housing suited to their needs in the communities where they would like to live.[27]

Every presidential commission on housing over the last forty years has highlighted the need for regulatory reform. In 1968 and 1969, the Douglas Commission (The National Commission on Urban Problems) and the Kaiser Committee (The President's Committee on Housing) issued reports that highlighted the substantial impact government regulations have on the cost and availability of housing. Despite these warnings, government at all levels has continued to expand regulatory control of housing. The Douglas Commission recommended greater centralization of land use regulatory authority, reductions in incentives for fiscal and exclusionary zoning, and fairer allocation of land-use costs between the government and the developer.[28] Venturing even further, the Kaiser Committee recommended that the federal government preempt local zoning and other land-use regulations in controlling federal construction projects and low-income housing development. It favored state review of local zoning ordinances to ensure that they did not interfere with satisfying housing needs in metropolitan areas. The committee also concluded that "given the widespread abuses, and the need for low-cost housing, local prerogative should yield somewhat in this instance."[29]

More than a decade later, in 1982, the President's Commission on Housing reached very similar conclusions: "In hearings across the country, the commission was told repeatedly that unnecessary regulations at all levels of government have seriously hindered the production of housing, increased its cost, and restricted opportunities for mobility."[30] The commission report

---

[26] Advisory Commission on Regulatory Barriers to Affordable Housing, "Not in My Backyard," 3.
[27] Ibid.
[28] National Commission on Urban Problems, "Building the American City."
[29] The President's Committee on Urban Housing, A Decent Home, 144.
[30] President's Commission on Housing, *Report of the Commission,* 180.

found that regulation can hinder the efficient operation of the marketplace by denying consumers a wide range of housing choices and denying owners and developers the freedom to use property efficiently: "Regulation has unnecessarily pushed up cost in some localities by as much as 25% of the final sales price, and. . . . regulation often limits flexibility in housing construction, both by inhibiting the substitution of available materials, labor, land, and capital in response to changes in prices, and by impeding the rate at which new products and building systems can be introduced."[31]

More recent is a report to HUD Secretary Jack Kemp and President George Bush in 1991. After studying the problem for well over a year, the commission, assembled by Secretary Kemp, found that excessive regulation increased housing prices by 20% to 35% in the most severely affected areas of the country.[32] The commission went on to highlight regulatory barriers in suburbs and cities, and the challenges of environmental regulations that impact affordable housing. The problem, as noted by the commission, involves competing public policy objectives: "Numerous federal, state, and local regulations that intended to achieve specific, admirable goals turn out to add negative consequences for affordable housing. The impact on housing cost may not have been considered when the regulations were promulgated."[33] Another part of the problem, as identified by the commission, is the fragmented structure of government land-use and development regulations. To address these problems, the commission called on all levels of government to work with the private sector to remove barriers. It recommended that the federal government play a major role in stimulating regulatory reform and in integrating barrier removal into federal housing programs. It further recommended a wide range of reform at the state and local levels and that HUD monitor the implementation of these efforts.

Unfortunately, regulatory barriers to building affordable housing still exist. While this author served as a member of a congressional housing commission, the Millennial Housing Commission, between 2001 and 2002, the commission heard numerous concerns about excess government regulations and the barriers they raise for people trying to find affordable housing. Such issues will not be overcome without concerted effort at all levels. The Department of Housing and Urban Development should en-

---

[31] Ibid.
[32] Advisory Commission on Regulatory Barriers to Affordable Housing, "Not In My Backyard," 4.
[33] Ibid., 8.

courage both the White House and Congress to recognize and focus on this problem. Creative efforts at the state and local levels are even more essential. If the cost of housing can be lowered by 10% or 15% through the removal of regulatory barriers, it will make an important difference in the availability of affordable housing at all levels, and a modest dent in the needs of the nation's housing "have-nots."

The Challenges of Growth and the Environment

To the extent that housing is considered an item on the national policy agenda, the discussion usually centers on growth or environmental concerns related to the production and development of housing; affordable housing is usually left out of the dialogue. Sprawl, livability, and smart growth have become top-of-the-mind issues in some communities. For example, a national voter attitude survey conducted by the National Association of Home Builders in February 1999 asked a sample of 1,209 registered voters what they thought was the most important issue facing their community, and housing was not raised per se. Education and schools and roads and traffic were first and third, respectively. In fact, issues of expanding development and sprawl often translate as concerns related to schools, the quality of education, and the fact that traffic has risen and infrastructure is inadequate.

As with any public policy topic, there are multiple sides to the debate. On the one hand, there are those who raise this topic and talk about protecting the environment, smart growth, or fighting sprawl with the primary purpose of stopping growth. Such advocates would use these concerns as reasons to stop all development. On the other hand, there are legitimate concerns about growth that must be addressed. The environment needs to be protected. Traffic congestion and problems with schools and infrastructure, as well as general notions of livability, need to receive focus at the community, state, and even national levels. However, discussions of smart growth should not be turned into discussions of no growth, and should take into consideration housing affordability and meeting on-going demographic demand. Placing limits on the quantity and the type of housing will only make meeting the needs of the housing "have-nots" and of a growing population more difficult. Constraints that raise building costs and limit growth will make it more difficult to produce new affordable housing, raise the cost of existing housing in established communities, and increase discrimination through exclusion. It is impossible today to sidestep the issues of growth and the environment, but the trade-offs should be dealt with explicitly. The challenges that must be faced in the twenty-first century cannot be addressed without a balance between housing affordability and smart growth.

Finally, it is worth noting that issues of "growth" and "no growth" generally rise and fall with the economy. Strong demand for housing when the economy is good often leads to efforts to slow things down. For example, in the latter part of the 1990s, we saw an unprecedented period of solid economic development and strong housing production, and with it came cries to slow down housing production in many communities. However, when the economy slows down and people become concerned about jobs and economic growth, the country looks to housing as a way to stimulate the economy and create jobs.

Achieving Common Ground

How can we best address the housing challenges of the twenty-first century? The problems after World War II were significant, and the nation has done a remarkable job to meet many of them. However, our very success in the past complicates our ability to address the problems of the future. If we are to succeed, it will be essential for those who are involved in housing to work together to achieve common ground. It is easy enough to identify the challenges; the real need is to reach consensus on solutions that can be implemented.

The people who deal with housing represent a wide variety of interests. At times they come together to work with Congress and the White House to establish housing priorities and programs. Oftentimes, though, each group or person represents a somewhat different view, and it is very difficult to reach a solution that has the votes to become law and to be signed by the president. However, achieving common ground will be essential if we are ever to address the nation's housing challenges before us.

CONCLUSION

The United States is one of the best, if not the best housed nation in the world. To some, such a statement implies that the job is done, but that is not the case! Significant gaps and problems remain, especially for the housing "have-nots." The housing challenges of the future may be greater in many respects than they were fifty years ago because our national priorities have shifted. However, as we think of the challenges that lie ahead, the words of President Franklin D. Roosevelt ring loud: "The test of our progress is not whether we add more to the abundance of those who have much; it is whether we provide enough for those who have too little."[34]

---

[34] President Franklin D. Roosevelt, Second Inaugural Address (January 20, 1937).

PART II

Achieving Common Ground
in the
Twenty-First Century

Chapter 7

ACHIEVING COMMON GROUND: THE REALITIES AND THE PARTICIPANTS

Over time, the consensus reflected in the Housing Act of 1949 has shifted, and in many respects, housing issues have become far more complex. It is more difficult now to achieve common ground. This chapter will outline the realities of the twenty-first century. One of these realities is the complexity of the process of providing affordable housing, and the large number of participants involved, many of whom have very different perspectives. However, a review of the complexities of the housing delivery system should help one better understand the formulation and implementation of housing policy in the future.

THE NATION'S HOUSING FOCUS SHIFTS

During the depths of the depression, one of the areas around which President Franklin Delano Roosevelt chose to rally the American people was housing. In his second inaugural address in 1937, he spoke of three basic needs — housing, clothing and food — and said of a traumatized nation, "I see one-third of a nation ill-housed, ill-clad, ill-nourished." In response, a number of federal housing initiatives, such as the Federal Housing Administration (FHA), the Federal Home Loan Bank system, and the public housing system, were established, and the foundation was laid for dramatic improvements in the nation's housing delivery system.

At the end of World War II, with the return of soldiers and war-related workers, people needed places to live, and housing was revived as a national priority. Providing a decent home, and therefore suitable living environment for every American, filled a national need and was one small way to recognize the sacrifice's of our veterans. The range of government programs was expanded, beginning with the 1949 Housing Act, but even more important was the revitalization of the private housing market.

Between 1950 and 2000, 77 million single-family and multifamily housing units were added to the overall housing stock, and more than 65% of our current housing stock has been built within the last fifty years. This is not to say that at the end of World War II there were not debates among housing advocates and industry leaders as to the best way to meet America's housing needs. However, from the depths of the depression to the 1970s — whether through public housing, urban renewal, the Federal Housing Administration, support for the nation's housing finance system, efforts to lower downpayments, or many other approaches — the debate was over means not ends, and there was a clear national "call to action."

As America moved into the 1970s, though, other national priorities began to rise.[1] With the war in Vietnam, urban unrest, and general societal upheaval, national priorities and concerns pushed beyond the search for housing, clothing, food, and prosperity. Environmental advocates highlighted the pollution of our land, air, and water, the elimination of hazardous waste, and the protection of endangered species and wetlands. Questions were also raised about growth as well as residential and commercial development. More recently, traffic congestion, smart growth, and suburban sprawl have come to the forefront of housing and land-use policy debates. In addition, the development and housing approval process — which was already complex — has become even more onerous in many areas of the country. Once people secure their own housing they often seek to exclude others, thus the "not in my backyard" (NIMBY) syndrome. Regulation at the national, state, and local levels has escalated, driving up the cost of homes and making it more difficult to provide affordable housing. In a study on affordable housing in the mid-1980s, Kenneth Rosen wrote, "The extreme difficulty determining whether a minimum standard or requirement is necessary or excessive is the fundamental problem in analyzing land use controls. Many controls are necessary or desirable in providing amenities and preserving the quality of the living environment. As such, they are quite properly reflected in higher housing costs, however, it is generally believed that subdivision ordinances frequently impose standards for improvements that add costs beyond those needed for the protection of public health and safety."[2] Rosen's point was valid in 1984, and the dilemma is even greater today.

With the rise in the number of divergent views which began in the 1970s, it has become more difficult for people to work together to achieve

---

[1] Field, "Building Consensus for Affordable Housing."
[2] Rosen, *Affordable Housing: New Politics in Housing and Mortgage Markets,* 86.

common ground. When individuals and groups have a clear and common perspective, it makes it easier for them to come together to work toward a common cause. However, if those perspectives are divergent, then the incentive to work together decreases significantly. This is the environment in the twenty-first century, and the many actors and their divergent perspectives, which are outlined in this chapter, demonstrate the complexity of the housing policy process.

THE REALITIES IN THE TWENTY-FIRST CENTURY

Even before September 11, 2001 and the subsequent war on terrorism, policy areas such as education, crime, social security, and health care were higher priorities than housing. Concern over terrorism and homeland security pushes housing concerns even more to the background. To the extent that there is a public outcry related to housing, it tends to be around suburban sprawl, traffic congestion and growth issues, all of which can actually make providing affordable housing even more difficult. Also, the "have-nots" — the 4.9 million "worst case" Americans described earlier, and the 13 million Americans who pay more than 50% of their income on housing or live in severely inadequate housing, whether they rent or own — plus young families and immigrants who seek affordable housing, have relatively little political clout, and certainly far less influence than mainstream Americans, who are well-housed and focused on other issues.

Our ability to achieve common ground and to address housing challenges in the twenty-first century has been further complicated by a seemingly growing trend toward partisanship. If we are going to address the nation's housing problems we must cut across traditional interests and differences, and we must recognize market, political, and other realities. As we go forward in the twenty-first century, at least four major realities must be recognized; in some cases these realities overlap with the six housing policy challenges discussed in Chapter 6.

First, the challenges of the housing "have-nots" and the working poor are not an academic story. These are real people living in real housing, often in poor condition, which they cannot afford. Poverty and discrimination still exist. The difficulties of providing affordable housing are real.

The second reality is that the national commitment to housing is no longer robust. The paradox is that the nation continues to spend, primarily through tax expenditures, but also through direct costs, significant federal (as well as state and local) resources on housing. Further, in national surveys, homeownership continues to be highly valued and is still identified as a primary goal for a majority of Americans. Also, in a survey sponsored by the Fannie Mae Foundation in 2002, Americans identified the lack of affordable homes for low- and moderate-income working families as second only to lack of affordable health care as a problem. (37% said the lack of affordable housing was a very, or fairly big problem, and 43% identified lack of affordable health care as a very big or fairly big problem.) Affordable housing outnumbered job loss and unemployment (36%), crime (23%), and a polluted environment (21%) as a problem to those surveyed.[3] Further, for working families, the lack of affordable housing was the number one issue (41%), ranked just above health care (39%), and above job loss and unemployment (34%), crime (20%), and polluted environment (16%).[4] However, housing is no longer a top issue to many of the members of Congress or to many among the American public — especially those who already have achieved adequate housing. This must be recognized and addressed as we formulate the nation's housing policy.

The third reality we must deal with is the marketplace. Each year there is an estimated net migration of at least 800,000 people into the United States, not including those who come into the country illegally.[5] With this as a base, and considering the impact of immigration, births, and household change, the Harvard Joint Center for Housing Studies projects that the number of households will grow by 12.7 to 13 million between 2000 and 2010. In turn, this will create a need for 1.3 to 1.5 million housing starts per year, and the consumer is going to drive what the private market produces. During my years at NAHB, it was fascinating to meet with groups that accused home builders of creating sprawl. Builders build the homes, but those who want to stay in business build to consumer demand and are very careful to watch and follow that demand. If they build homes that the consumer does not want, the homes will not be sold, and they will go out of business. Home builders influence what happens in the marketplace, but in large part, they do not lead the market, they follow it. This is reflected by the fact that consumers are generally happy with the housing and the communities in which they live. In a 1999 national consumer attitude survey conducted by the National Association of Home Builders,

---

[3] Fannie Mae Foundation, Hart and Teeter, "Results of the Fannie Mae Foundation Affordable Housing Survey," 1.

[4] Ibid., 2.

[5] The U.S. Bureau of Census, Current Population Report, p. 25–1095, p. 25–130, estimates net migration at 820,000 per year from 1998–2050, also see U.S. Department of Commerce, Statistical Abstract of the United States, 1998.

with a sample size of 1,209 people, when voters were asked how they felt about the community they lived in, 90.5% said they were satisfied (50.9% said they were very satisfied, and 39.9% were somewhat satisfied)[6] with the community in which they live. This is despite all of the discussion in the newspapers about sprawl and the publicity about growing discontent among suburban home owners

The fourth reality is the wide variety of actors and competing interests found in the housing and urban policy arena. Each player views the world from his own perspective. The process of building and producing housing is complex, beginning with concept and land acquisition, and including land development, building and constructing, buying, financing, closing, owning and renting, maintaining and remodeling, and selling. Each step of the way there are new participants in both the private and the public sectors. Because of this confluence of actors and forces, it is extremely difficult to establish one set national housing policy. To understand the challenges created by this fourth reality, it is essential to discuss the actors and participants involved.

UNDERSTANDING THE HOUSING DELIVERY SYSTEM

The process of producing and consuming housing is often long and complex, but ten stages can be identified (see Figure 7.1). The first is land acquisition. Prior to land acquisition, a developer, builder, or community leader will undoubtedly envision how the land might be used, and community plans may be developed to provide an overall framework for land use. But the real process begins when somebody acquires the land with the intent to build.

The second stage is development. This can be a complex process in and of itself. Specific plans must be developed, decisions are made related to zoning and land use, and agreement must be reached, especially with the local jurisdiction, as to the requirements that must be met. Once all variances, permits, and approvals are achieved, construction can begin for the roads, sewers, water, and other infrastructure that will support the housing project.

Once the land is developed and specific lots are subdivided, parcels can be sold to a builder or kept by the builder/developer, and the third stage — the actual building — can begin. However, before construction can start, specific plans must be prepared and a building permit issued, and once again, a wide variety of participants are included in the decision-making

---

[6] National Association of Home Builders, public opinion survey.

FIGURE 7.1
Housing Production/Consumption Chain

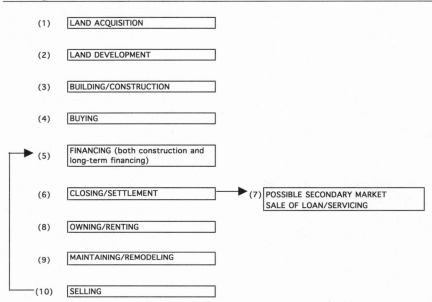

process. The actual building, of course, involves numerous components; many workers and manufacturers make the parts that go into a home, such as rugs, cabinets, paint, windows, roof trusses, nails, appliances, and so on. If the cost of lumber rises, the price of the house or apartment will likely rise. If labor shortages exist, they will impact the cost of building and the ultimate price. Any number of variables may arise which potentially impact the final price of the house.

The fourth step is that someone — the home buyer or apartment owner — buys the house or apartment. It goes without saying that the buyer is essential to the housing delivery process. Without the hope and expectation of finding a buyer, the builder would never build. And the preferences and financial capabilities of the home buyer and the renter have a major influence on the kinds of homes, apartments, and eventually communities that are built.

The fifth stage is financing, which includes not only the long-term financing for the home, but also financing for the acquisition and development of the land and the construction of the home. Before a house is built or sold (a home or apartment is seldom built or purchased with cash), financing must be arranged. In the sixth stage, the house is "closed" and a settlement occurs. Final financing arrangements are a key part of the closing, and at the time of closing, the ownership and title of the home is transferred from the builder/developer to the owner. Once the loan is closed, the lender has the option to sell the loan in the secondary market and/or to sell the servicing for the loan, and this possible sale constitutes the seventh stage in the housing production/consumption chain.

At this point, the eighth stage, owning or renting, begins for the consumer. With owning or renting comes the ninth stage, maintaining the property and, over time, perhaps remodeling the house or apartment. The tenth stage in the housing production/consumption chain involves selling the house, and with the sale of the house, the chain goes back to the fifth stage — financing — and the process recycles over and over again through stages five through ten with the sale of existing houses or apartments.

At each stage along the housing production/consumption chain, a variety of participants are involved. To help understand who they are, they can be divided into people who work in the private sector and those who work in the public sector. Figure 7.2 identifies many of the participants in the private sector, and Figure 7.5 highlights some of the key players in the public sector.

Private Sector

In the private sector, at least eight different groups or participants can be identified (see Figure 7.2). The first is developers. These are the people who buy the land and install the infrastructure — roads, sewers, water, electricity, and so on. Sometimes home builders will be developers, and other times the building and development functions are completely separate.

The second group is home builders and architects. These are the people who design and oversee the building of homes. A large home building company can build 30,000 homes a year, and in 2001, the 100 largest home building companies built 24.5% of all the houses in America and 27.8% of the single-family housing starts. But the majority of home builders build fewer than twenty-five homes a year; some "custom home builders" focus on five or ten homes at most annually. Many custom homes involve an architect, and at the high end of the market, some home builders will only build architect-designed homes. Many builders now design the homes they build, sometimes hiring architects or working with architectural firms. A number of sophisticated computer design models can also be used in designing a home.

The third group is subcontractors and construction workers. Most home builders subcontract out the large majority of the labor to framers, bricklayers, painters, and so on. Some of the construction workers are union

FIGURE 7.2
Private Sector Participants in the Housing Production/Consumption Chain

Participants

1. Developers

2. Home Builders and Architects

3. Construction Workers and Subcontractors

4. Lenders/Secondary Market Participants
   - Mortgage Banks
   - Savings and Loan Associations
   - Commercial Bankers
   - CreditUnions
   - Mortgage Brokers
   - Fannie Mae
   - Freddie Mac
   - Federal Home Loan Banks

5. Suppliers of a Wide Range of Home Related Products
   - As an example, see list of the members of
     NAHB's National Council of the Housing Industry
     (NCHI) (Figure7.3)

6. Realtors, Housing Advocates, Insurers and other Key Facilitators to the Housing Delivery System
   - Realtors
   - Housing Advocates
   - Private Mortgage Insurers
   - Title Companies
   - Appraisers
   - Other Insurance Companies

7. Home Buyers, Renters, and Other Interested Parties
   - Home Buyers
   - Renters
   - Community Leaders
   - Neighbors
   - Consumers

8. Environmental Groups
   - National Environmental Groups
   - Local and State Environmental Groups

labor, although the majority of workers in the home building industry do not belong to unions. Union workers are much more predominant in commercial and high-rise residential construction.

The fourth group is lenders and secondary market participants. Some of the key players include mortgage bankers, savings and loan associations, commercial banks, mortgage brokers, and credit unions. Although the government-sponsored enterprises, Freddie Mac and Fannie Mae, do not provide direct lending, they buy loans in the secondary market, and because of their size and importance in the market, they play a key role in determining underwriting guidelines and other mortgage parameters.

Suppliers of home products make up the fifth important group. There are literally thousands of parts in a home, and they are supplied by almost as many manufacturers and producers. They supply wood, kitchen fixtures, rugs, bricks, cement, roof trusses, and all the other items that go into the building of the house or apartment. To illustrate the number of suppliers, when the NAHB holds its annual convention and suppliers are asked to demonstrate their products, over 1,000 exhibitors participate in the show, and the exhibits cover more than twenty acres, and this is only a portion of the potential suppliers who participate. The NAHB has a National Council of the Housing Industry (NCHI) made up of the larger producers of building products and the membership in 2002 was close to ninety (see Figure 7.3)

The sixth group comprises realtors, housing advocates, insurers, title companies, and others who facilitate the mortgage transaction. Realtors are involved in most transactions, even the sale of new homes, and many builders are also realtors. Private mortgage insurance companies play an important role in insuring a portion of the mortgage, often for first-time home buyers who can afford only a low down payment. In addition, private mortgage insurance or FHA insurance is required for Fannie Mae and Freddie Mac to purchase a mortgage when the down payment is less than 20%. Appraisers, title companies, and other insurers are also involved in the mortgage transaction at the sale of the home, and in the closing/settlement process. Throughout the process, a wide range of housing advocates seek to achieve various programs to meet the nation's housing needs.

The seventh group includes home buyers, renters, and an array of other interested parties. Home buyers and renters are the consumers, and their preferences, expectations and financial capabilities drive the process. Community leaders and neighbors often express their opinions of housing projects. The providers of roads and schools are also closely linked to home building, and taxpayers from all walks of the community are often concerned about the level of housing production in a particular neighborhood or county.

Finally, the eighth group comprises environmental groups. They could join several of the categories noted above, but in recent years, they have played an increasing role in commenting on development projects and what has come to be known as smart growth. They also are deeply involved in conservation issues including conservation of wetlands and endangered species, which can have a major impact on the building process.

All homes are built locally, not nationally, and the participants highlighted above are involved in the decisions that affect the type, price, and quality of housing that gets built. At the local level, and often at the state level, there are literally hundreds of participants involved in the housing production/consumption chain. However, at the national level, most of these participants are represented by a trade association or a national organization. Many of these trade associations or national organizations also

FIGURE 7.3
Members of the NAHB National Council of the Housing Industry (as of 4/15/02)

2–10 Home Buyers Warranty	MH2 Technologies
Alcoa Building Products	Manufactured Housing Institute
American Gas Association	Marvin Windows
American Standard, Inc.	Masco Corporation
Andersen Windows, Inc.	Masonite International Corporation
Armstrong World Industries	Maytag (Jenn Air, Magic Chef)
Brick Industry Association	McGraw-Hill Construction Information GRP
Broan-Nutone, LLC	Moen, Inc. (Fortune Brands Home Products)
Builder Magazine	NAIMA (North American Insulation Manufacturers Association)
Carrier Corporation	NASFA (North American Steel Framing Alliance)
Certainteed Corporation	Noveon, Inc.
Channelinx.com, Inc.	NREL (National Renewable Energy Laboratory)
Congoleum Corporation	Overhead Door Corporation
Copper Development Association, Inc.	Owens-Corning Corporation
Craftmaster Manufacturing, Inc.	Pactiv Corporation
Crossville Porcelain Stone/USA	Pella Corporation
Cultured Stone Products Corporation	Portland Cement Association
Dal-Tile Corporation	Price Pfister
Dryvit System, Inc.	Professional Builder Magazine
E.I. Dupont De Nemours & Co., Inc.	Professional Warranty Corporation
Eldorado Stone	SBR, Inc. (Metallon)
Gaf Materials Corporation	Sears Contract Sales
GE Appliances	Senco Products, Inc.
Genesis Homes	Silver Line Building Products Corp.
Georgia-Pacific Corporation	Southern Forrest Products Association
GM Fleet and Commercial Group	Square D Company
Gorell Enterprises, Inc.	Stanley Works
Hearth, Patio & Barbecue Association	Sterling Plumbing Group, Inc.
Hearth Technologies Inc. (Heatilator, Heat-N-Glo)	Sub-Zero Freezer Company, Inc.
Home & Garden Television Network	Superior Walls of America
Homesphere	Temple-Inland Forest Products Corp.
Honeywell, Inc.	Therma-Tru Corporation
Icynene, Inc.	Timberlake Cabinet Company
In-Sink-Erator (Emerson Electric Co.)	Timberline Software Corporation
Jacuzzi Whirlpool Bath	The Trane Company
James Hardie Building Products, Inc.	Triangle Pacific Flooring Group
Johns Manville International, Inc.	US Gypsum Corporation
Kohler Company	Velux-America, Inc.
Kolbe & Kolbe Millwork Co., Inc.	Vent-Free Gas Products Alliance
Kwikset Locks	Viking Range Corporation
Lennox Industries Inc.	Weather Shield Mfg., Inc.
Louisiana Pacific Corporation	Whirlpool Corporation
Mannington Mills, Inc.	Wilsonart International

operate at the state and local level. For example, the National Association of Home Builders comprises more than 202,000 member firms, with employees in these firms numbering over 8 million. It also includes state associations in forty-nine states and close to 800 local associations. Many trade associations, including NAHB, are federations, in which the national organization provides a charter for the local associations, and if members join at the local level, they automatically become members at the state and national level. However, the exact structure and representation of each trade association or national association varies significantly. Figure 7.4 identifies some of the trade associations and organizations that are part of the housing production/consumption chain in each of the eight private sector groups. The list is not intended to be all inclusive, but to illustrate the fact that many different private sector participants are involved in the housing production/consumption chain.

Public Sector

Of course, homes are not built without significant involvement from the public sector. As Figure 7.5 illustrates, numerous actors at the federal, state, and local levels influence the housing production/consumption process. At the federal level, the Congress, working with the White House, sets the broad policy. Numerous agencies are involved, including the Department of Housing and Urban Development, the Environmental Protection Agency, the Army Corps of Engineers, the Interior Department, the Transportation Department, and the Agriculture Department. The White House plays a dual role, working with Congress to formulate policy, but also, oftentimes, exercising regulatory oversight, especially through the Office of Management of Budget (OMB). As noted in earlier chapters, HUD serves as a regulator in a variety of capacities, runs the FHA and GNMA programs, provides grants and subsidies under a variety of direct expenditure programs, and represents housing in the administration at the Cabinet level. The Army Corps of Engineers regulates wetlands in conjunction with the Environmental Protection Agency. Financial regulators include the Office of the Comptroller of Currency (OCC) which oversees commercial banks, and the Office of Thrift Supervision (OTS), which oversees the savings and loan associations. The Federal Deposit Insurance Corporation (FDIC) provides insurance for both banks and savings and loan associations, the Office of Federal Housing Enterprise Oversight (OFHEO), an independent part of HUD, oversees Freddie Mac and Fannie Mae, and the Federal Housing Finance Board (FHFB) oversees the twelve Federal Home Loan Banks. The federal courts play an important role in resolving differences in the interpretation of laws and in setting forth broad legal policy in areas such as property rights and land use.

At the state level, the governors set broad housing parameters, working with the state legislature. Under the Governor's direction are state agencies

FIGURE 7.4
Private Sector Participants and Organizations in the Housing Production/ Consumption Chain

Participants	Trade Associations and Other Organizations
1. Developers	☐ National Association of Home Builders (NAHB) ☐ Urban Land Institute
2. Home Builders and Architects	☐ National Association of Home Builders (NAHB) ☐ American Institute of Architects (AIA) ☐ National Multifamily Housing Council ☐ Urban Land Institute

3. Construction Workers and Subcontractors	☐ Unions— AFL-CIO
	☐ Building and Construction Trades
	☐ Numerous Subcontractor Organizations including:
	   - National Association of Plumbing-Heating-Cooling Contractors
	   - American Subcontractors Association
	   - Mechanical Contractors Association of America
	   - National Roofing Contractors of America
	   - Air Conditioning Contractors of America
	   - Painting and Decorating Contractors of America
	   - Sheet Metal and Air Conditioning National Association
	   - National Electrical Contractors Association

4. Lenders and Secondary Market Participants - Mortgage Banks - Savings and Loan Associations - Commercial Bankers	☐ Mortgage Bankers Association ☐ America's Community Bankers ☐ American Bankers Association ☐ Independent Bankers ☐ National Bankers Association
- Credit Unions	☐ Credit Union National Association ☐ National Association of Federal Credit Unions ☐ American Credit Union Mortgage Association ☐ National Federal of Community Development Credit Unions
- Mortgage Brokers - Fannie Mae - Freddie Mac - Federal Home Loan Banks	☐ National Association of Mortgage Brokers

5. Suppliers of a Wide Range of Home Related Products
 - As an example —see list of the members of
   NAHB's National Council of the Housing Industry
   (NCHI) (Figure 7.3)
	☐ Many of these organizations have their own Washington office legislation and regulation to influence.

6. Realtors, Housing Advocates, Insurers and other Key Facilitators to the Housing Delivery System - Realtors - Housing Advocates - Private Mortgage Insurers - Title Companies - Appraisers - Other Insurance Companies	☐ National Association of Realtors ☐ National Housing Conference ☐ Low Income Housing Coalition ☐ Mortgage Insurance Companies Association ☐ American Land Title Association ☐ Real Estate Settlement Services Providers ☐ Appraisal Institute
7. Home Buyers, Renters and Other Interested Parties - Home Buyers - Renters - Community Leaders - Neighbors - Consumers	☐ Neighborhood Associations ☐ Homeowner Associations ☐ Renter Associations ☐ Consumer Federation of America
8. Environmental Groups - National Environmental Groups - Local and State Environmental Groups	☐ Audubon Society ☐ Green Peace ☐ Legal Defense Fund ☐ National Resource Defense Council ☐ Nature Conservancy ☐ Sierra Club ☐ Thousand Friends ☐ Wildlife Society

FIGURE 7.5
Public Sector Participants and Organizations in the Housing Production/Consumption Chain

Participants	Organizations Representing Participants
FEDERAL	
U.S. Congress	
U.S. president, administration & regulators	
White House	
- Housing and Urban Development (HUD)	
- Environmental Protection Agency (EPA)	
- Corp of Engineers	
- Department of Agriculture (Natural Resources	
Conservation Service (NRCS)	
- Department of Interior (Fish and Wildlife Service (FWS)	
- Department of Transportation	
- Office of Management and Budget (OMB)	
- Financial Regulators including:	
Office of the Comptroller of the Currency (OCC)	
Office of Thrift Supervision (OTS)	
Federal Deposit Insurance Corporation (FDIC)	
Office of Federal Housing Enterprise Oversight (OFHEO)	
Federal Housing Finance Board (FHFB)	
Federal Courts	
STATE	
Governor	☐ National Governors Association (NGA)
State legislators	☐ National Council of State Legislatures
State housing finance agencies	☐ National Council of State Housing Agencies (NCSHA)
Other state agencies in housing, planning, and community and	
development	
State Courts	
LOCAL	
Mayors	☐ U.S. Conference of Mayors
County executives	☐ National Association of Counties Officials (NACO)
City managers	☐ International City Managers Association (ICMA)
Planners	☐ American Planners Association (APA)
Code Officials	☐ International Code Council (ICC)
Zoning Officials	☐ Building Officials and Code Administrators International (BOCA)
	☐ International Conference of Building Officials (ICBO)
	☐ Southern Building Code Congress International (SBCCI)

that — depending on the structure within the state — oversee housing, housing finance, planning, and community development. Forty-seven states have established housing finance agencies; these agencies are often deeply involved in framing state housing policy, and they participate in many housing programs, such as mortgage revenue bonds or the low-income tax credit program. In the early days of housing policy and implementation, going back to 1949, most of the activity took place at the federal level. However, over the last several decades, programs have increasingly emerged at the state level, and there is clearly a devolution of both responsibility and creativity underway from the national level to state and local jurisdictions.

At the local level, the number of jurisdictions expands exponentially. Of course, we have cities and counties, and often the boundaries overlap. The roles and specific functions of cities and counties are established by state legislatures, but within that overall structure, mayors, county executives, planners, and city managers all play a role, depending on the community. There are major differences between local jurisdictions in terms of their view toward providing housing, especially affordable housing, and in terms of specific regulatory and growth policies. Some communities are strongly antigrowth; others encourage growth and development and promote affordable housing. Still others try to strike a balance between the two. If a large home builder is involved in several states and local jurisdictions, he or she must learn to adapt to the philosophy and legal structure of each community, and sometimes to the whims and obstacles within that community.

Once again, many of the participants identified in Figure 7.5 are represented by organizations at the state and national levels (see Figure 7.5). These local and state participants want to ensure that the policies they feel are appropriate are implemented at the national level. At the national level, one set of groups is particularly involved in representing what is happening at the state and local level. They are often referred to as "public interest groups" (PIGs). Among them are the National Association of County Officials (NACO), the National Governors Association (NGA), the U.S. Conference of Mayors, the International City Managers Association (ICMA), and the state housing agencies represented by the National Council of State Housing Agencies (NCSHA).

WHAT CAN WE LEARN FROM VIEWING THE FRAMEWORK FOR THE HOUSING DELIVERY SYSTEM?

The participants involved in the housing production/consumption process form a complex system for building, financing, buying, selling, and reselling homes. It is a challenge to illustrate the confluence of participants in the housing production/consumption chain, especially when participants from both the private and the public sectors are included. Figure 7.6 is intended to provide only a summary. Literally hundreds of different people and groups determine national housing policy, influence legislation, affect regulations issued at the national level, and fight out differences in the courts. At the local and state levels, not only do these same participants interact to determine the broad policies being set, but they impact the specific decisions that are being made concerning where houses will be built and what requirements have to be met. The confluence of participants is still growing, and the complexity is enormous, at times even mind-boggling. It is amazing that the system works as well as it does, but it has evolved over time, and technology provides increasing assistance. Beyond the complexity, though, what can we learn from reviewing this framework?

FIGURE 7.6
Housing Production/Consumption Chain

Private Sector Participants	Public Sector Participants

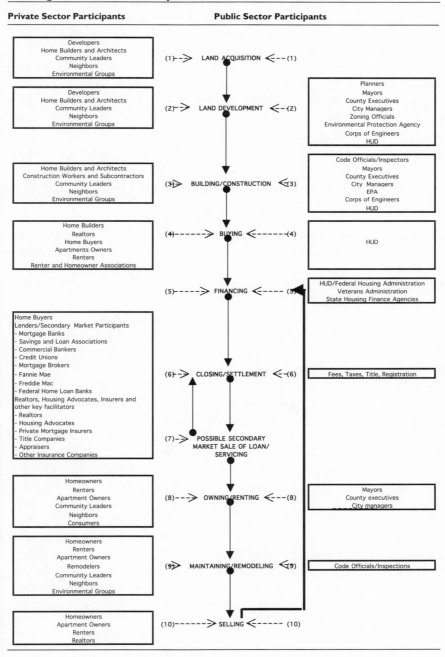

First, the many participants naturally tend to focus on their own special interests. Depending upon the overlap of interests, they may be willing to meet, compromise, and reach agreement, and people who agree may form coalitions. However, when conflicts arise, positions usually harden. Given the large number of participants, the potential for conflict is high.

Second, whether at the national, state, or local level, it is far easier for parties to stop something than it is to make something happen. For example, at the national level, it is often easier to defeat a piece of legislation or to oppose a regulation than it is to try to enact a new congressional direction. Competing interests often cancel each other out, and therefore make action more difficult. At the local level, a strong group of dissenters can have a major impact on years of planning. This is not to say that dissenters do not raise good issues, but it is almost always easier to block a proposal than it is to initiate action that will create affordable housing.

Third, given the array of participants, misunderstanding and miscommunication frequently lead to conflict and compound the difficulties of achieving common ground. To the extent that the people trying to reach agreement are "friends" working together in the housing industry, special care should be made for such housing advocates to listen carefully to each other and to avoid misunderstanding.

Fourth, it is rare for a leader to emerge at the national, state, or local level who can articulate a common vision. Because there are so many actors and forces, one clear national housing policy is almost impossible. Rather, housing policy is sorted through on an issue by issue basis. National housing policy is the sum total of a series of housing policy debates and efforts that in most cases focus on specific issues and specific programs.

Fifth, there are very few forums in the housing policy arena where different views can be raised and meaningful, on-going discussion of housing issues can take place. Participants may actually be willing to work together to compromise, but without a forum for reasoned discussion and exchange where differences and similarities can be explored and understood, it is difficult to do so. The large number of groups compounds matters. In some cases, the HUD secretary can convene a policy dialogue, but HUD secretaries are often too engaged in the debate as participants to provide a meaningful forum for discussion.

Sixth, coalitions are common, but they usually come together to achieve a particular goal. Further, most coalitions are made up of like-minded groups; it is unusual for groups with different points of view to sit down and hammer out their differences.

CONCLUSIONS

Housing is a complex issue, and there are few simple solutions. In the 1950s and 1960s there was a general agreement as to the vision for decent, affordable housing. The debatee was over the means of getting there. Most of the active parties in the debate had some involvement with housing, and the importance of obtaining decent and affordable housing was a vision shared by essentially all the parties. However, with the 1970s and later, a wide range of additional groups entered the fray — environmental organizations, community-based groups, tax organizations, etc. Many of these groups did not hold housing as their end goal; rather, their interests lay elsewhere — environmental protection, stopping community growth, decreasing tax burdens, etc. Further, they saw that the provision of housing could come in conflict with their interests, and that unchecked housing activity could be counterproductive to meeting their favored ends. The result is that two dynamics are taking place. First, there is an increase in the number of parties that see housing affecting their interests, and just the growth in the number of participating parties adds complexity and the possibility of conflict. Second, to the extent that these groups have different visions as to the importancee of housing, at least some conflict is inevitable.

However, if we are going to meet the housing challenges of the twenty-first century, it is the premise of this book that greater effort must be made to overcome this conflict. Failure to achieve common ground — especially among thosee who are advocates for affordable housing — could lead to the loss of sorely needed federal revenues to other national priorities, and a further diminution in the role and importance of HUD. Opponents have already talked at length about abolishing HUD. In addition, unless we achieve common ground, the issues around housing affordability are likely to get worse, and the challenges faced by the housing "have-nots" will increase. Further, the process for developing land and building homes will become even more difficult and time consuming. Home builders and developers, in the minds of some, already have a negative image. A failure of friends and advocates in the housing industry to come together at the local, state, and national levels will add to this image and make the challenges even greater.

With this in mind, the next four chapters outline a series of case studies. Each illustrates a different set of complexities in examining how and why we achieve or do not achieve common ground. Following the four cases, the question is asked in Chapter 12: Can we achieve common ground?

Chapter 8

A CASE STUDY ON ACHIEVING COMMON GROUND: OSHA REGULATIONS FOR THE HOME BUILDING INDUSTRY

The application of Occupational Safety and Health Administration (OSHA) regulations within the home building industry has been an issue for a number of years. On the one hand, home builders and workers desire worker safety. Workers obviously care about their health, and problems and actions on the job site are very time consuming and costly to builders. On the other hand, home builders feel that safety requirements to work on a single-family home job site are significantly different from those for a high-rise apartment or office construction project. The question, then, is how to find the appropriate balance between worker safety and eliminating excessive regulations that lead to unnecessary costs.

This chapter presents a case study on the application of safety standards to the home building industry. It describes an effort, involving a wide range of people and organizations, to achieve common ground. Overall, the case is an example of success.

SAFETY STANDARDS FOR THE HOME BUILDING INDUSTRY

The National Association of Home Builders (NAHB) began working with OSHA on these issues early in the Clinton administration, in 1993, when Joe Dear was appointed Assistant Secretary and Administrator at the Department of Labor for OSHA. Mr. Dear had previously worked in the state of Washington where he had headed the department responsible for worker safety. He therefore already understood the importance of involving a variety of parties in reaching reasonable decisions about construction safety. Mr. Dear expressed genuine interest to work with the home building industry, and early in his tenure, he visited a home building job site, where the builders identified the differences between high-rise construction and home building. This led to regular meetings between home builders and Mr. Dear. Efforts were made to identify areas — such as fall-protection, trenching, and fire extinguishers — in which home building safety requirements could be tailored to low-rise residential construction as compared to other safety construction standards. One of the best illustrations of these efforts relates to worker fall-protection.

Fall Protection and Home Building

On February 6, 1995, a far-reaching fall-protection regulation for the home building industry went into effect. Almost immediately, many builders, as well as many subcontractors, became concerned about the impact the new regulations would have on the cost of housing. Specifically, the new OSHA rules required the use of personal fall arrest systems to prevent employee falls at heights over six feet. The roofing industry was the most concerned, as requirements would essentially force all persons on roofs to "tie off" to the structure. Despite the fact that the roofing industry has one of the highest rates for workers' compensation in the construction industry — primarily because of injuries and fatalities related to falls — roofers were very much opposed to the government forcing safety precautions that added costs to building housing and that seemed unnecessary, especially in low-rise residential construction.

Both the NAHB and the National Roofing Contractors Association began to hear from their membership that the new requirements were intolerable and that OSHA should rescind them. In addition, NAHB determined that OSHA's final development of the fall protection regulation had failed to adequately address all the hazards associated with falls. NAHB also concluded that some of OSHA's new requirements were at times either infeasible or more hazardous than no fall protection at all. These specific problems with compliance, coupled with the overall growing concern over the roofing requirements, led to the involvement of Congress. At the urging of NAHB, the National Roofing Contractors Association, and individual home builders and roofers, language was attached to the Senate's 1996 Labor Appropriations Bill that rescinded the new fall protection requirements for the home building industry.

It should be noted that NAHB originally did not support the full repeal of the new worker protections. This was, in part, because the previous regulations were also infeasible. More important, though, NAHB believed that the majority of the new requirements would save lives. However, because NAHB supported some elements of the new OSHA rules and not others, it became difficult to explain to sympathetic members of the House and the Senate which sections should be rescinded and which should remain. Consequently, to make a clear statement and to force further negotiations, the language in the labor appropriations bill struck down the entire regulation.

Shortly after the 1996 appropriations bill passed the House, James Stanley, OSHA's Deputy Assistant Secretary, approached NAHB's safety director, Regina Solomon McMichael, about resolving the issue without further congressional action. NAHB informally agreed to request the removal of the appropriation language if an acceptable solution could be reached. Since the regulation was already in effect, OSHA could not just revert to the previous rule. Instead, OSHA would have to develop an interpretation of the final rule that addressed the concerns of the home building and roofing industries without violating any regulatory laws.

To prepare for the discussions with OSHA, NAHB held several meetings with builder members, including a number who had expressed concern over the new requirements. In turn, NAHB established what it referred to as a Builder Action Team to help determine what solutions would be accepted by OSHA and what areas were negotiable on the part of home builders. This information was then reviewed with OSHA to determine whether the options developed by the builders were acceptable. Numerous NAHB working meetings and several discussions with OSHA and the National Roofing Contractors Association yielded a document that the Builder Action Team believed the industry could accept. Most important in this negotiation was for the NAHB to develop an alternative requirement with which a builder or subcontractor would actually comply. Despite the fact that the new fall protection requirements had the potential to save lives and reduce injuries, ultimately they would save no lives if the industry refused to comply. In addition, since the number of OSHA inspectors nationwide pales next to the number of housing starts every year, many small-business home builders believed they would not be caught if they ignored the new rule.

After a series of meetings and discussions between NAHB and OSHA, a compromise was reached. In December of 1995, OSHA finalized revised rules (Std 3.1) for residential contractors. This interpretation relaxed many of the onerous requirements of fall-protection for roofing contractors while still protecting worker safety. It also clarified many sections of the original regulation that were infeasible or created a greater work hazard.

Why Did the Fall-Protection Effort Succeed?

This effort to alter a regulation after it was finalized would have been impossible without direct congressional intervention. Also, while NAHB had several members of Congress behind its efforts, many staff at OSHA also agreed that a regulation would be effective only if the companies were willing to comply. Because NAHB had a close working relationship with OSHA, and because McMichael was able to speak directly to OSHA staff like Jim Stanley and Bruce Swanson, OSHA's Director of Construction, lengthy delays were avoided. McMichael regularly met with Stanley and Swanson informally to ensure that all parties involved in the process continued toward resolution. If the attempt to change the rule had remained strictly in the hands of Congress or had become adversarial, the process likely would have failed. As a result of the general level of trust shared by NAHB and OSHA, many OSHA staff were helpful in working to determine how fall injuries and fatalities could be reduced without imposing a restrictive regulation that many small-business home builders and roofers would ignore. The feeling was that less restrictive regulations would be safer over the long-run than strict regulations that in theory would save everyone, but in fact would save few because few people would follow them.

The difficulties builders experienced with the OSHA fall-protection regulations emphasized to many in the home building industry that OSHA rules should be different for residential and commercial contractors. Many in the NAHB membership believed that OSHA should actually write new regulations for home builders that took into consideration the distinct differences in building practices. This option was discussed with OSHA on many occasions, and will be discussed later in this chapter. However, many impediments stood in the way of writing new regulations. As an alternative, Joe Dear, OSHA's director, and the home builders agreed that a simple no-nonsense guide to what OSHA expected from the home building industry would help contractors achieve compliance. Dear pledged to NAHB that a joint handbook would be developed that would tell builders and their subcontractors what OSHA really expected to see when it inspected a residential job site.

NAHB/OSHA Job Site Safety Handbook

Since the guide was just a guide, not a set of regulations it presented some unique challenges. NAHB staff spent countless hours working with

OSHA to develop a list of those safety requirements that should be included. One of the primary goals of the handbook was to simply state some of the most important safety rules that contractors must comply with on the job site. Keeping the handbook brief and illustrating it with photographs and drawings could help achieve the goal of teaching small-business home builders how to protect their employees. If the handbook became too large or complicated, most small contractors would ignore it and assume that, once again, government requirements were too complicated to follow. Because Joe Dear was an advocate for change and for simplifying OSHA rules, a joint effort seemed the perfect way to satisfy the industry's request for something unique for the residential construction industry. However, a joint effort between government and a trade association to develop a simple tool for compliance was a first and difficulties developed.

After several months of reviewing and rewriting the OSHA requirements, a final draft was ready for review by the Department of Labor's Solicitor's Office. Unfortunately, representatives from the Solicitors Office had not been involved in developing the handbook, and as a result, there was resistance to the groundbreaking idea of simplifying government regulations with the help of a trade association. Almost immediately, the Solicitor's Office indicated that NAHB was welcome to develop this handbook, but that OSHA would not be able to have its name or logo on the book or give "approval" to the document since it was not an official regulation. This ultimately became a major stumbling block. If the handbook was not developed through the formal regulatory process, then OSHA could not use the handbook as a tool for compliance.

Since the Solicitor's Office reported directly to the Secretary of Labor and not to OSHA, the desire of Joe Dear and NAHB to publish the document carried little weight. NAHB pushed repeatedly with Dear to get the handbook published. However, OSHA's response always included the Solicitor's Office restrictions on the project. NAHB could publish the document, but it could not be published jointly. However, Joe Dear believed in the project, and he never stopped trying. Ultimately, after almost eighteen months of ongoing efforts, Dear and his staff convinced the Secretary of Labor and the Solicitor that joint publication of the handbook would prove more helpful than harmful. This certainly appears to be the case. Since the first version of the handbook was published, over 40,000 copies have been distributed to federal and state OSHA staff, insurance companies, home builders, subcontractors, and many more.

Credit for the success of this effort goes primarily to OSHA's staff who decided to try something new with an industry stakeholder even if it was somewhat outside the realm of their regulatory mandate. Despite NAHB's insistence that the handbook be published as intended, if Joe Dear or other OSHA employees had given up on it, it would have just been another publication for sale by the NAHB. Instead, it was a government-produced document that bore the name of OSHA and NAHB, and therefore it could be very helpful on the job site for both home builders and OSHA inspectors.

SEPARATE OSHA STANDARDS FOR RESIDENTIAL CONSTRUCTION

Although the home building industry now had its own job site handbook that was generally easy to use, many in the industry still believed that separate OSHA regulations were the answer. Hence, as the relationship between NAHB and Mr. Dear evolved, one of the primary requests from the home building industry continued to be a separate compilation of standards for regulations related to home building as compared to other types of construction. The premise was that single-family residential construction was different from high-rise and other forms of heavy construction, and thus worker needs and requirements were different. Mr. Dear seemed sympathetic to the concept of a separate standard, but he also recognized the problems, challenges, and politics that might arise — for example, opposition from the trade unions. In addition, establishing a completely separate regulatory standard would take years, entailing a drawn out regulatory development and comment process that would have significant implications for OSHA in terms of labor and cost. As a result, the dialogue between Mr. Dear and NAHB continued to focus primarily on specific regulations such as fall-protection, and discussions of a separate standard, were put aside.

Recognizing the need to approach the issue at multiple levels, the National Association of Home Builders also talked to key people at the White House, including President Clinton, about a separate standard for residential construction. For example, in 1995, one of the elected officers of NAHB, Randy Smith, president of NAHB in 1996, and this author, then the executive vice president and chief executive officer of NAHB, met with President Clinton, along with a group of other business leaders. Each person was given the opportunity to raise a particular issue, and Randy

Smith focused on OSHA standards. He suggested to President Clinton that different standards were needed for single-family and high-rise construction, and President Clinton seemed sympathetic. In fact, he turned to one of his aides and said he would follow-up. However, despite several discussions with other staff in the White House and calls between NAHB, the White House, and the Labor Department, it became clear that general support at this level meant little because any real action would need to be spearheaded from the Department of Labor in general, and OSHA in particular, and such action was not forthcoming.

The Role of Congress

Realizing that the dialogue with the administration was going nowhere, the National Association of Home Builders decided to approach Congress during the 1996 appropriations process for the fiscal year 1997 federal budget. Bipartisan support was essential if anything was going to be done, so NAHB worked to generate interest with both Republicans and Democrats. NAHB began meeting with the Republican leadership in both the House and the Senate, then with both the Republican and Democratic leadership in the House and Senate Appropriations Committees that were responsible for developing the budget for the Department of Labor. In 1996, both the House and the Senate were under Republican control. NAHB had a working relationship with the Republican leadership in both the House and the Senate and was able to gain general support. The focus then turned in earnest to the House and Senate Appropriations Committees, and to the subcommittees responsible for dealing with the budget for the Department of Labor.

Since a bipartisan approach was crucial to success, NAHB also sought out key proponents among the Democrats — working closely in the House with Congressman Stenny Hoyer from Maryland, and in the Senate with Senator Harry Reid from Nevada. NAHB has a large grassroots network of builders throughout the country, and it drew upon these relationships to have home builders make direct contact with their representatives to seek support for NAHB's position. Since this effort was generally viewed by both Republicans and Democrats as an issue of achieving a reasonable balance regarding worker safety, it was possible to find bipartisan support.

As a result, NAHB convinced both the House and the Senate to appropriate $2 million to evaluate the idea of developing safety regulations specific to residential construction. The House report on the 1997 appropriation for the Labor Department (House Report 104-659) stated: "The bill includes $2 million for the purposes of evaluating the practical application of construction regulations under the Occupational Safety and Health Act to residential construction. The committee questions whether these regulations are appropriate for residential construction."[1] The comparable Senate report (Senate Report 104-368) stated: "The committee applauds the department for its desire to streamline construction and provides $2 million to the Office of the Secretary for the purposes of evaluating the practical application of construction regulations to residential construction."[2] In other words, the seed had been planted, and Congress had appropriated $2 million for the Department of Labor to examine and evaluate the application of OSHA construction regulations to residential construction. The funds were approved by Congress as part of the fiscal 1997 Appropriations bill for the Department of Labor, and it was signed into law by President Clinton in the fall of 1996. With the action of Congress and the President, NAHB could now go back to the administration, specifically OSHA and the Labor Department, and seek the implementation of the congressional action and appropriation.

However, just because Congress had acted, it did not mean that something would actually happen. Congress often authorizes and appropriates funds for particular actions, but the interpretation of what the legislation means precisely, and therefore the specific implementation, is left up to the administration. From NAHB's perspective, and most likely from the perspective of the members of Congress who had supported the measure, the intent was clear. But this was only one of many budget items related to the Department of Labor. It was now up to OSHA and the Department of Labor to determine exactly how the $2 million would be spent and what "evaluating the practical application of construction regulations under the Occupational Safety and Health Act to residential construction" actually meant.

Implementing the Intent of Congress

When the work was underway in Congress on the Labor Department appropriations bill, John Dunlop, a Harvard University professor, stopped by this author's office. Dunlop had been a longtime friend and colleague, but more important, he had served as the Secretary of Labor during the Ford administration from March 1975 through January 1976, and he had a

---

[1] House Appropriations Committee, House Report 104–659.
[2] Senate Appropriations Committee, Senate Report 104–368.

long history of very close relationships with the Department of Labor, the construction trade unions, and the home building industry. Over the years, he had worked on numerous projects as a mediator/facilitator, working with both unions and businesses to reach common ground through discussion and compromise. Thus he had extensive access to all levels of the Department of Labor. He was well acquainted with Joe Dear, the OSHA administrator, and he was a close friend of Bob Georgine, President of the Building and Construction Trades Department for the AFL-CIO.

One of the topics Dunlop raised at our meeting was whether the home building industry might be interested in distinct OSHA regulations for residential, but especially home building, construction. The answer, of course, was yes, and I explained the dialogue that had been held with Joe Dear on this topic and the discussions that were already underway with Congress. We decided that if NAHB succeeded in getting the $2 million appropriation included in the fiscal 1997 budget, perhaps Professor Dunlop could play a role in the implementation of this provision.

When the Labor Department appropriations bill was signed into law in the fall of 1996, a meeting was arranged between Dunlop, Joe Dear, Bob Georgine, and this author to discuss the possible uses of the $2 million and how the project might proceed. At the meeting, we agreed to establish a working group that would include high-level representatives from OSHA, the Construction Trades Department of the AFL-CIO, and NAHB. It was further agreed that Professor Dunlop would be asked by OSHA to facilitate the working group since he was a seasoned mediator/facilitator and was well respected by all parties.

A positive dialogue had begun, but soon thereafter, Joe Dear announced that he was leaving OSHA at the end of the year to return to his home state of Washington. This was a significant disappointment since Dear had established relationships with both the home building industry and the unions and was therefore in a solid position to move the project forward. With his pending departure, much of the momentum for the project was quickly lost.

Several months passed with no action. Then, in December, NAHB was informed by Bruce Swanson, OSHA's director of construction, that the Solicitor's Office in the Department of Labor had determined that the working group, made up of labor, the home builders, and OSHA (in essence, labor, management, and government), we had envisioned to implement the project was a violation of the Federal Advisory Committee Act (FACA). The working group could not provide information and advice to OSHA because it had not been formally established according to the requirements of FACA. OSHA had therefore decided that the project should be undertaken by a work group of the already existing OSHA Advisory Committee on Construction and Safety and Health (ACCSH). This work group would be open to all parties interested in participating. OSHA decided that the work group would be chaired by Dr. Knut Ringen, who served as the chairman of the full ACCSH. Ringen also worked on the staff of the Center to Protect Workers Rights, the research arm of the AFL-CIO Building and Construction Trades Department (BCTD).

NAHB was immediately concerned about this new development because historically such work groups address their tasks very slowly, and because the advisory committee members had a variety of different political agendas.[3] However, there was little choice, and NAHB decided that it would proceed under this new format.

The first meeting of the work group was held in January 1997 at OSHA. However, it did not go well — at least from NAHB's perspective. The open session was attended by a wide number of organizations, most of which did not focus on residential construction and had very little interest in separate standards for residential construction. Also, the participants from the unions were very negative about what such an effort might mean. The meeting did not follow a tight agenda. Although it was intended to focus on how to implement the legislation outlined in the fiscal 1997 appropriations bill, much discussion took place as to what Congress really meant by evaluating the practical application of constructing regulations to residential construction. The attendees were not able to agree.[4] Dr. Ringen chaired the meeting, and approximately twenty people attended. Attendees from NAHB were Regina Solomon McMichael, NAHB's Safety Director and the principal staff person working on the project, and two builder members of NAHB, Bob Masterson and Mike McMichael. John Dunlop was unable to attend the first meeting.

A second meeting was scheduled for February, and in the interim Professor Dunlop tried to open up the communication between the various parties. He had worked in the past with Knut Ringen and had an office at the Center to Protect Worker's Rights. However, when the February meeting took place, once again it was an open meeting attended by about twenty people from many organizations that did not represent residential construction. Discussion ranged from the true meaning of the congressional

---

[3] Memorandum from McMichael to Colton.
[4] Memorandum from Colton to the NAHB senior officers.

language related to the $2 million appropriation to whether it was appropriate to even begin an endeavor that might be unique to residential construction. A portion of the discussion, especially disconcerting to NAHB, revolved around whether OSHA had sufficient regulation to protect workers in the industry and whether OSHA should be determining if more regulations should be written. The union representatives, therefore, suggested that further research be conducted to determine what activities were causing injuries and fatalities in the residential construction industry. NAHB staff and member representatives pointed out that although further research is often worthwhile, this type of dialogue was a distraction, and it was not part of the congressional mandate. However, several others in the room seemed to agree that the topic of research was an important item for the work group to consider. Since this was an open meeting, it was not possible to limit the conversation, and in the end very little progress was made toward deciding how to spend the $2 million. The ACCSH work group scheduled the next meeting for March.

Based on the lack of progress at the February meeting and the concern that the project was being derailed, NAHB decided that it would not participate in the process until another venue was established to oversee the project. NAHB sent a letter to Cynthia Metzler, Acting Secretary of the Labor Department, and Gregory Watchman, the Acting Assistant Secretary of Labor for Occupational Safety and Health. (Watchman had been appointed as the interim administrator after Joe Dear left OSHA.) The letter read, in part:

> At the second meeting on February 24th, not only was there no resolution to the issue of congressional intent, but the tone of the meeting deteriorated to the point where NAHB's views were ignored. Attempts were made to illustrate NAHB's so-called "inflexibility" on the issue, when we are seemingly the only party interested in carrying out Congress' intent in a timely manner. . . .
>
> Furthermore, NAHB cannot take part in the process which is not consistent with the intent and purpose of identifying existing standards applicable to residential construction. As a result I have instructed my staff to no longer participate in this process until another venue is established to oversee the project that was intended, and until OSHA exercises more oversight of the process and the project is carried out as specified by Congress.
>
> I look forward to discussing this with you in person and hope we can schedule a meeting as soon as possible.[5]

---

[5] Letter from Colton to Metzler and Watchman.

The Role of the Facilitator

NAHB's position got the attention of Metzler, Watchman, and the Labor Department. In addition, John Dunlop — who attended the February meeting but was not in a position to be involved in the discussion — was informed of the letter, and he volunteered to arrange a meeting of Dunlop, Georgine, and me. Dunlop noted that a meeting of these three people (and Joe Dear) had been held in November 1996 and agreement had been reached as to the basic focus of the project. Given the distractions that had arisen, perhaps a quiet meeting among the three could help revive the common ground identified earlier.

During this period, the fact that $2 million had been appropriated seemed to help keep the process moving forward. Since the Labor Department and OSHA did not feel that the full sum would be needed to develop a set of standards related to residential development, discussions had already taken place about the possibility of using all or a portion of the money for training grants. OSHA was interested in the training grants, and both the AFL-CIO Building and Construction Trades Department and the NAHB felt they might be able to use some of those dollars for training their respective constituents. The existence of the money therefore served as a catalyst or a "carrot" to keep OSHA and the AFL-CIO interested in the project.

There was also concern that members of Congress might feel that the purpose of their appropriation request was being thwarted, and NAHB had already contacted members of Congress, particularly Congressman Stenny Hoyer's staff, about the problems at the two meetings. Congressman Hoyer was a friend of both the home building industry and the Building and Construction Trades Department of the AFL-CIO. Since he had been essential in establishing the initial legislation, he had a vested interest in keeping the project from going awry.

With all of these factors as background, John Dunlop was able to arrange a breakfast meeting on March 7 of Dunlop, Georgine, and this author. Based on the discussion that took place at that session, and recognizing that there had been common agreement earlier, a consensus was reached among the three as to how the project should proceed. In a confidential memorandum to Georgine and me, Dunlop summarized the process that had been agreed upon at the meeting:[6]

---

[6] Memorandum to Georgine and Colton from Dunlop, 1.

In accordance with our breakfast discussion on Friday morning, March 7, . . . Acting Secretary, Cynthia Metzler told me on Friday noon, on the telephone, that she would welcome meeting with the three of us, and I believe this is essential if anything useful is to happen. A further meeting would be necessary with the new Secretary upon confirmation. [Alexis Herman had been nominated by President Clinton to serve as the new Secretary of Labor, and in the interim, Cynthia Metzler was serving as the acting secretary.]

The Dunlop memorandum set forth a fast track for completing the project by the end of September, 1997. Since the fiscal year was already half over and the $2 million could be lost, quick action was appropriate. The approach that was agreed upon at the breakfast meeting was to review "the full universe of OSHA construction regulations," and from this review to "select those that have general application to single-family and multiple-family housing (not high-rise residential construction)." Once the "core standards" for single- and multiple-family housing were identified, each would be examined to ascertain "whether, and in what specifics, problems had been identified with regard to its application to single-family and multiple-family housing."[7] However, Dunlop went on to make clear that selecting those standards that had general application would not exempt others from potential OSHA regulation. In his memo, he clearly noted that this evaluation "does not by itself constitute any action to revise or alter any construction standard. Any such revision would have to be a separate activity undertaken in accordance with established procedures of OSHA."[8] However, it would highlight regulations most significant to residential construction (not high-rise) and therefore help streamline the process and help home builders understand how to better comply with OSHA regulations.

Once the core standards were identified, a book of standards applicable to residential construction could be published. In addition, it was agreed that a program should be developed for the period after September 30, 1997, utilizing the uncommitted portion of $2 million, to establish an education and training program for builders, contractors, and workers. Thus, if the project was able to proceed quickly, whatever funds remained could be used for training programs of interest to OSHA, the unions, and the home builders.

The memorandum also set forth that a contract of less than $25,000

---

[7] Ibid., 2.
[8] Ibid., 3.

should be written by the Office of the Secretary to John Dunlop to provide "travel, secretarial assistance, and modest compensation" for him to implement the program. In addition, the Department of Labor "should assign one or two staff to assist in identifying construction standards and experience within OSHA" to work with Dunlop. The newly appointed work group of the Advisory Committee on Construction Safety and Health "should be continued, although responsibility for a report to the Secretary of Labor by September 30, 1997, should be solely that of John T. Dunlop." In other words, the work group could continue to meet and be available for periodic discussions of the substantive issues of the program outlined above, and should be entitled to comment to the secretary on the report, but it would not be able to slow down progress on the project. Dunlop's memo noted that "the subcommittee was unable to agree upon a common agenda previously."[9]

In essence, then, this agreement created a process to identify the standards (within the existing OSHA construction standards) that would be applicable to residential construction, and to do it within the context of the Federal Advisory Committee Act (FACA). As a contractor, Dunlop would consult with all of the relevant parties, but there would not be the formal dialogue among the three parties that had been suggested earlier, that is, OSHA, labor, and the home builders. The work group of the advisory committee would continue to meet, but primarily in a consulting role rather than an implementation role. Dunlop would prepare the report to the Secretary of Labor. A separate document would be developed to serve as a streamlined reference by which home builders could identify regulations especially applicable to residential construction. Once the book of standards was complete, a training program could be implemented, using any remaining funds, to educate home builders, workers, and OSHA inspectors as to the regulations and their applicability in the home building industry. As noted before, the unions were interested in receiving funding to help conduct such an educational effort, and so was OSHA. However, the only way they would receive any of these dollars for training was if the book of standards was published.

Reaching Common Ground

In the meantime, while the first two meetings of the work group were being held, NAHB approached Congressman Hoyer and his staff for assistance

9 Ibid., 3.

to encourage action by OSHA and the Department of Labor. With this in mind, Congressman Hoyer held a hearing in April at which acting OSHA head Greg Watchman was asked what he had done to implement the portion of the fall 1996 appropriations bill related to residential construction. As a follow-up, Congressman Hoyer sent a letter to Watchman. In his letter he noted:

> As you know, I am a strong supporter of OSHA and will continue to support the agency in its ongoing efforts to ensure safe working conditions for American workers.
>
> I look forward to your response to my questions on how OSHA will conduct this systematic review of current OSHA construction standards. Furthermore, I want to impress upon you the importance of ensuring that this project is conducted while keeping in mind the original intent and specific report language in last year's appropriations bill. Specifically, I mean that current standards are reviewed and categorized by their application to the residential construction industry and further, whether home builders can practically comply with the applicable regulations. I am aware that OSHA has concluded that several standards, including fall-protection and trenching, are difficult for residential contractors to comply with, and has begun a thorough review of them.
>
> I understand that interested parties have met and are seeking a way to move this project forward. Furthermore, they believe that your personal involvement and leadership would greatly assist in the ultimate success of this effort. As I told you at the hearing, I hold OSHA and the leadership throughout the Department of Labor ultimately responsible for seeing to it that this project is completed by the end of the fiscal year.[10]

The combination of John Dunlop's efforts to achieve common ground and the strong support of Congressman Hoyer put the project back on track. A document based on the agreement between Dunlop, Georgine, and me was prepared and sent to Cynthia A. Metzler, Acting Secretary of the Department of Labor, and a meeting between her and the three parties was held. Figure 8.1 outlines the process decided upon at the meeting. In addition, a coordinated response was sent from Greg Watchman to Congressman Hoyer outlining the plan of action:

1. Identification of the construction safety and health standards that address the hazards most commonly found at residential construction sites, after consultation with the National Association of Home Builders, the building trades, and other affected stakeholders.

---

[10] Letter from Hoyer to Watchman.

FIGURE 8.1
Process for Residential Home Builders Booklet

1. Contractor given task order to look at full universe of OSHA construction regulations and select those that have general application and are generally appropriate to single-family and multiple-family housing (not high-rise residential construction).

2. Contractor meets separately with OSHA's Directorate of Construction, representatives of the National Association of Home Builders, representatives of the building trades, and any other stakeholders for their recommendations of items to be included.

3. Contractor delivers compilation of OSHA regulations by July 7.

4. OSHA Directorate of Construction reviews compilation.

5. On July 14, compilation delivered to national home builders and building trades and is made available to other interested stakeholders.

6. July 28 national home builders and building trades communicate any disagreements with the compilation to mediator. The mediator will have five working days to negotiate a consensus.

7. Mediator submits consensus compilation to OSHA assistant secretary on August 4.

8. OSHA delivers a booklet to a printer by August 18 and gives copies to training grant awardees outlined below for use in developing the training.

9. Printer produces XX copies, which are distributed to the residential home building industry on October 1.

10. Training and Outreach: May 12 place Federal Register Notice requesting bids for training on residential home building for three training programs (residential home builders, OSHA inspectors, and building trade members).

    July 1, bids are due.

    August 4, training grants are awarded and awardees are given advance copies of the compilation.

    August 8, money is obligated.

    November 15, begin training sessions nationwide.

SOURCE: Handout at meeting held with Cynthia A. Metzler, Acting Secretary of the Department of Labor, Bob Georgine, John Dunlop, and Kent Colton, 30 April 1997.

2. The compilation of the residential construction industry regulations will be published containing the full text of the standards identified in step one as most commonly applicable to residential construction. It will be published in English and Spanish. Both of these activities will be finished by late August or early September.

3. To accompany the compilation of regulations addressing residential construction, there will be a very extensive training outreach program wherein employers and employees engaged in residential construction will be trained on residential safety and health. These training seminars are expected to last from six to ten hours

and will be offered free of charge throughout the United States. One series of at least twenty seminars will be directed to residential contractors and their employees. Another series of seminars will be delivered to building trades members employed in residential construction. A third series of training seminars will be held for OSHA compliance staff who perform inspections of residential building sites. These seminars, which will be funded from the appropriation which you sponsored, will be conducted over the next year.[11]

Shortly after this, Alexis Herman was confirmed as the new Secretary of Labor, and Dunlop arranged a meeting with her to reconfirm the plan of action and to assure her ongoing support. Secretary Herman agreed with the overall project as well as with the goal of completing it before the end of the fiscal year.

Common ground had been reached among Dunlop, Georgine representing the AFL-CIO, this author representing the NAHB, the Acting Assistant Secretary for OSHA, the Acting Secretary of the Labor Department, and the Secretary of the Labor Department. Further, a framework had been established to meet the congressional intent established in the fall, 1996.

Implementing the Agreement

Based on the agreements that were reached, a contract was entered into with Dunlop. In an effort to carry out this assignment, Dunlop invited each of the organizations that had expressed an interest in the applicability of OSHA construction regulations to residential home building to meet with him for a detailed separate discussion of these issues. Each organization was also asked, if interested, to mark the 1996 OSHA document "Safety and Health Standards for The Construction Industry" (OSHA 3149, 1996) to indicate which sections, subsections, or paragraphs they felt were not generally applicable to single-family and multi-family (not high rise) residential construction.

Dunlop met with a variety of groups (See Figure 8.2), some of them more than once.[12] They included the NAHB, a number of specialty and subcontract associations (who elected to submit a common response as to the construction regulations applicable to home construction), the Associated Buildings and Contractors, and a number of people from the Building

---

[11] Letter from Watchman to Hoyer.
[12] Dunlop, *Report to the Secretary of Labor,* 2–3.

FIGURE 8.2
Organizations and Representatives Involved in Discussions
with John T. Dunlop Related to Residential Construction Standards

The following is a listing of organizations and representatives involved in these consultations without significance in the order of listing:

1. National Association of Home Builders: Regina Solomon McMichael, Director, Labor, Safety & Health Services; a committee of the NAHB comprised of three builders: Stuart E. Price, Granor Price Homes; Bob Masterson, The Ryland Group, Inc.; and Mike McMichael, The McMichael Company; Kent W. Colton, Executive Vice President and C.E.O.

2. Specialty and subcontractor associations:

   -National Association of Plumbing-Heating-Cooling Contractors — Claudia Harris
   -American Subcontractors Association — Brian Pallasch
   -Mechanical Contractors Association of America — Peter Chaney
   -National Roofing Contractors of America — Tom Shanahan
   -Air Conditioning Contractors of America — Ellen Larson
   -Painting and Decorating Contractors of America — Marc Freedman
   -Sheet Metal and Air Conditioning National Association — David DeLorenzo
   -National Electrical Contractors Association — Dave Potts

   These associations elected to submit a common response as to the construction regulations typically applicable to single- and multiple-family home building construction.

3. Associated Builders and Contractors, Inc.: Charles E. Hawkins III, Executive Vice President, and Charles Maresca, Director of Legal and Regulatory Affairs.

4. Building and Construction Trades Department, AFL-CIO: Sandra Tillett, Acting Director, Health and Safety; Health and Safety representatives of various national unions including:

Asbestos Workers	John Griffiths
Roofers	Robert Krul
Laborers	George Macaluso
Teamsters	Azita Mashayekhi
Carpenters	Vernon McDougall
Operating Engineers	Shannon Ramsby
United Association	William Rhoten
Electrical Workers	John Widener
Occupational Health	Christina Trahan
Foundation	
United Brotherhood of	Frank "Bronco" Hollis
Carpenters, Health and	
Safety Fund	

Robert A. Georgine, President, Building and Construction Trades Department, AFL-CIO

SOURCE: Dunlop, "Report to the Secretary of Labor," 2–3.

and Construction Trades Department of the AFL-CIO. In meeting with these groups, Dunlop found great diversity in their responses. This diversity is outlined below as it was set forth in the report Dunlop submitted to Secretary Herman.

The various groups of organizations . . . consulted as to the appropriate compilation of standards applicable to hazards regularly or typically found in single-family and multiple-family (not high-rise) residential construction have expressed quite different views regarding such a listing.

The unions proposed to delete a relatively few construction standards for this single-family and multiple-family (not high-rise) construction compilation, in part because they appear to regard most all construction standards as applicable to some home building.

The NAHB recommended a reduced list of standards, and parts of standards, as typically relevant to single-family and multiple-family (not high-rise) residential construction.

The subcontractor associations by letter of July 8, 1997, submitted a restricted list of deletions, of full standards only, stating in part: "Because all standards will still apply in certain situations, there is not relief or benefit to excluding infrequently used standards. Further, we do not believe that compliance will be improved by omitting some of the regulations." These associations also emphasized that a "tremendous amount of construction activity occurs in the residential sector on renovation and remodeling projects." Subsequently the subcontractor associations submitted a revised list of deletions in book form including sections and parts of construction standards.

The National Association of Plumbing, Heating, and Cooling Contractors, one of the group of responding subcontractor associations, by letter of June 27, 1997, emphasized that "specialty contractors are at the heart of today's building industry, performing most of the work on residential building sites." This association expressed similar views to those cited by the group of subcontractor associations. On July 16, 1997, the Air Conditioning Contractors of America also wrote supporting the submission of the group of subcontractor associations and stressed the importance of "service, repair, and replacement" work.

The Associated Builders and Contractors expressed the view that home building is so interrelated with other types of construction such as commercial work, that there is little purpose in a separate home building compilation of OSHA standards. Both contractors and workers move frequently among home building, commercial, and other types of construction.

Thus, there are widespread differences over the content, the objectives, and value of the assignment to provide a compilation of OSHA standards most commonly applicable to hazards found in single- and multiple-family (not high-rise) residential construction.[13]

Despite the diversity expressed by the various groups and the fact that many of the groups felt that such a compilation was not necessary or appropriate, Dunlop concluded that the assignment as set forth in the legislation, and in the agreement reached with the acting secretary of labor, was

---

[13] Ibid., 2–3.

clear. A listing of the regulations that were applicable to single-family and multi-family (not high-rise) residential construction could be developed, but such a listing would not replace or alter any construction standard that was otherwise applicable. Professor Dunlop concluded that his task was "to provide residential builders and subcontractors, their supervisors and employees, labor organizations, their staff and members, and OSHA inspectors, with the compilation of applicable standards applicable to hazards regularly or typically found in the residential construction industry."[14] This compilation could then be used to facilitate training and on-the-job activities.

Dunlop presented his report to Secretary of Labor Alexis Herman on time, on August 4, 1997. It included a fourteen-page report outlining the assignment, the process, diverse responses, precedent for specialized compilation of OSHA construction regulations, questions related to the document, a discussion of the absence of appropriate data, and Dunlop's findings and recommendations. Also attached was a copy of OSHA's "Safety and Health Standards for the Construction Industry (OSHA 3149, 1996)" marked to highlight applicable areas. This marked-up volume could therefore provide the basis for the publication of a shorter document of regulations that were applicable to the home building industry. Presenting his report, Dunlop once again made it clear that the marked-up document was "not an exercise in rulemaking or in rewriting," nor was it an effort in "simplification of any rule." Rather, it was a listing of existing construction standards generally applicable in residential home building. He also stated that, to avoid any ambiguity, the document should include the following preface.

> To provide residential construction employers and employees with a useful compilation of the standards applicable to the hazards most commonly found at work sites in the residential construction industry, the Occupational Safety and Health Administration (OSHA) has reviewed its standards applicable to the construction industry and has identified those that are likely to have the most significant positive impact on the safety and health practices of contractors within the residential construction industry.
>
> While every effort has been made to identify those standards which are most commonly applicable to hazards found in residential construction, OSHA notes that other standards not included in this book also apply. Whenever situations arise in which hazards exist which are beyond the scope of the standards herein identified but are covered by other OSHA

---

[14] Ibid., 5.

safety or health standards, those standards remain applicable and abatement
actions must be implemented by the contractor.

OSHA is retaining a reference in this compilation to those construction
standards not included in this book so that users may refer readers to the
complete text published in the *Code of Federal Regulations,* Part 29, should
the need arise and should the user wish to review the text of standards not
included in this book.[15]

This kind of clarification was essential in order to highlight the nature
of the project. However, the very existence of a shorter document would
now play an important role in allowing more effective training, as well as
communication, on OSHA requirements related to home building. In his
report, Dunlop also cited that there were precedents for providing such
specialized publications of applicable OSHA construction regulations, re-
ferring to work that had been done both by the government and by various
trade associations. It was therefore his premise that such a document
should be published quickly, as had been determined in the agreement
with Acting Secretary Cynthia Metzler.

Publication of the Report and Training

Once Dunlop's report was received by the Secretary of Labor, the project continued to move quickly. Within several months, OSHA published
Selected Construction Regulations for the Home Building Industry
(SCOR). The new book was, in its entirety including appendices, 186
pages long, while the larger volume of construction standards was 932
pages. The preface states, "This publication does not itself alter or determine compliance responsibilities as contained in OSHA standards, and
the Occupational Safety and Health Act of 1970. Consequently OSHA
notes that other standards not included in this document remain applicable
to the residential construction industry and abatement actions must be implemented by the contractor."[16]

This new, shorter document was significantly less intimidating to the
home building industry, and it allowed home builders to initially focus on
the rules and regulations that they most needed to follow to comply with
OSHA guidelines. The book was divided into the same subparts as the
larger volume, starting with the general and moving to specific rules related to fire protection, tools, electrical, scaffolds, fall protection, cranes,

---

[15] Ibid., 3–4.
[16] U.S. Department of Labor, *Selected Construction Regulations for the Home Building Industry,*
viii.

stairways and ladders, toxic and hazardous substances, and so on. If further information was needed, builders could refer to the larger document, but an easier frame of reference had been established. Most important, this new book did not contain confusing extraneous information; and regulations concerning nonresidential construction practices, such as high-voltage wiring and commercial diving, were excluded.

With the applicable standards published, it was now possible to use the $2 million for training outreach. This money, as noted earlier, had served as an important "carrot" for the AFL-CIO to support the project. It was also a resource for OSHA to be proactive in preventing accidents. The charge, outlined in the earlier agreement, was for OSHA to undertake an extensive training outreach program whereby employers and employees engaged in residential construction would be trained on residential safety and health, using the new standards publication as a framework. These courses were expected to last from six to ten hours, and because of the $2 million, they could be offered free of charge throughout the United States. A series of seminars could be directed to residential contractors and their employees, another series to the members of the Building and Trades Union employed in residential construction, and a third series to OSHA compliance staff who perform inspections of residential building sites. On September 29, 1997, less than two months after Dunlop's report was delivered to the Secretary of Labor, and one day before the end of the fiscal year, the Department of Labor announced $2 million in grants to four organizations for safety and health training in residential construction. The press release noted that more than 17,500 union and nonunion residential contractors, subcontractors, supervisors, and workers, as well as 700 OSHA compliance officers, would be trained under the program. Acting Assistant Secretary of Labor, Greg Watchman stated in the press release, "These programs will go a long way toward reducing injuries and illness in this very important sector of the construction industry." He added that "the training will supplement a soon to be published book on selected OSHA construction standards for the home building industry."[17]

The recipients of the $2 million and the amounts they received were: 1) The National Association of Home Builders Research Center, Inc., $900,000 to conduct a comprehensive national training and education program on construction safety for nonunion residential contractors, subcontractors, their supervisors and their workers. This grant was designed to

---

[17] U.S. Department of Labor, news release, 1.

train 10,000 people nationwide. 2) The Occupational Health Foundation, the foundation of the AFL-CIO Building and Construction Trades Department, $700,000. The goal of this grant was to train about 7,550 union workers in the residential construction sector. (3) The National Safety Council-Safety Institute and the United Brotherhood of Carpenters Health and Safety Fund of North America, $400,000. These two organizations were to jointly develop and conduct a course specifically designed to help OSHA compliance officers understand job-site hazards, procedures to control the hazards, and the specific OSHA standards pertinent to the home building industry.[18] The recipients of these grants were charged to work together so that the training programs would be consistent and relate together as a whole.

WHY DID THIS EFFORT SUCCEED?

Why did this effort to achieve common ground succeed when so many others fail? Six factors seem of particular importance.

First: The original proposal was a "good idea" that could stand the test of close scrutiny and be sold to a bipartisan group. In other words, to succeed, an idea must make basic sense. The concept of having a set of regulations focused especially on the needs of single-family and multi-family (not high-rise) residential development was well received by a number of people, especially those not deeply involved in the issue. It seemed to make good sense, and it could be sold — whether to the President of the United States, a Republican or Democrat member of Congress, or an academic. The fact that the idea could pass the "sense" test allowed the project to go forward, even when it was opposed by particular groups or individuals. The logic held up over time.

Second: A great deal of education and perseverance was required to communicate with all the appropriate parties, including members of Congress, individuals in the White House, labor unions, other subcontractors and trade groups, and key staff in the Department of Labor and OSHA. Without education and dialogue, understanding and compromise would have been impossible. Achieving common ground takes time, and it takes a lot of work. People who have different perspectives will work to protect their interests. If they are going to change their minds or be willing to consider different priorities,

---

[18] Ibid., 2.

it is essential that relevant information and analysis be made available and that the advocates take the time to explain their perspective to others.

Third: In this case, there was a willingness among the key parties to work together, at least at a small group level. When the attempt was made to establish a work group of the already existing OSHA Advisory Committee on Construction Safety and Health (ACCSH), it failed miserably. In that setting, with a large number of parties at the table, no one was willing to change his perspective. However, in a small group — such as the initial meeting of OSHA Administrator Joe Dear, John Dunlop, Bob Georgine from the AFL-CIO, and this author from NAHB — it was relatively easy to reach agreement. It was this initial agreement among four key parties that drove the effort, and it was the willingness of three of those parties to meet again and to compromise when things went awry that eventually led to success.

Fourth: "Carrots," or incentives, encouraged key people to participate in the process. In this case, $2 million in potential funding for training kept the AFL-CIO involved. It was also an important incentive for OSHA to continue to move forward. When the discussions broke down in the early part of 1997, no one wanted to lose the money Congress had appropriated. This was an important motivator to keep the process moving forward and to achieve common ground.

Fifth: Perhaps most important, was the presence of an honest broker, a facilitator who was respected by everyone and who could bring together the various parties, including the unions, the home builders, OSHA, and the highest levels within the Department of Labor. In this case, that facilitator was John Dunlop. Without his involvement, common ground would not have been possible. At several stages in the process, there was resistance to using a facilitator. For example, as late in the dialogue as April 1997, after OSHA had appeared before Stenny Hoyer's committee and it was clear that it needed to move forward on the project or face adverse consequences from Congressman Hoyer, OSHA was still thinking about developing the separate set of standards primarily on its own, without utilizing a third-party negotiator.[19] However, as the key players met (Dunlop, Georgine, and me), all three were absolutely convinced that without Dunlop, the project would not succeed. It had been shown several times that

---

[19] This was outlined in an NAHB Internal Memorandum from Regina Solomon McMichael to Bob Brown and Mike O'Brien, April 16, 1997. Ms. McMichael notes that OSHA was considering proceeding without the assistance of John Dunlop and that "OSHA, with the assistance of the National Association of Home Builders, will identify the construction, safety, and health standards that address the hazards most commonly found at residential construction sites."

OSHA alone was not able to keep the project moving forward due to the array of perspectives and interests involved. One has only to recall the diversity of opinions that Dunlop highlighted when he submitted his report to realize that without his extensive efforts, it would have been very difficult to reach agreement on what items should be included in the book of applicable standards. Without Dunlop providing a solid draft of the book, the effort undoubtedly would have taken significantly longer, and perhaps the book never would have been completed and published. The work of a person who had the respect of all sides and at the same time held a perspective that was free from specific biases and commitments was absolutely essential.

Sixth: Achieving common ground does not mean that players cannot take tough stands in the process. In fact, in this case, the tough stand taken by the National Association of Home Builders was essential. Although the idea of a "separate standard" had conceptual interest within the administration, it never would have happened without congressional action in the fiscal 1997 Labor Appropriations Bill. The bill, and further congressional involvement, then provided the guidance that was needed both to get the project started and to keep it on track when the dialogue faltered. Also, when the first attempts at implementation began to disintegrate, NAHB took a hard stand that the congressional intent was not negotiable. In this case the NAHB was backed by Congressman Stenny Hoyer. At the same time, though, its position was not without flexibility. Even as the letter was sent to the Labor Department indicating that NAHB would have to withdraw if things did not change, informal efforts were made to continue the project, through John Dunlop, along the lines originally planned. In this case, then, a hard stand, coupled with more flexible informal negotiations, was key to achieving common ground.

Chapter 9

A Case Study on the Challenges of Achieving Common Ground: Raising the Loan Limit for the Federal Housing Administration

In 1998, after much debate, the loan limit for the Federal Housing Administration (FHA) was raised. This is an interesting case because it primarily involves members of the housing industry — people who often work together on housing issues and who generally are committed to providing affordable housing. However, different perspectives emerged during the course of the debate. Friends were lined up against friends. The debate became heated, and as a consequence, emotions rose and positions hardened.

In the end, the loan limit was raised — from 75% to 87% of the loan limit for Fannie Mae and Freddie Mac, with the "floor" raised from 38% to 48% of the Fannie Mae/Freddie Mac limit. To the extent that a legislative compromise took place, it could be argued that common ground was reached. However, because the positions became so strong, and compromise was not achieved through quiet discussion but through a sometimes contentious political process, there were clear winners and losers. Further, negative feelings lingered. The outcome therefore had a broader impact on housing policy discussions. The case illustrates the challenge of achieving common ground even among people who have common roots and are committed to affordable housing.

BACKGROUND AND OVERVIEW

In 1980, the loan limits for Fannie Mae and Freddie Mac (often referred to as the conforming loan limit) and the Federal Housing Administration were very close: $93,751 and $90,000 respectively (see Figure 9.1). The

FIGURE 9.1
Change in Government Loan Limits

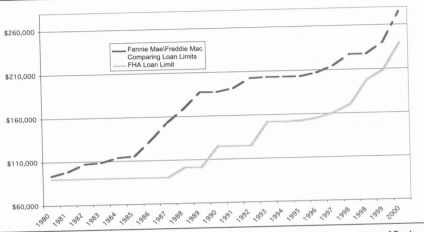

SOURCES: *Inside Mortgage Finance,* HUD, VA, Commerce Department, National Association of Realtors.

Fannie Mae/Freddie Mac limit was based on an index, prescribed in legislation, drawing on data gathered by the Federal Home Loan Banks and
was allowed to rise as the index rose. The FHA loan limit, however, was
set by Congress and remained constant until it was raised by legislative
action. From 1980 to 1987, the FHA loan limit remained at $90,000, while
the Fannie Mae/Freddie Mac limit rose from $93,751 to $153,100. In
1988, the FHA limit was raised to $101,250 for two years, and then it was
raised again to $124,875, where it remained from 1990 through 1992. In
1993, it was raised once again, to $151,725, and stayed at that level for
two years.

In 1994, HUD Secretary Henry Cisneros proposed that the FHA limit be
changed to 80% of the Fannie Mae/Freddie Mac limit. His proposal was to
set the ceiling at 80%, the floor at 50%. (The FHA loan limit includes both
a ceiling and a floor, while the Fannie Mae/Freddie Mac limit includes only
a ceiling.) He did not achieve his full proposal, but the FHA loan limit was
set at 75% of the confirming loan limit and the floor at 38%. Consequently,
from 1995 on, the FHA loan limit moved in proportion to the Fannie Mae/
Freddie Mac limit, and so by 1998, the Fannie Mae/Freddie Mac limit was
up to $227,150, and the FHA loan limit ceiling to $170,362.

Over the years, then, various proposals have been made — supported
and opposed by a variety of interests and perspectives — to raise the FHA

loan limit to bring it even with, or closer to, the Fannie Mae/Freddie Mac limit. When Andrew Cuomo was confirmed as HUD secretary in January, 1997 by a Senate vote of ninety-nine to zero, the stage was set, once again, for the consideration of a loan limit rise.

A variety of factors were involved in the debate to raise the FHA loan limit. Advocates of the FHA program wanted to make FHA mortgages more feasible in high-cost areas. In addition, raising the loan limit would expand the market for the FHA program and therefore increase the FHA premiums that would come in as revenue to the federal government. This revenue could be used to offset federal expenditures, especially related to housing. For example, in January of 1997, the federal budget proposal for HUD sought to raise the FHA ceiling to match the Fannie Mae/Freddie Mac loan limit as a way to pay for a $500,000 exclusion from capital gains for profits on home sales proposed by the Clinton administration. Although from the outset it was not expected that the administration would make a serious effort to raise the loan limit, the proposal allowed Clinton and Cuomo to present a more balanced budget. The proposal to raise the FHA ceiling in 1997 received little support and never became a serious policy issue.

However, in the fall of 1997, Cuomo began to consider what proposals he would push for in 1998. He had moved quickly after his confirmation to address overall issues related to low-income housing such as expanding the HUD budget for housing vouchers. The FHA loan limit was an issue that involved a different group of housing advocates and would broaden the secretary's focus. Since the budget needs to be prepared well in advance of its formal presentaton, HUD first developed the proposal to raise the FHA ceiling in the Summer of 1997 as a revenue enhancement, and in early 1998, Secretary Cuomo formally proposed that the FHA limit be set to conform to the same indexes as the Fannie Mae/Freddie Mac limit.

The 1998 proposal was supported by home builders, mortgage bankers, realtors, and a number of other smaller groups. Lining up on the other side were conservative Republicans, who usually opposed any expanded federal involvement in the housing sector, private mortgage insurers, who viewed FHA as a competitor, and Fannie Mae and Freddie Mac, who were also concerned about FHA competition. Fannie Mae, in particular, became involved in what became a divisive debate.

In the end, Senator Kit Bond (R-MO) and Congressman Jerry Lewis (R-CA), the respective chairmen of the Senate and House HUD/Veteran's Administration (VA) appropriations committees, sought and achieved a compromise to raise the FHA ceiling limit to 87% of the Fannie Mae/

Freddie Mac conforming loan limit, with 48% of the conforming limit as the FHA floor. As a result, in 1998 the FHA loan limit was raised to $197,620 with $109,032 as the floor. In 1999, the Fannie Mae/Freddie Mac conforming loan limit rose to $240,000, and the FHA limit was raised accordingly to $208,800, with the floor set at $115,200. The FHA loan limit continues to rise with the conforming loan limit. Effective January 1, 2001, the conforming loan limit rose to $275,000, and the FHA loan limit rose to $239,250 in high-cost areas, with a minimum floor of $132,000 elsewhere; and effective January 1, 2002, the conforming loan limit rose to $300,700, and the FHA loan limit rose to $261,609 in high cost areas, with a minimum floor of $144,336 elsewhere.

THE DEBATE

As noted earlier, Andrew Cuomo was confirmed as HUD Secretary without a single negative vote. He had served as the assistant secretary for community planning and development and knew the department well. As secretary, he moved quickly and aggressively to establish himself as an active leader in the housing industry. One issue that had been on the table for several years and required serious attention was the potential for long-term deficits related to HUD-subsidized housing programs. Secretary Cuomo immediately addressed what became known as the "mark-to-market" issue: the intention was to allow HUD-subsidized housing project rents to adjust to market-rates, which would free up future federal budget commitments, but at the same time preserve as much of the housing stock as possible for low-income families. Cuomo also moved vigorously in 1997 to expand the number of housing vouchers, something that was strongly supported by advocates for low-income housing.

As Cuomo began to set his agenda for 1998, raising the FHA loan limit began to rise in importance. The issue had a different, more business-oriented constituency than many of the issues he had highlighted in 1997. Mortgage bankers, home builders, and Realtors were three groups that were interested in affordable housing but spent less time focusing on subsidized housing programs.

As noted earlier, the FHA loan limit had been discussed on a number of occasions, sometimes with serious intent, and other times as a way of helping to advocate a more balanced budget. In the summer of 1997, as the budget began to be assembled, the HUD leadership included raising the loan limit to match the Fannie Mae/Freddie Mac conforming loan limit as a part of their budget proposal, but primarily as a revenue enhancer. Office of Management and Budget (OMB) hearings were held on the HUD budget in September and October of 1997, and the loan limit proposal was kept as a part of the budget. In November of 1997, Secretary Cuomo met OMB Director, Franklin Raines (who later became the Chairman and CEO of Fannie Mae), and once again, primarily for revenue enhancement, the proposal to raise the FHA loan limit remained part of the budget.[1] However, Cuomo now needed to decide whether this would simply be a budget ploy or a serious issue.

Word of the proposal to raise the FHA loan limit leaked out in Washington, and Cuomo began to receive "push back" from Fannie Mae and other groups, such as private mortgage insurers, who expressed serious opposition to raising the loan limit. Secretary Cuomo realized that he would have to pay a price to raise the loan limit. Did he want to go forward with what could become a fight, and would the benefits justify the cost? Cuomo met with other groups who had traditionally supported raising the limit to see what kind of support he would have. Also, having focused on the "mark-to-market" and voucher issues in the first year, he recognized that he might be typecast as "just a liberal." Trying to raise the FHA loan limit might be a good way to work with other groups such as the Mortgage Bankers Association (MBA), the National Association of Home Builders (NAHB), and the National Association of Realtors (NAR). It would broaden his agenda and therefore broaden his constituency in dealing with other housing issues.[2]

As he met with the MBA, NAHB, and NAR, he realized that he would have their support. The mortgage bankers felt this was their number one issue, and the realtors and home builders were strongly supportive. For example, in January 1998, Cuomo met with NAHB Representatives Danny Pincus, 1997 president, Don Martin, 1998 president, and this author to discuss the HUD agenda for 1998 and to review issues of prime concern to NAHB. Cuomo indicated that he was considering raising the loan limits and wanted to know where the home builders would stand on the issue. Danny Pincus noted that although this would not be the only issue for NAHB that year, NAHB would strongly support raising the FHA loan limit in 1998. Such a move would be especially helpful for mortgage lending in high-cost loan areas that FHA's current programs could not reach.

---

[1] Retsinas, Nicholas, interviewed by author, Cambridge, MA, 11 June 2001.
[2] Apgar, Bill, interviewed by author, Cambridge, MA, 11 June 2001.

Based on this kind of feedback, as well as other housing policy and political considerations, Cuomo decided to make the FHA loan limit a top priority. On January 17, 1998, he publicly announced the administration's proposal to raise the FHA loan limit at an NAHB convention. Once the loan limit was included in President Clinton's budget to Congress, Cuomo had already won a victory. This was his first HUD budget, and raising the FHA loan limit would secure additional revenue for vouchers and other programs. Even more important, he had now made a strong public commitment that this issue would be a top priority.[3]

Once Secretary Cuomo returned from the NAHB convention, he gathered the mortgage bankers, realtors, and home builders to discuss their support for the legislation. HUD could not lobby Congress directly, but the MBA, NAR, and NAHB could. Once Cuomo decided that this would be a worthy fight, he became the chief strategist. Nic Retsinas had served as the FHA commissioner from 1993 to 1998 with Secretary Cisneros and for Secretary Cuomo's first year, but in February of 1998 he left the department. Art Agnos, the former mayor of San Francisco, became acting FHA commissioner, and from his first day he was given the job of coordinating the loan limit effort. Weekly meetings with supporters were held throughout the legislative process, and when Bill Apgar, who was already serving at HUD as the Assistant Secretary for Policy Development and Research, was announced in May to be Cuomo's choice for the new FHA Commissioner, he was already deeply involved in the loan limit effort. Apgar was not confirmed by the Senate until October, but throughout the legislative process, he played a key role in providing research, analysis, and coordination, and he worked closely with Cuomo. In addition, Cuomo was actively calling members of Congress and others to build support.[4]

In early February, President Clinton formally proposed his fiscal 1999 budget, including the FHA loan limit increase as a part of the HUD budget. The battle had already begun, but it was now official.

Once Cuomo announced his proposal in January, a number of opponents began to emerge with vigor. Private mortgage insurance companies (PMIs) insure mortgages when the down payment is less than 20%, and so they compete directly with FHA low down payment programs. Over the years, they have argued that the private market can meet the nation's mortgage insurance needs and that FHA should be limited or "privatized" so as

---

[3] Retsinas, Nicholas, interviewed by author, Cambridge, MA, 11 June 2001.

[4] Apgar, Bill, interviewed by author, Cambridge, MA, 11 June 2001.

to not compete directly with the private market. Therefore, they strongly opposed raising the FHA loan limit.

Also lining up in opposition were conservatives (generally Republicans) who over the years had sought to limit the role of the federal government in housing. For example in February 1998, the National Tax Payers Union, a group with 300,000 members that generally opposes expanded federal programs, came out in opposition to raising the FHA loan limit. Conservative Republicans, such as James A. Leach (R-IA), chairman of the House Committee on Banking, Housing, and Urban Affairs, Rick Lazio (R-NY), chairman of the Housing Subcommittee in the House, and Don Nichols (R-OK), part of the Republican leadership in the Senate, also announced their opposition.

Fannie Mae, led by its Chairman and CEO, Jim Johnson, was one of the early opponents. Johnson met with Don Martin, NAHB's 1998 president, and this author, in late 1997 to discuss the home builders' agenda for 1998. Afterward he invited us into his office to privately discuss his concern about raising the FHA loan limit. He thought that raising the loan limits would be bad for Fannie Mae's business because it would increase competition from FHA and said Fannie Mae would oppose the proposal. He wanted to assure NAHB that he was in agreement on numerous issues, but in this area, Fannie Mae and NAHB agreed to disagree.

Freddie Mac, while also concerned about the possible rise in the FHA loan limit, chose not to get too deeply involved in the debate. It was clear on Capitol Hill that they generally agreed with Fannie Mae.

Another opponent was Gail Cincotta, Chairperson, National People's Action, and co-founder and Executive Director, National Training and Information Center. Cincotta had a long history of concern about the impact of FHA — and especially FHA-foreclosed properties — on communities around the country. In this case, she also felt that the attempt to raise the loan limit indicated that HUD was forgetting its basic mission to support low-income housing and trying to "go upscale" to the higher end of the market.[5] In an effort to neutralize her opposition, Cuomo and HUD senior staff tried to work with her in other areas to assure her that FHA and HUD would not neglect their basic mission.

Between February and June 1998, a great deal of discussion of the FHA loan limit took place in the housing industry. The advocates held weekly meetings to plan strategy and coordinate action, and similar meetings

---

[5] Ibid.

were probably underway among the opponents. HUD did a detailed analysis for each Congressional district on how a higher loan limit would benefit potential home buyers in that district and in the state. In some policy discussions a Cabinet secretary will advocate policy but stay removed from much of the debate, but in this case, Cuomo was very engaged personally and held a number of meetings and made numerous phone calls.

In the spring of 1998, hearings were held in the House appropriations subcommittee for HUD/VA chaired by Congressman Jerry Lewis. Secretary Cuomo was called to testify. A number of members of the House raised questions, including Jim Walsh (R-NY), Mark Neuman (R-WI), and Carrie Meek (D-FL). The testimony was heated and good questions were asked, but Cuomo was prepared and stood his ground along with the advocates of the proposal.[6]

In turn, Fannie Mae, the private mortgage insurance industry, and the fiscal conservatives led the opposition. The opposition of the PMI's and the conservatives was expected, but it became clear that Fannie Mae, led by its strong and dynamic Chairman and CEO, Jim Johnson, had taken on the battle with vigor. Fannie Mae had made contacts throughout the country, and people who worked with Fannie Mae had been asked for their support. The debate became particularly heated between Johnson and the 1998 President of the Mortgage Bankers Association, Mark Smith. Johnson argued that a rise in the FHA loan limit was not needed to address affordable housing needs, and Smith contested his premises. This led to an exchange of letters between the two in the *National Mortgage News,* a national trade publication on housing finance.

By late spring 1998, the fight in Congress was underway, and there was little effort to achieve common ground. Given that many of the people engaged in the debate were housing advocates and friends within the housing industry, why was a greater effort not made to achieve common ground? The reason is that the positions were already staked out, and neither side wanted to move. It does appear that there was a meeting around March 1998 between Secretary Cuomo and Jim Johnson. By this time, Cuomo realized that it was going to be a tough fight, and the likelihood of a complete victory (in which the FHA loan limit was raised to 100% of the Fannie Mae/Freddie Mac conforming limit) was slight. There was even a chance that he could lose the fight entirely. He was therefore looking for a compromise. However, Johnson, believing that the opponents were going

---

[6] Ibid.

to win, felt that there was no need to compromise, so the debate continued.[7]

In April, the two House Republicans who had the lead on the authorization side — James Leach and Rick Lazio — both came out in opposition. They sent a letter to Speaker Newt Gingrich saying that they opposed the plan and would introduce a bill to that end.[8] It was clear that the only way the FHA loan limit would be raised would be through the appropriations process. There were several reasons for this strategy. First, the chairmen of the two appropriations subcommittees for FHA/VA, Congressman Jerry Lewis in the House and Senator Kit Bond in the Senate, were both more favorably disposed to the idea. In addition, raising the loan limits, as discussed earlier, would add revenue, which could be used to fund budget requests for Veteran's Administration hospitals, NASA, and other requests. To turn down a raise in the FHA loan limit would mean an important loss in potential revenue.

On the downside of this strategy, there was a general precedent in Congress not to authorize legislation that changes public policy through the appropriations process. Those on the authorizing committees, for example Congressman Rick Lazio or Congressman James Leach, could argue that adjusting the loan limit was not an appropriations matter, but rather a matter of policy and should therefore be dealt with first in the authorizing committee. However, over the last several decades, Congress has often broken policy stalemates by using the appropriations process, since the budget has to pass each year. Despite the risks, the only remaining approach for the advocates was to go to the appropriations committees, and fortunately for the advocates, the two chairmen of the HUD/VA subcommittees, Congressman Lewis and Senator Bond, decided to play a major role in brokering an agreement on this issue.

The first major breakthrough came on June 12, 1998, when the Senate Appropriations Committee approved the fiscal 1999 HUD appropriations bill, including the increase in the FHA single-family mortgage limit. The ceiling, which had been 75% of the conforming loan limit, or $170,362, was raised to 87% or $197,620. The floor, which had been at 38% ($86,317), was raised to 48% ($109,032). With the passage of this compromise, Senator Bond noted, "We have tried to strike a reasonable balance,"

---

[7] Retsinas, Nicholas, interviewed by author, Camridge, MA, 11 June 2001. Apgar, Bill, interviewed by author, Cambridge, MA, 11 June 2001. Johnson, Jim, interviewed by author, Washington, D.C., 30 January 2002. In the Jim Johnson interview, Johnson indicated that he did not recall the meeting specifically, but it was perfectly possible that it took place.

[8] *American Banker,* 29 April 1998.

and Senator Al D'Amato (R-NY), chairman of the Senate Banking, Housing, and Urban Affairs Committee, called it "a great step in expanding homeownership."[9]

This breakthrough was not an easy one. For some time during the spring of 1998, it was uncertain what Bond would do. To make matters worse, during the debate, Secretary Cuomo traveled to Missouri and spoke in opposition to Bond's candidacy for the Senate. On the one hand, such a speech was natural because Cuomo represented President Clinton and a Democratic administration. On the other hand, Bond was very upset, and the timing of the speech — in the middle of the loan limit debate — caused serious problems. However, eventually, because Bond needed revenue for the appropriations process, and because he felt that some compromise was appropriate, he continued to meet with a variety of people regarding the loan limits. For example, the staff of the NAHB provided Senator Bond and his staff with a detailed analysis of the impact of the benefits and revenues of the various alternative proposals. Eventually he decided to raise the loan limit from 75% to 87%, and the compromise was passed by Senator Bond's Appropriations Subcommittee and then the full Senate Appropriations Committee. Given that the loan limit could have been completely lost, Cuomo embraced the compromise as an important step toward victory. And other advocates, such as the home builders, realtors, and mortgage bankers, heralded the Senate action as important progress. Most of the opponents considered it a defeat, but for Fannie Mae, it went a long way in reducing their business concerns. According to Jim Johnson, Fannie Mae's analysis of the competitive threat drove much of its opposition. Although Fannie Mae felt a rise in the loan limit was questionable public policy, its analysis showed that a rise to 100% of the conforming loan limit would make 7% of its business vulnerable to competition from FHA. When the rise was cut to 87%, the competitive threat dropped to 1%. Although this analysis was not discussed publicly, it gave Fannie Mae some room to ease up on the intensity of its opposition.[10]

On the House side, the battle was even more difficult. Congressman Jerry Lewis favored the increase as a point of housing policy and certainly desired the revenue. However, he was opposed by the Republican leadership of the House, and since in the past he had been identified as being somewhat moderate, he was in a difficult position. Once the loan limit increase was included in the Senate appropriations bill, though, it gave him

---

[9] *Housing and Development Reporter,* 15 June 1998.
[10] Johnson, Jim, interviewed by author, Washington, D.C., 30 January 2002.

further impetus. With the momentum of the Senate, Lewis was able to get the increase approved by his FHA/VA Appropriations Subcommittee, and was able to win a positive vote in the full House Appropriations Committee on July 8, 1998.

The challenge now was keeping the FHA loan limit increase as a part of House FHA/VA Appropriations bill. Since a number of key members of the House — including Congressman James Leach and Congressman Rick Lazio — felt that this was a case of authorizing legislation as a part of the appropriations process, it was likely that when the bill was being debated on the floor of the House that they would raise a "point of order" to that effect, and therefore have the FHA loan limit increase removed from the bill. The only way to avoid this was to have a "rule" from the House Rules Committee that such a point of order could not be raised. Congressman Lewis felt he had the votes to obtain such a "rule," but the House leadership decided to get involved, and such protection was not included in the "rule." Congressman Lewis became upset and resolved to fight. In essence, he decided to oppose the "rule" of the House Rules Committee, and he gathered sufficient votes to do just that. He then took the issue to the floor of the House where he said that if such a protecting procedure was not included in the "rule" that he had the votes to defeat the "rule" and would therefore not allow the HUD/VA Appropriations bill to come to the floor for a vote. With this show of strength, the House leadership backed down, and the protecting clause was added on the floor of the House, and the opponents were not able to raise a point of order. This type of action on the House floor was fairly unprecedented, and it showed Congressman Lewis' strong resolve and committment to raise the loan limit. As a consequence of Congressman Lewis' strong efforts, the House then passed the HUD/VA Appropriations bill on July 29, including the loan limit increase.

The final fight in the Senate took place on the Senate floor in July. Senator Don Nichols (R-OK) rose with an amendment to strike the increase. Nichols had opposed the measure from the beginning. As a member of the Republican leadership, and backed by the private mortgage industry, Fannie Mae, and others, he decided to go to the floor for one last fight. The advocates rallied, however, and the amendment was tabled sixty-nine to twenty-seven.[11] The Senate then voted on July 17, 1998, to boost the FHA loan limit and approve the appropriations bill.

In September, the House and the Senate established conferees to conference on the VA/HUD appropriations bill, and by this point, the loan

---

[11] *Housing and Development Reporter,* 27 July 1998.

limit issue had been decided. Other important housing issues were included in this appropriations bill, such as a reform of public housing. Once compromises were reached on all of these issues, the VA/HUD appropriations bill sailed through Congress. The House approved the conference report on October 6 by a vote of 409 to 14, and the Senate, on October 8, 1998, by a vote of 96 to 1.

The FHA loan limit had been raised, and on October 19, 1998, Secretary Cuomo announced the higher FHA loan limit for communities around the country. The loan limit ceiling in high cost areas rose from 75% to 87% or to $197,620, with the floor going from 38% to 48% or a level of $109,032. Since the FHA limit was now a percent of the overall conforming market, it climbed again in January 1999 and January 2001, and in January 2002 it rose to $261,609 in high-cost areas, with a floor of $144,336 elsewhere. Consequently, FHA business increased. When Secretary Cuomo spoke around the country in 1999 and 2000, he would often cite the fact that FHA business had risen, in part due to the loan limit increase.

WHY DID THE HIGHER LOAN LIMIT PASS?

First, a higher FHA loan limit was generally viewed to be a positive means of supporting homeownership and affordable housing. FHA helps home buyers, especially first-time buyers, to purchase a home, especially in areas of the country where the cost of housing has risen significantly. A higher loan limit allows FHA financing to reach those buyers. Certainly there were some who felt that raising the loan limit was more helpful to those with moderate incomes and was therefore not focused directly on what they felt was the primary mission of HUD: providing housing for the poor. But in the end, the majority of the members of Congress, both Republicans and Democrats, and a large number of housing advocates, agreed that providing affordable housing to more home buyers was a reasonable mission for the FHA.

Second, an important part of the passage of the loan limit was the coalition that was formed and the leadership provided by HUD Secretary Andrew Cuomo. Although past HUD secretaries had supported raising the limit, Secretary Cuomo played a highly visible and instrumental role in forming and maintaining the coalition, even though he realized that it could have some political cost. For a variety of reasons, he felt that this issue deserved his personal attention, and without his strong support, the legislation would not have passed. Also, the issue became a part of his overall effort to build a broader constituency to support affordable housing. His strategy of going for a loan limit equal to 100% of the conforming loan limit also proved to be effective because it left room for compromise. In addition, Cuomo was good at keeping his strategy "close to the vest."[12] He eventually was willing to compromise, but did not expose his bottom line too early. When the point of compromise was established by Senator Bond in the Senate appropriations process, Cuomo was willing to accept the compromise and work for its eventual success.

Third, support for the higher loan limit was broad and cut across party lines. Cuomo, of course, represented the Clinton administration and was able to work with the Democrats in the House and Senate. In addition, many of his coalition partners, especially NAHB and the National Association of Realtors, had close ties with Republican members of the House and Senate. The advocates were therefore able to assemble a bipartisan coalition of support.

A fourth reason for the measure's success was strong congressional leadership from key people. Raising the FHA loan limits was a tough political battle, and it would not have happened without strong leadership on the part of Senator Kit Bond and Congressman Jerry Lewis. Senator Bond was instrumental in determining the point of compromise and then leading the Senate Appropriations Subcommittee in passing the measure. In crafting the compromise, which eventually stood the test of time, he balanced the interests of all sides. Once he crafted the compromise, he held firm and was able to get bipartisan support despite the fact that some conservative Republicans rose in opposition. On the House side, Jerry Lewis was instrumental in gathering a group of congressmen who were willing to take a stand against the Republican leadership in the House, even on the floor of the House, to overturn the rule in order to assure that the measure was kept as a part of the House HUD/VA appropriations package. Without his efforts, the proposal would not have passed the House.

Fifth, the compromise worked out by Senator Bond helped ease the intensity of Fannie Mae's opposition. According to Jim Johnson, when the competitive threat to Fannie Mae's business dropped from 7% to 1%, the political dynamics changed: "To be at war with your friends on a policy issue is not a good idea. But to be at war with friends on 7% of your business is a different matter."[13] Fannie Mae did not acknowledge his shift publicly because, as Johnson observed, "Sometimes common ground is

---

[12] Apgar, Bill, interviewed by author, Cambridge, MA, 11 June 2001.
[13] Johnson, James, interviewed by author, Washington, D.C., 30 January 2002.

more positive if it is not a negotiated settlement. It may mean more to the other side if they beat us than to negotiate a conclusion."

Finally, it is important to recognize that the measure passed Congress because it had an important incentive — revenues that could be used for other purposes. In past years OMB has had concerns about increasing the FHA loan limit on philosophical grounds because it would expand the activities of the public sector in housing. However, President Clinton's campaign platform included raising the FHA loan limit. The proposal was therefore supported by the White House, and OMB included the measure in various proposals throughout the 1990s. Undoubtedly, though, OMB's support was strengthened by the desire for additional revenues. When Secretary Cuomo went to OMB with the proposal to raise the loan limit in the summer of 1997, it was to provide revenue to help support programs that he felt were necessary, such as the housing voucher program. Once he decided to take on the issue, the budget was no longer the driving force, but it was still important. The House and Senate Appropriations Subcommittees were also very interested in the increased revenue to help support Veterans Administration hospitals and NASA, as well as HUD. As former FHA Commissioner Nic Retsinas noted, "The FHA loan limits moved in part because of the needed dollars for the budget. In one way, you could say the FHA loan limits passed because of VA hospitals."[14]

CONSEQUENCES OF THE FAILURE TO ACHIEVE COMMON GROUND

At first blush, it might seem that common ground was achieved through congressional compromise. After all, the final FHA loan limit rise was halfway between the existing limit and the HUD proposal. Those who favored the increase claimed the compromise to be a success, and many of the participants recognized from the outset that some type of compromise was inevitable. However, because the opponents fought hard and to the end — for example, the last efforts in the Senate by Senator Nichols to strike the loan limits from the HUD/VA appropriations bill — it became a "win-lose" situation rather than a compromise with at least a partial "win-win."

During the debate, the discussion became heated among several of the parties, and groups that generally work together could not agree. Some ef-

---

[14] Retsinas, Nicholas, interviewed by author, Cambridge, MA, 11 June 2001.

fort was made to reach a compromise early in the process, but it did not succeed. Perhaps most importantly, the intensity of the debate led to lingering feelings of distrust and animosity. Toward the end of 1998, after the loan limit had passed, Fannie Mae Chairman Jim Johnson called NAHB and asked that they host a meeting to bring together the MBA, NAR, NAHB, and Fannie Mae and Freddie Mac. The meeting helped smooth over some of the differences, but the distrust was deep and in some cases lasting. In particular, the tension between Fannie Mae and HUD seemed to continue through most of Cuomo's tenure as HUD Secretary.

Further, in later years, the residue of the fight over FHA made it more difficult for housing interests to come together on a series of policy issues and debates. One such debate was over the roles of Fannie Mae and Freddie Mac. Congressman Richard Baker (R-LA) proposed legislation that would have curtailed Fannie Mae's and Freddie Mac's powers and provided significant regulatory shifts (see Chapter 4). In addition, HUD raised Fannie Mae's and Freddie Mac's affordable housing goals significantly. It would be hard to trace an absolute correlation between the battle to raise the FHA loan limit and the housing finance debates of 1999 and 2000. However, there is no question that a tone of disagreement was set in 1998, and housing interests that usually worked together for affordable housing were pitted against each other.

This case illustrates that the lines on housing issues are not always drawn between Republicans and Democrats. Rather they are drawn based on the different special interests within the housing sector. This is part of the democratic process, but it also raises questions about our ability to achieve common ground on housing issues in the twenty-first century.

Perhaps a compromise could have been reached earlier in the process if competing interests had been willing to shift their positions and to find common ground. The result might have been the same — a compromise rise in the loan limit in high-cost areas — but the animosity might have been avoided. The potential was there, but the various parties were not willing. As noted in the OSHA case study (Chapter 8), parties must be willing to step back and find areas of mutual benefit. It does not mean that one side has to win entirely and the other lose entirely — rather both parties can reach an agreement that will be better for each than the alternative. However, the FHA case demonstrates that, given the nature of personalities, politics, and public debate, achieving such a "win-win" can be difficult.

Chapter 10

A CASE STUDY ON THE INABILITY TO ACHIEVE COMMON GROUND: WETLANDS REGULATION IN THE UNITED STATES

Achieving a balance between home building and environmental concerns has posed a critical challenge for housing policy. On the one hand is the need to build adequate affordable housing, and on the other hand is the desire to protect the environment. Finding the appropriate balance between the two interests and meeting both concerns has proved to be one of the most fascinating and difficult aspects of housing policy in recent years. This case study examines the regulation and protection of wetlands as it has affected the home building industry over the last twenty-five years. Whereas the OSHA case displayed successful mediation and, ultimately, the achievement of common ground, this case is an example of failure to find a balance point amid the clash of interests.

The controversy over wetlands began in the 1970s, after the passage of the Clean Water Act. The legislation refers only to the "navigable waters of the United States," and it does not use the term "wetlands." However, through broad interpretations of the law, wetlands have become regulated under the act. One source of current conflict is the vagueness of the original law regarding the definition of wetlands and the process for regulating wetlands. Further, the Clean Water Act — in particular, Section 404, which has become the legislative framework for regulating wetlands — covers an array of activities and regulates a diverse cross-section of businesses and individuals in the process. The act regulates activities ranging from building an addition on a single-family home to drainage activity for new developments across many acres; it affects large industrial businesses as well as small businesses and individuals. This stands in marked contrast to most other environmental programs which tend to regulate only large businesses and municipalities. The initial ambiguity about how wetlands fit into the act and the unique scope of the act have resulted in a great deal of confusion regarding wetlands law (and regulation). This has been compounded by numerous legal battles and disputes over the last three decades between government agencies, business concerns, builders and developers, trade organizations, states and local governments, property owners, and environmental organizations.

Another aspect of the problem is that, scientifically speaking, wetlands are difficult to define. This makes it more challenging to devise adequate regulatory policies, and it means there are often different interpretations of whether certain pieces of land should be classified as wetlands. There are also many competing opinions about the current status of wetlands — some data sources reveal that wetlands continue to be destroyed, others report that wetlands remain stable, and still others report gains in wetlands. All of this contributes to the complexity and confusion surrounding the wetlands issue in the United States today.

A common misperception is that wetlands were rapidly destroyed due to home building and other development activities. From a historical perspective, building has certainly contributed to wetlands losses; however, for many years agriculture was the greater cause for wetlands destruction in the United States. Yet the wetlands debate has often been framed as a battle between builders and environmentalists, leaving the issue of the effect of agricultural practices on wetlands outside the discussion. This changed in 1985 with the passage of the "Swampbuster" provision of the Food Security Act of 1985 (16 United States Code Annotated [USCA], Section 3821) which eliminated Department of Agriculture financial assistance to farmers on any land which was converted from wetlands to farmlands.

The wetlands case exemplifies a highly polarized ideological and political situation. Agencies, organizations, and individuals have been unable to move beyond their specific perspectives to find common ground. The controversy is a useful case study for housing policy, but it is also an example of how difficult it can be to find common ground in the wider policy arena.

OVERVIEW OF THE WETLANDS CASE: 1972 TO 2000

The roots for many of today's wetlands problems lies in the text of the Clean Water Act (CWA) and in the design of the Section 404 permit program. The permitting process is cumbersome, and the government is frequently challenged about definitions of wetlands, how to navigate the permit program, and jurisdiction. A series of attempts to reduce confusion and hassle have been made; these attempts include the Nationwide Permit Program, wetlands delineation manuals, and administrative appeals. Despite efforts to reduce conflict, serious issues remain because of the wide gulf between participants and the failure of some to compromise. Thirty years of ineffective maneuvering have only made both sides more resolute in their views and more unwilling to come together.

The Clean Water Act

Early in the nation's history, wetlands were seen in a different light than they are today. They were considered unattractive health hazards that ought to be "reclaimed" — drained and filled to serve more useful purposes. This viewpoint shifted as scientists came to understand that wetlands are a critical piece of the larger ecosystem. Wetlands help preserve water quality, reduce flood damage, and provide important habitats for fish and wildlife. Yet for a long time, wetlands were being destroyed at a rapid rate. According to the National Research Council, by the mid-1980s, 117 million acres of wetlands in the United States — nearly half the original total — had been converted to alternative uses.[1]

Prior to the 1970s, federal policies were geared toward the increasing economic productivity of land, and they were not focused on conservation efforts. For many people, the goal was to make wetlands more economically productive by converting the land to agricultural use. With the rise of the environmental movement in the 1960s and 1970s, popular perceptions of wetlands and other environmental systems began to change. The effects of pollution and unregulated activities were evident across the country, and this reality, along with a growing scientific understanding of the environment, spurred change.

One of the major reflections of changing attitudes about the environment was the passage of legislation that has come to be known as the Clean Water Act. This legislation was passed to address pollution and a growing public concern about the environment; it was not originally designed to monitor wetlands. Before the passage of the Clean Water Act, there were no comprehensive safeguards to protect our lakes or rivers, and the problems were significant. For example, the Cuyahoga River in Ohio was catching on fire, Lake Erie was considered dead, and a number of lakes and rivers in the country were not swimmable or fishable. In 1972,

---

[1] National Research Council, *Wetlands: Characteristics and Boundaries*, 1.

Congress passed the Federal Water and Pollution Control Act Amendments to more adequately protect the waters of the United States. These amendments to the 1948 Federal Pollution Control Act provided the necessary enforcement mechanisms to monitor water use and potential pollution problems. These amendments are collectively referred to as the Clean Water Act. This legislation was the first to make protection of waterways a national commitment, and the first to address discharge of industrial pollutants into the nation's lakes and rivers. The CWA also casts the government in the role of trying to mediate between environmental and business concerns, and this has proven to be particularly challenging.

When the CWA was passed in 1972, the term "wetlands" was not used in the text of the law. The act refers to "waters of the United States" and discusses the regulation of "navigable waters." Further, there is no clear definition of wetlands. This lack of definition is in part a reflection of the lack of consensus among wetlands ecologists about what criteria should be used, since wetlands are so diverse in their characteristics. For example, some wetlands areas may actually be dry for years if water levels are low; still, such areas are deemed to be wetlands. Other wetlands remain saturated year-round and are more like swamp areas. In effect, it requires a great deal of scientific sophistication to formulate a useful definition. This sets up a troubling scenario: wetlands are difficult to define from a scientific standpoint, yet without a clear definition, builders will not know where they can or cannot build.

Section 404 of the CWA gave the U.S. Army Corps of Engineers (USACE or Corps) and the Environmental Protection Agency (EPA) joint authority to regulate the pollution of the nation's waterways. Section 404 regulates the placement of dredged or fill material in any waters of the United States.[2] This joint authority is another major flaw in the wetlands policy process. Both agencies were given responsibilities under the act, yet neither was given absolute authority. A split system of administration and management, in the words of Virginia Albrecht, a Washington, D.C. lawyer with extensive wetlands regulatory and judicial experience, is a "cardinal management sin."[3] The EPA (which was a new agency, also established in 1972) formulates the guidelines for the Section 404 program. The Corps then uses these guidelines to make permit decisions and is actually in charge of issuing individual permits for the discharge of dredged or fill material in waters or wetlands, but the EPA has the power to overrule the Corps on the granting of permits.

Since the passage of the Rivers and Harbors Act of 1899, the Corps has

---

[2] The details of the Section 404 Program are addressed later in the chapter.
[3] Albrecht, "The Wetlands Debate," 21.

had a program in place to regulate navigational impacts in traditionally navigable waters and their boundaries. The Corps's regulatory function was enhanced by the passage of environmental laws in the late 1960s, especially the National Environmental Policy Act (NEPA) of 1969. When the Clean Water Act was passed in 1972, the Corps was the logical agency to manage the Section 404 permitting program. However, the EPA had just been created, and its primary function was to protect the environment; Congress wanted to give EPA responsibilities and the ability to be involved in environmental protection. The EPA's mission was most clearly related to protecting U.S. waters, but the Corps had an important bureaucracy and management system already in place. In the end, a congressional compromise split the responsibility for administration and enforcement of the program.[4]

These flaws in the CWA legislation had an enormous impact almost immediately, and in many respects, they continue to fuel the tension surrounding wetlands regulation today.

Interpreting the Law: the Corps, the EPA, the Public, and the Courts

Shortly after the passage of the Clean Water Act, the EPA and the Corps each took a different approach to the legislation. The Corps stated that the act should not include wetlands, while the EPA insisted that wetlands should be regulated as part of the act. The Corps began by narrowly interpreting the law and regulating only traditionally navigable waters, not wetlands. Since the definition of a "wetland" was unclear, deciding the meaning of the law fell to the courts. In 1975, the National Resources Defense Council (NRDC) challenged this narrow interpretation and filed a lawsuit. In the ensuing legal case, *National Resources Defense Council (NRDC) v. Calloway,* the court ruled that the term "waters of the U.S." should be interpreted broadly. The court "held that Congress intended to assert federal jurisdiction over the nation's waters to the maximum extent permitted under the Commerce Clause of the Constitution."[5] After this ruling, the Corps altered its approach and redefined "waters of the U.S." to "include navigable waters and their tributaries, non-navigable intrastate waters whose use or misuse could affect interstate commerce, and all freshwater wetlands adjacent to other waters protected by the statute."[6]

---

[4] Liebesman, *Developer's Guide to Wetlands Regulation,* 3.
[5] Liebesman, Court ruling as found in "Overview of the Clean Water Act, iii.
[6] Salvesen, Regulatory ruling by the Corp of Engineers as found in *Wetlands: Mitigating and Regulating Impacts,* 28.

The inclusion of "adjacent wetlands" vastly expanded the scope of the Section 404 permit program.

In 1977, more amendments were passed as part of the commitment made by Congress to conduct ongoing assessments of the Clean Water Act.[7] It was in 1977 that the phrase "Clean Water Act" was first used to refer to the amendments of the Federal Water Pollution Control Act. It was also at this time that the term "wetlands" was incorporated into the text and given a definition. As Section 404 [Corps' 33 C.F.R. 328.3(b) and EPA's 40 C.F.R. 230.3(t)] reads:

> The term "wetlands" means those areas that are inundated or saturated by surface or ground water at a frequency and duration sufficient to support, and that under normal circumstances do support, a prevalence of vegetation typically adapted for life in saturated soil conditions. Wetlands generally include swamps, marshes, bogs and similar areas.[8]

From this definition, a piece of land is defined as a wetland if it has the following three characteristics: 1. wetland hydrology (presence of water at or near the surface for a period of time); 2. hydrophytic vegetation (wetland plants); and 3. hydric soils (periodically anaerobic soils resulting from prolonged saturation or inundation).

While the new definition finally gave some guidance, problems persisted. Much of the early legal haggling and debate about what defines a wetland was between the EPA and the Corps. Yet other organizations and agencies have added their own wetlands definitions. One particularly broad alternative definition comes from the U.S. Fish and Wildlife Service (FWS), which uses any one of the above three attributes to define a wetland. The Corps's 1977 definition was frequently challenged in the courts, and once again, because of the unclear definition and split jurisdiction, the courts became the place where decisions were made about wetlands regulation. Most notably, in *U.S. v. Riverside Bayview Homes, Inc.,* the Corps's definition was challenged and upheld by the Supreme Court in 1985. Riverside Bayview Homes had begun filling several acres near its property in Michigan when the Corps instructed them to stop on the grounds it did not have the appropriate permits to fill the land. The Corps claimed this area was classified as an adjacent wetlands; Riverside Bayview Homes argued that the presence of aquatic vegetation on the property was not a result of frequent flooding from nearby navigable waters and therefore

---

[7] Muskie, "Meaning of the 1977 Clean Water Act."
[8] Dennison, and Berry, *Wetlands: Guide to Science,* 5.

should not be regulated by the Corps.[9] The Supreme Court upheld the Corps's position, which ultimately gave the Corps an expanded wetlands jurisdiction. In explaining the impacts of the court case in an Urban Land Institute publication, David Salvesen writes: "Now wetlands do not have to be wet, connected to or flooded by navigable waters to fall within the Corps' purview; they must only be saturated frequently enough to support wetlands vegetation and have some connection to interstate commerce. The Supreme Court required only that wetlands be hydrologically connected with navigable waters."[10]

This decision greatly expanded the regulatory function of the Corps related to wetlands. It also highlighted how challenging it is for nonspecialists to identify a wetland. Yet, it still did not completely clarify the situation. The *Riverside* case neglected to address whether isolated wetlands could be regulated by the Corps. In 1985, the EPA issued a statement indicating that "waters of the United States" can include isolated waters that are or could potentially be used as habitat by migratory birds that are protected by treaties, that cross state lines, or that are endangered species. This in turn was used by the Corps when ascertaining its regulatory functions throughout the country. The inclusion of isolated wetlands in the regulatory framework was challenged by both *Tabb Lakes, Ltd. v. United States* in 1988–1989 and *Hoffman Homes, Inc., v. Administrator, U.S. EPA* in 1993. In the first case, the court rejected the Corps's use of the migratory bird rule on procedural grounds, yet in the second, the court upheld the Corps's ability to regulate the isolated wetlands. Isolated wetlands remain an important part of the debate, and will be discussed later in the chapter.

What emerges from this examination is a series of layers of tension and complexity. The first layer is the bifurcation of power between the EPA and the Corps, which led to each agency taking a different approach to the law. The next layer is public response from the many parties involved, including small businesses, individual landowners, large companies, and environmental groups. Challenges to wetlands regulations have covered the entire spectrum, ranging from accusations that the regulations do not protect wetlands enough to concerns that they go too far. The third layer is the persistent problem surrounding the precise nature of a wetlands.[11]

---

[9] Salvesen, *Wetlands: Mitigating and Regulating Impacts*, 28.
[10] Ibid.
[11] For an example of this debate see "Defining Wetlands: Science or Politics," *National Wetlands Newsletter*, 10.

Even within the courts there are layers of interpretation stemming from a number of different decisions which have been made at different levels of the court system. Lower courts and appeals courts may have different opinions, the Supreme Court may disagree with a lower court, and so on. In the short term, different decisions made by different courts tend to add to the confusion rather than resolve it. Also, the court process can take years to fully address even one lawsuit related to wetlands. The courts are the only place where firm decisions are being made, yet over time even they have not made consistent decisions about wetlands regulation, and differing interpretations continue to abound.

The Section 404 Permit Program

Section 404 was part of the first series of "clean water" amendments passed in 1972. However, it is most useful to discuss Section 404 in light of the 1977 changes and addition of the term "wetlands." Examining the pieces of Section 404 also illustrates how the program is divided between the two governmental agencies, and exactly how and why the dual jurisdictional role has contributed to the problems. The main provisions of the Section 404 permit program include:

- *Section 404(a)*: Authorizes the Corps to issue permits related to filling navigable waters, including wetlands. (The act gave the Corps the ability to issue permits, but it did not provide guidelines to evaluate them.)
- *Section 404(b)*: States the Corps is to issue permits according to guidelines developed by the EPA.
- *Section 404(c)*: Authorizes the EPA to veto a decision by the Corps to issue a permit to fill a wetland.
- *Section 404(e)*: Authorizes the Corps to issue general permits on a state, regional, or nationwide basis for wetlands activities that will cause minimal negative effects.
- *Section 404(f)*: Exempts certain activities from the permit requirements, including those related to silviculture, established farming, or ranching.
- *Section 404(g)*: Authorizes states to assume the permit program from the Corps if the state's program is approved by the EPA.
- *Section 404(q)*: Requires the Corps to enter into a memorandum of agreement (MOA) with other federal agencies to minimize

excessive paperwork related to the permitting process. This section also provides a mechanism for resolving disputes among the agencies involved in the process.[12]

These are the primary provisions in the statute. Effectively, no one is allowed to discharge dredged or fill material into a wetland without first receiving a permit from the Corps. Again, the EPA has veto power to stop the issuing of a permit, although it has rarely used this ability. For a permit to actually be granted, the following criteria must be met: 1. Discharge generated cannot have significant environmental impacts; 2. There can be no practicable upland alternative to the wetland site available for the proposed non-water-dependent activity; 3. The proposed activity must generally be water dependent.[13]

The Section 404 program is federally run, however Section 404(g) of the Clean Water Act allows individual states to assume responsibility to administer the permits. A state may apply to the EPA for approval of its program, and if approval is granted, the state can issue the Section 404 permits directly. Copies of all permits issued by states must be sent to the EPA, and the EPA retains the right to veto a permit and also to withdraw approval of a state's program if statutory and regulatory requirements are not followed correctly.[14] To date, only two states, Michigan and New Jersey, have assumed full responsibility for the 404 program. Although the process can be political and initially frustrating, Michigan and New Jersey show that state assumption of the program can provide an alternative approach to regulation.[15] In addition, some suggest that state assumption of the program could be the solution to the wetlands debate.[16]

Problems with the Permit Process

For many home builders, developers, and individual landowners, the biggest challenge of wetlands regulation is the Section 404 permitting process, which tends to be lengthy, costly, and complicated.

Figure 10.1 outlines the permitting process from filling out the application through the final decision to either grant or deny a permit. The figure displays the complexity of each stage of the process and the multiple requirements involved. It also reveals that at each stage of the process, a

---

[12] For a more detailed discussion of the Section 404 permit program see Salvesen, *Wetlands: Mitigating and Regulating Impacts,* 25–26.

[13] Gaddie and Regens, *Regulating Wetlands Protection,* 38.

[14] Dennison and Berry, *Wetlands: Guide to Science,* 226.

[15] Gaddie and Regens, *Regulating Wetlands Protection,* 80.

[16] Ibid., 57.

FIGURE 10.1
The Section 404 Permit Process

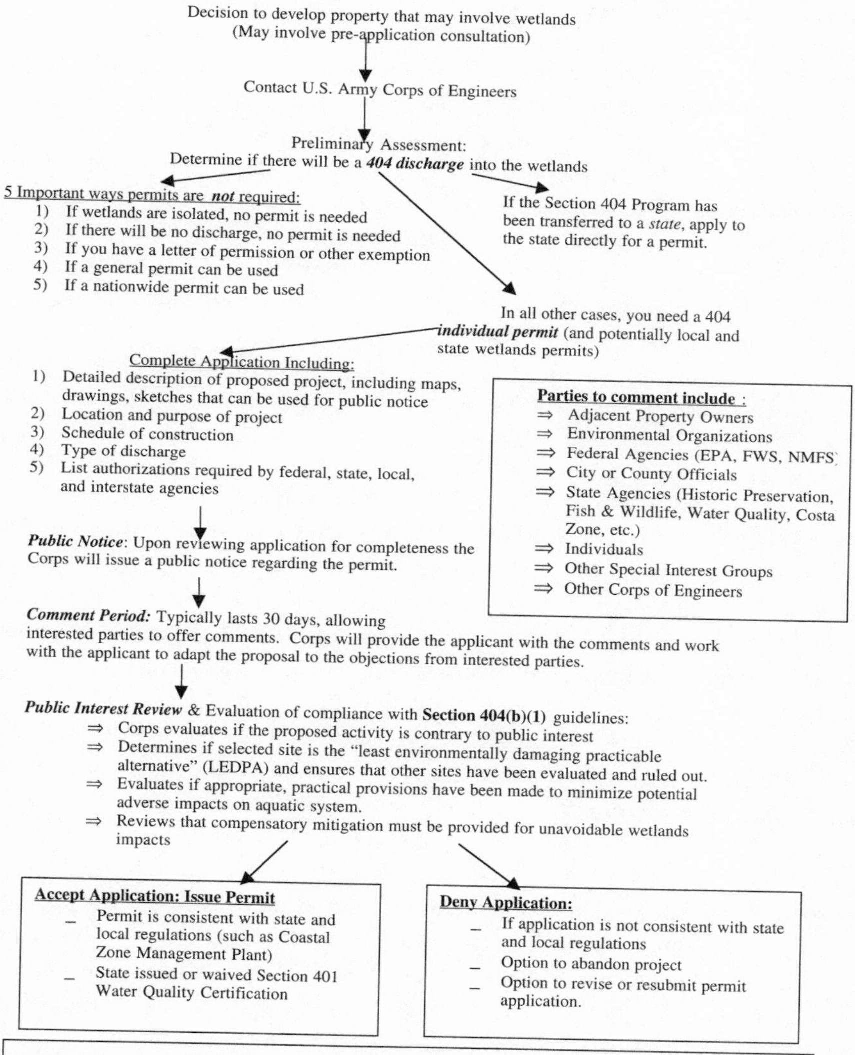

Decision to develop property that may involve wetlands
(May involve pre-application consultation)

Contact U.S. Army Corps of Engineers

Preliminary Assessment:
Determine if there will be a *404 discharge* into the wetlands

5 Important ways permits are *not* required:
1) If wetlands are isolated, no permit is needed
2) If there will be no discharge, no permit is needed
3) If you have a letter of permission or other exemption
4) If a general permit can be used
5) If a nationwide permit can be used

If the Section 404 Program has
been transferred to a *state*, apply to
the state directly for a permit.

In all other cases, you need a 404
individual permit (and potentially local and
state wetlands permits)

Complete Application Including:
1) Detailed description of proposed project, including maps,
   drawings, sketches that can be used for public notice
2) Location and purpose of project
3) Schedule of construction
4) Type of discharge
5) List authorizations required by federal, state, local,
   and interstate agencies

Parties to comment include :
⇒ Adjacent Property Owners
⇒ Environmental Organizations
⇒ Federal Agencies (EPA, FWS, NMFS)
⇒ City or County Officials
⇒ State Agencies (Historic Preservation,
    Fish & Wildlife, Water Quality, Costa
    Zone, etc.)
⇒ Individuals
⇒ Other Special Interest Groups
⇒ Other Corps of Engineers

Public Notice: Upon reviewing application for completeness the
Corps will issue a public notice regarding the permit.

Comment Period: Typically lasts 30 days, allowing
interested parties to offer comments. Corps will provide the applicant with the comments and work
with the applicant to adapt the proposal to the objections from interested parties.

Public Interest Review & Evaluation of compliance with **Section 404(b)(1)** guidelines:
⇒ Corps evaluates if the proposed activity is contrary to public interest
⇒ Determines if selected site is the "least environmentally damaging practicable
    alternative" (LEDPA) and ensures that other sites have been evaluated and ruled out.
⇒ Evaluates if appropriate, practical provisions have been made to minimize potential
    adverse impacts on aquatic system.
⇒ Reviews that compensatory mitigation must be provided for unavoidable wetlands
    impacts

Accept Application: Issue Permit
– Permit is consistent with state and
   local regulations (such as Coastal
   Zone Management Plan)
– State issued or waived Section 401
   Water Quality Certification

Deny Application:
– If application is not consistent with state
   and local regulations
– Option to abandon project
– Option to revise or resubmit permit
   application.

Sources: Salvesen, *Wetlands: Mitigating and Regulating Development Impacts;* and NAHB, "The Truth
About America's Wetlands." 1994.

great deal of time is allotted for review and comment. The public hearing phase allows for comments from multiple sources, including the Corps, EPA, special interest groups, state agencies, and adjacent property owners. After the hearing, the Corps works with the applicant to address the community-wide concerns and objections into the plan (if possible). The Corps then reviews the application again to ensure that it meets Section 404(b)(1) guidelines and is not contrary to the public interest.

Many people who have gone through the process complain that the permitting procedure is unnecessarily lengthy. The Corps lists 127 days as the average for going through the entire permit process, but Virginia Albrecht and Bernard Goode contest this figure based on their study of the time required to grant a permit. They write: "The 127-day figure for individual permits is misleading. It does not count all of the time the applicant is in the process, it includes non-wetland applications, and it only counts permits that are issued and thus excludes the majority of applications — those that are withdrawn or denied."[17] Albrecht and Goode point out that the majority of the applications for Section 404 permits were withdrawn between 1988 and 1993. According to their review, 38% were granted, 5% denied, and 57% withdrawn.[18] Figure 10.2 emphasizes these challenges and reveals that far more permits are denied or withdrawn than are granted. It also suggests that the processing system may not be working.

The length of time and multiple stages to obtain a permit make the process particularly costly. At several points, there is significant cost to the applicant for consultations, mapping, and plans. Building cannot take place until the permit is acquired, which means that any other plans or permits related to the project as a whole must be put on hold until the wetlands permit is obtained. There is significant financial risk involved, especially considering that applications may be denied. By this time, the builder has put time, money, and effort into the process and must decide whether to accept the loss and cancel building plans or adapt the plans to meet federal, state, or local permit requirements that were not met. The latter means starting the process over again, adding more cost and time to the entire project. These costs and delays can be particularly difficult for smaller businesses and individuals seeking to do small-scale projects. Again, wetlands regulations are unique in that they affect a diverse array of businesses and individuals. A cumbersome permit process which ap-

---

[17] Albrecht and Goode, "All is Not Well With Section 404," 14.
[18] Ibid., 15.

FIGURE 10.2

Processing Time for Wetland Permits

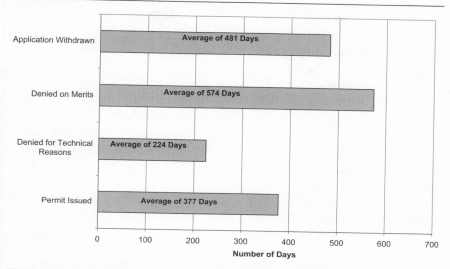

SOURCE: NAHB, "The Truth About America's Wetlands." 1994. (Data from Virginia S. Albrecht and Bernard Goode, "Wetland Regulation in the Real World," February 1994.)

plies to all applicants, large and small, tends to affect smaller businesses and individuals more.

The permit process is an attempt to provide compromise between development and environmental interests, but it is extremely cumbersome. For those who want to protect the environment, the ultimate goal is no disturbance and no construction; on the other side, those seeking to use their property to build a home for personal use or for profit would prefer minimal environmental review. This is not to say that an environmentalist is incapable of seeing the need to adapt wetlands protection when homes need to be built, or that a builder or developer cannot see the importance of environmental protection. However, their perspectives start and end with very different ideological views. The 404 permit program is designed to be a compromise between these two interests, but the complexity of the process and the negative reactions over time signal the very real difficulties of bridging the gap.[19]

---

[19] Gaddie and Regens, *Regulating Wetlands Protection,* 37.

Nationwide Permits

Many of the problems related to wetlands regulation arose in the years immediately after the initial round of clean water laws were passed. Confusion ran high among the public and the two agencies running the 404 program. The government faced a great deal of pressure from communities that, not having faced regulation previously, suddenly found their activities impinged upon in a very distinct and often costly manner. Congress sought to address the concerns of communities facing sudden, extensive regulation while attempting to preserve the integrity of the legislation, with new policies to help reduce unnecessary review and regulation of building projects. The result was the implementation of general permits, and what has come to be known as the Nationwide Permit (NWP) program.

Part of the dilemma of the early years of Section 404 was how the government could quickly move from a position of no regulation to a serious, intensive review process. The transition was not smooth, especially as concerns arose over what could be regulated and how to classify diverse wetlands areas. The Corps quickly realized that the regulatory functions it was assuming were beyond its capacities. It was unable to monitor all the projects and review permits in a timely fashion. This was magnified after the *NRDC v. Callaway* decision in 1975, by which the Corps gained an even greater regulatory role. Builders were frustrated by the new and cumbersome permitting process, and the Corps was overwhelmed with its new role. In the critical years between 1972 and 1977, it became clear that the process would have to be streamlined so the Corps could administer the program properly. Environmental protection had to be ensured, yet an excessive burden could not fall on the public (specifically, builders).

In 1975, the concept of "general permits" was offered as a solution to the problem. In effect, if a planned project satisfied all the guidelines, then the discharge was deemed authorized without a project-specific review by Corps personnel.[20] NWPs are issued by the Corps headquarters in Washington, D.C., and are effective in all states. Shortly after the Corps adopted this program, Congress amended the Clean Water Act to ratify the use of NWPs in Section 404(e) in 1977. Section 404(e) authorizes the Corps "to issue 'general' permits on a state, regional, and nationwide basis for any category of activities which are similar in nature and will have only minimal individual and cumulative environmental impacts."[21]

---

[20] National Association of Home Builders, "History of the Nationwide Permit Program," 1.
[21] Dennison and Berry, *Wetlands: Guide to Science*, 238.

NWPs were an attempt to allow the Corps to focus on the projects with the most ecological impact. They were meant to prevent the government from overregulating and bogging down the building process. This was a benefit for builders and developers, who could proceed with projects that had little negative impact. It provided manageable guidelines that the builder could understand and implement in a timely fashion; in this way, builders learned how to satisfy wetlands requirements and complete their projects. In addition, NWPs gave Corps personnel more time to focus on complicated wetlands permits rather than deal with every single wetlands issue. It was a means of empowering and informing the public about how to comply without a government agency watching over every project.

Despite this, many environmental organizations had strong reactions to NWPs. The concern was that allowing wetlands to be filled without a project-specific review from the government would mean that wetlands that should be regulated would be ignored. Such critics viewed the NWP program as a shirking of the agency's responsibilities and suggested that the administrative process should have been expanded rather than turning to a general permitting process.[22]

Perhaps the most significant NWP is Nationwide Permit 26, which affects isolated wetlands and headwaters. Most NWPs relate to categories of activities rather than to categories of wetlands. For example, NWP 1 relates to construction of aids to navigation and regulatory markers, NWP 5 is about scientific measurement devices, and NWP 20 is about oil spill cleanup activities. NWP 26 relates to the filling of a wetland based on its position in the drainage network rather than on the activity itself.[23] It is unique in that it authorizes the filling of relatively small areas as long as the procedure is consistent with CWA regulations. NWP 26 exempted individuals from acquiring a permit for discharge of dredged or fill material as long as the following requirements were met: (1.) the discharge did not cause the loss of more than ten acres of waters; (2.) the Corps district was notified of the discharge and loss; (3.) the discharge was part of a single and complete project.[24] NWP 26 received the most criticism of all the NWPs. The Audubon Society condemned it, contending that it had been the largest source of permitted wetlands loss in the country. In the 1990s,

---

[22] For such a critical assessment, see for example, Ortman, 'The Corps' Stealth Permit Program," 10.

[23] National Research Council, *Wetlands: Characteristics and Boundaries,* 155.

[24] Dennison and Berry, *Wetlands Guide to Science,* 240.

efforts were mounted to eliminate NWP 26 entirely. As a result, the acreage requirements were reduced from ten to three.[25]

Because the NWPs had endured so much controversy, in the mid-1990s the Corps reviewed the NWP program. As part of this review process, the Corps asked environmental organizations and trade organizations to provide input as to how the NWP program should be restructured. The Corps took this information and eventually issued its own set of new guidelines for the NWP program. From the perspective of NAHB and other building-oriented organizations, the changes to the program went too far and were more restrictive than Congress had intended when it approved the NWP program. From the environmental side, the alterations had not gone far enough. The National Resources Defense Council (NRDC), along with other environmental organizations, sued the Corps in 1998 with the aim of dismantling the NWP system. In *NRDC et al. v. West,* NRDC's main argument was that by sanctioning the NWP program, the Corps allowed more than minimal impacts upon the environment. In response to this, NAHB asked to be a codefendant with the Corps, since from NAHB's perspective, NWPs provided a greater balance in the regulatory process and needed to be retained.[26]

The lawsuit ended in 1999 with a restructuring of the NWP system. In place of NWP 26, five replacement permits were established, each of which corresponded to a particular type of building. For example, one permit was for residential construction, one for shopping malls, one for recreational facilities, and so on. This made the process more specialized and eliminated the ease with which builders had been able to operate under NWP 26. Also, the overall acreage limit for NWPs was reduced from three acres to one-half acre. (When NWPs were originally introduced in 1977 there was a ten acre limit.)

From NRDC's perspective, the breaking apart of what it viewed as the most damaging NWP was a major victory. The dismantling of the general permitting system would clearly increase the barriers to building and filling activities.

However, from NAHB's perspective, the outcome of the court case was the result of a negotiation done in bad faith and was a prime example of how wetlands regulation has been fought in the courts with the various participants simply trying to perpetuate their positions rather than trying to find common ground. The court asked all the parties in the case — the

[25] Environmental News Network, "Battle Brews."
[26] National Association of Home Builders. "Builders Intervene In NRDC Wetlands Lawsuit."

Corps of Engineers (the defendant), the NRDC (the plaintiff), and NAHB (the co-defendant) — to try to negotiate a settlement. A mediator was appointed, and the negotiations began. However, in the end it was NAHB's perspective that the Corps opted to deal privately with the NRDC to find a settlement that they were willing to accept, and in doing so, the Corps neglected to confer with its co-defendant, the NAHB.[27] Rather than negotiating with all parties in good faith to find common ground, NAHB felt that the government maneuvered to work with only one party, effectively alienating the other side.

In response to the outcome of the case and the issuing of the replacement permits in March of 2000, NAHB sued the government. NAHB argued that standard procedures had been violated and that on a substantive level the new replacement permits were not rationally justified. Further, NAHB argued that there was no statutory backing for the deletion of NWP 26, and that the insertion of these new permits into the case was an arbitrary move by the government without legislative authority.

Although NWPs have become a further hindrance to finding common ground, they were initially devised by Congress as a means to achieve balance. They also represent virtually the only time Congress has stepped in to affect wetlands regulation in a significant, committed way since the passage of the CWA. Congress attempted to expedite the permitting process for those projects with little impact in the hopes that larger projects with more far-reaching effects would be the focus of the Corps's permitting and regulatory control. The goal was to follow through with the intent of the CWA, to protect areas of major ecological significance in a sophisticated way, and to prevent environmental degradation — not to protect and regulate every wetland. However, the fact that NWPs only further antagonized the tensions among the participants indicates the true difficulty of finding common ground over this issue. NWPs were Congress's attempt to sort out the wetlands regulatory mess. Congress has not acted on wetlands since, yet many people suggest that Congress is the only place where true change can occur at this point. However, the inability to achieve common ground on these issues exists in Congress as well, and thus the issue remains unresolved as we enter the twenty-first century.

Delineation Manuals

The next major evolution in wetlands regulation was the creation of delineation manuals. After several court cases and discussions about the

---

[27] J. Michael Luzier interviewed by author and Amy E. Rowe, Washington, D.C., 25 January 2001.

problems with the permitting process, it became apparent to many people involved that something more needed to be done. A disconnect between the definition of a wetland and how to apply this definition remained despite efforts to streamline the process. From the environmental perspective, delays and confusion tended to be beneficial because they halted building projects and meant that fewer wetlands were being disturbed. However, throughout the 1980s pressure was building to do something about the consistent and pervasive problem. In 1977, NWPs were the policy approach to this pressure; in the mid-1980s, delineation manuals appeared as the newest option to reduce the confusion and conflict.

Delineation manuals are comprehensive guides that help people identify wetlands out in the field according to predetermined criteria. Given that there was ongoing confusion about what wetlands were and what should and should not be regulated, the EPA, the Fish and Wildlife Service (FWS), the Corps, and the Natural Resources Conservation Service (NRCS) (formerly the Soil Conservation Service, SCS; part of the U.S. Department of Agriculture) all confirmed that it was necessary to develop delineation manuals. Thus the EPA and the Corps set about to craft them. However, rather than collaborating on the project, each agency created its own manual, and each had a different process for delineation. The creation of these manuals therefore proved to be a continuation of the problem, not a solution.

As mentioned earlier, the 1977 definition adopted and used by both the EPA and the Corps required that wetlands have three characteristics: water, substrate, and biota — or, as they are often referred to, hydrology, soils, and vegetation.[28] Of these three, hydrology, or the presence of water in the soil, is the hardest to measure. The challenge lies in determining how far down in the soil water must be present to classify the area as a wetland. Thus, the definition still remained too general and unclear to be used directly. Shortly after the 1977 definition was adopted, the Environmental Laboratory at the Waterways Experiment Station (WES) began to work on a delineation manual. This evolved into a manual adopted by the Corps, which was finally published in January of 1987 as the "U.S. Army Corps of Engineers Wetlands Delineation Manual" (referred to as the 1987 Corps manual). The manual provided detailed guidance for Corps staff to perform wetlands delineation.

In 1988, the EPA issued its own manual, known as the "Wetland Identification and Delineation Manual." While EPA and the Corp work from the

---

[28] National Research Council, *Wetlands: Characteristics and Boundaries,* 70.

same three principles, namely that wetlands regulation is based on hydrology, soils, and vegetation, the EPA manual allows delineators to focus on vegetation alone for routine delineations and when obligate wetlands or upland species are dominant.[29] The FWS and the NRCS/SCS also adopted their own manuals. Thus there were four separate manuals in the federal system, all of which explained how to delineate wetlands, and none of which followed the same technical recommendations. No one — developers, property owners, or environmental groups — could effectively grasp the federal government's regulatory stance and how to identify wetlands. There was a desire for common understanding, yet the inability of the government to act swiftly with a sound policy to permanently resolve the conflict meant that the actors involved were not brought together to work toward compromise.

The Corps's manual had the most conservative procedures, the FWS had the most liberal and encompassing procedures (to protect the most area possible), and the NRCS and EPA manuals fell between these two extremes.[30] Given this problematic situation, the four organizations came together in 1989 to develop a joint manual for delineating wetlands. This manual was called "Federal Manual for Identifying and Delineating Jurisdictional Wetlands," and it reflected a compromise. The hope was that this joint manual (also referred to as the interagency manual) would put an end to the ongoing controversies regarding which areas were regulated wetlands.

The result, however, was far from a peaceful resolution, largely due to the reactions from the regulated community to the new joint manual. As David Salvesen writes in an Urban Land Institute publication: "The manual was greeted with rancorous outcry from the development community, farmers, and the oil industry, who claimed that the new approach dramatically expanded the Corps' jurisdiction into some lands not previously considered wetlands. EPA received over 100,000 comments on the 1989 delineation manual."[31] Perhaps the most significant issue was the hydrology criterion — water had to be present at eighteen inches under the ground. The manual had been devised by scientists from each of the agencies with little public input, and the new eighteen-inch rule was much more extensive than had been applied in the past. In the Corps 1987 manual, which took into consideration the growing season and the plants present in a given area (plants that required a certain level of ground saturation

---

[29] Ibid., 71.
[30] Salvesen, *Wetlands: Mitigating and Regulating Impacts*, 30.
[31] Ibid., 31.

to grow), the hydrology criterion was set at twelve inches. This correlates
to the root zone of plants in the soil. By extending the zone for hydrology
by 6 inches, the joint 1989 manual could greatly expand lands that could
be defined as wetlands. Given the strong reactions, the four agencies continued to discuss the problem.

In 1991, revisions to the 1989 manual were proposed. In true form, the
Corps issued one set of revisions, the EPA another. The Bush administration became involved at this time because of a speech given by President
George Bush in which he made a commitment to wetlands protection. The
main issue at hand when the Bush administration stepped in was the hydrology criterion — how long a piece of land had to be wet to be defined
as a wetland, and the depth of the saturation of the soil. President Bush's
cabinet worked with the EPA administrator, William Reilly, on a solution.
However, the proposed revisions were also criticized and in the end were
not adopted. Congress stepped in and forbade use of the 1989 manual and
directed the Corps to use its 1987 manual. The EPA agreed to also use the
1987 Corps manual as the standard manual for delineating wetlands. Figure 10.3 is a comparison of four delineation manuals. It shows the three
discussed thus far, and also a later manual used by the National Resources
Conservation Service. Again, this highlights the confusion, especially

FIGURE 10.3
Comparison of Delineation Manuals: Hydrology

Characteristic	1987 (Corps Manual)	1989 (Interagency Manual)	1991 (Proposed Revisions)	NFSAM (A manual used by National Resources Conservation Service)
Hydrologic Threshold	Inundation or saturation at surface for > 12.5% or 5-12.5% of growing season with other evidence	Inundation or saturation at surface for at least 7 days of growing season	Inundation at surface 15 days; saturation at surface 12 days during growing season	Inundation at surface for 15 days for most areas; 7 days for potholes, playas, or pocosins
Critical depth	Root Zone (12 in; 30 cm)	0.5 to 1.5 ft (15-46 cm); depending on soil	Surface	Surface
Growing Season	Frost-free days, based on air temperature	Biological zero (41 degrees F; 5 degrees C) 20 in. (50 cm) below soil surface; soil temperature zones estimated	Three weeks before to three weeks after last killing frost	Biological zero, estimated from frost-free days.

SOURCE: National Research Council, *Wetlands: Characteristics and Boundaries.*

given that hydrology — which is just one of three criteria — poses such a major challenge in the delineation process.

In 1992, Congress commissioned the National Academy of Sciences (NAS) to prepare an analysis of wetlands delineation. Congress put the issue to the academy because the agencies had gone around and around on the subject, and a definitive decision had not been reached. By 1995, NAS reached the conclusion that the 1987 Corps manual was "scientifically sound" and officially adopted it.[32] Subsequently, some came to believe that the1987 Corps manual evolved into a text more akin to the 1989 manual in the sense that over time it came to allow more extensive regulation of wetlands. The appendix of the 1987 Corps manual lists indirect measurements, or "indicators" that help the delineator determine whether a piece of land is a wetland. Some of these indicators include water-stained leaves, hairs on roots, and buttressing of trees. In effect, these indicators have made it easier to find jurisdiction, and hence the manual has come to function more like the regulation-oriented 1989 manual.[33]

The delineation manuals represent a further inability to achieve consensus around wetlands regulation. For nearly eight years, there was no clear and final decision about which manual would be the federal manual. Environmentalists and developers alike were frustrated with the lack of public involvement in the process. Congress was the only option for helping alleviate the situation because no other framework for finding common ground existed. The fiasco only built upon the previous problems, which in turn heightened the tensions surrounding wetlands.

Administrative Appeals

Another major critique of wetlands regulation has been that the Section 404 program does not allow for administrative appeals of the Corps's decisions. There has been no way to hold the government responsible for its decisions regarding wetlands permits. NWPs and delineation manuals were efforts to reduce the government's broad regulatory ability and put more decision making in the public sector. Yet when the government does regulate, its decisions are final. A permit applicant has no opportunity to challenge a jurisdictional determination made by the Corps because it is not a final agency action until it is denied by the Corps. Some people, especially builders, have pushed for implementation of administrative appeals to allow for the public to contest Corps jurisdictional determinations and hold it accountable for its actions.

---

[32] Davis, "A More Effective and Flexible Section 404," 7.

[33] J. Michael Luzier interviewed by author and Amy E. Rowe, Washington, D.C., 25 January 2001.

Historically, one requested a permit for a piece of land, and the outcome would be either an acceptance or a denial (see Figure 10.1). If someone was denied a permit, the only recourse was to contest the issue in court. There was no other way or time to challenge the process. Many concerned parties noted that at the stage of jurisdictional determination, there should be an opportunity to challenge the government. Jurisdictional determination is the stage at which the Corps issues a letter to a property owner stating whether there are any waterways or wetlands on that property that the government has the right to regulate. (In Figure 10.1 this is referred to as the preliminary assessment phase). Many property owners have wanted the right to challenge the government at this point, before entering into the Section 404 permit process without going to court, which involves a great deal of time, money, and effort. Concerned parties have articulated the need for an administrative appeals process and have expressed the desire to contest the Corps' initial assessment that a given piece of property has wetlands on it.[34]

The Corps itself recognized the need for administrative appeals and asked Congress for money to implement the appeals process. There was some speculation that if the Corps received money, it would begin investigating how to implement the appeals process but, in the end, spend the money on other Corps projects. At the end of the 1990s, bills such as the House of Representatives Energy and Water Appropriations Bill (H.R. 2605) included provisions to create an administrative appeals process for wetlands regulation. Congress finally approved the provision to create an appeals system in March of 1999. However, rather than craft an administrative appeals system for jurisdictional determination, the Corps developed a system whereby administrative appeals were tacked onto the Section 404 permitting process. The applicant could appeal only after a permit was denied.[35] Further, the new provisions did not allow for appeals of jurisdictional disputes, or determinations of what is considered a wetland.

This appeals system was not what permit applicants, property owners, and many members of Congress had been expecting. Adding administrative appeals at the permit denial level simply added another layer to the process, and it did not meet the primary goal, which was to challenge the government's ability to determine whether a piece of land should be classified as a wetland. NAHB, the American Roads and Transportation

[34] Environmental News Network, "Battle Brews."
[35] American Society of Agronomy, "Administrative Appeals Rule for Wetlands."

Builders Association (ARTBA), and others complained that the Corps had not established the administrative appeals process that was required and expected. The Corps had only partially complied with the directive to create an appeals system, and then it claimed it was not given enough money to fully implement the program.[36] The Corps's inability to create an administrative appeals process was viewed by many as a stalling technique that prevented the appeals process from actually working to the benefit of property owners and home builders.

In March of 2000, though, the Corps finally issued a rule incorporating into its existing administrative appeals process the appeal of wetlands jurisdictional determinations. Any determination of jurisdiction by the Corps under Section 404 of the Clean Water Act or Section 10 of the Rivers and Harbors Act made after March 28, 2000, can be appealed within the Corps to a level above the official who determines such jurisdiction.[37] This decision has been of significant help to the building process and has empowered the public to question government decisions. However, environmentalists view administrative appeals negatively, demonstrating once again that any attempt to alter a faulty system often only serves to further polarize the participants.

MAJOR ACTORS INVOLVED IN THE WETLANDS CASE

In reviewing the long history of wetlands regulation, highlighting the role of particular groups and individuals emerges as another way to understand the overall process. The primary participants can be thought of as either part of the government or as outside players. The three government players are the executive branch (including the president and the federal agencies) Congress, and the court system. The two major outside players are the trade organizations, which represent the perspectives of the home builders and a variety of others involved in the development process, and the environmental organizations.

Presidential Administrations and Agencies

From the passage of the CWA to the present, the Corps and the EPA have undergone many changes in leadership. Each time a new president is

---

[36] American Roads and Transportation Builders Association, "ARTBA/NWC Strategize.
[37] American Roads and Transportation Builders Association, "Corps of Engineers Adds New Appeals Process."

elected, the top officials in each federal agency are replaced so the federal administration will be cohesive. As a result, there is often little continuity from one administration to the next, and the leadership of the agencies varies significantly over time. This situation is of particular importance in the case of wetlands because of the unique relationship between the Corps and the EPA under Section 404. When new political appointees are brought in, these two agencies must manage not only their own internal changes, but also shifts in leadership at the other agency. The difficulties of administering the Section 404 program are compounded by the fact that political appointments make it hard to sustain agreements and relationships between the two agencies over time. Any networking that the two agencies initiate is always threatened by a shift in power.

During the 1980s, the divide between actors on both sides of the wetlands case was deep and growing. When Ronald Reagan took office, many government activities were tagged for reform, including the Section 404 program. Specifically, the Reagan administration sought to streamline the permitting process in relation to wetlands. Also, there was a desire to remove the ten-acre requirement from NWP 26. However, environmental groups reacted strongly to these changes, particularly to the effort to remove the acreage requirements. With such a swift, decisive, and organized response on the part of environmental groups, the Reagan administration was unable to move ahead on wetlands regulation reform.

When George Bush took office, his administration acknowledged the problems related to wetlands permits. During his 1988 campaign, Bush highlighted the need for change in the wetlands regulation program, and he followed through with this upon entering office. He adopted the "no net loss" strategy of the Conservation Foundation as a national goal. The overall goal was to prevent loss of wetlands through government acquisition of wetlands, through wetlands restoration and creation, and by expanding research on national wetlands trends.[38] President Bush made a bold move when seeking to prevent further wetlands losses, which had been the trend for most of the nation's history. His strategy was not about blaming builders or environmentalists; rather, keeping the number of wetlands stable. Many agencies set about investigating how this could be implemented. Thus the Bush administration provided a new focal point for the wetlands debate.

The Clinton administration made some decisions that radically shifted the balance in relation to wetlands policy. President Clinton appointed

---

[38] Liebesman, *Developer's Guide to Wetlands Regulation,* 18.

Mike Davis, who formerly worked at the EPA, as the deputy director of the Corps. Davis was thus in charge of the Section 404 permitting program. This meant that someone who had strong environmentalist/EPA political perspectives was now in charge of the agency responsible for all wetlands permitting. The Corps had historically been the more conservative of the two agencies, tending to err on the side of granting a permit and allowing for building. The former balance of power between the more conservative Corps and the proregulation EPA was dismantled. There has been a great deal of speculation that many of the court cases and decisions in the 1990s were heavily influenced by the fact that a pro-EPA person was in charge of the Corps. This shifted again in 2001 when President George W. Bush took office, yet the legacy of Davis leading the Corps in the Clinton years profoundly marked the debate.

Clinton continued the "no net loss" strategy, and in 1993 he announced a comprehensive wetlands protection plan. The plan would change federal wetlands policy by:

- increasing cooperation with private landowners to protect and restore wetlands;
- increasing public participation and state and local government involvement in wetlands protection;
- streamlining wetlands permitting programs; and
- basing wetlands protection on good science and sound judgment.[39]

As a result of this wetlands plan, the Corps, the Natural Resources Conservation Service (NRCS), EPA, and FWS signed an interagency agreement to develop consistent wetlands policy. Clinton issued an executive order in August of 1993 stating that the NRCS of the U.S. Department of Agriculture would be the lead agency for all wetlands delineation of agricultural lands.[40]

Wetlands mitigation is a key component of the "no net loss" strategy. Mitigation refers to the requirement that developers either restore or replace any wetlands they adversely affect. Mitigation is part of the permitting process and is evaluated by the Corps. Some examples of mitigation compliance include redirecting storm-water runoff, readjusting lot lines, and altering development plans so as not to touch the most sensitive wetlands in the project area. Mitigation is not specifically mentioned in Section

---

[39] Dennison, *Wetland Mitigation: Mitigation Banking and Other Strategies,* 9.
[40] National Research Council, *Wetlands: Characteristics and Boundaries,* 158.

404, but it is found in other federal laws that require mitigation for all federal actions that adversely affect the environment.[41] With the recent promotion of "no net loss," mitigation has become a more stringent requirement. Mitigation is particularly costly and takes a great deal of planning, funding, and supervision to do correctly.

One creative way to manage wetlands restoration and comply with "no net loss" is mitigation banking, where a builder who has to replace wetlands being converted for building can pay an organization to create wetlands in another area.[42] Often, these new wetlands are created in an area where wetlands already exist, but can be enhanced. A mitigation technique might be to remove debris from an area so water can flow through the land, creating a more highly functioning wetland. Such projects are often done on public lands, and thus private dollars are being used to create public benefits. The needs of the builder are being met, and at the same time, wetlands are being created. Much guidance on mitigation banking techniques exists, and the builder can know the cost in advance, which facilitates planning and cost estimates. However, environmentalists who are concerned about mitigation banking start from the perspective that all natural wetlands are good and should not be disturbed, and that man-made wetlands are not a sufficient substitute. Another drawback on the implementation side is that mitigation banking that enhances existing wetlands will only work in certain regions of the country. Also, wetland enhancement or restoration only works in certain water networks, and often these are larger networks extending over many miles. Thus mitigation is important and useful, especially in light of efforts to achieve "no net loss," but it cannot be the only solution offered.

In addition to examining the role of presidential administrations and the relationships between these administrations and the federal agencies, it is helpful to reflect upon the different orientations of the Corps and the EPA in order to ascertain why even these two agencies have had trouble coordinating their wetlands efforts.

The EPA as a whole has a mandate from Congress to protect the environment. All EPA functions relate to this primary concern. The agency has a vested interest in limiting land use that will excessively alter the natural

---

[41] Such federal acts include: National Environmental Policy Act (NEPA) and Fish and Wildlife Coordination Act. Dennison, *Wetland Mitigation: Mitigation Banking and Other Strategies,* 90.

[42] In the early 1980s, the concept of mitigation banking was first promoted as a means of improving mitigation techniques while reducing the cost to the regulated community. In 1990, a joint Corps/EPA Memorandum of Agreement (1990 MOA) approved of mitigation making as an acceptable form of compensatory mitigation. See Dennison, *Wetland Mitigation: Mitigation Banking and Other Strategies,* 130.

landscape. Another EPA goal is to conduct research and inform the public about the importance of the natural environment and about the harmful effects of unregulated land use and pollution. The EPA's Office of Water is in charge of wetlands concerns. Its mission statement reflects the wetlands-orientation of the agency:

> The enduring mission of the program is to encourage and enable *others* to act effectively in protecting and restoring the nation's wetlands and associated ecosystems, including shallow open waters and free-flowing streams. In doing so, the program engages in two principal categories of activities — establishing national standards and assisting others to meet them.[43]

The EPA functions to encourage other federal agencies, state and local agencies, businesses, and organizations to protect wetlands. As stated on the EPA's website the agency acts

1. as a partner, providing support for both regulatory and nonregulatory wetlands protection efforts;
2. as a promoter and distributor of sound wetlands science as the technical basis for effective wetlands decision making;
3. in an advisory capacity for state and tribal wetlands programs and for Clean Water Act Section 404 permit decisions;
4. as the developer of national wetlands standards and policies; and
5. as a regulator to back up our state and local partners and ensure that national standards are lawfully applied.[44]

The Corps has a decidedly different approach. The Corps is a branch of the U.S. Army, and it has one of the oldest regulatory programs in the federal government. The original function of its regulatory program was "to protect and maintain the navigable capacity of the nation's waters." Thus the orientation of the Corps is to protect the nation and manage waterways for that purpose. With the passage of the CWA, the Corps was designated to run the regulatory permitting process largely because it already had a regulatory and permitting function. It must be emphasized that, although Corps personnel are directly involved with permit applications and reviews, at the outset the overarching goal of the Corps was not environmental protection. Over the years, though, the Corps has adapted its stance to include environmental protection, and has made a strong commitment to protecting the nation's aquatic environment, including wetlands.[45] Still,

---

[43] Environmental Protection Agency, "About the Wetlands Program."
[44] Ibid.
[45] U.S. Army Corps of Engineers, "Regulatory Program: Goals."

Corps personnel are concerned with multiple goals — protection of the nation, ensuring navigability of waterways, and environmental protection.

Two other agencies involved in wetlands are the U.S. Department of the Interior's Fish and Wildlife Service (FWS) and the U.S. Department of Commerce's National Marine Fisheries Service (NMFS). The FWS is primarily concerned with the protection of freshwater waterway and wetland resources, especially as related to recreational activities. The FWS provides comments and advice to the Corps during the Section 404 permit review process.[46] The NMFS's responsibilities are virtually the same except they refer to coastal and marine waters. The FWS is far more oriented toward environmental protection, and the agency describes its goal as "conserving, protecting, and enhancing" fish, wildlife, plants, and their habitats for the American public.[47] These two agencies together preserve the environment for recreation, sports, and commercial activities such as fishing.

Clearly the federal government has a wide array of interests spread throughout its agencies. Some agencies fall more to the environmental protection end of the spectrum, while others support the land-use needs and property-use goals of builders. A review of the different mandates, goals, and structures of the agencies involved with wetlands reveals that common ground is difficult to achieve within the federal government itself.

Congress

Wetlands regulation was born in Congress through amendments made to the Federal Pollution Control Act in 1972. At the time, members of Congress were primarily concerned with serious examples of industrial pollution in the nation's waterways and with major development activities that caused environmental degradation. Wetlands were not perceived to be the focal point around which much of the CWA would turn. It is very likely that Congress did not foresee the multiple technicalities and difficulties related to wetlands regulation that arose as a result of the CWA. As two long-term observers of the wetlands debate, Mark S. Dennison and James F. Berry, suggest: "While Congress intended the Clean Water Act to reach a broad range of waters and wetlands, Congress never intended to regulate all wetlands as 'waters of the United States.' Congress' primary

---

[46] Liebesman, *A Developer's Guide to Wetlands Regulation,* 4.
[47] U.S. Fish and Wildlife Service, "Conserving Wildlife and Habitats."

concern was waters used in interstate commerce and waters that together form a 'hydrologic chain.' "[48] However, as the legislation has proved difficult to understand and implement, divergent perspectives have made it impossible for Congress to redefine or clarify the situation.

As highlighted earlier in the chapter, the two major faults of the legislation are the lack of definition of wetlands and the decision to split the administration of the Section 404 program between the Corps and the EPA. Also problematic is the fact that in the legislation Section 404 is very general compared to other similar environmental regulatory programs, or even to other sections of the Clean Water Act, such as Section 402.[49] Most programs are more detailed and have numerous pages of guidance, leaving little room for guesswork about how and why certain things should be regulated. Similarly, the set of wetlands regulations growing out of the CWA is unique when compared with other environmental legislation because of the diverse array of people and companies it affects. Much environmental legislation is targeted at large industrial and municipal users, both of which have resources, money, and bargaining power. When environmental regulations are imposed on these organizations, they have the capacity to react, negotiate, and often find compromises that fulfill their goals while meeting the environmental standards. However, the CWA affects municipalities, large development companies, small private landowners, and small businesses. The broad reach of this act has made it particularly hard to manage because it puts individual home owners seeking to clear their land or build a driveway on their land in the same regulatory category as a national development company.

As concern over wetlands regulation arose after the passage of the CWA, Congress heard a range of reactions, positive and negative. Perhaps the most proactive step Congress took was to approve the NWP program as an attempt to formulate a compromise. Again, the goal was for the Corps and the EPA to focus on large projects having the most impact on the nation's waterways, rather than spend countless hours in a lengthy permitting process for small projects. NWPs were thought to meet the needs of the CWA and to bring together the two sides. Yet this effort has generally failed, and Congress has been unable to achieve any significant steps to find common ground.

Many people view congressional action as the only way to fully clarify the terms of the debate. During the Clinton administration, revisions to the

---

[48] Dennison and Berry, *Wetlands: Guide to Science,* 218.
[49] Mark Weisshaar, interviewed by Amy E. Rowe, phone conversation, 22 February 2001.

CWA were debated in Congress, but the politics became too divisive and revisions were not made. With changing administrations and changes in Congress, it is always possible that some action may occur. However, past experience has shown that the chances of success are very low. Small compromises can be made on wetlands regulation at the local level on a case-by-case basis, but at the national level, achieving any kind of compromise in Congress is virtually impossible. Moving forward in the twenty-first century, the paradox is the reality: Congress is unlikely to act on this issue, yet any real clarification can only come through congressional action.

The Courts

The courts have been the primary place to resolve the many issues inherent in the wetlands regulations. Yet the court system is often a poor place to achieve common ground. Usually, one side is the "winner" and the other, the "loser." Also, court disputes are very lengthy, with decisions followed by appeals. In one sense, court decisions are definitive, but they also lead to further suits and appeals.

To further complicate matters, different participants have tended to ignore court decisions — even Supreme Court decisions — on regulatory matters. One example of this is in the Tulloch case. This case will be discussed later in the chapter, but in brief, the courts declared that in relation to the "Tulloch Rule" the Corps did not have the ability to regulate excavation activities. Nevertheless, the Corps continued to use Tulloch-like arguments to pursue regulatory activities in certain scenarios. Further court cases ensued, the courts continued to say the Corps could not regulate, and the Corps continued to ignore the courts. Despite a clear court decision, the federal agency continued to act in its own interest. If wetlands regulatory battles continue to be played out primarily in U.S. courtrooms, it will be difficult to achieve common ground.

Trade Organizations

Many trade organizations who represent the perspective of home builders and others involved in the development process have questioned the range of the government's regulatory activities. There is a great deal of interest in wetlands related to private property. Property owners want to exert their property rights to build homes, expand existing buildings, create roads, clear swamp areas, and so on, and they do not want to be excessively monitored by the government. Environmental protection is an important concern, but from the land owners' point of view it must be balanced with reasonable requests for land use and the need for affordable housing.

The primary trade organizations involved in the wetlands case are the National Association of Home Builders (NAHB), the National Mining Association, the National Association of Realtors, and the National Wetlands Coalition. Each of these trade organizations represents a large constituency that has been affected by wetlands regulation. NAHB, for example, conducted a survey that found that regulatory costs associated with home building were around 10% of the total cost of building.[50] Many of the builders who responded noted that permitting processes caused considerable delay and that the longer the delay, the greater the cost. Wetlands permits were identified as one of the primary reasons for delay.

The National Association of Realtors, NAHB, and others were involved in the push for the Corps to create administrative appeals in 1999, and each of these organizations lobbied Congress and the administration to make regulatory changes such as the administrative appeals decision. The National Wetlands Coalition is another organization that contests the current breadth of the government's jurisdiction over wetlands. The coalition comprises both public and private sector members who seek to create a more balanced regulatory scheme. The coalition acknowledges that regulation is necessary and supports many of the government's programs, but it also emphasizes the importance of private property and questions the government's power to cast such a wide net.[51]

Environmental Organizations

Environmental groups have also played a pivotal role in shaping the wetlands regulatory process. It was largely through grassroots environmental efforts that the CWA was first passed, and shortly after, it was NRDC's 1975 court case that expanded the Corps's Section 404 abilities. The environmental perspective on wetlands is that they should not be disturbed, if possible, and are a valuable part of the larger ecosystem. Environmentalists focus on wetlands for their own value and for their natural functions, not for the money that can be made from developing the land. This perspective is fundamentally different from that of the trade organizations.

---

[50] National Association of Home Builders, "The Truth About Regulatory Barriers."
[51] National Wetlands Coalition.

Some of the environmental organizations who have been particularly visible in the wetlands debate are the NRDC, the Sierra Club, and the National Wildlife Federation. NRDC is particularly concerned with the core principles of the CWA and emphasizes that environmental regulation should come before concerns about property rights in relation to wetlands.[52] The Sierra Club has also taken a lead position in terms of organizing, petitioning, and distributing information about wetlands. The Sierra Club promotes reform within the Corps and coordinates efforts to protect wetlands. Its policy statement regarding wetlands is as follows:

> The Sierra Club advocates a consistent public policy to preserve and restore the hydrologic, biologic, and aesthetic values of wetlands as public assets. We place highest priority on the protection of existing natural wetlands. Because our goal is to reverse, not merely slow, the trend of wetlands destruction and degradation, we also support restoration of degraded wetlands. Wetlands protection should be promoted further by increased public understanding and enjoyment of wetland values through compatible uses.[53]

Finally, the National Wildlife Federation seeks to prevent further loss of wetlands, and there are many examples of this national foundation teaming up with local groups to preserve wetlands. In particular, the federation monitors activities around the country to ensure that the no net loss policy is being implemented.[54]

Each of these organizations works to ensure that government regulations for wetlands are as comprehensive and far-reaching as possible. From the environmentalist perspective, preservation of existing natural wetlands is the ideal, and building activities negate this value. While efforts at mitigation and wetland restoration are important, for many environmentalists, it is most important to stop growth and to continue to extend the parameters of Section 404.

CURRENT STATUS OF THE WETLANDS DEBATE

As we look to the future, wetlands regulation remains a challenging topic at both the federal and state levels, and people continue to be strongly divided between the home building/affordable housing perspective and the environmental perspective. One fact that characterizes the discussion

---

[52] National Resources Defense Council, "Brief History of Clean Water Act."
[53] Sierra Club, "Wetlands Policy."
[54] National Wildlife Federation, "Wetlands."

FIGURE 10.4
Average Annual Net Wetland Loss Over Time
(for the conterminous United States)

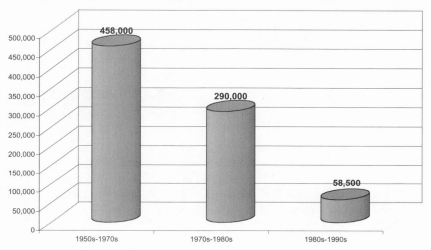

SOURCE: U.S. Fish and Wildlife Service, *Status and Trends of Wetlands in the Conterminous United States 1986 to 1997,* 2000.

today is that far fewer wetlands are being lost currently than prior to the passage of the Clean Water Act. Figure 10.4 shows a significant decline in the number of wetlands being lost over time. From the 1950s to the 1990s, there has been a major reduction in the number of wetlands being converted to agricultural or development use.

Another aspect of this shift is that wetlands are being "gained" as well as lost. Figure 10.5 shows that for all the wetlands lost, 69,000 acres were "gained," making the net loss of wetlands, from 1986 to 1997, 32,000 acres. When wetlands are gained, this typically refers to mitigation techniques that revive a former wetland or create an entirely new one. Most often, land that was once a wetland is converted by means of removing dams or clearing buildup in streams to allow the land to become a wetland area once again. All in all, Figures 10.4 and 10.5 point out that the situation today — while still highly charged politically — is very different than it was in 1972. There are disputes about the actual number of wetlands lost or gained, and various organizations and federal agencies use different techniques for gathering data, making it difficult to ascertain just how many wetlands once existed in the U.S. and how many have been lost

FIGURE 10.5
Wetlands Losses and Gains, 1986–1997

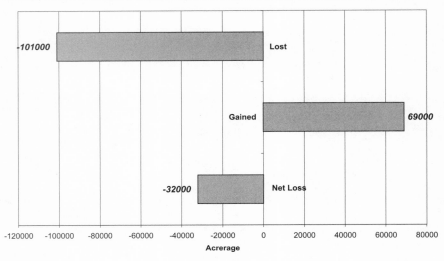

SOURCE: National Resources Conservation Service, *USDA National Resources Inventory (NRI).* http://www.nhq.nrcs.usda.gov/NRI.

or gained over time. What does emerge is the fact that far fewer wetlands are being lost, and many more are being created.

Today, despite strides in the protection and sustainable mixed-use of wetlands areas, the debate over regulation remains polarized and is typified by numerous court cases. The two sides hold fundamentally different viewpoints, and while some agreement can be found on general ideas, the implementation of regulations that are acceptable to all has proved near impossible to date. Two major wetlands issues illustrate this point: the "Tulloch Rule" case, relating to whether the Corps can regulate material that enters a wetland during excavation; and the SWANCC case, regarding isolated wetlands.

The Tulloch Rule

One of the primary court cases related to wetlands regulation is *North Carolina Wildlife Federation v. Tulloch.* This case deals with an important detail of Section 404 of the Clean Water Act. Section 404 focuses on the regulation of filling wetlands, yet it does not explicitly discuss the excavation of material. Developers in North Carolina had excavated wetlands areas to build, pointing out that the Corps had no authority to regulate their activity because they were excavating — not filling — a wetland. The North Carolina Wildlife Federation sued the Corps in 1993 for failing to regulate this excavation activity in a wetlands area. The resulting ruling has come to be known as the "Tulloch Rule." This rule states that the Corps has the right to regulate excavation activities because "when material is dredged out of a wetland, some of that material falls back down into the wetland, technically creating a discharge — and therefore within the Corps' jurisdiction."[55] This ruling represents a clever use of the language of the law to make areas that were being excavated subject to federal regulation.

The "Tulloch Rule" was an attempt to further expand the range of activities regulated by the government. In 1993, the National Mining Association, the American Road and Transportation Builders Association, the National Aggregates Association, The National Association of Home Builders, and the American Forest and Paper Association sued the Corps over this rule. On January 23, 1997, the U.S. District Court for the District of Columbia ruled that the Army Corps of Engineers had exceeded its authority under the Clean Water Act. In explaining the decision, the court said that any material that fell back in the process of excavation was incidental and therefore should not be subject to regulation.[56] The government appealed the ruling, and in June of 1998, the U.S. District Court for the District of Columbia upheld the decision.

In both cases, the court called for a reversal of the "Tulloch Rule," stating that in fact the process of excavating materials from a wetland does not simultaneously produce a fill in the same wetland. The following is an excerpt from the 1998 decision:

> We agree with the plaintiffs, and with the district court, that the straightforward statutory term "addition" cannot reasonably be said to encompass the situation in which material is removed from the waters of the United States and a small portion of it happens to fall back. Because incidental fallback represents a net withdrawal, not an addition, of material, it cannot be discharge. As we concluded recently in a related context, the nearest evidence we have for definitional intent by Congress reflects, as might be expected, that the word "discharge" contemplates the addition, not the withdrawal, of a substance or substances.[57]

---

[55] Corps of Engineer statement of the Tulloch Rule as reported in Sierra Club, "Wetlands: Tulloch Planet Article."

[56] *Federal Register,* 10 May 1999, 25120.

[57] National Mining Association, et al., v. U.S. Army Corps of Engineers, et al.,8.

Despite these rulings, the Corps continued to use Tulloch-related arguments to exercise its regulatory abilities. In particular, the Corps pushed to make the removal of material from a wetland equal to the addition of material to a wetland. The result was an EPA determination on January 9, 2001, that brought the Tulloch rule back to life. As a press release from the EPA explains:

> The new rule modifies the definition of "discharge of dredged material" in order to clarify what types of activities EPA and the Corps believe are likely to result in discharges that should be regulated. The Corps and EPA regard the use of mechanized earth moving equipment to conduct landclearing, ditching, channelization, in-stream mining, or other earth-moving activity in waters of the U.S. as resulting in a discharge of dredged material, unless project-specific evidence shows that the activity results in only "incidental fallback." The rule also provides a definition of what constitutes non-regulable incidental fallback that is consistent with the recent District of Columbia Circuit court decision.[58]

For the trade organizations who won earlier rulings stating that the "Tulloch Rule" should not be applicable, this new regulation was one more example of the government ignoring the court ruling. Robert Mitchell, 2000 President of NAHB, noted that the Corps and the EPA were disregarding the law, yet again, and using any measure possible to ensure stringent regulations.[59]

The "Tulloch Rule" stands as a testament to the agenda of the Corps and the EPA during the Clinton administration. The fact that a government agency ignored multiple court rulings symbolizes how wide the gap is between the perspectives involved. The Tulloch case continues to be a major point of contention and it is likely to remain that way for a long time.

The SWANCC Case

The government's ability to administer isolated wetlands was questioned again in the late 1980s, when the Solid Waste Agency of Northern Cook County (SWANCC) was formed. SWANCC is a consortium of twenty-three municipalities that came together to develop a long-range plan to dispose of garbage in an efficient, cost-effective, and environmentally sound manner.[60] In 1990, SWANCC purchased a former strip mine

---

[58] Environmental Protection Agency, "Clinton-Gore Administration Takes Action."
[59] National Association of Home Builders, "Builders Believe Tulloch Rule Will Prove Illegal."
[60] Business Wire, "Solid Waste Agency of Northern Cook County."

where it proposed to deposit garbage, and at this point the Corps intervened. The Corps claimed that the mine contained a wetland where migratory birds were present and insisted upon its right to regulate this area, using the migratory bird rule previously mentioned. SWANCC disagreed with the Corps, arguing that the CWA did not grant the Corps the ability to regulate isolated intrastate ponds not connected in any way to navigable waters. SWANCC supporters noted that by using the Corps's migratory bird rule, the federal government could regulate any and all waters — an overstepping of federal boundaries.

This case dragged on throughout the 1990s, and finally, on January 9, 2001, the Supreme Court ruled in favor of SWANCC. The Court denied the Corps's claim that it could regulate this isolated wetland. A *Washington Post* article details the Supreme Court's ruling:

> The government had argued that the act allowed it to protect the wetlands, where a group of counties wanted to build a garbage dump, because they serve as a nesting ground for migratory birds. The court, however, held by a five to four margin that the so-called migratory bird rule on which the government relied exceeded the law, which gives the federal government authority only over "navigable waters." The isolated pools in question do not fit that description, the court held, so the federal government has no jurisdiction over them just because the migratory birds make use of them.[61]

This decision clearly stated that the Corps cannot regulate isolated wetlands and noted that Congress had not explicitly given the Corps the ability to regulate based on the migratory bird rule. This decision helped limit the government's ability to regulate wetlands. Environmentalists and others, including the four dissenting Supreme Court justices, view this decision as opening the door for environmental degradation. Yet for others, especially organizations like SWANCC that are trying to manage difficult issues such as disposal of garbage from a metro area, it creates more feasible options for land use. Although this ruling was intended to clarify the law and to limit the Corps's reach, some suggest that the Corps will continue to try to find means to regulate areas such as the one in the SWANCC case;[62] For example, they may find other rules, such as the adjacent wetlands scenario to hault future projects. This remains to be seen, yet given the history of wetlands regulation, it is certain that major disputes regarding isolated wetlands will continue to arise.

---

[61] "A Blow to Clean Water," *Washington Post* editorial.
[62] J. Michael Luzier, interviewed by author and Amy E. Rowe, Washington, D.C., 25 January 2001.

Looking Ahead

Given the current status of wetlands and the ongoing court battles, the future of wetlands regulation is unclear. There are few immediate solutions, and ultimately it will be up to Congress to make real clarifying changes. One modest success is mitigation banking. While this technique is not the answer for the entire "problem" and will not work everywhere, it is a solution for some areas and may provide a positive alternative in the wetlands debate.

Mitigation banking is the process by which mitigation credits are sold to permit applicants who want to offset development activities with off-site mitigation.[63] An applicant can fulfill mitigation requirements by purchasing credits at the "bank," which in turn creates new wetlands or restores wetlands for the applicant in a different geographical location. The quality of the wetlands impacted by a particular project affects the price a permit applicant must pay to a mitigation bank, because wetlands of comparable quality must be created to compensate for building impacts.

The primary advantages of mitigation banking, as outlined in a book by Mark Dennison, include maintaining the integrity of the equatic ecosystem to consolidate compensating mitigation into a single large parcel or contiguous parcels, bringing together financial resources to increase the long term potential of successful mitigation, reducing permit processing time for qualifying projects, reducing the loss of wetlands by implementing mitigation in advance of actual wetland reductions, and helping to achieve the goal of "no net loss" of the nation's wetlands.[64] These advantages point out that wetlands gains can continue to be made, and can counteract losses due to building activity.

However, the downside of mitigation banking is that it is only successful in certain ecological environments. It cannot be done in certain regions of the country due to specific geographic conditions and the need for large-sites (for example, a streambed network covering several miles). Mitigation banking has been successful in Florida, but it is not as easy to implement in the Northeast. In addition, sometimes the function and value of a wetland is specific to its exact geographic space, and its disturbance by building or other activity would destroy its uniqueness. Mitigation

---

[63] Dennison, *Wetland Mitigation: Mitigation Banking and Other Strategies,* 31.

[64] Such advantages are discussed in greater detail in Dennison, *Wetland Mitigation: Mitigation Banking and Other Strategies,* 135–136.

techniques in another area cannot compensate for the loss of such wet-lands. Finally, mitigation banking sometimes results in the creation of the easiest and cheapest types of wetlands.[65] Given both the advantages and challenges, although mitigation is not always the right option, it is a viable technique that many states are in the process of reviewing and im-plementing.

CONCLUSIONS: WHY HAVE EFFORTS TO ACHIEVE COMMON GROUND FAILED?

Wetlands regulation has proved to be an area where the groups and indi-viduals involved have been unable to find common ground. For nearly thirty years, the participants — including government agencies, trade as-sociations, and environmental organizations — have gone around and around in debate over these issues. Their very different ideological groundings are a primary hindrance to achieving consensus. The terms of the debate are very different today than they were in 1972. Environmental protection has become widely accepted and promoted. At the same time, wetlands are no longer in crisis; many are being restored and even, through mitigation techniques, created. However, major differences still exist, and there are several key reasons why those involved with wetlands regulation have been unable to find common ground.

First: When the Clean Water Act was originally drafted, it was inade-quate regarding wetlands. Wetlands were never defined, which led to im-mediate problems, and the court case *NRDC v. Calloway* challenged the scope of the law. The result of this case was to require regulation of wetlands adjacent to waters of the United States under the Clean Water Act. This led to a push to determine what wetlands were, and in 1977, an attempt was made to define wetlands. Despite this later insertion of a defi-nition, continued disagreement has marred the regulatory process over the last three decades.

Second: The administration of the CWA Section 404 program was divided between two federal agencies, and this has led to an ongoing struggle between the U.S. Army Corps and the EPA. The EPA is far more fo-cused on protection and conservation to the exclusion of development activi-ties, while the Corps has historically been more amenable to development

---

[65] Ibid., 139.

and building activities as long as they follow federal guidelines. Many have described the sharing of administrative responsibilities between the two agencies as a major organizational blunder.

Third: Given the fact that major problems exist in definition and jurisdiction, the only place to go for resolution is the courts, and the court process is by definition adversarial. Congress has been unable to clarify the regulatory framework, so the courts are the only place where wetlands regulation can be contested, challenged, reconfigured, and reinterpreted. In the OSHA case (Chapter 8) one of the strong points was that a number of people on both sides were willing to come together to resolve their concerns in a mutually beneficial way. There were also incentives for both sides to create a space for dialogue and to find common ground. With wetlands, after years of court battles, the two sides are deeply divided and frustrated. There is little goodwill and no incentive to come together. If Congress could act, a new middle ground might be possible, but the sides are too divided and the politics too divisive for Congress to reach agreement. The courts will continue to provide the primary forum for dispute resolution.

Fourth: Each time the government has attempted to streamline the regulatory process, efforts have only further polarized the actors involved. The NWP program and the delineation manuals are two examples of failed efforts to find a balance. Rather than serving as areas of compromise, the NWP program and the effort to prepare a single delineation manual only perpetuated, rather than resolved, the wetlands conflict.

Fifth: Throughout the wetlands process, there has never been the equivalent of an "honest broker" — an individual or organization able to win the respect of all the participants — as there was in the OSHA case. Due to the serious tensions and the lack of trust between the parties, no such broker ever emerged. In *NRDC et al. v. West,* which involved the Corps, the NRDC, and NAHB, a mediator was actually appointed to help the participants achieve some type of agreement, but in the eyes of at least some of the participants, good faith negotiations never occurred.

Sixth: The perspectives of the participants involved, especially those of the trade and environmental organizations, are fundamentally different and virtually irreconcilable. Continual court cases from either side have only widened the gap that already existed. Further, in the literature of the various parties involved, the debate is usually framed in terms of victories or losses, loopholes or excessive regulation. There is no common ground in the terminology, the rhetoric is high, and the debate is always framed in black or white.

Seventh: Wetlands regulation is unique in that it affects a vast range of people, land, and different land uses. Under the Clean Water Act, an individual landowner who wants to alter a small piece of land can be subject to the Section 404 permit process the same as a development company that wants to build a new subdivision on 100 acres of land. It is not just an issue for big business; this regulation affects people at all levels. Thus, the CWA, and by extension wetlands regulation, has a broad scope that has made it even more challenging to bring people together. It places a heavy regulatory and permitting process on a diverse group of people, and in the end it does not serve anyone well.

The wetlands case illustrates a difficult situation in which policy makers and interested parties cannot find common ground. Differences will continue to be battled out at the regulatory and congressional levels, and to the extent that differences are resolved, they will be resolved with heavy reliance on the judicial process.

Chapter 11

A CASE STUDY ON ACHIEVING COMMON GROUND: HABITAT FOR HUMANITY INTERNATIONAL

In the spring of 1999, amid concrete blocks, wooden frames, and volunteers spreading mortar, former U.S. President Jimmy Carter and former Philippines President Corazon Aquino inspected homes being built in Maragondon in the Philippines. What brought these two former world leaders together, wearing work clothes and volunteer ID badges? Habitat for Humanity International (HFHI, or simply Habitat), one of the most recognizable nonprofit groups in the world. At the end of fiscal 2001, Habitat had 1,603 affiliates in the United States and more than 410 affiliates worldwide.[1] In the fall of 2000, Habitat completed its 100,000th house and set an ambitious goal of building its next 100,000 by 2005.

Habitat for Humanity was founded in 1976 by Millard Fuller. It is a grassroots home building organization that focuses on combining action with faith. The organization is broadly Christian, drawing upon religious concepts to motivate action, but it welcomes the participation of people of all faiths, traditions, or backgrounds. Habitat's vision is a world without poverty housing, and to fulfill this vision, it builds homes for people who would not otherwise have them. Habitat works with poor families and individuals who may be living in substandard housing, in public housing, or renting with little chance to save money to purchase a house. The organization identifies people who have the skills, motivation, and ability to become home owners and then provides the opportunity for them to do so. Emphasis is placed on helping the working poor, who, for various reasons — be it location, low salary, or unexpected expenses — may be unable to

---

[1] Habitat for Humanity International. *Annual Report 2001*. Note: HFHI's fiscal year runs from July 1 to June 30.

purchase a house. Habitat homes are sold at no profit, and no interest is charged on the mortgage. Habitat's model is one of partnership; the new home owner builds his or her new home alongside volunteers. Habitat serves as the facilitator and draws in a broad network of help.

By 2002, Habitat had a presence in 3,000 communities in 83 countries around the world and its local affiliates had built and sold more than 125,000 homes.[2] Habitat is growing at a very rapid rate, and it is on track to celebrate the completion of its 200,000[th] home by 2005. In 2001, it was the fifteenth largest home builder in the United States.[3] The organization's strength lies in its ability to be a grassroots, mission-oriented organization, and at the same time to build coalitions between groups that are sometimes in conflict, such as government officials, home builders, lenders, realtors, faith-based groups, youth organizations, and new Habitat home owners.

HABITAT'S APPROACH TO BUILDING SUPPORT AND CONSENSUS

HFHI is an example of an individual home building organization that has successfully fostered common ground within the housing community. Habitat is known for its ability to build consensus and form lasting partnerships, and coalition building is a trademark of the organization. Habitat achieves common ground in a number of unique ways, and seven approaches seem particularly important. They include creating a tangible product, addressing a basic human need, allowing for flexibility within the Habitat framework, encouraging the capacity to incorporate other issues into its mission, developing and encouraging coalitions, relying on volunteers to help keep costs low, and cultivating the support of the media and prominent public figures. This case study examines these approaches as Habitat has worked to achieve common ground. It also reviews Habitat's origins and founding principles, its operations at the national and international levels, and the challenges it faces in light of rapid growth.

THE ORIGINS OF HABITAT

Habitat's roots and its founding vision remain central to its goals. The life trajectory of Habitat's founder, Millard Fuller, and the activities on

---

[2] Millard Fuller, interviewed by author and Amy E. Rowe, 16 May 2001 and updated with later conversations with Millard Fuller and Habitat for Humanity.

[3] "Endangered Species," 134.

Koinonia Farm were both crucial to the creation of Habitat. The story that follows remains fundamental within the Habitat community and provides a key backdrop for its public message.

Millard Fuller and the Experiment of Koinonia

Habitat was founded by Millard and Linda Fuller in 1976. Yet the events prompting the creation of Habitat extend back much further and are tightly linked to the Fuller's personal lives and to their experiences at Koinonia Farm, a small Christian community in rural Georgia. Fuller grew up in Alabama, attended law school, and swiftly became a successful entrepreneur in the early 1960s. He worked constantly and rarely saw his family. As a result, the family came to a point of crisis. To save their family, the Fuller's decided to give up their wealth and establish a new lifestyle.

Fuller moved with his family to Koinonia Farm after meeting its charismatic founder, Clarence Jordan. Jordan had founded Koinonia Farm in 1942 on more than 400 acres of land in rural Sumter County, Georgia. He was a Southern Baptist preacher with a doctorate in scripture studies. Jordan was convinced that the New Testament espoused values of communal living, shared wealth, and fraternity.[4] In particular, he promoted equality, and Koinonia was a racially integrated Christian community. This drew a lot of negative attention from many others living in Sumter County, and Koinonia residents even suffered attacks from the Ku Klux Klan because of their emphasis on integration.[5] Despite this, the community persevered, and Jordan continued to preach his understanding of Christian values.

Jordan swiftly became a mentor to Fuller. During this critical time spent at Koinonia and in a subsequent job fund-raising for Tougaloo College, a predominantly black school in Mississippi, Fuller became increasingly concerned with the racial problems that were at the center of American public life in the 1960s.[6] Slowly, and with Jordan's help Fuller began to formulate a plan for applying the values of Koinonia in the broader society. The two decided on three main goals: spreading the social message of the Bible to the broader public, instructing concerned citizens at Koinonia, and assisting the poor in the area surrounding Koinonia.[7] The latter was a means of putting their values into action. The idea was to allow lower-

---

[4] Gaillard, *If I Were a Carpenter,* 8.
[5] Fuller, *Theology of the Hammer,* 3.
[6] Bagget, *Habitat for Humanity: Building Private Homes, Building Public Religion,* 44.
[7] Ibid., 45.

income people open access to the resources at Koinonia — they could, for example, farm the land or work for its mail-order business — and establish a "partnership housing" program.

To complete this work, Jordan and Fuller established a "Fund for Humanity" that dispensed no-interest loans to those in need. The goal was not to provide a handout, but rather to allow rich and poor to live together. Those with access to funds and the ability to raise money could help provide loans to the poor, doing so without profit. This notion of no-interest loans and no profit on Habitat homes is rooted in the Bible, specifically in Exodus and Leviticus, which state that no interest should be taken on a loan.[8] Not taking interest on a loan is an important concept in three of the major world religions — Christianity, Islam, and Judaism — a fact that has helped Habitat to expand around the world.[9]

Koinonia quickly became a center of activity for planning the construction of homes and for establishing cottage industries aimed at improving the lives of poor people. Sumter county had an especially large number of substandard homes. Most were dilapidated shacks lacking running water or electricity. Due to the great need, the idea of building better homes for the poor people living right near Koinonia caught on very rapidly. The home building activities made possible by the Fund for Humanity made great progress, and by the early 1970s, a series of families were successfully making their mortgage payments, and more were signing up for home loans.

Testing the Model

In 1973, Millard and Linda Fuller were ready for a new challenge. They had traveled in Zaire in the 1960s and decided to return. Working as missionaries for the Disciples of Christ, the Fullers sought to organize a community-development project that would create housing for those in need.[10] For three years, the Fuller family lived in Zaire and worked to create a Fund for Humanity that would function in the same way as the one at Koinonia Farm. They succeeded — homes were built, people readily volunteered, materials were donated, and the financing worked out smoothly. Most importantly, the experience taught them that the Fund for Humanity model could be transplanted to different settings. Fuller returned to the

---

[8] Trostel, "Love in the Mortar Joints," 110.

[9] Jones, Tom, and Amy Randall, HFHI Washington, D.C., office, correspondence with author and Amy E. Rowe, January–August 2001.

[10] Gaillard, *If I Were a Carpenter,* 21.

United States and hosted a conference, inviting Christian friends to hear his ideas and to provide input. Out of this meeting came the plans and a name for organization — Habitat for Humanity. "Habitat" came from a United Nations "Habitat Conference" held that same year, and "Humanity" came directly from Koinonia.[11] The name for the new organization represented a bridge, connecting the Koinonia model with the U.N.'s emphasis on providing shelter for needy people worldwide.[12]

Habitat for Humanity was designed as a grassroots organization based upon volunteerism and partnership. While guided by Christian principles and values, Habitat was designed from the outset to be an interdenominational, interfaith endeavor. Affiliates would be organized around the country, each with its own Fund for Humanity. From the start, Habitat for Humanity had several identities — as a volunteer-based nonprofit organization, as a home building federation, as a grassroots model designed to be implemented in various settings, and as a faith-based organization with faith-oriented goals. The organization was committed to building tangible homes and solid communities. It's original slogan reflected these commitments: "A decent house in a decent community for God's people in need."[13]

The Culture of Habitat

Although Habitat is focused on building homes for low-income households, its effects are far-reaching and extend beyond constructing houses. Many who have been involved with HFHI say it has transformed them — Habitat activities are "catching" and life-changing. This is true for both home owners and volunteers. Many people who have been touched by Habitat return to volunteer for the organization and help spread its message. Millard Fuller captures this sentiment in his book *More Than Houses*: "It is increasingly obvious [that we] are building so much more than houses. . . . We are building people. We are building relationships. We are breaking down barriers. We are bringing people together. We are promoting love and understanding. We are building and revitalizing neighborhoods, we are activating faith and planting hope in the hearts of people."[14] All of this refers to something that might be called the culture

---

[11] Millard Fuller, interviewed by author and Amy E. Rowe, 16 May 2001.

[12] Ibid.

[13] Ibid.

[14] Fuller, *More Than Houses*, xiii.

of Habitat. There are three key components to this culture: theology, oral tradition, and symbolism.

As a faith-based organization, Habitat draws upon theological principles and its identification as a religious organization inspires many people to volunteer. In a book about Habitat, Parker Trostel describes Habitat as a ministry to the poor in deserving need of a home and a ministry to the affluent who are looking for opportunities to help God's people in need.[15] Responding to human need without seeking profit is another basic Habitat principle.[16] The emphasis is on assisting the poor and sharing resources. Another key component of Habitat's message is the "theology of enough."[17] Habitat's home designs are simple and targeted to meet a family's basic needs, and Habitat has proven that affordable homes can be built for low-income families in the United States.

Habitat's pivotal theological principle is the "Theology of the Hammer." As Fuller writes in his book, *Theology of the Hammer,* "This theology is . . . about bringing a wide diversity of people, churches, and other organizations together to build houses and establish viable and dynamic communities."[18] Fuller sees the point of action — the actual construction of homes — as the space where common ground can be fostered, where there is little room for disagreement. By moving from the level of rhetoric to the level of action, people can thrust aside religious, political, and ideological differences.[19]

Oral tradition is the second aspect of Habitat culture. As a grassroots organization focused on action, HFHI kept few records in its early years. People ran the organization by relying on memory and Bible stories, and by retelling how Habitat was founded. Home owner testimonies are a key part of this oral tradition; they provide the proof that the Habitat model works. Fuller himself keeps impeccable track of home owner families, recalling people all over the world who have been changed by partnering with Habitat. He often refers back to the story of the first family whose home was built using the *Fund for Humanity* at Koinonia, and he has maintained a close relationship with this family. Given that Habitat has grown considerably in recent years, these testimonies are now being recorded in various ways, including Fuller's books, Habitat's website, videos, news clips, and photographs.

---

[15] Trostel, "Love in the Mortar Joints," 19.
[16] Habitat for Humanity International, "Habitat as a Christian Ministry."
[17] Fuller, *Theology of the Hammer,* 31.
[18] Ibid., 7.
[19] Habitat for Humanity International, "Habitat as a Christian Ministry."

Symbols are the third component of Habitat culture. One symbol is Habitat terminology: "Habitat house" or "Habitat home owner," or more broadly, "sweat equity," a term that is closely linked with Habitat. Also, Habitat tries to label its projects and link them to significant events or people. Major building initiatives are referred to as building "blitzes," and sometimes Habitat launches major blitzes or new projects at symbolic times of the year, for example during the Christian holy week at Easter time. Jimmy Carter has lent his name each year to a Habitat project known as the Jimmy Carter Work Projects (JCWP). Other examples include projects such as Houses the Congress Built and Houses the Senate Built, in which the goal was to have every member of the House of Representatives and the Senate help build a Habitat house in their home community or state.

The culture of Habitat promotes a sense of internal coherence, and an ethos of success, and it allows people to envision the organization as one that will continue to grow. The theology, oral tradition, and symbolism of Habitat all contribute to the organization's ability to stimulate partnership and cooperation and to achieve common ground.

THE NATIONAL LEVEL: HABITAT IN THE AMERICAN CONTEXT

Habitat has spread extensively around the United States since its founding. HFHI's headquarters are located in Americus, Georgia. Habitat is linked together as an organization by affiliates — local organizations that have their own nonprofit status and their own locally elected board, but are part of the larger organization. Further, the work of the U.S. affiliates is distinct from Habitat initiatives internationally.

Americus and Affiliates Around the United States

The first homes built using the Fund for Humanity model were in Sumter County, Georgia, near Koinonia Farm.[20] The offices in nearby Americus are the primary coordinating entity for U.S. affiliates, linking them to one another and to activities and affiliates abroad. The headquarters is not involved in day-to-day home building; rather, it manages the entire operation, stores information, serves as a place for volunteers to

---

[20] The first experiments at home building using the *Fund for Humanity* model were tried out in Sumter County and then in Zaire. After Habitat for Humanity was founded in 1976, the very first Habitat home was built in San Antonio, Texas.

congregate, hosts conferences, and serves as a symbol of origin for the organization. Although it might be more efficient to move the headquarters to an urban center such as Atlanta, there has been a very conscious effort to keep the HFHI headquarters in this small, rural Georgia town near the Koinonia Farm, where it all started.

HFHI's Washington office was opened in 1991 to represent the organization and its many public, private, and nonprofit partners in the nation's capital.[21] The Washington office has many roles, including being the national and international presence for the organization. It makes connections and keeps in contact with the wide variety of persons and groups in Washington who are interested in Habitat and in building housing for low-income families. Representatives in this office counsel HFHI decision-makers regarding federal legislation and other Washington activities. They also represent HFHI in Congress, the administration, embassies, and many other agencies and organizations.[22]

There are Habitat affiliates in every state in the U.S., and eight regional support centers.[23] Habitat is intentionally designed to be decentralized. Each affiliate is a separately incorporated, nonprofit organization governed by its own volunteer board and with its own 501(c)3 status. Each is run completely at the local level, with the affiliate coordinating all the fund raising, publicity, hiring, volunteer recruitment, building site selection, selection of families, house construction, and mortgage financing.[24] This flexibility helps Habitat build consensus. It allows many different individuals to get involved and allows different types of affiliates to form in diverse areas. Further, having local boards means representatives are community members who have a deep understanding of local conditions.[25]

The critical link between each affiliate and the Americus office is the document known as the Affiliate Covenant (see Figure 11.1). Each affiliate signs the covenant and through this act is bound to abide by Habitat's central principles. This procedure is HFHI's means of protecting its brand name, and ensuring that affiliates using the Habitat name do so according to the mission and principles that HFHI was founded upon. For example, affiliates must build houses with no-interest mortgages and must not accept government funding for building. The affiliates gain access to

---

[21] Jones, Tom, and Amy Randall, HFHI Washington, D.C., office, interviews and correspondence with the author and Amy E. Rowe, January–August 2001.

[22] Ibid.

[23] Regional support centers in the U.S.: Bend, OR, Oakland, CA, Waco, TX, Nashville, TN, Chicago, IL, West Chester, PA, Easley, SC, and Jacksonville, FL.

[24] Habitat for Humanity International, "Fact Sheet" (3 August 2000).

[25] U.S. Department of Housing and Urban Development, *Making Homeownership a Reality.*

FIGURE 11.1
Affiliate Covenant

Preface

Habitat for Humanity International and the Habitat for Humanity affiliate work as partners in this ecumenical Christian housing ministry. The affiliate works with donors, volunteers and homeowners to create decent, affordable housing for those in need, and to make shelter a matter of conscience with people everywhere. Although Habitat for Humanity International will assist with information resources, training, publications, prayer support and in other ways, the affiliate is primarily and directly responsible for the legal, organizational, fund-raising, family selection and nurture, financial and construction aspects of the work.

Mission Statement

Habitat for Humanity works in partnership with God and people everywhere, from all walks of life, to develop communities with God's people in need by building and renovating houses, so that there are decent houses in decent communities in which God's people can live and grow into all that God intended.

Method of Operation

Habitat for Humanity sponsors projects in habitat development by constructing modest but adequate housing. Habitat also seeks to associate with other organizations functioning with purposes consistent with those of Habitat for Humanity International and the affiliate, as stated in the Articles of Incorporation of both Habitat organizations.

Foundation Principles

1. Habitat for Humanity seeks to demonstrate the love and teachings of Jesus Christ to all people. While Habitat is a Christian organization, it invites and welcomes affiliate board members, volunteers and donors from other faiths actively committed to Habitat's Mission, Method of Operation, and Principles. The board will reflect the ethnic diversity of the area to be served.
2. Habitat for Humanity is a people-to-people partnership drawing families and communities in need together with volunteers and resources to build decent, affordable housing for needy people. Habitat is committed to the development and uplifting of families and communities, not only to the construction of houses.
3. Habitat for Humanity builds, renovates, and repairs simple, decent and affordable housing with people who are living in inadequate housing and who are unable to secure adequate housing by conventional means.
4. Habitat for Humanity selects homeowner families according to criteria that do not discriminate on the basis of race, creed, or ethnic background. All homeowners contribute "sweat equity"; they work as partners with the affiliate and other volunteers to accomplish Habitat's mission, both locally and worldwide.
5. Habitat for Humanity sells houses to selected families with no profit or interest added. House payments will be used for the construction or renovation of additional affordable housing.

Figure 11.1 (continued)

6. Habitat for Humanity is a global partnership. In recognition of and commitment to that global partnership, each affiliate is expected to contribute at least 10 percent of its cash contributions to Habitat's international work. Funds specifically designated by a donor for local work only may be excluded from the tithe.

7. Habitat for Humanity does not seek and will not accept government funds for the construction of houses. Habitat for Humanity welcomes partnership with governments that includes accepting funds to help set the stage for construction of houses, provided it does not limit our ability to proclaim our Christian witness, and further provide that affiliates do not become dependent on or controlled by government funds thus obtained. Setting the stage is interpreted to include land, houses for rehabilitation, infrastructure for streets, utilities and administrative expenses. Funding from third parties who accept government funds with sole discretion over their use shall not be considered as government funds for Habitat purposes.

Agreement to Covenant

In affirmation of the Mission, Method of Operation, and Principles state in this Covenant, we, _____, a Habitat for Humanity affiliate, covenant with other affiliates and Habitat for Humanity International to accomplish our mission. Each partner commits to enhancing that ability to carry out this mission by: supporting effective communication among affiliate, Habitat for Humanity International and regional offices; sharing annual reports; participating in regional and national training events; and participating in a biennial review and planning session between each affiliate and the regional office.

This Covenant is valid upon approval by each member of the affiliate board of directors and a designated representative of Habitat for Humanity International.

Habitat's brand name and to the organization's resources, yet they are autonomous, support themselves financially, designate their own priorities, and decide their own structure. For newly formed affiliates, HFHI provides informational resources such as the *Affiliate Operations Manual*, promotional materials, and strategies for how to partner with other community groups and local municipal bodies.[26]

The most common way affiliates are created is through partnerships of various denominations of Christian churches. One of the major tasks of HFHI's headquarters is to connect with new churches and maintain relationships with existing partners.[27] HFHI sends partner affiliates brochures and videos about how to sponsor house building, descriptions of the theological principles, logos, T-shirts, signs, brochures, billboards, and a quarterly newsletter. The organization also sends affiliates worship service suggestions to use at ground breaking and dedication services, sermon

---

[26] Baggett, *Habitat for Humanity: Building Private Homes, Building Public Religion*, 76.
[27] Habitat for Humanity International, "Church Relations."

outlines, devotions to use on different occasions, and mission moments (short explanations of Habitat's ministry designed to be presented over several weeks). Another growing partnership arena is high schools and colleges. In 1987, HFHI established its first college chapter at Baylor University. Shortly thereafter, Habitat began its Collegiate Challenge, a program in which college students spend their school breaks working on Habitat projects. These are two examples of how HFHI establishes affiliates. Given the diverse array of churches and colleges in the United States, Habitat is able to extend its message into many unique contexts by partnering with these institutions. These examples support the common ground themes of coalition building and adaptability — Habitat can partner with different groups, everyone benefits from the process, and people bring their unique issues into the mix while getting the job done.

Habitat Home Owners

Habitat affiliates identify potential home owners according to the following three criteria: a need for better housing, a willingness to become partners in the program, and the ability to repay a no-interest loan.[28] Habitat chooses families very carefully, and the primary emphasis in the selection process is on partnership with each Habitat home owner.

Each affiliate has a Family Selection Committee whose task is to select potential home owners. First, to qualify for a Habitat home, a household must be living in what is defined as substandard housing and unable to qualify for a conventional home loan. The second criterion is that the family must be willing to work in partnership with affiliate staff and volunteers. A major part is the new home owner's willingness to put in "sweat equity" hours — meaning that the family will work alongside the Habitat volunteers to work on other habitat homes and to complete their home. Typically, home owners spend between 200 and 500 hours helping with tasks such as hammering together the frame of their home, putting windows in place, or working on the roof. The goal is to help the new owners feel that they are contributing to the construction of their home, not just paying for it. This also furthers the understanding that the project is a partnership, not a handout.

The third criterion is the ability of potential home owners to pay their mortgage. Habitat families usually have incomes below 80% of area me-

---

[28] Habitat for Humanity International, "How Are Partner Families Selected?"

dian income, although affiliates have great latitude when setting income-eligibility standards.[29] While Habitat targets poor households, it must be cautious in the selection process. As Jerome Baggat writes in his book about Habitat: "A family's need. . . . cannot be so extreme that they are unprepared for the financial burdens of home ownership, which include paying the costs of the mortgage, taxes, insurance, and utilities."[30] To pay a mortgage, a household must have a steady income over a twenty- to thirty-year period. This typically means that home owners who are selected are working poor; their wages are low, but constant over time. Some affiliates require a down payment and closing costs, but many take care of these costs and consider "sweat equity" a sufficient contribution by the home owner.[31] Selecting families who will be able to pay off a twenty- or thirty-year no-interest mortgage helps reduce the likelihood of home owners defaulting on their loans. The families pay their loans back to the affiliate's Fund for Humanity, which in turn enables the organization to continue building houses. Careful selection of families allows Habitat to sustain itself and ensure its own continuity.

Habitat affiliates, through a Family Nurture Committee, typically offer counseling to inform the potential owners of their responsibilities and of the laws related to ownership, and to suggest ways to budget to pay the mortgage. Habitat home owners often maintain a relationship with the affiliate after the house is completed, continuing this counseling and community building. Some affiliates also require the new home owners to put funds in an escrow account for property taxes, maintenance, and insurance premiums as a means of easing them into their new responsibilities and to prepare them for unanticipated expenses.[32] In addition, Habitat home owners often become volunteers for Habitat as part of their ongoing willingness to partner with the organization.

As stated in the Affiliate Covenant (Figure 11.1), affiliates cannot discriminate according to race, ethnic background, or religion when selecting home owners. There seems to be a tendency to choose families (with either two parents or a single parent with children) rather than individuals to be Habitat home owners. Some suggest that this is because by targeting families with children, Habitat can have a multigenerational effect.[33]

---

[29] U.S. Department of Housing and Urban Development, *Making Homeownership a Reality,* ii–5.
[30] Bagget, *Habitat for Humanity: Building Private Homes, Building Public Religion,* 79.
[31] U.S. Department of Housing and Urban Development, *Making Homeownership a Reality,* iii–9.
[32] Ibid., iii–10.
[33] Ibid., vi–1.

The Flow of Funds

Each U.S. Habitat affiliate is responsible for raising money to support its activities. The affiliates do not receive funding from HFHI headquarters. Rather, they conduct local fund-raising campaigns. Each affiliate has a Fund for Humanity, into which all money it raises is deposited. The Fund for Humanity is used for home loans, construction costs, and other costs related to building and organizing. Land for homes is often donated, or it is sold to the affiliate at a low price. In urban areas where land is more scarce, affiliates sometimes depend on local governments to make foreclosed or abandoned properties available to them at a low cost.[34]

Sponsors may donate materials rather than money (tools, wood, supplies, windows, roofing materials, appliances and so on). For example, for Habitat's More Than Houses Campaign (designed to build 100,000 more homes in just five years), Whirlpool Corp. made a $25 million commitment to put a stove and refrigerator in every Habitat house built in the United States and Canada through 2005.[35] Other key partners that provide materials and/or financial contributions include: Dow Chemical, the *Oprah Winfrey Show,* Home Depot, Maxwell House Coffee Company, United Airlines, Fannie Mae, Freddie Mac, the Federal Home Loan Banks, Mobil Oil, the National Association of Home Builders, the National Association of Realtors, the Mortgage Bankers, American Airlines, Larson Manufacturing, Ethan Allen, Charles Schwabb, Citigroup, and many others.[36] Often these corporate sponsors work directly with HFHI headquarters, but as founder Millard Fuller notes, local affiliates benefit from these partnerships.[37] Over the years, Habitat has shown a remarkable ability to build coalitions nationally and locally and to draw individuals together in unique partnership.

While U.S. affiliates are essentially self-sufficient, affiliates abroad are partially supported by HFHI funds. Each Habitat affiliate is asked to "tithe," meaning it gives 10% of its total annual revenue to HFHI. These funds are carefully directed to international affiliates, not HFHI administrative activities. Tithes, in addition to money HFHI headquarters raises primarily through direct-mail fundraising, provide the bulk of the financial support for all Habitat activities. HFHI is also supported by government grants for land and development costs and by corporate donations. Figure 11.2 outlines how money flows through HFHI. Figure 11.3 shows the amount of money

---

[34] Baggett, *Habitat for Humanity: Building Private Homes, Building Public Religion,* 74.

[35] Habitat for Humanity International, "More Than Houses: Rebuilding Our Communities."

[36] Habitat for Humanity International, "Corporate Partners."

[37] Millard Fuller, interviewed by author and Amy E. Rowe, 16 May 2001.

FIGURE 11.2
HFHI Flow of Funds

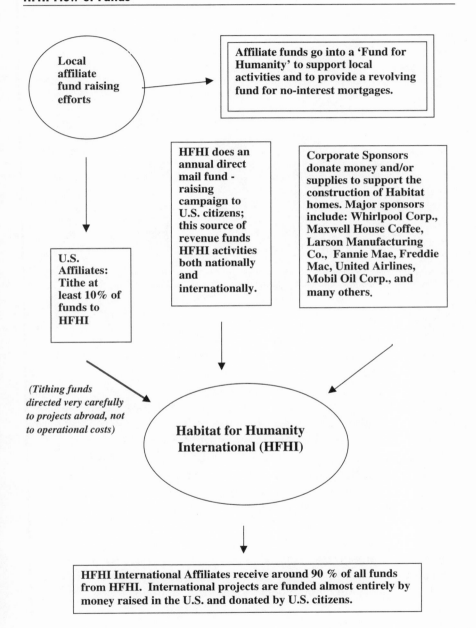

FIGURE 11.3
Total Amount of Tithes from U.S. Affiliates

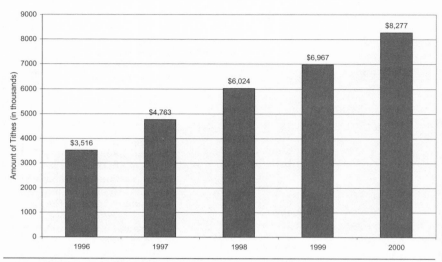

Source: Habitat for Humanity International, 2000 U.S. program statistics, 8 February 2001.

raised from U.S. affiliates' tithes from 1995 to 2000. These dollar amounts indicate that the bulk of the fund-raising activity is done within the U.S. This links back to the concept of wealth-sharing articulated at Koinonia Farm and also to Habitat's second approach to achieving common ground — meeting a basic human need. Habitat seeks to address the enormous housing needs abroad by drawing upon wealth and resources in the United States. HFHI funding also links to the sixth theme, that of service and volunteerism. Charitable donations are a form of service, and this is a well-established activity in America, one that is supported through tax benefits.

Habitat views the government as an important partner in addressing poverty housing. However, it does not accept government funding for housing construction. It does accept government funds for land, infrastructure, and community building. Habitat does not accept government money for construction because it might carry stipulations that could counteract the organization's principles. Affiliates are also wary of the red tape associated with government funding which could potentially interfere with their primary function to build homes and community.[38] While Habi-

---

[38] Baggett, *Habitat for Humanity: Building Private Homes, Building Public Religion,* 63.

tat maintains this principle, since the late 1980s, there has been a shift in where the line is drawn. The policy now is that government funds can be used to "set the stage" for building, as Millard Fuller put it, but not for actual building.[39] Stage setting includes land, houses for rehabilitation, infrastructure for streets, utilities, and administrative expenses.[40] For example, CDBG funds might be used to clear land, and then this land is made available for Habitat homes. In 1994, the HFHI board allowed government grants to be used for hiring staff and administrative expenses.[41] One way Habitat has benefited from staffing grants is through the AmeriCorps program. In this program, the federal government provides the salary, and the individual serves HFHI for a designated period of time.[42]

In the last five years, a major government resource through which Habitat sets the stage for building has been SHOP funds. The Self-help Homeownership Opportunity Program, authorized by Congress as part of the Housing Opportunity Program Extension Act of 1996,[43] is a competitive program whereby nonprofit organizations apply for grants to help low-income households that are unable to purchase a home. SHOP is designed to provide $10,000 per unit for land acquisition and infrastructure improvements. HFHI has received SHOP funds every year. These funds go directly to HFHI, which then runs a competitive application program for all U.S. Habitat affiliates.[44] HFHI has received $58.2 million in SHOP funds since 1996; these funds have substantially offset affiliates' costs and allowed them to direct more of the money they raise individually to home building. A second important government grant source is HUD's capacity building (known as CB) grants. CB grants are available to all U.S. affiliates and are used for innovative technical assistance and training programs.[45] As with SHOP, the funds are allocated to HFHI headquarters, which determines how the money will be used. HFHI has used CB grants to establish field support centers with staff who are specialists in particular fields; their presence in the regional offices allows them to partner with and be readily accessible to local affiliates.[46]

---

[39] Millard Fuller, interviewed by author and Amy E. Rowe, 16 May 2001.

[40] Habitat for Humanity International, "Fact Sheet" (15 June 2001).

[41] Baggett, *Habitat for Humanity: Building Homes, Religion,* 63.

[42] For more information see: "Habitat for Humanity Americorps" at www.habitat.org/hr/americorps.html.

[43] U.S. Department of Housing and Urban Development, "Self-Help Homeownership Opportunity Program."

[44] Habitat for Humanity International, "SHOP: Building on Success."

[45] Habitat for Humanity International, "Capacity Building: Investing in the Future."

[46] Ibid.

Finding a Niche in the Housing Market

Habitat has identified a particular niche in the housing market where it has been able to make important changes and thrive. It has specialized in meeting the needs of working families that are just barely outside of the home ownership market. Habitat gets these households into the ownership cycle by extending the entry point. Habitat home owners tend to be low-income minorities, and often single mothers.[47] Many government programs and other nonprofit housing organizations serve the same demographic community; however, Habitat takes a unique approach and has a high rate of success.

First, Habitat makes a strong statement about what constitutes decent, adequate housing. Over the last several decades, the emphasis in the U.S. has been on larger homes with more amenities. Each year, the average square footage for new homes rises. Habitat provides a strong counter to this trend.[48] The average cost of a Habitat home in the U.S. in 2001 was $48,000, far below market rates for similar homes.[49] Habitat is proving that through innovative approaches and very basic design, homes can be more affordable.

Habitat is also making strides in the U.S. housing market through the sustained success of its home owners. As noted earlier, Habitat affiliates have a detailed family selection process and also maintain relationships with home owners. As a result, the default rate on Habitat loans is very low.[50] Although little direct data on default rates is available, it is widely known that the rates are low and that Habitat home owners are generally very successful in their new responsibilities. This is remarkable given that many Habitat families would be considered "high risk" (likely to default or even foreclose on their property) if they applied for housing through federal programs. Additionally, Habitat home owners tend to be living in better conditions in their new homes without spending a larger percentage of their income on housing. As a 1998 HUD report explains: "While priced comparably to their previous homes in terms of monthly housing costs, the Habitat homes to which homebuyers moved are typically lower density, substantially less crowded, and in better physical condition than

---

[47] Tom Jones, and Amy Randall, interviewed by author and Amy E. Rowe, 25 January 2001.
[48] Husock, "It's Time to Take Habitat for Humanity Seriously," 42.
[49] Amy Randall, HFHI Washington Office, correspondence with Amy E.Rowe.
[50] U.S. Department of Housing and Urban Development. *Making Homeownership a Reality,* vi–3. Note: The conclusions drawn in the HUD publication are based on an in-depth survey of nineteen HFHI affiliates around the United States.

the dwelling units in which families lived previously."[51] Habitat home owners confirm that they would not have been able to buy a home without Habitat's assistance.

Accommodating Growth

HFHI first experienced growth-related pressures in the early 1990s. In its early years, HFHI did not focus on precise record keeping or well-developed plans, but on grassroots action. As it added more and more affiliates, it ran into an increasing array of problems. The lack of bureaucracy was beginning to prevent Habitat from managing its assets, fundraising, and contacting affiliates effectively. Seeing that the balance between mission and organization was not being well maintained, in 1990 the board of directors brought in a new operational leader, Jeff Snider.[52]

Snider and the board recognized that new techniques had to be implemented for Habitat to survive and continue to expand. The organization began to define headquarters' role more concretely, assess human resources, implement better record keeping, bring in employees with specific areas of expertise (fund-raising, marketing, financial management), and propose realistic growth objectives.[53] At the same time, efforts were made to diversify the board. Prior to this time, board members had been volunteers who had devoted their lives to Habitat. It was clear that to address the needs of a nonprofit of Habitat's size, new expertise was needed on the board.

This shift toward a more bureaucratized Habitat marked the organization during the 1990s, and it has helped increase Habitat's efficiency. Newfound direction and leadership as a result of these changes has further propelled growth. Figure 11.4 provides an extended overview of Habitat's building in the U.S, which further highlights the major increases in the 1990s. An estimated 33,247 houses have been built in the U.S. since Habitat's founding.[54] 31,012 of these were built since 1990, meaning that over 93% of Habitat homes in the U.S. were built in the ten years between 1990 and 2000. This suggests that HFHI has been increasing its efficiency and partnerships as it has added more affiliates. Figure 11.5 indicates the level

---

[51] U.S. Department of Housing and Urban Development. *Making Homeownership a* Reality, vi–1.

[52] Slavitt, "Habitat for Humanity International" 4.

[53] Ibid., 6.

[54] Please note that because HFHI's fiscal year runs from July 1 to June 30, the number of homes built per year in Figure 5 is calculated differently than in Figure 11.4, where homes built per year are from January 1 to December 31.

FIGURE 11.4
Total HFHI Building in the U.S., 1976–2000

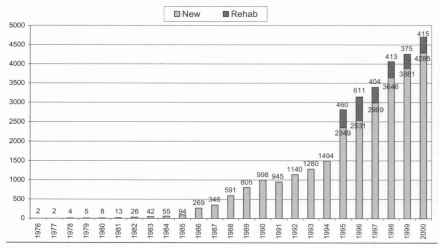

SOURCE: Habitat for Humanity International, 2000 U.S. program statistics, 8 February 2001.

of building by region in 2000. The most building occurred in the southeast (near Habitat's origins), with a total of 1,108 houses.

As the number of national and international affiliates has increased, HFHI headquarters has taken on an increasingly important role as a clearinghouse for funds, resources, and guidance. As with other multisite nonprofits, when affiliates are established, the original entity must convert its role to a national office and increasingly become a service provider to affiliates.[55] Habitat in Americus now manages hundreds of affiliates every year, and it is becoming more bureaucratized and more organized out of sheer necessity. It must be emphasized that the affiliates across the U.S. are incredibly diverse (some affiliates build many homes while others build two or three), and more are being formed. It is likely Americus will continue to serve as a place for volunteers to congregate and as a symbol for the organization, and will also increasingly become a quality-control clearinghouse if Habitat continues to expand at its current rate.

---

[55] Grossman and Rangan, "Managing Multi-Site Nonprofits," 2.

FIGURE 11.5
HFHI Building in U.S. Regions, 2000

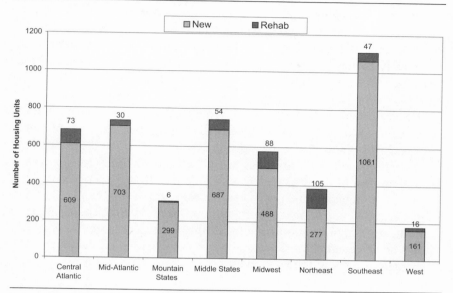

SOURCE: Habitat for Humanity International, 2000 U.S. program statistics, 8 February 2001.

HABITAT IN THE GLOBAL ARENA

Habitat for Humanity has had an international component and emphasis since its founding. The early experiments with the Habitat model were conducted in Georgia and Zaire, and the model proved to be successful in these two divergent contexts. There are important differences in how the Habitat model functions in the U.S. and how it functions in other nations. The movement of funds through HFHI shows a clear commitment to encouraging the wealthy countries to help those living in impoverished regions of the world. Once Habitat had successfully formed affiliates in each of the fifty states, even more emphasis was placed on expanding Habitat abroad.

International Partners

Habitat is currently present in seventy-nine countries around the world. Poverty housing is a worldwide problem, and Habitat seeks to draw together people around the world to address this shared problem. Millard Fuller explains that Habitat has been able to expand around the world by using the "Christian family" as the base of support — through missionary networks and in regions where there are well-established Christian populations.[56] Figure 11.6 shows the extensive expansion of Habitat internationally during the 1990s: between 1990 and 2000, the number of countries partnered with Habitat, through affiliates or otherwise, more than doubled.

HFHI establishes partners internationally through the National Covenant which is similar to the Affiliate Covenant used in the United States. Just as in the U.S., this document allows HFHI to protect its brand name by requiring new affiliates to follow key principles, yet again there is a great deal of flexibility allowed within the structure. For example, although the Habitat standard is a single-family detached home, home designs are modified to make them appropriate in various countries. HFHI tries to use "appropriate technology" that keeps construction costs low, limits environmental impacts, and is in keeping with local customs.[57] Still, new ideas are being transported abroad, such as support for home ownership.

Construction of Habitat homes abroad is far less expensive than in the U.S. This is due to lower construction and utility costs and fewer regulations. In some countries, the cost to build a Habitat house is as little as $800 U.S. dollars.[58] As noted, most of HFHI's activities abroad are funded by U.S. affiliates through the tithes. In some cases, HFHI provides specific funding grants to affiliates in developing countries to aid with special projects or helps raise money for those projects.[59] Americans further Habitat endeavors abroad by volunteering. In the Global Village program, people travel to sites abroad for one to three weeks at a time. In these ways, wealth-sharing goals are achieved and common ground is created through volunteering and supporting the ideal of service abroad.

Diversification and the New Expertise

HFHI has divided the globe into five major international areas: 1) Africa/Middle East with offices in Pretoria, South Africa; 2) Asia/Pacific with offices in Bangkok, Thailand; 3) Europe/Commonwealth of Indepen-

---

[56] Millard Fuller, interviewed by author and Amy E. Rowe, 16 May 2001.
[57] Habitat for Humanity International, *Annual Report 1999*, 5.
[58] Habitat for Humanity International, "Fact Sheet," (2 April 2001).
[59] Habitat for Humanity International, "Fact Sheet," (15 June 2001).

FIGURE 11.6
Number of Countries Partnered with HFHI, 1976–2001

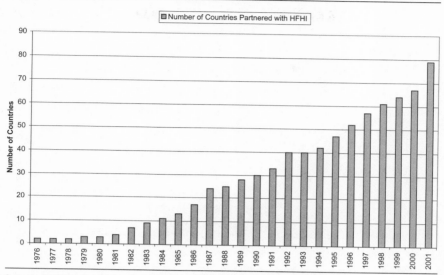

SOURCE: Habitat for Humanity International, "The History of Habitat" (photo time line) www.habitat.org/how/history.html, for 1976–2000. 2001 data from Washington, D.C., HFHI office, July 2001.

dent States with offices in Budapest, Hungary; 4) U.S.A. and Canada; and 5) Latin America/Caribbean with offices in San Jose, Costa Rica. Figure 11.7 provides a breakdown of houses built in each region of the world in fiscal 1999 and fiscal 2000. Until very recently, the international regions were run from HFHI headquarters in Americus. The creation of regional offices in San Jose, Bangkok, Budapest, and Pretoria is illustrative of HFHI's changing strategies. Given the proliferation of international affiliates, by the late 1990s, there was a growing need for more localized guidance and support. The new regional offices allow volunteers and directors to be in better touch with the local groups, to oversee projects more effectively, and to better monitor the pulse of activities around the world. It is likely that HFHI will continue to decentralize in order to stay current with regional events and to ensure quality control among the international affiliates.

Another revealing shift within Habitat has been its effort to diversify its board. All board members must be Christian, and there has been an effort to keep the board linked to Habitat's origins. The board consists of Millard Fuller plus twenty-seven church, community, and business leaders. This is

FIGURE 11.7
Total Units Built by HFHI at End of FY 2000

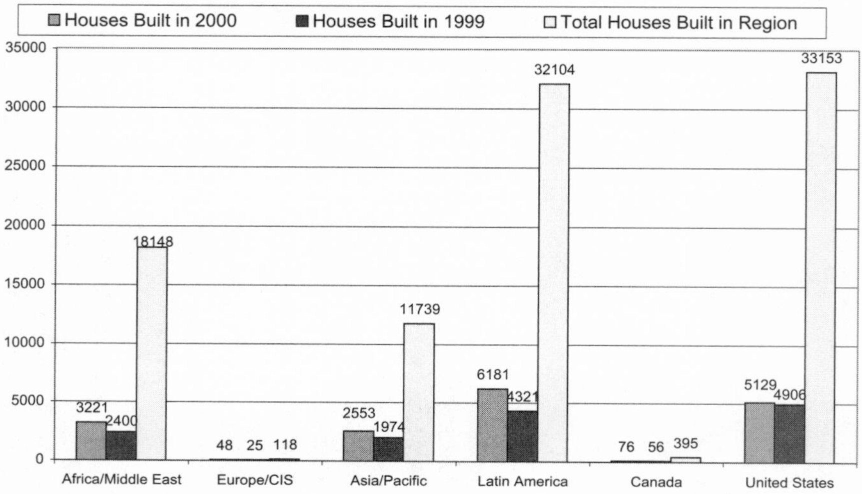

| | ■ Houses Built in 2000 | ■ Houses Built in 1999 | □ Total Houses Built in Region |

SOURCE: Habitat for Humanity International, *Annual Report 1999* and *Annual Report 2000*. Note: Habitat's fiscal year runs from July 1 to June 30. In the fall of 2000, Habitat built its 100,000th house, which will be reflected in the FY2001 Annual Report.

the same number that came to Habitat's first conference in 1976.[60] Most of the current board members are in fact of Euro-American ancestry and have some kind of family missionary background within the international regions they represent. The goal is to shift the balance so that approximately half of the board represents U.S. affiliates and half international affiliates. The other component of this is to move toward choosing international members who are native to the region they represent (though still Christian). The idea is to include people who have a solid sense of what is happening in their region of the world.

There is also an effort to bring more business leaders with professional expertise onto the board. Originally, Habitat board members were people who had devoted their lives to the organization and whose work on the board was a natural extension of their total commitment. In the 1990s, the board sought to add people with specialized knowledge who could provide diverse perspectives and help lead HFHI into the next century. Business leaders who had worked in the housing sector, in finance, or in

[60] Baggett, *Habitat for Humanity: Building Private Homes, Building Public Religion,* 69.

international nonprofit organizations were asked to join. For many of these people, Habitat is not their sole passion and activity. There are still those on the board for whom Habitat is their major life commitment, but the dynamic has clearly changed in recent years.

CHALLENGES AND NEXT STEPS

Habitat continues to face the challenges of its own growth and the pervasiveness of poverty housing around the world. Each of the strategies discussed in this section reflect Habitat's commitment to fostering common ground and drawing people together in partnership in the housing industry.

Twenty-First Century Challenge

Millard Fuller believes that Habitat has a "mandate from God to end poverty housing."[61] To accomplish this, Habitat is taking on new advocacy roles and renewing long-standing commitments to building community through its new program, the 21st Century Challenge. Habitat recognizes that it cannot end poverty housing single-handedly; new partnerships will be necessary. The strategy is for affiliates to bring a challenge to their communities and lead the effort to create an initiative partnership. Local support then draws assistance from HFHI and other nationally supported housing groups."[62]

The 21st Century Challenge sets forth a call to action to communities to eliminate substandard housing in their area within a designated time by first determining the amount of substandard housing in the community, then organizing a local initiative to address the issue, raise funds, set a date by which the goals will be achieved, and develop the resources to meet those goals.[63] The thrust here is on repairing communities. While not explicitly stated, this new program seems to be moving toward making communities more stable and healthy, which in turn may prevent the development of poverty housing. The program seeks to bring the entire housing stock up to a certain standard and to set aside funds to prevent the stock from becoming dilapidated in the future. The first initiative, in Sumter County, Georgia, was deemed a success.

---

[61] Millard Fuller, interviewed by author and Amy E. Rowe, 16 May 2001.

[62] Habitat for Humanity International, "21st Century Challenge: Eliminating Substandard Housing."

[63] Ibid.

Habitat recognizes that just building houses will not change the lives of everyone in a community. As Fuller states, "We are not a 'Lottery for Humanity.' We are building for everybody. We need to develop these initiative partnerships to address the whole problem so that we do not become a lottery."[64] This new project is an effort to expand Habitat's message and impact. It is a prime example of how Habitat is striving to create common ground around housing needs within communities. As an HFHI 21st Century Challenge publication states: "Foremost is the opportunity to engage your whole community — churches, civic clubs, businesses and individuals of every race, creed, age and color — in a community-wide stand against substandard housing. A strong collaborative effort restores hope to a community. As residents work side by side to erase substandard housing locally, the same model of cooperation follows them into other facets of community life."[65]

The 21st Century Challenge is emblematic of broader changes within HFHI. Habitat is grappling with issues of scale and globalization; it is making new alliances and examining problems linked to housing. Habitat affiliates have long acknowledged that housing is not the only problem low-income people face. Many do not have stable jobs or access to health care. As Andrew Slavitt explained in a 1993 case study of Habitat:

> In the effort to serve an impoverished community, Habitat could not avoid confronting the many other problems its homeowner families faced. While not a traditional strength, many of Habitat's local volunteers did have backgrounds in other areas of community development . . . . [and because] each affiliate supported itself, it was able to establish its own priorities, as long as it abided by the Affiliate Covenant. As a result, many affiliates more broadly defined their role as outreach organization within their community. Many devoted varying amounts of attention to issues such as hunger, health care, day care, drug prevention, education, and community building.[66]

Habitat has long addressed a wide range of concerns that impact low-income households, and Habitat has often defined its work as community development, not just home building.[67] This echoes Habitat's first slogan: "A decent home in a decent community for all God's people in need." Habitat is therefore trying to step up its efforts to adequately address the multiple problems that affect low-income people in order to create decent communities around the United States.

---

[64] Ibid.
[65] Habitat for Humanity International, "What is the 21st Century Challenge?" 4.
[66] Slavitt, "Habitat for Humanity International," 9.
[67] Austin and Woolever, "Voluntary Association Boards, 183.

These commitments are reflected in HFHI's strategic plan for 2000 to 2005. The plan explains that Habitat wants to implement a "holistic" approach, acknowledging that HFHI must designate partners at each level (international, area, regional, national, affiliate) and that housing needs of low-income households are tied to other key needs (such as health care, jobs, education, and transportation).[68] Habitat is taking on a new advocacy role, and in doing so is forging a wider space for common ground. The 21st Century Challenge with its community emphasis and the strategic plan's holistic partnership approach are both examples of how Habitat orchestrates different groups, with their specialized concerns to work together for positive change.

Habitat University

One HFHI idea for addressing rapid growth is to establish a Habitat University. HFHI is currently discussing how a university could sustain the mission-oriented aspects of the organization. Habitat University would be a place to train Habitat leaders, volunteers, and others interested in the problem of poverty housing. The goal would be to teach students both the mission of Habitat and the specific skills related to home building, coalition building, volunteer management, community development, housing finance, and so on.[69] The university would educate those involved with Habitat and those interested in housing issues, create a space for ongoing dialogue and training, and sustain the links between itself and alumni over time.

Another aspect of the University would be to conduct research related to affordable housing, community building, and other topics critical to Habitat's mission.[70] A Habitat University could serve as a focal point for creating, testing, implementing, and exporting Habitat's educational approaches. It could be the place where workshops are devised, and then graduates or professors could travel to affiliates around the world conducting training sessions. HFHI already has departments dedicated to education and training, and their existing projects could serve as the foundation for a university.

Habitat University would draw upon multiple funding sources, including grants, government assistance, and HFHI subsidy. It would seek to build relations with other academic institutions, development organizations, and

---

[68] Habitat for Humanity International, *Strategic Plan 2000–2005: Building the Next 100,000 Homes*, 33
[69] Habitat for Humanity International, "DRAFT: Concept Paper for Habitat University," 1.
[70] Ibid., 2.

indigenous agencies in order to provide a diverse array of learning opportunities for students.[71] In essence, it would be another arena in which Habitat could make new alliances and train people to build coalitions around housing topics.

At this stage, Habitat University is just a concept, but HFHI is in the process of hiring a consulting company to develop a work plan, budget, and timeline. Some Habitat participants believe that the establishment of a university is the only viable means to preserve the mission intact and continue the momentum of HFHI. Others are not certain if a university is the best option, or even if it is a feasible one. The future of Habitat University is unclear, but, the fact that HFHI is discussing such an option signifies that the organization recognizes that new challenges require new solutions.

Unique Challenges in Urban Settings

The Habitat model has proved successful in many different contexts — rural farm areas, small towns, industrial cities, central cities, and suburban areas. However, it has been most successful in rural areas. In rural areas, such as Sumter County, acquiring land and materials is a relatively streamlined process. In urban areas, land is more expensive, and, there are often stricter building codes, extensive state and federal regulations, and higher utility costs. Additionally, land tends to be more scarce, and often the only way to increase the affordable housing stock is to rehabilitate existing units. These problems tend to be magnified in the older, industrial cities of the Northeast. Despite the difficulties of working in urban areas, the Habitat approach is thriving in cities such as Minneapolis, St. Paul, Atlanta, Miami, Dallas, Fort Worth, and Houston.[72] In cities such as Los Angeles, Newark, Chicago, Boston, and Detroit, the Habitat model works, but with greater challenge.[73]

Some of this can be attributed to structural issues and to the layouts of particular U.S. cities. Millard Fuller notes that in Newark and Chicago, many of the potential Habitat leaders and volunteers live in the suburbs and are not as connected to the inner cities where they go to work on Habitat homes on the weekends.[74] There is a disconnect between the leadership pool and the low-income households that need housing. Partnerships have

---

[71] Ibid., 3.
[72] Millard Fuller, interviewed by author and Amy E. Rowe, 16 May 2001.
[73] Ibid.
[74] Ibid.

proven more challenging, but not impossible, to create in these areas. In the mid-1990s, Habitat sought to do more work in New York City. It did this in part by deviating from the traditional fund-raising approach whereby the affiliate raises money for all its local activities and then tithes a portion of it. Instead, money was taken directly from HFHI's central funds to help support the New York affiliate. This provided the necessary funding for home building in this dense, costly urban setting. It is unlikely that HFHI donating money to urban affiliates will be a sustainable means of making progress in urban areas. Yet at the same time, it shows that Habitat is willing to target certain areas and wants to make a greater commitment to urban areas. Habitat's strategic plan for 2000 to 2005 indicates that Habitat staff are preparing a study on how Habitat can "impact housing needs in complex urban environments,"[75] and this is another arena where Habitat will seek to generate more partnerships in the future.

HABITAT AS A CATALYST: BUILDING COALITIONS AND ACHIEVING COMMON GROUND

There are currently more than 1,600 Habitat affiliates around the United States.[76] In fiscal 2000 (July 1, 1999 to June 30, 2000), Habitat affiliates built 5,129 homes in the United States.[77] Much of Habitat's growth is due to its ability to facilitate partnerships and create a space for common dialogue. Habitat actively draws other organizations into its work. It has kept its message simple, which has allowed it to pull in participants who would be unlikely to work together in other settings. This section reviews three examples of how Habitat has brought the housing community together.

Involving the Public Sector: The Houses the Senate Built

HFHI has sought to create common ground by involving public representatives. In recent years, Habitat has sponsored The Houses That Congress Built, The Houses the Senate Built, The Houses the Assembly Built (for state general assemblies), and The First Ladies Build (first ladies and women state governors, past and current). This is an example of how Habitat builds common ground by garnering support from high-profile

---

[75] Habitat for Humanity International, *Strategic Plan 2000–2005,* 10.

[76] Correspondence with HFHI Washington, D.C., office, 19 June 2001.

[77] Habitat for Humanity International, *Annual Report 2000,* 15. Note: The 5,129 figure (as with all HFHI annual report numbers) is an estimate based on new, rehab, and repairs for the fiscal year.

figures and the media. It is also a means by which important coalitions have been formed, as many corporations and organizations agree to sponsor builds precisely because of the media attention given to the events.

On June 9, 2000, the U.S. Senate established The Houses the Senate Built with the unanimous passage of Senate Resolution 319. In passing this resolution, each Senator agreed to the concept of working with a Habitat affiliate in his or her home state to build a house. The other component of the resolution was for the Senate to build two houses in the Washington, D.C., area. On March 7, 2001 the U.S. senators' build was held in Capitol Heights, Maryland. The event drew together senators (including then Majority Leader Trent Lott and Minority Leader Tom Daschle), their spouses, and other government representatives, including HUD Secretary Mel Martinez. The senators and their spouses raised the walls and worked the full day, and throughout the spring, the senators returned periodically to see the project to completion. In the first week of June 2001, during National Homeownership Week, the two houses were dedicated. The focus of this partnership between HFHI and the U.S. Senate was to strengthen neighborhoods and communities by bringing the senators together with local Habitat affiliates, sponsors, volunteers, and new home owner families.

In addition to the senators and their spouses, a number of housing industry leaders were present. Among the building partners for this event were Fannie Mae, Freddie Mac, the Council of Federal Home Loan Banks, the National Association of Home Builders, the National Association of Realtors, and the Mortgage Bankers Association of America.[78] Other sponsors included the Mortgage Insurance Companies of America, the Corporation for National Service, America's Community Bankers, the American Bankers Association, and the U.S. Department of Housing and Urban Development (HUD).[79]

In other settings, these senators argue over policy concerns, and it can often be difficult to find agreement. Yet in this instance, Habitat was able to reduce partisanship and put people in a setting where they could leave other arguments aside; cooperation and common ground could be forged through the act of building a home for two families in need. Similarly, the groups that sponsored the event have different approaches and solutions to issues of affordable housing. However, all of these groups were able to come together to build a Habitat home. Perhaps, in a small way, this event

---

[78] Habitat for Humanity International, "The Houses the Senate Built."
[79] Ibid.

will serve as a catalyst for the senators and representatives and for other groups to bring this cooperation into other housing arenas.

Promoting Community, Homeownership, and Acceptability: Fairfax County

Habitat has established itself as an organization that promotes community and civic responsibility, and selects home owner families carefully. As a result, Habitat can sometimes provide affordable housing where others have failed. In many neighborhoods, the construction of affordable housing can be a challenging undertaking. Residents are often concerned that households living in more affordable units may negatively affect overall property values in the area or may not take care of their property. Due to Habitat's reputation and attention to detail, affiliates around the U.S. have been able to generate widespread community support for affordable housing, and do so in areas where local housing authorities or other non-profit housing advocates may not have been able to achieve common ground.

One illustration is in Fairfax County, Virginia. Since 1998, Fairfax County has had an inclusionary zoning ordinance requiring that a certain number of housing units be set aside as affordable units. This is known as the Affordable Development Unit (ADU) Ordinance. As part of this program, the Fairfax County Redevelopment and Housing Authority (FCRHA) has the exclusive right to purchase up to one-third of the affordable units in a development (in both for-sale and rental developments).[80] However, the FCRHA has faced difficulty implementing the stipulations of the ADU ordinance. In one instance of public outcry, the local Habitat affiliate was able to come into the community where FCRHA had encountered major opposition and generate partnership and support for the construction of affordable homes for low-income families.

In working to expand the number of affordable units under the ADU ordinance, the FCRHA in 1999 sought to move some of its units targeted for public subsidy from a public housing development known as The Green (today called Westglade) to designated ADUs elsewhere in the county. The FCRHA decided that a housing development known as Westbrook would need to comply with the ADU ordinance and offer units to households receiving public subsidy.[81] Westbrook consists of about eighty

---

[80] Fairfax County Redevelopment and Housing Authority, "ADU Program."
[81] The Westbrook development is located near the intersection of Route 29 and Waples Mill Road.

apartments and owner-occupied condominiums; the typical resident is a first-time home buyer. The FCRHA sought to purchase three units for rental to low-income families receiving public subsidy.[82]

When the FCRHA announced its plans, Westbrook residents had a very negative reaction. They were opposed to this purchase on the grounds that the people who would move into the affordable units would be "renter types" not suited to the community. They would not take care of their apartments, and that they would "not be like us."[83] Westbrook residents repeatedly referred to potential renters of the ADUs as "those people" and decided to publicly oppose the FCRHA in its attempts to purchase the three units. Residents marched on FCRHA meetings, vehemently expressing their views and doing all they could to halt the creation of ADUs in Westbrook.[84] The entire process had become tainted and divisive, and as a result, the FCRHA decided against the purchase.[85] The degree of public resentment was too much to handle, so the FCRHA opted to look for an alternative site.

In the meantime, the Habitat affiliate in the area, known as Habitat for Humanity of Northern Virginia (HFHNV), was looking to build affordable units. The FCRHA owned a 1.6-acre piece of property zoned for affordable housing. In 2000 it sold this land to the Northern Virginia Habitat affiliate for $450,000, so that Habitat could build across the street from the Westbrook housing development. Eighteen affordable townhouses will be built on the site by 2003.[86] On February 10, 2001, the ground breaking ceremony was held. A diverse group of more than 100 civic leaders, project sponsors, prospective volunteers, and Fairfax County housing officials attended.[87] Many of those who attended were Westbrook residents who, in this case, were very supportive of Habitat building affordable units in the area.

Habitat was able to bring the community together in partnership and consensus because of its home owner selection process and because the lower-income households were to be home owners, not renters. The Westbrook residents were able to find common ground with the new Habitat home owners because they too would be owners with similar commit-

---

[82] Conrad Egan, interviewed by Amy E. Rowe, 21 June 2001.
[83] Ibid.
[84] Ibid.
[85] Ibid.
[86] Habitat for Humanity of Northern Virginia, "Presentations and Dedications: HFHNV Breaks Ground at Stevenson Street."
[87] Ibid.

ments to the community and to maintaining their property. However, the families selected by the Habitat affiliate to move into the new townhouses essentially had the same incomes as the families who would have moved into the Westbrook ADUs. The low-income households in Fairfax County are primarily working families who, due to very high home prices and rental rates, struggle to find adequate housing.[88] Conrad Egan, chairman of the FCRHA, suggests that it is primarily working families who use public subsidies for renting in the area, and these same families are likely to be chosen by the Northern Virginia Habitat affiliate to become Habitat home owners.[89] Thus, Westbrook residents are living with and welcoming the same people they had previously prevented from moving into the area.

In this case, Habitat was able to gain public acceptance when the housing authority was not. It shows Habitat's ability to bring people together in the construction of affordable housing — affordable housing that will provide home ownership. Habitat is known for the values it generates; it not only builds homes, but also builds character, responsibility, and community values and teaches people how to finance and maintain their homes. The FCRHA was pleased because affordable units were being built, and the Westbrook community members were pleased because they felt the new families would be an asset to the neighborhood.

Habitat Brings a Good Face: Working With the Housing Community in Phoenix

Habitat has been able to create partnerships and support housing in community disputes. As evidenced in the Fairfax County example, Habitat can bring a positive face to many challenging situations because of its reputation. Habitat can also function as a partner in complex policy situations. One example of this is the stance that the Habitat affiliate in Phoenix, Arizona, took in regards to antigrowth legislation.

In 1998 Arizona passed the Growing Smarter Act, a law designed to promote "smart growth" as the state develops at a rapid pace. In 2000 a coalition of environmental advocates and community groups known as Citizens for Growth Management drafted a proposal, Proposition 202, to

---

[88] Note: The median home price in Fairfax County is more than $200,000. Source: Habitat for Humanity of Northern Virginia. "Presentations and Dedications: HFHNV Breaks Ground at Stevenson Street."

[89] Conrad Egan, interviewed by Amy E. Rowe, 21 June 2001.

be included on the November 2000 ballot. Their efforts were referred to as the Citizens for Growth Management Initiative (CGMI), or as the Sierra Club Initiative because of the Sierra Club's prominent involvement in drafting and supporting Proposition 202. The proposition required each municipality to have an enforceable growth management plan by 2003. The plan would include urban growth boundaries and would limit development and new city services outside of these boundaries. As a result, developers would have to bear the costs associated with all-new developments, such as water supply.

The proposition caused considerable community reaction and, as in the wetlands case discussed in Chapter 10, the environmental, antidevelopment side and the housing side were unable to find common ground. From the perspective of CGMI members, open space should be protected at all cost and, as the Sierra Club notes, developers ought to pay for transit, roads, utilities, and emergency services linked to housing developments.[90] To housing companies, developers, and mortgage lenders, the stipulations outlined in Proposition 202 were so stringent that they amounted to a no-growth initiative. Indeed, one of the provisions would have put a two-year moratorium on new construction in municipalities of more than 2,500 people.[91] The lines were drawn, and as Phoenix City Councilman Phil Gordon pointed out, the debate made it clear that there was not a community consensus on the issue of growth in Arizona.[92]

Amid growing controversy in the fall of 2000, the Phoenix Habitat affiliate (Habitat for Humanity: Valley of the Sun) entered the public debate by joining with other housing groups in opposing Proposition 202. It did so because strict growth management in the state would negatively affect middle- and lower-income households by escalating property values and rental rates, making it even harder for poorer households to become home owners. This has been the pattern in other parts of the country where anti-growth measures have been implemented. As one observer of these debates, John K. Carlisle wrote: "The growing anti-sprawl crusade imperils the significant social and economic gains made by minorities in recent years. Wherever anti-sprawl policies have been aggressively implemented, the cost of housing has soared and diminished low- to moderate-income families' access to affordable housing."[93] Along the same lines,

---

[90] Sierra Club, "Bulldozing Our Vanishing Sonoran Desert."
[91] Mortgage Bankers Association of America, "Proposition 202 — A No-Growth Initiative."
[92] Gordon, "Councilman Phil Gordon's Letter to the Editor, Nov. 8, 2000."
[93] Carlisle, "Suburban Snob Politics Fuels 'Smart Growth' Land-Use Movement."

Robert J. Framnciosi notes that growth control policies often produce "highly attractive and environmentally friendly places where only the affluent can afford to live."[94] After reviewing Proposition 202, the mayor of Tuscon, Robert Walkup, wrote: "Its passage will unfairly place the burden and risk of upscale environmental protection on Tuscons's low- and middle-income working families. Proposition 202 will make it even more difficult for tens of thousands of Tuscon families to own their own homes and build strong neighborhoods."[95]

Habitat did not want to support legislation that would be a detriment to the very population it serves and that would make it very challenging to construct affordable housing. Habitat therefore stood alongside other businesses and homebuilding organizations to publicly denounce Proposition 202. Habitat's presence in the mix helped provide an alternative voice and diversity among the opponents and showed that it was not just wealthy developers wanting to avoid the cost burdens of Proposition 202 who were opposed. Habitat and other groups against Proposition 202 suggested that the state should pursue a different environmental protection plan, one that would not severely polarize constituents and would take into consideration the effects of antisprawl measures on lower-income households.

Proposition 202 was defeated. Habitat was able to provide an alternative voice and help fellow home building and housing organizations. Habitat can often promote housing issues from a different perspective, and the integrity and visible success of the organization adds credibility to the pro-housing position.

HABITAT: ACHIEVING COMMON GROUND

During fiscal 2000 (for Habitat, from July 1, 1999, to June 30, 2000), Habitat constructed 17, 208 homes worldwide, the most productive twelve-month period in its history, and a 25% increase in construction from the previous fiscal year.[96] This growth continues, with Habitat building at a pace to complete its 200,000th home in 2005. Clearly, Habitat is doing something right. It is one of the most highly recognized nonprofit organizations in the United States. As a home building organization, it is

---

[94] Franciosi, "Of Regressions and Regressivity: What Growth Controls Do to Housing Prices."
[95] Walkup, "I Have Reviewed Proposition 202."
[96] Habitat for Humanity International, *Annual Report 2000,* 1.

unique in its ability to draw people together. Seven factors seem particularly important as Habitat generates a "win-win" for everyone.

Creating a tangible product. Habitat is centered around action and the creation of new, safe, adequate homes. Volunteers and funders are not simply giving money or discussing ideas — they are creating a home, and they see the results of their efforts as they work with the new home owner family. As Habitat founder Millard Fuller comments, "Volunteers can hug the new home owner family and take a photograph of the house."[97] People latch on to the Habitat model precisely because they can see, touch, and feel the results of their efforts. Fuller's Theology of the Hammer concept emphasizes that when individuals come together, pick up a hammer, and create a house alongside the family that will inhabit it, disagreements can be left aside. Fuller refers to Habitat's methodology as "radical common sense." The creation of a home is something everyone can agree upon; it is simply the right thing to do.[98] In a sense, Habitat is selling a product for everyone. A house is literally sold to the Habitat family, yet everyone gains a "product" in the sense that volunteers gain new building skills, foster teamwork, form new friendships, and feel good about doing public service and good work for the community.

Addressing a basic human Need and fulfilling the American Dream. Habitat draws individuals and organizations together because it addresses a very essential, basic concern — decent, affordable, safe shelter. Habitat relies on the notion that people should help each other fulfill basic life standards and work to eliminate poverty housing as a matter of conscience.

Equal access to shelter, and ownership in particular, is an important component of the American Dream. The fact that HFHI has emphasized home-ownership has helped the organization gain legitimacy, and many organizations support its activities. HFHI helps lower-income households get a foothold in the ownership market. Families (and their children) are then often able to continue moving upward in the housing market.

Allowing for flexibility within the Habitat framework. HFHI is decentralized; affiliates are all independent nonprofit organizations. HFHI is held together by key principles, yet it allows for flexibility and diverse approaches among its affiliates. Affiliates are able to determine local needs and define their methods of operation in terms of fund-raising, publicity, and family selection, yet they simultaneously benefit from the well-

---

[97] Millard Fuller, interviewed by author and Amy E. Rowe, 16 May 2001.
[98] Ibid.

respected brand name that HFHI has created. A Harvard Business School case study on multisite nonprofits revealed how effectively HFHI has marketed its method and its name: "Many of [the Habitat affiliates] told us that without the pull of the Habitat name, they would be unable to raise the amount of funds and other donations to sustain their work."[99] Affiliates continue to be created around the United States precisely because they can behave as local housing organizations, while benefiting from their association with HFHI.

Capacity to incorporate other issues. Habitat's message is about meeting the human need for shelter. It is about minimum standards and a faith-based obligation to meet these standards. The key is that individuals can funnel their own concerns and ways of doing things into the Habitat model; anyone can bring their approach to the table. For example, Habitat has sponsored all-women's builds and homes built entirely by people with disabilities, and it has a "green team" that studies how Habitat homes can be built in more energy-efficient ways. In each of these examples, specific issues are brought to the forefront while a house is being built for a low-income family. Habitat has proven that it can adapt to different settings and incorporate a range of issues while continuing to meet its primary goal of providing shelter for those in need. Habitat's willingness and ability to incorporate a variety of issues into its activities has proven to be an important technique for fostering common ground.

Coalition building. Habitat builds coalitions around housing issues by providing important outcomes for everyone involved. If a youth group or employees from a local business volunteer together they will promote unity and team-building within their group as well as provide an important service for the family who will receive the Habitat home. Jerome Bagget relates participants' response to one Habitat project: "Volunteers from sponsoring corporations spoke of the public-relations and team-building gains that were derived from the experience, both of which could redound in future profits. Church groups, in somewhat parallel fashion, marveled about their heightened sense of fellowship. Individuals listed a number of considerations, including. . . . desire to challenge themselves, a hankering to acquire carpentry and home-maintenance skills, a longing for adventure and, of course, their commitment to serve and care for others."[100]

When people come together to build a Habitat home, the cooperation can be carried over into other arenas. Also, HFHI values partnership with

---

[99] Grossman and Rangan, "Managing Multi-Site Nonprofits," 18.
[100] Bagget, *Habitat for Humanity: Building Private Homes, Building Public Religion,* 38.

all peoples and emphasizes minority representation. In a review of local affiliate boards and general affiliate membership, Austin and Woolever confirm that Habitat affiliates are "fairly representative of the larger community in which they function."[101]

Volunteering for the common good. One of the most impressive aspects of Habitat's methodology is the organization's ability to recruit volunteers and to rely on volunteer labor. Habitat has been successful in extending homeownership opportunities to lower-income families in part because affiliates keep designs simple, supply costs are low (largely through reduced prices and donations), and labor is free because nearly all workers are volunteers. The notion of volunteering, of giving one's time for a greater cause, is an important theme in American public and religious life. It is also a means for wealthier people to extend their services and resources to others. By specifically working through religious groups, Habitat taps preexisting volunteer networks. Also, Habitat projects benefit both the volunteer and the Habitat home owner. It is volunteering with people, not for people; it is helping people help themselves rather than providing a handout.

Public figures and media attention. Habitat's ability to bring people together is due in part to its famous participants and its media attention. Habitat can bring a good face to negotiations precisely because its leaders have worked hard to publicize its good work. Habitat's founder, Millard Fuller, has been instrumental in making Habitat a household name, and his drive continues to push HFHI in new directions. In some sense, Habitat is like a family-owned business. Fuller can recall the first activities of the organization, knows which tactics have worked best, and he has personally created many of the relationships with influential organizations that have bolstered HFHI.

In the early 1980s, Fuller gained the support of former President Jimmy Carter, and Carter became the public face of HFHI. Carter and his wife, Rosalyn, have been active participants, working hard in their home state of Georgia (Carter grew up not far from Koinonia Farm) and traveling around the United States and abroad to spread the Habitat message. In lending his support to HFHI, Carter has endorsed its tactics and frequently comments on what a personal pleasure it is to work for the organization. Carter helps to emphasize, as Fuller does, that this work can be a joy and has the potential to change everyone's values and perspective. Other major figures such as President George W. Bush, former president Bill Clinton,

---

[101] Austin and Woolever, "Voluntary Association Boards," 191.

former vice president Al Gore, former HUD secretaries Jack Kemp, Henry Cisneros, and Andrew Cuomo, former speaker of the house Newt Gingrich, and HUD Secretary Mel Martinez have all worked on Habitat homes. They may disagree in the political arena, but they all agree on Habitat as a way of building affordable housing. Endorsements by such individuals, and many more, spread Habitat's word and generate widespread approval.

The participation of these high-profile figures garners media attention. Further, local affiliates often use newspaper and TV coverage when completing and dedicating Habitat homes. But it is not just the publicity that is key; it is the message. Habitat emphasizes that it is building a community, and so the completion of a home should be a public affair. All of this helps spread Habitat's message and methodology, and in the end enables Habitat to draw people together out of concern for the basic need for decent, affordable shelter. Perhaps the lessons learned from Habitat can be applied more broadly as we work to achieve common ground in meeting the housing challenges of the twenty-first century.

PART III

Framework for the Future

Chapter 12

ACHIEVING COMMON GROUND IN THE TWENTY-FIRST CENTURY

As we look to the future of housing in the twenty-first century we face a paradox. Since the enactment of the Housing Act of 1949, the nation has seen remarkable progress. However, needs and priorities have shifted, and today common ground is more elusive. The paradox of housing policy is that housing is no longer a top issue to many in the public or in Congress, at least in part because of the success of the last fifty years in housing. Sixty-eight percent of the nation's households are homeowners, and once a person obtains their own home, the focus on housing diminishes and priorities often shift. However, housing still receives significant federal resources from both direct expenditures and tax benefits. Also, housing is a significant part of the nation's economy, with direct investment in housing construction contributing to over 4% of GDP, and all housing related investment, consumption, and spending totaling over 21% of the nation's GDP. Further, when surveyed, the American public recognizes that the lack of affordable housing is a big and growing problem for some American families. In a 2002 survey sponsored by the Fannie Mae Foundation and conducted by Peter Hart and Robert Teeter, working families identified the lack of affordable housing as a problem as big or bigger than the lack of health care.[1]

The challenge, then — given this paradox of mixed signals and mixed priorities related to housing policy — is to develop a coherent approach — a framework for housing policy in the twenty-first century. The 2002 Fannie Mae Foundation survey concluded that "given the extent to which Americans view housing as a significant problem for working families, it is not surprising that a strong majority believes that government should be involved."[2] However, housing advocates often make it

---

[1] Hart and Teeter, "Lack of Affordable Housing Rivals Health Care as a Problem for Working Families."

[2] Hart and Teeter, "Results of the Fannie Mae Foundation Affordable Housing Survey," 8.

easy for Congress or for state or local governments to do little to address the nation's housing needs because they cannot agree on how we should proceed.

If we are to achieve common ground in order to address the nation's housing challenges in the twenty-first century, two elements of discussion are essential. The first relates to the process of achieving common ground. What does it mean to achieve common ground, and is it possible? What are the principles important to reach consensus? The second element relates to the substance of national housing policy. What should be the housing policy framework for the future, and what are the building blocks that will move us forward in the twenty-first century? Both of these elements will be discussed in this concluding chapter.

ACHIEVING COMMON GROUND: CAN WE SUCCEED?

Common ground does not mean unanimous agreement. Housing policy is set within a democratic system with a variety of interests and perspectives. Unanimous agreement is rare, and it is not expected that common ground will be achieved among parties that are completely at odds. Rather, the hope is that parties that have a common interest in housing will be able to compromise and build consensus so that key housing issues can be identified, agreed upon, promoted, and implemented. It is also unrealistic to expect that housing policy will come solely from HUD or Congress. Housing policy involves an array of participants, and no one party is able to establish or even dominate it. National policy is sorted through issue by issue, and it combines numerous actions and decisions at the state, local, and national levels.

In May of 2001, the Millennial Housing Commission held a roundtable discussion in Washington, D.C., to focus on the need for federal programs to encourage and stimulate the production of low- and moderate-income housing. Eight groups were invited, including private sector builders and organizations dealing with local, state, and national government programs. All agreed that more affordable housing was essential and that some type of federal assistance was appropriate, but there were eight different opinions as to what should be done. This failure to reach agreement heightens the paradox noted above and strengthens the hand of those that would do little or nothing to address the nation's housing challenges or even seek to dismantle some of the housing programs and successes that have evolved over the years. It also heightens the importance of achieving common ground on housing issues. If all parties instrumental in providing housing could come to a place of general agreement, they would likely be able to establish and implement reasonable programs at the federal, state, and local levels, as long as the costs were not too high. However, disagreements abound, and without consensus the process is often stalled. If the housing challenges we face are to be met, they must be met within today's realities. This means those who are committed to providing affordable housing must come together more effectively to focus on solutions. Can we succeed? Yes, but only if we can more effectively achieve common ground.

Establishing and Implementing Common-Ground Approaches to Housing

What lessons can be learned from the foregoing case studies, and what general principles can be identified? The wetlands case shows that it is extremely difficult to reach agreement on some issues. The perspective of the environmental community is very different from that of the home building community. In this case, the gaps were just too broad, especially given the history of disputes among the parties. The case on raising the FHA loan limit shows that on some critical issues, people who normally agree can clearly disagree, and that such disagreement can have significant impacts. A compromise was reached through the congressional political process, but the failure to achieve common ground outside of the battleground of Congress created lingering distrust.

However, the OSHA case shows that it is possible to achieve common ground. In this situation, different perspectives were brought together even though there were several points at which agreement could easily have fallen apart. Professor John Dunlop of Harvard University was instrumental as a facilitator, holding together agreement among diverse parties and developing core OSHA standards for residential construction. The Habitat for Humanity case reinforces the notion that common ground can be achieved, demonstrating that providing affordable housing to those in need can gain widespread support. Whether at the local level or through national partnerships, Habitat has marshaled the support of diverse segments of the housing industry. Home builders work side by side with lenders, low-income-housing advocates, manufacturers of building products, and many others to help build affordable housing for working families or individuals with a willingness to work. All of this is made possible by a focused vision which a wide range of individuals and groups can hold in common, and by an execution that minimizes controversy — an important prescription for achieving common ground.

General Principles for Achieving Common Ground

Recognizing that these four cases are very different, in terms of both subject and process, it is still possible to identify common themes. What lessons can be gleaned as we seek to achieve common ground in the twenty-first century? Nine principles seem particularly important as we look to the future.

1. A GOOD IDEA

To achieve common ground, the program or policy must be a "good idea" where people can share a vision that is focused enough to withstand close scrutiny over time and to receive at least some bipartisan support. Since housing is not a top national issue, it is unlikely that we will see sweeping reform or large-scale public policy changes at the federal level. More likely, changes occur at the margin, and often through the appropriations process — for example, the increase in the FHA loan limit. If a program or policy is to be implemented, it must be a solid proposal that can stand the test of time and be sold to a bipartisan group. The 1949 Housing Act set in motion a series of sweeping changes at the national level: urban renewal, changes in public housing, new and revised subsidized housing programs, an expansion of Fannie Mae, the creation of Freddie Mac, and the list goes on. Now, however, housing programs must usually be dealt with one at a time, and on a smaller scale. Granted, when a crisis occurs, like the savings and loan debacle, sweeping legislation is enacted. But generally, solutions and legislation at the national level will occur on a smaller scale.

The OSHA case is a good illustration of this principle. Establishing core safety standards for single-family residential construction that differed from those for high-rise construction made sense to a number of people, and the issue was specific enough to mobilize a range of supporters. It was a good idea and the supporters could share a common vision; it therefore gained the momentum it needed to be propelled through the maze of congressional action and administrative implementation.

Raising the FHA loan limit was also a very specific issue, and although not all of the participants could agree, the issue was focused enough that — with the right political circumstances — congressional action was possible. The idea was considered to be a good one among enough people to achieve some bipartisan support and to form a political coalition strong enough to pass an increase in the loan limit. Because the issue related to the budget and actually raised revenue, it could pass as a part of the appropriations process. Agreement would have been impossible through the housing authorization process.

Habitat for Humanity also demonstrates the importance of a good idea and shared vision that is focused so a range of parties can agree. This focus has made it possible for Habitat to avoid the sting of partisanship. The Habitat goal of homeownership for low- and moderate-income individuals who are willing to work hard is a clear, tangible theme. It is a good idea, and it allows diverse parties to come together to achieve the goal. The shared vision is that of a first-time owner of a Habitat house receiving the keys to their new home. In a narrow, but very real way, Habitat is an excellent illustration of achieving common ground.

2. TIME AND PERSUASION

Achieving common ground usually takes time, and a great deal of education and persuasion may be necessary for consensus to emerge. Even a case as focused as developing guidelines for safety standards for single-family home building took a number of years to reach a consensus among members of Congress, individuals in the White House, labor unions, subcontractors, and key staff in the Department of Labor and OSHA. Without time and a long-term process for education and dialogue, compromise would have been impossible. People with different perspectives want to protect their interests. If they are going to change their minds, or even consider different proposals, time to educate and inform is essential, and relevant information and analysis must be made available.

The passage of a higher FHA loan limit required dialogue over several years. Although the new limit was officially proposed in January 1998 and enacted into law in October of the same year, many of HUD's key decisions were actually made by the middle of the summer of 1997, and there had been dialogue about the loan limit throughout the 1990s. The issue was not new when it came to the forefront early in 1998. In fact, a number of the positions had already been established in advance of HUD's formal announcement.

The development of the nation's housing finance system — particularly the secondary market — also illustrates the importance of time and persuasion. Although it was clear in the early 1980s that major problems existed and that a broader-based, more resilient housing finance system was essential if the nation's housing needs were to be met, the development and implementation of new proposals took time. The President's Commission on Housing began meeting in the summer of 1981, and recommendations were not set forth until the next year. The commission concluded its work in July of 1982, but the Secondary Mortgage Market Enhancement Act (SMMEA), which implemented many of the commission's proposals, was not passed until 1984. However, by the time Congress began to consider the legislation, a number of interested parties had already reached a consensus, and passage of SMMEA was relatively uncontroversial.

3. HONEST BROKER

To achieve common ground, it is helpful to have an honest broker — a facilitator who is respected by the parties and who has the ability to bring people together. This was clearly demonstrated in the OSHA case. Without John Dunlop, who was considered an honest broker, it is unlikely that the book outlining core standards for residential construction would ever have been published. When the dialogue broke down, he was able and willing to bring the key players — the unions, the home builders, and OSHA — back together. He was also essential in facilitating dialogue at the highest levels of the Labor Department to ensure that the framework that had been agreed upon was implemented.

Looking to the future, the HUD secretary may be able to play such a role in national housing policy. The secretary obviously can participate directly in the process of developing housing policy, as Andrew Cuomo demonstrated in raising the FHA loan limit. However, depending on personality and mode of operation, the secretary, with the prestige of the office, can also play a major role in bringing people together. Secretary Henry Cisneros was able to do this. Early in his administration in 1993, Cisneros identified homeownership as an area where significant progress might be made during his tenure and where he might play a key role in bringing together people committed to homeownership. Rather than encourage a partnership outside of HUD, Cisneros convened the National Partners in Home Ownership, working closely with key staff such as FHA Commissioner Nic Retsinas and partnership director Craig Nickerson, bringing them together on a regular basis (see Chapter 2). Although the partnership did not develop a specific legislative agenda of its own, it helped coordinate homeownership activities throughout the country. The partnership established Homeownership Week, initially designated as the first week in June, during which the president of the United States, the HUD secretary, members of Congress, and others focused the nation on the importance of homeownership and the need to expand homeownership opportunities — especially for those who are outside the homeownership circle. The "homeownership gap" based on race and income was highlighted, and to the extent that federal, state, or local programs could help to narrow this gap, members of the partnership were encouraged to take action.

Did the homeownership partnership achieve common ground? From the perspective of this writer, yes, and resoundingly so. Although one cannot document a cause and effect relationship between the partnership and the significant growth in the national homeownership rate in the 1990s, the National Partners in Home Ownership helped highlight the growth, brought people together for a common cause, and gave everyone involved a sense of accomplishment and purpose beyond their own interests. It also helped to elevate the importance of homeownership in the minds of the president, the Congress, and the American public, and consequently, the HUD secretary and his lead staff were able to influence national housing policy.

In the housing field, federal commissions have often played an important role in achieving common ground. Although their role differs from that of an individual facilitator, commissions have been able to bring together a variety of people with different perspectives to identify common issues and elevate key ideas and a variety of proposals. The housing industry will not automatically unite behind a commission's recommendations, but over the years, housing commissions have provided an important framework for future action. The Kaiser Commission (The President's Commission on Urban Housing) and the Douglas Commission (The National Committee on Urban Problems) completed their work in 1968, and their recommendations resulted in housing and urban legislation. The President's Commission on Housing, in 1981 to 1982, set forth recommendations that led to significant modifications in the secondary market for housing finance and called for greater emphasis on housing vouchers rather than the production of low-income housing. These recommendations provided the framework for housing programs in the 1980s and 1990s. In 1987, the Senate created the National Housing Task Force, often called the Rouse/Maxwell Task Force because it was chaired by James W. Rouse and David O. Maxwell, both prominent in the housing field. Its report spurred the 1990 Cranston-Gonzales National Affordable Housing Act, which emphasized the role of state and local governments in affordable housing and created the HOME program, administered by HUD, to foster government-private partnerships to create affordable housing. And in 2000, Congress established the Millennial Housing Commission to examine the importance of housing, particularly affordable housing, to analyze possible methods for increasing the role of the private sector in providing affordable housing, and to review whether existing HUD programs worked in conjunction with one another to provide better housing opportunities for families, neighborhoods, and communities. The Millennial Housing Commission completed its report to Congress at the end of May 2002. A commission does not guarantee the achievement of common ground, but it can certainly help move the process forward.

4. KEEP THE RHETORIC LOW

To achieve common ground it is very helpful to keep the rhetoric as low as possible. Negotiations often generate strong emotions. If emotions run high and the rhetoric rises, the dialogue may become personal, and bipartisanship and compromise become difficult. Further, before parties are able to compromise, it may be necessary to overcome past feelings and emotions. This is often the case in partisan political debates. People speak about the need for bipartisanship and their desire to reach agreement, but as tensions mount and the political stakes rise, emotions may get the better of one party or the other, and the stakes rise to a point where it is difficult to reach agreement without "losing face" or "giving in." When this occurs, a winner or a loser is often identified, either by the press or by the people involved. One way to keep the rhetoric low is to approach a conversation with an attitude of listening first to learn. What does the other party mean? What motivates them? Listening carefully puts a person in a better position both to advocate and to compromise.

In the battle to raise the FHA loan limit, once the debate became public, people were identified as being on one side or the other. In some cases, disagreements became highly public, and emotions and rhetoric rose. In the end, what might have been perceived as a compromise became a political victory for one side and a loss for the other. The wetlands case shows this outcome even more dramatically. Because each side is so clearly staked, it is almost impossible to achieve compromise. Congress is also split on the issue — so much so that a political solution through Congress is no longer feasible. Each side can usually block the other. If one party disagrees with a decision made by the administration at the regulatory level, then the battleground often moves to the courts. The rhetoric is usually high on both sides, and it is difficult for one on the outside to know where the truth lies, or where an appropriate balance point can be found.

On the other hand, the OSHA case illustrates how the rhetoric can be kept down. When disagreements arose, it would have been easy for either side to pull away from the table and blame the other party. The National Association of Home Builders came close to doing so when it threatened to withdraw from the discussions because it felt that Congressional intent was not being followed. Fortunately, a credible third-party facilitator was able to bring everyone back to the table in a quiet, diplomatic approach. People listened before they acted. The rhetoric was allowed to cool, and an agreement was eventually achieved.

One of the basic premises of Habitat for Humanity is to concentrate on positive goals and to stay focused on the benefits of homeownership and eliminating poverty housing. This is true at the national level, where Habitat participates in coalitions toward this end, but Habitat is usually careful not to get involved in issues where the rhetoric is high and there is a risk of losing sight of the primary focus. At the local level, Habitat often succeeds because of its focus on homeownership and its good name. This is illustrated by the Habitat project in Fairfax County, Virginia, as discussed in Chapter 11. When the local housing authority proposed making affordable housing part of a particular housing project, the neighborhood was immediately up in arms. The proposed scatter-site public housing became too controversial, so the county sold the land to Habitat for Humanity. Because the neighbors felt positively about Habitat and believed in its cause of homeownership, they welcomed the Habitat project. Habitat is often viewed as creating value by helping people to help themselves, and it is therefore able to keep the rhetoric down and avoid the "not in my backyard" debate that often occurs at the local level.

5. INCENTIVES

In an effort to craft a situation in which both sides feel that they have won, incentives are often helpful. Incentives proved to be extremely valuable in the effort to provide separate standards for single-family residential housing in the OSHA case. The existence of $2 million of potential funding for training workers was essential to keeping the AFL-CIO involved in the process. It was also an important incentive for OSHA to keep the project moving forward. From OSHA's perspective, the $2 million appropriated by Congress, would be lost if the project did not proceed. Although the money alone could not have persuaded the parties to agree, it was an important carrot that kept everyone at the negotiating table.

In the case of raising the FHA loan limit, the incentives were clear for one side: home owners, lenders, home builders, and realtors would benefit if the limit was raised to allow greater participation in FHA loans, especially by first-time home buyers in high-cost areas or in areas where the floor for FHA loans was too low. However, there were few incentives for the opponents. Fannie Mae and the private mortgage insurers viewed a higher limit as competition, and therefore as a threat to their livelihood. However, this lack of incentives for the opponents was offset by an important incentive for members of Congress: raising the FHA loan limit created revenues that could be used to finance other government appropriations needs. To Senator Kit Bond and Congressman Jerry Lewis, the chairmen of their respective Senate and House HUD/VA Appropriations Subcommittees, this was an important motivation.

6. MARKET REALITIES

Common ground must be based on a clear understanding of market realities if success is to be achieved over the long term. This principle is tied to the first principle, the importance of having a good idea. A program or policy is only good if it can work in the marketplace. This was true for the OSHA standard for residential construction. Identifying the differences between high-rise construction and single-family construction not only made sense conceptually, but it could also be implemented by developing a core standard for the residential environment. Different sets of fall protection requirements for workers on single-family homes and workers on high-rise complexes made sense to members of Congress and could be implemented within the market realities of the residential workplace.

"Smart growth" must also be based on market realities. In today's environment, much discussion centers around a definition of smart growth and how it can be implemented. The term is used by both those who would stop development and advocates for greater development. Who can be against "smart" growth? Who can be against livable communities? However, specific proposals must be put to the test of market realities. Bringing residential housing back to the urban core has strong, widespread support. It brings housing closer to transportation and to jobs, often helps stimulate the revitalization of downtown areas, and increases vitality during the day as well as the evening. However, if market realities do not support urban housing, then efforts to build housing in the downtown will fail. Placing market housing in a neighborhood where the economics do not support housing growth and where market values are still deteriorating may lead to frustration for residents when they buy a house only to see its value drop. In turn, if community leaders and developers encourage housing where the demand is low, it will lead to frustration as well as unfilled promises at a high cost.

The same kinds of realities apply to suburban development. City planners may want to direct housing toward the inner city and to transportation corridors, but in the end, consumers have their own desires in mind when they decide where to live and what kind of house to own. The American Dream, for many, is still the single-family house with a yard, detached from other houses. Some people may never be satisfied until they achieve this dream, even if it means living farther out in the suburbs — thus suburban sprawl. In turn, a home builder will naturally try to build where there is demand in order to earn a living and to make a profit. Attempts to stop such growth through onerous growth controls only distort the market. Existing homes rise in value, making them unaffordable for many who do not already own a house. If demand exists and growth controls limit development in certain areas, home buyers and builders are forced to seek a location to build outside these areas, and therefore create even greater sprawl. Since planning and local growth controls are usually implemented one community at a time, regional planning is complex. Further, all wisdom does not reside with a regional planning authority. Smart growth can be positive, but it must be based on a clear understanding of market realities.

7. HUMAN DYNAMICS AND PERSONALITIES

Efforts to achieve common ground must be sensitive to human dynamics and to the personalities of the key participants. It is often difficult to separate the participants from the issues. Each person at the negotiating table brings not only the interests of his party, but his personal style, which may determine his ability to work toward compromise. HUD Secretary Andrew Cuomo and Fannie Mae Chairman Jim Johnson were both dynamic leaders with track records of success. As the conflict on FHA loans approached, it was difficult for either person to step back, because both had strong personalities and were vested in what they were trying to accomplish.

An individual's strengths are oftentimes closely related to their weaknesses. A strong leader may provide dynamic direction, but it may also make compromise more difficult. When people become personally involved, the stakes rise and the ability to compromise decreases. The presence of a facilitator or third-party negotiator often helps to overcome these challenges, but only if people are ultimately willing to negotiate and compromise.

8. TOUGH STANDS CAN BE OK — BUT NOT WITHOUT COMPROMISE

Achieving common ground does not mean that interested parties cannot take tough stands, but in the end, people must be willing to deal in good faith, and at some point there must be a willingness to compromise. The

OSHA case is probably the best illustration of this principle. Although a separate standard for residential construction received interest within the Clinton administration, it never would have come into being without congressional action in the fiscal 1997 labor appropriations bill. This legislation provided the guidance the project needed to get started and to keep moving when the dialogue faltered. When the efforts to implement the congressional mandate began to disintegrate, the NAHB took a hard stand that the congressional intent, as outlined in the legislation, was not negotiable. NAHB was backed by Congressman Stenny Hoyer (D-Maryland); however, NAHB took its position with an eye to compromise. Although NAHB sent a letter to the Labor Department indicating that it would withdraw from the efforts if the congressional focus was not maintained, at the same time, private, informal discussions were underway through John Dunlop to continue the project around the framework of compromise originally discussed by OSHA, the AFL-CIO, and NAHB. In this case, more flexible, informal negotiations kept the project moving forward in the face of a tough stand.

The wetlands case also illustrates the point, but to the other extreme. In the late 1990s, the Army Corps of Engineers undertook an examination of the nationwide wetlands permit program. In response to the Corps' action, the National Resources Defense Council (NRDC) sued the Corps of Engineers. NAHB asked to be a codefendant with the Corps. In the negotiations, the Corps worked privately with NRDC to find a compromise; and NAHB felt excluded from those discussions. When, as a part of the lawsuit, NRDC, NAHB, and the Corps were brought together to see if a negotiated settlement could take place, the Corps presented a solution that was significantly different from what NAHB felt had been discussed at the bargaining table. The result was that all sides took tough stands, and compromise was impossible. Further, NAHB, believing that the negotiations had been done in bad faith, filed a lawsuit against the Corps.

The case on raising the FHA loan limits further illustrates the pros and cons of taking a strong stand. Fairly early in the loan limit debate, it appears, HUD Secretary Andrew Cuomo and Fannie Mae Chairman Jim Johnson sat down to discuss the issue. At that point, it seemed that the secretary was willing to compromise, but Johnson thought it was unlikely that Congress would pass an increase in the loan limit. Based on their respective assessments of the political realities, a compromise was not reached until Congress forged one through the political process. If an agreement had been negotiated earlier, it is conceivable that some of the hard feelings that resulted from the debate could have been avoided. Perhaps the lesson learned is that a tough stand might be appropriate as part of an overall negotiating strategy, but in the interest of achieving common ground among friends of varying interests, it may be best to couple such a stand with an ongoing willingness to discuss and negotiate the issues at hand.

9. STRIVE TO FIND A WIN-WIN, OR A COMPROMISE THAT IS BETTER THAN OTHER REALISTIC ALTERNATIVES

Strive to find a win-win, or if a true win-win is not possible, a compromise that is better for each party than other realistic alternatives. The ideal in the art of achieving common ground is to find a compromise that benefits all parties — a true win-win. In the OSHA case, the eventual solution was positive for all the major participants — although none of the parties achieved everything they might have hoped for at the outset of the process. With many Habitat for Humanity projects, the parties come to the table with a common purpose, and a true win-win is straightforward — people who otherwise would not be able to qualify for a house obtain an affordable, quality home, and Habitat and those involved achieve public support and positive publicity. However, it may be difficult to achieve a true win-win in every circumstance, and finding common ground is often elusive. The wetlands debate is a prime illustration of this reality. Regulatory or legislative actions are described by both sides in battle terms — wins or losses.

If common ground is to be achieved among friends in the housing area, it will be necessary for all parties to compromise at times and to seek solutions that may not be the best for them, but are better than other realistic alternatives. (Realistic alternatives include actions parties can take to satisfy their interests absent consent from other parties in the negotiation.) With that perspective, perhaps some of the rhetoric and the tension among friends could have been avoided in the FHA loan limit case. The effort to achieve such a compromise is referred to by some as "principled negotiation."

The primary creators and proponents of the principled negotiation approach are Roger Fisher, William Ury, and their colleagues at the Harvard program on negotiation.[3] Principled negotiation, then, is a methodology to try to help two parties, or even numerous parties, reach a negotiated agreement that is good for all sides. Charles Field, a major proponent of the application of this approach to affordable housing, suggests, "Principled negotiation offers a practical and conceptually useful approach to problem solving. . . . This approach to negotiation has been widely applied to

---

[3] See Fisher and Brown, *Getting Together*; Fisher and Ury, *Getting to Yes*, Ury. *Getting Past No.*

conflicts ranging from business disagreements to environmental land disputes. It has been applied only on a limited basis to housing and community disputes."[4] Principled negotiation relies on a specific conceptual framework that has seven elements: interest, options, standards of legitimacy, communication, relationships, commitment, and alternatives. At the outset of the negotiation, the various parties agree to make explicit, to the extent possible, their *interests* in the negotiation. Based on these interests, the parties develop a range of possible *options* for consideration and *standards of legitimacy* that they can agree upon to try to fairly evaluate the various options. Open and honest *communication* is key in discussing and reviewing the options, and the parties must develop workable *relationships* if they are going to reach agreement. As the participants in a negotiated settlement work together, they may reach a *commitment* or agreement among themselves, or they may pursue *alternatives* outside the negotiation. The intent, of course, is to find an agreement within the negotiation that is good for all sides, and that is better for all sides than what they could have achieved if they went outside the negotiation. However, for such an effort to succeed, the parties must be realistic about their alternatives beyond a negotiated settlement. If they have unrealistic expectations about what they can achieve outside of a specific negotiation, they are obviously not going to stay in the negotiation, because they feel that they can do better otherwise. But, if an agreement really is better than the outside alternatives, then people are able to negotiate an agreement without "giving in."[5]

These principles are similar to those for achieving common ground outlined earlier. However, principled negotiation draws on a more structured conceptual framework to provide the parameters for the parties involved in the negotiation. When it is possible to utilize such a structure, it can be a powerful tool in achieving common ground on housing policy objectives. However, it is not a panacea, and, as Field notes, it does not guarantee an agreement.[6] It can provide a framework for bringing parties together to help them understand and discuss issues. As people come to fully understand their own interests, as well as the interests of others, the potential for compromise grows. Sometimes it is even possible for parties to look for actions which they can take together that will help satisfy their respective interests. Further, much of principled negotiation and achieving common

---

[4] Field, "Building Consensus for Affordable Housing," 821.

[5] Fischer, Ury and Patton's book on this topic is entitled: *Getting to Yes: Negotiating Agreement Without Giving In,* and they outline in detail the seven elements of principled negotiation.

[6] Ibid., 816.

ground is common sense: trying to reach a solution that is best for everyone. However, the case studies demonstrate that the practical application of principled negotiation, or trying to achieve a win-win, is often complex. In some cases, the interactions are such that the appropriate setting for compromise, let alone a negotiated settlement, never materializes. In the heat of a policy debate, opposite parties are usually not inclined to negotiate their best alternative compared to other realistic options. The goal is usually to win outright, and the potential of high costs is often ignored. If people working together in the housing industry are willing to step back, even slightly, from their own interests, perhaps it will be possible to accomplish more, to reach a compromise that is better for everyone than the alternatives.

FRAMEWORK FOR THE FUTURE

With the passage of the Housing Act of 1949, the nation declared that every American should have a "decent home and suitable living environment." As we look to the future, the goal should be similar: every American should have the opportunity to live in a decent and affordable home in a suitable, safe environment. However, today's housing challenges are very different from those following World War II. The key challenges, outlined in Chapter 6 include: meeting the needs of the housing have-nots and working families; meeting the housing needs of a growing population; overcoming the complacency of our own success; overcoming regulatory barriers that delay and add cost to housing; dealing with the challenges of growth and the environment; and achieving common ground. As we strive to address these challenges, ten building blocks for housing policy have been identified: homeownership; the production and preservation of affordable rental housing; a focus on the housing "have-nots" and working families; a strong housing finance system; a tax system to support housing; removing the barriers to building and remodeling affordable housing; strong state and local leadership and the continued devolution of responsibility to the state and local levels; a strong supporting and coordinating role at the federal level; harnessing the strength of the private sector by encouraging creativity, public-private partnership, and a focus on community; and smart growth based on market realities.

These ten building blocks provide a framework for housing policy in the twenty-first century. Although some specific ideas and approaches are mentioned as illustrations within the various building blocks, the book intentionally does not outline a series of specific programs to be implemented. Rather, the purpose is to highlight these ten areas as a framework for the nation's housing policy around which specific legislative and regulatory programs can be developed, based on the consensus of key parties, members of Congress, and the administration. Some of the ideas set forth are from the findings of the Millennial Housing Commission, which reported to Congress at the end of May 2002. Since this author served as an active member of that commission, it is only natural that there is a clear tie between some of the ideas in this book and the commission report. Still, the purpose of this concluding chapter is not to focus on specific programs, but to provide a framework for discussion to build a consensus on specific legislation, regulation, and action in the marketplace. This framework will only succeed if it is implemented within the context of an effort to achieve common ground, and hopefully the lessons learned from the four case studies will motivate the participants to this end. If we are to address the challenges we face, it will require compromise, consensus, and coordinated effort.

I. Homeownership

Homeownership has been a key part of the nation's housing strategy over the last fifty years. Strong support for homeownership should continue as a primary element of ongoing efforts to address housing needs. The public supports homeownership, both as a lifestyle that fosters societal and family priorities and as a housing policy strategy. Chapter 2 highlights the rise of homeownership over the last fifty years and documents the benefits of homeownership to family and society. Homeownership is more than housing; it helps create better education outcomes for the children who live in owned homes, encourages economic opportunity, and fosters political stability within a community. Chapter 2 also sets forth possible strategies to strengthen homeownership. The mortgage interest deduction is a primary support for homeownership, although the benefits are greater for those who are in the middle- and upper-income categories. A strong housing finance system is also essential to homeownership, including efforts to lower down payments, reduce monthly costs, and expand the number of people who qualify for a mortgage.

One of the greatest homeownership challenges is the homeownership gap between white Americans and the nation's minority population. For example, the homeownership rate for white Americans is more than 25% higher than that for Hispanic and African American households. The mortgage interest deduction provides some incentive for minorities, but the primary benefits go to middle- and upper-income households. To expand minority homeownership, special focus is needed to lower down payments, decrease monthly payments, and expand the number of people who qualify for a mortgage. In his 2000 campaign, President George W. Bush proposed a homeownership tax credit. In his State of the Union address on January 29, 2002, he called for "broader homeownership, especially among minorities."[7] And on June 17, 2002, President George W. Bush announced "America's Homeownership Challenge" to increase minority homeowners by at least 5.5 million before the end of the decade. He also expressed his support for a new Single Family Affordable Housing Tax Credit to provide approximately $2.4 billion over five years to encourage the production of 200,000 affordable homes for low- and moderate-income homeowners.

The Millennial Housing Commission also recommended that a new homeownership tax credit be established and administered by the states, modeled on the success of the low-income housing tax credit.[8] States would be able to use this flexible credit under a qualified allocation plan for two related purposes. First, in census tracks where the cost to build or rehabilitate a home is greater than the appraised value of the home, states could use the credit to offset for developers the difference between the cost of production and the fair market value of the property, up to 50% of the total development cost. Used in this manner, the credit would help support community development as well as homeownership. Second, the states could allocate the credit to lenders in an effort to provide lower-cost mortgages to qualified buyers. The purpose of the homeownership tax credit in both cases would be to extend the benefits of homeownership to low-income households and to make homeownership available in communities where these people choose to live.

Continued incentives and strategies for increasing homeownership — especially for minorities and low- to moderate-income families — are an important building block in the nation's housing policy.

2. The Production and Preservation of Affordable Rental Housing

Housing policy in the twenty-first century must also focus on the production and preservation of affordable rental housing for both those who

---

[7] President George W. Bush. State of the Union Address, House of Representatives, Washington, D.C., 29 January 2002.

[8] Millennial Housing Commission, Final Report, 29–31.

are priced out of the homeownership circle and those who choose not to own and prefer to rent. Affordability is the single greatest challenge: one in eight households report spending more than half of their income on housing, and hundreds of thousands of Americans go homeless on any given night. Spending more than 30% of income on housing is generally considered to be a moderate cost burden; more than 50% is considered to be a severe cost burden. By these definitions, according to the Millennial Housing Commission, 13.4 million American renter households and 14.5 million owner households bear moderate to severe housing cost burdens.[9] Housing affordability problems are especially severe for those who have extremely low incomes (ELI) where they earn less than 30% of the local area median income and for those with very low income (VLI) between 30% and 50% of the median income. (Low-income households are considered to be between 50% and 80% of the median income, and moderate-income households are between 80% and 120% of median income.)

The nation's 8.5 million extremely-low-income (ELI) renter households constitute one-quarter of its 34 million rental households.[10] The issue is not just affordability, though; there is also a severe supply problem. Only 6.7 million housing units are affordable to ELI rental households, a shortage of 1.8 million units.[11] Supply problems, however, are not limited to those with extremely low incomes. Between 1985 and 1999, the number of units affordable to people earning between 60% and 120% of area median income decreased sharply, with a loss of nearly 1 million units affordable to those earning 60% to 80% of median income and nearly 1.5 million units affordable to those earning 80% to 100% of median income.[12] With the situation deteriorating, and with very little production of new affordable housing stock, there is a strong need to both preserve the existing stock and increase the supply.

To preserve the existing housing stock, special attention should be paid to public and subsidized housing. Public housing projects throughout the country are a valuable resource for the future and should be maintained and in some cases converted to mixed-income residential developments. Further, preserving the stock of subsidized rental housing should be a central focus of our federal housing policy in the twenty-first century, with the goal being to achieve the long-term sustainability of as many of these projects as possible. One tool that appears essential to maintaining this ex-

[9] Ibid., 15.
[10] Ibid., 17.
[11] Ibid., 17.
[12] Ibid., Figure 7,19.

isting housing stock is some type of "exit tax relief" that will allow owners of existing subsidized units to avoid high taxes if they sell to some entity that will be committed to preserving these units as affordable housing.[13]

To produce affordable units in the future, two types of government programs are appropriate. One should focus on the production of extremely-low-income units. Several proposals already exist. One calls for a national housing trust fund to provide the resources to produce and rehabilitate low-income housing units. As of July 2002, the proposal for a National Housing Trust Fund had 189 cosponsors in the U.S. House of Representatives (H.R. 2349) and 27 cosponsors in the Senate (S. 1248). If the legislation is enacted it would establish a fund to build and preserve 1.5 million units of rental housing for the lowest income families over a ten-year period.[14] Another recommendation, set forth by the Millennial Housing Commission, suggests a direct capital subsidy or capital grant that would be used to produce new units or preserve existing units by eliminating the debt on those units.[15] The capital grant would be allocated to the portion of a mixed-income housing project that was for extremely-low-income households, so there would be no debt on those low-income units, and, in essence, rents would be calculated to cover only operating costs. The grant would be in the form of a 100% capital subsidy for construction or rehabilitation, and the extremely-low-income units would be produced as part of a mixed-income housing project.

The second type of government program should focus on moderate-income housing. The approach advocated by the Millennial Housing Commission is to remove the limits on the ability of states to issue tax exempt debt for specific multifamily properties, with a condition that eligible properties dedicate at least 20% of the units to families with incomes below 80% of the median income.[16] Such production would be under the direction of state housing finance agencies, and states would be required to establish parameters and criteria using some type of allocation plan similar to that required under the low-income tax credit program. State agencies could require that more than 20% of the units be dedicated to moderate-income housing. The clear intent of such a program would be to provide mixed-income properties. According to the proposal made by the Millennial Housing Commission, at least half of units set aside for

---

[13] Such exit tax relief is called for by the Millennial Housing Commission; Ibid., 31–36.
[14] See for example, National Low Income Housing Coalition, "The National Housing Trust Fund Campaign," *www.nhtf.org,* August, 2001.
[15] Millennial Housing Commission, Final Report, 37–39.
[16] Ibid., 39–40.

families with incomes below 80% of the median should be available to extremely-low-income households through project-based vouchers, housing choice vouchers, or capital grants.

Another way to stimulate the production of rental housing is through revitalization of the Federal Housing Administration (FHA) Multifamily program. FHA has provided an important backdrop for financing multifamily projects in the past, and its role can continue to be significant if it is given greater flexibility.[17]

The private market is also an important part of the nation's rental housing stock, providing choice for households that are highly mobile or choose to rent. As we address the nation's future needs, rental housing is a key component of a long-term balanced housing policy, through both production and preservation.

3. Creating a Focus on the Housing "Have-Nots" and Working Families

The success over the past fifty years helps to hide the disparity between the housing "haves" and the housing "have-nots." If the issue of affordable housing for those at the low end of the scale is ever to be addressed, some way must be found to create broader support. The importance of meeting the needs of low- and moderate-income households must be highlighted, especially given that many people who have their own housing are no longer concerned about others' needs. This problem deserves renewed focus, and it will require going beyond housing, since homelessness and housing for the very poor also relate to income, health, mental health, geographic location, discrimination, education, job access, and other concerns.

HUD's Worst Case Housing Needs reports, discussed in Chapter 6, point out the nation's continuing housing gap. If we are going to address the housing challenges of the twenty-first century, the "haves" of the housing community must be more concerned about the "have-nots." Perhaps those in the housing industry who are concerned about these issues can develop an approach to expand public knowledge and generate support. The private sector must become more involved. To achieve this, the barriers to building affordable housing in the inner city and elsewhere must be addressed. The challenge is daunting, especially in light of political realities. Obviously, a significant allocation of new resources would help. However, given budget realities, such an allocation is not likely. Continued

---

[17] For a proposal to revitalize the FHA see Millennial Housing Commission, Ibid., 49–54.

work on these issues one step at a time, with ideas such as those outlined in this framework is imperative. The success of the last fifty years is a great compliment to this nation's capacity to deal with housing issues. This resolve should continue now as it relates to those who have the greatest need.

4. A Strong Housing Finance System

Over the last fifty years, the housing finance system has become a strong means for supporting affordable housing (see Chapter 4). It is essential that it continue as the lifeblood and circulatory system for the housing delivery system. The United States is the primary country in the world with a 30-year fixed-rate mortgage without significant prepayment penalties. The reason is our robust housing finance system and the strong role the secondary market plays. Lenders will no longer hold long-term fixed-rate mortgages in their portfolio without significant hedging capacity, so the large majority of fixed-rate mortgages are sold in the secondary market, where they are securitized or divided into a variety of different financial instruments. For the consumer, though, the benefit is a long-term mortgage instrument with relatively low interest rates, which gives stability and a fixed cost while other sources of income and revenue rise. Further, as the equity for the home appreciates, home owners are able to take out wealth with a second mortgage and use the money for longer-term needs, such as education, home remodeling, or other consumer expenditures. Increased equity is a source of wealth and, in fact, a strong stimulant to the economy.

Housing has played a major role in the economy, especially during the recession at the end of the '90s and the beginning of the twenty-first century. While the rest of the economy faltered, housing remained amazingly strong. In the March 30 to April 5, 2002, issue of the *Economist,* the front page feature story was entitled "The Houses That Saved the World." The article asks the question, "Why has the world recession been so mild?" The answer: "Because there has been a surprising house price boom in many rich countries, most notably America."[18] In a related article entitled "Safe at Home: The New Role of Housing in the U.S. Economy," Todd Buchholz argues that housing has taken on a new role of stability. It served as a bulwark during the economic downturn of 2000 and 2001 and will likely play a major role in reviving the economy during 2002. He also

---

[18] "The Homes that Saved the World," 11. "Going Through the Roof," 65–67.

concludes that the wealth gained in housing during the 1990s, resulting from home price appreciation, has been more widely distributed than gains in the stock market and has played an important role in the overall economy.[19]

Much of the framework for this unique role for housing has come from the support and stability of the housing finance system. The robust nature of the system — especially during periods of stable and moderate interest rates — has helped to provide a steady source of capital for housing, and many of the constraints on buying a house have been decreased through lower down payments, and lower monthly payments, with a greater number of people qualifying to buy a house.

The federal role in the housing finance system has been significant in this shift. The Federal Housing Administration (FHA), the Veterans Administration (VA), and the Farmers Home Programs should continue as important support mechanisms. The Millennial Housing Commission calls for an increased role for the FHA, major reforms in the operation of its multifamily and single-family programs, and a new structure as a public corporation within HUD.[20] Whether or not such reform takes place, the full faith and credit of the federal government is a powerful tool for FHA and for housing finance, and it should continue in the years ahead.

The secondary mortgage market — strongly supported by the government-sponsored enterprises, Fannie Mae, Freddie Mac, and the Federal Home Loan Bank system — already plays a central role in the transformed housing finance system. Fannie Mae and Freddie Mac have been essential for innovations that have helped to bring down the cost of mortgages to the consumer, and the benefits of secondary market technology have empowered home buyers as never before, slashing information costs and providing greater access to mortgage credit. With the growth of the secondary market, a debate has also arisen about the role and influence of Fannie Mae and Freddie Mac. While concerns about competition and assuring minimal risks to the federal government are important, they should be considered alongside the benefits of the secondary market to the home buying public. Fannie Mae and Freddie Mac need to be safe and sound, and significant steps have already been taken to ensure their stability and financial security with the implementation of a risk-based capital rule and a variety of other commitments. However, it is very important that these institutions also be allowed to innovate, and the benefit to the consumer

[19] Buchholz, "Safe at Home: The New Role of Housing."
[20] Millennial Housing Commission, Final Report, 72–78.

should play an important role in driving and defining the debate. Freddie Mac and Fannie Mae need to operate within their charters, but they should also be allowed to continue to push the envelope in order to bring down the cost of housing and to make improved information available to the consumer.

The Federal Home Loan Bank system plays a major role as a backstop for housing lenders, and this role should continue. FHL banks can also play a larger role in such areas as establishing a secondary market for construction and development lending and in enhancing the housing finance delivery system. Competition among the GSEs is generally positive, as long as it is done with a clear sense of safety and soundness.

The nation's housing finance system has evolved over the last fifty years, and today it is, by many counts, the envy of the world. This system should be allowed to continue and flourish, and it is essential that the nation's housing policy in the twenty-first century be built around a strong housing finance framework.

5. A Tax System to Support Housing

A variety of tax incentives for housing are an essential part of the nation's housing policy. This support is crucial in the future. For example, the mortgage interest deduction is a key support for homeownership, and any change in this deduction could cause a major disruption of property values. The middle class is the primary beneficiary of the deduction, and some argue that these dollars would be best used for more direct housing programs for low- and moderate-income households. While some may agree with such an approach philosophically, it is politically naive. At some point in the future, Congress may reduce or eliminate the mortgage interest deduction, but if this were to occur, the dollars saved would be used to decrease the deficit or fund other priorities, not for low-income housing. The political will to redirect those tax expenditures to other housing needs is simply not there. In addition, a large majority of Americans have benefited from the deduction, and polls continually demonstrate constant and strong support.

Of course, the mortgage interest deduction is not the only part of the tax system that supports housing. The low-income tax credit, mortgage revenue bonds, depreciation treatment for rental housing, the property tax deduction, exclusion of capital gains, and tax credits for the rehabilitation of historic structures are all important components of the framework for housing policy in the future.

The low-income tax credit has proven to be a particularly efficient way to provide subsidies to build and rehabilitate low-income rental housing. In conjunction with other federal, state, local, and private sector efforts, it has lead to the production and rehabilitation of 50,000 to 100,000 housing units each year. This program should be strengthened in the years ahead, and other efforts to use the tax system to help stimulate the production of affordable housing should be considered. For example, as noted earlier, the Millennial Housing Commission has recommended that the limits be taken off states' ability to issue tax-exempt debt for multifamily properties, with the condition that eligible properties dedicate at least 20% of the units to families with incomes below 80% of median income.[21] Also, further improvements can be made in the low-income tax credit by, for example, updating outdated rules and regulations relating to the operation of the HOME program in conjunction with the low-income tax credit program.[22]

6. Removing the Barriers to Build and Remodel Affordable Housing

To provide affordable housing for this nation, we must do more to find effective ways to remove the barriers to build and remodel affordable housing. Building codes set a threshold on housing quality, but they can also impact and, in some cases, limit affordability. Zoning standards provide an important framework for land use, but they can also be used to exclude affordable housing and to prevent higher-density projects from going forward. Real wetlands must be protected, but if the standards are completely confusing and regulatory agencies can't agree on how they should be implemented, then such regulations will be a barrier to building affordable housing. A balance must therefore be struck on regulatory issues in order to provide quality housing, protect the environment, serve the community, and at the same time produce affordable housing. One way to do this is to require a "housing impact statement" on any federal regulation that will impact the production of affordable housing.[23] Such an approach was passed by the U.S. House of Representatives in 2000 (H.R. 3899), but it was not passed by the Senate. Yes, a housing impact statement would require additional time and effort for agencies to respond. But, just as an environmental impact statement requires a builder or developer to focus on and mitigate a project's impact on the environment, a housing impact

---

[21] Ibid., 39–40.
[22] Ibid., 62–67.
[23] Ibid., 75–76.

statement would help highlight how federal regulations will impact affordable housing.

Of course, the primary responsibility for removing the barriers to affordable housing rests at the local level. Once again, balance is key. Long-term planning to balance needed growth, transportation, affordable housing, and sensitivity to the environment is essential. Trade-offs are required, and not every building project should proceed. However, communities need to recognize that affordable housing is an essential part of community growth. *A job needs a place to sleep at night.* If the person who holds that job cannot find a reasonable place to live, he or she will have to look elsewhere for employment. Housing is more than shelter; it is an integral part of the community. Local leaders must seek to remove regulatory barriers if they desire to provide affordable housing in their community.

7. Strong State and Local Leadership and the Continued Devolution of Responsibility to the State and Local Level

All three levels of government are important in a coherent housing delivery system, and the best strategies for producing and preserving affordable housing are often a collaboration between the federal, state, and local level. However, in many cases, state and local governments are best positioned to identify the challenges that need to be met and to appropriately allocate resources and programs. All homes are built at the local level, and ultimately it is state and local governments that can work most closely with neighborhood and community leaders and the private sector to address specific community housing problems.

Just as housing is more than shelter for a family, affecting its long-term strength and stability, housing is an important element in communities and neighborhoods. The type and nature of housing within a community is an important part of its fabric. Understanding the dynamics of what is happening at the community level is essential in achieving long-term solutions to housing challenges.[24]

At the state level, it is important to recognize that housing needs do not exist in a vacuum. Rather, the broader context of jobs, commercial development, smart-growth initiatives, health delivery challenges, and a broad

---

[24] See, for example, a discussion of the dynamics of housing and neighborhood change, Rolf Goetze and Kent W. Colton, "The Dynamics of Neighborhoods, A Fresh Approach to Understanding Housing and Neighborhood Change," *Journal of the American Planning Association*, 184–194.

range of community development issues require state leadership, planning, and administration. States are therefore in a strong position to help allocate and coordinate the use of housing resources with other federal funding streams. State housing finance agencies, in many cases, have proved to be a creative means for addressing issues and concerns both statewide and locally. The low-income tax credit program requires that state housing finance agencies develop a "Qualified Allocation Plan" (QAP) as a framework for building and rehabbing low-income housing. Although not a guarantee for good planning, such a framework helps to ensure that housing is built within the community context to meet overall community needs in a location that will, among other things, hopefully complement jobs.

While state government can provide an overall state and regional framework for the allocation of resources, local governments are in a prime position to assess and address specific affordable housing needs. Local governments and housing authorities currently receive the bulk of their funding from block grants, public housing, and housing choice vouchers, and they play a key role in neighborhood revitalization, where affordable housing can be one of the most effective tools. A partnership between the state, local, and federal government is therefore essential to address housing issues. In recent years, a group of entrepreneurial mayors has emerged and made a difference in urban and housing issues. Michael Stegman, director of the Center for Community Capitalism at the University of North Carolina, Chapel Hill, has argued that it is time to "shatter the myth that American business cannot realize competitive returns by investing in emerging inner cities . . . Business can do good and do well by investing in the inner city."[25] In the same article, Stegman points to a new generation of entrepreneurial mayors who are reducing regulatory barriers, improving infrastructure, and forming joint ventures with business and community organizations in the inner city. Partnerships between the public and private sectors are essential. For example, under the coordination and leadership of HUD, the National Association of Home Builders worked with the U.S. Conference of Mayors and other public leaders, along with a range of other groups, on building homes in the inner city. Resources from the federal government are clearly required, but the leadership and responsibility for allocating and implementing those resources should continue to devolve to the state and local levels.

---

[25] Stegman, "America's Inner Cities as Emerging Markets," 52.

8. A Strong Supporting and Coordinating Role at the Federal Level

The federal government provides essential resources for housing. Federal systems that support housing and community development, such as the Community Development Block Grant and the HOME program, should be maintained as efficiently as possible. The role of the Federal Housing Administration has already been discussed as an important part of an effective housing finance delivery mechanism. Without direct federal resources, much of what has been accomplished at the local and state levels would not have been possible.

Recognizing that the growth of the direct federal budget for housing will be limited in the future, the federal government should focus where it can make the greatest difference. To provide a framework for the allocation of its resources, the federal government should set overall affordable housing goals, and establish performance measures. It should also ensure that resources are fairly and effectively delivered. To accomplish this, HUD should establish broad performance requirements for the delivery of housing assistance for both entitlement programs (such as HOME and CDBG) and competitive programs (such as Homeless Assistance and HOPE VI). HUD should specify acceptable outcomes, but it should not be too deeply involved in setting procedural requirements other than those necessary to see that objectives are met.

It is also important to maintain a cabinet-level agency to speak for housing within the federal government. HUD can serve as a catalyst and facilitator. A creative, energetic HUD secretary can frame the debate for housing policy and focus the dialogue on housing policy in the twenty-first century. The federal government does not need to be the answer to housing problems at all levels, but it can be a catalyst and a strong advocate. The HUD secretary, as the nation's chief spokesman for housing, should highlight the importance of affordable housing, recognize that housing makes a difference to individuals, families, and communities, and continually call for the removal of regulatory barriers.

9. Harness the Strengths of the Private Sector by Encouraging Creative Public-Private Partnerships and A Focus on Community

The large majority of houses that are built and remodeled are done so by the private sector. If we are ever to achieve significant increases in the production of affordable housing, it will be essential to harness the strengths of the private sector. We have already discussed unleashing the private sector by removing the barriers to build affordable housing, especially at the local and state level. Undoubtedly, this would increase the affordable housing produced and available in America. However, being realistic, it is unlikely that major changes will be made over the next few years to reduce these barriers; and in fact, many of the pressures which exist in the marketplace, such as those to stop or limit growth, would actually add to the barriers.

Nevertheless, there are a number of creative activities which are already underway which show the potential and strength of the private sector. These efforts utilize the private sector through such activities as public-private partnerships, a focus on the community, and creative leadership to bring people together.

AMERICAN CITYVISTA

American CityVista, headed by Henry Cisneros, the former HUD secretary, is a private sector initiative established to provide large scale communities of affordable housing in the inner neighborhoods of cities. It was launched August 7, 2000 as a partnership between American CityVista (ACV) where Cisneros serves as the Chairman and CEO, and KB Homes, one of the nation's largest private home builders, chaired by Bruce Karatz. Cisneros and Karatz developed the concept for a community-oriented company focused on affordable housing to work closely with a large scale high production builder in order to produce affordable housing at a scale large enough to create a small community within a larger community. The focus of ACV is to produce large scale communities of new homes in the inner city — a concept which they describe as "Villages Within The City."[26] (In this case large scale means more than 100 units in a development — large enough to create a unique environment.) American CityVista communities are intended to consist of new homes with state of the art designs, materials, technologies, floor plans, and amenities. The premise is that people want to live in central areas, but they clearly also want to live in pleasant communities. A major attempt is made to keep the house price at an affordable range. For example, in Texas communities such as San Antonio, Laredo, and Dallas, prices start from mid-$70,000 to mid-$80,000. The intent is to price homes within the range of families with average incomes at or below the area median home price.

No direct government subsidy is involved in producing the housing, and the developments are not intended to be low-income housing or upscale

---

[26] Cisneros, "Building Villages Within American Cities."

gentrification. Local communities may provide some write-downs in the form of reduced land cost or infrastructure improvements, and those benefits are passed on to the home buyer through lower prices. An effort is made to work with local and national lenders involved in providing affordable housing, and Fannie Mae has been a financing partner in a number of the American CityVista projects.

An effort is also made to link the neighborhoods which are built by American CityVista to the larger community by coordinating development plans with plans for schools, civic institutions, and churches. According to Cisneros "we push the planning dialogue beyond issues of physical design to connections we refer to as 'the architecture of community.'"[27]

By the middle of 2002, American CityVista had over 1,300 units in execution at five different projects in Texas and California. They also had plans to build at least 1,200 to 1,500 homes per year going forward. KB Homes is generally the builder on most of the sites, and they are able to help produce houses which are at or below the median home price because of the economies which come from their large scale high production techniques. Speaking of American CityVista, Cisneros talked about the importance of housing and homeownership in the community.

> Over the years of my work as Mayor of San Antonio and as Secretary of the Department of Housing and Urban Development, I saw how intensely important homeownership is for families. And the last two years I have seen from a new vantage point the pride of parents, the joy of children, and the enthusiasm of new home owners of all ages on the day they move into their homes. Weeks later when I visit the communities, I see them working in their yards, playing with their children, adding finishing touches to their decorating, or simply enjoying the evening breeze on their front porches. I have seen the broad smiles and bright eyes of people who are living in new homes, in new communities they never imagined could exist. It is at such moments that I know that our concept has transcended the realm of a normal business transaction. We have created maximum value for an achievable price and built the places where family members will experience the events which profoundly touch their lives: their homes.[28]

AMERICA'S HOMEOWNERSHIP CHALLENGE

On June 17, 2002 President George W. Bush announced a public-private sector initiative to increase the number of minority homeowners by at least 5.5 million before the end of the decade. The intent of the

---

[27] Ibid., 1.
[28] Ibid., 2.

presidential action was to help dismantle the barriers to homeownership through a variety of techniques such as downpayment assistance, increasing the supply of affordable homes, increasing support for self-help homeownership programs, simplifying the home buying process, and increasing education.

The president also issued what was referred to as "America's Homeownership Challenge" to the real estate and mortgage finance industries to join in the effort to increase the number of minority homeowners by taking concrete steps to tear down the barriers to homeownership that face minority families. Speaking in Atlanta the president said "this is not just a federal responsibility — that's why I've challenged the industry leaders all across this country to get after it for this goal, to stay focused, to make sure that we achieve a more secure America, by achieving the goal of 5.5 million new minority home owners. I call it America's Homeownership Challenge."[29]

The initiative highlights the fact that overall homeownership is at an all time high, around 68%, but there is a clear and persistent homeownership gap. (For example, in the second quarter of 2002 non-Hispanic whites had a 74.3% homeownership rate while African Americans had a 48% rate and Hispanics a 47.6% rate.) Barriers that were identified included a lack of inventory of affordable single-family housing for sale in many areas where a majority of the residents are minority families, the need for downpayment assistance, a lack of access to affordable mortgage credit, a lack of understanding of the home buying process, weak credit histories often arising from poor financial understanding (and highlighting the need for financial counseling), and language difficulties or "cultural differences."

In order to address these issues at the federal level, the president called for downpayment assistance through a proposal for $200 million annually for the American Dream Downpayment Fund to help roughly 40,000 families a year with their downpayment and closing costs, a Single Family Affordable Housing Tax Credit which would provide approximately $2.4 billion over five years to encourage the production of 200,000 affordable homes for sale to low- and moderate-income families, increasing the funding for self-help homeownership programs for organizations such as Habitat for Humanity through such programs as Sweat Equity and Volunteerism in their communities, simplifying the home buying process, and increasing education for potential home owners. Looking to the private sector, the president also announced a variety of efforts which are under way.

---

[29] Bush, President George W., The White House, June 17, 2002, <www.whitehouse.gov>.

They include substantial increases, by at least $440 billion, from the government-sponsored enterprises (Fannie Mae, Freddie Mac, and the Federal Home Loan Banks) specifically targeted towards the minority market, launching a wide variety of different local initiatives across the nation geared toward eliminating specific home owner barriers faced by minority families in those communities, raising $750 million in below market investments by 2007 which would work in collaboration with local home-ownership initiatives and be targeted to heavily minority program areas, pursuing strategic partnerships in twenty top housing markets between home builders, lenders, local officials and community leaders to develop approaches that address the local challenges to building homes for minority families living in urban centers, and establishing faith-based housing partnerships between the participants and at least 100 churches, mosques, synagogues, and other faith-based institutions.

The president's initiatives included federal programs along with a major effort to harness and encourage the private sector to be involved in providing minority home ownership. The focus was on communities and what can be done at the local and state level, but many of the resources would come from the federal government, government-sponsored enterprises, and a wide variety of public and private efforts.

HABITAT'S TWENTY-FIRST CENTURY CHALLENGE

One of the early Habitat slogans established by their founder, Millard Fuller, was "A Decent Home and a Decent Community for all God's People in Need." With this goal in mind, Habitat's 21st Century Challenge, which was discussed previously in Chapter 11, expands Habitat's effort to build affordable housing within a broader community approach. The intent is to bring communities and housing proponents together to eliminate poverty housing, and "a successful effort requires partnerships with other housing providers and interest groups. Local Habitat authorities bring the challenge to their communities and lead the effort to create an initiative."[30] The first effort to eliminate poverty housing by Habitat took place in Sumter County, Georgia, the home of Habitat for Humanity. It is referred to it as the Sumter County Initiative. This was an effort to eliminate all substandard housing in the county, and according to Habitat for Humanity, the goal has been met.

---

[30] Habitat for Humanity International. "21st Century Challenge: Eliminating Substandard Housing in the 21st Century."

The intent with the 21st Century Challenge was to take this effort forward throughout the United States and eventually to other countries. Habitat affiliates are encouraged to serve as a catalyst, working with the broad community, especially people who are concerned about affordable housing and eliminating substandard housing. The partnership obviously involves numerous groups in the private sector and certainly close coordination and partnership with local and state governments. As the Habitat 21st Century Challenge publication states: "foremost is this opportunity to engage your whole community — churches, civic clubs, businesses and individuals of every race, creed, age, and color — in a community-wide stand against substandard housing. A strong collaborative effort restores hope to a community. As residents work side by side to erase substandard housing locally, the same model of cooperation follows them into other facets of community life."[31]

These are just three illustrations of many efforts which are under way throughout the country to try to harness the private sector to build affordable housing and to encourage public-private partnerships. These kinds of efforts must be encouraged. The common ingredient is a variety of people working together to address affordable housing, utilizing a broad range of tools. A clear emphasis is placed on the private and the public sectors working together with a recognition that the private sector is essential if affordable housing needs are to be successfully addressed. There is no one prescription for success, but the clear focus is on the community and developing projects which will succeed within the local environment.

10. Smart Growth Based on Market Realities

As the nation's population increases, where will the housing be built? Chapter 6 highlights Census Bureau projections that the U.S. population could grow by 25 million to a total of 305 million people by 2010. The National Association of Home Builders projects that the number of households will grow by around 12.5 million between 2001 and 2010, which means that over a million more households will be formed in that decade than in the 1990s. Where will these people live? Given the patterns of the past decade, it is expected that much of this growth will be in the west and the south, with almost half being in three states, California, Texas, and Florida. Issues of sprawl, congestion, transportation planning, and ade-

---

[31] Habitat for Humanity International. "What is the 21st Century Challenge?" 4.

quate schools are therefore high on the agendas of many growing communities. When housing becomes a top community issue, the debate often centers on issues of growth. How do we balance the demands of a growing population and the need for affordable housing with the desire for livable communities and ongoing concerns to protect the environment?

The term "smart growth" has become the buzzword, and who can be against "smart" growth? But the issue is complex. Powerful and partisan forces exist on all sides of the debate. The government and the interest groups discussed earlier must base policy decisions on market realities, recognizing that demographic and consumer preferences drive housing demand. Efforts to fully control where people live are doomed to failure. According to a survey of home buyers cosponsored by the National Association of Home Builders (NAHB) and the National Association of Realtors (NAR), price and home size were far more important to home buyers than proximity to work or minimizing the commute. For example, given three statements to choose from, 62% of home buyers indicated that the top concern was price, 31% indicated that finding a home in the right neighborhood was the top priority, and only 7% said that being close to work and minimizing the commute was really important.[32] Nevertheless, the housing industry, including home builders, realtors, land developers, and others, must focus on working with the community to achieve solutions to real problems of traffic congestion, the quality of schools, and unsightly sprawl.

Smart growth means, among other things, preserving open space and protecting the environment, providing for compact development, revitalizing downtowns, funding infrastructure including transportation and schools, and providing realistic housing choices based on an understanding of market forces and neighborhood dynamics. One community's solutions will be very different than another's. Smart growth may mean different things to different people, but the ABCs of smart growth, based on the experiance of this author, should be: Affordability, Balance, and Choice.

CONCLUSION — A NEW PARADIGM FOR ACHIEVING COMMON GROUND

Fifty years ago, millions of young families needed homes, and large portions of the nation's housing stock were in poor condition. With government policy and strong demand as catalysts, home builders, lenders,

---

[32] National Association of Home Builders, "Smart Growth, Smart Choices."

suppliers of housing products, realtors, and other members of the housing industry came together to address the need. Millions of new homes were built, including housing for the poor through public housing and subsidized housing programs. The achievements over the last fifty years in homeownership, housing quality, and housing finance are remarkable. However, with success comes complacency, and the urgency of the past no longer exists at the federal level. Addressing the housing concerns of working families and those that are more severely disadvantaged will therefore be harder. Resources are limited, the challenges of poverty go beyond housing, and we face a paradox of mixed signals and mixed priorities related to housing policy. Further, new battles have arisen over housing, land use, smart growth, and environmental balance, and these new issues will undoubtedly be a central part of the housing debate in the years ahead.

This housing policy paradox is further highlighted by David Broder in an op-ed piece he wrote for the *Washington Post* on June 9, 2002. Writing about housing and the Millennial Housing Commission, he noted that from a national perspective housing was on the "back burner," although at the local level the urgency was still strong. "You can call it the forgotten issue — except for the fact that in almost every city I've visited this year, from Sacramento to Tallahassee to Boston, the shortage of affordable housing is close to the top of people's concerns. It's mainly in Washington, D.C. — the federal government, not the local government — that housing is a chronically neglected subject.[33]

The normal paradigm in a democracy is that everyone looks after their own interest. However, if we are going to address the realities of housing in the twenty-first century and implement the framework for the future outlined above, a renewed effort must be made to achieve common ground among the various interests involved in developing and influencing the nation's housing policies and programs. In fact, we need more than principles in achieving common ground, we need a new paradigm where the focus is on agreement. The best proposals mean nothing if they are never implemented.

In a recent meeting among industry leaders, a dialogue evolved over where we should be going in national housing policy. A variety of proposals were put forth, but they were all different. Finally, in exasperation, one of the attendees said: "If we want to keep fighting forever we can, but if we ever want to get anywhere, we need to start working together." Partisanship and the temptation of many groups to focus only on their own interests will severely limit the ability to reach agreement. A new paradigm is

---

[33] Broder, "Housing on the Back Burner," *The Washington Post,* June 9, 2002, B7.

required where parties focus on where they can agree, and efforts are made to implement starting from a common denominator of consensus. It is very unlikely that we will ever reach agreement in certain areas, such as wetlands. It is therefore essential that on other less controversial issues the various parties, outlined in Chapter 7, focus on finding areas for common agrement. For example, at the end of May 2002, the Millennial Housing Commission released its Report to Congress outlining why housing is important and setting forth a series of recommendations for the future. Perhaps this report can help provide a policy guide for the twenty-first century. Participants in the housing policy process will not agree on every item, but if a few items can be selected and implemented, it will be a first step in moving forward. The Secretary of the Department of Housing and Urban Development could also play a key role in helping to build consensus. Obviously the secretary will be a key participant in the policy process, but one of the most important things that can be done is to frame the debate by convening people to discuss the future and to develop bipartisan support for future action.

Further, the nation's housing policy will no longer be dictated from the federal level. Rather, policy will be framed incrementally through multiple specific local, state, and national policy actions and debates. As this proceeds, it will be essential to identify the new issues and realities we face and achieve common ground as we address them. Many people might agree that housing is more than bricks and mortar, and homeownership is more than shelter; but if housing advocates cannot agree among themselves on policy, it will be impossible to carry these themes forward or to reach any kind of national agreement.

The framework for the future outlined earlier is based on the realities of achieving common ground. Existing federal housing programs that support homeownership and affordable rental housing, a strong housing finance system, and housing tax incentives will continue to provide the foundation for the nation's housing policy in the twenty-first century. We should continue to support these programs and resources. Efforts to funnel new resources to address the needs of the housing "have-nots" and working families are also needed, but it is only realistic to recognize that federal dollars will be limited. We must therefore focus on the most efficient delivery mechanisms possible, which means greater responsibility for states and local communities. The federal government is still essential in providing resources, leadership, and guidance, but the actual implementation of the programs is often best undertaken at the state and local levels. The ten building blocks for housing policy set forth previously provide a framework for the future, but they do not outline a final program — that program should be developed through discussion and compromise. The new housing challenges of the twenty-first century will only be addressed with a renewed focus on achieving common ground.

The case studies have shown that there is no magic prescription for reaching agreement, although the principles for achieving common ground outlined earlier should be helpful. Democracy does not provide for a simple policy making process. Special interests will try to implement the programs and policies that benefit them the most. However, as we strive to achieve common ground, we cannot let the complexity of the process stop our efforts.

The world of public policy rarely yields an ideal solution; rather, we muddle through the process and eventually reach decisions.[34] This chapter has outlined nine principles for muddling through the process of achieving common ground, but efforts to compromise are both formal and informal. They can utilize the more structured techniques of principled negotiation, or they can simply be based on the instincts of participants who recognize that compromise will be necessary to move forward.

The housing community in Washington, or in any given state or community, comprises hundreds of participants. Still, this is a relatively small community in which individual actors can be identified by name, personality, and interests. To the extent that this housing community has a desire to meet the nation's housing needs as we continue the rallying cry of 1949 to provide a decent home and suitable living environment for all Americans, continued and greater efforts must be made to reach a new paradigm in order to achieve common ground. Some would argue that the problem with democracy is that there are too many special interests. I disagree. The problem is when special interests are not willing to compromise. Disagreement should be expected on major political issues where partisan differences exist not only on programs, but on objectives. In the housing area, though, it should be easier to reach agreement, at least among housing proponents and advocates. As we look to the future, we must therefore focus not only on the substance of developing and implementing housing policy, but also on the process.

The challenges are real and there is no one magic answer or silver bullet solution. Rather, the solution will come from a variety of public and private actions and a combination of federal, state, local, and private sector initiatives. Leadership and resources are needed at the federal level, but the answer will not come from the top; rather it will come community by community, and sometimes one home at a time.

---

[34] See, for example, Charles Lindboom, "The Science of Muddling Through," 79–88.

Bibliography

"A Blow to Clean Water." editorial. www.washingtonpost.com/wp-dyn/articles/A45045-2001Jan10.html (12 January 2001).

Advisory Commission on Regulatory Barriers to Affordable Housing. "Not in My Backyard: Removing Barriers to Affordable Housing." Report to President Bush and Secretary Kemp. Washington, D.C.: 1991.

Alba, Richard D. "Assimilation and Stratification in the Homeownership Patterns of Racial and Ethnic Groups." *International Migration Review.* Vol. 26, no. 4 (100). 1989.

Albrecht, Donald. *World War II and the American Dream.* Cambridge, MA: The MIT Press, 1995.

Albrecht, Virginia. "The Wetlands Debate." *Urban Land* (May 1992).

Albrecht, Virginia S., and Bernard N. Goode. "All Is Not Well With Section 404." *National Wetlands Newsletter* (March/April 1996).

Alexander, Barbara, "The U.S. Homebuilding Industry: A Half-Century of Building the American Dream," John T. Dunlop Lecture, Harvard University, 12 October 2000.

American Banker article on FHA (29 April 1998).

American Roads and Transportation Builders Association. "ARTBA/NWC Strategize on Wetlands Permitting." www.artba-hq.org/public/docs/enviro/articles/Article%20on%20NWC.html (22 January 2001).

American Roads and Transportation Builders Association. "Corps of Engineers Adds New Administrative Appeals Process for Wetlands Jurisdictional Determinations." www.artba-hq.org/public/docs/enviro/articles/042400.html (22 January 2001).

American Society of Agronomy/Crop Science Society of America/Soil Science Society of America. "Administrative Appeals Rule for Wetlands." www.asa-cssa-sssa.org/dbrief/324991625.html (22 January 2001).

Apgar, William C., George S. Masnick, and Nancy McArdle. *Housing in America: 1970–2000: The Nation's Housing Needs for the Balance of the 20th Century.* Cambridge, MA: Joint Center for Housing Studies, Harvard University, 1991.

Apgar, William C., and H. James Brown. Press release introducing *State of the Nation's Housing: 1988.* Cambridge, MA: Joint Center for Housing Studies, Harvard University, 17 March 1988.

Armijo, Gretchen A., David W. Berson, Mark H. Obrinsky, and Bragi Valgeirsson. "Demographic and Economic Trends." *Journal of Housing Research.* Vol.1, issue1 (1991): 21–42.

Austin, Mark D., and Cynthia Woolever. "Voluntary Association Boards: A Reflection of Member and Community Characteristics." *Nonprofit & Voluntary Sector Quarterly.* Vol. 21, no. 2 (Summer 1992): 181–193.

Bagget, Jerome P. *Habitat for Humanity: Building Private Homes, Building Public Religion.* Philadelphia: Temple University Press, 2001.

Beidle, Richard. *National Mortgage News.* Needham, Massachusetts: Tow Group (14 February 2000).

Belsky, Eric., Paper prepared for the Millennial Housing Commission on commission themes. Harvard Joint Center for Housing Studies. November 2001.

Belsky, Eric, and Thalia Brown. "Federal Housing Assistance." A report prepared for the Millennial Housing Commission, Housing Program Tutorial, May 2001.

Beyer, G. *Housing and Society.* New York: MacMillion, 1965.

Black, J. Thomas. *Opportunity & Challenge: Multifamily Housing in Mixed Use Activity Centers.* Washington, D.C.: National Multi Housing Council, 1998.

Boehm, Thomas P. "Does Homeownership by Parents Have an Economic Impact on Children?" *Journal of Housing Economics.* Vol. 8, (1999): 217–232.

Bogdon, Amy S. and Carol A. Bell. "Making Lending a Reality in the New Millennium." *Fannie Mae Foundation Proceedings,* June 30, 1999. Washington, D.C.: Fannie Mae Foundation, 2000.

Bogdon, Amy S., and James R. Follain. "Multifamily Housing: An Exploratory Analysis Using the 1991 Residential Finance Survey." *Journal of Housing Research.* Vol. 7, issue 1 (1996): 79–116.

"Bonner and Associates Survey of Business Issues in the New Congress." Princeton, New Jersey: The Gallop Organization, Inc., 9 December 1992.

Broder, David S., "Housing on the Back Burner," *The Washington Post,* June 9, 2002, B7.

Brueggeman, William B., and Jeffrey D. Fisher. *Real Estate Finance and Investments, 10th edition.* New York: Irwin McGraw-Hill, 1997.

Buchholz, Todd G. "Safe at Home: The New Role of Housing in the U.S. Economy." Homeownership Alliance, Washington, D.C. (March 2002).

Buist, Henry, Isaac F. Megbolugbe, and Tina R. Trent. "Racial Homeownership Patterns, the Mortgage Market, and Public Policy." *Journal of Housing Research.* Vol. 5, issue 1, (1994).

Buist, Henry, Peter D. Linneman, and Isaac F. Megbolugbe. "Residential-Mortgage Lending Discrimination and Lender-Risk-Compensating Policies." *Real Estate Economics.* Vol. 27, no. 4 (1999): 695–717.

Burchell, Robert W., and David Listokin. "Influences on United States Housing Policy." *Housing Policy Debate.* Vol. 6, issue 3 (1995): 559–617.

Bureau of Economic Analysis, Survey of Current Business, September 2001.

Burt, Martha, and Barbara Cohen. *America's Homeless: Number, Characteristics, and Programs that Serve Them.* Washington, D.C.: The Urban Institute, 1989.

Burt, Martha, *Helping America's Homeless,* Washington, D.C.: The Urban Institute, 2001.

Bush, President George W., State of the Union Address, January 29, 2002, House of Representatives, Washington , D.C.

Bush, President George W., The White House, June 17, 2002. <www.whitehouse.gov>.

Business Wire, 30 October 2000. "Solid Waste Agency of Northern Cook County v. Army Corps of Engineers Goes Before Supreme Court Tomorrow." biz.yahoo.com/bw/001030/il_dilensc.html (23 January 2001).

Carlisle, John K. "Suburban Snob Politics Fuels 'Smart Growth' Land-Use Movement." www.nmagriculture.org/suburban_snob_politics_fuels.htm (3 July 2001).

Center for Housing Policy/National Housing Conference. "Paycheck to Paycheck: Working Families and the Cost of Housing America." *New Century Housing.* Vol. 2, issue 1 (June 2001).

Cisneros, Henry, American CityVista, "Building Villages Within American Cities," 2002, <www.americancityvista.com>.

Clay, Phillip. "Homeownership for the Poor: The Experience and Opportunities." MIT Center for Real Estate Development. Working Paper No.10, May 1987.

Coan, Carl A.S. "Introduction to Federal Housing Programs: Background of the Community Development Block Grant and HOME Programs." American Bar Association Forum on Affordable Housing and Community Development Law. Presented at 3rd Annual Conference on Affordable Housing and Community Development Law, Washington, D.C., April 28–29, 1994.

Coates & Jarratt, Inc. *The Future of the Apartment Industry.* Washington, D.C.: National Multi Housing Council, 1995.

Colean, Miles L. *American Housing: Problems and Prospects: The Factual Analysis.* New York: The Twentieth Century Fund, 1994.

Collignon, Kate. *Expiring Affordability of Low-Income Housing Tax Credit Properties: The Next Era in Preservation.* Cambridge, MA: Joint Center for Housing Studies and the Neighborhood Reinvestment Corporation, 1999.

Collins, Michael J., Eric S. Belsky, and Nicholas P. Retsinas. "Towards a Targeted Homeownership Tax Credit." Working Paper No. W98-5. Cambridge, MA: Joint Center for Housing Studies, Harvard University, November 1998.

Colton, Kent W. "Housing at the Millennium." John T. Dunlop Lecture, Joint Center for Housing Studies, Harvard University, 4 May 1999.

Colton, Kent W. "The Report of the President's Commission on Housing: The Nation's System of Housing Finance." *Journal of the American Real Estate and Urban Economics Association.* Vol. 11, no. 2 (Summer 1983).

Colton, Kent W., David A. Crowe, and Paul Emrath. *The Benefits of Multifamily Housing.* Washington, D.C.: National Association of Home Builders, 1998.

Colton, Kent W., Letter to Cynthia A. Metzler, Acting Secretary of Labor, and Gregory R. Watchman, Acting Assistant Secretary of Labor for Occupational Safety and Health, Letter (27 February 1997).

Colton, Kent W., Memorandum to NAHB senior officers, Memorandum (17 January 1997).

Congressional Research Service Report. "A Chronology of Housing Legislation and Selected Executive Actions, 1892–1992." Prepared for the Committee on Banking, Finance, and Urban Affairs and the Subcommittee on Housing and Community Development, House of Representatives. Washington, D.C.: U.S. Government Printing Office, December 1993.

Cummings, Jean L., and Denise DiPasquale. *Building Affordable Rental Housing: An Analysis of the Low-Income Housing Tax Credit.* Boston, MA: City Research, 1998.

Danforth, David P. "Online Mortgage Business Puts Consumers in the Drivers Seat." *Secondary Mortgage Markets.* Vol. 16, no 1 (April 1999).

Daskal, Jennifer. *In Search of Shelter: The Growing Shortage of Affordable Rental Housing.* Washington, D.C.: Center on Budget and Policy Priorities, 1998.

Davis, Michael L. "A More Effective and Flexible Section 404."

"Defining Wetlands: Science or Politics." Editorial. *National Wetlands Newsletter* (November/December 1991).

Dennison, Mark S. *Wetland Mitigation: Mitigation Banking and Other Strategies for Development and Compliance.* Rockville, Maryland: Government Institutes, 1996.

Dennison, Mark S., and James F. Berry. *Wetlands: Guide to Science, Law and Technology.* Park Ridge, New Jersey: Noyes Publications, 1993.

Devaney, John. *Tracking the American Dream: 50 Years of Housing History from the Census Bureau.* Current housing reports. Washington, D.C.: U.S. Census Bureau, 1994.

DiPasquale, Denise, and Edward L. Glaeser. "Incentives and Social Capital: Are Homeowners Better Citizens?" *Journal of Urban Economics.* Vol. 45 (1999).

DiPasquale, Denise, and Jean L. Cummings. "Financing Multifamily Rental Housing: The Changing Role of Lenders and Investors." *Housing Policy Debate.* Vol. 3, issue 1 (1992): 77–116.

Doan, Mason C. *American Housing Production: 1880–2000: A Concise History.* Latham, Maryland: University Press of America, Inc., 1997.

Dolbeare, Cushing N., "Changing Priorities: The Federal Budget and Housing Assistance, 1976–2006," National Low-Income Housing Coalition, May 2001.

Dolbeare, Cushing N. "Housing Affordability: Challenge and Context." Unpublished paper, 2000.

Downing, Paul B., and Richard D. Gustav. "The Public Service Costs of Alternative Development Patterns: A Review of the Evidence." *Local Service Pricing Policies and Their Effects on Urban Spatial Structures.* Vancouver, B.C.: University of British Columbia Press, 1997.

Dreier, Peter. "Labor's Love Lost? Rebuilding Unions' Involvement in Federal Housing Policy." *Housing Policy Debate.* Vol. 11, issue 2 (2000): 327–392.

Dreier, Peter. "Why America's Workers Can't Pay the Rent." *Dissent.* (Summer 2000).

Duda, Mark, and Eric S. Belsky. "The Anatomy of the Low-Income Homeownership Boom in the 1990s." Joint Center for Housing Studies. Paper from Symposium on Low-Income Homeownership as an Asset Building Strategy, November 14–15, 2000.

Dunlop, John T., to Bob Georgine and Kent Colton, Memorandum (10 March 1997), 1–3.

Dunlop, John T. *Report to the Secretary of Labor, "Housing and Construction Health and Safety Standards"* (4 August 1997).

"The Durable Expansion." *New York Times,* (7 February 2000): A18.

Ehrenreich, Barbara. *Nickled and Dimed" On (Not) Getting by in America.* New York, NY: Metropolitan Books, Henry Holton, 2001.

"Endangered Species." *Builder Magazine.* Vol. 25, issue 6 (May 2002).

Environmental News Network. "Battle Brews Over House Wetlands Riders." www.enn.com/enn-news-archive/1999/08/082099/wetlandrider_5132.asp (22 January 2001).

Environmental Protection Agency. "About the Wetlands Program." www.epa.gov/owow/wetlands/about.html#anchor1093687 (7 January 2001).

Environmental Protection Agency. "Clinton-Gore Administration Takes Action to Protect the Nation's Wetlands." EPA press release. www.epa.gov/owow/wetlands/dredgedmat/dredmat.html (16 January 2001).

Fairfax County Redevelopment and Housing Authority. "ADU Program." www.co.fairfax.va.us/gov/rha/ADUPROGRAM_files/ADUProgram.htm (2 July 2001).

Fannie Mae. "Fannie Mae National Housing Survey 1999." www.fanniemae.com (2 August 2000).

Fannie Mae. "Fannie Mae National Housing Survey 2000." www.fanniemae.com (8 August 2000).

Fannie Mae. "Fannie Mae: Who We Are." *www.fanniemae.com/company/who_we_are. html* (2 June 2000).

Fannie Mae. *National Housing Survey 2000.* Washington, D.C.: Fannie Mae, 2000.

Fannie Mae. "Our History." www.fanniemae.com/company/history.html (12 July 2001).

Fannie Mae Foundation, Peter Hart and Robert Teeter, Survey by Peter D. Hart Research Associates and the Coldwater Corporation, "Results of the Fannie Mae Foundation Affordable Housing Survey," May/June, 2002: 1–2.

Federal Deposit Insurance Corporation, Historical Data on Banking, www2.fdic.gov/hsob.

Federal Housing Finance Board. "About Us." www.fhfb.gov/Aboutus/aboutus.htm (16 July 2001).

Federal Register. Vol. 64, no. 89 (10 May 1999).

Federal Reserve Flow of Funds Accounts, Table B.100 www.federalreserve.gov/releases/z1.

Field, Charles G. "Building Consensus for Affordable Housing." *Housing Policy Debate.* Vol. 8, issue 4. Fannie Mae Foundation, 1997.

Fisher, Roger, and Scott Brown. *Getting Together: Building Relationships as We Negotiate.* New York: Penguin, 1988.

Fisher, Roger, and William Ury, with Bruce Patton, ed. *Getting to Yes: Negotiating Agreement without Giving In.* New York: Penguin, 1991.

Forester Research. "E-Commerce Continues to Gain a Hold in the Mortgage Industry." *National Mortgage News.* (12 January 2000).

Franciosi, Robert J. "Of Regressions and Regressivity: What Growth Controls Do to Housing Prices." www.nmagriculture.org/of_regressions_and_regressivity_.htm (3 July 2001).

Freddie Mac. "About Freddie Mac." www.freddiemac.com/corporate/about/ (12 July 2001).

Freddie Mac. "Conventional Mortgage Home Price Index." www.freddiemac.com/news/archives2000/2q00hpi.htm (31 May 2000).

Freddie Mac. "Conventional Mortgage Home Price Index: Press Release." www.freddiemac.com/news/archives2000/2q00hpi.htm (5 September 2000).

Freddie Mac. "Twelve Frequently Asked Questions About Freddie Mac." www.freddiemac.com/corporate/about/twlvquest.html#BM9 (12 July 2001).

Fuller, Millard. *Bokotola.* Piscataway, NJ: Association Press, 1977.

Fuller, Millard. *More Than Houses: How Habitat for Humanity Is Transforming Lives and Neighborhoods.* Nashville, TN: Word Publishing, 2000.

Fuller, Millard. *A Simple, Decent Place to Live: The Building Realization of Habitat for Humanity.* Dallas, TX: Word Publishing, 1995.

Fuller, Millard. *The Theology of the Hammer.* Macon, GA: Smyth & Helwys, 1994.

Fuller, Millard, and Diane Scott. *Love in the Mortar Joints: The Story of Habitat for Humanity.* Piscataway, NJ: Association Press, 1980.

Fuller, Millard, and Diane Scott. *No More Shacks! The Daring Vision of Habitat for Humanity.* Waco, TX: Word Books, 1986.

Fuller, Millard, and Linda Fuller. *The Excitement Is Building.* Dallas, TX: Word Publishing, 1990.

Gabriel, Stuart A. "Urban Housing Policy in the 1990s." *Housing Policy Debate.* Vol. 7, issue 4 (1996): 673–693.

Gaddie, Ronald Keith, and James L. Regens. *Regulating Wetlands Protection.* Albany, NY: State University Press of New York, 2000.

Gaillard, Frye. *If I Were a Carpenter: Twenty Years of Habitat for Humanity.* Winston-Salem, NC: John F. Blair, Publisher, 1996.

Gibson, Campbell J., and Emily Lennon. "Historical Census Statistics on the Foreign-born Population of the United States: 1850–1990" Population Division, Working Paper no. 29. Washington, D.C.: U.S. Census Bureau, 1999. www.census.gov/population/www/documentation/twps0029/twps0029.html.

Goetze, Rolf and Kent W. Colton. "The Dynamics of Neighborhoods, A Fresh Approach to Understanding Housing and Neighborhood Change." *Journal of the American Planning Association.* Vol. 46, no. 2 (April 1980): 184–194.

"Going Through the Roof." *The Economist* (30 March to 5 April 2002): 65–67.

Goodman, Jack. "The Changing Demography of Multifamily Rental Housing." *Housing Policy Debate.* Vol. 10, issue 1 (1999): 31–58.

Gordon, Phil. "Councilman Phil Gordon's Letter to the Editor, Nov. 8, 2000." www.ci. phoenix.az.us/DISTLTRS/d4letr01.html (3 July 2001).

Green, Richard, and Andrew Reschovsky. "Using Tax Policy to Increase Homeownership Among Low- and Moderate-Income Households." Final report submitted to the Ford Foundation (Grant number 0990-1035-1), November 2001.

Green, Richard K., and Michelle J. White. "Measuring the Benefits of Homeowning: Effects on Children." *Journal of Urban Economics.* Vol. 41, (1997).

Grossman, Allen, and V. Kasturi Rangan. "Managing Multi-Site Nonprofits." Working Paper, 99-095. Social Enterprise Series No. 8. Boston: Division of Research, Harvard Business School, 1999.

Gyourko, Joseph, and Peter Linneman. "Affordability and the American Dream: An Examination of the Last 30 years." *Journal of Housing Research.* Vol. 4, issue 1, (1993).

Habitat for Humanity Americorp. www.habitat.org/hr/americorps.html.

Habitat for Humanity International. *Annual Report 1999.*

Habitat for Humanity International. *Annual Report 2000.*

Habitat for Humanity International. *Annual Report 2001.*

Habitat for Humanity. "A Brief Introduction to Habitat for Humanity International." *www. habitat.org/how/tour/1.html* (15 July 2000).

Habitat for Humanity International. "Capacity Building: Investing in the Future." www. habitat.org/gov/cb.html (18 June 2001).

Habitat for Humanity International. "Church Relations." www.habitat.org/cr/ (13 June 2001).

Habitat for Humanity International. "DRAFT: Concept Paper for Habitat University." September 2000. Provided by Nicolas Retsinas, HFHI Board Member and Chair of Habitat University Planning Group.

Habitat for Humanity International. "Corporate Partners." <*http://www.habitat.org/cp/list. html*> (18 June 2001).

Habitat for Humanity International. "Fact Sheet." www.habitat.org/how/factsheet.html (3 August 2000).

Habitat for Humanity International. "Fact Sheet." www.habitat.org/how/factsheet.html (2 April 2001).

Habitat for Humanity International. "Fact Sheet." www.habitat.org/how/factsheet.html# select (15 June 2001).

Habitat for Humanity International. "Habitat as a Christian Ministry." www.habitat.org/ how/christian.html (3 March 2001).

Habitat for Humanity International. "The History of Habitat." www.habitat.org/how/ history.html.

Habitat for Humanity International. "The Houses the Senate Built." www.habitat.org/ build/senate.html (4 June 2001).

Habitat for Humanity International. "How Are Partner Families Selected?" www. habitat.org/how/factsheet.html#select (18 June 2001).

Habitat for Humanity International. "More Than Houses: Rebuilding Our Communities." www.habitat.org/build/mth/ (20 March 2001).

Habitat for Humanity International. "SHOP: Building on Success." www.habitat.org/gov/shop.html (18 June 2001).

Habitat for Humanity International. *Strategic Plan 2000–2005: Building the Next 100,000 Homes.*

Habitat for Humanity International. "21st Century Challenge: Eliminating Substandard Housing in the 21st Century." www.habitat.org/build/21st/ (19 June 2001).

Habitat for Humanity International. "What is the 21st Century Challenge?" Brochure. HFHI, Washington, D.C., regional office, October 2000.

Habitat for Humanity of Northern Virginia. "Presentations and Dedications: HFHNV Breaks Ground at Stevenson Street." www.hfhnv.org/habitat_w/files?grndbreak1.html (2 July 2001).

"Habitat for Humanity Pushed As Policy Model." *Christian Century*. Vol. 110 (28 April 1993): 448.

Hart, Peter and Robert Teeter, "Lack of Affordable Housing Rivals Health Care as a Problem for Working Families," Press Release, 16 June 2002, Fannie Mae Foundation, Washington, D.C.

Hart, Peter and Robert Teeter "Results of the Fannie Mae Foundation Affordable Housing Survey," May/June 2002: 8.

Haurin, Donald R., Toby L. Parcel, and R. Jean Haurin, "The Impact of Homeownership on Child Outcomes." Unpublished paper. Ohio State University, 24 January 2001.

Hays, R. Allen. *The Federal Government and Urban Housing: Ideology and Change in Public Policy.* Albany, New York: State University of New York Press, 1995.

Hendershott, Patric H. "The Tax Reform Act of 1986 and Real Estate." Working paper, MIT Housing Policy Project, MIT Center for Real Estate Development. Cambridge, MA: Massachusetts Institute of Technology, 1988.

Herbert, Christopher E. "Assessing the Potential for Increasing Black Homeownership in the 1990s." Working Paper N95-3. Cambridge, MA: Joint Center for Housing Studies, Harvard University, November 1995.

Herbert, Christopher E., Abt Associates, Inc. "An Assessment of the Availability and Cost of Financing Small Multifamily Properties." prepared for the U.S. Department of Housing and Urban Development, 17 January 2001.

"The Homes That Saved the World." *The Economist* (30 March to 5 April 2002):11.

House Appropriations Committee, Labor Department Subcommittee. House Report 104–659, 1996.

Housing and Development Reporter (15 June 1998): 94.

Housing and Development Reporter (27 July 1998): 189.

Housing and Development Reporter, The Housing and Community Development Electronic Library (CD-Rom), West Group, February 2002.

Housing Assistance Council. "Information about Rural Housing Assistance Programs." www.ruralhome.org/pubs/infoshts/info521.htm (16 July 2001).

Hoyer, Congressman Stenny, to Greg Watchman, Acting Assistant Secretary for OSHA, Letter (18 April 1997).

Husock, Howard. "It's Time to Take Habitat for Humanity Seriously." *City Journal*. Vol. 5, no. 3 (Summer 1995): 35–43.

Husock, Howard. "Standards Versus Struggle: The Failure of Public Housing and the Welfare-State Impulse." *Social Philosophy & Policy*. Vol. 14, no. 2 (Summer 1997): 69–94.

Hutchinson, Janet. "Building for Babbitt: The State and the Suburban Home Ideal." *Journal of Policy History*. Vol. 9, no. 2, (1997).

Immigration and Naturalization Services, U.S. Department of Justice. "Legal Immigration, Fiscal Year 1998." In *Office of Policy and Planning Annual Report*. www.ins.usdoj.gov/graphics/aboutins/statistics/index.htm.

Ip, Greg. "The new Data Paint Darker Pictures of the Economy. *The Wall Street Journal*. (1 August 2002): A1–2.

Jackman, Mary R., and Robert W. Jackman. "Racial Inequalities in Homeownership." *Social Forces*. Vol. 58, no. 4, (June 1980).

Jackson, Kenneth T. *Crabgrass Frontier: The Suburbanization of the United States*, New York: Oxford University Press, 1985.

Johnson, James A. *Showing America a New Way Home: Expanding Opportunities for Home Ownership*. San Francisco, CA: Jossey-Bass Publishers, 1996.

Joint Center for Housing Studies. *Housing America's Seniors*. Cambridge, MA: Joint Center for Housing Studies, Harvard University, 1999.

Joint Center for Housing Studies. *Housing America's Seniors*. Cambridge, MA: Joint Center for Housing Studies, Harvard University, 2000.

Joint Center for Housing Studies. *Improving America's Housing: The Remodeling Futures Program*. Cambridge, MA: Joint Center for Housing Studies, Harvard University, 1999.

Joint Center for Housing Studies. *State of the Nation's Housing: 1999*. Cambridge, MA: Joint Center for Housing Studies, Harvard University, 1999.

Joint Center for Housing Studies. *State of the Nation's Housing 2000*. Cambridge, MA: Joint Center for Housing Studies, Harvard University, 2000.

Joint Center for Housing Studies. *State of the Nation's Housing: 2001*. Cambridge, MA: Joint Center for Housing Studies, Harvard University, 2001.

Jones, Tom and Amy Randall, HFHI Washington, D.C. Office. Correspondence with author and Amy E. Rowe, January–August 2001.

Krivo, Lauren J. "Homeownership Differences Between Hispanics and Anglos in the United States." *Social Problems*. Vol. 23, no. 4 (April 1986).

Lacayo, Richard. "Suburban Legend: William Levitt." *Time Magazine* (7 December 1998): 148.

Legal Information Institute. "U.S. Code: Clean Water Act" www4.law.cornell.edu/uscode/unframed/33/404.html (3 December 2000).

Liebesman, Lawrence R. *A Developer's Guide to Federal Wetlands Regulation*. Washington, D.C.: National Association of Homebuilders, 1993.

Liebesman, Lawrence R. "Overview of the Clean Water Act: Section 404 Program." Linowes and Blocher LLP, Silver Spring, MD, 1996.

Lindbloom, Charles. "The Science of Muddling Through." *Public Administration Review*. Vol. 19 (Spring 1959).

Lipman, Barbara J. "Paycheck to Paycheck: Working Families and the Cost of Housing in America." *New Century Housing*, Center for Housing Policy/National Housing Conference. Vol. 2, issue 1 (June 2001).

Listokin, David. "Federal Housing Policy and Preservation: Historical Evolution, Patterns, and Implications." *Housing Policy Debate*. Vol. 2, issue 2 (1991).

Long, James E., and Steven B. Caudill. "Racial Differences in Homeownership and Housing Wealth, 1970–1986." *Economic Inquiry*. Vol. 30 (January 1992).

Lore, Kenneth G. "Challenges and Opportunities for the Federal Role in Affordable Housing: A Presentation to the Millennial Housing Commission." Swidler Berlin Shereff Friedman, LLP, 23 January 2001.

Martinez, Sylvia C. "The Housing Act of 1949 and the American Dream of Homeownership." *Housing Policy Debate*. Vol. 11, issue 2 (2000). 467–487.

Marvell, Thomas B. *The Federal Home Loan Bank Board*, (1969).

Masnick, George. "Citizenship and Homeownership Among Foreign Born Residents in the U.S." Working Paper N97-1. Cambridge, MA: Joint Center for Housing Studies, Harvard University, August 1997.

Masnick, George S., Nancy McArdle, and Eric S. Belsky, "A Critical Look at Rising Homeownership Rates in the United States Since 1994." Working Paper No. W99-2 Joint Center for Housing Studies, Harvard University, January 1999.

Masnick, George S., Nancy McArdle, and William C. Apgar. "U.S. Household Trends: The 1990s and Beyond." Joint Center for Housing Studies, Harvard University, Working Paper No. W96-2, July 1996.

Mason, Joseph B. *History of Housing in the U.S., 1930–1980*. Houston, TX: Gulf Publishing Company, 1984.

Matthews, Mary Lockwood, *Elementary Home Economics,* 1931 (as found in Jackson, Kenneth T., *Crabgrass Frontier: The Suburbanization of the United States,* 45).

Maudlin, Michael G. "God's Contractor: How Habitat for Humanity's Millard Fuller Persuaded Corporate America to do Kingdom Work." *Christianity Today*. Vol. 43 (June 14, 1999) 44–47.

McArdle, Nancy. "Foreign Immigration and Homeownership: A Summary." Working Paper N95-2. Cambridge, MA: Joint Center for Housing Studies, Harvard University, November 1995.

McArdle, Nancy. "Outward Bound: The Decentralization of Population and Employment." Working Paper Series, W99-5. Cambridge, MA: Joint Center for Housing Studies, Harvard University, 1999.

McEvoy, John. "Statement of the National Council of State Housing Agencies on the Role of State Housing Agencies in Delivering Federal Housing." Presented before the Millennial Housing Commission, 23 July 2001.

McMichael, Regina Solomon, NAHB staff, to Kent W. Colton, Memorandum (11 December 1996).

McMichael, Regina Solomon, NAHB staff, to Bob Brown and Mike O'Brien, NAHB staff, Memorandum (16 April 1997).

Meyerson, Ann. "The Changing Structure of Housing Finance in the United States," in *Housing Issues of the 1990s*. Sara Rosenberry and Chester Hartman, eds., 155–189. New York: Praeger, 1989.

Millennial Housing Commission Final Report, Washington, D.C., May 2002.

"Minorities Do Well on HMDA." *National Mortgage News*. Vol. 24, no. 47, (14 August 2000).

Mortgage Bankers Association of America. "Proposition 202 — A No-Growth Initiative." www.mbaa.org/wash_update/lib2000/FF1018.html (3 July 2001).

"Multifamily Finance: A Pathway to Housing Goals, A Bridge to Commercial Mortgage Market Efficiency." Paper presented at the Mid-Year Meeting of the American Real Estate and Urban Economics Association, 30 May 2000.

Munnell, Alicia H., Geoffrey M.B. Tootell, Lynn E. Browne, and James McEneaney. "Mortgage Lending in Boston: Interpreting HMDA Data," *American Economic Review,* Vol. 86 (March 1996), 25–53.

Muolo, Paul. "Top 10 Servicers Pass 50% Share," *National Mortgage News.* Vol. 26, no. 33 (13 May 2002).

Muskie, Edward. "The Meaning of the 1977 Clean Water Act." History Office, U.S. Environmental Protection Agency. www.epa.gov/history/topics/cwa/04.htm (3 December 2000).

National Association of Home Builders. "Builder 100." *Builder Magazine.* Vols. 13–24 (1989–2001).

National Association of Home Builders. "Builders Believe New Tulloch Rule Will Prove Just as Illegal as Old Rule." www.nahb.org/news/newtulloch.htm (20 January 2001).

National Association of Home Builders. "Builders Intervene in NRDC Wetlands Lawsuit, Ask Court To Have NAHB Named Co-Defendant." *www.nahb.net/press_releases/1998/NS52-98.html* (23 January 2001).

National Association of Home Builders. *The Future of Home Building.* Washington, D.C.: National Association of Home Builders, 1996.

National Association of Home Builders. "History of the Nationwide Permit Program." internal memo, June 1999.

National Association of Home Builders. "Housing's Impact on the Economy." Report of the National Association of Home Builders, submitted to the Millennial Housing Commission, November 2001.

National Association of Home Builders. *Low- & Moderate-Income Housing: Progress, Problems, & Prospects.* Washington, D.C.: National Association of Home Builders, 1986.

National Association of Home Builders. *The Next Decade For Housing.* Washington, D.C.: National Association of Home Builders, 2001. www.nahb.com.

National Association of Home Builders. Public Opinion Survey, January 1999.

National Association of Home Builders. *Smart Growth: Building Better Places to Live, Work and Play.* Washington, D.C.: National Association of Home Builders, 1999.

National Association of Home Builders. "Smart Growth, Smart Choices." Survey of 2000 home buyers who purchased a primary residence within the last 48 months (April 2002); also at www.nah/news/smartsurvey202.htm.

National Association of Home Builders. "The Truth About America's Wetlands." Washington, D.C.: National Association of Home Builders, 1994.

National Association of Home Builders. "The Truth About Regulatory Barriers to Housing Affordability." www.nahb.org/housing_issues/regulate.pdf (19 January 2001).

National Association of Real Estate Investment Trusts 1999.

National Association of Realtors. "Community Involvement: National Partners in Homeownership." *nar.realtor.com/community/housing/ownership.htm* (22 June 2000).

National Center for Health Statistics. *National Vital Statistics Report.* Vol. 7, no. 13, 1998.

National Coalition for the Homeless. Nch.ar.net/numbers.html.

National Commission on Urban Problems. "Building the American City." Part III. Washington, D.C.: U.S. Government Printing Office, 1968.

National Council of State Housing Finance Agencies. *Annual Reports,* 1992–1999.

National Law Center on Homelessness and Poverty. *Out of Sight – Out of Mind? A Report on Anti-Homeless Laws, Litigation, and Alternatives in 50 United States Cities.* Washington, D.C.: National Law Center on Homelessness and Poverty, 1999.

National Low Income Housing Coalition. "The National Housing Trust Fund Campaign." <www.nhtf.org> (August 2001).

National Mining Association, et al, v. U.S. Army Corps of Engineers, et al,. 97/F.5099 (1998).

National Multi Housing Council. *Growing Smarter with Apartments.* Washington, D.C.: National Multi Housing Council, 1999.

National Multi Housing Council, *Research Notes,* "Residents of Newly Built Apartments," Washington, D.C.: National Multi Housing Council, September 1997: 1–2.

National Research Council. *Wetlands: Characteristics and Boundaries.* Washington, D.C.: National Academy Press, 1995.

National Resources Conservation Service, USDA National Resources Inventory (NRI). http://www.nhq.nrcs.usda.gov/NRI.

National Resources Defense Council. "A Brief History of the Clean Water Act." www.nrdc.org/water/pollution/hcwa.asp (23 January 2001).

National Wetlands Coalition. *www.thenwc.org/nwc.htm* (21 January 2001).

National Wildlife Federation. "Wetlands." www.nwf.org/wetlands/ (9 December 2000).

Nelson, Kathryn P. "Whose Shortage of Affordable Housing?" *Housing Policy Debate.* Vol. 5, issue 4 (1994): 401–441.

Nenno, Mary K. "Changes and Challenges in Affordable Housing and Urban Development," In *Affordable Housing and Urban Redevelopment in the United States,* Willem van Vliet, ed., 1–21. Thousand Oaks, CA: Sage Publications Ltd., 1997.

Office of the Comptroller of the Currency (OCC). "About the OCC." www.occ.treas.gov/aboutocc.htm (16 July 2001).

Office of Federal Housing and Enterprise Oversight. "About OFHEO." www.ofheo.gov/about/ (13 July 2001).

Office of Thrift Supervision. www.ots.treas.gov/ (16 July 2001).

Ortman, David E. "The Corps' Stealth Permit Program." *National Wetlands Newsletter* (March/April 1995).

Passel, Jeffrey S., and Barry Edmonston, "Immigration and Race: Recent Trends in Immigration to the U.S."

President's Commission on Housing. *The Report of the President's Commission on Housing.* William F. McKenna, chair, Carla A. Hills, vice chair. Washington, D.C.: President's Commission on Housing, 1982.

The President's Committee on Urban Housing. "A Decent Home." Washington, D.C.: U.S. Government Printing Office, 1969.

Randall, Amy with Amy E. Rowe, HFHI Washington, D.C. office, correspondence with Amy E. Rowe, (20 July 2001).

Ratner, Mitchell S. "Many Routes to Homeownership: A Four-Site Ethnographic Study of Minority and Immigrant Experiences." *Housing Policy Debate.* Vol. 7, issue 1, 1996.

Report of the National Housing Task Force. "A Decent Place to Live," Washington, D.C., March 1988.

Retsinas, Nicholas P. "Beyond the Bully Pulpit." *National Housing Conference News* (Spring 1999): 15–17.

Rohe, William M., George McCarthy, and Shannon Van Zandt. "The Social Benefits and Costs of Homeownership: A Critical Assessment of the Research." Working Paper No. 00-01. *Research Institute for Housing America,* May 2000.

Rohe, William M., and Leslie S. Stewart. "Homeownership and Neighborhood Stability." *Housing Policy Debate.* Vol. 7, issue 1 (1996).

Rohe, William M., and Michael A. Stegman. "The Effects of Homeownership on the Self-Esteem, Perceived Control and Life Satisfaction of Low-Income People." *Journal of the American Planning Association.* Vol. 60, no. 2 (Spring 1994).

Roosevelt, President Franklin D., Second Inaugural Address, January 20, 1937.

Rosen, Kenneth T. *Affordable Housing: New Politics in Housing and Mortgage Markets.* Cambridge, MA: Ballenger Publishing Company, 1984.

Rossi, Peter H,. and Eleanor Weber. "The Social Benefits of Homeownership." *Housing Policy Debate.* Vol. 7, issue 1 (1996).

Russell, Cheryl. *Americans and Their Homes: Demographics of Homeownership.* Ithaca, New York: New Strategist Publications, Inc., 1998.

Salvesen, David. *Wetlands: Mitigating and Regulating Development Impacts.* Washington, D.C.: The Urban Land Institute,1994.

Sandler O'Neill Research. *National Mortgage News* (14 February 2000): 23.

Savage, Howard A., "Who Could Afford to Buy a House in 1995?" Current Housing Reports, H121/99-1, U.S. Census Bureau, August 1993: 3.

Schnare, Ann B. "The Impact of Changes in Multifamily Housing Finance on Older Urban Areas." A discussion paper prepared for the Brookings Institution Center on Urban and Metropolitan Policy and the Harvard Joint Center for Housing Studies, June 2001.

Segal, Lewis M., and Daniel G. Sullivan. "Trends in Homeownership: Race, Demographics and Income." *Economic Perspectives.* Second quarter, 1998.

Seiders, David F. "Residential Mortgage and Capital Markets." *The Handbook of Mortgage Banking, A Guide to the Secondary Market,* James M. Kinney and Richard T. Garrigan, Dow Jones: Irwin, Homewood, Illinois: 1985.

Senate Appropriations Committee, Labor Department Subcommittee. Senate Report 104–368, 1996.

Sierra Club. "Bulldozing Our Vanishing Sonoran Desert." arizona.sierraclub.org/conservation/growth_management.asp (3 July 2001).

Sierra Club. "Wetlands Policy." www.sierraclub.org (23 January 2001).

Sierra Club. "Wetlands: Tulloch Planet Article." www.sierraclub.org/wetlands/tulloch/planet.asp (2 December 2000).

Simmons, Patrick A. "The Homeownership Boom of the 1990s: Characteristics and Implications." Housing Statistics of the United States, Third Edition. Washington, D.C.: Bernan Press, 2000.

Simmons, Patrick A., ed. *Housing Statistics in the United States.* Second Edition. Washington, D.C.: Bernan Press, 1998.

Slavitt, Andrew. "Habitat for Humanity International." Harvard Business School Case Study, 1993.

Smith, Barton A, and Zahra Saderion. "Home Owning in the 1990s." *Society* (September/October 1992).

Stegman, Michael. "America's Inner Cities as Emerging Markets." Kenan-Flager Business School, University of North Carolina at Chapel Hill. Kenan-Flager Alliance: 52 (Fall 1988).

Stegman, Michael A. "Recent U.S. Change and Policy Initiatives." *Urban Studies.* Vol. 32, no. 10 (1995).

Stegman, Michael, Roberto G. Quercia, and George McCarthy. "Housing America's Working Families." *New Century Housing.* Vol. 1, issue 1 (June 2000).

Steinbach, Carole F. "The Hourglass Market." *National Journal* (10 March 1990).

Sternlieb, George, and James W. Hughes. "Structuring the Future." *Society* (March/April 1994).

"Tax Report." *Wall Street Journal* (20 May 1998).

"The 1980s: Too Easy Money Fuels a Building Boom." *National Real Estate Investor* (30 September 1999): 40.

Thomas, Craig C. "Policy Thicket Complicates Efforts to Take Lending Online." *Secondary Mortgage Markets*. Vol. 16, no. 1 (April 1999).

Trostel, Parker. "Love in the Mortar Joints." *Architecture Minnesota*. Vol. 13 (May-June 1987): 19, 110, 114.

Urban Land Institute. *The Case for Multifamily Housing*. Washington, D.C.: Urban Land Institute, 1991.

Urban Land Institute. *ULI on the Future: Smart Growth*. Washington, D.C.: The Urban Land Institute, 1998.

Ury, William. *Getting Past No: Negotiating with Difficult People*. New York: Bantam, 1991.

U.S. Advisory Commission on Regulatory Barriers to Affordable Housing. "Not In My Back Yard: Removing Barriers to Affordable Housing." Washington, D.C.: U.S. Department of Housing and Urban Development, 1991.

U.S. Army Corps of Engineers. "Regulatory Program: Goals." www.usace.army.mil/inet/functions/cw/cecwo/reg/goals.htm (22 January 2001).

U.S. Census Bureau. "American Housing Survey, 1997." www.census.gov/hhes/www/housing/ahs/ahs97/tab29.html.

U.S. Census Bureau. "American Housing Survey, 1997." www.census.gov/hhes/www/housing/ahs/97adtchrt/tab3-1.html   and   www.census.gov/hhes/www/housing/ahs/97bdtchrt/tab4-1.html (13 September 2000).

U.S. Census Bureau. "Census of Housing and Population." *www.census.gov*.

U.S. Census Bureau. "Characteristics of Families and Subfamilies in the United States in April 1947." Current Population Reports, Population Characteristics, Series P-20, no. 17 (1948).

U.S. Census Bureau. "Characteristics of New Housing: 1998." "Current Construction Reports, Series C25." www.census.gov/prod/www/abs/c25.html.

U.S. Census Bureau. Current Population Report: 25-1095.

U.S. Census Bureau. Construction Reports, Series C-25.

U.S. Census Bureau. Construction Reports: Expenditures for Residential Improvements and Repairs, Series C-50.

U.S. Census Bureau. Current Population Survey/Housing Vacancy Survey, Series H-111, 2000.

U.S. Census Bureau. "Geographic Areas Reference Manual," www.census.gov/geo/www/garm.html.

U.S. Census Bureau data as presented by Eric Belsky, Harvard Joint Center for Housing Studies. Paper presented to the Joint Center's Advisory Committee, 30 October 2001.

U.S. Census Bureau. "The Hispanic Population in the United States: March 1999." *www.census.gov/prod/2000pubs/p20-527.pdf*.

U.S. Census Bureau. "Historical Census of Housing Tables: Homeownership." *www.census.gov/hhes/www/housing/census/historic/owner.html* (7 August 2000).

U.S. Census Bureau. Historical Census of Housing Tables and Housing Vacancies/Homeownership for 2000. www.census.gov/hhes/www/housing/hvs/annual00/ann00t9.html.

U.S. Census Bureau. *Historical Statistics of the United States, Colonial Times to 1970*. Washington, D.C.: U.S. Dept. of Commerce, Bureau of the Census, 1975.

U.S. Census Bureau. *Historical Statistics of the United States, Colonial Times to 1970*, Vols. 1, 2. White Plains, N.Y.: Kraus International Publications, 1989.

U.S. Census Bureau. "Home Sweet Home: America's Housing, 1973 to1993." Statistical brief, SB/95-18. Washington, D.C.: U.S. Dept. of Commerce, Economics and Statistics Administration, U.S. Census Bureau, 1995.

U.S. Census Bureau. "Homeownership Rates by State: 1984 to 1999" Housing Vacancies and Homeownership, Annual Statistics, 1999. *www.census.gov/hhes/www/housing/hvs/annual99/ann99t13.html* (7 September, 2000).

U.S. Census Bureau. "Homeownership Rates for the U.S. and Regions: 1965 to Present." *www.census.gov/hhes/www/housing/hvs/historic/histt14.html* (6 September 2000).

U.S. Census Bureau. "Households by Tenure, Race, and Hispanic Origin: 1970 to Present." *www.census.gov/population/socdemo/hh-fam/htabHH-5.txt* (7 August 2000).

U.S. Census Bureau. "Households by Type, 1940 to Present." www.census.gov/population/socdemo/hh-fam/htabHH-1.txt (13 September 2000).

U.S. Census Bureau. "Housing Brief: In and Around the Home." American Housing Brief, AHB/99-1, 1997. http://www.census.gov/prod/www/abs/ahb.html.

U.S. Census Bureau. "Housing Then and Now: 50 Years of Decennial Censuses." Historical Census of Housing Tables. www.census.gov/hhes/www/housing/census/histcensushsg (May 2000).

U.S. Census Bureau. "Housing Vacancies and Homeownership." www.census.gov/hhes/www/hvs.html.

U.S. Census Bureau. "Housing Vacancies and Homeownership Annual Statistics (1999)." *www.census.gov/hhes/www/housing/hvs/annual99/ann99t12.html*.

U.S. Census Bureau. "Housing Vacancies and Homeownership: First Quarter 2001." *www.census.gov/hhes/www/housing/hvs/q100prss.html*.

U.S. Census Bureau. "Housing Vacancies and Homeownership: Second Quarter 2000." www.census.gov/hhes/www/housing/hvs/hvsgraph.html (29 August 2000).

U.S. Census Bureau. "Housing Vacancy Survey." www.census.gov/hhes/www/housing/hvs/historic/index.html.

U.S. Census Bureau. "Moving to America — Moving to Homeownership." *www.census.gov/hhes/www/housing/homeown/tab5.html* (16 July 2000).

U.S. Census Bureau. Population Projections Program, Population Division. www.census.gov/population/projections/nation/summary.

U.S. Census Bureau. www.census.gov.

U.S. Census Bureau. *Statistical Abstract of the United States: 1992*. 119th edition. Washington, D.C.: U.S. Census Bureau, 1992.

U.S. Census Bureau. *Statistical Abstract of the United States: 1998*. Washington, D.C.: U.S. Census Bureau, 1998.

U.S. Census Bureau. *Statistical Abstract of the United States: 1999*. Washington, D.C.: U.S. Census Bureau, 1999.

U.S. Census Bureau. *Statistical Abstract of the United States: 2000*. Washington, D.C.: U.S. Census Bureau, 2000.

U.S. Census Bureau. "Survey of Construction, Series C-20." www.census.gov/const/www.

U.S. Census Bureau. Technical Paper 29, Table 1. www.census.gov/population/www/documentation/twps0029/twps0029.html.

U.S. Census Bureau. "Urban and Rural Population, 1900–1990." Selected Historical Census Data: Urban and Rural Definitions Data. www.censusdata/ur-det.html.

U.S. Department of Housing and Community Affairs. "Mission & History." www.hud.gov/library/bookshelf18/mission.cfm (2 August 2001).

U.S. Department of Housing and Urban Development. "Affordable Housing and Home-ownership." *www.hud.gov/cpd/home1.html#home* (5 September 2000).

U.S. Department of Housing and Urban Development, Office of Policy Development and Research. *Making Homeownership a Reality: Survey of Habitat for Humanity (HFHI), Inc. Homeowners and Affiliates.* Chicago: Applied Real Estate Analysis (AREA), Inc., April 1998.

U.S. Department of Housing and Urban Development, Office of Policy Development and Research. *National Analysis of Housing Affordability, Adequacy, and Availability: A Framework for Local Housing Strategies.* Washington, D.C.: U.S. Dept. of Housing and Urban Development, 1994.

U.S. Department of Housing and Urban Development. "Public Housing Reform Act." www.hud.gov/pih/legis/titlev.html (11 July 2001).

U.S. Department of Housing and Urban Development. "Rental Housing Assistance — the Crisis Continues." 1997 Report to Congress on Worst Case Housing Needs. Office of Policy Development and Research, April 1998.

U.S. Department of Housing and Urban Development. "A Report on Worst Case Housing Needs in 1999: New Opportunity Amid Continuing Challenges." Executive summary. Office of Policy Development Research, January 2000.

U.S. Department of Housing and Urban Development. "A Report on Worst Case Housing Needs in 1999: New Opportunities Amid Continuing Challenges." Office of Policy Development and Research, January 2001.

U.S. Department of Housing and Urban Development. "Self-Help Homeownership Opportunity Program." www.hud.gov:80/progdesc/selfhelp.cfm (15 June 2001).

U.S. Department of Housing and Urban Development. *Survey of Mortgage Lending Activity.* Annual Tables, table 4.

U.S. Department of Labor. Alexis M. Herman, Secretary, Occupational Safety and Health Administration, Gregory R. Watchman, Acting Assistant Secretary. *Selected Construction Regulations for the Home Building Industry,* 1997.

U.S. Department of Labor, News release, Occupational Safety and Health Administration (30 September 1997).

U.S. Department of Veteran Affairs. "Legislative History of the VA Loan Guaranty Program."*www.homeloans.va/gov/doc/HISTORY.doc* (4 September 2000).

U.S. Fish and Wildlife Service. "Conserving Wildlife and Habitats." /www.fws.gov/conwh.html (22 January 2001).

U.S. Fish and Wildlife Service. *Status and Trends of Wetlands in the Conterminous United States 1986 to 1997,* 2000.

U.S. Immigration and Naturalization Service. "Fact Sheet." www.ins.gov/graphics/index.htm.

U.S. Immigration and Naturalization Service. "INS Announces Legal Immigration Figures for FY 1998." www.ins.gov/graphics/publicaffairs.

Van Vliet, Willem. *The Encyclopedia of Housing.* Thousand Oaks, CA: SAGE Publications, 1998.

Vandell, Kerry S. "Multifamily Finance: A Pathway to Housing Goals, a Bridge to Commercial Mortgage Market Efficiency." Paper presented at the Mid-Year Meetings of the American Real Estate and Urban Economics Association, Washington, D.C., 30 May 2000: 5.

Vandell, Kerry S. *Strategic Management of the Apartment Business in a "Big REIT" World.* Washington, D.C.: National Multi Housing Council, 1998.

Ventura, S.J., J.A. Martin, B.E. Hamilton, Dr. Fay Menacker, and M.M. Park. *Births: Final Data for 2000.* National Vital no 5. Hyattsville, Maryland: National Center for Health Statistics, February 2002.

Von Hoffman, Alexander. "Home Building Patterns in Metropolitan Areas." Working Paper W99-9. Cambridge, MA: Joint Center for Housing Studies, Harvard University, December 1999.

Von Hoffman, Alexander. *Housing Heats Up: Home Building Patterns in Metropolitan Areas.* Washington, D.C.: The Brookings Institution, December 1999.

Von Hoffman, Alexander. "A Study in Contradictions: The Origins and Legacy of the Housing Act of 1949." *Housing Policy Debate.* Vol. 11, no. 2, 2000.

Vuyst, Alex. "Self-Help for the Homeless." *Humanist.* Vol. 49, no. 3 (May-June 1989): 13, 49.

Walkup, Robert. "I Have Reviewed Proposition 202" www.nmagriculture.org/i_have_reviewed_proposition_202.htm (3 July 2001).

The Wall Street Journal. 25 October 2001: 1.

Watchman, Greg, Acting Assistant Secretary of OSHA, to Congressman Stenny Hoyer, Letter (May 1997).

Weicher, John C. *Housing, Federal Policies and Programs.* Washington, D.C.: American Enterprise Institute for Public Policy Research, 1980.

Wellner, Alison S. "Gen-X Homes In." *American Demographics* (August 1999).

Williams, Grant. "Habitat for Humanity Survives a Bitter Power Struggle but still must Confront Problems Created By the Crisis." *Chronicle of Philanthropy.* Vol. 3 (2 July 1991): 31, 37.

Interviews

Apgar, Bill, HUD FHA Commissioner 1998 to 2001. Interviewed by author, Cambridge, MA (11 June 2001).

Egan, Conrad, Chairman, Fairfax County Redevelopment and Housing Authority. Interviewed by Amy E. Rowe (21 June 2001).

Fuller, Millard, HFHI Founder. Interviewed by author and Amy E. Rowe, (16 May 2001).

Johnson, James, Chairman and CEO of Fannie Mae 1990 to 2000. Interviewed by author, Washington, D.C. (30 January 2002).

Jones, Tom & Amy Randall, HFHI Washington D.C. Office. Interviewed by author and Amy E. Rowe (25 January 2001).

Luzier, J. Michael. Interviewed by author and Amy E. Rowe, Washington, D.C. (25 January 2001).

Retsinas, Nicolas. HFHI Board Member. Continued Correspondence with author and Amy E. Rowe (January–August 2001).

Retsinas, Nicholas, HUD FHA Commissioner 1993 to 1998. Interviewed by author, Cambridge, MA (11 June 2001).

Weisshar, Mark. Interviewed by Amy E. Rowe, phone conversation (22 February 2001).

Index

493

Reid, Harry, 326
Reilly, William, 378
REITs. *See* real estate investment trusts
remodeling, 14, 15–17
rental housing
    affordability, 64, 121, 133–38, 457–60
    single-family homes, 50–51, 82, 118, 128
    See also multifamily rental housing
Rental Housing Development Grant (HoDAG), 221,
    222
renters
    characteristics, 119, 120, 124–28
    factors in choice to rent, 119, 120, 121–22, 124,
        127–28
    immigrants, 61, 106, 125, 131–32
    incomes, 124–25, 126, 132–33, 139
    low-income, 136, 458
    middle market, 128, 288
    mobility, 125, 126
    priority housing problems, 136
    proportion of income spent on rent, 134, 458
    single people, 125, 128
    spending on housing services, 266
    See also multifamily rental housing
Rent Supplement Program, 216
residential fixed investment (RFI), 264–65
Resolution Trust Corporation (RTC), 145, 151–52
RESPA. *See* Real Estate Settlement Procedures Act
Retsinas, Nicholas, 71–72, 350, 358, 446
RHS. *See* Rural Housing Service
Ringen, Knut, 329
Riverside Bayview Homes, 365–66
Rohe, William, 77, 93
Roosevelt, Franklin D., 70, 172, 173, 175, 299, 303
Rosen, Kenneth, 304
Rouse, James W., 65, 222, 447
Rouse/Maxwell Task Force, 65, 222, 447
RTC. *See* Resolution Trust Corporation
rural areas
    affordable housing, 235
    jobs in, 11, 13
    population losses, 10–11, 27
Rural Housing Service (RHS), 235

S&Ls. *See* savings and loans
safety regulations. *See* OSHA home building regu-
    lations
Salvesen, David, 366, 377
Sandler O'Neill and Partners, 205
savings and loans (S&Ls)
    crisis of 1980s, 30, 144–45, 151–52, 186, 234
    deposit insurance, 174–75
    Federal Home Loan Banks and, 171–72
    financing of multifamily housing, 144–46
    mortgages, 178–79
    regulation of, 187
    See also thrift institutions
Schlottmann, Alan, 78

secondary mortgage market
    background, 177–82
    benefits to consumers, 190, 210–11, 462
    development of, 174, 182–85, 231, 445–46
    financing of multifamily housing, 146–48, 150–
        51, 155
    in future, 462–63
    government agencies, 62–63
    growth of, 185–97, 210
    legal and regulatory environment, 183, 184–85
    liquidity, 190–91
    share of mortgages funded in, 188–89
    See also Fannie Mae; Freddie Mac
Secondary Mortgage Market Enhancement Act
    (SMMEA), 184–85, 446
Section 8 program, 219–20
    existing, 219–20, 221
    new construction, 219, 236
    number of units, 236
    passage of, 219
    provisions, 157
    reforms, 223
    Substantial Rehabilitation, 219, 236
Section 235 program, 177, 217, 218
Section 236 program, 157, 159, 161, 217, 218
Section 404. *See* Clean Water Act,
    Section 404
Securities and Exchange Commission, 183
segregation, 92, 93, 290
*Selected Construction Regulations for the Home
    Building Industry*, 340–41
    See also OSHA home building regulations
Self-Help Homeownership Opportunity Program
    (SHOP), 415
shortages, housing
    in postwar period, 25–27, 214
    See also affordable housing; demand for housing;
        housing stock
Sierra Club, 390, 432
single-family homes
    growth in, 31
    investment in, 264–65
    ownership, 50–51, 81–82
    prices, 24, 28–29, 308
    as proportion of housing stock, 5–7
    rented, 50–51, 82, 118, 128
    See also homeownership; housing quality
single people
    homeowners, 102, 110
    households headed by, 130
    renters, 125, 128
Slavitt, Andrew, 424
smart growth
    balancing affordable housing with, 432–33
    based on market realities, 450–51, 472–73
    debates on, 297–98, 431–33
    development costs, 432
    laws, 431–33